Teacher's Edition

by
Barbara A. Trautman
David H. Trautman

AGS Publishing
Circle Pines, Minnesota 55014-1796
1-800-328-2560
www.agsnet.com

About the Authors

Barbara A. Trautman has taught English and social studies for more than thirty years at the elementary, secondary, and college levels. In addition, she has taught curriculum and methods courses for several universities. She holds a Ph.D. in curriculum and has served as curriculum coordinator in the United States and for American Overseas Schools sponsored by the State Department in Central America and Africa. She has also modeled the teaching of English as a second language in China.

David H. Trautman has been a professional writer of technical materials for industry and instructional materials for education. He holds a master's degree in education and has taught English, journalism, composition, and math to international students in Central America, Africa, and China.

Photo credits for this textbook can be found on page 304.

The publisher wishes to thank the following educators for their helpful comments during the review process for *English to Use*. Their assistance has been invaluable.

Patricia Baylis, Coordinator of Special Education, School District of Kansas City, Kansas City, MO; **Bonnie Gebhardt,** English Department Chairperson, El Cajon Valley High School, El Cajon, CA; **Pamela Kinzler,** Special Education Teacher, Penn Hills Senior High School, Pittsburgh, PA; **Virginia Malling,** Special Education Teacher, Oak Ridge High School, Oak Ridge, TN; **Suzanne Roth,** ELD Department Chairperson, La Quinta High School, Westminster, CA; **Susan West,** D/HH Instructor, Costa Mesa High School, Costa Mesa, CA

Publisher's Project Staff

Director, Product Development: Karen Dahlen; Associate Director, Product Development: Teri Mathews; Senior Editor: Julie Maas; Assistant Editor: Emily Kedrowski; Development Assistant: Bev Johnson; Senior Designer: Daren Hastings; Design Manager: Nancy Condon; Purchasing Agent: Mary Kaye Kuzma; Marketing Manager/Curriculum: Brian Holl

Editorial and production services provided by The Mazer Corporation.

Printed in the United States of America

ISBN 0-7854-3057-1

Product Number 93602

A 0 9 8 7 6 5 4 3 2 1

Contents

Overview

English to Use Overview T4
AGS Worktexts T5
Other AGS English Textbooks T6
English to Use Student Text Highlights T8
English to Use Teacher's Edition Highlights T10
English to Use Teacher's Resource Library Highlights T14
Skill Track Software T15
Skills Chart for *English to Use* T16
Learning Styles T18

Lesson Plans

How to Use This Book: A Study Guide x
Introduction xvi
Chapter 1 Building Sentences 3
Chapter 2 Adding Prepositions 27
Chapter 3 Using Compound Parts 49
Chapter 4 Direct Objects 67
Chapter 5 Practice with Parts of Speech 91
Chapter 6 More Sentence Patterns 113
Chapter 7 Sentences with Linking Verbs 131
Chapter 8 Verbs Tell Time 157
Chapter 9 Be Exact 179
Chapter 10 Making Sentences Work 199
Chapter 11 Writing for Others 219
Chapter 12 Spelling 241
Chapter 13 Fine-Tuning Your Writing 261
Appendix A: The Writing Process 280
Appendix B: ASL Illustrations 287
Glossary 292
Index 296

Teacher's Resources

Midterm and Final Mastery Tests 305
Teacher's Resource Library Answer Key 308
   Activities 308
   Alternative Activities 315
   Workbook Activities 321
   Diagramming Activities 329
   Community Connection 333
   English in Your World 333
   Self-Study Guide 333
   Tests 333

English to Use

English to Use is designed to meet the communication needs of secondary school students and adults who are reading below grade level or learning English as a second language. Grammar and usage are integrated into each lesson to facilitate an understanding of rules and their practical application to the patterns of written and spoken English. Students practice and apply each language skill in a variety of settings, from identification and classification to evaluative thinking and application.

The search for ways to communicate with others is universal. Many people learn to speak more than one language, which gives them more than one way to communicate through speech. Some people learn sign language and are able to communicate with others through signing. Sign language is featured throughout *English to Use*. By providing these illustrations, we hope to make the connection between the spoken word and signing. However, it is not the intention of this text to provide a total program in signing—only an awareness of it.

English to Use presents instructions, examples, directions, and exercises in a systematic, controlled manner. Particular attention is given to organizing the instruction so that only a single rule or a single concept is presented at one time, each accompanied by at least one practice exercise. Numerous practice exercises allow frequent review of students' understanding so that teachers can provide appropriate instructional intervention. Lessons build upon each other throughout the book. New skills are introduced in practical, real-life settings that students understand. This textbook provides the English grammar and usage skills people need to help them succeed in school, in the workplace, and in life.

Check Out AGS Worktexts! AGS offers additional language arts materials to help you tailor instruction to meet the diverse needs of your students. Each worktext contains 96 pages of information and motivating skill lessons with numerous opportunities for practice and reinforcement. These texts can be used with a basal program or as the core instructional tool.

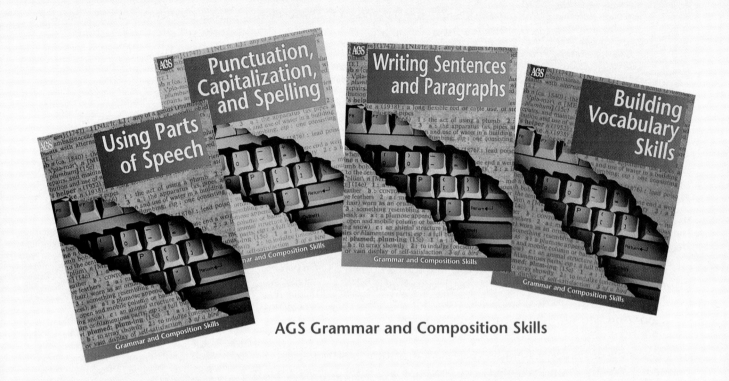

AGS Grammar and Composition Skills

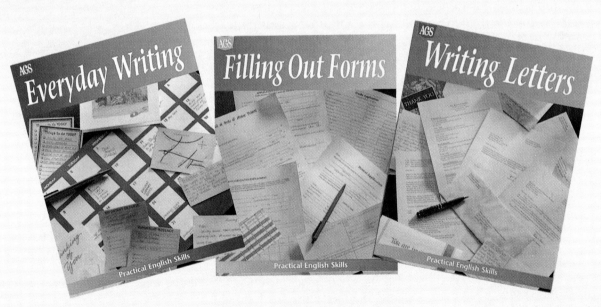

AGS Practical English Skills

AGS English Textbooks

Basic English is designed to build and reinforce basic language skills. Written at a lower reading level, the program is ideal for students and adults who need extra help with language concepts, or those who are learning English as a second language.

The program provides clear instruction of the basics of English usage. Lessons are constructed so that succeeding activities incorporate previous instruction. Concepts introduced earlier are reinforced and assimilated in combination with new material. Plenty of skills practice reinforces lessons on parts of speech, writing skills, and advanced skills such as developing themes and ideas. High-interest content and life-relevant examples and activities appeal to older students.

Reading Level: 3.9 Spache
Interest Level: Grades 6–12, ABE, ESL

Basic English Grammar is designed to help secondary students and adults develop English grammar and usage skills. Written at a lower reading level, the program is designed for students who need help with grammar and usage concepts, or those who are learning English as a second language. Interviews with teachers, supervisors, and students across the country were conducted prior to development of this text. A need was identified for a textbook that would present grammatical rules and concepts one at a time and provide sufficient opportunities for appropriate practice.

All aspects of the text are carefully controlled, including instructions, examples, directions, and activities. The sentence structure and vocabulary are clear and straightforward, which helps lower-level readers access the material more easily than they could with traditional grammar textbooks. In addition, the high-interest content of the activities appeals to older students.

Reading Level: 3.2 Spache
Interest Level: Grades 6–12, ABE, ESL

Basic English Composition is designed to help secondary students and adults develop practical writing skills. Throughout the text, comprehension is enhanced through the use of simple sentence structure and low-level vocabulary. To add motivational interest, the instruction and activities revolve around a group of high school students experiencing a typical school year.

Prior to development of this text, the author conducted a series of interviews with teachers, curriculum supervisors, and students across the country. As a result, *Basic English Composition* reflects the needs by emphasizing writing sentences, then paragraphs, followed by reports and other projects. All were identified as important skills for students to have.

Reading Level: 3.8 Spache
Interest Level: Grades 6–12, ABE, ESL

The major goal of *Life Skills English* is to develop language skills that young people and adults need in their everyday life. The content in this textbook is based on feedback from interviews with teachers, supervisors, and students across the country.

Life Skills English teaches students how to seek and evaluate information. Students learn how to find information, how information is organized, and how to use reference tools to locate information. Students learn how to develop and use skills that they can apply to other subjects and everyday life.

Sentence structure and vocabulary are controlled throughout the text. This allows students to concentrate on content mastery. Chapter openers, examples, and exercises focus on relevant and practical applications. For example, students are taught how to read a food label, read the yellow pages, follow recipe directions, and read the want ads.

Reading Level: 3.7 Spache
Interest Level: Grades 6–12, ABE, ESL

English for the World of Work develops communication skills that are essential for deciding on a career, obtaining a job, keeping a job, and being prepared for promotions.

Students prepare a career portfolio, which they can use later during their job searches. This textbook is intended for secondary students and adults who are planning to enter the working world soon after the course.

Content is practical and relevant. Activities and exercises are patterned after situations in the working world and are designed to develop better reading, writing, speaking, and listening skills. Effort has been made to keep the reading level below the fourth grade. Some concepts are dealt with at a slightly higher level than others. The Teacher's Edition provides suggestions for directing students' reading to help them achieve full comprehension.

Reading Level: 3.6 Spache
Interest Level: Grades 6–12, ABE, ESL

For more information on AGS worktexts and textbooks:
call 1-800-328-2560, visit our Web site at www.agsnet.com, or e-mail AGS at agsmail@agsnet.com.

Student Text Highlights

◆ Each lesson is clearly labeled to help students focus on the skill or concept to be learned.

◆ Content is introduced and then followed by example boxes and activities.

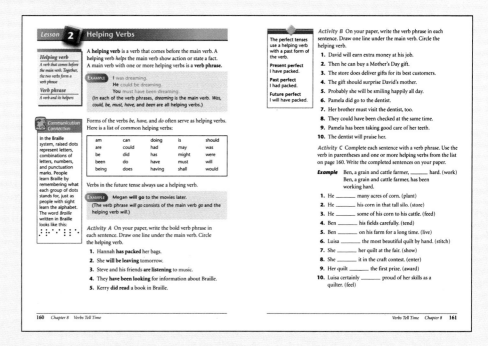

◆ Goals for Learning at the beginning of each chapter identify learner outcomes.

Goals for Learning

◆ To use verbs in past, present, and future forms

◆ To use helping verbs and negative adverbs

◆ To use correct forms of irregular verbs

◆ To identify and use contractions

◆ Focused activities give students opportunities to practice information they have just learned. Activities parallel the instruction and examples in each lesson.

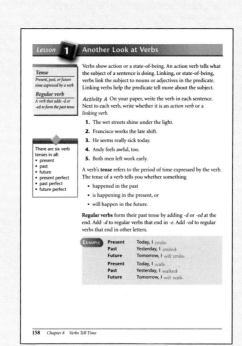

◆ Vocabulary terms are bold-faced and then defined in the margin at the top of the page and in the Glossary.

Tense

Present, past, or future time expressed by a verb

Regular verb

A verb that adds -d or -ed to form the past tense

B

U

S

Soon

Coming

Will

The bus will be
coming soon.

The perfect tenses
use a helping verb
with a past form of
the verb.

Present perfect
I have packed.

Past perfect
I had packed.

Future perfect
I will have packed.

**Communication
Connection**

In the Braille
system, raised dots
represent letters,
combinations of
letters, numbers,
and punctuation
marks. People
learn Braille by
remembering what
each group of dots
stands for, just as
people with sight
learn the alphabet.
The word *Braille*
written in Braille
looks like this:

**Using
What
You've
Learned**

Review a
classmate's story.
Do the verbs agree
in number with
their subjects? Are
negatives correct?
Are past forms
of irregular verbs
correct? Give
suggestions for
corrections. Share
ideas about other
ways to improve
the story.

Writing Tip

We often use
contractions
when speaking.
For this reason,
we think of them
as informal. In
general, you
should avoid
using contractions
in formal writing,
such as reports
and essays.

◆ Reminder notes and
tips help students
recall and apply
what they already
know.

◆ Targeted chapter
exercises encourage
students to practice
something taught in
the chapter.

◆ Communication
features focus on
the ways people
communicate.

◆ American Sign
Language (ASL)
illustrations in each
chapter provide
signs for words
or sentences that
appear in the
lessons.

◆ Chapter Reviews allow
students and teachers to
check for skill mastery.
Multiple-choice items are
provided for practice in
taking standardized tests.

◆ Test-Taking Tips at the end
of each Chapter Review
help reduce text anxiety
and improve test scores.

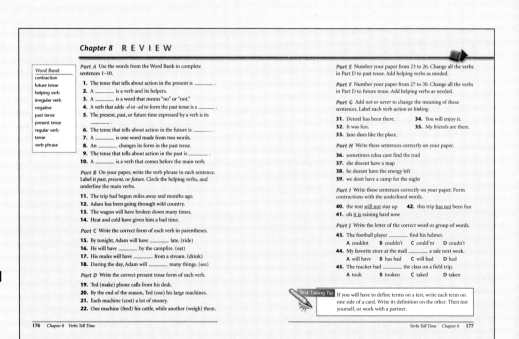

Teacher's Edition Highlights

The comprehensive, wraparound Teacher's Edition provides instructional strategies at point of use. Everything from preparation guidelines to teaching tips and strategies is included in an easy-to-use format. Activities are featured at point of use for teacher convenience.

◆ Quick overviews of chapters and lessons save planning time.

◆ Lesson objectives are listed for easy reference.

◆ Page references are provided for convenience.

◆ Easy-to-follow lesson plans in three steps save time: Warm-Up Activity, Teaching the Lesson, and Reinforce and Extend.

◆ Relevant Web sites are listed in Online Connections.

◆ Career, Community, Home, and Global applications relate lessons to the world outside of the classroom.

Lesson at a Glance

Chapter 8 Lesson 8

Overview This lesson challenges students to practice verb tenses in creative writing activities.

Objectives
■ To apply the writing process
■ To practice writing creatively

Student Pages 172–173

Teacher's Resource Library TRL
Workbook Activity 71
Activity 71
Alternative Activity 71

 Warm-Up Activity

Discuss with students the types of subjects that they enjoy writing about and have them give examples of writing projects they have enjoyed. Then ask them about writing projects that they have found difficult. Ask them to explain why certain projects have been frustrating, while others have given them a feeling of success. Tell students that all writers work hard and that even for professional writers, writing can be a difficult task.

 Teaching the Lesson

Remind students that they will probably be less frustrated about writing if they do not try to do the entire project all at once. Review the steps in the writing process—prewrite, write, rewrite, and edit—and ask students which of these steps they find most difficult or most enjoyable. Have students share strategies that have helped them work through these steps in the past.

Tell students that being interested in a topic can greatly improve the writing experience. Have students brainstorm ideas for Activity A, discussing different ways that they could approach writing a children's story about a dragon. Help students see that there are many approaches to such a story and discuss with them how they could write it as a mystery, a comedy, or a love story.

172 *Chapter 8 Verbs Tell Time*

Lesson 8 Writing Practice

Your writing should create images in the minds of others. A good writer can make readers think they are taking part in the story.

Activity A Write a children's story about a dragon. Have your story take place in the past. Follow the four steps in the writing process.

1. **Prewrite.** Think about stories that children enjoy. Think about dragons, and pretend they really did exist sometime in the past.

   > **List words to describe the dragon. Ask:**
   > Is the dragon friendly? clumsy? brave or not? Does it have a funny tail? fiery breath? Does it laugh? giggle? growl?

2. **Write.** Give your dragon a name. Write about what it saw and where it went. Write about what it did. Use your list of describing words.

   > **Example of a beginning:**
   > howard was a sily dragon with a funny tail. he meets a little boy who wanted a ride.

3. **Rewrite.** Look at what you wrote. Would a young child enjoy your story? Is it exciting? funny? scary? Can you make it more interesting?

   > **Example of a beginning rewrite:**
   > Once upon a time, a very sily dragon named howard meets a little boy. the boy looks at the big dragon and says in a small brave voice may I have a ride.

4. **Edit.** Check to make sure that the verbs are all in the past tense. Check for spelling, end marks, and commas.

172 *Chapter 8 Verbs Tell Time*

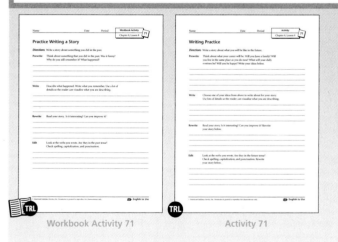

Workbook Activity 71   Activity 71

T10 *English to Use*

Using What You've Learned

Review a classmate's story. Do the verbs agree in number with their subjects? Are negatives correct? Are past forms of irregular verbs correct? Give suggestions for corrections. Share ideas about other ways to improve the story.

Example of an edited beginning:
Once upon a time, a very silly dragon named Howard met a little boy. The boy looked at the big dragon and said in a small, brave voice, "May I have a ride?"

Activity B Write a story about something that is happening right now. Follow the steps of the writing process.

1. **Prewrite.** Think about a man driving a car, a woman working, or a child playing a game. Choose one of these people to be the main character in your story.

2. **Write.** Write about what the person is doing now. Where is the person? What's happening? Is the person happy or sad? laughing or crying? running or sitting? eating or sleeping? What will happen to the person by the end of the story?

3. **Rewrite.** Read your story. Is it interesting? Can you improve it? Try to make it better.

4. **Edit.** Look at the verbs you wrote. The story happens in the present time. Are your verbs all in present tense? Check spelling, end marks, and commas.

Activity C Write a story that takes place in the future. Follow the steps of the writing process.

1. **Prewrite.** Think about ways people will travel in the future. Think about spaceships. Pretend a spaceship will take tourists to Jupiter.

2. **Write.** Write about a trip to Jupiter. Who will be on the trip? What funny or scary things will happen on the way?

3. **Rewrite.** Read your story. Is it exciting? Can you make it more interesting? Rewrite sentences to improve your story.

4. **Edit.** Look at the verbs you wrote. Your story takes place in the future. Are your verbs correct? Check spelling, end marks, and commas.

Activity A Answers

Stories will vary. Make sure that students have used past tense verbs correctly.

Activity B Answers

Stories will vary. Make sure that students have used present tense verbs correctly.

Activity C Answers

Stories will vary. Make sure that students have used future tense verbs correctly.

Using What You've Learned

Discuss with students different strategies for reviewing other people's stories. For example, students might want to read the story through once, looking only at the punctuation. They may want to skim the story a second time as they check the verbs. Remind students that checking all of the elements of mechanics and punctuation would be difficult to do in one reading.

3 Reinforce and Extend

LEARNING STYLES

Auditory/Verbal
Arrange for students to read their dragon stories to children and their other stories to appropriate audiences. Discuss with students how they can modulate their voices—speeding up, slowing down, speaking more loudly or softly—to maintain audience interest.

ONLINE CONNECTION

The National Council of Teachers of English site has a list of teaching ideas submitted by teachers and selected from NCTE publications. To see their suggestions for writing activities, visit *www.ncte.org/teach/write.shtml.*

◆ Speaking and Writing Practice activities provide additional reinforcement of content covered in the Student Text.

◆ Learning Styles provide teaching strategies to help meet the needs of students with diverse ways of learning. Modalities include Auditory/Verbal, Body/Kinesthetic, Interpersonal/Group Learning, Logical/Mathematical, and Visual/Spatial. Additional teaching activities are provided for LEP/ESL students.

◆ Answers for all activities in the Student Text appear in the Teacher's Edition. Answers to the Teacher's Resource Library and Student Workbook appear at the back of this Teacher's Edition and on the TRL CD-ROM.

◆ Activity, Workbook, and Test pages from the Teacher's Resource Library are shown at reduced size at point of use.

◆ The Planning Guide saves valuable preparation time by organizing all materials for each chapter.

◆ A complete listing of lessons allows you to preview each chapter quickly.

◆ Assessment options are highlighted for easy reference. The options include Chapter Reviews, Chapter Mastery Tests A and B, and Midterm and Final Tests.

Chapter 8

Planning Guide
Verbs Tell Time

	Student Pages	Student Text Lesson		Language Skills		
		Vocabulary	Practice Activities	Identification Skills	Writing Skills	Punctuation Skills
Lesson 1 Another Look at Verbs	158–159	✔	✔	✔	✔	
Lesson 2 Helping Verbs	160–161	✔	✔	✔	✔	✔
Lesson 3 The Present Tense	162–163	✔	✔	✔	✔	✔
Lesson 4 The Past Tense	164–165	✔	✔	✔	✔	✔
Lesson 5 The Future Tense	166–167	✔	✔	✔	✔	✔
Lesson 6 Negatives	168–169	✔	✔	✔	✔	✔
Lesson 7 Verbs That Change Form	170–171	✔	✔	✔	✔	✔
Lesson 8 Writing Practice	172–173		✔	✔	✔	✔
Lesson 9 Writing Mechanics	174–175	✔	✔	✔	✔	✔

Chapter Activities

Teacher's Resource Library
Community Connection 8:
Talk with Your Neighbors About
Improvements in the Community
English in Your World 8:
Using Action Verbs

Assessment Options

Student Text
Chapter 8 Review

Teacher's Resource Library
Chapter 8 Mastery Tests A and B

156A

Communication Connection	Notes	Using What You've Learned	Writing Tips	Teacher Alert	Online Connection	Applications (Home, Career, Community, Global)	Speaking Practice	Writing Practice	Auditory/Verbal	Body/Kinesthetic	Interpersonal/Group Learning	Logical/Mathematical	Visual/Spatial	LEP/ESL	Workbook Activities	Activities	Alternative Activities	Sentence Diagramming Activities	Self-Study Guide
	✔								159						64	64	64		✔
160	✔												161		65	65	65		✔
			✔	163	163									163	66	66	66	39	✔
	✔				165			165			165				67	67	67	40	✔
			✔		167					167					68	68	68	41	✔
							169				169				69	69	69		✔
									171					171	70	70	70		✔
		173			173				173						71	71	71		✔
			✔		175							175			72	72	72		✔

Student Text Features · **Teaching Strategies** · **Learning Styles** · **Teacher's Resource Library**

- Page numbers of Student Text and Teacher's Edition features help teachers customize lesson plans.

- Many teaching strategies and learning styles are listed to help include students with diverse needs.

- All activities for the Teacher's Resource Library are listed.

- A Pronunciation Guide is provided to help teachers work with students to pronounce difficult words correctly.

Pronunciation Key

a hat	e let	ī ice	ô order	ů put	sh she
ā age	ē equal	o hot	oi oil	ü rule	th thin
ä far	ėr term	ō open	ou out	ch child	ŦH then
â care	i it	ò saw	u cup	ng long	zh measure

ə { a in about / e in taken / i in pencil / o in lemon / u in circus }

Alternative Activities

The Teacher's Resource Library (TRL) contains a set of lower-level worksheets called Alternative Activities. These worksheets cover the same content as the regular Activities but are written at a second-grade reading level.

Skill Track Software

Use the Skill Track Software for English to Use for additional reinforcement of this chapter. The software program allows students using AGS textbooks to be assessed for mastery of each chapter and lesson of the textbook. Students access the software on an individual basis and are assessed with multiple-choice items.

156B

TRL All of the activities you will need to reinforce and extend the text are conveniently located in the Teacher's Resource Library (TRL) CD-ROM. All of the reproducible activities pictured in the Teacher's Edition are ready to select, view, and print. Additionally, you can preview other materials by linking directly to the AGS Web site.

Workbook

Workbook Activities are available to reinforce and extend skills from each lesson of the textbook. A bound workbook format is also available.

Activities

Activities for each lesson of the textbook give students additional skill practice.

Alternative Activities

These activities cover the same content as the Activities but are written at a second-grade reading level.

Community Connection/English in Your World

Relevant activities connected to real-life situations help reinforce concepts and skills students have learned in class.

Self-Study Guide

An assignment guide provides the student with an outline for working through the text independently. The guide provides teachers with the flexibility for individualized instruction or independent study.

Mastery Tests

Chapter, Midterm, and Final Mastery Tests are convenient assessment options.

Answer Key

All answers to reproducible activities are included in the TRL and in the Teacher's Edition.

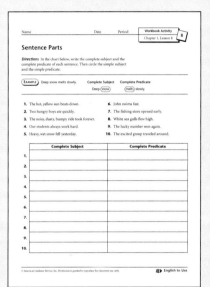

Workbook Activities

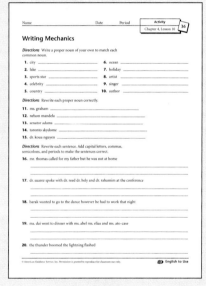

Activities

Community Connection

Mastery Tests

Skill Track Software

The Skill Track software program allows students using AGS textbooks to be assessed for mastery of each chapter and lesson of the textbook. Students access the software on an individual basis and are assessed with multiple-choice items.

Students can enter the program through two paths:

Lesson
Six items assess mastery of each lesson.

Chapter
Two parallel chapter assessment forms are provided to determine chapter mastery. The two forms are equal in length and cover the same concepts with different items. The number of items in each chapter assessment varies by chapter, as the items are drawn from content in each lesson of the textbook.

The program includes high-interest graphics that accompany the items. Students are allowed to retake the chapter or lesson assessments over again at the instructor's discretion. The instructor has the ability to run and print out a variety of reports to track students' progress.

Skills Chart

English to Use

Identification Skills

Parts of Speech

Skill	1	2	3	4	5	6	7	8	9	10	11	12	13
Nouns	1	2	3	4	5	6	7	8	9	10	11	12	13
Pronouns		2		4	5	6	7	8	9	10	11	12	13
Adjectives	1	2	3	4	5	6	7	8	9	10	11	12	13
Verbs	1	2	3	4	5	6	7	8	9	10	11	12	13
Adverbs	1	2	3	4	5	6	7	8	9	10	11	12	13
Prepositions		2	3	4	5	6	7	8	9	10	11	12	13
Conjunctions			3	4	5	6	7	8	9	10	11	12	13
Interjections					5	6	7	8	9	10	11	12	13

Phrases

Skill	1	2	3	4	5	6	7	8	9	10	11	12	13
Adjective		2	3	4	5	6	7	8	9	10	11	12	13
Adverb		2	3	4	5	6	7	8	9	10	11	12	13
Prepositional		2	3	4	5	6	7	8	9	10	11	12	13
Verb								8	9	10	11	12	13

Clauses

Skill	1	2	3	4	5	6	7	8	9	10	11	12	13
Dependent										10	11	12	13
Independent										10	11	12	13

Sentences

Skill	1	2	3	4	5	6	7	8	9	10	11	12	13
Subject	1	2	3	4	5	6	7	8	9	10	11	12	13
Predicate	1	2	3	4	5	6	7	8	9	10	11	12	13
Complete	1	2	3	4	5	6	7	8	9	10	11	12	13
Incomplete/Fragments	1												
Compound			3	4	5	6	7	8	9	10	11	12	13
Complex										10	11	12	13
Compound-Complex										10	11	12	13
Direct Object				4	5	6	7	8	9	10	11	12	13
Indirect Object						6	7	8	9	10	11	12	13
Nominative Pronoun				4	5	6	7	8	9	10	11	12	13
Object Complement						6	7	8	9	10	11	12	13
Objective Pronoun				4	5	6	7	8	9	10	11	12	13
Subject Complement							7	8	9	10	11	12	13
Patterns	1	2	3	4	5	6	7	8	9	10	11	12	13
Purposes									9	10	11	12	13
Appositives						6	7	8	9	10	11	12	13
Articles	1	2	3	4	5	6	7	8	9	10	11	12	13
Degrees of Comparison							7	8	9	10	11	12	13
Direct/Indirect Quotations										10	11	12	13
Gender							7						
Verb Forms								8	9	10	11	12	13
Verb Tenses								8	9	10	11	12	13

Grammar Skills

Skill	1	2	3	4	5	6	7	8	9	10	11	12	13
Definitions	1	2	3	4	5	6	7	8	9	10	11	12	13
Spelling	1	2	3	4	5	6	7	8	9	10	11	12	13
Irregular Spellings								8	9	10	11	12	13
Phrases		2	3	4	5	6	7	8	9	10	11	12	13
Clauses										10	11	12	13

CHAPTER

Skill	1	2	3	4	5	6	7	8	9	10	11	12	13
Contractions								8	9	10	11	12	13
Abbreviations									9	10	11	12	13
Questions										10	11	12	13
Singular												12	13
Plural												12	13
Subject-Verb Agreement													13
Punctuation Skills													
Capitalization	1	2	3	4	5	6	7	8	9	10	11	12	13
Period	1	2	3	4	5	6	7	8	9	10	11	12	13
Question Mark	1	2	3	4	5	6	7	8	9	10	11	12	13
Exclamation Point	1	2	3	4	5	6	7	8	9	10	11	12	13
Comma	1	2	3	4	5	6	7	8	9	10	11	12	13
Quotation Marks			3	4	5	6	7	8	9	10	11	12	13
Semicolon			3	4	5	6	7	8	9	10	11	12	13
Apostrophe					5	6	7	8	9	10	11	12	13
Colon									9	10	11	12	13
Addressing Envelopes											11		
Parts of a Letter											11		
Writing Skills													
Sentences	1	2	3	4	5	6	7	8	9	10	11	12	13
Paragraphs					5	6	7	8	9	10	11	12	13
Topic Sentences											11	12	13
Comparisons							7		9				
Conclusions and Summaries											11	12	13
Transitions											11	12	13
Writing Process					5	6	7	8	9	10	11	12	13
Writing Mechanics	1	2	3	4	5	6	7	8	9	10	11	12	13
Types of Writing													
Addresses											11		
Descriptive Paragraphs	1				5				9		11		13
Dialogue										10	11		
Directions											11		
Invitations											11		
Memos											11		
Messages											11		
Narratives									9		11		
News Stories											11		
Personal Letters			3			6					11		
Persuasive Paragraphs											11		
Process Paragraphs											11		
Reviews											11		
Research and Study Skills													
Using Reference Materials												12	
Understanding Instructions	1	2	3	4	5	6	7	8	9	10	11	12	13
Following Written Instructions	1	2	3	4	5	6	7	8	9	10	11	12	13
Taking Notes									9				
Using Technology	1	2	3			6	7						
Critical Thinking Skills													
Applying Information	1	2	3	4	5	6	7	8	9	10	11	12	13
Classifying and Categorizing	1	2	3	4	5	6	7	8	9	10	11	12	13
Drawing Conclusions	1	2	3	4	5	6	7	8	9	10	11	12	13
Organizing Information	1	2	3	4	5	6	7	8	9	10	11	12	13

Learning Styles

The learning style activities in the *English to Use* Teacher's Edition provide activities to help students with special needs understand the lesson. These activities focus on the following learning styles: Visual/Spatial, Auditory/Verbal, Body/Kinesthetic, Logical/Mathematical, Interpersonal/Group Learning, LEP/ESL. These styles reflect Howard Gardner's theory of multiple intelligences. The writing activities suggested in this student text are appropriate for students who fit Gardner's description of Verbal/Linguistic Intelligence.

The activities are designed to help teachers capitalize on students' individual strengths and dominant learning styles. The activities reinforce the lesson by teaching or expanding upon the content in a different way.

Following are examples of activities featured in the *English to Use* Teacher's Edition.

LEP/ESL

Students benefit from activities that promote English language acquisition and interaction with English-speaking peers.

LEARNING STYLES

LEP/ESL
Different languages use a variety of styles to express ongoing action and present tense forms. Invite students who speak a different language to translate the sentences in the example and to write the translations on the board. Discuss the ways that different languages express the concept of tenses and ongoing action.

Visual/Spatial

Students benefit from seeing illustrations or demonstrations beyond what is in the text.

LEARNING STYLES

Visual/Spatial
Provide students with magazines, and ask them to find pictures that illustrate different types of actions. Have students cut out the pictures and tape them to the board. Next, have each student write a sentence using the picture instead of the main verb. Students will need to fill in helping verbs and add *-ed* for past tenses. When students have finished, have them read their sentences to the rest of the class.

Auditory/Verbal

Students benefit from having someone read the text aloud or listening to the text on audiocassette. Musical activities appropriate for the lesson may help auditory learners.

LEARNING STYLES

Auditory/Verbal
Ask students to choose one or two of the irregular verbs from the chart on page 170 and write sentences in the past tense, present tense, and future tense with helping verbs. Have students say the sentences aloud. As students read their sentences, have them identify verb forms that are particularly difficult for them to use correctly. In addition, students can indicate when nonstandard verb forms may "sound" more correct. Give special time and attention to these problem verb forms and have students model the correct forms more than once.

Logical/Mathematical

Students learn by using logical/mathematical thinking in relation to the lesson content.

LEARNING STYLES

Logical/Mathematical
Help students understand contraction patterns by asking them to create word clusters around the omitted letters. Have students make a list of the letters that are missing from words used in contractions: for example, the *o* from *not*, the *ould* from *would*, *should*, and *could*, and the *i* from *is*. Then have students list as many words that include that deleted letter as they can.

Body/Kinesthetic

Learners benefit from activities that include physical movement or tactile experiences.

LEARNING STYLES

Body/Kinesthetic
Have students work in groups of three to write a short story that involves past, present, and future tenses. Assign each student one of the verb tenses to act out when he or she uses the tense in the story. Each student should read aloud the sentence that includes his or her verb tense, using gestures to show the action, if appropriate.

Interpersonal/Group Learning

Learners benefit from working with at least one other person on activities that involve a process and an end product.

LEARNING STYLES

Interpersonal/Group
Ask each student to write a positive sentence and then to exchange his or her paper with a partner. Have partners rewrite the original sentences as negative statements. Ask students to read both versions aloud for class critique or in writing response groups.

English to Use

by
Barbara A. Trautman
David H. Trautman

AGS Publishing
Circle Pines, Minnesota 55014-1796
1-800-328-2560

About the Authors

Barbara A. Trautman has taught English and social studies for more than thirty years at the elementary, secondary, and college levels. In addition, she has taught curriculum and methods courses for several universities. She holds a Ph.D. in curriculum and has served as curriculum coordinator in the United States and for American Overseas Schools sponsored by the State Department in Central America and Africa. She has also modeled the teaching of English as a second language in China.

David H. Trautman has been a professional writer of technical materials for industry and instructional materials for education. He holds a master's degree in education and has taught English, journalism, composition, and math to international students in Central America, Africa, and China.

Photo credits for this textbook can be found on page 304.

The publisher wishes to thank the following educators for their helpful comments during the review process for *English to Use*. Their assistance has been invaluable.

Patricia Baylis, Coordinator of Special Education, School District of Kansas City, Kansas City, MO; **Bonnie Gebhardt,** English Department Chairperson, El Cajon Valley High School, El Cajon, CA; **Pamela Kinzler,** Special Education Teacher, Penn Hills Senior High School, Pittsburgh, PA; **Virginia Malling,** Special Education Teacher, Oak Ridge High School, Oak Ridge, TN; **Suzanne Roth,** ELD Department Chairperson, La Quinta High School, Westminster, CA; **Susan West,** D/HH Instructor, Costa Mesa High School, Costa Mesa, CA

Publisher's Project Staff

Director, Product Development: Karen Dahlen; Associate Director, Product Development: Teri Mathews; Assistant Editor: Emily Kedrowski; Development Assistant: Bev Johnson; Senior Designer: Daren Hastings; Graphic Designer: Diane McCarty; Design Manager: Nancy Condon; Desktop Publishing Manager: Lisa Beller; Purchasing Agent: Mary Kaye Kuzma; Marketing Manager/Curriculum: Brian Holl

ASL Consultant: Daun-Teresa Wahl; ASL Illustrator: Judy King
Editorial and production services provided by The Mazer Corporation.

Printed in the United States of America
ISBN 0-7854-3056-3
Product Number 93600

A 0 9 8 7 6 5 4 3 2 1

Contents

How to Use This Book: A Study Guide . . . . **x**

Introduction . . . . **xvi**

Chapter 1   Building Sentences **3**

Lesson 1   Sentences 4

Lesson 2   Nouns 6

◆ ASL Illustration 7

Lesson 3   Adjectives 8

Lesson 4   Action Verbs 10

Lesson 5   Adverbs 12

Lesson 6   Adverbs Tell "When" 14

Lesson 7   Adverbs Tell "Where" 16

◆ Communication Connection 17

Lesson 8   Complete and Simple Sentence Parts 18

◆ ASL Illustration 19

Lesson 9   Sentence or Fragment? 20

Lesson 10 Writing Mechanics 22

◆ Using What You've Learned 23

◆ Chapter Review 24

◆ Test-Taking Tip 25

Chapter 2   Adding Prepositions **27**

Lesson 1   Prepositional Phrases 28

◆ ASL Illustration 29

Lesson 2   Adjective Prepositional Phrases 30

Lesson 3   Confusing Subjects 32

Lesson 4   Adverb Prepositional Phrases 34

◆ ASL Illustration 35

Lesson 5   Preposition or Adverb? 36

◆ Communication Connection 37

Lesson 6   Two or More Prepositional Phrases 38

Lesson 7   Hidden Verbs 40

◆ Using What You've Learned 41

Lesson 8   All Kinds of Prepositional Phrases 42

Lesson 9   Writing Mechanics 44

◆ Chapter Review 46

◆ Test-Taking Tip 47

Chapter 3   **Using Compound Parts** **49**

Lesson 1   Conjunctions 50
Lesson 2   Compound Subjects 52
◆ ASL Illustration 53
Lesson 3   Compound Predicates 54
Lesson 4   Compounds and Prepositions 56
Lesson 5   Compound Sentences 58
◆ ASL Illustration 59
Lesson 6   Sentences with Compounds 60
Lesson 7   Writing Mechanics 62
◆ Communication Connection 62
◆ Using What You've Learned 63
◆ Chapter Review 64
◆ Test-Taking Tip 65

Chapter 4   **Direct Objects** **67**

Lesson 1   What Is a Direct Object? 68
◆ ASL Illustration 69
Lesson 2   Compound Direct Objects 70
Lesson 3   More Compounds 72
Lesson 4   Direct Objects and Prepositional Phrases 74
Lesson 5   Nouns in a Sentence 76
Lesson 6   Pronouns in a Sentence 78
◆ Using What You've Learned 79
Lesson 7   Using Pronouns 80
◆ Communication Connection 80
Lesson 8   Pronoun or Adjective 82
Lesson 9   *This, That, These, Those* 84
Lesson 10 Writing Mechanics 86
◆ ASL Illustration 87
◆ Chapter Review 88
◆ Test-Taking Tip 89

Chapter 5   **Practice with Parts of Speech** **91**

Lesson 1   Assorted Parts of Speech 92
Lesson 2   Using Owner Words 94
◆ ASL Illustration 95
Lesson 3   Owner Pronouns 96
◆ Communication Connection 97
Lesson 4   More Than One Owner 98
Lesson 5   Hidden Subjects 100
Lesson 6   More About Adverbs 102
Lesson 7   Interjections 104
◆ ASL Illustration 105
Lesson 8   The Writing Process 106
Lesson 9   Writing Mechanics 108
◆ Using What You've Learned 109
◆ Chapter Review 110
◆ Test-Taking Tip 111

Chapter 6   **More Sentence Patterns** **113**

Lesson 1   Indirect Objects 114
◆ ASL Illustration 115
Lesson 2   Indirect Objects in Long Sentences 116
Lesson 3   Object Complements 118
◆ ASL Illustration 119
Lesson 4   Object Complements in Long Sentences 120
Lesson 5   Appositives 122
Lesson 6   Writing Practice 124
Lesson 7   Writing Mechanics 126
◆ Communication Connection 126
◆ Using What You've Learned 127
◆ Chapter Review 128
◆ Test-Taking Tip 129

Chapter 7

Sentences with Linking Verbs **131**

Lesson 1   Noun Subject Complements 132

Lesson 2   Nouns That Give New Names 134

Lesson 3   Adjective Subject Complements 136

Lesson 4   Adjectives Always Describe Nouns 138

◆ ASL Illustration 139

Lesson 5   Adjective or Adverb? 140

◆ Communication Connection 140

Lesson 6   Subject Complements in Long Sentences 142

Lesson 7   Pronouns in Subject Complement Sentences . . 144

Lesson 8   More Pronouns 146

Lesson 9   Reviewing Sentence Patterns 148

Lesson 10 Writing Practice 150

Lesson 11 Writing Mechanics 152

◆ ASL Illustration 153

◆ Using What You've Learned 153

◆ Chapter Review 154

◆ Test-Taking Tip 155

Chapter 8

Verbs Tell Time **157**

Lesson 1   Another Look at Verbs 158

◆ ASL Illustration 159

Lesson 2   Helping Verbs 160

◆ Communication Connection 160

Lesson 3   The Present Tense 162

Lesson 4   The Past Tense 164

Lesson 5   The Future Tense 166

◆ ASL Illustration 167

Lesson 6   Negatives 168

Lesson 7   Verbs That Change Form 170

Lesson 8   Writing Practice 172

◆ Using What You've Learned 173

Lesson 9   Writing Mechanics 174

◆ Chapter Review 176

◆ Test-Taking Tip 177

Chapter 9

Be Exact **179**
Lesson 1   Writing for Yourself. 180
Lesson 2   *Accept, Except; Teach, Learn* 182
Lesson 3   Pronouns or Contractions? 184
◆ ASL Illustration 185
Lesson 4   *Lie, Lay; Sit, Set; Rise, Raise* 186
Lesson 5   *To, Too, Two; Let, Leave* 188
Lesson 6   Say *No* Only Once 190
◆ Communication Connection 190
Lesson 7   Writing Practice. 192
Lesson 8   Writing Mechanics 194
◆ ASL Illustration 195
◆ Using What You've Learned 195
◆ Chapter Review 196
◆ Test-Taking Tip 197

Chapter 10

Making Sentences Work **199**
Lesson 1   Tone of Voice 200
Lesson 2   What Sentences Can Do 202
Lesson 3   Questions. 204
◆ ASL Illustration 205
Lesson 4   Compound and Complex Sentences 206
Lesson 5   More About Complex Sentences 208
◆ Communication Connection 209
Lesson 6   Punctuating Quotations. 210
Lesson 7   Writing Practice. 212
Lesson 8   Writing Mechanics 214
◆ ASL Illustration 215
◆ Using What You've Learned 215
◆ Chapter Review 216
◆ Test-Taking Tip 217

Chapter 11	**Writing for Others** **219**
	Lesson 1 Write the Facts.......................... 220
	Lesson 2 Facts Make News 222
	◆ ASL Illustration 223
	Lesson 3 Writing a Paragraph to Describe 224
	Lesson 4 Writing a Process Paragraph................ 226
	◆ ASL Illustration 227
	Lesson 5 Writing a Paragraph to Persuade 228
	Lesson 6 Writing a Story.......................... 230
	Lesson 7 Writing a Review 232
	◆ Communication Connection......................... 233
	Lesson 8 Writing a Letter to a Friend 234
	◆ Using What You've Learned 153
	Lesson 9 Writing Mechanics 236
	◆ Chapter Review.................................. 238
	◆ Test-Taking Tip 239

Chapter 12	**Spelling** **241**
	Lesson 1 Practice Spelling 242
	Lesson 2 Homonyms–Words That Sound Alike 244
	Lesson 3 More Homonyms 246
	Lesson 4 Plurals–Two or More...................... 248
	Lesson 5 Other Word Endings...................... 250
	◆ ASL Illustration 251
	Lesson 6 Words with *ie* or *ei*................... 252
	Lesson 7 Words That Look Similar 254
	◆ Using What You've Learned 255
	Lesson 8 Writing Mechanics 256
	◆ Communication Connection......................... 256
	◆ ASL Illustration 257
	◆ Chapter Review.................................. 258
	◆ Test-Taking Tip 259

Chapter 13	**Fine-Tuning Your Writing** **261**
	Lesson 1 Subject-Verb Agreement. 262
	◆ ASL Illustration 263
	Lesson 2 More About Subject-Verb Agreement 264
	Lesson 3 Verb Agreement with Pronoun Subjects 266
	Lesson 4 Pronoun-Noun Agreement 268
	◆ ASL Illustration 269
	Lesson 5 *Don't* and *Doesn't* 270
	Lesson 6 Misplaced Words and Phrases 272
	◆ Communication Connection 273
	Lesson 7 Standard English 274
	Lesson 8 Writing Mechanics 276
	◆ Using What You've Learned. 277
	◆ Chapter Review 278
	◆ Test-Taking Tip 279

Appendix A: The Writing Process **280**

Appendix B: ASL Illustrations **287**

Glossary **292**

Index **296**

How to Use This Book: A Study Guide

How to Use This Book: A Study Guide

Overview

This section may be used to introduce grammar skills, to preview the book's features, and to review effective study skills.

Objectives

- To introduce grammar skills
- To preview the student textbook
- To review study skills

Student Pages x–xv

Teacher's Resource Library

How to Use This Book 1–7

Introduction to the Book

Have volunteers read aloud the three paragraphs on page x. Ask students why it is important to know grammar skills such as those listed in the first paragraph.

How to Study

Read aloud the bulleted statements, pausing to discuss with students why each recommendation is a good study habit. Have students identify where, when, and how they study at home. Then have them consider whether their methods for studying follow the recommendations given on page x. If they do not, have students suggest ways to change their study habits so that they follow the recommendations.

How to Use This Book: A Study Guide

Welcome to *English to Use*. This book includes many of the grammar skills you will need now and later in life. You may be wondering why you should study English grammar. Think about the world around you. When you write, read, or speak, you draw on your knowledge of grammar. Knowing how to write sentences correctly will help you communicate more effectively, both in writing and speaking. Knowing how words fit together in sentences will help you understand what you read. We use language every day when we write, read, and speak. In this book, you will learn about the different parts of speech. You will learn about word placement and punctuation. You will put words together to create sentences and paragraphs.

As you read this book, notice how each lesson is organized. Information is presented and then followed by examples and activities. Read the information. Then practice what you have read. If you have trouble with a lesson, try reading it again.

It is important that you understand how to use this book before you start to read it. It is also important to know how to be successful in this course. The first section of the book can help you to achieve these things.

How to Study

These tips can help you study more effectively:

- ◆ Plan a regular time to study.
- ◆ Choose a quiet desk or table where you will not be distracted. Find a spot that has good lighting.
- ◆ Gather all the books, pencils, paper, and other equipment you will need to complete your assignments.
- ◆ Decide on a goal. For example: "I will finish reading and taking notes on Chapter 1, Lesson 1, by 8:00."
- ◆ Take a five- to ten-minute break every hour to keep alert.
- ◆ If you start to feel sleepy, take a break and get some fresh air.

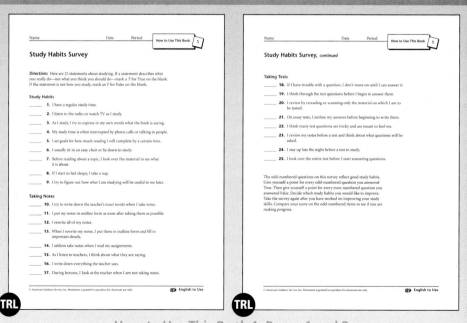

How to Use This Book 1, Pages 1 and 2

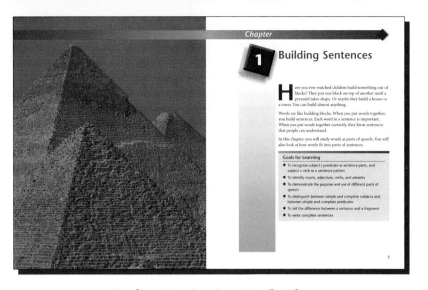

Before Beginning Each Chapter

◆ Read the chapter title and study the photograph. What does the photo tell you about the chapter title?

◆ Read the opening paragraphs.

◆ Study the Goals for Learning. The Chapter Review and tests will ask questions related to these goals.

◆ Look at the Chapter Review. The questions cover the most important information in the chapter.

Note these Features

Writing Tip
Quick tips to help improve writing skills

Writing Tip

Beware of double comparisons. Do not add *more* or *most* when you use the *-er* or *-est* form of an adjective.

Note
Hints or reminders that point out important information

Look for this box for helpful tips!

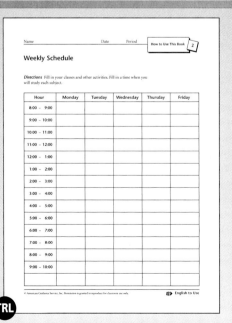

Provide an opportunity for students to become familiar with the way the chapters and lessons are organized in the textbook. On the board, list the following book features: Table of Contents, Chapter Opener, Lesson, American Sign Language, Communication Connection, Using What You've Learned, Chapter Review, Glossary, and Index.

Have students skim their textbooks to find each listed feature. Ask volunteers to tell the page numbers on which they found the features and have the other students check to see that the features do appear on those pages.

Before Beginning Each Chapter

When students begin their study of Chapter 1, you may wish to have them read aloud and follow each of the bulleted suggestions on page xi. At the beginning of other chapters, refer students to page xi and encourage them to follow the suggestions.

In addition to the suggestions on page xi, the text in the Teacher's Edition that accompanies each Chapter Opener offers teaching suggestions for introducing the chapter. The text also includes a list of Teacher's Resource Library materials for the chapter.

Note these Features

Use the information on pages xi and xii to identify features provided in each chapter. As a class, locate examples of these features in Chapter 1. Read the examples and discuss their purposes.

Before Beginning Each Lesson

Read aloud the information in "Before Beginning Each Lesson" on page xii. Ask students whether they have used in other books the text features listed. Then have students discuss how each bulleted item could help them learn the information in a lesson. You might ask questions such as these: *What are some different ways to organize text? How can photos contribute to a lesson's meaning?*

Then divide the class into pairs or small groups. Assign each pair or group one of the 10 lessons in Chapter 1. Have each group restate the lesson title in the form of a question and list the features in the lesson. After surveying its lesson, each pair or group should report its findings to the class.

Write five sentences comparing two or more movies, TV programs, or books. Compare the items with adjectives. When you have finished writing, check to make sure that you have used the correct comparative or superlative form of each adjective.

Using What You've Learned
An exercise that practices something taught in the chapter

Communication Connection
Body language is communicating by moving your body parts. It includes crossing your arms, tapping your feet, and eye contact.

Communication Connection
Information about various ways people communicate with each other

Before Beginning Each Lesson

Read the lesson title and restate it in the form of a question.

For example, write: *What is writing mechanics?*

Look over the entire lesson, noting the following:
◆ bold words
◆ text organization
◆ exercises
◆ notes in the margins
◆ photos

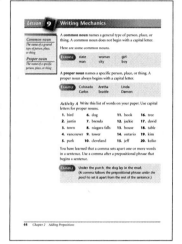

As You Read the Lesson

◆ Read the major headings.
◆ Read the paragraphs that follow.
◆ Read the content in the Example boxes.
◆ Before moving on to the next lesson, see if you understand the concepts you read. If you do not, reread the lesson. If you are still unsure, ask for help.
◆ Practice what you have learned by doing the activities in each lesson.

Using the Bold Words

Bold type

Words seen for the first time will appear in bold type

Glossary

Words listed in this column are also found in the glossary

Knowing the meaning of all the boxed words in the left column will help you understand what you read.

These words appear in **bold type** the first time they appear in the text and are often defined in the paragraph.

A **common noun** names a general type of person, place, thing, or idea.

All of the words in the left column are also defined in the **glossary**.

Common noun—(kom´ ən noun) The name of a general type of person, place, thing, or idea. (p. 44)

Word Study Tips

◆ Start a vocabulary file with index cards to use for review.
◆ Write one word on the front of each card. Write the chapter number, lesson number, and definition on the back.
◆ You can use these cards as flash cards by yourself or with a study partner to test your knowledge.

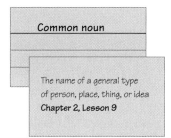

Common noun

The name of a general type
of person, place, thing, or idea
Chapter 2, Lesson 9

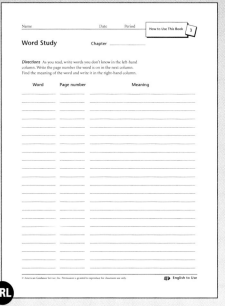

As You Read the Lesson

Read aloud the bulleted items on page xiii. Have students preview lessons in Chapter 1 and note headings and activities. Encourage students to identify these text features as they study each lesson.

Using the Bold Words

Read aloud the information on page xiii. Make sure students understand what the term *bold* means. Explain that words that appear in bold type are important vocabulary terms. Then ask students to look at the boxed words on page 4. Have a volunteer read the first vocabulary word (*sentence*) and then find and read the sentence in the text in which that word appears in bold. Then ask another volunteer to read the definition of the word from the word box.

Point out that boxed words may appear on a page other than the first page of a lesson. Have students turn to page 5 and look at the boxed word on that page (*sentence pattern*). Explain that this word appears in a box because it is used on this page as a vocabulary word. Have volunteers find and read the sentence in the text in which the vocabulary word appears. Then have students turn to the Glossary at the back of the book and ask a volunteer to find and read the definition of the word.

Word Study Tips

Have a volunteer read aloud the "Word Study Tips" on page xiii. You may wish to demonstrate how to create a vocabulary card with the word *common noun* and its definition (page 44).

Using the Reviews

Have students turn to pages 24 and 25. Point out that Chapter Reviews allow students to focus on and review the key terms and skills presented in a chapter before students are tested on the material. Suggest that students complete the review after they have studied their notes, vocabulary lists, and worksheets.

Preparing for Tests

Encourage students to offer their opinions about tests and their ideas on test-taking strategies. How do they study for a test? List their comments on the board. Then read the bulleted statements on page xiv. Add these suggestions to the list on the board if they are not already there.

Discuss how each suggestion could help students when taking a test. Lead students to recognize that following these suggestions and the Test-Taking Tips in the textbook will improve their test-taking skills.

Have students turn to the Chapter Review at the end of any chapter in the textbook and find the Test-Taking Tip. Ask several volunteers to read aloud the tips they find in the Chapter Reviews. Discuss how using the tips can help students study and take tests more effectively.

Writing Practice

Read aloud the statements in the section "Writing Practice" on page xiv. Have students preview Appendix A beginning on page 280. Tell students that they can use the steps of the writing process as outlined in Appendix A to complete writing projects and assignments in this book.

Using the Reviews

- ◆ In the Chapter Reviews, answer the questions about vocabulary under Part A. Study the words and definitions. Say them aloud to help you remember them.
- ◆ Answer the questions under the other parts of the Chapter Reviews.
- ◆ Review the Test-Taking Tips.

Preparing for Tests

- ◆ Complete the activities in each lesson. Make up similar activity questions to practice what you have learned. You may want to do this with a classmate and share your questions.
- ◆ Review your answers to lesson activities and Chapter Reviews.
- ◆ Test yourself on vocabulary words and key ideas.
- ◆ Use graphic organizers as study tools.

Writing Practice

- ◆ Read and review Appendix A: The Writing Process at the back of this book.
- ◆ Follow the directions outlined in each step of the process. For example, read the information under Prewriting. Choose a topic you feel strongly about. Gather information to develop a paper about that topic.
- ◆ Write a first draft on your topic. Then revise and proofread your draft.
- ◆ Share your draft with others and ask for their opinions. Using your comments and your readers' comments, rewrite your draft.
- ◆ Read and revise your second draft. Proofread it and revise it again as needed.
- ◆ When your paper is final, share it with others. Also, take the time to evaluate what you have written. Ask yourself, "What would I do differently next time?"

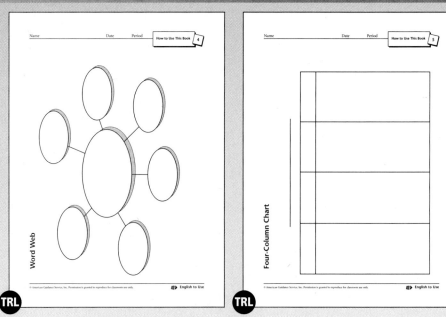

xiv   *How to Use This Book: A Study Guide*

How to Use This Book 4 and 5

American Sign Language (ASL) Illustrations

Many people with hearing impairments rely on hand signs and gestures to communicate. They use a language called American Sign Language (ASL). In each chapter, you will learn some ASL signs for words or sentences that appear in the lessons. Look at the word order in the ASL sentences. It is different than sentences in the English language. ASL has grammar rules that are different from the English language. Read and review Appendix B: ASL Illustrations.

Using Graphic Organizers

A graphic organizer is a visual representation of information. It can help you see how ideas are related to each other. A graphic organizer can help you study for a test or organize information before you write. Here are some examples.

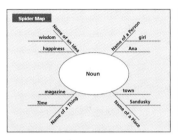

Spider Map

The Spider Map shown here can be used to connect related ideas to a central idea or concept. Write the main or central idea or concept in the circle in the center. Identify related ideas and write them on the lines that angle out from the circle. Write examples that support the ideas on the horizontal lines that are attached to the angled lines.

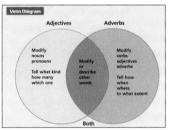

Venn Diagram

The Venn diagram shown here can be used to compare and contrast two things. For example, this diagram compares and contrasts adjectives and adverbs. List the characteristics for adjectives in the left circle. List the characteristics for adverbs in the right circle. In the intersection of the two circles, list the characteristics that both have.

American Sign Language (ASL) Illustrations

Invite a volunteer to read aloud the paragraph at the top of page xv. Ask students whether they are familiar with American Sign Language. Ask volunteers who know ASL to sign some words for the class. Then have students preview Appendix B beginning on page 287. As students move through the textbook, encourage them to practice forming the ASL signs in each chapter.

Using Graphic Organizers

Explain that graphic organizers allow students to organize information visually to make it easier to understand and remember. Emphasize that there are many different kinds of graphic organizers including Venn diagrams, spider maps, word webs, and charts.

Tell students that they can use a variety of organizers to record information for different purposes. For example, a Venn diagram is useful for comparing and contrasting information. Draw a Venn diagram on the board. Show students how to use the diagram to compare and contrast two items, such as a ball and a globe. Discuss how the diagram clearly shows the similarities and differences between the two items.

Display other organizers, such as a spider map, word web, and chart. Ask volunteers to suggest ways that they could use these organizers to record information. Then encourage students to record information on graphic organizers and use them as study tools.

Have students refer back to the pages in this section, "How to Use This Book" as often as they wish while using this textbook.

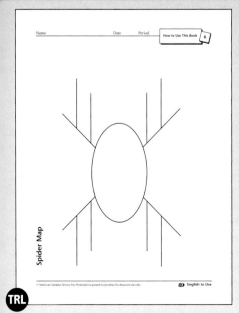

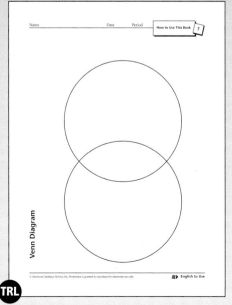

Introduction

Whenever you speak or write, you use language to communicate. The English language is made up of letters and sounds arranged in patterns to form words. Words are arranged in patterns to form sentences. Groups of sentences form paragraphs. Groups of paragraphs form stories, articles, reports, letters, and so on. Using the English language correctly will help you to communicate correctly.

Each word in the English language is a part of speech. In this book, you will learn about:

Nouns	Words that name people, places, and things
Pronouns	Words that take the place of nouns
Verbs	Words that show action or state-of-being
Adjectives	Words that describe nouns or pronouns
Adverbs	Words tell about verbs, adjectives, or other adverbs
Prepositions	Words that relate nouns and pronouns to other words in a sentence
Conjunctions	Words that connect words and ideas
Interjections	Words that show strong feelings

As you learn about the parts of speech, you will learn how they work in sentences. You will also learn how to arrange the parts of speech to form different sentence patterns. Sentence variety adds interest to any type of writing you do.

Communication is important. Hearing people use spoken words to communicate in the English language. Many people with hearing impairments rely on hand signs and gestures to communicate. They use a language called American Sign Language (ASL). Each chapter of this book will help you to communicate better in English. In each chapter, you will also learn some ASL signs for words or sentences that appear in the lessons. Appendix B shows the ASL alphabet and many of the words or sentences you will learn in sign language. Clear communication can connect people with one another both in words and in signs.

Introduction

Discuss with students different ways that people communicate and different methods of communication (for example, speaking, writing, and using sign language; through signs and signals; and by telephone, letter, and e-mail). Take a survey of the different languages your students know. Ask students: *What special difficulties do students who are learning English as a second language have with the English language? What problems in grammar and usage do English-speaking students have?*

Explain to students that each chapter in this book addresses basic and important elements of the English language. Tell students that as they study the information presented in the text and complete the lesson activities, they will learn more about the English language and build on their language skills.

GLOBAL CONNECTION

People in different parts of the world use internationally accepted visual signs that communicate without printed words. Ask students to name some of the most common (a circle with a line through it, meaning "Don't do something," or the image of a man or a woman on a restroom door). Have them look for other signs without words that people around the world would understand and make a list of them. As a class, discuss the signs that students find.

Planning Guide
Building Sentences

	Student Pages	Student Text Lesson		Language Skills		
		Vocabulary	Practice Activities	Identification Skills	Writing Skills	Punctuation Skills
Lesson 1 Sentences	4–5	✔	✔	✔	✔	✔
Lesson 2 Nouns	6–7	✔	✔	✔	✔	
Lesson 3 Adjectives	8–9	✔	✔	✔	✔	
Lesson 4 Action Verbs	10–11	✔	✔	✔	✔	
Lesson 5 Adverbs	12–13	✔	✔	✔	✔	
Lesson 6 Adverbs Tell "When"	14–15		✔	✔	✔	
Lesson 7 Adverbs Tell "Where"	16–17		✔	✔	✔	
Lesson 8 Complete and Simple Sentence Parts	18–19	✔	✔	✔	✔	
Lesson 9 Sentence or Fragment?	20–21	✔	✔	✔	✔	✔
Lesson 10 Writing Mechanics	22–23	✔	✔	✔	✔	✔

Chapter Activities

Teacher's Resource Library
Community Connection 1:
What's in a Name?
English in Your World 1:
Sentence Fragments

Assessment Options

Student Text
Chapter 1 Review

Teacher's Resource Library
Chapter 1 Mastery Tests A and B

ASL Illustration	Communication Connection	Notes	Using What You've Learned	Writing Tips	Teacher Alert	Online Connection	Applications (Home, Career, Community, Global)	Speaking Practice	Writing Practice	Auditory/Verbal	Body/Kinesthetic	Interpersonal/Group Learning	Logical/Mathematical	Visual/Spatial	LEP/ESL	Workbook Activities	Activities	Alternative Activities	Sentence Diagramming Activities	Self-Study Guide
		✔			5	5										1	1	1	1	✔
7									7	7						2	2	2	2	✔
		✔								9					9	3	3	3	3	✔
				✔			11									4	4	4	4	✔
				✔			13									5	5	5	5	✔
												14	15			6	6	6	6	✔
	17													17		7	7	7	7	✔
19											19					8	8	8	8	✔
				✔			21	21								9	9	9		✔
			23		25										23	10	10	10		✔

Pronunciation Key

a	hat	e	let	ī	ice	ô	order
ā	age	ē	equal	o	hot	oi	oil
ä	far	ėr	term	ō	open	ou	out
â	care	i	it	ȯ	saw	u	cup

ù	put	sh	she
ü	rule	th	thin
ch	child	ᴛH	then
ng	long	zh	measure

ə {
a in about
e in taken
i in pencil
o in lemon
u in circus
}

Alternative Activities

The Teacher's Resource Library (TRL) contains a set of lower-level worksheets called Alternative Activities. These worksheets cover the same content as the regular Activities but are written at a second-grade reading level.

Skill Track Software

Use the Skill Track Software for English to Use for additional reinforcement of this chapter. The software program allows students using AGS textbooks to be assessed for mastery of each chapter and lesson of the textbook. Students access the software on an individual basis and are assessed with multiple-choice items.

Chapter at a Glance

Chapter 1: Building Sentences
pages 2–25

Lessons

1. **Sentences**
   pages 4–5

2. **Nouns**
   pages 6–7

3. **Adjectives**
   pages 8–9

4. **Action Verbs**
   pages 10–11

5. **Adverbs**
   pages 12–13

6. **Adverbs Tell "When"**
   pages 14–15

7. **Adverbs Tell "Where"**
   pages 16–17

8. **Complete and Simple Sentence Parts**
   pages 18–19

9. **Sentence or Fragment?**
   pages 20–21

10. **Writing Mechanics**
    pages 22–23

Chapter 1 Review
pages 24–25

Skill Track Software for English to Use

Teacher's Resource Library **TRL**

Workbook Activities 1–10

Activities 1–10

Alternative Activities 1–10

Sentence Diagramming Activities 1–8
(Optional sentence activities accompany lessons.)

Community Connection 1

English in Your World 1

Chapter 1 Self-Study Guide

Chapter 1 Mastery Tests A and B

(Answer Keys for the Teacher's Resource Library begin on page 308 of this Teacher's Edition.)

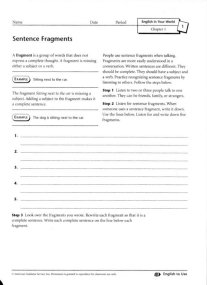

TRL Community Connection 1

TRL English in Your World 1

1 Building Sentences

Have you ever watched children build something out of blocks? They put one block on top of another until a pyramid takes shape. Or maybe they build a house or a tower. You can build almost anything.

Words are like building blocks. When you put words together, you build sentences. Each word in a sentence is important. When you put words together correctly, they form sentences that people can understand.

In this chapter, you will study words as parts of speech. You will also look at how words fit into parts of sentences.

Goals for Learning

◆ To recognize subject | predicate as sentence parts, and subject + verb as a sentence pattern

◆ To identify nouns, adjectives, verbs, and adverbs

◆ To demonstrate the purpose and use of different parts of speech

◆ To distinguish between simple and complete subjects and between simple and complete predicates

◆ To tell the difference between a sentence and a fragment

◆ To write complete sentences

3

Introducing the Chapter

Draw students' attention to the blocks that make up the pyramids in the photograph. Discuss how words are building blocks for language. Tell students that this chapter will help them look at some of the building blocks that make up sentences: parts of speech that include nouns, verbs, adjectives, and adverbs. Discuss how parts and pieces often make the most sense when you join them together. Point out that sentences consist of word parts that work together.

TEACHER'S RESOURCE

The AGS Teaching Strategies in English Transparencies may be used with this chapter. The transparencies add an interactive dimension to expand and enhance the *English to Use* program content.

CAREER INTEREST INVENTORY

The AGS Harrington-O'Shea Career Decision-Making System–Revised (CDM) may be used with this chapter. Students can use the CDM to explore their interests and identify careers. The CDM defines career areas that are indicated by students' responses on the inventory.

Writing Tips and Notes

Ask volunteers to read the tips and notes that appear in the margins throughout the chapter. Then discuss them with the class.

CHAPTER PROJECT

Speeches or writing with fragments and grammatical errors will not make a good impression. Ask students to conduct a chapter project in which they ask professionals or people in the community to identify situations that require especially good sentence skills. Students should ask for examples of good and bad speaking and writing and then share their findings with the class.

Name _____ **Date** _____ **Period** _____ *SELF-STUDY GUIDE*

CHAPTER 1: Building Sentences

Goal 1.1 *To recognize subject | predicate as sentence parts*

Date	Assignment	Score
_____	**1.** Read pages 3–4. Complete Activities A–B on page 4.	_____
_____	**2.** Read page 5. Complete Activities C–D on page 5.	_____
_____	**3.** Complete Workbook activity 1.	_____

Comments:

Goal 1.2 *To identify nouns, adjectives, verbs, and adverbs; to demonstrate the purpose and use of different parts of speech; and to identify subject + verb as a sentence pattern*

Date	Assignment	Score
_____	**4.** Read page 6. Complete Activities A–B on page 6 and Activity B on page 7.	_____
_____	**5.** Complete Activities C–E on page 7.	_____
_____	**6.** Complete Workbook activity 2.	_____
_____	**7.** Read page 8. Complete Activities A–B on page 8.	_____
_____	**8.** Read page 9. Complete Activities C–D on page 9.	_____
_____	**9.** Complete Workbook Activity 3.	_____
_____	**10.** Read page 10. Complete Activities A–B on page 10.	_____
_____	**11.** Complete Activities C–E on page 11.	_____
_____	**12.** Complete Workbook Activity 4.	_____
_____	**13.** Read page 12. Complete Activity A on page 12.	_____
_____	**14.** Complete Activities B–D on page 13.	_____
_____	**15.** Complete Workbook Activity 5.	_____
_____	**16.** Read page 14. Complete Activity A on page 14.	_____
_____	**17.** Read page 15. Complete Activities B–C on page 15.	_____
_____	**18.** Complete Workbook Activity 6.	_____
_____	**19.** Read page 16. Complete Activity A on page 16.	_____
_____	**20.** Complete Activities B–C on page 17.	_____
_____	**21.** Complete Workbook Activity 7.	_____

Comments:

© American Guidance Service, Inc. Permission is granted to reproduce for classroom use only. *English to Use*

(TRL)

Name _____ **Date** _____ **Period** _____ *SELF-STUDY GUIDE*

CHAPTER 1 Building Sentences, continued

Goal 1.3 *To distinguish between simple subjects and simple predicates and complete subjects and complete predicates*

Date	Assignment	Score
_____	**22.** Read page 18. Complete Activity A on page 18.	_____
_____	**23.** Complete Activities B–D on page 19.	_____
_____	**24.** Complete Workbook Activity 8.	_____

Comments:

Goal 1.4 *To tell the difference between a sentence and a fragment*

Date	Assignment	Score
_____	**25.** Read page 20. Complete Activity A on page 20.	_____
_____	**26.** Complete Activities B–C on page 21.	_____
_____	**27.** Complete Workbook Activity 9.	_____

Comments:

Goal 1.5 *To write complete sentences*

Date	Assignment	Score
_____	**28.** Read page 22. Complete Activity A on page 22.	_____
_____	**29.** Complete Activities B–D on page 23.	_____
_____	**30.** Complete Workbook Activity 10.	_____
_____	**31.** Complete the Chapter 1 Review, Parts A–F on pages 24–25.	_____

Comments:

Student's Signature _____ Date _____

Instructor's Signature _____ Date _____

© American Guidance Service, Inc. Permission is granted to reproduce for classroom use only. *English to Use*

(TRL)

Lesson at a Glance

Chapter 1 Lesson 1

Overview This lesson provides basic information to aid students' identification of a subject, predicate, sentence, and the subject + verb sentence pattern.

Objectives

■ To name the two parts of a sentence

■ To identify the subject and verb as a sentence pattern

Student Pages 4–5

Teacher's Resource Library

Workbook Activity 1

Activity 1

Alternative Activity 1

Sentence Diagramming Activity 1

Vocabulary

capital letter
exclamation point (!)
period (.)
predicate
question mark (?)
sentence
sentence pattern
subject

 Warm-Up Activity

Write these sentences on the board: *Leaves fall. Children grow. Wind blows.* Ask students to tell what these three items have in common besides the same number of words. (All are sentences.)

 Teaching the Lesson

Tell students that a sentence is a complete idea that contains an action and tells who or what does or receives that action. Tell students that even long groups of words are not complete without both a subject and a predicate. Then ask students to complete the exercises.

Sentence
A group of words that forms a complete thought; a sentence begins with a capital letter and ends with a period, question mark, or exclamation point

Subject
The part of a sentence that tells who or what the sentence is about

Predicate
The part of a sentence that tells what the subject is doing

Capital letter
A letter that is uppercase. A is a capital or uppercase letter; a is a lowercase letter

Period (.)
The punctuation mark ending a sentence that makes a statement or gives a command

Question mark (?)
A punctuation mark that ends a sentence asking a question

Exclamation point (!)
A punctuation mark showing strong feeling

People speak and write in sentences. A **sentence** is a group of words that tells a complete idea. A sentence has a **subject** and a **predicate.** The subject is the part of a sentence that tells who or what the sentence is about. The predicate is the part of a sentence that tells what the subject is doing.

Every sentence begins with a **capital letter,** or uppercase letter. Every sentence ends with a **period (.),** a **question mark (?),** or an **exclamation point (!).**

> **EXAMPLE**
> **Sentence**   Teams win.
> **Sentence parts**   subject | predicate
> (*Teams* is the subject of the sentence. *Teams* tells what the sentence is about. *Win* is the predicate in the sentence. *Win* tells what the subject is doing.)

Activity A Write these sentences on your paper. Label the subject and predicate in each sentence.

1. Birds sing.   **4.** Cars run.

2. Cats climb.   **5.** Teams play.

3. Tools break.

Activity B Write a different one-word predicate for each of these subjects. Write the complete sentences on your paper.

1. Boys _____ .   **4.** Waves _____ .

2. People _____ .   **5.** Wolves _____ .

3. Women _____ .

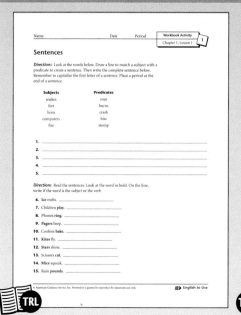

Workbook Activity 1

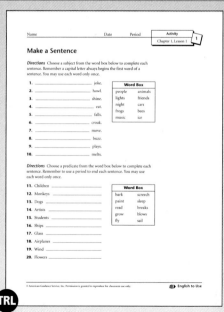

Activity 1

Sentence pattern
The basic form of a sentence

Activity C Write a different one-word subject for each of these predicates. Write the complete sentences on your paper.

1. _____ grow.
2. _____ sit.
3. _____ roar.
4. _____ walk.
5. _____ sing.

To find the subject of a sentence, first look for the verb. Then ask who or what is doing the action.

The order of words in a sentence is important. The English language has patterns of word order in sentences. In this lesson, you have been reading and writing the first **sentence pattern,** subject and verb. A sentence pattern is the basic form of a sentence.

EXAMPLE | Sentence | Teams win.
Sentence pattern | subject + verb

Activity D Copy the sentences. Fill in the blanks on your paper.

1. A sentence has two parts. The two parts are the _____ and the _____ .

2. Read this sentence:
Students write.

Students is the _____ of the sentence, and *write* is the _____ of the sentence.

3. The sentence pattern is _____ + _____ .

These students write their test answers.

Building Sentences Chapter 1 **5**

Activity A Answers

1. S—Birds; P—sing 2. S—Cats; P—climb 3. S—Tools; P—break 4. S—Cars; P—run 5. S—Teams; P—play

Activity B Answers

Predicates will vary. Check to ensure that each predicate makes sense with the given subject.

Activity C Answers

Subjects will vary. Check to ensure that each subject makes sense with the given predicate.

Activity D Answers

1. subject, predicate 2. subject, predicate 3. subject + verb

3 Reinforce and Extend

ONLINE CONNECTION

For further resources, visit the Purdue University Online Writing Lab at *owl.english.purdue.edu.* The site offers additional resources for teachers, as well as exercises for additional student practice.

TEACHER ALERT

Some textbooks may identify five different sentence patterns, while others identify seven. The difference arises because some texts combine patterns into subcategories. *English to Use* combines the two types of sentences with object complements into one pattern because that type of pattern is rare. This text provides separate patterns for the two types of subject complements, which are more common.

Name _____ Date _____ Period _____ | Sentence Diagramming Activity 1 | Chapter 1, Lesson 1

Diagram Your Sentences

Sentence Pattern 1: Subject + Verb

Step 1 The simple subject (a noun or pronoun) is written on the line on the left side. The simple predicate (a verb or a verb phrase) is written on the line on the right side.

Directions Look at the steps above and the example below. Diagram the sentences below using the blank diagrams.

EXAMPLE People sing. _____ People | sing _____

1. Dogs bark. _____ + _____

2. Birds chirp. _____ + _____

3. Children play. _____ + _____

4. People talk. _____ + _____

5. Stores open. _____ + _____

© American Guidance Service, Inc. Permission is granted to reproduce for classroom use only. 📖 English to Use

Sentence Diagramming Activity 1

Chapter 1 Lesson 2

Overview This lesson defines noun as a part of speech and explains its use as a subject of a sentence.

Objectives

- To identify a noun as the name of a person, place, or thing
- To identify nouns in two-word sentences and three-word groups

Student Pages 6–7

Teacher's Resource Library

Workbook Activity 2

Activity 2

Alternative Activity 2

Sentence Diagramming Activity 2

Vocabulary

noun

 1 Warm-Up Activity

Write a list of nouns on the board. Ask students what each word names. Then review the definition of *noun*.

Have students work in pairs to see how many nouns they can name in two minutes. Then have them analyze their lists to see how many words are *persons*, *places*, or *things*.

 2 Teaching the Lesson

Discuss how word order can help students identify parts of speech. Review the subject + verb sentence pattern.

Activity A Answers

1. Leaders 2. Clowns 3. Artists
4. Children 5. Swimmers

Activity B Answers

1. author 2. nation 3. man 4. table
5. tape

Lesson 2 Nouns

Noun
A word that names a person, place, or thing

Every word in the English language is a part of speech. A **noun** is a part of speech. Nouns are words that name. A noun names a person, a place, or a thing. The subject of a sentence is usually a noun.

EXAMPLE

Sentence	Citizens vote.
Sentence parts	subject | predicate
Sentence pattern	subject + verb

(*Citizens* is a noun that tells the name of persons.)

Sentence	Towns grow.
Sentence parts	subject | predicate
Sentence pattern	subject + verb

(*Towns* is a noun that tells the name of places.)

Sentence	Telephones ring.
Sentence parts	subject | predicate
Sentence pattern	subject + verb

(*Telephones* is a noun that tells the name of things.)

Activity A Find the nouns in these sentences. Write the nouns on your paper.

1. Leaders plan.
2. Clowns laugh.
3. Artists paint.
4. Children play.
5. Swimmers float.

Activity B Find the noun in each group. Write the nouns on your paper.

1. write author sing
2. build govern nation
3. man eat find
4. table sit think
5. buy tape remember

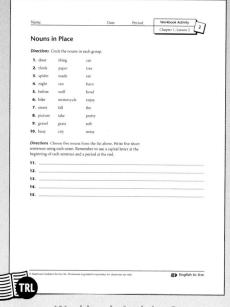

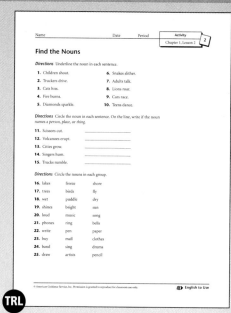

Towns

Telephones

Activity C Write each sentence on your paper. Underline the nouns.

1. Fires burn.
2. Trumpets blare.
3. Mice squeak.
4. Trees grow.
5. Winds blow.
6. Lightning strikes.
7. Snow falls.
8. Glass breaks.
9. Flowers droop.
10. Needles hurt.

Activity D Find the nouns in these sentences. Write each noun on your paper and tell whether it names a *person, place,* or *thing.*

1. Chains rattle.
2. Pilots fly.
3. Stereos play.
4. Cities grow.
5. Leaders speak.

Activity E Answer each of these items on your paper.

1. Nouns tell the names of persons, _____ , or _____ .

2. Write the nouns in this list:

house	car	did	flowers
day	driver	streets	teacher
books	person	cloud	town
horse	chairs	tell	sit

3. Write five nouns of your own that name places.

4. Write five nouns of your own that tell the names of persons.

5. Write five nouns of your own that name things.

Writing Practice

Have each student write a short paragraph that describes what he or she saw on the way to school. After students have completed their paragraphs, organize them into groups. In groups, students should trade papers and then underline all the nouns they find in the paragraphs. When students have finished, count the number of *person, place,* and *thing* nouns in each group's writing.

Activity C Answers

1. <u>Fires</u> burn. 2. <u>Trumpets</u> blare. 3. <u>Mice</u> squeak. 4. <u>Trees</u> grow. 5. <u>Winds</u> blow. 6. <u>Lightning</u> strikes. 7. <u>Snow</u> falls. 8. <u>Glass</u> breaks. 9. <u>Flowers</u> droop. 10. <u>Needles</u> hurt.

Activity D Answers

1. Chains—things 2. Pilots—persons 3. Stereos—things 4. Cities—places 5. Leaders—persons

Activity E Answers

1. places, things 2. house, day, books, horse, car, driver, person, chairs, streets, cloud, flowers, teacher, town 3. Answers will vary. 4. Answers will vary. 5. Answers will vary.

3 **Reinforce and Extend**

LEARNING STYLES

Body/Kinesthetic Learning
As students work through the lesson, remind them that often nouns are things that they can identify through the senses—by seeing, hearing, tasting, smelling, and touching. Have students take turns picking up items in the classroom and identifying the sense they can use to identify that object.

ASL ILLUSTRATION

Have students practice making the ASL signs for "towns" and "telephones." Ask students how they imagine these signs developed. Would they have recognized the signs without the captions? Have students explain their responses.

Name ___ Date ___ Period ___ Sentence Diagramming Activity **2** Chapter 1, Lesson 2

More Short Sentences to Diagram

Sentence Pattern 1: Subject + Verb

Step 1 The simple subject (a noun or pronoun) is written on the line on the left side. The simple predicate (a verb or a verb phrase) is written on the line on the right side.

Directions Look at the steps above and the example below. Diagram the sentences below using the blank diagrams.

(EXAMPLE) Ladies talk. Ladies | talk

1. Stars shine.
2. Horses trot.
3. Deer run.
4. Babies sleep.
5. Dogs howl.

© American Guidance Service, Inc. Permission is granted to reproduce for classroom use only. ⏺ English to Use

TRL

Lesson at a Glance

Chapter 1 Lesson 3

Overview This lesson introduces adjectives, including articles.

Objectives
- To identify an adjective's purpose in describing a noun
- To locate an adjective in a three-word sentence
- To identify articles as a specific type of adjective

Student Pages 8–9

Teacher's Resource Library **TRL**

Workbook Activity 3

Activity 3

Alternative Activity 3

Sentence Diagramming Activity 3

Vocabulary
adjective
article

 Warm-Up Activity

Point to objects in the classroom and have students tell you what the objects look, smell, sound, or feel like. Write the words on the board as students provide them. Then review the definition of *adjective* and explain how adjectives provide more information about nouns.

 Teaching the Lesson

Have students review the example. Point out to them that the word *good* answers the question "what kind of team?" As students work through the activities, have them first identify the nouns in the exercises. Then they can answer the question "what kind of?" to locate the adjective.

Activity A Answers
1. (Little) birds sing. 2. (Hungry) wolves howl. 3. (White) clouds float. 4. (Big) ships sail. 5. (Empty) cars sit.

Adjective
A word that describes a noun

An **adjective** is a part of speech. Adjectives describe nouns. An adjective gives information about a noun.

EXAMPLE

Good teams win.
| | | |
adjective noun verb

Parts of speech	*adjective noun verb*
Sentence parts	subject | predicate
Sentence pattern	subject + verb

(*Teams* is a noun. *Good* is an adjective used to describe the noun *teams*. *Good* tells what kind of teams.)

Activity A Write each sentence on your paper. Circle the adjectives. Draw a line under each noun. All these sentences use the subject + verb pattern.

1. Little birds sing.
2. Hungry wolves howl.
3. White clouds float.
4. Big ships sail.
5. Empty cars sit.

Nouns can have many adjectives that describe them.

EXAMPLE Friendly, happy, noisy children played.

Activity B Write each sentence on your paper. Circle the adjectives. Draw a line under each noun.

1. Long, yellow pencils break.
2. Ripe, red apples fall.
3. Strong, young women win.
4. Loud cars race.
5. Weary men sleep.

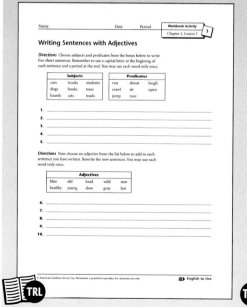

Workbook Activity 3

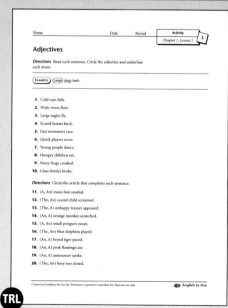

Activity 3

Article
A word that points out a noun

A, *an,* and *the* are **articles.** Articles are adjectives. Articles point out nouns. Use *an* before words beginning with *a, e, i, o, u,* and sometimes *h.* Use *a* before words beginning with the other letters. Use *the* before any letter.

EXAMPLE An ant crawls.   A frog jumps.   The wind blows.

Use *an* before words beginning in *h* only when the *h* is silent. Use *a* before words beginning in *h* when the *h* is pronounced.

Activity C Write the article that belongs with each sentence on your paper.

1. (A, An) deer runs.
2. (An, A) old man sleeps.
3. (An, The) best team wins.
4. (The, A) egg hatches.
5. (The, An) summer breeze blows.

Activity D Add an adjective to each sentence. You may choose from the list below or think of your own. Write the complete sentences on your paper.

a	good	loud	the
an	great	old	tired
big	healthy	pretty	wild
brave	little	strong	young

1. _____ sirens squeal.
2. _____ people walk.
3. _____ bug crawls.
4. _____ flowers bloom.
5. _____ horses run.
6. _____ artist draws.
7. _____ soldiers fight.
8. _____ farmers plant.
9. _____ athletes run.
10. _____ singers perform.

Building Sentences   Chapter 1   **9**

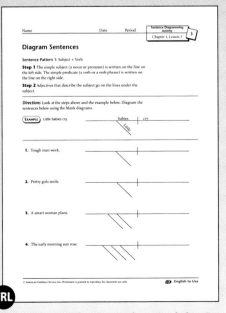

Activity B Answers
1. Long, yellow pencils break.
2. Ripe, red apples fall. 3. Strong, young women win. 4. Loud cars race. 5. Weary men sleep.

Activity C Answers
1. A 2. An 3. The 4. The 5. The

Activity D Answers
Answers will vary.

 Reinforce and Extend

LEARNING STYLES

Auditory/Verbal
Discuss with students the way in which many different words can describe the state or condition of an object. For example, you might describe an object that is extremely large as *big, huge,* or *gigantic.* Organize the class into small groups and have each group pick an object to describe. Have the group first identify the object's general characteristics. Then ask the group to think of other words that have similar meanings. Each group should pick a volunteer to write the adjectives the group generates. When the groups have finished identifying adjectives, have them compare their lists with the rest of the class.

LEARNING STYLES

LEP/ESL
Point out to students that the use of *a* and *an* depends on the sounds that beginning letters make. Discuss examples of words that begin with the letter *h,* such as *hungry* and *honest,* and help language learners hear the difference in the *h* sounds. Discuss with students any letters that might have more than one sound in their own language or that have a different sound when used in English. Model the letter *j* in Spanish and discuss the contrast between its pronunciation in Spanish and English.

Chapter 1 Lesson 4

Overview This lesson defines *verb* and *action verb* and explains the use of verbs in the predicate of a sentence.

Objectives

■ To identify an action verb in a very short sentence

■ To create sentences with one-word predicates

■ To review adjectives and nouns

Student Pages 10–11

Teacher's Resource Library

Workbook Activity 4

Activity 4

Alternative Activity 4

Sentence Diagramming Activity 4

Vocabulary

action verb

verb

---

1 Warm-Up Activity

Have students complete the following statement and write their responses on the board: "After school I like to _____ and _____." Tell students that the words they use to complete the statement are action verbs. Emphasize that a verb indicates what the subject of a sentence does.

2 Teaching the Lesson

Invite volunteers to act out some of the sentences. Review the strategies students used to find the subject of a sentence. Discuss how they can locate the verb by asking, "What does the subject do?"

Activity A Answers

1. <u>crows</u> 2. <u>rises</u> 3. <u>clangs</u> 4. <u>sings</u>
5. <u>dawns</u>

Verb
A word that shows action

Action verb
A word that tells what the subject of a sentence does

A **verb** is a word that shows action. Verbs tell what is happening in a sentence. The predicate of a sentence always has a verb.

Action verbs tell what the subject does.

 EXAMPLE

	Good teams win.
Parts of speech	adjective noun verb
Sentence parts	subject | predicate
Sentence pattern	subject + verb

(*Win* tells what the teams do. *Win* is an action verb.)

Activity A Write each sentence on your paper. Draw a line under each action verb.

1. The red rooster crows.   4. A lonely bird sings.
2. The golden sun rises.   5. A new day dawns.
3. An old, rusty bell clangs.

Action verbs do not always show action or movement.

EXAMPLE The tired child sleeps.
(*Sleeps* is an action verb. It does not show action or movement, but it still tells what the child—the subject—does.)

Activity B Write each sentence on your paper. Draw a line under each action verb.

1. The gray kitten breathes.   4. An athlete rests.
2. The drowsy owls stare.   5. Little children dream.
3. A wise old man sits.

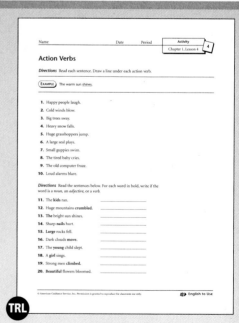

Workbook Activity 4   Activity 4

Writing Tip

Choosing colorful words helps your writing come alive for readers. When you write, use an on-line thesaurus to find vivid verbs to tell about actions.

Activity C Complete each sentence with an action verb that makes sense. Choose one of the verbs in the box below or think of your own. Write the complete sentences on your paper.

cries	strikes	sets	laughs
rises	hops	reads	jokes
grows	races	studies	plays

1. The white rabbit _____ .

2. The red sun _____ .

3. A lost child _____ .

4. The student _____ .

5. Bright lightning _____ .

Activity D Write each sentence on your paper. Label each word a noun (*n.*), an adjective (*adj.*), or a verb (*v.*).

Example An eel slithers.
              adj. n.   v.

1. The young racehorse trots.

2. A fat robin chirps.

3. An owl sleeps.

4. A friend waves.

5. A black kitten drinks.

Activity E Write the answer to each question.

1. What does a noun tell?

2. What does an adjective tell?

3. What three words are articles?

4. What does a verb tell?

5. What does an action verb tell?

Building Sentences   *Chapter 1*   **11**

Activity B Answers

1. breathes 2. stare 3. sits 4. rests
5. dream

Activity C Answers

Answers will vary.

Activity D Answers

1. Adj.—The, young; N—racehorse;
V—trots 2. Adj.—A, fat; N—robin;
V—chirps 3. Adj.—An; N—owl;
V—sleeps 4. Adj.—A; N—friend;
V—waves 5. Adj.—A, black;
N—kitten; V—drinks

Activity E Answers

1. the name of a person, place, or thing 2. tells about a noun 3. *a*, *an*, and *the* 4. tells about action 5. what the subject of a sentence does

3 Reinforce and Extend

GLOBAL CONNECTION

Ask students who are familiar with other languages to describe how other languages use verbs. Compare this usage with English. For example, some languages do not have the same verb tenses; other languages place verbs in a special place in the sentence. Ask volunteers to model a verb from another language and then compare it with English usage.

IN THE COMMUNITY

Have students gather information about businesses in the school neighborhood. Students can find the names of businesses from newspapers, the telephone book, or by walking around the school. After students have made a list of businesses, have them choose verbs to describe what each business does. When students have completed their lists, have them copy the lists on the board. Note that more than one verb may describe some businesses, for example, *Lee's Restaurant cooks and bakes.* You may have students compile their lists into a local directory.

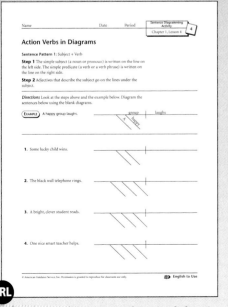

TRL

Sentence Diagramming Activity 4

Building Sentences   *Chapter 1*   **11**

Lesson at a Glance

Chapter 1 Lesson 5

Overview This lesson introduces adverbs as words that add meaning to a verb, focusing on those adverbs that answer the question "how?"

Objectives

- To identify adverbs that tell how an action happened
- To identify adverbs as part of the predicate
- To identify *good* as an adjective and *well* as an adverb

Student Pages 12–13

Teacher's Resource Library **TRL**

Workbook Activity 5

Activity 5

Alternative Activity 5

Sentence Diagramming Activity 5

Vocabulary

adverb

---

1 Warm-Up Activity

Write these sentences on the board: *She finished the project _____. He worked on his experiment _____.*
Ask students to think of words that complete the sentences. Tell students that the words that fit in the blank are adverbs. They describe verbs, adjectives, and other adverbs.

2 Teaching the Lesson

As students work through Activities C and D, have them discuss other strategies for locating adverbs. Write a list of easily confused adverbs and adjectives on the board, including *good/well, bad/badly,* and *real/really.* Have students take turns using these words in sentences.

Adverb
A word that describes a verb, an adjective, or another adverb

An **adverb** is a word that describes a verb, an adjective, or another adverb. When an adverb describes a verb, it tells how, when, or where. In this lesson, adverbs tell *how* about verbs.

EXAMPLE

	Good teams practice eagerly.
Parts of speech	*adj. noun verb adverb*
Sentence parts	subject | predicate
Sentence pattern	subject + verb

(The adverb *eagerly* tells **how** good teams practice. *Eagerly* is an adverb that describes the verb *practice*. *Eagerly* is part of the predicate.)

Activity A Write each sentence on your paper. Circle each adverb. Draw a line under the verb it tells about.

1. The brown deer ran swiftly.
2. The train whistle blows loudly.
3. The snow falls quickly.
4. The bus moves rapidly.
5. The couple dances gracefully.

All of the adverbs in Activity A come after the verb. Adverbs do not always come after a verb. An adverb that describes the verb is always part of the predicate, no matter where the adverb is in the sentence.

EXAMPLE

	The red fox | ran swiftly.
Parts of speech	*adj. adj.noun verb adverb*
Sentence parts	subject | predicate

subject

Swiftly, \| the red fox \| ran.

predicate

(The adverb *swiftly* tells **how** about the verb *ran* in both sentences. *Swiftly* is separated from the verb *ran* in the second sentence, but it is still part of the predicate.)

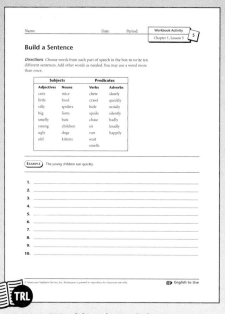

Activity B Write the Activity A sentences again. This time, begin each sentence with the adverb.

All of the adverbs in Activity A end in -*ly*. Some examples of adverbs that do not end in -*ly* are *fast, hard,* and *well.* These adverbs usually come after the verb.

Activity C Write each sentence on your paper. Draw a line under the verb. Circle the adverb.

1. The whole team plays hard.
2. The track star runs fast.
3. The man dresses well.
4. The teacher spoke fast.
5. The young people work hard.

People sometimes mix up the words *good* and *well. Good* is usually an adjective. *Well* is usually an adverb.

Activity D In these sentences, *well* is an adverb and *good* is an adjective. Write these sentences on your paper. Label each word a noun (*n.*), a verb (*v.*), an adjective (*adj.*), or an adverb (*adv.*).

Example   The new car runs well.
                  adj. adj. n.   v. adv.

1. A good idea does well.
2. Good steak cooks well.
3. A good old recipe works well.
4. A good student learns well.
5. A good car drives well.

Writing Tip

Besides *good* and *well,* people often confuse *bad* and *badly* and *real* and *really. Bad* and *real* are adjectives. *Badly* and *really* are adverbs.

Activity A Answers

1. The brown deer ran (swiftly.)
2. The train whistle blows (loudly.)
3. The snow falls (quickly.) 4. The bus moves (rapidly.) 5. The couple dances (gracefully.)

Activity B Answers

1. Swiftly, the brown deer ran.
2. Loudly, the train whistle blows.
3. Quickly, the snow falls.
4. Rapidly, the bus moves.
5. Gracefully, the couple dances.

Activity C Answers

1. The whole team plays (hard.)
2. The track star runs (fast.) 3. The man dresses (well.) 4. The teacher spoke (fast.) 5. The young people work (hard.)

Activity D Answers

1. Adj.—A, good; N—idea; V—does; Adv.—well 2. Adj.—Good; N—steak; V—cooks; Adv.—well 3. Adj.—A, good, old; N—recipe; V—works; Adv.—well 4. Adj.—A, good; N—student; V—learns; Adv.—well 5. Adj.—A, good; N—car; V—drives; Adv.—well

3 Reinforce and Extend

AT HOME

Ask students to cut out a picture from a magazine or newspaper and list nouns, adjectives, verbs, and adverbs that could describe the scene. Have students bring the pictures and lists to class. Have each student use these materials to write a short paragraph or story about the picture.

Name _____ Date _____ Period _____   **Sentence Diagramming Activity** 5
                                          Chapter 1, Lesson 5

Diagram Sentences with Adverbs

Sentence Pattern 1: Subject + Verb

Step 1 The simple subject (a noun or pronoun) is written on the line on the left side. The simple predicate (a verb or a verb phrase) is written on the line on the right side.

Step 2 Adjectives that describe the subject go on the lines under the subject.

Step 3 Adverbs that tell about the verb go on the lines under the verb.

Directions Look at the steps above and the example below. Diagram the sentences below using the blank diagrams.

(EXAMPLE) Wet clothes dry slowly.   clothes | dry

1. The old movie theater opened early.

2. Little Nikki runs fast.

3. The three men dress well.

4. Cold, wet rain fell yesterday.

© American Guidance Service, Inc. Permission is granted to reproduce for classroom use only.   **English to Use**

TRL

Chapter 1 Lesson 6

Overview This lesson focuses on the study of adverbs that answer the question "when?"

Objectives

■ To identify adverbs that tell when an action happened

■ To review adverbs as part of the predicate, regardless of position in the sentence

Student Pages 14–15

Teacher's Resource Library

Workbook Activity 6

Activity 6

Alternative Activity 6

Sentence Diagramming Activity 6

 Warm-Up Activity

Explain that this lesson focuses on adverbs that answer the question "when?" about verbs. Discuss the sentence in the example box and explain that *daily* tells *when* the teams practice. Ask students to think of other words that could tell *when* in this sentence (*weekly, often, frequently*).

 Teaching the Lesson

Review with students what they have learned about adverbs. Point out that all the rules about adverbs that tell *how* apply to adverbs that tell *when*.

 Reinforce and Extend

LEARNING STYLES

Interpersonal/ Group Learning

Have students work in small groups to expand the two-word sentences they analyzed in Lesson 1. Ask student groups to add *how* or *when* adverbs to the sentences in Activity A. When student groups have finished, have them read their sentences aloud to the rest of the class.

Adverbs tell how, when, or where an action happens. In this lesson, adverbs tell *when* about verbs.

EXAMPLE

The good teams practice daily.

Parts of speech	*adj.*	*adj.*	*noun*	*verb*	*adverb*
Sentence parts	subject	predicate			
Sentence pattern	subject + verb				

(*Daily* is an adverb that describes the verb *practice*. *Daily* tells **when** the good teams practice.)

Activity A Write each sentence on your paper. Circle each adverb. Draw a line under each verb.

1. The jet plane lands today.
2. The wide river floods often.
3. The guest arrives tomorrow.
4. The old bus stops twice.
5. The TV show runs late.
6. A good worker tries again.
7. The mail comes early.
8. The morning paper comes late.
9. A good friend arrives today.
10. The clock stops sometimes.
11. The store closes soon.
12. The sick child coughs often.
13. A little girl laughs first.
14. A kind nurse visits daily.
15. The angry dog barks now.

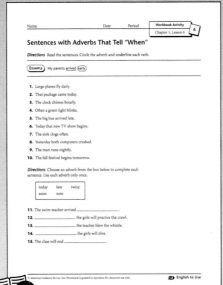

Workbook Activity 6

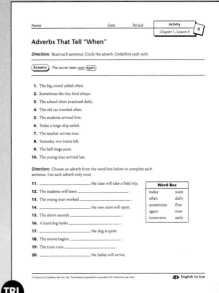

Activity 6

As you learned in Lesson 5, adverbs do not always come after the verb. Some sentences begin with adverbs.

EXAMPLE   Today, the helicopter lands.
(*Today* is an adverb telling when the helicopter lands.)

Activity B   Write the Activity A sentences again. Begin each sentence with the adverb. Write the new sentences on your paper.

Sometimes adverbs come right before the verb.

EXAMPLE   The detectives often travel.
(*Often* is an adverb telling when the detectives travel.)

A sentence can have more than one adverb. Adverbs can begin or end a sentence. An adverb can come before or after the verb.

EXAMPLE   The train always arrives late. Travelers wait sometimes. Often travelers leave.

Activity C   Write each sentence on your paper. Circle each adverb. Draw a line under each verb. Some sentences may have more than one adverb.

1. The baseball game starts late.
2. The pitcher suddenly throws.
3. The batter swings once.
4. A player runs fast.
5. Soon the best team wins.
6. The band sometimes practices daily.
7. Often, the drummer arrives first.
8. Twice, the guitar player came early.
9. The band always practices late.
10. Tomorrow, the band has a show.

Activity A Answers

1. The jet plane <u>lands</u> (today.) **2.** The wide river <u>floods</u> (often.) **3.** The guest <u>arrives</u> (tomorrow.) **4.** The old bus <u>stops</u> (twice.) **5.** The TV show <u>runs</u> (late.) **6.** A good worker <u>tries</u> (again.) **7.** The mail <u>comes</u> (early.) **8.** The morning paper <u>comes</u> (late.) **9.** A good friend <u>arrives</u> (today.) **10.** The clock <u>stops</u> (sometimes.) **11.** The store <u>closes</u> (soon.) **12.** The sick child <u>coughs</u> (often.) **13.** A little girl <u>laughs</u> (first.) **14.** A kind nurse <u>visits</u> (daily.) **15.** The angry dog <u>barks</u> (now.)

Activity B Answers

1. Today, the jet plane lands.
2. Often, the wide river floods.
3. Tomorrow, the guest arrives.
4. Twice, the old bus stops. **5.** Late, the TV show runs. **6.** Again, a good worker tries. **7.** Early, the mail comes. **8.** Late, the morning paper comes. **9.** Today, a good friend arrives. **10.** Sometimes, the clock stops. **11.** Soon, the store closes.
12. Often, the sick child coughs.
13. First, a little girl laughs.
14. Daily, a kind nurse visits.
15. Now, the angry dog barks.

Activity C Answers

1. The baseball <u>game</u> <u>starts</u> (late.) **2.** The pitcher (suddenly) <u>throws</u>. **3.** The batter <u>swings</u> (once.) **4.** A player <u>runs</u> (fast.) **5.** (Soon) the best team <u>wins</u>. **6.** The band (sometimes) <u>practices</u> (daily.) **7.** (Often,) the drummer <u>arrives</u> (first.) **8.** (Twice,) the guitar player <u>came</u> (early.) **9.** The band (always) <u>practices</u> (late.) **10.** (Tomorrow,) the band <u>has</u> a show.

LEARNING STYLES

Logical/Mathematical Learning

Have students work in pairs to describe how to perform a task, such as tying shoelaces or performing a computer function. Students should describe a series of steps from beginning to end, all done in the proper sequence. As students develop the sequence for the tasks, they should note which adverbs they use to tell *when*. Ask volunteers to perform their descriptions for the class and have the audience write the words they hear that tell *when*.

Chapter 1 Lesson 7

Overview This lesson continues the study of adverbs, focusing on adverbs that answer the question "where?"

Objectives

■ To identify adverbs that tell where an action happened

■ To distinguish among adverbs that tell *how, when,* or *where*

Student Pages 16–17

Teacher's Resource Library **TRL**

Workbook Activity 7

Activity 7

Alternative Activity 7

Sentence Diagramming Activity 7

1 Warm-Up Activity

Ask students to complete this sentence with adverbs that tell *where:* "I walked the dog _____." Have students take turns completing the sentence and write their answers on the board. Explain that this lesson will help students identify a third type of adverb, one that tells *where.*

2 Teaching the Lesson

With the class, read the example and go over the parts of speech. Make sure that students understand that the word *there* answers the question "Where did the teams play?"

Activity A Answers

1. V—goes; Adv.—on 2. V—falls; Adv.—down 3. V—drives; Adv.—nearby 4. V—sits; Adv.—downstairs 5. V—flies; Adv.—above 6. V—goes; Adv.—out 7. V—rests; Adv.—upstairs 8. V—discuss; Adv.—here 9. V—barks; Adv.—outside 10. V—speed; Adv.—by 11. V—stays; Adv.—inside 12. V—points; Adv.—there 13. V—flew; Adv.—around 14. V—follows; Adv.—along 15. V—goes; Adv.—below

---

Lesson	7	Adverbs Tell "Where"

Adverbs tell how, when, or where an action happens. In this lesson, adverbs tell *where* about verbs.

> **EXAMPLE**
>
> The good teams play there.
> | | | | | |
> Parts of speech   *adj. adj. noun verb adverb*
> Sentence parts   subject | predicate
> Sentence pattern subject + verb
> (*There* tells where the good teams play. *There* is an adverb that describes the verb *play.*)

Activity A Write each sentence on your paper. Circle the adverb. Draw a line under the verb.

1. Life goes on.
2. A football player falls down.
3. The fire truck drives nearby.
4. The computer sits downstairs.
5. An airplane flies above.
6. A young couple goes out.
7. A sick man rests upstairs.
8. We discuss new topics here.
9. A big dog barks outside.
10. The days speed by.
11. The cat stays inside.
12. The tall woman points there.
13. A small plane flew around.
14. The group follows along.
15. The sleepy captain goes below.

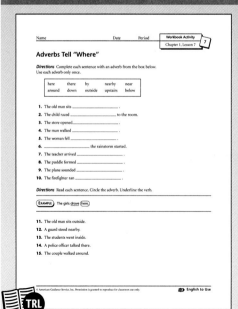

Workbook Activity 7

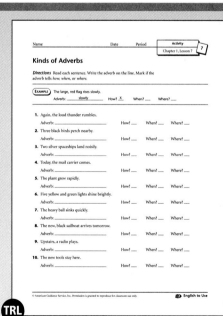

Activity 7

Activity B Read each sentence and find each adverb. Write each adverb on your paper. Write whether the adverb tells *how, when,* or *where.* Some sentences may have more than one adverb.

1. Suddenly, news arrives.
2. People often talk.
3. News travels fast.
4. Ships rarely sink.
5. Often, planes arrive early.
6. Space shuttles speed skyward.
7. Good news reads well.
8. Trains run slowly.
9. Speed records move up quickly.
10. Sometimes, the computer screen goes blank.

Activity C Number your paper from 1 to 10. Read each sentence and find all the adverbs. Write the adverbs on your paper. Some sentences may have more than one adverb.

1. Tonight, the late TV show starts early.
2. The old movie stars act well.
3. The pilot flies alone.
4. His instruments work poorly.
5. His fuel runs low.
6. Suddenly, a rescue ship comes.
7. The pilot leaves safely.
8. Finally, he smiles happily.
9. Then the TV show ends quickly.
10. The silly ad runs twice.

Activity B Answers

1. Suddenly—how 2. often—when
3. fast—how 4. rarely—when
5. Often—when, early—when
6. skyward—where 7. well—how
8. slowly—how 9. up—where, quickly—how 10. Sometimes—when

Activity C Answers

1. Tonight, early 2. well 3. alone
4. poorly 5. low 6. Suddenly
7. safely 8. Finally, happily 9. Then, quickly 10. twice

 Reinforce and Extend

LEARNING STYLES

 Visual/Spatial
Display a large map in front of the class and point to your city or state. Then point to other cities and states on the map and have students suggest adverbs that describe the location of these places in relation to your location. Students should identify adverbs such as *below, beside, near, far, up,* and *down.* Ask a volunteer to keep a list of the *where* adverbs on the board.

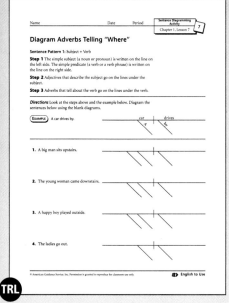

Sentence Diagramming Activity 7

Lesson at a Glance

Chapter 1 Lesson 8

Overview This lesson explains complete and simple subjects and complete and simple predicates.

Objectives

- To identify simple and complete subjects
- To identify simple and complete predicates

Student Pages 18–19

Teacher's Resource Library

Workbook Activity 8

Activity 8

Alternative Activity 8

Sentence Diagramming Activity 8

Vocabulary

complete predicate
complete subject
simple predicate
simple subject

----

 1 Warm-Up Activity

On the board, write several two-word sentences. Ask students to identify the parts of speech. Tell students that these nouns and verbs are all that they need to form sentences. Then ask students how they could make the sentences more interesting and ask them to suggest adjectives and adverbs to add to the sentences. Compare the new sentences to the original ones.

 2 Teaching the Lesson

Review both the examples on page 18, going over the differences between simple subjects and predicates and complete subjects and predicates. Review the way in which words describing the simple subject will be part of the complete subject. Similarly, words that describe the simple predicate will be part of the complete predicate.

Lesson 8 — Complete and Simple Sentence Parts

Complete subject	The whole part of a sentence that tells who or what the sentence is about
Simple subject	One or more subject nouns or pronouns in a sentence
Complete predicate	The whole part of a sentence that tells what the subject is doing
Simple predicate	One or more verbs in a sentence

You have learned that every sentence has a subject and a predicate. The **complete subject** is the whole part of the sentence that tells who or what the sentence is about. The **simple subject** is the one or more main nouns or pronouns in the sentence.

The **complete predicate** is the whole part of the sentence that tells what the subject is doing. The **simple predicate** is the one or more main verbs in the predicate.

EXAMPLE   Good, strong teams play hard.
Sentence parts   subject | predicate
(*Teams* is the simple subject. *Good, strong teams* is the complete subject. *Play* is the simple predicate. *Play hard* is the complete predicate.)

Sometimes the simple subject is also the complete subject. Sometimes the simple predicate is also the complete predicate.

EXAMPLE   Teams play.
Sentence parts   subject | predicate
(*Teams* is the simple subject and also the complete subject. *Play* is the simple predicate and also the complete predicate.)

Activity A Write each sentence on your paper. Draw a line under the complete subject. Circle the complete predicate.

1. The rusty car clatters loudly.
2. A skilled worker finishes quickly.
3. The old bicycle breaks suddenly.
4. The tired men work hard.
5. The summer sun shines brightly.

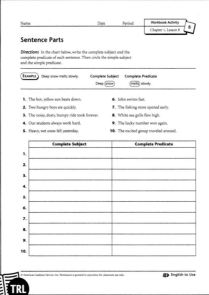

Workbook Activity 8

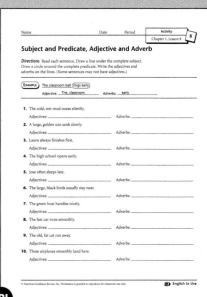

Activity 8

Teams

play.

Teams play.

Activity B The complete subject is underlined in each of the following sentences. Number your paper from 1 to 5. Write the simple subject in each complete subject.

1. <u>The black smoke</u> drifts up.
2. <u>A red car</u> stops suddenly.
3. <u>The new clothes</u> fit nicely.
4. <u>A hungry cat</u> eats quickly.
5. <u>A graceful white swan</u> swims fast.

Activity C The complete predicate is underlined in each of the following sentences. Number your paper from 1 to 5. Write the simple predicate in each complete predicate.

1. The kind teacher <u>grades easily</u>.
2. The sharp pencil <u>writes well</u>.
3. The old jeans <u>fade nicely</u>.
4. The large theater <u>quickly fills</u>.
5. The orange leaves <u>fall slowly</u>.

Activity D Copy these sentences on your paper. Underline the complete subject once and the complete predicate twice. Circle the simple subject and simple predicate.

1. The large mall fills quickly.
2. A bright, young couple shops carefully.
3. The small child cries loudly.
4. Shiny, new products sell easily.
5. A polite guard helps quietly.

Activity A Answers

1. <u>The rusty car</u> clatters loudly.
2. <u>A skilled worker</u> finishes quickly.
3. <u>The old bicycle</u> breaks suddenly.
4. <u>The tired men</u> work hard. 5. <u>The summer sun</u> shines brightly.

Activity B Answers

1. smoke 2. car 3. clothes 4. cat
5. swan

Activity C Answers

1. grades 2. writes 3. fade 4. fills
5. fall

Activity D Answers

1. <u>The large</u> mall fills quickly.
2. <u>A bright, young</u> couple shops carefully.
3. <u>The small</u> child cries loudly.
4. Shiny, new products sell easily.
5. A polite guard helps quietly.

3 ## Reinforce and Extend

LEARNING STYLES

Body/Kinesthetic
In Activity D, assign each student a word from sentences 1–5. Then have students arrange themselves to form human "sentences." After students have arranged themselves in order, have the students in the "sentences" first tell their part of speech and then "read" themselves aloud. After students have "read" their sentence, the students who are the simple subjects and simple predicates should step forward and identify themselves. Then the students who are the complete subjects and complete predicates should organize into two groups. Students in the audience may want to question individual "words" to find out why they are in one group or the other.

ASL ILLUSTRATION

Have the class practice together making the ASL sign illustrated on page 19. Have students keep a list of the ASL signs they learn in a notebook. Later in the year, students may want to combine the signs they have learned to hold short conversations.

TRL

Sentence Diagramming Activity 8

Lesson at a Glance

Chapter 1 Lesson 9

Overview This lesson presents the concept of sentence fragments and contrasts them with complete sentences.

Objectives
- To identify complete sentences
- To create complete sentences from fragments

Student Pages 20–21

Teacher's Resource Library
Workbook Activity 9
Activity 9
Alternative Activity 9

....

Vocabulary
fragment

....

 1 Warm-Up Activity

Begin a discussion about a popular topic. Speak in incomplete sentences, perhaps leaving out verbs or subjects. Ask students whether they are confused. Then tell them that a sentence fragment does the same thing: it leaves out vital information and confuses readers.

 2 Teaching the Lesson

Have students study the examples and consider the reasons these groups of words are fragments and not sentences. Then have students suggest words that will convert the example fragments to complete sentences.

Activity A Answers

1. Kites fly. 4. Other people watch.
7. The boys play. 9. The wind blows.
10. Children run. 11. It goes far.
14. Cars race. 16. Friends cheer.
17. The day ends. 18. Adults relax.
20. Everybody sleeps.

Lesson 9 Sentence or Fragment?

Fragment
A group of words that is not a complete sentence

Not every group of words tells a complete idea. A group of words that does not tell a complete idea is a **fragment.** A fragment is missing a subject or a predicate. Because a fragment does not tell a complete idea, it is not a sentence.

EXAMPLE　**Fragment**　　Good, strong teams.
(What happened to *Good, strong teams?* This fragment is missing a predicate.)
Fragment　　Play hard.
(Who or what *Play hard?* This fragment is missing a subject.)
Sentence　　Good, strong teams play hard.

Activity A On your paper, write the groups of words that are complete sentences. Begin each sentence with a capital letter. End each sentence with a period.

1. kites fly
2. the young people
3. small, distant kites
4. other people watch
5. long kite string
6. flying high
7. the boys play
8. clear, sunny day
9. the wind blows
10. children run
11. it goes far
12. fun there
13. new cars
14. cars race
15. the finish line
16. friends cheer
17. the day ends
18. adults relax
19. a dark night
20. everybody sleeps

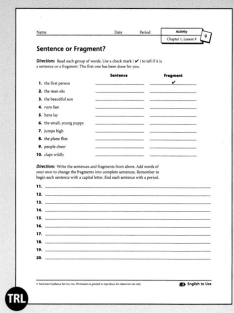

Workbook Activity 9　　　　　**Activity 9**

Activity B Decide whether each group of words is missing a subject or a predicate. Complete each fragment and write it as a sentence on your paper.

1. a tall, thin boy

2. drove yesterday

3. dropped quickly

4. the happy woman

5. big, white waves

Activity C Read the short passage. Then follow the directions.

A big, red kite. An old green kite rises slowly. Suddenly, the long string breaks. Disappears quickly.

1. Find two fragments in the passage. Copy them on your paper. Next to each fragment, write whether it is missing a subject or a predicate.

2. Complete each fragment to make it a sentence. Add a subject or predicate. Write the new sentences on your paper.

3. Find two complete sentences in the passage. Copy them on your paper.

4. Underline the complete subject once and the complete predicate twice in each of the complete sentences. Circle each simple subject and simple predicate.

5. On your paper, rewrite the passage using your new sentences.

Activity B Answers

Sentences will vary, but all should add either a subject or a predicate to the fragment. Check to see that each sentence begins with a capital letter and ends with a period, question mark, or exclamation point.
1. missing predicate 2. missing subject 3. missing subject
4. missing predicate 5. missing predicate

Activity C Answers

1. A big, red kite.—missing predicate; Disappears quickly.—missing subject 2. Sentences will vary. 3. An old green kite rises slowly. Suddenly, the long string breaks. 4. An old green kite rises slowly. Suddenly, the long string breaks. 5. Passages will vary.

Speaking Practice

Discuss with students the way in which sentence fragments often appear in informal speech. For example, people respond to a question such as "Where are you going?" with a fragment such as "to the store" or "back to school." Ask students to listen for sentence fragments at home and in school and to write them down. When students bring their sentence fragments to class for discussion, have them explain how the fragments did or did not make sense in the context of the conversation.

 3 **Reinforce and Extend**

 CAREER CONNECTION

Point out to students that the confusion caused by sentence fragments could be costly, or even dangerous, in the workplace. Have students identify some jobs that require clear and precise written instructions. Then have students work in pairs to dramatize a scene in which a fragment causes confusion in the workplace. Make sure that students explain why their particular workplace requires clear instructions.

Chapter 1 Lesson 10

Overview This lesson reviews the mechanics of writing sentences and explains when to use commas with adjectives and adverbs.

Objectives

■ To capitalize the first letter in a sentence

■ To punctuate with periods and commas

Student Pages 22–23

Teacher's Resource Library TRL

Workbook Activity 10

Activity 10

Alternative Activity 10

Vocabulary

comma (,)
punctuation

1 Warm-Up Activity

With a volunteer, act out buying a bottle of juice at a store. Use customary greetings and courtesy words. With another volunteer, act out the same scenario, leaving out the greetings and courtesy words. Discuss with students how *hello, goodbye, please,* and *thank you* indicate a conversation, marking when we start and stop.

Tell students that writing mechanics are markers that tell readers whether they are at the beginning, middle, or end of a sentence.

2 Teaching the Lesson

Discuss how commas add types of pauses in sentences. Have a volunteer read the first example without the comma. Discuss how *new* seems to describe *red*, which does not make sense. Show students how the added comma tells readers that *new* describes *truck*.

Punctuation

Marks in a sentence that tell readers when to pause or stop

Comma (,)

A punctuation mark used to set apart one or more words

You have learned that each sentence begins with a capital letter and ends with a period, a question mark, or an exclamation point. These marks are types of **punctuation.** Punctuation marks are marks that tell readers when to pause or stop.

Commas are another kind of punctuation. We use them in a sentence to set apart one or more words. A comma tells you to pause briefly.

A comma can separate two or more adjectives in a sentence.

EXAMPLE   The new, red truck crashed.
(The comma separates *new* and *red*. New and *red* are two adjectives that tell about the noun *truck*.)

Activity A Write each sentence on your paper. Add commas to separate adjectives.

1. A beautiful sunny day dawned.

2. The young lean athlete ran.

3. The excited friendly crowd cheered.

4. A new happy coach watched.

5. The bright shiny medal sparkled.

You can use a comma after an adverb at the beginning of a sentence.

EXAMPLE   Cheerfully, the bird sang.
(The comma separates the adverb *cheerfully* from the rest of the sentence.)

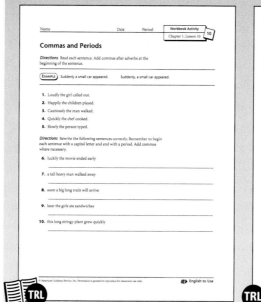

Workbook Activity 10

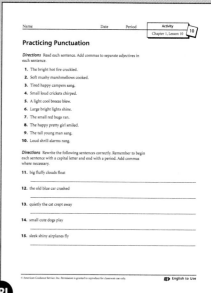

Activity 10

Activity B Write each sentence on your paper. Add commas after adverbs at the beginning of sentences.

1. Sadly the lost boy cries.

2. Immediately a police officer arrives.

3. Soon a crowd gathers around.

4. Nervously the parents search.

5. Happily the family hugs.

Activity C Write each sentence on your paper. Add commas where necessary.

1. The long winding road curves sharply.

2. Usually people drive slowly.

3. A new young driver crashes.

4. Luckily the driver walks away.

5. Softly the driver apologizes.

Activity D Write the following sentences on your paper. Begin each sentence with a capital letter. End each sentence with a period. Add commas where necessary.

1. dark heavy clouds gather

2. loud noisy thunder crashes

3. soon lightning strikes

4. the scared worried people rush inside

5. suddenly rain falls

Lightning strikes Earth fifty to one hundred times every second of the day.

Activity A Answers

1. beautiful, sunny 2. young, lean
3. excited, friendly 4. new, happy
5. bright, shiny

Activity B Answers

1. Sadly, the lost boy cries.
2. Immediately, a police officer arrives. 3. Soon, a crowd gathers around. 4. Nervously, the parents search. 5. Happily, the family hugs.

Activity C Answers

1. The long, winding road curves sharply. 2. Usually, people drive slowly. 3. A new, young driver crashes. 4. Luckily, the driver walks away. 5. Softly, the driver apologizes.

Activity D Answers

1. Dark, heavy clouds gather.
2. Loud, noisy thunder crashes.
3. Soon, lightning strikes. 4. The scared, worried people rush inside.
5. Suddenly, rain falls.

Using What You've Learned

After students have finished their descriptions, have them present the descriptions to the class. Ask presenters to share with the class their interest in the activity described. Then have students explain how and why they chose particular action verbs and adverbs. Allow students to explain any special types of rules or movements in the activities they chose to describe and have them discuss why particular verbs and adverbs might be necessary in order for an audience to fully understand or appreciate the activity.

3 Reinforce and Extend

LEARNING STYLES

LEP/ESL
Ask English language learners to share examples of punctuation in other languages. Discuss the ways in which other types of punctuation can tell readers to stop, pause, or begin a new sentence. Invite volunteers to write on the board examples of different types or styles of punctuation.

Chapter 1 Review

Use the Chapter Review to prepare students for tests and to reteach content from the chapter.

Chapter 1 Mastery Test

The Teacher's Resource Library includes parallel forms of the Chapter 1 Mastery Test. The difficulty level of the two forms is equivalent. You may wish to use one form as a pretest and the other form as a posttest.

REVIEW ANSWERS

Part A

1. exclamation point **2.** sentence pattern **3.** predicate **4.** article **5.** period **6.** verb **7.** action verb **8.** subject **9.** question mark **10.** comma

Part B

11. The bright, blue truck slows down.

12. A young doctor studies quietly.

13. The new car stops suddenly.

14. The sleepy dog lies down.

Part C

15. N.: station; Adj.: The, radio; Adv.: softly (how) **16.** N.: videos; Adj.: Rock, music; Adv.: everywhere (where) **17.** N.: speakers; Adj.: The, old, worn-out, stereo; Adv.: loudly (how) **18.** N.: guitars; Adj.: New, electric; Adv.: well (how)

Chapter 1 REVIEW

Word Bank
action verb
article
comma
exclamation point
period
predicate
question mark
sentence pattern
subject
verb

Part A Use the words from the Word Bank to complete sentences 1–10.

1. A punctuation mark showing strong feeling is an _____ .

2. A _____ is the basic form of a sentence.

3. The part of a sentence that tells what the subject is doing is the _____ .

4. An _____ is a word that points out a noun.

5. A punctuation mark ending a sentence that makes a statement or gives a command is a _____ .

6. A _____ is a word that shows action.

7. A word that tells what the subject of a sentence does is an _____ .

8. The part of a sentence that tells who or what the sentence is about is the _____ .

9. A _____ is a punctuation mark that ends a sentence asking a question.

10. A _____ is a punctuation mark used to set apart one or more words.

Part B Write each sentence on your paper. Underline the complete subject. Circle the complete predicate.

11. The bright, blue truck slows down.

12. A young doctor studies quietly.

13. The new car stops suddenly.

14. The sleepy dog lies down.

Part C List the nouns, adjectives, and adverbs in these sentences on your paper. Some sentences may have more than one adjective. For each adverb, write whether it tells *how*, *when*, or *where*.

15. The radio station plays softly.

16. Rock music videos entertain everywhere.

17. The old, worn-out stereo speakers crackle loudly.

18. New electric guitars play well.

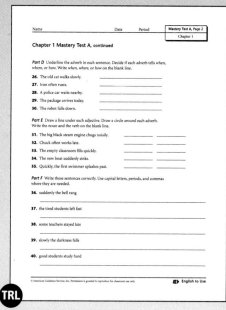

Chapter 1 Mastery Test A

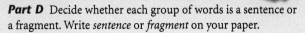

Part D Decide whether each group of words is a sentence or a fragment. Write *sentence* or *fragment* on your paper.

19. New music videos.

20. A new lamp.

21. Rusty hinges creak.

22. Computer software helps.

Part E Write each sentence correctly on your paper. The sentences need capital letters and end punctuation. Some sentences need commas.

23. the skillful builder works hard

24. the tired worker tries again

25. suddenly the new saw breaks

26. carefully the worker saws again

Part F On your paper, write the letter that correctly identifies the simple subject or simple predicate in each sentence.

27. The young boy shouts loudly. (simple subject)

    A The young boy   **C** young boy

    B boy   **D** shouts

28. The cold, hard wind blows. (simple subject)

    A The cold, hard wind   **C** cold, hard wind

    B blows   **D** wind

29. The wild wolves suddenly howl. (simple predicate)

    A The wild wolves   **C** howl

    B wolves   **D** suddenly howl

30. Slowly, snow falls. (simple predicate)

    A Slowly   **C** snow

    B Slowly falls   **D** falls

 **Test-Taking Tip** When answering multiple-choice questions, first identify the answers you know are incorrect.

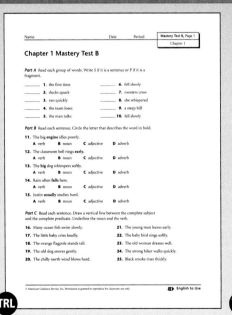

Planning Guide

Adding Prepositions

	Student Pages	Vocabulary	Practice Activities	Identification Skills	Writing Skills	Punctuation Skills
		Student Text Lesson			Language Skills	
Lesson 1 Prepositional Phrases	28–29	✔	✔	✔	✔	
Lesson 2 Adjective Prepositional Phrases	30–31	✔	✔	✔	✔	✔
Lesson 3 Confusing Subjects	32–33		✔	✔	✔	✔
Lesson 4 Adverb Prepositional Phrases	34–35	✔	✔	✔	✔	
Lesson 5 Preposition or Adverb?	36–37		✔	✔	✔	✔
Lesson 6 Two or More Prepositional Phrases	38–39		✔	✔	✔	
Lesson 7 Hidden Verbs	40–41	✔	✔	✔	✔	✔
Lesson 8 All Kinds of Prepositional Phrases	42–43		✔	✔	✔	✔
Lesson 9 Writing Mechanics	44–45	✔	✔	✔	✔	✔

Chapter Activities

Teacher's Resource Library
Community Connection 2:
Write a Journal About
Your Community
English in Your World 2:
Using Prepositions to Give Directions

Assessment Options

Student Text
Chapter 2 Review

Teacher's Resource Library
Chapter 2 Mastery Tests A and B

Student Text Features					Teaching Strategies					Learning Styles						Teacher's Resource Library				
ASL Illustration	Communication Connection	Notes	Using What You've Learned	Writing Tips	Teacher Alert	Online Connection	Applications (Home, Career, Community, Global)	Speaking Practice	Writing Practice	Auditory/Verbal	Body/Kinesthetic	Interpersonal/Group Learning	Logical/Mathematical	Visual/Spatial	LEP/ESL	Workbook Activities	Activities	Alternative Activities	Sentence Diagramming Activities	Self-Study Guide
29							29					29				11	11	11	9	✔
								31			31					12	12	12	10	✔
		✔											33		33	13	13	13	11	✔
35							35									14	14	14	12	✔
	37						37									15	15	15	13	✔
				✔					39	39						16	16	16	14	✔
			41			41										17	17	17	15	✔
				✔	43	43										18	18	18	16	✔
														45	45	19	19	19		✔

Pronunciation Key

a	hat	e	let	ī	ice	ô	order	ù	put	sh	she		a	in about
ā	age	ē	equal	o	hot	oi	oil	ü	rule	th	thin		e	in taken
ä	far	ér	term	ō	open	ou	out	ch	child	ŦH	then	ə	i	in pencil
â	care	i	it	ȯ	saw	u	cup	ng	long	zh	measure		o	in lemon
													u	in circus

Alternative Activities

The Teacher's Resource Library (TRL) contains a set of lower-level worksheets called Alternative Activities. These worksheets cover the same content as the regular Activities but are written at a second-grade reading level.

Skill Track Software

Use the Skill Track Software for English to Use for additional reinforcement of this chapter. The software program allows students using AGS textbooks to be assessed for mastery of each chapter and lesson of the textbook. Students access the software on an individual basis and are assessed with multiple-choice items.

Chapter at a Glance

Chapter 2: Adding Prepositions
pages 26–47

Lessons

1. **Prepositional Phrases**
   pages 28–29

2. **Adjective Prepositional Phrases**
   pages 30–31

3. **Confusing Subjects**
   pages 32–33

4. **Adverb Prepositional Phrases**
   pages 34–35

5. **Preposition or Adverb?**
   pages 36–37

6. **Two or More Prepositional Phrases**
   pages 38–39

7. **Hidden Verbs**
   pages 40–41

8. **All Kinds of Prepositional Phrases**
   pages 42–43

9. **Writing Mechanics**
   pages 44–45

Chapter 2 Review
pages 46–47

Skill Track Software for English to Use

Teacher's Resource Library (TRL)

Workbook Activities 11–19

Activities 11–19

Alternative Activities 11–19

Sentence Diagramming
   Activities 9–16
   (Optional sentence activities
   accompany lessons.)

Community Connection 2

English in Your World 2

Chapter 2 Self-Study Guide

Chapter 2 Mastery Tests A and B

(Answer Keys for the Teacher's
Resource Library begin on page 308
of this Teacher's Edition.)

2 Adding Prepositions

Have you ever thought about the words you use to give directions or to explain a process? You might tell someone that the kitchen is *down* the hall or *beside* the dining room. Perhaps you have explained how to make a sandwich. You might have used words such as *of, on, under,* and *in.* These words show the relationships between the items on the sandwich. You might have said, "First, get two slices *of* bread. Put a slice *of* cheese *on* the bread. Then, place some lettuce *under* the tomato. Now hold the sandwich *in* your hands."

In Chapter 2, you will learn about prepositions—words that show the relationships between things. You will also discover how prepositional phrases make sentences more interesting by telling *which one, what kind, how, when,* and *where.*

Goals for Learning

◆ To identify and use prepositions and prepositional phrases

◆ To state the use of prepositional phrases

◆ To tell the difference between prepositions and adverbs

◆ To identify state-of-being verbs

◆ To use capital letters with proper nouns

◆ To use a comma to set off an introductory prepositional phrase

27

Introducing the Chapter

Ask students what types of food they have made in the kitchen and how they prepared these dishes. Where did they chop ingredients? How did they mix ingredients? As they describe how they cooked, list their prepositional phrases on the board: *on the cutting board, with a mixer.* Tell students that the words they used to describe locations—such as *in, on, with*—are prepositions. The groups of words they used are prepositional phrases.

TEACHER'S RESOURCE

The AGS Teaching Strategies in English Transparencies may be used with this chapter. The transparencies add an interactive dimension to expand and enhance the *English to Use* program content.

CAREER INTEREST INVENTORY

The AGS Harrington-O'Shea Career Decision-Making System–Revised (CDM) may be used with this chapter. Students can use the CDM to explore their interests and identify careers. The CDM defines career areas that are indicated by students' responses on the inventory.

Writing Tips and Notes

Ask volunteers to read the tips and notes that appear in the margins throughout the chapter. Then discuss them with the class.

CHAPTER PROJECT

Ask each student to keep a log of instructions, directions, or other information that he or she can read on a regular basis. Ask students to note examples of writing that presents information clearly, and record examples that they find confusing. Ask students to bring in their examples on a specified day, and review them as a class.

Lesson at a Glance

Chapter 2 Lesson 1

Overview This lesson introduces prepositions as words that tie groups of words to a sentence.

Objectives

- To identify words used as prepositions
- To choose prepositions to begin phrases

Student Pages 28–29

Teacher's Resource Library

Workbook Activity 11

Activity 11

Alternative Activity 11

Sentence Diagramming Activity 9

Vocabulary

object of the preposition
preposition
prepositional phrase

 1 Warm-Up Activity

Point to people and objects around the classroom, and have students describe where these objects are located: for example *on the desk,* or *beside the bookshelf.* Tell students that their descriptions are prepositional phrases.

 2 Teaching the Lesson

Read the definition of *preposition* and *prepositional phrase,* and discuss how prepositions help clarify one thing's relationship to another. Ask students to locate their school, going from a general description (*in Ottawa*) to a specific one *near the park.*

> **Preposition**
> *A word that ties or relates a noun or pronoun to another part of the sentence*
>
> **Prepositional phrase**
> *A group of words that begins with a preposition and ends with a noun or pronoun*
>
> **Object of the preposition**
> *The noun or pronoun that follows the preposition in a prepositional phrase*

A **preposition** is a word that ties or relates a noun or pronoun to another part of the sentence.

A **prepositional phrase** is a group of words that begins with a preposition and ends with a noun or pronoun. The noun or pronoun that follows the preposition is the **object of the preposition.**

EXAMPLE

Natasha looked at the truck.

Parts of speech   *noun   verb   prep. adj.   noun*

(The preposition *at* begins the prepositional phrase *at the truck.* The noun *truck* is the object of the preposition *at.*)

Different prepositions show a different relationship between words in a sentence. Notice how the meaning of the sentence changes when the preposition changes.

EXAMPLE

Natasha looked inside the truck.
Natasha looked under the truck.
Natasha looked behind the truck.

Here are some common prepositions.

aboard	behind	from	since
about	below	in	through
above	beneath	inside	to
across	beside	into	toward
after	between	near	under
against	beyond	of	until
along	by	off	up
among	down	on	upon
around	during	outside	with
at	except	over	within
before	for	past	without

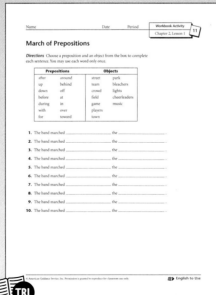

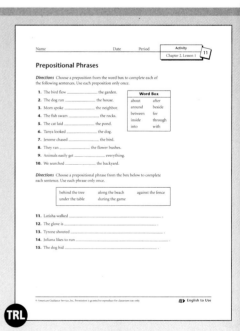

With

In

Between

Across

Activity A Add a different preposition to each of the following sentences. Write each sentence on your paper.

1. Arturo walked _____ the woods.
2. They talked _____ the music video.
3. We sat _____ the shady tree.
4. The plane flew _____ the clouds.
5. The principal spoke _____ the new students.
6. Lisa jumped _____ the big puddle.
7. The dog ran _____ the yard.
8. A boy waited _____ the park bench.
9. Pete looked _____ the little house.
10. They watched _____ their friends.

As you have seen, prepositions help you add more information to your sentences. Prepositional phrases make your sentences complete and more interesting.

> **EXAMPLE** The girls swam.
> The girls swam in the pool.
> (The prepositional phrase *in the pool* adds information to the sentence *The girls swam.*)

Activity B Add a prepositional phrase from the box to each sentence. Write the new sentences on your paper. Use each phrase only once.

near the car	along the shore	with her best friend
for two hours	around the block	

1. We searched.
2. Rain fell.
3. They talked.
4. Matt drove.
5. Kim walked.

Answers will vary. Possible answers follow. **1.** Arturo walked through the woods. **2.** They talked about the music video. **3.** We sat under the shady tree. **4.** The plane flew above the clouds. **5.** The principal spoke to the new students. **6.** Lisa jumped over the big puddle. **7.** The dog ran toward the yard. **8.** A boy waited on the park bench. **9.** Pete looked at the little house. **10.** They watched for their friends.

Activity B Answers

Answers will vary. Possible answers follow. **1.** We searched along the shore. **2.** Rain fell for two hours. **3.** They talked near the car. **4.** Matt drove around the block. **5.** Kim walked with her best friend.

3 **Reinforce and Extend**

LEARNING STYLES

Interpersonal/Group
Have students work in pairs to act out the prepositions on page 28. Students may want to show relationships with objects

GLOBAL CONNECTION

Ask students who know another language to translate into that language some of the prepositions on page 28. Then place a chair at the front of the room. Ask a student to choose a preposition from the list on page 28 and take the position in relation to the chair that the preposition describes (*near* the chair). Students who know other languages can say the same sentence in those languages.

ASL ILLUSTRATION

As students practice making the signs, have them notice how the gestures indicate relationships between objects, just as prepositions tie nouns to the rest of a sentence in written language.

Name _____ Date _____ Period _____

Sentence Diagramming Activity
Chapter 2, Lesson 1   9

Diagram Prepositional Phrases

Sentence Pattern 1: Subject + Verb

Step 1 The simple subject (a noun or pronoun) is written on the line on the left side. The simple predicate (a verb or a verb phrase) is written on the line on the right side.

Step 2 Adjectives that describe the subject go on the lines under the subject.

Step 3 Adverbs or prepositional phrases that tell about the verb go on the lines under the verb.

Directions Look at the steps above and the example below. Diagram the sentences below using the blank diagrams.

EXAMPLE Dogs howl at the moon.

1. Planes fly through clouds.

2. People sleep during the night.

3. Children play near the house.

4. A dog crawled under the porch.

© American Guidance Service, Inc. Permission is granted to reproduce for classroom use only.   English to Use

TRL

Lesson at a Glance

Chapter 2 Lesson 2

Overview This lesson describes and defines adjective prepositional phrases so that they can be identified within sentences.

Objectives

- To identify adjective prepositional phrases
- To review adjectives
- To review parts of speech and the subject + verb sentence pattern

Student Pages 30–31

Teacher's Resource Library TRL

   Workbook Activity 12

   Activity 12

   Alternative Activity 12

   Sentence Diagramming Activity 10

....

Vocabulary

adjective prepositional phrase

....

1 Warm-Up Activity

Write on the board the words *lines* and *paper*. Ask students to look at a piece of lined notebook paper and suggest a prepositional phrase that connects the two words, such *as lines on paper* or *paper with lines*. Then ask students to write a sentence using the prepositional phrase.

2 Teaching the Lesson

Review the definitions of *adjective* and *prepositional phrase*. Discuss how a prepositional phrase can do the same work as an adjective, that is, describe nouns in a sentence. Write the sample sentence on the board: *The woman in the car laughed.* Have students make up prepositional phrases to describe *woman* and *car*.

Lesson **2** **Adjective Prepositional Phrases**

Adjective prepositional phrase

A prepositional phrase that describes a noun

A prepositional phrase can be an adjective phrase or an adverb phrase.

An **adjective prepositional phrase** acts like an adjective in a sentence. Like an adjective, an adjective prepositional phrase describes a noun. It answers the questions *which one* or *what kind* about a noun.

> **EXAMPLE**
>
> The red pencil with an eraser broke.
> **Parts of speech**   *adj. adj. noun prep. adj. noun verb*
> (The preposition *with* shows the relationship of *eraser* to *red pencil*. *With an eraser* is an adjective prepositional phrase that answers the question *which red pencil broke?* The red pencil with an eraser broke.)
>
> The woman in the car laughed.
> **Parts of speech**   *adj. noun prep.adj. noun verb*
> (The preposition *in* shows the relationship of *car* to *woman*. *In the car* is an adjective prepositional phrase that answers the question *which woman laughed?* The woman in the car laughed.)

Remember that the complete subject is the whole part of the sentence that tells who or what the sentence is about. The simple subject is the one or more subject nouns or pronouns in a sentence.

An adjective prepositional phrase that tells about the simple subject is part of the complete subject.

> **EXAMPLE**
>
> **Sentence parts**   complete subject   predicate
> The woman in the car laughed.
> simple subj. adj. prep. phrase
> (The adjective prepositional phrase *in the car* describes the simple subject *woman*, a noun.)

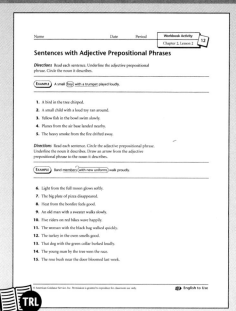

Workbook Activity 12

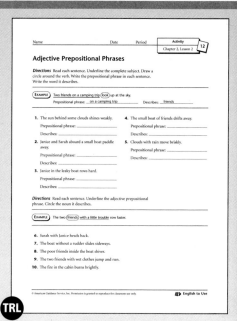

Activity 12

Activity A Each of these sentences has an adjective prepositional phrase that describes the simple subject. Write each sentence on your paper. Underline the adjective phrase. Circle the noun it describes.

Example A small (boy) with glasses spoke softly.

1. A dog inside the house barked.
2. A scared woman with a child hurried outside.
3. The firefighters from town arrived quickly.
4. A big player with the ball ran swiftly.
5. People in the stands cheered loudly.

A prepositional phrase includes the preposition, the object of the preposition, and all of the words in between. Adjectives that come between a preposition and its object tell about the object.

> **EXAMPLE** A green parrot in the tall palm tree blinked.
>
> **Prepositional phrase** in the tall palm tree
> | | | | |
> **Parts of speech** *prep. adj. adj. adj. noun*
> (The adjectives *the, tall,* and *palm* all tell about the noun *tree,* the object of the preposition *in.* The adjectives *A* and *green* tell about the noun *parrot,* the simple subject of the sentence.)

Activity B Write each sentence on your paper. Underline the adjective prepositional phrase. Circle the noun it describes. Draw an arrow from each adjective to the noun it describes.

Example Small (shadows) under the large tree danced.

1. The strong men in the canoe paddled quickly.
2. Smoke from the big, bright fires drifted upward.
3. The huge pile of wood disappeared.
4. Small boys with happy faces ran swiftly.
5. Three small children on the blanket watched quietly.

Activity A Answers

1. A (dog) inside the house barked.
2. A scared (woman) with a child hurried outside.
3. The (firefighters) from town arrived quickly.
4. A big (player) with the ball ran swiftly.
5. (People) in the stands cheered loudly.

Activity B Answers

1. The strong (men) in the canoe paddled quickly.
2. (Smoke) from the big, bright fires drifted upward.
3. The huge (pile) of wood disappeared.
4. Small (boys) with happy faces ran swiftly.
5. Three small (children) on the blanket watched quietly.

Speaking Practice

Have students work with partners, and tell them to practice *which one* and *what kind* questions using the sentences in Activities A and B. After one partner has read a sentence, have the other partner ask a *which one* or *what kind* question. The first partner then answers the question. For example, after the first partner reads Sentence 1 in Activity A, the second partner asks *Which dog?* The first partner then answers by saying *A dog inside the house.*

3 Reinforce and Extend

> **LEARNING STYLES**
>
> **Body/Kinesthetic Learning**
> Help students see the relationship between adjective prepositional phrases and the nouns they describe by writing several nouns and prepositional phrases on small pieces of paper. Students can physically manipulate the adjective prepositional phrases, matching the phrases with different nouns to create different types of sentences.

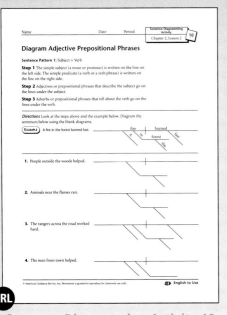

TRL

Sentence Diagramming Activity 10

Lesson at a Glance

Chapter 2 Lesson 3

Overview This lesson explains the difference between the simple subject and the object of a preposition, both of which are nouns in the complete subject.

Objectives

- To identify adjective prepositional phrases and simple subjects in subject + verb sentences
- To differentiate between a collective noun used as a simple subject and the object of a preposition

Student Pages 32–33

Teacher's Resource Library **TRL**

Workbook Activity 13

Activity 13

Alternative Activity 13

Sentence Diagramming Activity 11

---

1 Warm-Up Activity

Write the following sentence on the board and read it aloud: *The woman near the flag waved.* Have students locate the nouns; ask which of those nouns can wave. When students determine that both *woman* and *flag* can wave, ask which noun is the subject of the sentence. Tell students that finding the subject can be confusing because the prepositional phrase comes between the subject and the verb.

2 Teaching the Lesson

Review the example sentence. Discuss how students might mistakenly think the noun *nearest* the verb is the subject of the sentence. Choose sentences from Activity A, and point out that the noun closest to the verb cannot be the subject of the sentence. Then model for students how to identify the prepositional phrase that appears in each selected sentence.

Prepositional phrases often come between the simple subject and the verb in a sentence. Don't let the noun or pronoun that is the object of the preposition confuse you. The object of a preposition is *never* the subject of a sentence.

To find the simple subject of a sentence, follow these steps.

1. Find the verb.
2. Ask who or what is doing the action.
3. Find the noun or pronoun that answers the who or what question about the verb.
4. Do not include nouns or pronouns that are part of a prepositional phrase.

A prepositional phrase can sometimes act as a noun and act as the subject of a sentence.

Example Behind the chair is a good hiding place.

EXAMPLE

Sentence parts   *complete subject*   *complete predicate*

The man with the hat sings well.

simple subject   *verb*

(The words *man* and *hat* are nouns in the complete subject. To find out which noun is the simple subject, ask the question *who sings well?* The man with the hat sings well. *Man* is the simple subject. *Hat* is the object of the preposition *with*. The adjective prepositional phrase *with the hat* describes the noun *man*.)

Activity A Write each sentence on your paper. Circle the prepositional phrase. Underline the simple subject.

1. The plant with yellow leaves died.
2. The yellow leaves of the dead plant fell gently.
3. The plant near the window grew well.
4. Light from the big window shines brightly.
5. Flowers on the plant opened wide.

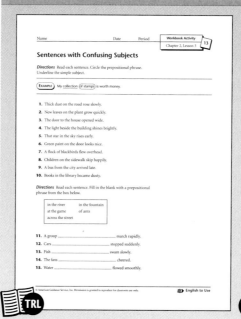

Workbook Activity 13

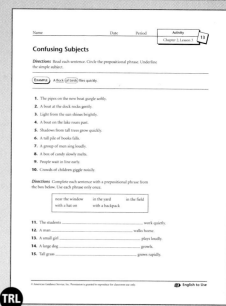

Activity 13

Some nouns name groups of people or things.

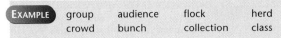

EXAMPLE	group	audience	flock	herd
	crowd	bunch	collection	class

When an adjective prepositional phrase follows a word that names a group, you may become confused about which noun is the subject. Remember, the object of a preposition is *never* the subject of a sentence.

EXAMPLE

Sentence parts

           complete subject   complete predicate

A small school of fish swam past.

   simple subject obj. of prep. verb

(*What swam past?* Although *fish* answers the question, *fish* cannot be the subject because it is the object of the preposition *of*. The noun *school* is the simple subject. The adjective prepositional phrase *of fish* describes the noun *school*.)

> A *quartet* is a group of four.

Activity B Write each sentence on your paper. Circle the prepositional phrase. Underline the simple subject.

1. The quartet of men sang loudly.

2. The silent herd of cows moved slowly.

3. A large group of students gathered.

4. The collection of fine jewels sparkled.

5. Packs of wild dogs howled.

Activity C Write each sentence on your paper. Fill in the blank with a prepositional phrase to fit the sentence. Underline the simple subject.

1. A team _____ arrived.

2. The happy crowd _____ yelled wildly.

3. A swarm _____ buzzed.

4. A big flock _____ flew away.

5. The fans _____ cheered loudly.

Activity A Answers

1. The plant (with yellow leaves) died. 2. The yellow leaves (of the dead) (plant) fell gently. 3. The plant (near) (the window) grew well. 4. Light (from the big window) shines brightly. 5. Flowers (on the plant) opened wide.

Activity B Answers

1. The quartet (of men) sang loudly. 2. The silent herd (of cows) moved slowly. 3. A large group (of) (students) gathered. 4. The collection (of fine jewels) sparkled. 5. Packs (of wild dogs) howled.

Activity C Answers

Answers will vary. Possible answers follow. 1. A team of experts arrived. 2. The happy crowd of fans yelled wildly. 3. A swarm of bees buzzed. 4. A big flock of geese flew away. 5. The fans of the team cheered loudly.

3   Reinforce and Extend

LEARNING STYLES

LEP/ESL

Have students who speak other languages illustrate other language patterns. Ask students to translate some of the sentences in Activity A or B, and discuss how that language conveys the information in the prepositional phrase.

LEARNING STYLES

Logical/Mathematical

Copy the sentences in Activity B. Have students read them and use a marker or colored pencil to underline the nouns. Next, ask students to use a different color to underline prepositions and then use a third color to underline nouns that appear *after* the prepositions. Explain that the noun following the preposition is its object and cannot be the subject of a sentence.

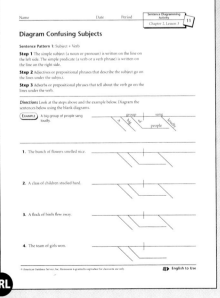

Sentence Diagramming Activity 11

Lesson at a Glance

Chapter 2 Lesson 4

Overview This lesson describes and defines adverb prepositional phrases.

Objective

■ To identify adverb prepositional phrases

Student Pages 34–35

Teacher's Resource Library

Workbook Activity 14

Activity 14

Alternative Activity 14

Sentence Diagramming Activity 12

Vocabulary

adverb prepositional phrase

1 Warm-Up Activity

Remind students that adjective prepositional phrases describe nouns. Tell students that adverb prepositional phrases provide similar information but that they describe verbs.

Write these words on the board: *grows, wall.* Ask students to create a prepositional phrase that connects the two words, such as *grows beside the wall.* Have the class write sentences using this phrase.

Tell students that they can identify adverb prepositional phrases with the questions *how, when, where.* Model the questions with the sentences that the class created: The tree grows *where?* The tree grows beside the wall.

2 Teaching the Lesson

Have students identify the subject and verb in the example sentence (*athletes, run*). Help them see that *on the track* is an adverb because it answers the question *where* about the verb *run.*

Remind students that adverb prepositional phrases focus on the action part of a sentence. Review strategies to locate verbs and identify action.

34 *Chapter 2 Adding Prepositions*

Adverb prepositional phrase

A prepositional phrase that describes a verb

An **adverb prepositional phrase** acts like an adverb in a sentence. Like an adverb, an adverb prepositional phrase answers the questions *how, when,* and *where* about a verb.

EXAMPLE

Many athletes run quickly on the track.

Parts of speech adj. noun verb adv. prep. adj. noun

(The preposition *on* shows the relationship of *track* to *run. On the track* is an adverb prepositional phrase that answers the question *where do many athletes run quickly?* Many athletes run quickly on the track.)

The four students left during the play.

Parts of speech adj. adj. noun verb prep. adj. noun

(The preposition *during* shows the relationship of *play* to *left. During the play* is an adverb prepositional phrase that answers the question *when did the students leave?* The students left during the play.)

You have learned that the complete predicate is the whole part of the sentence that tells what the subject is doing. The simple predicate, or verb, is the main verb in the predicate.

An adverb prepositional phrase that tells about the verb is part of the complete predicate.

EXAMPLE

Sentence parts subject complete predicate

Many athletes run at top speed.

verb prep. phrase

(The adverb prepositional phrase *at top speed* describes the simple predicate *run.* It answers the question *how did the athletes run?* The athletes ran at top speed.)

34 *Chapter 2 Adding Prepositions*

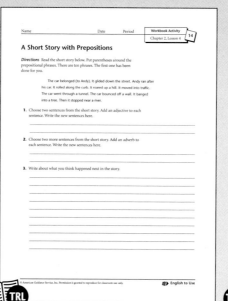

Workbook Activity 14

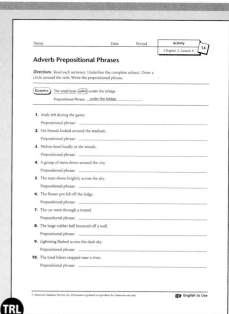

Activity 14

The sun rises

above

the mountains.

The sun rises above
the mountains.

Activity A Each of these sentences has an adverb prepositional phrase. Write each sentence on your paper. Underline the adverb phrase. Circle the verb it describes. Next to each sentence, write whether the adverb phrase answers *when* or *where* about the verb.

Example The cowhands (camped) near the mountain.
Where?

1. The campfire burns brightly during the meal.
2. The tired cowhands talk after dinner.
3. Night creeps over the land.
4. Stars shine across the sky.
5. A hot meal bubbles in the pot.
6. Wolves howl through the still night.
7. Embers glow until morning.
8. The sun rises above the mountains.
9. The birds sing in the trees.
10. Another day begins on the range.

Activity B Write each sentence on your paper. Fill in the blank with an adverb prepositional phrase that answers the question in parentheses about the verb. Then underline each verb.

1. Rick drove directly _____ . (Where?)
2. My mom works _____ . (When?)
3. The talented musician played _____ . (How?)
4. That woman shops daily _____ . (Where?)
5. The newborn kitten crawled _____ . (Where?)

Adding Prepositions   Chapter 2   **35**

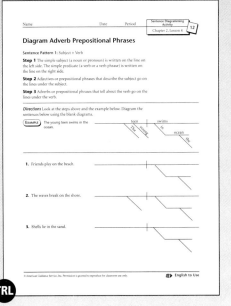
Activity A Answers

1. The campfire (burns) brightly <u>during the meal</u>. When 2. The tired cowhands (talk) <u>after dinner</u>. When 3. Night (creeps) <u>over the land</u>. Where 4. Stars (shine) <u>across the sky</u>. Where 5. A hot meal (bubbles) <u>in the pot</u>. Where 6. Wolves (howl) <u>through the still night</u>. When 7. Embers (glow) <u>until morning</u>. When 8. The sun (rises) <u>above the mountains</u>. Where 9. The birds (sing) <u>in the trees</u>. Where 10. Another day (begins) <u>on the range</u>. Where

Activity B Answers

Prepositional phrases will vary. Possible sentences follow:
1. Rick <u>drove</u> directly to the store.
2. My mom <u>works</u> every Saturday.
3. The talented musician <u>played</u> with great feeling. 4. That woman <u>shops</u> daily at the market.
5. The newborn kitten <u>crawled</u> beneath its mother.

 Reinforce and Extend

At Home

 When people give directions, they usually use prepositional phrases, such as *around the corner, down the street, on the right,* and *up the stairs.* Ask students to sketch a map of the route they walk or ride home from school. Then have them describe their route, either orally or in writing, using prepositional phrases. Tell students to use a format similar to "First I go _____ ," or "I always turn _____ ."

ASL Illustration

Ask students to practice the signs illustrated on page 35. Have students describe how the signs describe the concepts in the sentence and how closely they think the signs relate to the ideas. Ask students whether they think the preposition above is a more difficult concept to convey than the idea of "sun rises" or "mountains."

Adding Prepositions   Chapter 2   **35**

Lesson at a Glance

Chapter 2 Lesson 5

Overview This lesson identifies words that can be prepositions or adverbs.

Objectives

- To identify adverbs and prepositions
- To distinguish between adverb phrases and adjective phrases

Student Pages 36–37

Teacher's Resource Library **TRL**

Workbook Activity 15

Activity 15

Alternative Activity 15

Sentence Diagramming Activity 13

1 Warm-Up Activity

Write on the board: *My father looked up. My father looked up the mountain.* Tell students that because *up* has an object in the second sentence, it is a preposition, not an adverb. Have students form similar sentences.

2 Teaching the Lesson

Model the first pair of sentences in Activity A. Make sure students know the different meanings of *around*.

Activity A Answers

1. adverb 2. preposition
3. preposition 4. adverb
5. preposition

Activity B Answers

1. V—slows, Adv.—down 2. V—stops, Adv.—across, prep. phrase—from our house 3. V—sits, Adv.—up, prep. phrase—on a jack 4. V—rattles, Adv.—by, prep. phrase— past the car. 5. V—comes, Adv.—along, prep. phrase—after a few minutes

---

Lesson 5 Preposition or Adverb?

Some words that are prepositions can also be adverbs. Remember, a preposition always has an object. An adverb does not have an object.

> **EXAMPLE**
> **Adverb** The football players ran around.
> **Adverb prepositional phrase** The football players ran around the field.
> (In the first sentence, *around* does not have an object. It is an adverb that describes how the football players ran. In the second sentence, *around* has an object—*field*. *Around* is a preposition that introduces the adverb prepositional phrase *around the field.*)

Activity A Write each word in bold on your paper. Write whether it is an *adverb* or a *preposition*.

1. The cat looked **around.**
2. The bus traveled **around** the block.
3. The car parked **outside** the gate.
4. The girls waited **outside.**
5. The ball rolled **down** the stairs.

Activity B Write the sentences on your paper. Draw one line under the adverb. Draw two lines under the prepositional phrase. Circle the verb.

Example The woman (goes) out for dinner.

1. The driver of the car slows down in seconds.
2. The car stops across from our house.
3. The car sits up on a jack.
4. A bus rattles by past the car.
5. A tow truck comes along after a few minutes.

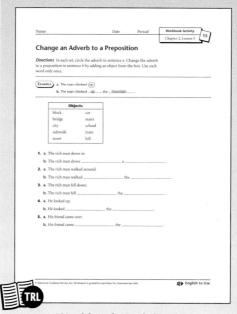

Workbook Activity 15

Activity 15

Activity C On your paper, complete each sentence with a word from the box. First use the word as an adverb. Then use the word as a preposition that introduces an adverb prepositional phrase. Do not use a word more than once.

after	before	down	near	outside
around	behind	inside	out	up

Example We drove _____ .
We drove around.
We drove around the town.

1. The curious boy looked _____ .
2. The happy children walked _____ .
3. A small, green frog jumped _____ .
4. The painter climbed _____ .
5. The clumsy clown fell _____ .

Communication Connection

Instant messaging is a way to communicate directly and quickly with others on the computer. People use it at home to chat with friends or family members. At work, people use it to share and discuss the latest news and information with people in distant places.

Activity D Write each sentence on your paper. Circle the prepositional phrase. Above each phrase, write whether it is an adjective phrase or an adverb phrase. Draw an arrow to the subject or the verb that each phrase tells about.

Example
           Adv. phrase
A baby yelled loudly (at midnight.)

           Adj. phrase
A box (of popcorn) spilled outside.

1. The kind doctor from the village sent his friend an instant message.
2. The good friend responded immediately with a greeting.
3. The strong swimmer dove beneath the waves.
4. Ten boxes of books arrived.
5. A small, green bird whistled loudly for its mate.

Activity C Answers

Answers will vary. Possible answers follow. **1.** The curious boy looked around; around the corner. **2.** The happy children walked inside; inside the park. **3.** A small, green frog jumped near; near the rock. **4.** The painter climbed up; up the ladder. **5.** The clumsy clown fell down; down the stairs.

Activity D Answers

1. The kind doctor (from the village) ADJ. PREP. PHRASE sent his friend an instant message.

2. The good friend responded immediately (with a greeting.) ADV. PREP. PHRASE

3. The strong swimmer dove (beneath the waves.) ADV. PREP. PHRASE

4. Ten boxes (of books) arrived. ADJ. PREP. PHRASE

5. A small, green bird whistled loudly (for its mate.) ADV. PREP. PHRASE

3   Reinforce and Extend

IN THE COMMUNITY

People often describe the location of places in relation to the location of community landmarks. Have students reverse this procedure. Ask them to choose a landmark in their community and describe its location in relation to other places around it, using prepositional phrases. Students might use expressions like these: *The courthouse is across the street from_____, down the street from____, around the corner from _____.*

Sentence Diagramming Activity 13

Lesson at a Glance

Chapter 2 Lesson 6

Overview This lesson reviews adjective and adverb prepositional phrases that modify other phrases.

Objective

■ To identify prepositional phrases and the words they modify

Student Pages 38–39

Teacher's Resource Library

Workbook Activity 16

Activity 16

Alternative Activity 16

Sentence Diagramming Activity 14

1 Warm-Up Activity

Ask students to list prepositional phrases describing the position of your desk: *on the floor, in front of the board, beside the window.* Then ask them to form sentences using two of the phrases: *The desk sits beside the window in front of the board.* Write the new sentence on the board. Tell students that because the prepositional phrases describe where the desk sits, they are adverb prepositional phrases.

Next, list prepositional phrases describing the desk itself: *with the large drawers, with the shiny surface.* Tell students that because these prepositional phrases describe the desk, they are adjective prepositional phrases.

2 Teaching the Lesson

Discuss the text and examples with students. After discussing the examples, write each example sentence on the board, but replace the prepositional phrases with other adjective or adverb prepositional phrases. For example: *The flower grows <u>in the garden beside the tree.</u>*

Remind students that this lesson builds on information they already have learned about adjective and adverb prepositional phrases.

Sentences often have more than one prepositional phrase. Sometimes the phrases describe the same word.

A sentence may have more than one adjective phrase.

> **EXAMPLE** The girl with blonde hair in the first seat waved.
>
> | Phrases | adjective | adjective |
> | Sentence parts | subject | predicate |
>
> (Both adjective phrases describe *girl.* Both phrases tell which girl waved.)

A sentence may have more than one adverb phrase.

> **EXAMPLE** The flower grows on the porch in the flowerpot.
>
> | Phrases | adverb | adverb |
> | Sentence parts | subject | predicate |
>
> (Both adverb phrases describe *grows.* Both phrases tell where the flower grows.)

A sentence may have adjective phrases and adverb phrases.

> **EXAMPLE** The girl in the first seat waved to me.
>
> | Phrases | adjective | adverb |
> | Sentence parts | subject | predicate |

You have learned about adjective prepositional phrases that describe subjects. An adjective prepositional phrase may also describe the noun object of another prepositional phrase.

> **EXAMPLE** The flower grows in the middle of the flowerpot.
>
> | Phrases | adverb | adjective |
> | Sentence parts | subject | predicate |
>
> (The adjective phrase *of the flowerpot* describes *middle. Middle* is the noun object of the preposition *in.*)

---

38 Chapter 2 *Adding Prepositions*

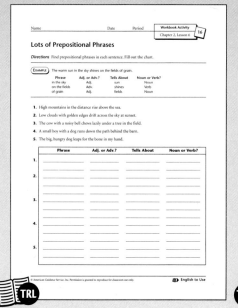

Workbook Activity 16

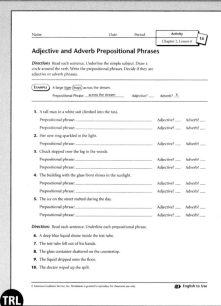

Activity 16

Activity A On your paper, write each prepositional phrase. Then write the word each phrase describes.

1. Ducks swam through the pond toward the grass.
2. Flowers sit beneath the window in the garden.
3. People waited against the fence after the game and talked among themselves.
4. A lazy cat sleeps beside the pillow on the big bed.
5. The old TV broke in the middle of a good show.
6. The car with the number on the side stopped.
7. The man walked down the street into the park.
8. The people stood in the hall outside the door.
9. The dog ran between the tree and the bush on the hill.
10. The new computer sits among the other packages in the lab.

Activity B On your paper, write the prepositional phrases in each sentence. Next to each phrase write *adjective phrase* or *adverb phrase* and the word the phrase describes.

Example Shoppers with heavy coats hurry to the stores in the city.

with heavy coats—adjective phrase, shoppers
to the stores—adverb phrase, hurry
in the city—adjective phrase, stores

1. A clerk with a smile on his face works quietly at the computer.
2. Another clerk sorts through a stack of paper carefully.
3. A huge amount of work for other people piles on the desks.
4. A long line of people waits nervously for reports on the new project.
5. The computer clerks in the office work hard through the long hours of the day.

Activity A Answers

1. through the pond—swam; toward the grass—swam 2. beneath the window—sit; in the garden—sit 3. against the fence—waited; after the game—waited; among themselves—talked 4. beside the pillow—sleeps; on the big bed—pillow 5. in the middle—broke; of a good show—middle 6. with the number—car; on the side—number 7. down the street—walked; into the park—walked 8. in the hall—stood; outside the door—hall 9. between the tree and the bush—ran; on the hill—bush 10. among the other packages—sits; in the lab—packages

Activity B Answers

1. with a smile—adjective phrase, clerk; on his face—adjective phrase, smile; at the computer—adverb phrase, works 2. through a stack—adverb phrase, sorts; of paper—adjective phrase, stack 3. of work—adjective phrase, amount; for other people—adjective phrase, work; on the desks—adverb phrase, piles 4. of people—adjective phrase, line; for reports—adverb phrase, waits; on the new project—adjective phrase, reports 5. in the office—adjective phrase, clerks; through the long hours—adverb phrase, work; of the day—adjective phrase, hours

Writing Practice

Ask students to write additional sentences with prepositional phrases that describe the object of a previous prepositional phrase. They may use sentences from the lesson as models.

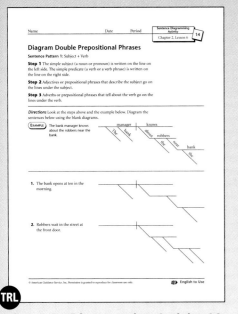

TRL
Sentence Diagramming Activity 14

3 Reinforce and Extend

LEARNING STYLES

Auditory/Verbal Learning
Ask a volunteer to tell how to get to a familiar neighborhood spot or how to perform a familiar task. As the volunteer says aloud the directions or explanation, have the rest of the class listen for prepositional phrases. Have the volunteer stop at the end of each sentence so that you can write the prepositional phrases that the rest of the students identified and the words that the prepositional phrases describe.

Lesson at a Glance

Chapter 2 Lesson 7

Overview This lesson introduces state-of-being verbs.

Objectives

■ To identify state-of-being verbs

■ To locate state-of-being verbs and prepositional phrases within sentences

Student Pages 40–41

Teacher's Resource Library **TRL**

Workbook Activity 17

Activity 17

Alternative Activity 17

Sentence Diagramming Activity 15

....

Vocabulary

state-of-being verb

....

 1 Warm-Up Activity

Write on the board: *All of the students are in the room.* Ask students to identify the prepositional phrases (*of the students, in the room*). Draw a line through each. Identify the remaining words: *All*, the subject, and *are*, the verb. Explain that verbs like *are* indicate existence, not action—we do not know what the students are doing. We know only that they are in the room.

 2 Teaching the Lesson

Review the list of commonly used state-of-being verbs. Tell students that their knowledge of prepositional phrases will help them distinguish prepositions from verbs such as *am, are, is,* and *was.*

Activity A Answers

1. is(behind)the tree. 2. am (in big trouble.) 3. remained 4. appear 5. is(under the desk.)

Hidden Verbs

> *State-of-being verb*
>
> *A verb that tells that the subject exists, but does not show action*

You have learned that an action verb is a word that shows action. There is another kind of verb. It is a **state-of-being verb.** A state-of-being verb tells that the subject exists in some way. A state-of-being verb does not show action.

The most commonly used state-of-being verb is *to be.* Here are some forms of the verb *to be.*

am	is	were
are	was	will be

Here are some other state-of-being verbs.

appear	feel	remain
become	look	seem

Because a state-of-being verb does not show action, you may have difficulty finding the verb when it is followed by an adverb prepositional phrase. Remember:

- A verb is never part of a prepositional phrase.
- A prepositional phrase always begins with a preposition.

EXAMPLE

The team is on the field.

Sentence parts	*subject verb adverb phrase*	
Sentence pattern	subject + verb	

(*Is* is a verb. The verb *is* does not show action. It tells that the team exists. It is a *state-of-being verb.* The preposition *on* begins the prepositional phrase *on the field.*)

Activity A Write each sentence on your paper. Underline the state-of-being verb. Circle the prepositional phrase.

1. Jack is behind the tree.
2. I am in big trouble.
3. The car remained clean.
4. They appear friendly.
5. His book is under his desk.

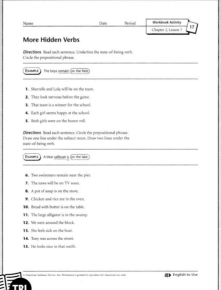

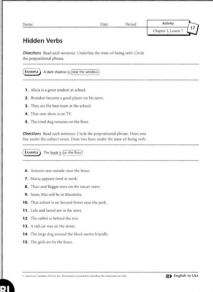

Workbook Activity 17

Activity 17

Using What You've Learned

Look in a newspaper or a magazine article for five sentences with state-of-being verbs. Could an action verb make any of these sentences more interesting? Write the five sentences that you chose on your paper. Replace the state-of-being verbs with action verbs and rewrite the sentences.

Activity B Write each sentence on your paper. Circle the prepositional phrases. Draw one line under the subject noun. Draw two lines under the state-of-being verb.

Example   A <u>can</u> (of beans) <u><u>was</u></u> (on the shelf.)

1. A loaf of bread is in the oven.
2. My friends were in the other room.
3. The smell of the warm bread is in the air.
4. My parents were in the basement.
5. Soon, only bread crumbs will be on the plate.

Good writers often use action verbs instead of state-of-being verbs. Action verbs make sentences clearer and more interesting than state-of-being verbs do.

EXAMPLE

State-of-being verb   The runner is on the track.
Action verb   The runner races on the track.
(The action verb *races* gives readers a clearer picture of what the runner is doing on the track.)

Activity C Write these sentences on your paper. Circle the state-of-being verb in each sentence. Then write the sentence again, using an action verb in place of the state-of-being verb. Try to use a different action verb in each sentence.

1. The pitcher is on the mound.
2. The catcher is behind the plate.
3. Yesterday, Jane was in center field.
4. I am in the stands.
5. Other players are in their dugouts.

Activity B Answers

1. A <u>loaf</u> (of bread) <u><u>is</u></u> (in the oven.)
2. My <u>friends</u> <u><u>were</u></u> (in the other) (room.)
3. The <u>smell</u> (of the warm bread) <u><u>is</u></u> (in) (the air.)
4. My <u>parents</u> <u><u>were</u></u> (in the basement.)
5. Soon, only bread <u>crumbs</u> <u><u>will be</u></u> (on the plate.)

Activity C Answers

Sentences will vary. Sample sentences follow.

1. The pitcher (is) on the mound. The pitcher stands on the mound.
2. The catcher (is) behind the plate. The catcher crouches behind the plate.
3. Yesterday, Jane (was) in center field. Yesterday, Jane stood in center field.
4. I (am) in the stands. I cheer in the stands.
5. Other players (are) in their dugouts. Other players wait in their dugouts.

3 Reinforce and Extend

Using What You've Learned

When students have rewritten their five sentences from newspapers and magazines, have them read their new sentences aloud to the rest of the class. Then have them read aloud the original sentences that used state-of-being verbs. Ask the class to compare the two sentences, discussing which type of sentence is more meaningful or lively. Alert students to the possibility that they may have changed or added meanings to the original sentence when they inserted action verbs.

Sentence Diagramming Activity 15

Lesson at a Glance

Chapter 2 Lesson 8

Overview This lesson examines the placement of prepositional phrases in sentences and presents examples of confusion caused by misplaced phrases.

Objectives

■ To analyze sentences that contain prepositional phrases and determine their modifiers

■ To evaluate sentences with misplaced prepositional phrases

Student Pages 42–43

Teacher's Resource Library

Workbook Activity 18

Activity 18

Alternative Activity 18

Sentence Diagramming Activity 16

1 Warm-Up Activity

Write the following sentence on the board: *In the morning on her way to work, the woman thinks about her plans for the day.* Help students identify the prepositional phrases and the words they modify. As students look at the example, ask them whether there is a place in the sentence where a prepositional phrase *cannot* fit.

2 Teaching the Lesson

Rewrite the example sentence, shifting the prepositional phrases to read *Near our school on the street, a bus stops with a flat tire.* Ask students to compare this sentence with the example sentence. Why is the example sentence easier to understand?

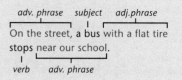

Lesson 8 All Kinds of Prepositional Phrases

Prepositional phrases may come anywhere in a sentence. An adjective phrase usually follows the noun it describes. An adverb phrase may come before or after the verb it tells about.

EXAMPLE

Sentence parts

          adv. phrase   subject   adj.phrase

On the street, a bus with a flat tire stops near our school.

                verb   adv. phrase

Activity A Write each sentence on your paper. Circle each prepositional phrase. Draw an arrow from the phrase to the word it describes.

Example (On the sidewalk,) a woman (with a briefcase) waits.

1. In the front yard of the house, the big dog growls.
2. The mother of the man appears on the porch of the house.
3. A short man in a black coat walks toward the door.
4. The big, old dog lies in the shade.
5. In the house, the young man visits with his mother.

When you write sentences with prepositional phrases, put each phrase where it makes the most sense.

Writing Tip

To express the meaning you want, place prepositional phrases as close as possible to the words they describe.

Activity B Read the facts. Decide which sentence makes more sense. Write the letter of the sentence that makes more sense on your paper.

1. **Facts** The bike has a horn. The bike is missing.
   - **A** The bike with a horn is missing.
   - **B** The bike is missing with a horn.
2. **Facts** The man had a dog. The man laughed at a joke.
   - **A** The man laughed at a joke with the dog.
   - **B** The man with the dog laughed at a joke.

42 *Chapter 2 Adding Prepositions*

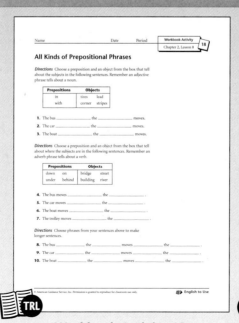

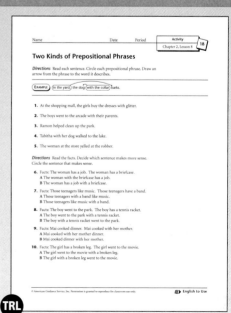

Workbook Activity 18   Activity 18

Activity C Copy the following chart on your paper. Then read each sentence and fill in the chart. Like the example, some sentences have more than one prepositional phrase.

Example A runner with strong legs ran quickly around the track.

Phrase	Adj. or Adv.	Describes Which Word	Noun or Verb
with strong legs	adj.	runner	noun
around the track	adv.	ran	verb

1. Yesterday, a small, yellow airplane landed at the airport.
2. The young tiger leaps through the air in the jungle.
3. The dark blue car with large tires parked in the garage.
4. The runners with colored batons headed to the finish line.
5. The woman with the yellow shirt ran in the race.
6. The woman with the blue baton won the race.
7. The store on the corner opened during the weekend.
8. A duck with a yellow tail swam in the river.
9. A talented little girl sang in a concert at the park.
10. A friend of my mom's writes for a newspaper.

The runners with colored batons race around the track.

Adding Prepositions   Chapter 2   43

3 Reinforce and Extend

CAREER CONNECTION

Students who enjoy clear, lively, and well-written texts may be interested in journalism careers. Have students tell about the different types of journalistic careers that interest them. They can get their information through the Internet or by reading through a newspaper and describing its different features. Ask students to bring those sections of a newspaper to class and to discuss their choices.

| Name | Date | Period | Sentence Diagramming Activity 16 |

Chapter 2, Lesson 8

Diagram All Sorts of Prepositional Phrases

Sentence Pattern 1: Subject + Verb

Step 1 The simple subject (a noun or pronoun) is written on the line on the left side. The simple predicate (a verb or verb phrase) is written on the line on the right side.

Step 2 Adjectives or prepositional phrases that describe the subject go on the lines under the subject.

Step 3 Adverbs or prepositional phrases that tell about the verb go on the lines under the verb.

Directions Look at the steps above and the example below. Diagram the sentences below using the blank diagrams.

EXAMPLE Outside the school, parents wait for good news.

1. Inside the classroom, children smile at the teacher.
2. A cousin of mine waits for me.
3. My parents waited at home.

© American Guidance Service, Inc. Permission is granted to reproduce for classroom use only.   English to Use

Sentence Diagramming Activity 16

TEACHER ALERT

The chart in Activity C may be useful for other types of assignments. Graphic organizers help students create new arrangements of details. Spatially oriented students may especially benefit from such structures.

Chapter 2 Lesson 9

Overview This lesson introduces common nouns, proper nouns as words that require capital letters, and the use of commas following introductory prepositional phrases.

Objectives

■ To distinguish common nouns from proper nouns

■ To capitalize proper nouns

■ To put commas after introductory prepositional phrases

Student Pages 44–45

Teacher's Resource Library

Workbook Activity 19

Activity 19

Alternative Activity 19

....

Vocabulary

common noun
proper noun

....

 Warm-Up Activity

Write on the board the following list:
street   I know a street named _____.
teacher   I know a teacher named _____.
Ask students to fill in the blanks. Then ask what is different about the noun on the left and the noun they provided. Discuss *common* and *proper nouns.*

 Teaching the Lesson

Tell students that if they question whether a word is a common or a proper noun, they should check a dictionary.

Activity A Answers

The following nouns begin with capital letters: **2.** Justin **4.** Vancouver **7.** Brenda **8.** Niagara Falls **10.** Cleveland **12.** Jackie **14.** Ontario **15.** Jeff **17.** David **19.** Kim **20.** Keiko

---

A **common noun** names a general type of person, place, or thing. A common noun does not begin with a capital letter.

Here are some common nouns.

> **Common noun**
> *The name of a general type of person, place, or thing*
>
> **Proper noun**
> *The name of a specific person, place, or thing*

EXAMPLE

state	woman	girl
man	city	boy

A **proper noun** names a specific person, place, or thing. A proper noun always begins with a capital letter.

EXAMPLE

Colorado	Aretha	Linda
Carlos	Seattle	Damon

Activity A Write this list of words on your paper. Use capital letters for proper nouns.

1. bird	**6.** dog	**11.** book	**16.** tree
2. justin	**7.** brenda	**12.** jackie	**17.** david
3. town	**8.** niagara falls	**13.** house	**18.** table
4. vancouver	**9.** tower	**14.** ontario	**19.** kim
5. park	**10.** cleveland	**15.** jeff	**20.** keiko

You have learned that a comma sets apart one or more words in a sentence. Use a comma after a prepositional phrase that begins a sentence.

EXAMPLE   Under the porch, the dog lay in the mud.
(A comma follows the prepositional phrase *under the porch* to set it apart from the rest of the sentence.)

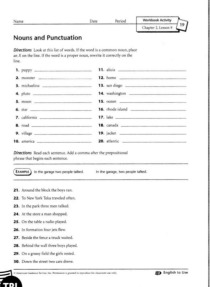

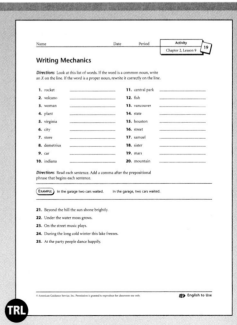

Workbook Activity 19

Activity 19

Activity B Write each sentence on your paper. Add a comma after the prepositional phrase that begins the sentence.

1. On the branch a bird perched.
2. In the hall friends chatted.
3. At the corner a car stopped.
4. Over the river a moose stood.
5. Beneath the water fish swim.

When writing sentences, remember to:

- Begin every sentence with a capital letter. End every sentence that makes a statement with a period.
- Begin proper nouns with capital letters.
- Do not begin common nouns with capital letters.
- Use a comma after a prepositional phrase that begins a sentence.

Activity C On your paper, write each sentence correctly with capital letters and commas. Put a period at the end of each sentence.

1. near the phone john waited silently
2. at the park karen skated
3. around the corner david talked with his friends
4. except for dwayne the members of the chorus sang
5. in the harbor the statue of liberty stands

The Statue of Liberty stands in New York Harbor.

Adding Prepositions Chapter 2 **45**

Activity B Answers

1. On the branch, a bird perched.
2. In the hall, friends chatted.
3. At the corner, a car stopped.
4. Over the river, a moose stood.
5. Beneath the water, fish swim.

Activity C Answers

1. Near the phone, John waited silently. 2. At the park, Karen skated. 3. Around the corner, David talked with his friends. 4. Except for Dwayne, the members of the chorus sang. 5. In the harbor, the Statue of Liberty stands.

 3 **Reinforce and Extend**

LEARNING STYLES

 Visual/Spatial Learning
Ask students to look at the photograph on page 45 and to identify it if they can. Have students discuss what they know about the Statue of Liberty. Then ask them to identify other important national or local monuments, such as the Washington Monument or their state capitol. Tell students to capitalize the names of important monuments because they are proper nouns. Tell students that capitalizing names gives readers a visual clue that the word they are reading is special and important.

LEARNING STYLES

 LEP/ESP
Rules for punctuating proper nouns vary in different languages. Ask students who speak other languages to offer examples of proper nouns from their native languages. Discuss how the rules for capitalization are different from or similar to the rules in English. You may want to have volunteers who speak other languages write some of the words in Activity A on the board in their native languages.

Chapter 2 Review

Use the Chapter Review to prepare students for tests and to reteach content from the chapter.

Chapter 2 Mastery Test

The Teacher's Resource Library includes parallel forms of the Chapter 2 Mastery Test. The difficulty level of the two forms is equivalent. You may wish to use one form as a pretest and the other form as a posttest.

REVIEW ANSWERS

Part A

1. proper noun 2. preposition
3. object of the preposition
4. common noun 5. adverb prepositional phrase 6. state-of-being verb 7. prepositional phrase 8. adjective prepositional phrase

Part B

Answers will vary. Possible answers follow. 9. over the tall building 10. to a distant corner
11. behind the little house
12. after a late dinner

Part C

13. with the long tail—adjective phrase; to me—adverb phrase
14. off the bus—adverb phrase
15. in your car—adverb phrase

Part D

16. B 17. A 18. C

Chapter 2   R E V I E W

Word Bank

adjective prepositional phrase

adverb prepositional phrase

common noun

object of the preposition

preposition

prepositional phrase

proper noun

state-of-being verb

Part A On a sheet of paper, write the correct word or words from the Word Bank to complete each sentence.

1. The name of a specific person, place, or thing is a _____.
2. A _____ is a word that ties or relates a noun or pronoun to another part of the sentence.
3. The noun or pronoun that follows the preposition is the _____ .
4. A _____ is a general type of person, place, or thing.
5. An _____ is a prepositional phrase that describes a verb.
6. A verb that does not show action is a _____ .
7. A _____ is a group of words that begins with a preposition and ends with a noun or pronoun.
8. A prepositional phrase that describes a noun is an ____.

Part B Add a different preposition to each phrase. Write each complete prepositional phrase on your paper.

9. _____ the tall building   11. _____ the little house
10. _____ a distant corner   12. _____ a late dinner

Part C Write each prepositional phrase on your paper. Tell whether it is an *adjective phrase* or an *adverb phrase*.

13. The dog with the long tail ran to me.
14. Melinda got off the bus.
15. I left my umbrella in your car.

Part D On your paper, write the letter of the simple subject of each sentence.

16. The students with good grades went to the park.
    A grades   B students   C went   D park
17. The school of fish swam down the stream.
    A school   B fish   C down   D stream
18. Everybody with a ticket can go into the theater now.
    A ticket   B theater   C Everybody   D now

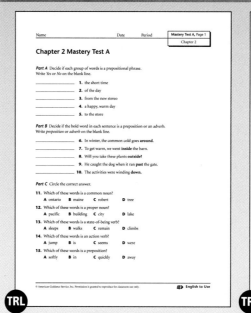

Chapter 2 Mastery Test A

Part E Read this paragraph about a race. Then answer the questions on your paper.

The sleek cars with skillful drivers race around the track. A green flag waves. The cars roar past. A black car is ahead. The excited crowd jumps up.

19. Find these words in the story. Tell what part of speech each one is: *sleek, with, black, past, up, ahead, cars.*

20. Rewrite the first sentence so that it begins with a prepositional phrase. Remember to use a comma.

21. List all the verbs. There are five.

Part F Write each sentence on your paper. Underline each state-of-being verb. Circle each action verb.

22. I go to football games.   **24.** The game is over.

23. We cheer for our team.

Part G Write the words in bold on your paper. Then write whether each word is a *preposition* or an *adverb.*

25. Please sit **down.**

26. I live **down** the street.

Part H On your paper, write each sentence correctly with capital letters and commas. Don't forget the periods. Underline each preposition and circle each prepositional phrase.

27. after the race on friday people cheer for maria

28. jamal smiles at maria with pride

29. she talks about the olympics

30. maria is in the winner's circle

 Before answering questions about a paragraph, reread the parts of the paragraph that contain the information you need to answer each question correctly.

REVIEW ANSWERS

Part E

19. sleek—adjective; with—preposition; black—adjective; past—adverb; up—adverb; ahead—adjective; cars—noun
20. Around the track, the sleek cars with skillful drivers race.
21. race, waves, roar, is, jumps

Part F

22. go; action verb **23.** cheer; action verb **24.** is; state-of-being verb

Part G

25. down, adverb **26.** down, preposition

Part H

27. (After the race)(on Friday,) people cheered (for)(Maria.)
28. Jamal smiles (at Maria)(with pride.)
29. She talks (about the Olympics.)
30. Maria is (in the winner's circle.)

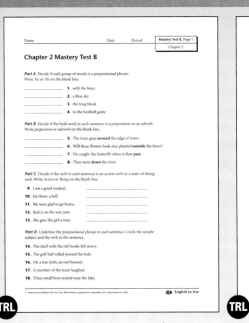

Chapter 2 Mastery Test B

3

Planning Guide

Using Compound Parts

		Student Text Lesson		Language Skills		
	Student Pages	Vocabulary	Practice Activities	Identification Skills	Writing Skills	Punctuation Skills
Lesson 1 Conjunctions	50–51	✔	✔	✔	✔	
Lesson 2 Compound Subjects	52–53	✔	✔	✔	✔	✔
Lesson 3 Compound Predicates	54–55	✔	✔	✔	✔	✔
Lesson 4 Compounds and Prepositions	56–57	✔	✔	✔	✔	✔
Lesson 5 Compound Sentences	58–59	✔	✔	✔	✔	✔
Lesson 6 Sentences with Compounds	60–61	✔	✔	✔		✔
Lesson 7 Writing Mechanics	62–63	✔	✔	✔	✔	✔

Chapter Activities

Teacher's Resource Library
Community Connection 3:
Talk with the Police About
Your Community
English in Your World 3:
Conjunctions in Newspapers
and Magazines

Assessment Options

Student Text
Chapter 3 Review

Teacher's Resource Library
Chapter 3 Mastery Tests A and B

	Student Text Features				Teaching Strategies					Learning Styles						Teacher's Resource Library				
ASL Illustration	Communication Connection	Notes	Using What You've Learned	Writing Tips	Teacher Alert	Online Connection	Applications (Home, Career, Community, Global)	Speaking Practice	Writing Practice	Auditory/Verbal	Body/Kinesthetic	Interpersonal/Group Learning	Logical/Mathematical	Visual/Spatial	LEP/ESL	Workbook Activities	Activities	Alternative Activities	Sentence Diagramming Activities	Self-Study Guide
		✔		✔			51								51	20	20	20	17	✔
53		✔		✔			53					53				21	21	21	18	✔
					55		55		55							22	22	22	19	✔
						57		57						57		23	23	23	20	✔
59				✔	59					59						24	24	24	21	✔
											61		61			25	25	25	22	✔
	62	✔	63				63									26	26	26		✔

Pronunciation Key

a	hat	e	let	ī	ice	ô	order	ù	put	sh	she		a in about
ā	age	ē	equal	o	hot	oi	oil	ü	rule	th	thin	ə	e in taken
ä	far	ėr	term	ō	open	ou	out	ch	child	ᵺ	then		i in pencil
â	care	i	it	ò	saw	u	cup	ng	long	zh	measure		o in lemon
													u in circus

Alternative Activities

The Teacher's Resource Library (TRL) contains a set of lower-level worksheets called Alternative Activities. These worksheets cover the same content as the regular Activities but are written at a second-grade reading level.

Skill Track Software

Use the Skill Track Software for English to Use for additional reinforcement of this chapter. The software program allows students using AGS textbooks to be assessed for mastery of each chapter and lesson of the textbook. Students access the software on an individual basis and are assessed with multiple-choice items.

Chapter 3: Using Compound Parts
pages 48–65

Lessons

1. **Conjunctions**
   pages 50–51

2. **Compound Subjects**
   pages 52–53

3. **Compound Predicates**
   pages 54–55

4. **Compounds and Prepositions**
   pages 56–57

5. **Compound Sentences**
   pages 58–59

6. **Sentences with Compounds**
   pages 60–61

7. **Writing Mechanics**
   pages 62–63

Chapter 3 Review
   pages 64–65

Skill Track Software for English to Use

Teacher's Resource Library

Workbook Activities 20–26

Activities 20–26

Alternative Activities 20–26

Sentence Diagramming
   Activities 17–22
   (Optional sentence activities
   accompany lessons.)

Community Connection 3

English in Your World 3

Chapter 3 Self-Study Guide

Chapter 3 Mastery Tests A and B

(Answer Keys for the Teacher's
Resource Library begin on page 308
of this Teacher's Edition.)

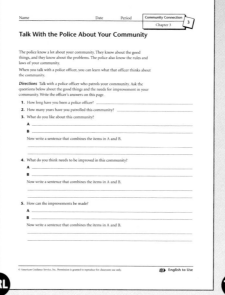

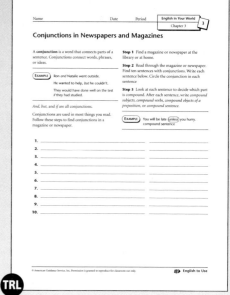

3 Using Compound Parts

Have you ever put together a puzzle together? When you first look at the tiny individual pieces, you might not be able to tell what the finished puzzle would look like. However, by matching and fitting together similar shapes and colors, you can eventually build the small pieces into a big picture that is complete and meaningful.

Sentences, like puzzles, are built of small parts that, when put together, have a larger meaning. In this chapter, you will study sentences with words that connect ideas.

Goals for Learning

◆ To introduce and use conjunctions

◆ To identify compound subjects, predicates, and objects of prepositions

◆ To combine two simple sentences to create a compound sentence

◆ To use commas and semicolons to punctuate sentences with compound parts

◆ To capitalize and punctuate titles correctly

49

Introducing the Chapter

Discuss with students how they unconsciously combine many types of information in the course of ordinary conversation. To illustrate, write this sentence starter on the board: *I will.* Have students complete the sentence by listing at least two activities they will do later in the day. Identify the connecting words. Tell students that words like *and, but,* and *or* are conjunctions that link the compound parts of a sentence. Tell the class that this chapter presents ways to use compound parts in sentences.

TEACHER'S RESOURCE

The AGS Teaching Strategies in English Transparencies may be used with this chapter. The transparencies add an interactive dimension to expand and enhance the *English to Use* program content.

CAREER INTEREST INVENTORY

The AGS Harrington-O'Shea Career Decision-Making System–Revised (CDM) may be used with this chapter. Students can use the CDM to explore their interests and identify careers. The CDM defines career areas that are indicated by students' responses on the inventory.

Writing Tips and Notes

Ask volunteers to read the tips and notes that appear in the margins throughout the chapter. Then discuss them with the class.

CHAPTER PROJECT

Have student pairs write 10 sentences containing conjunctions. As the class works through each lesson, have pairs modify those beginning sentences to include new types of compounds. Have pairs trade sentences with other pairs to review grammar and mechanics.

TRL   **TRL**

Chapter 3 Self-Study Guide

Chapter 3 Lesson 1

Overview This lesson introduces conjunctions as connecting words in sentences.

Objectives

■ To write conjunctions to connect words, phrases, and ideas in sentences

■ To identify conjunctions and the words they connect

Student Pages 50–51

Teacher's Resource Library TRL

Workbook Activity 20

Activity 20

Alternative Activity 20

Sentence Diagramming Activity 17

Vocabulary

conjunction

1 Warm-Up Activity

Put on the desk a group of similar items that can be classified in a number of different ways: for example, by color, size, and use. Ask students to create sentences describing the items (*The notebook and the eraser are red. The pencil and pen are small, but the book is large.*) Write on the board the conjunctions students use to join words. Tell students that they use conjunctions to show relationships between different things.

2 Teaching the Lesson

Help students identify the conjunctions in the example sentences and the words, phrases, or ideas that the conjunctions connect. Encourage students to create new sentences modeled on those in the example box.

> **Conjunction**
> A word that joins two or more words, phrases, or ideas in a sentence

A **conjunction** is a word that joins two or more words, phrases, or ideas in a sentence.

Here are some commonly used conjunctions:

and	but	yet
as well as	or	

EXAMPLE

Words	Larry and Anthony went to the store. She's my friend as well as my cousin.
Phrases	Did he go into the shop or down the sidewalk?
Ideas	He travels around the country, yet he longs for the beach. I tried hard, but I lost.

Activity A Write each sentence on your paper. Fill in the blank with a conjunction. Use *and, but, or, as well as,* or *yet.* More than one conjunction may make sense.

1. Tim _____ Lisa will call later.

2. The paper _____ the pencil are on the desk.

3. You should go to bed, _____ you will oversleep.

4. My sister _____ my mother arrived late.

5. The cat moved quickly _____ silently.

6. Cindy _____ Paul cleaned up.

7. His ancestors come from Spain _____ Portugal.

8. They traveled along wide city streets _____ narrow country roads.

9. A girl in running shorts _____ sneakers came to the door.

10. Slowly _____ violently, the storm swept through town.

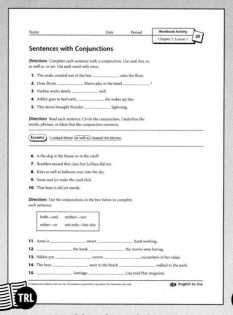

Workbook Activity 20

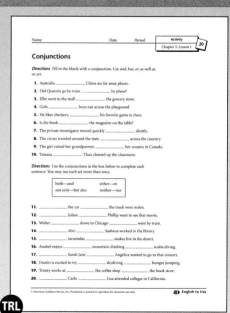

Activity 20

Writing Tip

Using many short sentences together can make your writing choppy. Conjunctions can help make your writing smoother. Use conjunctions to join short sentences.

The conjunctions that come in sets are *correlatives*. *Correlative* means "closely related." Correlatives are always used together.

Activity B Write each sentence on your paper. Circle the conjunction. Underline the words, phrases, or ideas that the conjunction connects in each sentence.

Examples   Her shoes umbrella are in the room.

We looked in the closet (as well as) on the counter.

I arrived late, (yet) I sat up front.

1. We spoke to Omar and Anita about the cleaning supplies.
2. Through the day and into the night, we worked.
3. Slowly but surely, the old house came to life.
4. Windows and floors sparkled.
5. The old yet sturdy house stood proudly.

These conjunctions come in sets, but they are separated in a sentence.

| both—and | not only—but also |
| either—or | neither—nor |

 EXAMPLE   Both the snow and the icicles melted.
Either Maya or I will drive.
Not only Alvaro but also his dad left early.
Neither my keyboard nor my monitor worked.

Activity C On your paper, write a set of conjunctions for each sentence.

1. Unfortunately _____ her books _____ her homework were at school.
2. The books were _____ in her locker _____ in the classroom.
3. Ama studied _____ in the evening _____ in the morning before school.
4. Ama _____ rode to school _____ walked.
5. She _____ did well on her homework _____ passed a quiz.

Using Compound Parts   Chapter 3   **51**

Activity A Answers

Answers will vary. Be sure that the conjunction used in each sentence makes sense.

Activity B Answers

1. Omar (and) Anita 2. Through the day (and) into the night 3. Slowly (but) surely 4. Windows (and) floors 5. old (yet) sturdy

Activity C Answers

Answers will vary, but all four conjunction sets should be used.

 3 Reinforce and Extend

LEARNING STYLES

LEP/ESL
Help language learners make connections between conjunctions in English and those in their native languages. Write translations of conjunctions in several languages on the board or ask volunteers to help you. Make sure that language learners know which conjunctions imply connections and which indicate exceptions.

IN THE COMMUNITY

Every community has a unique history of growth and change. Students may enjoy exploring the history of their community. Suggest that they check the library for books about the community. They also can talk to people whose families have lived in the area for a long time. As students discover facts, tell them to write sentences using conjunctions. For example: *Our library was once small, but now it includes several neighborhood branches.*

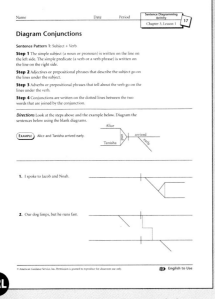

Sentence Diagramming Activity 17

Using Compound Parts   Chapter 3   **51**

Lesson at a Glance

Chapter 3 Lesson 2

Overview This lesson presents compound subjects and explains how to combine two or more sentences to create a more interesting sentence with a compound subject.

Objectives

■ To identify compound simple subjects

■ To write sentences with compound subjects

Student Pages 52–53

Teacher's Resource Library

Workbook Activity 21

Activity 21

Alternative Activity 21

Sentence Diagramming Activity 18

Vocabulary
compound subject

 Warm-Up Activity

Ask students to combine several short sentences that repeat the same information in the predicate into one sentence. Tell students that they have created a sentence with a compound subject.

2 Teaching the Lesson

Have students read the sentence in the example box and identify the conjunction and the simple subjects.

Activity A Answers

1. An alley(and)an empty store
2. Old products(and)dirty supplies
3. Men(and)women 4. The clean, empty street(and)store 5. The busy clerks(and)pleased shoppers

---

A sentence may have more than one subject. A **compound subject** is two or more subjects joined by a conjunction.

> **Compound subject**
> *Two or more subjects joined by a conjunction*

EXAMPLE Polar bears and reindeer live in the Arctic.

compound subject

(This sentence tells about two things that live in the Arctic—*polar bears* and *reindeer*. *Polar bears* and *reindeer* are two simple subjects that make up a compound subject when they are joined by the conjunction *and*. The complete subject is *polar bears and reindeer*.)

> Compound subjects share a verb.
> • Subjects joined by *and* take a plural verb.
> • Singular subjects joined by *or* or *nor* take a singular verb.

Activity A Write the complete subject in these sentences on your paper. Underline the simple subjects in the compound subject. Circle the conjunction.

1. An alley and an empty store lie ahead.
2. Old products and dirty supplies sit on the shelves in the store.
3. Men and women clean during the cool morning.
4. The clean, empty street and store fill with shoppers.
5. The busy clerks and pleased shoppers smile at the change in the street.

> **Writing Tip**
> You can avoid repeating words by combining the subjects of two or more short sentences into a compound subject. Creating a compound subject can make your writing better.

When writing sentences with compound subjects, make sure the sentences are clear and easy for readers to understand.

EXAMPLE Red tomatoes, purple grapes, yellow melons, and green beans are on sale.
(*Tomatoes, grapes, melons,* and *beans* are the simple subjects in the compound subject.)

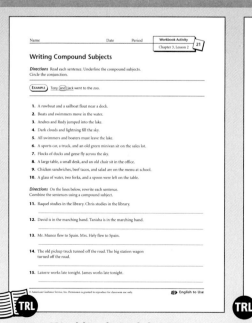

Workbook Activity 21

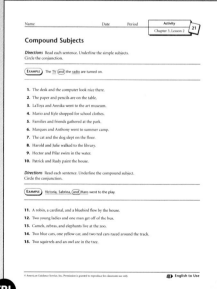

Activity 21

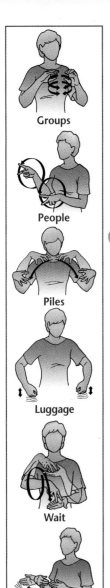

Groups

People

Piles

Luggage

Wait

Gate

Groups of people and piles of luggage wait at the gate.

Activity B Write the compound subject for each sentence. Underline each simple subject. Circle the conjunction.

1. A duck, a chicken, and a spotted pig stood in the yard.
2. A taxi, a bus, and an old truck drove around the block.
3. A tall lamp, a round table, and a large bed sat in the store window.
4. Kimi, Dawn, and Deepa step into the airplane.
5. Groups of people and piles of luggage wait at the gate.

You can often combine the subjects of two or more sentences into a compound subject and make the two sentences into one sentence.

> **EXAMPLE** Brandon talked. Hannah talked.
> Brandon and Hannah talked.
> Lakes can freeze. Rivers can freeze.
> Lakes and rivers can freeze.

Activity C Write each pair of sentences as one sentence with a compound subject.

1. Chris went to the movies. Marco went to the movies.
2. A tape played loudly. A CD played loudly.
3. The old table broke. The old chair broke.
4. The moon shone brightly. The stars shone brightly.
5. Ted works at the bank. Trish works at the bank.

Activity B Answers

1. A <u>duck</u>, a <u>chicken</u>, (and) a spotted <u>pig</u> 2. A <u>taxi</u>, a <u>bus</u>, (and) an old <u>truck</u> 3. A tall <u>lamp</u>, a round <u>table</u>, (and) a large <u>bed</u> 4. <u>Kimi</u>, <u>Dawn</u>, (and) <u>Deepa</u> 5. <u>Groups</u> of people (and) <u>piles</u> of luggage

Activity C Answers

1. Chris and Marco went to the movies. 2. A tape and a CD played loudly. 3. The old table and the old chair broke. 4. The moon and the stars shone brightly. 5. Ted and Trish work at the bank.

3 Reinforce and Extend

LEARNING STYLES

Interpersonal/Group
Ask students to form small groups and create sentences with compound subjects. Help the groups get started by asking them to list their names and complete this sentence: _____, _____, _____, _____, and _____ are in the group.

CAREER CONNECTION

Careers in such areas as food service, construction, and retail sales often require the ordering of supplies and merchandise. Ask each student to imagine that he or she works for a small company and must write a list of items to order. The list should include conjunctions and compound forms. For example, a student may write *six sweaters in blue, red, and yellow; ten jackets with collars, deep pockets, and hoods.*

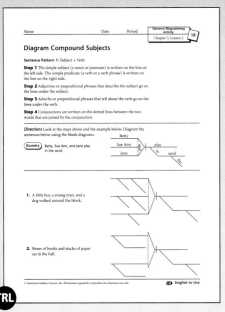

ASL ILLUSTRATION

Have students observe that the signs illustrated on page 53 do not include a conjunction. Ask students how they think ASL users make the connection between "groups of people" and "piles of luggage" without the use of "and." Have students practice making the signs and forming the sentence.

Sentence Diagramming Activity 18

Chapter 3 Lesson 3

Overview This lesson presents compound predicates and explains how to combine two or more sentences to create a more interesting sentence with a compound predicate.

Objectives

■ To identify compound simple predicates

■ To write sentences with compound predicates

Student Pages 54–55

Teacher's Resource Library

Workbook Activity 22

Activity 22

Alternative Activity 22

Sentence Diagramming Activity 19

Vocabulary

compound predicate

 1 Warm-Up Activity

Ask a volunteer to perform a series of actions. Ask the class to describe the individual actions. Have students combine the descriptions into one statement with a compound predicate.

 2 Teaching the Lesson

Review compound predicates. Emphasize that sentences with compound predicates contain two or more actions.

Activity A Answers

1. whistles and eases around the curve 2. bend and groan under the weight of the train 3. rattles and squeaks along the tracks 4. rise and settle on the road 5. sways and fades into the distance

---

A sentence may have more than one predicate. A **compound predicate** is two or more verbs joined by a conjunction.

Compound predicate
Two or more verbs joined by a conjunction

EXAMPLE The plastic melted and stuck to the table.

compound predicate

(This sentence tells about two things that the plastic did—*melted* and *stuck*. *Melted* and *stuck* form a compound predicate made up of two simple predicates, or verbs. They are joined by the conjunction *and*. The complete predicate is *melted and stuck to the table*.)

Activity A Write the complete predicate in these sentences on your paper. Underline the verbs in the compound predicate. Circle the conjunction.

1. A long train whistles and eases around the curve.
2. Tracks bend and groan under the weight of the train.
3. The slow train rattles and squeaks along the tracks.
4. Clouds of dust from the train rise and settle on the road.
5. The long train sways and fades into the distance.

Railroad cars are linked together. Conjunctions link the verbs of a compound predicate.

54 Chapter 3 Using Compound Parts

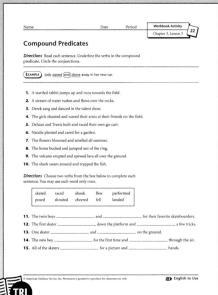

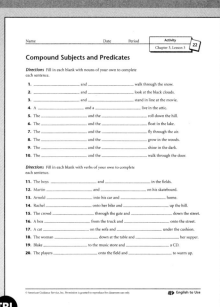

Workbook Activity 22   Activity 22

A conjunction may join two or more verbs in the predicate.

EXAMPLE   The crowd yelled, jumped, and cheered.
(*Yelled, jumped,* and *cheered* are the verbs in the compound predicate.)

Activity B Write the complete predicate for each sentence. Underline each simple predicate. Circle the conjunction.

1. Joe sits in the new car, drives along the street, and honks at friends.
2. The young man looks for a store, stops, parks, and walks down the street.
3. Joe goes into the store, looks at the shelves, and talks to the owner.
4. The young buyer laughs, jokes, and pays for a CD.
5. Joe gets into his car, roars past the park, and turns onto the highway.

You can often combine the predicates of two or more sentences into a compound predicate and make the two sentences into one sentence.

EXAMPLE   Amanda sat. Amanda groaned.
Amanda sat and groaned.
Ichiro made lunch. Ichiro sat at the counter.
Ichiro made lunch and sat at the counter.

Activity C Write each pair of sentences as one sentence with a compound predicate.

1. Mark ate at the counter. Mark drank at the counter.
2. Sue watched television. Sue went to bed.
3. The old dog barked. The old dog howled.
4. The brown rabbit jumped. The brown rabbit ran away.
5. The women sat at the table. The women talked at the table.

Activity B Answers

1. <u>sits</u> in the new car, <u>drives</u> along the street, (and) <u>honks</u> at friends
2. <u>looks</u> for a store, <u>stops</u>, <u>parks</u>, (and) <u>walks</u> down the street 3. <u>goes</u> into the store, <u>looks</u> at the shelves, (and) <u>talks</u> to the owner 4. <u>laughs</u>, <u>jokes</u>, (and) <u>pays</u> for a CD 5. <u>gets</u> into his car, <u>roars</u> past the park, (and) <u>turns</u> onto the highway

Activity C Answers

1. Mark ate and drank at the counter. 2. Sue watched television and went to bed. 3. The old dog barked and howled. 4. The brown rabbit jumped and ran away.
5. The women sat and talked at the table. *Or* The women sat at the table and talked.

3 Reinforce and Extend

GLOBAL CONNECTION

Explain that in some languages, the verb changes form when compound subjects are added to a sentence. Give students the following example from Spanish: *Carlos vivió en Guatemala* means "Carlos lived in Guatemala." *Carlos y Maria vivieron in Guatemala* means "Carlos and Maria lived in Guatemala."

Ask students with knowledge of other languages to give more examples of how verbs change when compound subjects are added to a sentence.

Writing Practice

Ask students to form small groups and create sentences with compound predicates. Help the groups get started by asking them to write each group member's name and then to complete a sentence with several verbs placed after the names.

TEACHER ALERT

If some students point out that they have seen very short compound sentences without commas, explain that some writers use commas only in long or confusing compound sentences.

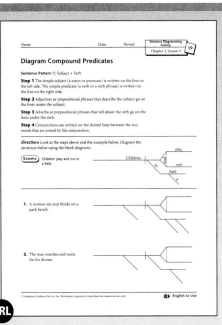

Lesson at a Glance

Chapter 3 Lesson 4

Overview This lesson presents a method for analyzing long sentences that contain compounds and prepositional phrases.

Objective

■ To identify compound subjects and compound objects of prepositions in long sentences

Student Pages 56–57

Teacher's Resource Library

Workbook Activity 23

Activity 23

Alternative Activity 23

Sentence Diagramming Activity 20

Vocabulary

compound object of preposition

 1 Warm-Up Activity

Use the sentence in the example box to teach the three steps of finding the subject in complicated sentences.

 2 Teaching the Lesson

Have students review the parts of a prepositional phrase. Ask students how they can identify a compound subject or a compound predicate in a sentence.

Activity A Answers

1. simple predicate: sat **2.** complete subject: The salad with oranges and nuts and the frozen yogurt in the pint container **3.** compound simple subjects: salad, yogurt; conjunction: and **4.** prepositional phrases in the complete subject: with oranges and nuts; in the pint container **5.** objects of prepositions: oranges, nuts, container

---

Lesson 4 Compounds and Prepositions

Compound object of preposition

Two or more objects of one preposition joined by a conjunction

Some sentences with compound subjects may also have adjective prepositional phrases. The object of a prepositional phrase may be compound, too.

EXAMPLE The man in the jacket and scarf and the boy with the bicycle spoke softly.

Compound subject	man and boy
Compound object of a preposition	jacket and scarf

It may seem difficult at first to locate the simple subjects in a sentence with a compound subject, prepositional phrases, and **compound objects of the preposition.** However, there are some steps you can follow to find the subjects.

1. Find the verb.
2. Ask who or what is doing the action. (The answer is more than one word if the subject is compound.)
3. Find the prepositions. Remember that the object of a preposition is never the subject.

Activity A Write this sentence on your paper. Then follow the directions.

The salad with oranges and nuts and the frozen yogurt in the pint container sat in the sun.

1. Draw a line under the simple predicate.
2. Draw two lines under the complete subject.
3. Write the simple subjects found in the compound subject. Circle the conjunction.
4. Put brackets [ ] around the prepositional phrases in the complete subject.
5. Circle the object or compound object of each preposition in the complete subject.

56   *Chapter 3 Using Compound Parts*

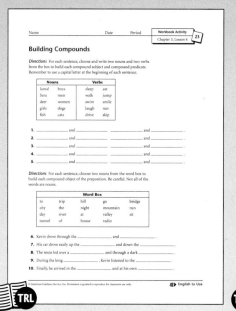

Workbook Activity 23

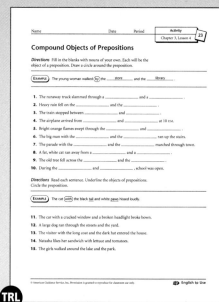

Activity 23

Activity B On your paper, write the simple subjects that make up the compound subject of each sentence.

1. Diane in a white sweater and Rosa in a blue coat wait outside a theater in the cool breeze.

2. The girls and a few other friends talk about the new movie and the actors.

3. Behind the girls, more men, women, and teenagers crowd onto the sidewalk and the street.

4. At the curb, a man in a dark suit and a woman in a pink dress arrive.

5. The girls and the large crowd of men and women cheer for the famous couple.

Activity C Write each sentence on your paper. Circle each preposition and underline each object of the preposition.

1. A yellow plane with a number on the wing and a silver plane with a blue design bounce along the rough ground.

2. The model plane with red and green lights glides high above the trees.

3. A wooden plane and a metal plane wait with their owners in the open field of short grass.

4. People with video cameras and reporters with microphones watch carefully.

5. The silver and blue plane flies high, soars above the trees, and wins easily.

The compound parts of sentences have similarities and differences like these two planes.

Activity B Answers

1. Diane, Rosa **2.** girls, friends
3. men, women, teenagers **4.** man, woman **5.** girls, crowd

Activity C Answers

1. Prep.—with, on, with, along; Obj. of Prep.—number, wing, design, ground **2.** Prep.—with, above; Obj. of Prep.—lights, trees
3. Prep.—with, in, of; Obj. of Prep.—owners, field, grass
4. Prep.—with, with; Obj. of Prep.—cameras, microphones
5. Prep.—above; Obj. of Prep.—trees

3 Reinforce and Extend

LEARNING STYLES

Visual/Spatial
Have students examine the photograph of the airplanes on page 57. Have each student identify at least two different elements about the planes. Then organize students in pairs, and ask partners to combine their observations into a sentence with a compound subject or a compound object of a preposition.

ONLINE CONNECTION

The English Department at the University of Calgary offers tutorials and interactive exercises that allow students to test their grammar skills. For a grammar exercise on compound sentences, visit *www.ucalgary.ca/UofC/eduweb/ grammar/course/sentence/2_5b.htm.*

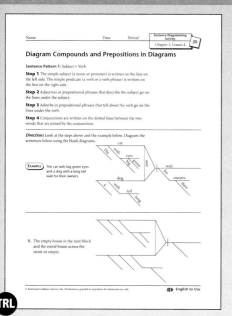

Speaking Practice

Long sentences containing compounds may be difficult to understand when read aloud because listeners may lose track of the subject or the verb. Have students take turns reading aloud the sentences in Activities B and C. Tell students to modulate their voices so that listeners can hear which parts of the sentence are most important—the subjects and verbs—and which parts are descriptive—the objects of the prepositions.

Lesson at a Glance

Chapter 3 Lesson 5

Overview This lesson explains compound sentences.

Objectives

- To identify complete ideas in compound sentences
- To identify sentence parts in compound sentences
- To construct compound sentences from two simple sentences

Student Pages 58–59

Teacher's Resource Library **TRL**

Workbook Activity 24

Activity 24

Alternative Activity 24

Sentence Diagramming Activity 21

Vocabulary

compound sentence

1 Warm-Up Activity

Write the following on the board: *Marcus plays the guitar well. He will not play for strangers. Marcus plays the guitar well, but he will not play for strangers.* Have a volunteer circle the conjunction that combines the sentences.

2 Teaching the Lesson

Emphasize that in a compound sentence, the information on both sides of the conjunction must be a complete sentence.

Activity A Answers

1. The winning car rolls across the finish line, (and) the driver smiles with joy. 2. In the stands, a friend cheers, (and) a brother grins. 3. The driver waves, (and) the crowd yells louder. 4. On the track, a black car crosses over the line, (and) a red car limps into the pit. 5. The race is done, (and) the race crews pack up all of their tools.

Lesson 5 Compound Sentences

Compound Sentence
A sentence made up of two or more complete sentences joined by a conjunction

A **compound sentence** is two or more sentences joined by a conjunction. A compound sentence joins two related ideas. Each part of a compound sentence has a subject and a verb.

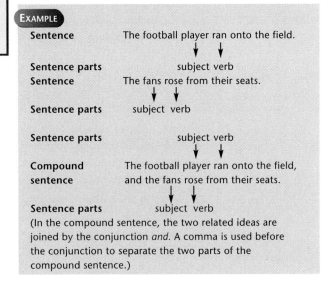

EXAMPLE

Sentence	The football player ran onto the field.
Sentence parts	subject verb
Sentence	The fans rose from their seats.
Sentence parts	subject verb
Sentence parts	subject verb
Compound sentence	The football player ran onto the field, and the fans rose from their seats.
Sentence parts	subject verb

(In the compound sentence, the two related ideas are joined by the conjunction *and*. A comma is used before the conjunction to separate the two parts of the compound sentence.)

Writing Tip

Using compound sentences helps you write more ideas in each sentence. This helps you include more information and gives your writing variety.

Activity A Write the sentences on your paper. Underline the two complete ideas. Circle the conjunction.

Example The day was long, (and) the competition was tough.

1. The winning car rolls across the finish line, and the driver smiles with joy.

2. In the stands, a friend cheers, and a brother grins.

3. The driver waves, and the crowd yells louder.

4. On the track, a black car crosses over the line, and a red car limps into the pit.

5. The race is done, and the race crews pack up all of their tools.

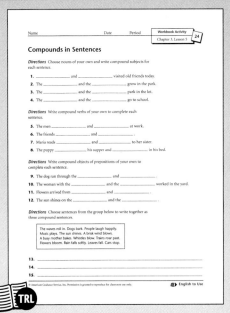

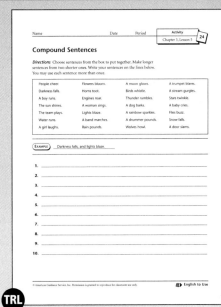

Rain

Happen, Occur

But

Ground

Dry

Stay

Activity B Write the subjects and verbs in these sentences on your paper. Write the conjunction that joins the sentence parts.

Example The rain falls, but the ground stays dry.

Subjects   rain, ground

Verbs   falls, stays

Conjunction   but

1. The man works on a puzzle, and the woman reads silently in the big chair.
2. The couple sits quietly, and the rain splashes against the window.
3. During the storm, the radio crackles, and the lights dim.
4. The long day passes, and darkness falls swiftly.
5. The power fails, but the couple sits by the fire.

Activity C Combine each pair of sentences into a compound sentence. Use the conjunction in parentheses. Don't forget to put a comma before the conjunction.

Example A dog barked in the distance.

Michael huddled in the corner. (and)

A dog barked in the distance, and Michael huddled in the corner.

1. Shadows moved across the wall. The door creaked softly. (and)
2. Michael sat up. The noise faded away. (but)
3. The wind died down. Michael tossed and turned. (yet)
4. The sun came up. The day began. (and)
5. Michael was tired. He went to school. (but)

The rain falls, but the ground stays dry.

Activity B Answers

1. Subjects: man, woman; Verbs: works, reads; Conj.: and
2. Subjects: couple, rain; Verbs: sits, splashes; Conj.: and
3. Subjects: radio, lights; Verbs: crackles, dim; Conj.: and
4. Subjects: day, darkness; Verbs: passes, falls; Conj.: and
5. Subjects: power, couple; Verbs: fails, sits; Conj.: but

Activity C Answers

1. Shadows moved across the wall, and the door creaked softly.
2. Michael sat up, but the noise faded away.
3. The wind died down, yet Michael tossed and turned.
4. The sun came up, and the day began.
5. Michael was tired, but he went to school.

3 Reinforce and Extend

LEARNING STYLES

Auditory/Verbal

Ask students to write pairs of short, related sentences. Have them exchange their sentences with partners who can combine sentences to form compound sentences. Ask students to read their compound sentences aloud.

TEACHER ALERT

When students begin to write their own compound sentences, they may link an independent clause with a dependent clause by mistake.

ASL ILLUSTRATION

Have students practice the sentence illustrated on page 59. Draw their attention to the sign for "but," and ask them to relate the gesture to its meaning. Help students see that the hands moving apart can illustrate a word that indicates opposition.

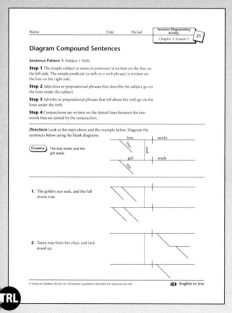

TRL

Sentence Diagramming Activity 21

Lesson at a Glance

Chapter 3 Lesson 6

Overview This lesson reviews compound parts of sentences and compound sentences.

Objectives
- To identify compounds
- To complete compounds
- To identify types of compounds

Student Pages 60–61

Teacher's Resource Library

Workbook Activity 25

Activity 25

Alternative Activity 25

Sentence Diagramming Activity 22

....

Vocabulary

compound

....

 1 Warm-Up Activity

Write on the board two nouns and two verbs. Instruct students to combine the subjects and verbs to form compound sentences or sentences that contain compounds.

 2 Teaching the Lesson

Read and discuss the definition of *compound.* Then ask volunteers for a variety of sentences that are compound, as well as sentences with compound parts.

Activity A Answers

Answers may vary, but each answer should make sense in the sentence.

Activity B Answers

1. parked and sat—V 2. grease and smoke—Obj. of Prep. 3. salads and pans—S 4. pole, boat, and motor—Obj. of Prep. 5. car and motor home—S

Lesson 6 Sentences with Compounds

Compound
Two or more words, phrases, or ideas joined by a conjunction

You have learned about compound subjects, compound predicates, compound objects of a preposition, and compound sentences.

Compounds are two or more words, phrases, or ideas joined by a conjunction. Some sentences have one compound part. Some sentences have two or more compound parts.

Activity A On your paper, write each sentence. Fill in the missing compound shown in parentheses.

1. Nurses watched over the patients during the day and _____ . (object of the preposition)
2. The _____ and men walked toward the bus stop. (subject)
3. The bus driver _____ and looked at the train crossing. (verb)
4. Alice and _____ waited for Belinda. (subject)
5. Belinda laughed and _____ to her friends. (verb)

Activity B Write the compounds found in each of these sentences. Write the kind of compound used.

Example A team of workers and volunteers drove steadily through the morning.

workers and volunteers—objects of the preposition

1. Alberto parked and sat on the pier with his fishing pole.
2. The window fan in the diner blew through the grease and smoke.
3. Crisp, green salads and long pans of tasty meats sat on the table.
4. The angler with a pole, boat, and motor fished in the middle of the river.
5. A car and a motor home turned into the park.

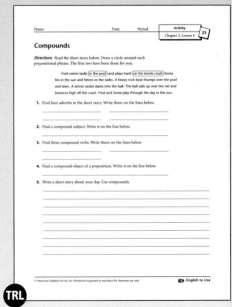

Workbook Activity 25   Activity 25

Activity C Read each sentence. On your paper, write the compound part of each sentence. Then write whether it is a *compound subject*, a *compound predicate*, a *compound object of a preposition*, or a *compound sentence*.

1. A gray cat climbed out through a window, and then he ran across the yard.

2. He jumped over the bushes and fence.

3. A small, red car braked and skidded to a sudden stop.

4. The cat jumped through the window of the car, and the driver screamed in fright.

5. The driver and a woman passenger in the car looked for the owner of the cat.

Activity D Read the paragraph. Then write the answer to each item on your paper.

> The fish pulled on the hook and line. The fishing rod bent, and the reel buzzed. The angler and the fish pulled hard. The angler bent and reached toward the fish. The smart fish scraped against a rock under the water. The angler stood up, and the fish splashed. Then the rain and wind picked up. Not only the angler but also the fish headed for home and safety.

1. Write the sentence that has no compounds.

2. What kind of compound does the first sentence have?

3. Write one of the two sentences that has a compound subject but no other compound parts. Underline the simple subjects.

4. Write the sentence that has a compound predicate. Underline the verbs.

5. Write one of the two compound sentences. Underline the two ideas. Circle the conjunction.

---

1. A gray cat climbed out through a window, and then he ran across the yard.—compound sentence
2. bushes and fence—compound object of a preposition **3.** braked and skidded—compound predicate
4. The cat jumped through the window of the car, and the driver screamed in fright.—compound sentence **5.** driver and passenger—compound subject

Activity D Answers

1. The smart fish scraped against a rock under the water. **2.** compound object of a preposition **3.** The angler and the fish pulled hard. *Or* Then the rain and the wind picked up. **4.** The angler bent and reached toward the fish. **5.** The fishing rod bent, (and) the reel buzzed. *Or* The angler stood up, (and) the fish splashed.

3 **Reinforce and Extend**

LEARNING STYLES

Body/Kinesthetic
Have students act out the work of "building" compound sentences. Write a subject on the board. Have groups of students write complete predicates on separate pieces of paper. Then have students "build" the sentence by ordering the predicates and placing commas and conjunctions as needed. Repeat the exercise by writing a verb on the board and having students form the complete subject.

LEARNING STYLES

Logical/Mathematical
You may want to develop a system of color-coding the parts of compound sentences. Provide students with colored highlighters, and help them mark the sentences according to the colors you have chosen.

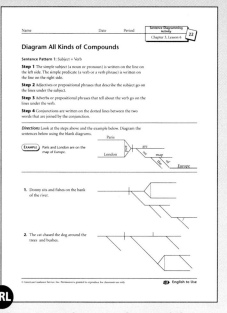

Lesson at a Glance

Chapter 3 Lesson 7

Overview This lesson explains how to use commas and semicolons to punctuate sentences with compound parts. It also explains how to punctuate the titles of long works and the parts of long works.

Objectives

■ To use commas and semicolons correctly to punctuate sentences with compound parts

■ To capitalize and underline titles and to enclose parts of works in quotation marks

Student Pages 62–63

Teacher's Resource Library

Workbook Activity 26

Activity 26

Alternative Activity 26

....

Vocabulary

quotation marks
semicolon

....

 1 **Warm-Up Activity**

Point out that no matter how skillful a writer is, readers may not be able to understand the writing if capital letters and punctuation are incorrect.

 2 **Teaching the Lesson**

Ask students why commas are needed in the sentence in the first example box. Help students identify the series of four verbs, and discuss why the items in the series must be separated by commas.

Use commas in sentences with three or more compound parts.

> **Semicolon (;)**
> A punctuation mark that separates two related ideas not connected by a conjunction

 EXAMPLE

	Cats often meow, purr, scratch, or hiss.
Parts of speech	noun adv. verb verb verb conj. verb
Sentence parts	subject │ compound predicate

Activity A On your paper, write each sentence. Add commas, capital letters, and periods.

> **Communication Connection**
>
> Today more people than ever use e-mail to communicate with others. Some experts predict that by the year 2005 people will send more than 36 billion e-mail messages per day.

1. carrots corn tomatoes beans and peas grow in the garden
2. spiders flies and mice wait in the basement
3. people eat sleep and rise again for another day
4. swings slides and monkey bars sat on the empty playground
5. cheerleaders bend jump dance and yell
6. toys books and clothes lie on the floor
7. bears snakes and monkeys live in the zoo
8. smoke sparks and flames pour from the chimney
9. I sent an e-mail to the coach the teacher and the principal
10. Computers TVs and keyboards are in that room

You have learned to use commas in compound sentences. Place a comma after the first complete idea, just before the conjunction. You can use a **semicolon** instead of a conjunction to separate two related ideas in a sentence.

EXAMPLE Some people sing, but other people dance.
Some people sing; other people dance.

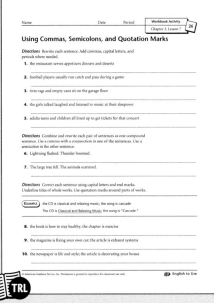

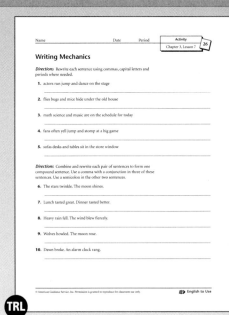

**Quotation marks
(" ")**

Punctuation used around the title of a part of a large work

Underline the titles of books, magazines, newspapers, and CDs when writing by hand.

Using What You've Learned

Imagine that you have recently read a magazine article about a CD that you like. Write a letter to a friend, telling about the article. In your letter, include the name of the magazine, the article, and the CD. Remember to write the titles correctly.

Activity B On your paper, write each pair of sentences as one compound sentence. Use a comma with a conjunction in three of the sentences. Use a semicolon in the other two.

1. Skaters glide. Bicyclists ride.
2. The night wind blew. The moon disappeared.
3. Dinner burned in the oven. The smoke alarm rang.
4. The sun shone. People headed toward the beach.
5. Time passed. Night fell.

You know that a proper noun begins with a capital letter. Titles are proper nouns. Titles begin with capital letters.

Titles of books appear in *italic* (or underlined). The same is true for the titles of magazines, newspapers, and CDs. Each is a complete work. Parts of works such as chapters, articles, and songs need **quotation marks** around them. Remember:

- The title of a large work should be printed in italic (or underlined).
- The title of a part of a large work should be in quotation marks.

> **EXAMPLE** The book is <u>World of Architecture.</u>
> The book is *World of Architecture.*
> The chapter is "Modern Buildings."

Activity C On your paper, correct each sentence. Use capital letters and periods. Underline titles of whole works. Use quotation marks around parts of works.

1. the newspaper is the daily news and information
2. the CD is songs of jazz; the song is a jazz evening
3. the book is canada cooking; the chapter is cooking chicken
4. the book is fix your car; the chapter is spark plugs
5. the magazine is surf and stuff; the article is surfing clubs

Using What You've Learned

Tell students that properly punctuating titles is a courtesy to readers. Proper punctuation helps readers find a work that they might want to read or learn more about. After each student has written a letter containing titles, have students exchange letters with partners. Then have each partner try to learn more about the magazine or CD by using either print materials or a computer search.

3 **Reinforce and Extend**

AT HOME

Correctly writing sentences that contain compounds and titles requires practice. Suggest that students observe the movements of family members or of people in their neighborhoods. Ask students to include compounds in the sentences they will write about what they see. Tell students to use titles as well.

Activity A Answers

1. Carrots, corn, tomatoes, beans, and peas grow in the garden.
2. Spiders, flies, and mice wait in the basement. 3. People eat, sleep, and rise again for another day.
4. Swings, slides, and monkey bars sat on the empty playground.
5. Cheerleaders bend, jump, dance, and yell. 6. Toys, books, and clothes lie on the floor. 7. Bears, snakes, and monkeys live in the zoo. 8. Smoke, sparks, and flames pour from the chimney. 9. I sent an e-mail to the coach, the teacher, and the principal. 10. Computers, TVs, and keyboards are in that room.

Activity B Answers

Answers will vary. Three sentences should have a comma and a conjunction; two should have a semicolon. Sentences are shown with commas. 1. Skaters glide, and bicyclists ride. 2. The night wind blew, and the moon disappeared. 3. Dinner burned in the oven, and the smoke alarm rang. 4. The sun shone, and people headed toward the beach. 5. Time passed, and night fell.

Activity C Answers

1. The newspaper is <u>The Daily News and Information</u>. 2. The CD is <u>Songs of Jazz</u>; the song is "A Jazz Evening." 3. The book is <u>Canada Cooking</u>; the chapter is "Cooking Chicken." 4. The book is <u>Fix Your Car</u>; the chapter is "Spark Plugs." 5. The magazine is <u>Surf and Stuff</u>; the article is "Surfing Clubs."

Chapter 3 Review

Use the Chapter Review to prepare students for tests and to reteach content from the chapter.

Chapter 3 Mastery Test

The Teacher's Resource Library includes two parallel forms of the Chapter 3 Mastery Test. The difficulty level of the two forms is equivalent. You may wish to use one form as a pretest and the other form as a posttest.

REVIEW ANSWERS

Part A

1. compound subject
2. quotation marks
3. compound 4. compound sentence 5. compound object of preposition 6. compound predicate 7. conjunction
8. semicolon

Part B

9. and; Janet, Maria 10. and; hot dogs, popcorn/and; ate, went 11. but; The roller coaster was noisy, it was the most fun 12. Neither, nor; Janet, Maria

Part C

13. Whitney <u>pulls</u> over in the car and <u>shouts</u> to her friends.
14. Irena <u>sings</u> and <u>dances</u> beautifully. 15. A <u>woman</u> with a briefcase and a <u>boy</u> in a football uniform got on the bus. 16. Juan went to the <u>store</u> and the <u>gym</u>.
17. <u>Gerald</u> and <u>Lisa</u> like to read.

Word Bank

compound
compound object of preposition
compound predicate
compound sentence
compound subject
conjunction
quotation marks
semicolon

Part A Read each sentence below. Fill in each blank with a vocabulary word that correctly completes the sentence.

1. A _____ is two or more subjects joined by a conjunction.
2. Place _____ around the title of part of a large work.
3. Two or more words, phrases, or ideas joined by a conjunction is a _____.
4. You can create a _____ by combining two or more complete sentences with a conjunction.
5. A _____ is two or more objects of one preposition joined by a conjunction.
6. Two or more predicates joined by a conjunction is a _____.
7. A _____ joins two or more words, phrase, or ideas.
8. Use a _____ to separate two related ideas not connected by a conjunction.

Part B Read the sentences. Write the conjunctions and the words they connect on your paper.

9. Janet and Maria spent the day at the fair.
10. They ate hot dogs and popcorn and then went to the rides.
11. The roller coaster was noisy, but it was the most fun.
12. Neither Janet nor Maria was scared in the haunted house.

Part C Write each pair of sentences as a single sentence. Use conjunctions to connect subjects, verbs, or objects of prepositions. Underline any compound subjects, predicates, and objects of prepositions.

13. Whitney pulls over in the car. She shouts to her friends.
14. Irena sings beautifully. Irena dances beautifully.
15. A woman with a briefcase got on the bus. A boy in a football uniform got on the bus.
16. Juan went to the store. Juan went to the gym.
17. Gerald likes to read. Lisa likes to read.

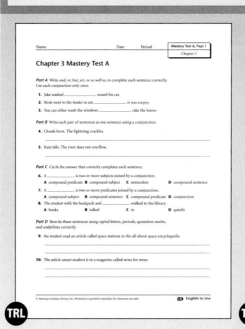
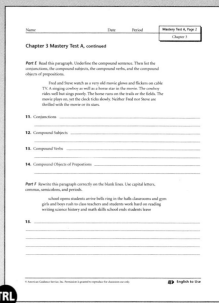

Chapter 3 Mastery Test A

Part D Read each sentence. Then answer the questions that follow. Write the letter of the sentences.

> **A** A man and a woman with a large trunk and a small box wait on a dusty bench inside the station.
> **B** At the station, the man and the woman climb into the train and sit down near a window.
> **C** The whistle blows, and the train moves.

18. Which sentence has a compound verb?

19. Which sentence has a compound object of a preposition?

20. Which sentence is a compound sentence?

Part E Write each pair of sentences as one compound sentence. Use a semicolon in one of the sentences.

21. The car stopped. The driver fixed the flat tire.

22. The team practiced. Reporters watched.

Part F Choose the correct way to write each underlined item.

23. The newspaper called <u>usa news</u> is on the table.
  A USA news   **C** *Usa News*
  B *USA News*   **D** "USA News"

24. The book has a chapter titled <u>the right machine.</u>
  A "the right machine."   **C** *The Right Machine.*
  B The Right Machine.   **D** "The Right Machine."

25. Find a recipe in the book <u>joys of grilling.</u>
  A *Joys of Grilling.*   **C** Joys of Grilling.
  B "joys of grilling."   **D** "Joys of Grilling."

If you know you will have to define terms on a test, write the term on one side of a card. Write its definition on the other side. Use the cards to test yourself.

REVIEW ANSWERS

Part D
18. B **19.** A **20.** C

Part E
21. The car stopped, and the driver fixed the flat tire. *Or* The car stopped; the driver fixed the flat tire. **22.** The team practiced, and reporters watched. *Or* The team practiced; reporters watched.

Part F
23. B **24.** D **25.** A

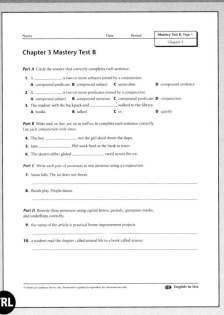

Chapter 3 Mastery Test B

Chapter 4

Planning Guide

Direct Objects

	Student Pages	Student Text Lesson			Language Skills	
		Vocabulary	Practice Activities	Identification Skills	Writing Skills	Punctuation Skills
Lesson 1 What is a Direct Object?	68–69	✔	✔	✔	✔	
Lesson 2 Compound Direct Objects	70–71	✔	✔	✔	✔	✔
Lesson 3 More Compounds	72–73		✔	✔	✔	
Lesson 4 Direct Objects and Prepositional Phrases	74–75		✔	✔	✔	
Lesson 5 Nouns in a Sentence	76–77	✔	✔	✔	✔	
Lesson 6 Pronouns in a Sentence	78–79	✔	✔	✔	✔	
Lesson 7 Using Pronouns	80–81		✔	✔	✔	
Lesson 8 Pronoun or Adjective?	82–83		✔	✔	✔	
Lesson 9 This, That, These, Those	84–85		✔	✔	✔	
Lesson 10 Writing Mechanics	86–87	✔	✔	✔	✔	✔

Chapter Activities

Teacher's Resource Library
Community Connection 4:
Visit the Chamber of Commerce
English in Your World 4:
Listening for Pronouns

Assessment Options

Student Text
Chapter 4 Review

Teacher's Resource Library
Chapter 4 Mastery Tests A and B

66A

	Student Text Features					Teaching Strategies					Learning Styles						Teacher's Resource Library				
ASL Illustration	Communication Connection	Notes	Using What You've Learned	Writing Tips	Teacher Alert	Online Connection	Applications (Home, Career, Community, Global)	Speaking Practice	Writing Practice	Auditory/Verbal	Body/Kinesthetic	Interpersonal/ Group Learning	Logical/Mathematical	Visual/Spatial	LEP/ESL	Workbook Activities	Activities	Alternative Activities	Sentence Diagramming Activities	Self-Study Guide
69		✔									69					27	27	27	23	✔
				✔				71				71				28	28	28	24	✔
						73								73		29	29	29	25	✔
						75							75			30	30	30	26	✔
		✔			77							77				31	31	31		✔
			79	✔		79				79						32	32	32	27	✔
	80	✔				81								81		33	33	33	28	✔
				✔		83								83		34	34	34		✔
									85						85	35	35	35		✔
87										87						36	36	36		✔

Pronunciation Key

a	hat	e	let	ī	ice	ô	order	u̇	put	sh	she
ā	age	ē	equal	o	hot	oi	oil	ü	rule	th	thin
ä	far	ėr	term	ō	open	ou	out	ch	child	ᴛʜ	then
â	care	i	it	ȯ	saw	u	cup	ng	long	zh	measure

ə { a in about / e in taken / i in pencil / o in lemon / u in circus }

Alternative Activities

The Teacher's Resource Library (TRL) contains a set of lower-level worksheets called Alternative Activities. These worksheets cover the same content as the regular Activities but are written at a second-grade reading level.

Skill Track Software

Use the Skill Track Software for English to Use for additional reinforcement of this chapter. The software program allows students using AGS textbooks to be assessed for mastery of each chapter and lesson of the textbook. Students access the software on an individual basis and are assessed with multiple-choice items.

Chapter 4:
Direct Objects
pages 66–89

Lessons

1. **What is a Direct Object?**
    pages 68–69

2. **Compound Direct Objects**
    pages 70–71

3. **More Compounds**
    pages 72–73

4. **Direct Objects and Prepositional Phrases**
    pages 74–75

5. **Nouns in a Sentence**
    pages 76–77

6. **Pronouns in a Sentence**
    pages 78–79

7. **Using Pronouns**
    pages 80–81

8. **Pronoun or Adjective?**
    pages 82–83

9. **This, That, These, Those**
    pages 84–85

10. **Writing Mechanics**
    pages 86–87

Chapter 4 Review
pages 88–89

Skill Track Software for English to Use

Teacher's Resource Library TRL

Workbook Activities 27–36

Activities 27–36

Alternative Activities 27–36

Sentence Diagramming
Activities 23–28
(Optional sentence activities
accompany lessons.)

Community Connection 4

English in Your World 4

Chapter 4 Self-Study Guide

Chapter 4 Mastery Tests A and B

(Answer Keys for the Teacher's
Resource Library begin on page 308
of this Teacher's Edition.)

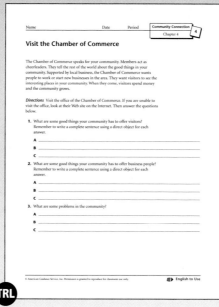

Community Connection 4   English in Your World 4

Chapter

4 Direct Objects

Have you ever watched an exciting soccer game? When you are watching a good game, it is sometimes hard to find the player who has the ball. You try to follow the ball from player to player. One player passes the ball. Another player kicks the ball. The forward passes the ball to a teammate. Sometimes a goalkeeper blocks the ball. The ball receives most of the action.

In this chapter, you will study words that take the action of the verb.

Goals for Learning

♦ To identify the *subject + verb + direct object* sentence pattern
♦ To identify simple and compound direct objects
♦ To use pronouns correctly in place of nouns
♦ To capitalize titles of people and abstract proper nouns
♦ To punctuate compound sentences correctly

67

Introducing the Chapter

Invite students to think of sentences that describe the moves in a soccer game. Write them on the board. Underline the verbs. Draw an arrow from the verbs to the words that receive the action of the verbs. Tell students that the words that receive the action of the verbs are called direct objects.

TEACHER'S RESOURCE

The AGS Teaching Strategies in English Transparencies may be used with this chapter. The transparencies add an interactive dimension to expand and enhance the *English to Use* program content.

CAREER INTEREST INVENTORY

The AGS Harrington-O'Shea Career Decision-Making System–Revised (CDM) may be used with this chapter. Students can use the CDM to explore their interests and identify careers. The CDM defines career areas that are indicated by students' responses on the inventory.

Writing Tips and Notes

Ask volunteers to read the tips and notes that appear in the margins throughout the chapter. Then discuss them with the class.

CHAPTER PROJECT

 After students have completed the chapter, invite them to identify all the grammatical concepts learned in this chapter in an excerpt from a story or book. Students may type the excerpt into a word processing program and use graphics such as color and formatting to highlight direct objects, prepositional phrases, and so on.

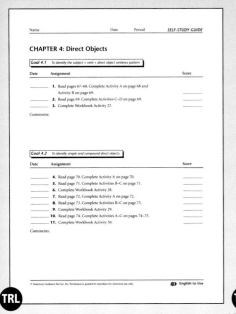

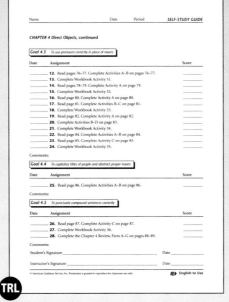

Chapter 4 Lesson 1

Overview This lesson introduces and explains direct objects.

Objectives

- To identify the direct object in sentences
- To write direct objects in sentences
- To identify sentence parts in sentences with direct objects

Student Pages 68–69

Teacher's Resource Library TRL

Workbook Activity 27

Activity 27

Alternative Activity 27

Sentence Diagramming Activity 23

Vocabulary

direct object

----

1 Warm-Up Activity

Say and write on the board: *Nathan opened the book.* Ask students to identify the subject and verb of the sentence. (Nathan, opened) Then ask "What did Nathan open?" Students should understand that Nathan opened the book. Explain that *book* is a direct object. Direct objects always receive action directly from the verb.

2 Teaching the Lesson

Write these sentences on the board: *The boy washed. The teacher read. The girls cheered.* Help students add direct objects to each sentence by asking "The boy washed *what*? The teacher read *what*? The girls cheered *what*?" Tell students to notice the difference in the patterns of the original sentences and the new ones.

Activity A Answers

1. DO—rain 2. DO—corn 3. DO—puddle 4. DO—water 5. DO—water

Direct object
A noun or pronoun that receives action directly from the verb

In earlier lessons, you focused on one sentence pattern: *subject + verb.* Now you will learn about a second sentence pattern: *subject + verb + direct object.*

A **direct object** is a noun or pronoun that receives action directly from the verb.

EXAMPLE   Yoshi watched.
Sentence pattern   subject | verb
            Yoshi watched the clock.
Sentence pattern   subject + verb + direct object
(The noun *clock* receives the action of the verb *watched.* Yoshi watched *what?* Yoshi watched the clock. *Clock* is the direct object.)

Here are more examples of sentences with action verbs and direct objects. Notice that in each sentence the noun receives action directly from the verb.

EXAMPLE   Lynda mailed the **letter.**
Sentence pattern   subject + verb + direct object
(Lynda mailed *what?* Lynda mailed the *letter. Letter* is the direct object.)

            The friends ate **lunch.**
(The friends ate *what?* The friends ate *lunch. Lunch* is the direct object.)

A direct object helps complete a thought in a sentence. To find the direct object, ask *what* or *whom.* Then look for the word or words that answer the question.

Activity A On your paper, write each sentence. Draw an arrow from the bold verb to the direct object.

Example The ball **hits** the net.

1. A farmer **watches** the rain.
2. The water **washes** the corn.
3. The rain **forms** a puddle.
4. The ground **swallows** the water.
5. The plant roots **drink** the water.

----

68 Chapter 4 Direct Objects

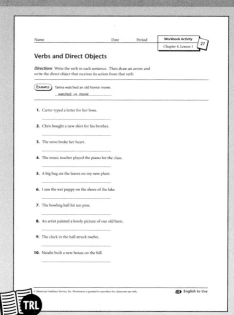

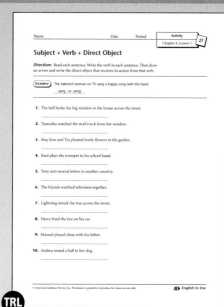

Workbook Activity 27   **Activity 27**

Lunch

Friend

Eat

Finish

The friends ate lunch.

Activity B Fill in the blank with a direct object. Write the completed sentences on your paper.

1. Jim opened the _____ .

2. The bat hit the _____ .

3. Bright sunlight lit the _____ .

4. A sharp saw cut the _____ .

5. The cat caught a _____ .

Adjectives can describe nouns that are direct objects.

EXAMPLE			The girls watched an old TV show.

Parts of speech   *adj. noun   verb   adj. adj. adj. noun*
Sentence pattern   subject + verb + direct object
(The adjectives *an, old,* and *TV* describe the direct object *show.*)

Activity C Write the sentences on your paper. Circle the direct object. Do not include adjectives. Draw an arrow from the verb to the direct object. The verb is in bold.

Example Thick clouds **surrounded** the quiet (city).

1. A scientist **pushed** two buttons.

2. Sparks **filled** the cold, dreary room.

3. The scientist **created** a giant monster.

4. The scientist **watched** his creation.

5. The monster **opened** the heavy steel door.

Activity D Write each sentence. Label the subject (*s.*), the verb (*v.*), and the direct object (*d. obj.*).

1. The farmer plowed the muddy field.

2. Ronald hit a long fly ball.

3. Sarah brought an old green book.

4. A brown squirrel climbed a tall oak tree.

5. The shivering boy closed the kitchen window.

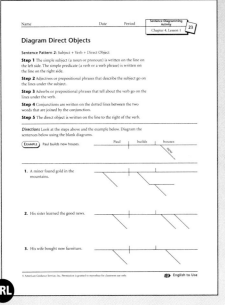

Answers will vary. Possible answers appear below. **1.** Jim opened the window. **2.** The bat hit the ball. **3.** Bright sunlight lit the room. **4.** A sharp saw cut the wood. **5.** The cat caught a mouse.

Activity C Answers

1. DO—buttons 2. DO—room
3. DO—monster 4. DO—creation
5. DO—door

Activity D Answers

1. The farmer plowed the muddy field. 2. Ronald hit a long fly ball. 3. Sarah brought an old green book. 4. A brown squirrel climbed a tall oak tree. 5. The shivering boy closed the kitchen window.

ASL ILLUSTRATION

Have students practice making the signs for *lunch* and *eat.* Invite them to imagine how these signs developed. Ask students whether they would have recognized the signs even without the captions. Have students explain their responses.

 Reinforce and Extend

LEARNING STYLES

Body/Kinesthetic
Allow students to work as partners to act out the sentences in Activities C and D. Acting out the sentences will help students find the verb and understand that the direct object receives the action of the verb. Partners should take turns acting out the sentences. The student who watches the enactment should try to identify the action and the direct object.

Lesson at a Glance

Chapter 4 Lesson 2

Overview This lesson introduces compound direct objects and compound sentences with a direct object in each clause. It also explains that the direct object is part of the complete predicate.

Objectives

- To identify compound direct objects
- To identify direct objects in compound sentences
- To identify the direct object in the complete predicate

Student Pages 70–71

Teacher's Resource Library

Workbook Activity 28

Activity 28

Alternative Activity 28

Sentence Diagramming Activity 24

Vocabulary

compound direct object

 1 Warm-Up Activity

Explain that a compound is a mixture of two or more things. For example, bread is a compound of flour, water, and yeast. Invite students to think of other compounds that they have learned about in other classes.

 2 Teaching the Lesson

Remind students that conjunctions show connections between the parts of a sentence. In completing the activities, students' first step should be to look for the conjunctions in the sentences and then figure out what the conjunctions are connecting—parts of a compound sentence, direct objects, and so on.

Remind students that a comma always precedes the conjunctions in compound sentences.

> **Compound direct object**
> Two or more direct objects joined by a conjunction

Direct objects can be compound. Two or more direct objects joined by a conjunction make a **compound direct object**.

EXAMPLE

The seamstress sewed the dress and the veil.

Parts of speech adj. noun verb adj. noun conj. adj. noun

Sentence pattern subject + verb + direct object

(The two nouns *dress* and *veil* receive the action of the verb *sewed*. The seamstress sewed *what?* The seamstress sewed the dress and veil. The nouns *dress* and *veil* make up the compound direct object. They are joined by the conjunction *and*.)

Activity A On your paper, write the compound direct object in each sentence. Do not include adjectives.

Example Winter brings ice and heavy snow.
compound direct object—ice, snow

1. The big storm floods streets and homes.
2. Water fills basements and yards.
3. Big tree limbs block the sidewalks and streets.
4. Cara watches the muddy water and floating branches.
5. A warm sun slowly dries the puddles and mud.

Two sentences with direct objects can be joined to form a compound sentence. Both ideas in the compound sentence will have direct objects.

EXAMPLE

Marina ordered a salad.
Todd got spaghetti.

Compound sentence Marina ordered salad, and Todd got spaghetti.

(Each part of the compound sentence has a direct object. Marina ordered *what?* She ordered a salad. *Salad* is the direct object of the verb *ordered*. Todd got *what?* He got spaghetti. *Spaghetti* is the direct object of the verb *got*. The two ideas are joined by the conjunction *and*.)

Workbook Activity 28

Activity 28

Activity B Write these compound sentences on your paper. Circle the direct object of each verb. The verbs are in bold.

Example Aman and Tony **wrote** poor (paragraphs), but they **wanted** good (grades).

1. Aman **reads** science fiction stories, but Tony **chooses** war stories.

2. Rosa **played** the piano, and Amy **read** a book.

3. One **likes** music, but the other **likes** books.

4. Rosa **played** loud music, and Amy **covered** her ears.

5. Amy **left** the room, and Rosa **pounded** on the piano keys.

The direct object follows the verb in a sentence. The direct object is always part of the complete predicate.

EXAMPLE
The class heard the important news yesterday.
Sentence parts   complete subject | complete predicate
Sentence pattern   subject + verb + direct object
(The complete predicate includes the verb *heard* plus the direct object *news* and its adjectives *the* and *important*. The adverb *yesterday* answers the question *when* about the verb. *Yesterday* is also part of the complete predicate.)

Activity C Write each sentence on your paper. Draw one line under the complete subject. Draw two lines under the complete predicate. Draw a circle around the direct object or compound direct object.

Example The TV news and the highway patrol warned (people) about a heavy flood.

1. Men, women, and children left the area in their cars.

2. The storm hit the coast and harbors suddenly.

3. The high waves rocked and damaged the boats.

4. Waves and strong winds sank one boat.

5. Thunder and lightning split the sky.

Activity A Answers

1. streets, homes 2. basements, yards 3. sidewalks, streets 4. water, branches 5. puddles, mud

Activity B Answers

1. Aman reads science fiction (stories,) but Tony chooses war (stories.) 2. Rosa played the (piano,) and Amy read a (book.) 3. One likes (music,) but the other likes (books.) 4. Rosa played loud (music,) and Amy covered her (ears.) 5. Amy left the (room,) and Rosa pounded on the piano (keys.)

Activity C Answers

1. Men, women, and children left the (area) in their cars. 2. The storm hit the (coast) and (harbors) suddenly. 3. The high waves rocked and damaged the (boats.) 4. Waves and strong winds sank one (boat.) 5. Thunder and lightning split the (sky.)

Speaking Practice

Have students read aloud the sentences in Activities B and C. Help students hear and express the differences between compound sentences and sentences with compound direct objects. Students should pause briefly when they come to commas in compound sentences. Explain that a slight pause at the comma helps listeners understand that the sentence is a compound sentence.

3 Reinforce and Extend

LEARNING STYLES

Interpersonal/ Group Learning

Encourage students to work in pairs or small groups to create sentences with compound direct objects and compound sentences with a direct object in each clause. Suggest that they model their sentences after those in Activities A, B, and C.

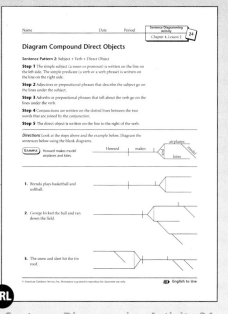

Chapter 4 Lesson 3

Overview This lesson explains the difference between a sentence with compound parts and a compound sentence. It also introduces the concept that each verb in a compound verb may have its own direct object or compound direct object.

Objectives

■ To distinguish between sentences with compound parts and compound sentences

■ To identify compound parts of sentences

Student Pages 72–73

Teacher's Resource Library TRL

Workbook Activity 29

Activity 29

Alternative Activity 29

Sentence Diagramming Activity 25

 Warm-Up Activity

Write the following sentences, side by side, on the board: *The husband and wife wrote and directed the play and the film. The husband and wife wrote the play, but another writer wrote and directed the film.* Ask students to identify all the nouns, verbs, conjunctions, and direct objects. Then ask students which sentence is a compound sentence.

 Teaching the Lesson

Guide students toward developing patterns like these: *Compound sentence:* S + V + DO <conjunction> S + V + DO; *Sentences with compounds:* Compound subjects: (S + S)+ V + DO; *Compound verbs:* S + (V + V) + DO; *Compound direct objects:* S + V + (DO + DO)

Students should consult these patterns as they complete Activities A, B, and C.

Activity A Answers

1. NC 2. C 3. NC 4. C 5. C

A sentence can have a compound subject, a compound verb, and a compound direct object. Do not confuse compound sentences with sentences that have compound parts. Remember, a compound sentence has two complete ideas joined by a conjunction.

EXAMPLE Fireworks and rockets thrill and excite families and friends.

Compound subject	Fireworks and rockets
Compound verb	thrill and excite
Compound direct object	families and friends

(Although the sentence has compound parts, it does not have two ideas joined by a conjunction. It is not a compound sentence.)

Compound sentence Fireworks and rockets thrill the crowd, but only some fireworks excite small children and their friends.

(This sentence is a compound sentence because it has two ideas joined by the conjunction *but*. The first part of the sentence has the compound subject *fireworks* and *rockets*. The second part of the sentence has the compound direct object *children* and *friends*.)

Activity A Number your paper from 1 to 5. Read each sentence. Decide whether it is a compound sentence. If it is compound, write *C*. If it is not compound, write *NC*.

1. Cats and dogs scratch and tear rugs and chairs.

2. Maria mowed the lawn, and Joe trimmed the hedge.

3. David and Mark washed and waxed the car and the truck.

4. The driver emptied the trunk, and his friend carried the boxes and bags inside.

5. The farmer and his son fed the pigs and cows, and their guest fed the horses.

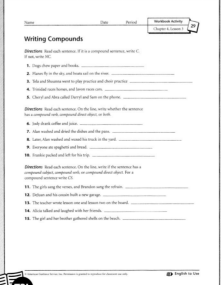

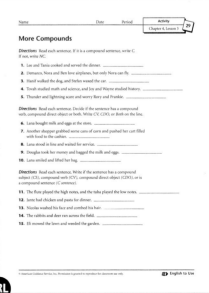

In sentences that have compound verbs, each verb may have its own direct object.

> **EXAMPLE** Jason made breakfast and cleaned the pots.
> **Compound verb** made and cleaned
> (*Breakfast* is the direct object of *made*. *Pots* is the direct object of *cleaned*.)

In sentences that have compound verbs, each verb may have a compound direct object.

> **EXAMPLE** Chris washed the sheets and towels and ironed the shirts and dresses.
> **Compound verb** washed and ironed
> (The compound direct object of *washed* is *sheets* and *towels*. The compound direct object of *ironed* is *shirts* and *dresses*.)

Activity B Number your paper from 1 to 5. Write whether the sentence has a *compound verb*, a *compound direct object*, or *both*.

1. Ben ordered pancakes and eggs.
2. Kim drank coffee and read the morning paper.
3. A server brought the pancakes and poured coffee and juice.
4. Along with his waffle, Eddie wanted strawberries and cream.
5. Ben finished breakfast and left the diner.

Activity C On your paper, write whether the sentence has a *compound subject*, a *compound verb*, or a *compound direct object*. If the sentence is a compound sentence, write *CS*.

1. The birds chirped tunes, and the squirrels gathered nuts.
2. A rabbit ate carrots and lettuce in the garden.
3. The boy and his sister caught fish for dinner.
4. The player removed his hat and glove.
5. Gerri washed the car and tuned the engine.

Activity B Answers

1. compound direct object
2. compound verb 3. both
4. compound direct object
5. compound verb

Activity C Answers

1. CS 2. compound direct object
3. compound subject 4. compound direct object 5. compound verb

 3 **Reinforce and Extend**

LEARNING STYLES

Visual/Spatial
Allow students to use colored pencils or highlighters to mark the lesson activity sentences. Students should assign a different color to each part of a sentence—subject, verb, direct object, and conjunction. Then students should mark each part with the appropriate color. The colors will make it easier for students to see the compound subjects, verbs, and direct objects, and to identify the compound sentences.

GLOBAL CONNECTION

Create a chart with several columns. As column heads use *English* and the names of other languages spoken by students in your class. Under *English*, list the conjunctions *and*, *but*, and *or*. Ask students who speak other languages listed in the chart to say the words for *and*, *but*, and *or* in their native languages and to write them in the chart in the appropriate columns. This activity will help ESL students more easily recognize *and*, *but*, and *or* as conjunctions.

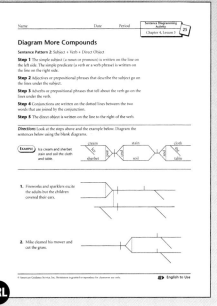

TRL
Sentence Diagramming Activity 25

Lesson at a Glance

Chapter 4 Lesson 4

Overview This lesson introduces direct objects with prepositional phrases.

Objectives

- To identify prepositional phrases that describe direct objects
- To distinguish between adjective and adverb prepositional phrases in sentences
- To review adjectives and nouns

Student Pages 74–75

Teacher's Resource Library

Workbook Activity 30

Activity 30

Alternative Activity 30

Sentence Diagramming Activity 26

1 Warm-Up Activity

List prepositions on the board, including *in, on, of,* and *with.* Remind students that a preposition relates a noun or pronoun to another word; then challenge them to think of other prepositions. After students have listed ten prepositions, invite students to think of hand movements or gestures that act out or give a sense of the direction of each preposition.

2 Teaching the Lesson

Write on the board: *Anna saw a movie about dinosaurs.* Ask students to identify the direct object by asking "Anna saw *what*?" (movie) Invite a volunteer to underline the prepositional phrase. Help students recognize that *about dinosaurs* describes the movie. It answers the question "What kind?" about the direct object *movie.* Therefore, *about dinosaurs* is also an adjective phrase.

Activity A Answers

1. <u>building</u> of offices 2. <u>boxes</u> of papers 3. <u>water</u> from a nearby hydrant 4. <u>walls</u> inside the building 5. <u>man</u> with a broken leg

---

Direct objects can have prepositional phrases.

> **EXAMPLE** The juice stained the dress with pink roses.
> **Sentence pattern** subject + verb + direct object + adjective prepositional phrase
> (The adjective prepositional phrase *with pink roses* describes the noun *dress,* the direct object.)

Activity A Write each sentence on your paper. Underline the direct object. Circle the prepositional phrase that tells about the direct object.

Example Brady read a <u>book</u> (about a detective).

1. A fire burned a tall building of offices.
2. Workers carried boxes of papers.
3. Firefighters sprayed water from a nearby hydrant.
4. Flames burned the walls inside the building.
5. A brave woman saved a man with a broken leg.

A prepositional phrase that follows a direct object may describe the direct object, or it may describe the verb. Some sentences may have prepositional phrases that describe the direct object *and* prepositional phrases that describe the verb.

> **EXAMPLE** The camper carries a bag with snacks.
> (The adjective phrase *with snacks* describes the direct object *bag.* It tells which bag.)
>
> The camper carries a bag on her back.
> (The adverb phrase *on her back* tells about the verb *carries.* It tells where the camper carries the bag.)
>
> The camper carries a bag with snacks on her back.
> (The adjective phrase *with snacks* describes the direct object *bag.* The adverb phrase *on her back* tells about the verb *carries.*)

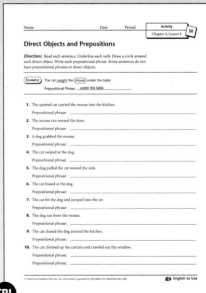

Workbook Activity 30

Activity 30

Activity B Write each sentence on your paper. Circle each prepositional phrase. Draw an arrow from each phrase to the word it describes.

Example The driver grabbed the wheel (of the car) (with his left hand).

1. The horse threw the rider during the rodeo.
2. The crowd cheered the brave rider on the ground.
3. The horse jumped the fence near the side gate.
4. The rider wiped the dust on his pants with his scarf.
5. Josie met a group of friends after the rodeo.

Activity C On your paper, make a chart of the prepositional phrases in these sentences. Write the type of prepositional phrase.

Example The girl with the hat pulled the boat with green sails toward the shore.

Prepositional Phrases	Adjective or Adverb?
with the hat	adjective
with green sails	adjective
toward the shore	adverb

1. The smart fish twisted the line of heavy nylon around a rock.
2. The man in the boat grabbed the line near the surface.
3. The fish pulled the angler with his gear from the boat.
4. A friend in another boat offered help to the man in the water.
5. The angler thanked his friend on the boat for rescuing him.

Saddle bronc riding was a popular activity long before rodeo became a sport.

1. The horse threw the rider (during the rodeo.) 2. The crowd cheered the brave rider (on the ground.) 3. The horse jumped the fence (near the side gate.) 4. The rider wiped the dust (on his pants) (with his scarf.) 5. Josie met a group of friends (after the rodeo.)

Activity C Answers

1. of heavy nylon—adjective; around a rock—adverb 2. in the boat—adjective; near the surface—adverb 3. with his gear—adjective; from the boat—adverb 4. in another boat—adjective; to the man—adverb; in the water—adjective 5. on the boat—adjective; for rescuing him—adverb

3 Reinforce and Extend

LEARNING STYLES

Logical/Mathematical

Have students create a list of questions based on the 5W-How? questions (*Who? What? Where? When? Why?* and *How?*) As students look at a sentence, they should run down the list of questions—*What happened? To whom did it happen? When did it happen? Where did it happen?* and so on. Students should realize that prepositional phrases answering the questions *What* and *To whom* are adjective phrases. Prepositional phrases answering the questions *Where, When, Why,* and *How much or how many* are likely to be adverb phrases. Have students construct a list of basic questions to use as a checklist as they complete this lesson's activities.

Name ___ Date ___ Period ___ Sentence Diagramming Activity 26
Chapter 4, Lesson 4

Diagram Direct Objects and Prepositional Phrases

Sentence Pattern 2: Subject + Verb + Direct Object

Step 1 The simple subject (a noun or pronoun) is written on the line on the left side. The simple predicate (a verb or a verb phrase) is written on the line on the right side.

Step 2 Adjectives or prepositional phrases that describe the subject go on the lines under the subject.

Step 3 Adverbs or prepositional phrases that tell about the verb go on the lines under the verb.

Step 4 Conjunctions are written on the dotted lines between the two words that are joined by the conjunction.

Step 5 The direct object is written on the line to the right of the verb.

Step 6 Adverbs or prepositional phrases that tell about the direct object go on the lines under the direct object.

Directions Look at the steps above and the example below. Diagram the sentences below using the blank diagrams.

EXAMPLE The two boys gave a party for their parents.

1. A man with a book reads a story about pirates.
2. The fish around the boat watched the angler with his rod.

© American Guidance Service, Inc. Permission is granted to reproduce for classroom use only.

English to Use

TRL

Sentence Diagramming Activity 26

ONLINE CONNECTION

Suggest that students log on to the Web site "The Tongue Untied," at *grammar. uoregon.edu* to learn more about prepositional phrases and direct objects. Have students go to the Table of Contents and select "Phrases." Invite a volunteer to read aloud the information, or print it out. Have students complete the short quiz on prepositional phrases.

Lesson at a Glance

Chapter 4 Lesson 5

Overview This lesson reviews the placement of nouns in sentences. It also defines abstract and concrete nouns.

Objectives

■ To identify nouns and their role in sentences

■ To identify abstract and concrete nouns

Student Pages 76–77

Teacher's Resource Library

Workbook Activity 31

Activity 31

Alternative Activity 31

Vocabulary

abstract noun
concrete noun

 1 Warm-Up Activity

Give students a randomly selected list of nouns, including people, places, things, and ideas. Invite students to classify the nouns. Then talk about how nouns that name real objects or people are easy to picture, while those that name ideas may be difficult to picture.

 2 Teaching the Lesson

Challenge students to identify five nouns that are ideas. Then have students read the definitions of concrete noun and abstract noun on page 77, and talk about the difference between the two types of nouns.

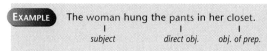

You have learned that nouns can appear in three places in sentences. A noun can be any of the following:

- the subject of a sentence
- the direct object of a sentence
- the object of a preposition

Some sentences have nouns in all three places.

> **EXAMPLE** The woman hung the pants in her closet.
> | | |
> subject   direct obj.   obj. of prep.

Activity A Write each noun in the following sentences on your paper. Next to each noun, write whether it is the *subject*, *direct object*, or *object of preposition* (Remember that nouns name persons, places, and things.)

1. The sleek car squealed away from the curb onto the freeway.

2. Craig hit third gear, and the engine howled.

3. A squirrel jumped off the road, away from the car.

4. The gauge on the dash showed an almost empty tank of gas.

5. Craig walked away from the car toward a gas station down the road.

6. People on the ship watched the lights of the city by the harbor.

7. The ship left the harbor and sailed toward the sea.

8. Lightning split the sky, and rain drenched the ship.

9. During the storm, a lamp fell from the table in a shower of sparks.

10. The captain steered the ship to another safe harbor.

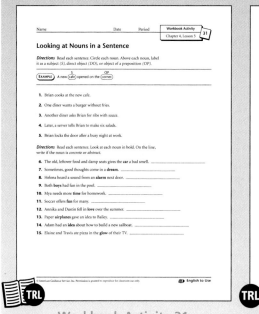

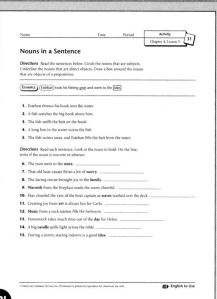

Workbook Activity 31   Activity 31

Concrete noun

A word that names something that can be seen or touched

Abstract noun

A word that names something that cannot be seen or touched

Many things that nouns name we can see and touch, such as *store*, *book*, and *dog*. Some things we cannot see or touch, such as *dream*, *idea*, and *time*. A **concrete noun** names something that we can see or touch. An **abstract noun** names something that we cannot see or touch. Here are some examples.

Concrete Nouns	Abstract Nouns
flame	warmth
tree	thirst
pen	truth
ball	action
camera	love

Concrete nouns are things you know about through your senses (sight, hearing, touch, taste, or smell). Abstract nouns name ideas, qualities, feelings, or characteristics.

How can you be sure a word is a noun? Remember that articles (*a*, *an*, and *the*) point out common nouns. If you can use an article with it, the word is a noun.

Activity B Write each noun in these sentences on your paper. Tell whether it is *concrete* or *abstract*.

1. Chuck had a dream about a horse.
2. The heat from the fire warmed the campers.
3. The bell on the wall made a sound.
4. Anita took time off from work.
5. Tom saw hunger in the eyes of the kitten.
6. Kisha liked the action and excitement of football.
7. Light from the TV filled the room.
8. Karen had an idea for a game.
9. Bill saw love in the eyes of the old dog.
10. The video filled Joe with fear.

Direct Objects   Chapter 4   **77**

Activity A Answers

1. S—car; Obj. of Prep.—curb, freeway 2. S—Craig, engine; DO—gear 3. S—squirrel; Obj. of Prep.—road, car 4. S—gauge; Obj. of Prep.—dash, gas; DO—tank 5. S—Craig; Obj. of Prep.—car, station, road 6. S—People; Obj. of Prep.—ship, city, harbor; DO—lights 7. S—ship; DO—harbor; Obj. of Prep.—sea 8. S—Lightning, rain; DO—sky, ship 9. Obj. of Prep.—storm, table, shower, sparks; S—lamp 10. S—captain; DO—ship; Obj. of Prep.—harbor

Activity B Answers

1. Chuck—concrete; dream—abstract; horse—concrete 2. heat—abstract; fire—concrete; campers—concrete 3. bell—concrete; wall—concrete; sound—abstract 4. Anita—concrete; time—abstract; work—abstract 5. Tom—concrete; hunger—abstract; eyes—concrete; kitten—concrete 6. Kisha—concrete; action—abstract; excitement—abstract; football—concrete 7. Light—concrete; TV—concrete; room—concrete 8. Karen—concrete; idea—abstract; game—concrete or abstract 9. Bill—concrete; love—abstract; eyes—concrete; dog—concrete 10. video—concrete; Joe—concrete; fear—abstract

3 Reinforce and Extend

TEACHER ALERT

Explain that in some contexts, nouns that are usually abstract can be concrete, and vice versa. For example, in sentence 4 of Activity B, *work* is an abstract noun, but the word *work* often refers to a particular piece of art, such as a sculpture. In that case, *work* is a concrete noun. Also, sentence 8 contains the noun *game*, which can be either concrete (for example, a board game) or abstract (for example, a guessing game). Challenge students to think of other examples of nouns that can be either concrete or abstract.

LEARNING STYLES

Interpersonal/ Group Learning

Allow students to work in small groups to decide whether the nouns in Activity B are abstract or concrete. Students should identify the nouns that they cannot classify and then offer their reasons for thinking that the noun could be either abstract or concrete. Students should consider all the reasons carefully before deciding. Have groups keep track of their decisions. Bring the groups together to compare their decisions.

Lesson at a Glance

Chapter 4 Lesson 6

Overview This lesson introduces pronouns. It also defines and explains nominative pronouns and objective pronouns.

Objectives

■ To choose the correct pronoun and identify its place in a sentence

Student Pages 78–79

Teacher's Resource Library

Workbook Activity 32

Activity 32

Alternative Activity 32

Sentence Diagramming Activity 27

Vocabulary

nominative pronoun
objective pronoun
pronoun

1 Warm-Up Activity

Begin the lesson by telling students a brief anecdote about yourself or your day, referring to yourself by name and avoiding the use of any pronouns. Challenge students to identify what was odd about the way you told your story. Invite partners to tell each other something about themselves without using the words *I, you, we, they, he, she,* or *it.* Ask students for their reactions to the exercise.

2 Teaching the Lesson

Discuss the information and examples presented in the text. Invite volunteers to take turns making up sentences. Have the class identify all the nouns in the sentences and then replace each noun with the appropriate pronoun. Ask a volunteer to write the sentences with pronouns. Finally, have students identify the pronouns in the sentences as nominative or objective.

Lesson 6   Pronouns in a Sentence

Pronoun
A word that takes the place of a noun
Nominative pronoun
A pronoun used as the subject of a sentence
Objective pronoun
A pronoun that is the direct object or object of the preposition

A **pronoun** is a word that replaces a noun in a sentence.

EXAMPLE   Food spoils quickly in the heat.
                 It spoils quickly in the heat.

Sentence parts   subject | predicate
Sentence pattern   subject + verb
(*Food* is a noun. *It* is a pronoun. In the second sentence, the pronoun *it* replaces the noun *food*.)

Pronouns have different forms, or cases.

	Pronouns	
	Nominative	**Objective**
One		
First person	I	me
Second person	you	you
Third person	he, she, it	him, her, it
Two or More		
First person	we	us
Second person	you	you
Third person	they	them

A **nominative pronoun** replaces a noun that is the subject of a sentence.

EXAMPLE   Rosalia celebrated Thanksgiving with her cousins.
                 She celebrated Thanksgiving with her cousins.

An **objective pronoun** replaces a noun that is the direct object or object of the preposition.

EXAMPLE   Rosalia celebrated Thanksgiving with her cousins.
                 Rosalia celebrated it with her cousins.
                 Rosalia celebrated Thanksgiving with her cousins.
                 Rosalia celebrated Thanksgiving with them.

78   *Chapter 4   Direct Objects*

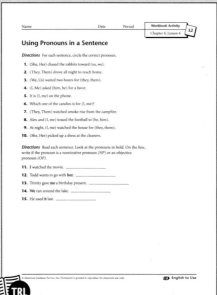

Workbook Activity 32

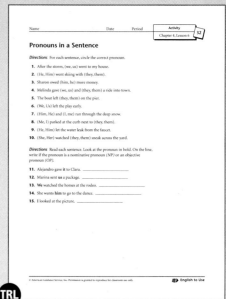

Activity 32

Writing Tip

Pronouns connected by the verb *be* should be in the same case. *It is me* sounds right because that is what people usually say. But *It is I* is correct.

We can use more than one pronoun in a sentence.

EXAMPLE She brought it for him.

Activity A For each sentence, choose the correct pronoun. Write the pronoun on your paper, and tell what part of the sentence it is.

Example   (We, Us) heard the bird sing.
　　　　　We—subject

1. (She, Her) looked through the window and saw (they, them) in the rain.

2. Quickly, (I, me) opened the door for (they, them).

3. (He, Him) waited for (we, us) at home.

4. The roof leaked water on (they, them) and dropped plaster on (she, her) and (I, me).

5. (We, Us) left the house, and dark storm clouds dumped rain on (we, us).

6. (We, Us) and (they, them) ran to the bus.

7. The bus dropped some of (they, them) off at the corner.

8. (We, Us) rode with (she, her) to another street.

9. The bus left (he, him) and (we, us) on the curb.

10. Then (he, him) and (I, me) walked through the rain to a shelter with (she, her).

Using What You've Learned

Write three or four sentences about a special occasion that you celebrate. First write the sentences with nouns as subjects and objects. Then rewrite the sentences, replacing each noun with a pronoun.

Direct Objects   Chapter 4   **79**

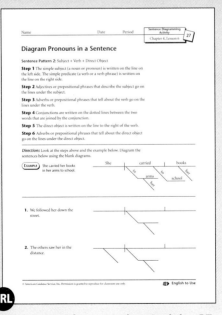

Activity A Answers

1. S—She; DO—them **2.** S—I; Obj. of Prep.—them **3.** S—He; Obj. of Prep.—us **4.** Obj. of Prep.—them; Compound Obj. of Prep.—her, me **5.** S—We; Obj. of Prep.—us **6.** Compound S—We, they **7.** Obj. of Prep.—them **8.** S—We; Obj. of Prep.—her **9.** Compound DO—him, us **10.** Compound S—he, I; Obj. of Prep.—her

Using What You've Learned

Have students work with partners to check their work. Then, if time allows, ask students to check previous writing assignments for the misuse of pronouns. Suggest that students correct any mistakes they find. Finally, have students write short journal entries about what they learned and how they plan to avoid similar mistakes in the future.

3 **Reinforce and Extend**

LEARNING STYLES

Auditory/Verbal

If students have trouble identifying the correct answers in Activity A, suggest that they work as partners and read the sentences aloud to each other. Readers should say the sentences at least twice, using each possible pronoun. Students may notice that they recognize correct English more easily when they hear it than when they see it written on the page.

IN THE COMMUNITY

Students who have mastered the concepts introduced so far in the book, including writing sentences with direct objects, may wish to share their grammar skills with students in lower grades or with students who are learning English as a second language. Suggest that capable students volunteer their time in community centers, adult literacy programs, or local grade schools.

Lesson at a Glance

Chapter 4 Lesson 7

Overview This lesson explains when to use pronouns to replace nouns in sentences. It also introduces reflexive, or *-self*, pronouns and pronouns that refer to general rather than specific people and things.

Objectives

- To replace nouns with pronouns
- To complete sentences with *-self* pronouns
- To identify pronouns and their uses in a sentence

Student Pages 80–81

Teacher's Resource Library TRL

Workbook Activity 33

Activity 33

Alternative Activity 33

Sentence Diagramming Activity 28

---

1 Warm-Up Activity

Write the following sentences on the board: *Today, something happened to somebody. Everybody is talking about everything.* Talk with students about the content of the sentences. Elicit that the sentences are too vague. Challenge students to rewrite the sentences in a way that makes them interesting.

2 Teaching the Lesson

Invite volunteers to read aloud the instructions, example sentences, and lists of pronouns in the lesson. Ask students to listen for the sentences that sound like the language people use in real life.

Activity A Answers

1. They 2. them 3. She 4. her 5. it

Pronouns help you avoid repeating the same nouns over and over again. They help your sentences sound better.

EXAMPLE Yoshi and Malcolm went for a walk Saturday morning. Suddenly, Yoshi and Malcolm spotted a rabbit in the street. Yoshi and Malcolm stopped and watched the rabbit.

Yoshi and Malcolm went for a walk Saturday morning. Suddenly, they spotted a rabbit in the street. They stopped and watched it.

(In the second group of sentences, pronouns replace the repeated nouns. The pronouns make the sentences sound more like natural speech.)

Do not use pronouns unless readers will know exactly which noun the pronoun is replacing. Sometimes, for clarity, it may be better to repeat the noun.

EXAMPLE Juan met Paulo at the library. He worked there. (*Who* worked at the library? Did Juan or Paulo work at the library? In this case, the pronoun makes the meaning of the sentence unclear. It would have been better to repeat the noun *Paulo*.)

Communication Connection

One out of every thousand people is born deaf. More than one-third of the U.S. population has a hearing problem by age 65.

Activity A Write each sentence on your paper. Change the words in bold to pronouns. Be sure to use the correct form for each pronoun. Look at the table in Lesson 6 on page 78 for help.

1. **Josh and Andrea** walked into the busy store and saw Maria and Carlos.
2. Josh signed "hello" to **Maria and Carlos.**
3. **Maria** bought a loaf of bread.
4. Carlos talked to **Andrea** about the soccer game.
5. The clerk filled the bag and gave **the bag** to Carlos.

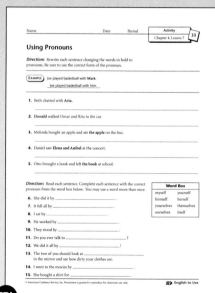

Workbook Activity 33   Activity 33

Some pronouns end with *-self* or *-selves.*

myself	herself	ourselves
yourself	yourselves	itself
himself	themselves	

Activity B Write each sentence on your paper. Fill in the blank with the correct *-self* pronoun.

1. I did it by _____ .
2. He did it by _____ .
3. You did it by _____ .
4. They did it by _____ .
5. We did it by _____ .

Some pronouns refer to things and people in general. No specific person or thing is pointed out.

Pronouns that do not refer to specific people or things are indefinite pronouns. *Indefinite* means "not defined or specific."

People		Things
someone	somebody	something
anyone	anybody	anything
everyone	everybody	everything
no one	nobody	nothing

Activity C Write each pronoun in these sentences on your paper. Write whether the pronoun is a *subject*, a *direct object*, or an *object of a preposition.*

1. In a small town, everyone knows everything about everybody.
2. In a big city, hardly anyone knows anything about anybody.
3. Someone knows everything about somebody.
4. Everyone knows something about somebody.
5. Everyone knows something about nothing.

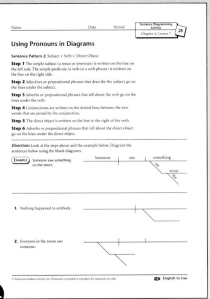

1. myself 2. himself 3. yourself or yourselves 4. themselves 5. ourselves

Activity C Answers

1. S—everyone; DO—everything; Obj. of Prep.—everybody 2. S—anyone; DO—anything; Obj. of Prep.—anybody 3. S—Someone; DO—everything; Obj. of Prep.—somebody 4. S—Everyone; DO—something; Obj. of Prep.—somebody 5. S—Everyone; DO—something; Obj. of Prep.—nothing

3 Reinforce and Extend

LEARNING STYLES

Visual/Spatial

If students have trouble assigning the correct number and gender to pronouns, have them stop after reading each activity item and imagine the scene. For example, in the first sentence in Activity A, students should picture four people, two boys and two girls, standing in the doorway of a grocery store. Once students picture the subjects and actions of the sentences, they may find it easier to identify the pronouns.

AT HOME

Ask students to watch the play-by-play action in a sports event on television and to listen to how the announcer uses sentences with pronouns and direct objects to describe the action. For example, an announcer might say, "Hobbs avoids the tackle; he runs for the goal." or "The pitcher faces the batter. She slams another home run over the fence." Have each student write his or her own play-by-play description of a real or imagined sports event, using sentences with pronouns and direct objects.

Lesson at a Glance

Chapter 4 Lesson 8

Overview This lesson presents words that can be both pronouns and adjectives. It also introduces two-word pronouns.

Objectives

■ To identify adjectives, pronouns, and nouns

■ To distinguish between adjectives and pronouns

■ To write sentences with adjectives and pronouns

Student Pages 82–83

Teacher's Resource Library

Workbook Activity 34

Activity 34

Alternative Activity 34

1 Warm-Up Activity

Write the following sentences and ask a volunteer to read them aloud: *Three bears lived in a cottage in the woods. All three liked porridge. One liked his porridge hot. Another liked her porridge warm. And the last one liked his porridge cold. Each bear thought the others were silly. But each loved the other two.* Underline each subject. Circle the adjectives that describe the subjects. Point out that some words can be both pronouns and adjectives.

2 Teaching the Lesson

Have a volunteer read aloud the instruction and examples on page 82. Challenge students to make up other sentences modeled on the first example's sentences.

Activity A Answers

1. Many—people; two—jobs
2. Some—men; several—jobs
3. Each—person; all—kinds
4. One—woman; ten—jobs
5. Another—woman; any—job

Some words in the English language can be more than one part of speech.

These words can be pronouns or adjectives.

all	few	other
another	many	several
any	one (or any	some
each	other number)	

EXAMPLE   Adjective   Some snow melted.
           Pronoun   Some melted.

(In the first sentence, *some* is an adjective that describes the noun subject *snow*. In the second sentence, *some* is a pronoun that takes the place of the noun subject *snow*. *Some* is the subject of the sentence.)

Some pronouns are two words.

each other	one another

EXAMPLE   Claudia and Brittany see each other every week.
           Claudia, Brittany, and Fiona see one another.

Activity A On your paper, write each adjective and the noun it describes.

1. Many people work two jobs.
2. Some men work at several jobs.
3. Each person tries all kinds of jobs.
4. One woman tried ten jobs.
5. Another woman wanted any job.

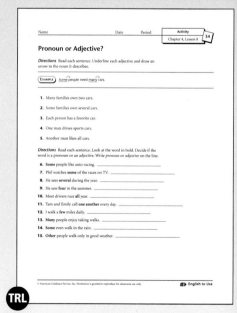

Activity B On your paper, copy each word in bold. Then tell whether it is an *adjective* or a *pronoun*.

1. **Some** people like football games.

2. I like a **few** of them.

3. Sarah likes **some** kinds of sports.

4. She saw **two** games in the fall.

5. Good players on a team play well and share the glory with **one another.**

Activity C On your paper, use each of these terms as a pronoun in a sentence.

1. each other
2. ten
3. anybody
4. several
5. everybody
6. another
7. one another
8. each
9. nothing
10. some

Activity D On your paper, use each of these words as an adjective in a sentence.

1. ten
2. several
3. another
4. each
5. some

Some college football stadiums have room for over 100,000 fans.

Activity B Answers

1. Some—adjective 2. few—pronoun 3. some—adjective 4. two—adjective 5. one another—pronoun (or one—adjective; another—pronoun)

Activity C Answers

Answers will vary. Remind students to use each word as a pronoun in a complete sentence.

Activity D Answers

Answers will vary. Remind students to use each word as an adjective in a complete sentence.

 3 Reinforce and Extend

LEARNING STYLES

 Logical/Mathematical

Invite students to work with partners or small groups to create a system of symbols or a new organization of the words that will help class members remember them. Ask students from each pair or group to share their system with the class.

CAREER CONNECTION

 Ask students to watch or talk to a group of workers and then write at least ten sentences about the tasks that the workers perform. Students' sentences should have direct objects as well as words that may be used as adjectives or as pronouns. For example: *He writes reports. Some send messages by e-mail. She interviews people. One makes all the decisions.* Ask students to share their sentences with the class. Ask volunteers to identify the direct objects, pronouns, and adjectives in the sentences.

Lesson at a Glance

Chapter 4 Lesson 9

Overview This lesson presents *this*, *that*, *these*, and *those* as adjectives and pronouns.

Objectives

- To identify *this*, *that*, *these*, and *those* as adjectives
- To distinguish between the use of *this*, *that*, *these*, and *those* as adjectives and pronouns
- To use *this*, *that*, *these*, and *those* appropriately in sentences

Student Pages 84–85

Teacher's Resource Library

Workbook Activity 35

Activity 35

Alternative Activity 35

---

1 Warm-Up Activity

Point to objects around the room, asking "What is this?" "What is that?" "What are these?" and "What are those?" Students should answer each question using *this*, *that*, *these*, or *those* as the subjects. Ask students to talk about the differences between the uses of *this*, *that*, *these*, and *those*.

2 Teaching the Lesson

Remind students that a word can be more than one part of speech. Then discuss the text and the example sentences on pages 84 and 85.

Activity A Answers

1. These **2.** That **3.** This, that
4. That **5.** Those, that

This, *that*, *these*, and *those* can be more than one part of speech. They can be either pronouns or adjectives.

> **EXAMPLE**   **Adjective**   That water boiled on the stove.
> **Pronoun**   That boiled on the stove.
>
> (In the first sentence, *that* is an adjective that describes the noun subject *water*. In the second sentence, *that* is a pronoun that takes the place of the noun subject *water*. *That* is the subject of the sentence.)

Activity A On your paper, write the adjective that describes each noun in bold.

1. These **stores** have many items for sale.
2. That **music box** plays a tune.
3. This **mirror** shines brightly in that **light.**
4. That **watch** keeps good time.
5. Those **lamps** go nicely with that **table.**

Activity B Copy each word in bold on your paper. Then write whether it is an *adjective* or a *pronoun*.

1. **That** book dropped to the floor.
2. I want **this.**
3. **These** belong on the shelf.
4. Tim will wrap **those** packages for you.
5. Julio lost **that** on the bus.
6. Ali caught **this** fish by herself.
7. **This** matches **that** jacket.
8. **Those** flowers look nice.
9. Nina sat on **that** chair.
10. **That** stands along the wall.

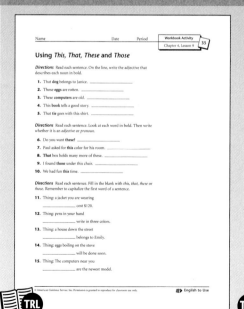

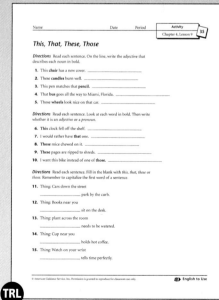

This, that, these, and *those* point out persons and things.

The word *this* points out one person or thing that is near. The word *that* points out one person or thing that is in the distance.

 EXAMPLE This boy beside me won the contest.
That girl by the tree entered the contest.

The word *these* points out more than one person or thing that is near. The word *those* points out more than one person or thing that is in the distance.

EXAMPLE These workers over here served the meal.
Those workers near the sink cleaned up.

Activity C Write each sentence on your paper. Fill in the blank with *This, That, These,* or *Those.*

Example Thing: mirror near you
___This___ hangs on the wall.

1. Thing: vase across the room
_____ sits on the table.

2. Thing: rug near you
_____ lies on the floor.

3. Thing: tall plants across the room
_____ stand in the corner.

4. Thing: curtains near you
_____ hang at the window.

5. Thing: clock near you
_____ goes on the shelf.

Activity B Answers

1. That—adjective 2. this—pronoun 3. These—pronoun 4. those—adjective 5. that—pronoun 6. this—adjective 7. This—pronoun; that—adjective 8. Those—adjective 9. that—adjective 10. That—pronoun

Activity C Answers

1. That 2. This 3. Those 4. These 5. This

Writing Practice

Point out that using the words *this, that, these,* and *those* as pronouns works better in speech than in writing. If the speaker and the listener are in the same room, the listener can figure out what the pronoun stands for by watching the speaker's expressions and gestures. Also, the listener can ask questions, such as "What do you mean by this?" Writing that uses *this, that, these,* and *those* regularly as pronouns is less effective. To illustrate this point, have students work in small groups to plan a short skit in which two characters talk briefly, using *this, that, these,* and *those* as pronouns. Students should also write a script for their skit. Have half of the groups perform their skits before reading their scripts aloud. Have the other half read their scripts aloud before performing. All students should notice that they understood the scripts better after they saw the skits. Challenge students to think of how they can make their writing more effective when using *this, that, these,* and *those.*

 3 Reinforce and Extend

 LEARNING STYLES

LEP/ESL
Take a moment to analyze the difference between standard and nonstandard speech. For example, *them* is an objective case pronoun that cannot be an adjective. The words *here* and *there* are adverbs that also cannot be adjectives. Therefore, sentences such as *Them there books belong to me* and *This here pen ran out of ink* are incorrect. Ask students to express the same ideas in sentences using standard English.

Lesson at a Glance

Chapter 4 Lesson 10

Overview This lesson focuses on the capitalization of proper abstract nouns and titles. It explains the use of semicolons and commas in compound sentences that use specific conjunctions.

Objectives

- To capitalize proper abstract nouns and titles
- To punctuate compound sentences

Student Pages 86–87

Teacher's Resource Library

Workbook Activity 36

Activity 36

Alternative Activity 36

Vocabulary

capitalize

---

 1 Warm-Up Activity

Write the following fill-in-the-blank sentence on the board, and ask students to copy it onto separate sheets of paper. (*Subject*) wanted (*adjective*) (*direct object*) (*prepositional phrase*). Then ask each student to fill in the blanks with appropriate nouns, pronouns, and prepositions. Remind students that some pronouns can be adjectives, and some pronouns can be subjects.

---

 2 Teaching the Lesson

Remind students to use correct capitalization and punctuation. Before students read the instruction and examples, review the concepts of abstract nouns, proper nouns, and compound sentences.

Activity A Answers

Answers will vary. Students should write a proper noun for each common noun.

Capitalize
To use capital letters

Proper nouns can be examples of abstract nouns. Remember that all proper nouns need capital letters.

Abstract Nouns	Proper Nouns
month	September
holiday	Presidents' Day
event	U.S. Open
country	Canada

Activity A On your paper, write a proper noun to match each common noun.

1. day
2. country
3. holiday
4. song
5. city
6. event
7. movie
8. language
9. sports team
10. book

The name of a person is a proper noun. A person's title is part of his or her name. **Capitalize** the first letter of each word in a person's title. To capitalize, use capital letters. When you use a short form, add a period.

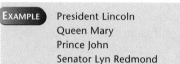

EXAMPLE

President Lincoln
Queen Mary
Prince John
Senator Lyn Redmond

Dr. Maria Chang
Ms. Lisa Waters
Mrs. Leslie Conners
Mr. Steven Arnold

Activity B Write this list of words. Capitalize each proper noun. Some of the words are common nouns. Common nouns do not begin with capital letters.

1. mr. smith
2. detroit
3. statue of liberty
4. school
5. monday
6. city
7. senator
8. dr. adams
9. day
10. president washington

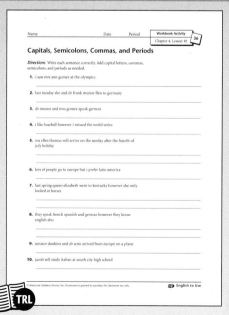

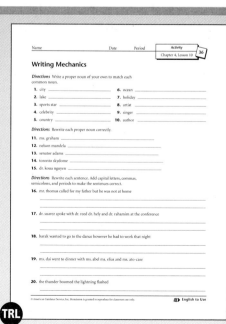

Workbook Activity 36

Activity 36

Canada

President

Day

Holiday

Detroit

Semicolons and commas must appear in compound sentences that use these conjunctions: *however, therefore, besides,* and *instead.*

A semicolon comes before the conjunction. A comma comes after the conjunction.

EXAMPLE The ice melted into a puddle; however, I wiped it up.

Activity C Write each sentence on your paper. Add capital letters, commas, semicolons, and periods to make the sentences correct.

1. it rained therefore we left early

2. he wanted candy instead he ate fruit

3. ann brought her car besides we rode with her before

4. the sun set a new moon rose

5. dr adams mr allen and ms romone met senator lopez in the park

6. mr samuels beeped the horn however ms tompkins and mrs west had already left

7. mrs gomez greeted senator andrews during the labor day parade

8. mr edwards and ms keller watched prince charles on television

9. dr finch opened the door therefore mr lee handed him the package for mrs finch.

10. senator larsen explained the problem to mr boyd ms lake mr shobe and dr connors

ASL ILLUSTRATION

Have students practice the signs for the proper nouns shown on page 87. Challenge students to incorporate at least two of the signs into a complete thought and to sign the sentence for the class.

Activity B Answers

1. Mr. Smith 2. Detroit 3. Statue of Liberty 4. school 5. Monday 6. city 7. senator 8. Dr. Adams 9. day 10. President Washington

Activity C Answers

1. It rained; therefore, we left early. 2. He wanted candy; instead, he ate fruit. 3. Ann brought her car; besides, we rode with her before. 4. The sun set; a new moon rose. 5. Dr. Adams, Mr. Allen, and Ms. Romone met Senator Lopez in the park. 6. Mr. Samuels beeped the horn; however, Ms. Tompkins and Mrs. West had already left. 7. Mrs. Gomez greeted Senator Andrews during the Labor Day parade. 8. Mr. Edwards and Ms. Keller saw Prince Charles on television. 9. Dr. Finch opened the door; therefore, Mr. Lee handed him the package for Mrs. Finch. 10. Senator Larsen explained the problem to Mr. Boyd, Ms. Lake, Mr. Shobe, and Dr. Connors.

3 Reinforce and Extend

LEARNING STYLES

Auditory/Verbal

Have students work in pairs to read aloud the sentences in Activity C to each other before adding the correct punctuation and capitalization. After students correct the sentences on paper, they should meet again with their partners. This time they should read their answers aloud, vocalizing the corrections they made. For example, a student might say "It (capital I) rained (semicolon) therefore (comma) we left early (period)" Both students should read their sentences aloud in this way. Then they should talk about any choices in punctuation and capitalization about which they disagree.

Chapter 4 Review

Use the Chapter Review to prepare students for tests and to reteach content from the chapter.

Chapter 4 Mastery Test

The Teacher's Resource Library includes parallel forms of the Chapter 4 Mastery Test. The difficulty level of the two forms is equivalent. You may wish to use one form as a pretest and the other form as a posttest.

REVIEW ANSWERS

Part A

1. objective pronoun 2. direct object 3. compound direct object 4. abstract noun 5. nominative pronoun 6. pronoun 7. capitalize 8. concrete noun

Part B

9. The students (cleaned) the vacant lot near the school. 10. They (collected) the trash on the ground. 11. Later, they (planted) some flowers in the dirt. 12. The students (made) a new park, and the neighbors (thanked) them with a party.

Part C

13. She didn't like it. She—subject, it—d. object 14. Studying for it was hard. It—obj. of the prep. 15. He studied with them. He—subject, them—obj. of the prep.

Part D

Answers for items 16 through 19 will vary. Remind students to write a proper noun for each common noun.

Word Bank

abstract noun
capitalize
compound direct object
concrete noun
direct object
nominative pronoun
objective pronoun
pronoun

Part A On a sheet of paper, write the correct word or words from the Word Bank to complete each sentence.

1. A pronoun used as an object is an _____ .
2. A _____ receives action directly from the verb.
3. A _____ is two or more direct objects joined by a conjunction.
4. A word that names something that you cannot see or touch is an _____ .
5. A pronoun used as the subject of a sentence is a _____ .
6. A _____ is a word that takes the place of a noun.
7. To use capital letters is to _____ .
8. A _____ names something that you can see or touch.

Part B Write each sentence. Underline the subject once, underline the prepositional phrase twice, circle the verb, and draw an arrow to the direct object. If a sentence is compound, write *C*.

9. The students cleaned the vacant lot near the school.
10. They collected the trash on the ground.
11. Later, they planted some flowers in the dirt.
12. The students made a new park, and the neighbors thanked them with a party.

Part C Write each sentence. Replace each noun in bold with a pronoun. Write what part of the sentence the pronoun is: *subject, direct object,* or *object of the preposition.*

13. **Sarah** didn't like the **homework.**
14. Studying for the **test** was hard.
15. **Greg** studied with **Franklin** and **Ramon.**

Part D Write a proper noun for each common noun. Be sure to capitalize each proper noun.

16. month
17. state
18. landmark
19. person

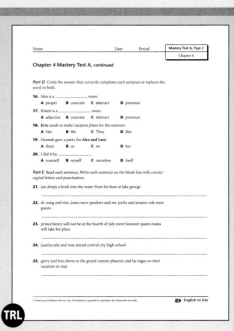

Chapter 4 Mastery Test A

Part E Write each sentence correctly.

20. ms cho met dr ray on monday march 17

21. i had an appointment however it was canceled

22. we grabbed our lunches ran out the door and got on the bus

Part F Read this paragraph. Then follow the directions for each item.

> Michelle plays the flute, and Lynda plays the guitar. The women often meet and practice music. Lynda and Michelle strum and toot songs and tunes. Sometimes a friend stops by, holds the music, and sings a tune with them. Michelle, Lynda, and the friend make a good sound and have fun during lazy summer nights.

23. Write the sentence that has a compound subject, compound verb, and compound direct object.

24. Write the compound sentence.

25. Find each of these words and tell its part of speech: *often, and, practice, with, lazy,* and *sometimes.*

26. Find three abstract nouns.

27. List the verbs along with any direct objects in the sentence that begins with an adverb.

Part G On your paper, write the letter that correctly completes the sentences or describes the word in bold.

28. Since Bo needed a tie, he bought one for _____ .

   A himself   **B** myself   **C** themselves   **D** ourselves

29. Please put _____ dishes near you on the counter.

   A that   **B** those   **C** this   **D** these

30. Helen took **that** suit to the cleaner.

   A pronoun   **B** noun   **C** adjective   **D** preposition

 **Test-Taking Tip** Answer all questions you are sure of first; then go back and answer the others.

REVIEW ANSWERS

Part E

20. Ms. Cho met Dr. Ray on Monday, March 17. **21.** I had an appointment; however, it was canceled. **22.** We grabbed our lunches, ran out the door, and got on the bus.

Part F

23. Lynda and Michelle strum and toot songs and tunes. **24.** Michelle plays the flute, and Lynda plays the guitar. **25.** often—adverb; and—conjunction; practice—verb; with—preposition; lazy—adjective; Sometimes—adverb **26.** Answers will vary. Check to make sure that all three nouns are used as abstract nouns. **27.** stops; holds—music; sings—tune

Part G

28. A **29.** B **30.** C

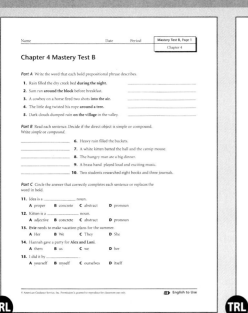

Chapter

5

Planning Guide

Practice with Parts of Speech

Lesson		Student Text Lesson			Language Skills	
		Student Pages	Vocabulary	Practice Activities	Identification Skills	Writing Skills	Punctuation Skills
Lesson 1	Assorted Parts of Speech	92–93		✔	✔	✔	
Lesson 2	Using Owner Words	94–95	✔	✔	✔	✔	✔
Lesson 3	Owner Pronouns	96–97	✔	✔	✔	✔	✔
Lesson 4	More Than One Owner	98–99		✔	✔	✔	✔
Lesson 5	Hidden Subjects	100–101	✔	✔	✔	✔	
Lesson 6	More About Adverbs	102–103		✔	✔		
Lesson 7	Interjections	104–105	✔	✔	✔		✔
Lesson 8	The Writing Process	106–107	✔	✔		✔	✔
Lesson 9	Writing Mechanics	108–109		✔	✔	✔	✔

Chapter Activities

Teacher's Resource Library
Community Connection 5:
Find Out About Social Service
Organizations
English in Your World 5:
Finding Interjections in a
Children's Book

Assessment Options

Student Text
Chapter 5 Review

Teacher's Resource Library
Chapter 5 Mastery Tests A and B

ASL Illustration	Communication Connection	Notes	Using What You've Learned	Writing Tips	Teacher Alert	Online Connection	Applications (Home, Career, Community, Global)	Speaking Practice	Writing Practice	Auditory/Verbal	Body/Kinesthetic	Interpersonal/Group Learning	Logical/Mathematical	Visual/Spatial	LEP/ESL	Workbook Activities	Activities	Alternative Activities	Sentence Diagramming Activities	Self-Study Guide
					93						93					37	37	37	29	✔
95					95		95					95				38	38	38	30	✔
	97			✔	96, 97											39	39	39		✔
		✔				99	99		99							40	40	40		✔
		✔					101								101	41	41	41	31	✔
					103					103						42	42	42		✔
105				✔			105	105						104		43	43	43	32	✔
				✔		107							107			44	44	44		✔
			109		109	109									109	45	45	45		✔

Pronunciation Key

a	hat	e	let	ī	ice	ô	order	ù	put	sh	she
ā	age	ē	equal	o	hot	oi	oil	ü	rule	th	thin
ä	far	ėr	term	ō	open	ou	out	ch	child	ᴙH	then
â	care	i	it	ȯ	saw	u	cup	ng	long	zh	measure

ə { a in about / e in taken / i in pencil / o in lemon / u in circus }

Alternative Activities

The Teacher's Resource Library (TRL) contains a set of lower-level worksheets called Alternative Activities. These worksheets cover the same content as the regular Activities but are written at a second-grade reading level.

Skill Track Software

Use the Skill Track Software for English to Use for additional reinforcement of this chapter. The software program allows students using AGS textbooks to be assessed for mastery of each chapter and lesson of the textbook. Students access the software on an individual basis and are assessed with multiple-choice items.

Chapter 5: Practice with Parts of Speech
pages 90–111

Lessons

1. **Assorted Parts of Speech**
   pages 92–93

2. **Using Owner Words**
   pages 94–95

3. **Owner Pronouns**
   pages 96–97

4. **More Than One Owner**
   pages 98–99

5. **Hidden Subjects**
   pages 100–101

6. **More About Adverbs**
   pages 102–103

7. **Interjections**
   pages 104–105

8. **The Writing Process**
   pages 106–107

9. **Writing Mechanics**
   pages 108–109

Chapter 5 Review
pages 110–111

Skill Track Software for English to Use

Teacher's Resource Library

Workbook Activities 37–45

Activities 37–45

Alternative Activities 37–45

Sentence Diagramming Activities 29–32
(Optional sentence activities accompany lessons.)

Community Connection 5

English in Your World 5

Chapter 5 Self-Study Guide

Chapter 5 Mastery Tests A and B

(Answer Keys for the Teacher's Resource Library begin on page 308 of this Teacher's Edition.)

Community Connection 5   English in Your World 5

Chapter

5

Practice with Parts of Speech

Do you remember how you learned to do something new? Maybe you just learned to drive. Maybe you learned how to use a new computer. Maybe you learned a new dance movement. At first the task seemed hard. It felt odd to be doing something you'd never done before. But it got easier each time you did it. The old saying "practice makes perfect" is true. It takes practice to master a new skill.

In this chapter, you will practice the parts of speech you have studied. You will study other parts of speech. You will also practice a four-step writing process.

Goals for Learning

◆ To identify parts of speech in different positions in a sentence

◆ To use owner nouns and pronouns correctly

◆ To use a variety of adverbs

◆ To recognize a sentence with an understood subject

◆ To identify and write interjections

◆ To apply the writing process

91

Introducing the Chapter

Ask students to discuss new skills they have learned recently and to talk about how they learned to master these skills. Have class members describe the process of practicing a new activity. Emphasize that practice requires setting a goal, trying repeatedly, and patience.

Explain that this chapter will provide students with the practice they need to build their writing skills.

TEACHER'S RESOURCE

The AGS Teaching Strategies in English Transparencies may be used with this chapter. The transparencies add an interactive dimension to expand and enhance the *English to Use* program content.

CAREER INTEREST INVENTORY

The AGS Harrington-O'Shea Career Decision-Making System–Revised (CDM) may be used with this chapter. Students can use the CDM to explore their interests and identify careers. The CDM defines career areas that are indicated by students' responses on the inventory.

Writing Tips and Notes

Ask volunteers to read the tips and notes that appear in the margins throughout the chapter. Then discuss them with the class.

CHAPTER PROJECT

Write a story as a class. Have the class select a topic, and ask students to talk about details supporting that topic. After students have completed prewriting, guide them through the next three steps of the writing process. Ask students to include elements that they have learned in Chapter 5, including hidden subjects, adverbs, and interjections.

TRL   **TRL**   Chapter 5 Self-Study Guide

Lesson at a Glance

Chapter 5 Lesson 1

Overview This lesson presents words that can be used as different parts of speech and explains how to determine a word's part of speech depending on its use in a sentence.

Objective

■ To determine the part of speech of words in sentences

Student Pages 92–93

Teacher's Resource Library

Workbook Activity 37

Activity 37

Alternative Activity 37

Sentence Diagramming Activity 29

1 Warm-Up Activity

Write on the board:

The paper has lines.
I put groceries in a paper bag.
She will paper her walls.

Ask students to identify the part of speech of the underlined word in each sentence. *(first sentence—noun, second sentence—adjective, third sentence—verb)* Explain that some words, such as *paper*, can be different parts of speech. See whether students can identify other words that can be more than one part of speech.

2 Teaching the Lesson

Review the seven parts of speech students have learned. On the board, write a sentence that contains all seven parts, such as *Yes, the cook slowly grills tasty vegetables for you and me.* Ask students to identify each part of speech in the sentence.

Lesson 1 Assorted Parts of Speech

Some words in the English language can be more than one part of speech. The part of speech that a word is depends on the use of the word in a sentence.

You have learned about words that can be either prepositions or adverbs. There also are words that can be either nouns or verbs. Some words can be either nouns or adjectives. Other words can be either nouns, verbs, or adjectives.

EXAMPLE

Adverb	The teacher looked inside. (*Inside* tells where the teacher looked.)
Preposition	The teacher looked inside the room. (*Inside* introduces the adverb prepositional phrase *inside the room*.)
Noun	Sam starred in the show. (*Show* is the object of the preposition *in*.)
Verb	Show me the picture. (*Show* is the simple predicate. What do you do? You *show*.)
Noun	The test will be easy. (*Test* is the subject. What will be easy? The *test* will be easy.)
Adjective	Claude will be a test subject. (*Test* describes the noun *subject*. It tells what kind of subject.)
Noun	They saw a statue made of iron. (*Iron* is the object of the preposition *of*.)
Adjective	Jorge and Kendall walked to the iron statue. (*Iron* describes the noun *statue*. It tells which statue.)
Verb	Teresa and Rick iron the wrinkled clothes. (*Iron* is the simple predicate. What do Teresa and Rick do? They *iron*.)

Workbook Activity 37

Activity 37

Activity A On your paper, write the part of speech for each word in bold.

1. Ben and Karen take a long **drive.**
2. Karen will **drive** during the trip.
3. Karen will **park** the car near the **park** entrance.
4. They **walk** in the **park.**
5. During the **walk,** they pass by a **park** bench.

Some forms of verbs can be used as adjectives.

 Verb
The water spilled.
(*Spilled* is the simple predicate. What happened to the water? It *spilled.*)

Adjective
The spilled water ruined the drawing.
(*Spilled* describes the noun *water.* It tells which water.)

Activity B On your paper, write the part of speech for each word in bold.

1. Jasmeen writes a **check** for $100.
2. The **check** is for the man in the **checkered** shirt.
3. The man will **check** his **watch** and **watch** for Jasmeen.
4. Jasmeen phoned the man and **checked** in with him.
5. Dennis **scaled** a fish and weighed it on a **scale.**

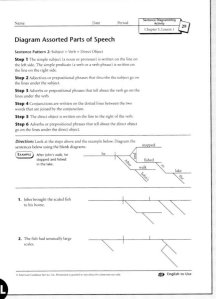

Ben and Karen walk in the park.

1. noun 2. verb 3. verb, adjective 4. verb, noun 5. noun, adjective

Activity B Answers

1. noun 2. noun, adjective 3. verb, noun, verb 4. verb 5. verb, noun

 3 Reinforce and Extend

TEACHER ALERT

Students may often hear nouns used as verbs in casual conversation; for example, "She right-fielded it," instead of "She hit it into right field." Tell students that the lesson examines a special group of words used in multiple ways; writers do not use verbs as nouns.

LEARNING STYLES

Body/Kinesthetic
Refer students to the photograph on page 93, in which a couple is *walking* (verb) and going for a *walk* (noun). Ask students to work in pairs to act out other words, such as *ride, run,* or *lie,* that can be used as more than one part of speech. Have the class identify the part of speech as each pair acts out a word.

Name _____ Date _____ Period _____ | Sentence Diagramming Activity | 29 |
Chapter 5, Lesson 1

Diagram Assorted Parts of Speech

Sentence Pattern 2: Subject + Verb + Direct Object

Step 1 The simple subject (a noun or pronoun) is written on the line on the left side. The simple predicate (a verb or a verb phrase) is written on the line on the right side.

Step 2 Adjectives or prepositional phrases that describe the subject go on the lines under the subject.

Step 3 Adverbs or prepositional phrases that tell about the verb go on the lines under the verb.

Step 4 Conjunctions are written on the dotted lines between the two words that are joined by the conjunction.

Step 5 The direct object is written on the line to the right of the verb.

Step 6 Adverbs or prepositional phrases that tell about the direct object go on the lines under the direct object.

Directions Look at the steps above and the example below. Diagram the sentences below using the blank diagrams.

EXAMPLE After John's walk, he stopped and fished in the lake.

1. John brought the scaled fish to his home.

2. The fish had unusually large scales.

© American Guidance Service, Inc. Permission is granted to reproduce for classroom use only. English to Use

TRL

Sentence Diagramming Activity 29

Lesson at a Glance

Chapter 5 Lesson 2

Overview This lesson introduces possessive nouns and explains how to form them by using an apostrophe plus -*s*.

Objective

■ To write common and proper possessive nouns

Student Pages 94–95

Teacher's Resource Library **TRL**

Workbook Activity 38

Activity 38

Alternative Activity 38

Sentence Diagramming Activity 30

Vocabulary

apostrophe
owner noun

 Warm-Up Activity

Ask several students to stand and have each of them hold a small object. Then ask the class to create sentences that tell about the students and objects; for example, *Julio has a pen.* Explain that students can show these relationships with *owner nouns.* Help students use the information in their sentences to form owner nouns, for example, *Julio's pen.*

2 Teaching the Lesson

Students who understand the concept of owner nouns may still have difficulty with the placement of 's. Tell students that all of the examples in this lesson are singular and form owner nouns by using an apostrophe plus -*s*. Write the sentences in the example boxes on page 94 on the board, but leave out the apostrophes. Have students tell you where to add the apostrophes in the sentences.

Owner noun
A noun that owns something in a sentence

Apostrophe (')
A punctuation mark in an owner's name

Some nouns show ownership. A noun that shows ownership in a sentence is an **owner noun.** An owner noun may be a proper noun or a common noun.

Use an **apostrophe** plus -*s* ('*s*) to form an owner noun that tells about only one owner.

EXAMPLE Roberta's car runs smoothly.
(Whom does the car belong to? The car belongs to Roberta. *Roberta* is a proper noun.)

The dog's toy rolled behind the tree.
(Whom does the toy belong to? The toy belongs to the dog. *Dog* is a common noun.)

The sink's drain leaks.
(What does the drain belong to? The drain belongs to the sink. *Sink* is a common noun.)

An owner noun may show ownership of a common noun or an abstract noun.

EXAMPLE We watched the singer's performance.
(Whose performance did we watch? We watched the singer's performance. *Performance* is a common noun.)

We discussed Kim's ideas.
(Whose ideas did we discuss? We discussed Kim's ideas. *Ideas* is an abstract noun.)

94 *Chapter 5 Practice with Parts of Speech*

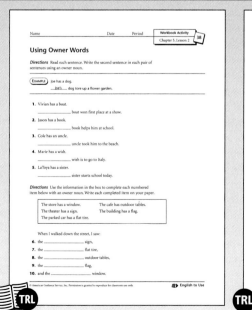

Workbook Activity 38

Activity 38

M

a

x

Max's cat

sleeps

in the sun.

Activity A On your paper, write the second sentence in each pair of sentences with an owner noun.

Example Maria has a sister.
<u>Maria's</u> sister took her to the game.

1. Max has a cat.
_____ cat sleeps in the sun.

2. Tomas has a car.
_____ car made a wrong turn.

3. Jamal has a cold.
_____ cold kept him home from work.

4. Megan had a dream.
_____ dream was scary.

5. Kate has a brother.
_____ brother bought a new car.

Activity B Use the information in the box to complete each numbered item below with an owner noun. Write each completed item on your paper.

The boy has a sleeping bag.
The child has a book.
The cat has a rubber mouse.
The neighbor has a rake.
The teenager has some tapes.
The television has a cord.

When I came home, I tripped on

Example the <u>neighbor's</u> rake,

1. the _____ rubber mouse,

2. the _____ book,

3. the _____ cord,

4. the _____ tapes, and

5. the _____ sleeping bag.

Max's cat sleeps in the sun.

Activity A Answers

1. Max's cat sleeps in the sun.
2. Tomas's car made a wrong turn.
3. Jamal's cold kept him home from work. **4.** Megan's dream was scary.
5. Kate's brother bought a new car.

Activity B Answers

1. the cat's rubber mouse, **2.** the child's book, **3.** the television's cord, **4.** the teenager's tapes, and **5.** the boy's sleeping bag.

3 Reinforce and Extend

LEARNING STYLES

Interpersonal/Group
Ask pairs of students to work together to write sentences with owner nouns similar to those they completed in Activity B. They might begin by writing a list of sentences like those in the box.

GLOBAL CONNECTION

The Spanish language doesn't use an apostrophe for possession. Instead, Spanish uses *de*, which means "of." For example, *el padre de Maria* literally means "the father of Maria" or *Maria's father*. Invite students who speak Spanish or another non-English language to give examples of phrases that show possession in these languages.

ASL ILLUSTRATION

Have students notice that the sentence illustrated on page 95 gives the signs for "Max" and "cat," followed by a sign for ownership. Have students practice combining other nouns and using the sign that shows possession.

TEACHER ALERT

Draw students' attention to item two in Activity A, a noun that ends in -'s. Form the possessive of *Tomas* with the class, and help students familiarize themselves with the -s's and -s' constructions.

Name _____ Date _____ Period _____

Sentence Diagramming Activity
Chapter 5, Lesson 2 30

Diagram Using Owner Words

Sentence Pattern 2: Subject + Verb + Direct Object

Step 1 The simple subject (a noun or pronoun) is written on the line on the left side. The simple predicate (a verb or verb phrase) is written on the line on the right side.

Step 2 Adjectives or prepositional phrases that describe the subject go on the lines under the subject.

Step 3 Adverbs or prepositional phrases that tell about the verb go on the lines under the verb.

Step 4 Conjunctions are written on the dotted lines between the two words that are joined by the conjunction.

Step 5 The direct object is written on the line to the right of the verb.

Step 6 Adverbs or prepositional phrases that tell about the direct object go on the lines under the direct object.

Directions Look at the steps above and the example below. Diagram the sentences below using the blank diagrams.

EXAMPLE My napkin dropped on the floor.

1. You forgot your coat on the bus.

2. He left his homework in my house.

© American Guidance Service, Inc. Permission is granted to reproduce for classroom use only.

English to Use

TRL

Sentence Diagramming Activity 30

Chapter 5 Lesson 3

Overview This lesson explains possessive pronouns and their use in sentences.

Objectives

- To identify possessive pronouns and the objects they possess
- To write possessive pronouns in sentences

Student Pages 96–97

Teacher's Resource Library

Workbook Activity 39

Activity 39

Alternative Activity 39

Vocabulary

owner object
owner pronoun

1 Warm-Up Activity

Write this sentence on the board: *Claire's school has a new roof.* Ask students to take turns using the different owner pronouns in the chart in place of the name in the sentence.

2 Teaching the Lesson

Review the concept of owner words. Discuss how to substitute owner pronouns for owner nouns. Have students practice identifying the objects following owner nouns and owner pronouns.

3 Reinforce and Extend

TEACHER ALERT

Students have not yet learned about linking verbs. When you create example sentences, remember to use action verbs.

Lesson 3 Owner Pronouns

Owner pronoun
A pronoun that owns something in a sentence

Owner object
A noun following an owner pronoun or owner noun

You have learned that pronouns can take the place of nouns in a sentence. Pronouns that show ownership in a sentence are **owner pronouns.** Owner pronouns do not use apostrophes.

Owner Pronouns	
One Owner	**Two or More Owners**
my	our
your	your
his	their
her	
its	

Writing Tip

Another way to show possesion is to use a prepositional phrase with the preposition *of.*

Example: the car's engine—the engine of the car.

The noun following the owner pronoun or owner noun is the **owner object.**

EXAMPLE Stephan placed *his* glass on the counter.
(The owner pronoun *his* takes the place of the proper noun *Stephan*. *His* shows that the glass belongs to Stephan. *Glass* is the owner object.)

The truck lost *its* mirror.
(The owner pronoun *its* takes the place of the common noun *truck*. *Its* shows that the mirror belongs to the truck. *Mirror* is the owner object.)

The visitors left *their* papers on the table.
(The owner pronoun *their* takes the place of the common noun *visitors*. *Their* shows that the papers belong to the visitors. *Papers* is the owner object.)

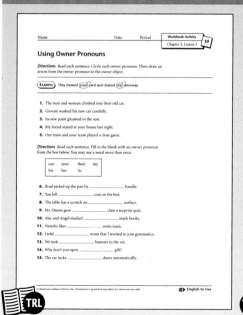

Workbook Activity 39

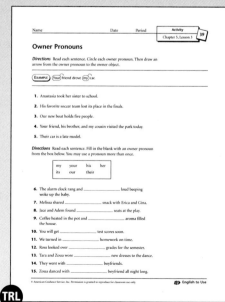

Activity 39

Activity A Read each sentence. Find all the owner pronouns, and write them on your paper. Next to each owner pronoun, write the owner object.

Example Her cousin went around the block on my new scooter.
Her—cousin
my—scooter

1. Martin and I saw his sister at the movie.
2. Her dog and our cat play in their yard.
3. Your bus, with its orange sign, stops at her house.
4. His brother gestures with his hands to talk to their neighbor.
5. My sweater, your glove, and her scarf are here.
6. This is her book about Braille.
7. The woman learned to read Braille from her cousin.
8. Kamilla had polished her old car carefully.
9. Its left wheel had a flat tire during their last ride.
10. Their car showed its age.

Activity B Write each sentence on your paper. Fill in the blank with an owner pronoun. Look at the list of owner pronouns on page 96 for help.

Example We visited Nate at the ranch and rode <u>his</u> horse.

1. Lin and I picked berries from _____ garden.
2. We made a fruit salad, and _____ bright colors tempted everyone.
3. Mom shared _____ cooking secrets with us.
4. Dad gave _____ opinion to the cooks.
5. Coleta's brothers washed _____ hands and came to the table.

Activity A Answers

1. his—sister 2. Her—dog; our—cat; their—yard 3. Your—bus; its—sign; her—house 4. His—brother; his—hands; their—neighbor 5. My—sweater; your—glove; her—scarf 6. her—book 7. her—cousin 8. her—car 9. Its—wheel; their—ride 10. Their—car; its—age

Activity B Answers

Answers will vary. Possible answers are given.

1. Lin and I picked berries from our garden. 2. We made a fruit salad, and its bright colors tempted everyone. 3. Mom shared her cooking secrets with us. 4. Dad gave his opinion to the cooks. 5. Coleta's brothers washed their hands and came to the table.

TEACHER ALERT

! Remind students not to confuse *its* with *it's*. Point out that *its* is a pronoun that shows ownership; *it's* is a contraction that means "it is."

Lesson at a Glance

Chapter 5 Lesson 4

Overview This lesson presents plural possessives and explains how to form them using -*s* apostrophe. It also explains how to replace collective nouns with pronouns.

Objectives

- To understand and write plural possessives
- To replace collective nouns with pronouns

Student Pages 98–99

Teacher's Resource Library

Workbook Activity 40

Activity 40

Alternative Activity 40

---

1 Warm-Up Activity

Write the following sentence on the board: *The boy's brother works for the girls' father.* Ask the class how many boys are referred to in the sentence (one) and how many girls (more than one). Ask students how they determined the number of boys and girls. Ask students how they knew this.

2 Teaching the Lesson

Review how to form singular possessives and possessive pronouns. Demonstrate how irregular plurals such as *men, women,* and *geese* form plural possessives.

Activity A Answers

1. kids' 2. parks' 3. horses'
4. kittens' 5. trucks'

You have learned that an owner noun can show ownership by one owner. Owner nouns can also show ownership by more than one owner.

Use -*s* apostrophe (*s*') to form most owner nouns that show ownership by more than one owner.

EXAMPLE	
One owner	The worker painted Mr. Jackson's house.
	(Mr. Jackson alone has a house.)
More than one owner	The worker painted the girls' cabinet.
	(Two or more girls share the cabinet.)

Owner pronouns can also show ownership by more than one owner.

EXAMPLE	
More than one owner	The pirates buried their treasure.
	(The owner pronoun *their* shows that the treasure belongs to more than one pirate.)

> Two people may own something together. For example, Kat and Jen may share a bedroom. To show this, add an apostrophe and -*s* to the last word in the word group: *Kat and Jen's room.*

Activity A Write each owner's name on your paper.

Example The performers have dances.
performers' dances

1. The kids have toys. _____ toys
2. The parks have paths. _____ paths
3. The horses have saddles. _____ saddles
4. The kittens have milk. _____ milk
5. The trucks have tires. _____ tires

---

98 Chapter 5 *Practice with Parts of Speech*

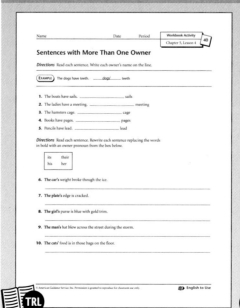

Workbook Activity 40

Activity 40

Be careful when using a pronoun to take the place of a noun that names a group, such as *team, crowd, army,* and *committee.* Use the pronoun *it* to take the place of a noun that names a group.

EXAMPLE	**Group noun** **Pronoun**	The stack of bricks fell. It fell. (Although many bricks fell, only one stack fell.)

Use the owner pronoun *its* to take the place of a group noun that shows ownership.

EXAMPLE	**Group noun** **Pronoun**	The band's singer wrote the song. Its singer wrote the song. (Although there are many musicians in the band, there is only one band.)

Activity B Write these sentences on your paper. Replace the words in bold with pronouns.

1. **The group** left early.
2. **The cheerleaders'** captain began a new cheer.
3. **The team** scored.
4. **A player** stole the ball from his opponent.
5. **The crowd** yelled.

Activity C Write these sentences on your paper. Replace the words in bold with owner pronouns.

1. **The group's** cheer made the rafters ring.
2. **The school's** score rose after the cheer.
3. **The team's** spirit rose, too.
4. **The crowd's** yells grew.
5. **The band's** music filled the gym.

Activity B Answers

1. It left early. 2. Their captain began a new cheer. 3. It scored. 4. He stole the ball from his opponent. 5. It yelled.

Activity C Answers

1. Its cheer made the rafters ring. 2. Its score rose after the cheer. 3. Its spirit rose, too. 4. Its yells grew. 5. Its music filled the gym.

Writing Practice

Ask students (in pairs or small groups) to use the ideas in Activities B and C to write paragraphs. Encourage students to use a variety of nouns and pronouns. Suggest that they add descriptive words and phrases to improve the sentences.

3 Reinforce and Extend

ONLINE CONNECTION

 For more practice with collective nouns, have students visit an ESL site at the College of San Mateo: *http://smccd.net/accounts/sevas/esl/ reviewlesson/agree2a.html.* The interactive lesson includes quizzes and references for additional support.

IN THE COMMUNITY

 Ask students to take a walk in their community and make lists of things that the community owns, such as parks, streets, sidewalks, and buildings. Have students use their lists to write sentences like the ones in Activities A and C. In class, ask students to change each owner's name to an owner pronoun (as requested in Activity C).

Lesson at a Glance

Chapter 5 Lesson 5

Overview This lesson explains how to identify the simple subject in sentences with prepositional phrases in the subject, when the subject is understood, and when the predicate comes before the subject.

Objectives

- To identify subjects, verbs, and direct objects in sentences with prepositional phrases in the subject and with understood subjects

- To rewrite sentences that appear in reverse order

Student Pages 100–101

Teacher's Resource Library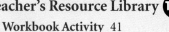

Workbook Activity 41

Activity 41

Alternative Activity 41

Sentence Diagramming Activity 31

....

Vocabulary

understood subject
understood you

....

 Warm-Up Activity

Write these sentences on the board: *A few of my friends have skates. Give this note to your teacher. Here comes the rain.* Read each sentence with students, helping them identify the subject, verb, and direct object. Begin by having volunteers delete prepositional phrases.

 Teaching the Lesson

Review the example sentences and explain that objects of prepositions can be easily confused with the subject of a sentence. Discuss how this confusion can lead to problems in subject-verb agreement.

Understood subject
A subject that cannot be seen in a sentence

Understood you
You as a subject that cannot be seen in a sentence

Every sentence has a subject. Prepositional phrases may make the subject hard to find. Just remember that the object of a preposition is *never* the subject of a sentence.

> **EXAMPLE**
>
> A lot of people waited.
>
> **Parts of speech**   *adj. noun prep. noun   verb*
> **Sentence parts**   subject with prepositional phrase | predicate
> **Sentence pattern**   subject + verb

Some sentences have **understood subjects.** For example, a sentence spoken to *you* means that *you* are being asked to do something. It is an **understood *you*.** The subject of the sentence is understood to be *you.*

> **EXAMPLE**
>
> Pick up that trash.
>
> **Parts of speech**   *verb adv. adj.   noun*
> **Sentence pattern**   (subject) + verb + direct object
> (*You* is the understood subject.)

The subject can be hard to find when the predicate comes before the subject of a sentence. These kinds of sentences often begin with the adverb *here* or *there*. To find the subject in these sentences, try turning the sentence around.

> **EXAMPLE**
>
> There goes the teacher.
>
> **Parts of speech**   *adv.   verb adj.   noun*
> (To find the subject, turn the sentence around.)
> The teacher goes there.
> (Who goes? The *teacher* goes.)
> **Sentence pattern**   subject + verb

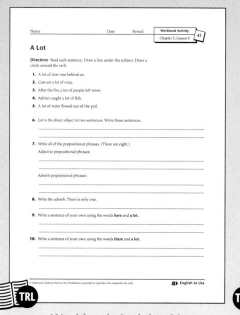

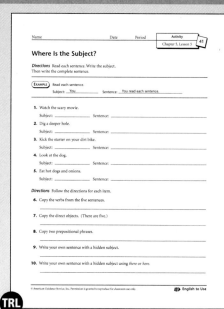

Workbook Activity 41   **Activity 41**

Activity A On your paper, write the subject, verb, and direct object (if there is one) for each sentence. If the subject is understood, write *you*.

1. Akili earned a lot of money.
2. Come to my house.
3. Take me to work on Tuesday.
4. A lot of money sat on the table.
5. Catch that amazing show.
6. Watch my bag.
7. Many people want a lot of money.
8. Sit quietly and listen.
9. Raise your hand.
10. Turn left at Maple Lane.
11. A lot of trees stand by the road.
12. Look at that paper's ad.
13. Call your parents.
14. A lot of people like Tyler.
15. Read the next chapter by Friday.

Activity B On your paper, write each sentence so that the subject comes first. Underline the simple subject.

1. Here comes Alice with her friends.
2. Away fly the birds.
3. Here comes the train from New York.
4. There goes the group of children.
5. There lies the problem.

Do not be fooled by *here* or *there* at the beginning of these kinds of sentences. As adverbs, they tell *where.* The fastest way to find the subject of a sentence is to ask *who* or *what* is doing the action.

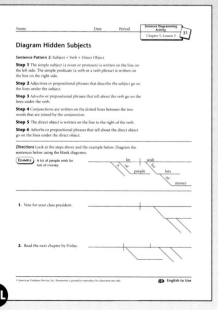

1. S—Akili; V—earned; D.O.—lot
2. S—you; V—Come **3.** S—you; V—Take; D.O.—me **4.** S—lot; V—sat
5. S—you; V—Catch; D.O.—show
6. S—you; V—Watch; D.O.—bag
7. S—people; V—want; D.O.—lot
8. S—you; V—Sit, listen **9.** S—you; V—Raise; D.O.—hand **10.** S—you; V—Turn **11.** S—lot; V—stand
12. S—you; V—Look **13.** S—you; V—Call; D.O.—parents **14.** S—lot; V—like; D.O.—Tyler **15.** S—you; V—Read; D.O.—chapter

Activity B Answers

1. <u>Alice</u> comes here with her friends.
2. The <u>birds</u> fly away. **3.** The <u>train</u> from New York comes here. **4.** The <u>group</u> of children goes there.
5. The <u>problem</u> lies there.

 3 Reinforce and Extend

LEARNING STYLES

 LEP/ESP
Some English language learners may need clarification regarding understood subjects. In many languages, the subject of a sentence is indicated by the form of the verb and does not appear separately in the sentence. Have English language learners write some of these verbs on the board. Then discuss with them the difference between these verbs with subjects and the English understood "you."

CAREER CONNECTION

 Work rules are frequently written as directives, with understood subjects. You may have rules for your classroom: *Bring your book, do your homework,* and so on. Discuss your classroom or school rules. Ask students to think about rules that might be important in a workplace. Such rules could include reference to safety, courtesy, and accuracy. Have them make a list of workplace rules. Ask volunteers to share their rules with the class.

Lesson at a Glance

Chapter 5 Lesson 6

Overview This lesson explains how adverbs can be used to modify adjectives and other adverbs. It also presents alternatives for *too* and *very*.

Objectives

■ To identify adverbs and the words they modify and their parts of speech

■ To write adverbs other than *too* and *very* in complete sentences

Student Pages 102–103

Teacher's Resource Library **TRL**

Workbook Activity 42

Activity 42

Alternative Activity 42

1 ◆ Warm-Up Activity

Write the following sentences on the board: *I _____ enjoyed the movie. I enjoyed the movie _____.* Challenge students to think of as many words as they can to fill in the blanks of the sentences above. Tell students that they can start with the adverb *very* but that they need to use other adverbs as well.

2 ◆ Teaching the Lesson

Read and discuss the text and the example sentence. Point out that there will be times when *very* and *too* are acceptable. Explain to students that they should be careful to avoid overusing those words when writing or speaking.

Activity A Answers

1. too—many, adjective
2. extremely—sharp, adjective
3. quite—often, adverb
4. unusually—bad, adjective
5. really—long, adjective

You have learned that adverbs describe verbs. Adverbs can also describe adjectives and other adverbs.

> **EXAMPLE**
>
> The very large package arrived too late.
>
> **Parts of speech** adj. adv. adj. noun verb adv. adv.
> **Sentence parts** subject | predicate
> (*Very* describes the adjective *large*. *Very* is an adverb. *Too* describes the adverb *late*. *Too* is an adverb.)

Try to avoid using *too* and *very* when another adverb will make your sentence more interesting. Here are some adverbs you can use in place of *too* and *very*.

almost	rather	terribly
awfully	really	totally
extremely	so	truly
quite	somewhat	unusually

Activity A On your paper, write the adverb in bold in each sentence. Then write the word it describes and its part of speech.

Example The taxi left the station **very** early.
       very—early, adverb

1. The driver spent **too** many hours on the road.
2. The route covered **extremely** sharp curves.
3. Snow comes **quite** often in the mountains.
4. The bus arrived in an **unusually** bad storm.
5. Alan waited a **really** long time for the bus.

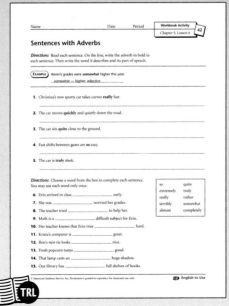

Workbook Activity 42

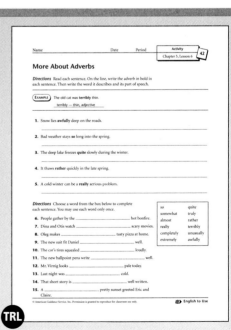

Activity 42

Activity B Choose a word other than *too* or *very* to fill in these blanks. Write the words on your paper.

1. Our _____ snowy winter made a good sports season.
2. Ice and snow made the ski trails _____ slick.
3. Skaters glide _____ fast across the frozen lake.
4. People need to be _____ careful in the winter.
5. The _____ cold winter damaged trees and shrubs.
6. Icy ruts made the roads _____ dangerous.
7. Some people stayed inside during the _____ long winter.
8. Fields of snow glared in the _____ bright sun.
9. _____ strong winds flattened the old barn.
10. _____ long chunks of ice hung from the roof.

Skiers enjoy the snowy weather.

Practice with Parts of Speech Chapter 5 **103**

Activity B Answers

Answers will vary. Check to see that students have used a variety of adverbs.

TEACHER ALERT

By avoiding *too* and *very*, students may fall into another trap: they might simply overuse another adverb, such as *terribly*, or they might use new adverbs in ways that sound awkward or stilted. Monitor students' use of adverbs and help them broaden their adverb use without making sentences that sound artificial.

3 Reinforce and Extend

LEARNING STYLES

Auditory/Verbal
Point out to students the picture on page 103. Have each student choose one of the words from the box on page 102 and use it in a sentence to describe what he or she sees in the picture. Then invite students to take turns saying their sentences aloud.

Chapter 5 Lesson 7

Overview This lesson introduces interjections. Adverbs and interjections are contrasted and used in sentences.

Objectives

■ To write interjections in sentences
■ To distinguish between interjections and adverbs in sentences

Student Pages 104–105

Teacher's Resource Library **TRL**

Workbook Activity 43
Activity 43
Alternative Activity 43
Sentence Diagramming Activity 32

Vocabulary

interjection

1 Warm-Up Activity

Write on the board: *I overslept. Yikes! I overslept!* Have students discuss how the word *Yikes!* expresses panic and concern.

2 Teaching the Lesson

Read and discuss the definition of *interjection* and the examples given. Have students share appropriate interjections that they hear in daily conversation.

Activity A Answers

Answers will vary.

3 Reinforce and Extend

LEARNING STYLES

Visual/Spatial

Encourage students to bring to class magazine or newspaper cartoons that demonstrate the use of interjections. Then ask students to create their own cartoons that use interjections.

Interjection
A word that shows feelings

An **interjection** is a word that expresses feeling. An interjection often comes first in a sentence.

EXAMPLE   Oh, the ice melted.
Hey! It's all over the carpet.
(*Oh* and *hey* are both interjections.)

Writing Tip

Interjections are a good way to make your writing more interesting. Use interjections only in informal writing.

Here are some words that are used as interjections:

hurray	good-bye	zap
hush	gee whiz	whoosh
hello	ah	boy
ouch	gosh	pow
wow	well	hey
oh	yuck	ha
yikes	aha	no

Activity A Write each sentence on your paper. Fill in the blank with an interjection from the list above.

1. _____! Antonio won a large amount of money.

2. _____! The new worker on the night shift works hard.

3. _____! That small airplane landed safely in the dense fog.

4. _____! The thick ropes snapped during the daring rescue at sea.

5. _____! A black motorcycle roared through the quiet streets.

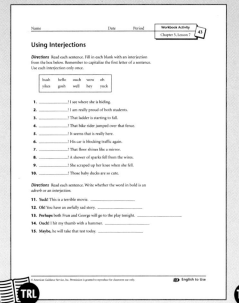

Workbook Activity 43

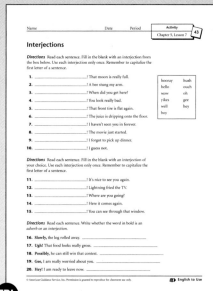

Activity 43

Oh

Ice

Melts

Finish

Oh, the ice melted.

Activity B Write each sentence on your paper. Fill in the blank with an interjection of your choice.

1. _____! I forgot to buy bread.
2. _____! Maybe I can stop at that store.
3. _____! Look at the huge bread selection
4. _____! I don't think I can make a decision.
5. _____! This bread is expensive.

Do not confuse interjections with adverbs that begin a sentence. Remember, adverbs tell about verbs, adjectives, or other adverbs. Interjections express feelings. They do not tell about any other word in the sentence.

> **EXAMPLE**
>
> **Adverb**   Honestly, Julie spoke to her mother. (*Honestly* is an adverb that tells about the verb *spoke*. How did Julie speak? She spoke *honestly*.)
>
> **Interjection**   Honestly! I did not break the window. (*Honestly* is an interjection that expresses the subject's feelings. *Honestly* does not tell about any other word in the sentence.)

Activity C Write whether the word in bold is an adverb or an interjection.

1. **Hush,** the baby is sleeping.
2. **Ugh!** I really disliked that movie.
3. **Perhaps** you did not understand it.
4. **Maybe,** Ravi left early.
5. **Oh,** I miss him.

Activity B Answers

Answers will vary.

Activity C Answers

1. interjection 2. interjection
3. adverb 4. adverb 5. interjection

Speaking Practice

After students have completed Activities A and B, have them read the sentences aloud, both with and without the interjections. Ask students to read the sentences expressively, and have them discuss how the sentences change after the interjection is added.

AT HOME

Tell students to note how family members, friends, and others use interjections to express strong feeling. Ask students to list new classroom-appropriate interjections in their personal journals for reference.

ASL ILLUSTRATION

Have students practice making the sign for the interjection "Oh!" Tell them to insert the interjection into other sentences they have learned so far in the text.

Diagram Interjections

Sentence Pattern 2: Subject + Verb + Direct Object

Step 1 The simple subject (a noun or pronoun) is written on the line on the left side. The simple predicate (a verb or a verb phrase) is written on the line on the right side.

Step 2 Adjectives or prepositional phrases that describe the subject go on the lines under the subject.

Step 3 Adverbs or prepositional phrases that tell about the verb go on the lines under the verb.

Step 4 Conjunctions are written on the dotted lines between the two words that are joined by the conjunction.

Step 5 The direct object is written on the line to the right of the verb.

Step 6 Adverbs or prepositional phrases that tell about the direct object go on the lines under the direct object.

Step 7 Interjections are placed on a separate line above the main diagram.

Directions Look at the steps above and the example below. Diagram the sentences below using the blank diagrams.

1. Hey! That is my bike.

2. Whoosh! The ball passed by me.

Sentence Diagramming Activity 32

Lesson at a Glance

Chapter 5 Lesson 8

Overview This lesson introduces the four steps in the writing process.

Objectives

■ To apply the four steps of the writing process to develop and present ideas

Student Pages 106–107

Teacher's Resource Library

Workbook Activity 44

Activity 44

Alternative Activity 44

Vocabulary

edit
prewrite
rewrite
write
writing process

 Warm-Up Activity

Have students describe the types of writing that give them satisfaction or pleasure and the types of writing that they find difficult to complete.

 Teaching the Lesson

Read with the class the explanation of the writing process on page 106. Arrange students in small groups, and have them share some of their thoughts about what makes them happy. Then ask each student to spend two or three minutes writing an informal, personal response to the group discussion. Tell students that they have completed the first part of the writing process.

Writing process

The use of four steps: prewrite, write, rewrite, and edit

Prewrite

Talking, thinking, or reading about a topic before writing

Write

Putting ideas on paper

Rewrite

Writing again until the meaning is clear

Edit

Checking written work for mistakes

Writing is a way to express your feelings and ideas. Writing well takes practice. The **writing process** can help you develop good ideas. It can help you focus your thoughts and present them clearly to your readers.

The writing process has four steps: **prewrite, write, rewrite,** and **edit.**

1. **Prewrite.** The first thing you do before writing is decide what you want to write about. Gather your thoughts. Write them down on paper or note cards. Then arrange your notes so that they make sense.

2. **Write.** Write a first draft, or copy. Write your ideas as clearly as you can, but don't worry about mistakes. You can correct mistakes later.

3. **Rewrite.** You want your writing to express your meaning. Go back and read what you wrote. Can it be improved? Rewrite any sentences that are unclear.

4. **Edit.** Now read your work and look for mistakes in spelling, punctuation, or sentence structure. Be sure to correct all the mistakes you find.

Activity A Read each group of sentences. Then choose one group. Add adverbs, adjectives, compounds, and prepositional phrases to the sentences to write a short story. Use the steps of the writing process.

1. **A** Andres and Regina sit.

  B Andres and Regina play chess.

  C People watch.

  D Regina wins the prize.

  E Regina and Andres leave.

---

106   *Chapter 5   Practice with Parts of Speech*

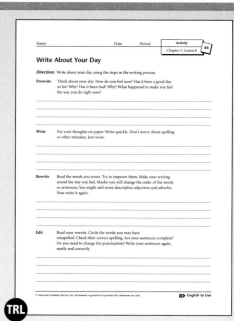

Workbook Activity 44   Activity 44

Writing Tip

When choosing a topic, you need to think about your audience and purpose. Ask yourself: For whom am I writing? Why am I writing?

2. **A** Rachel bakes rolls.

   B Rachel bakes bread.

   C Rachel slices bread.

   D Rachel serves bread.

   E Rachel sells baked goods.

3. **A** Fish swim.

   B Bruce wades.

   C Bruce casts.

   D Bruce reels.

   E Bruce catches fish.

4. **A** Eddie chases.

   B Nick runs.

   C Nick hides.

   D Eddie searches.

   E Nick waits.

5. **A** Kyle digs.

   B Kyle plants.

   C Sun shines.

   D Rain falls.

   E Tree grows.

ONLINE CONNECTION

The Old Dominion Web site offers additional information about the writing process, including instruction on generating ideas, proofreading and editing, and help with grammar and punctuation. Visit *web.odu.edu/AL/wts/process.htm*.

Activity A Answers

Answers will vary. Possible answers follow.

1. Andres and Regina sit quietly in the park. They play chess in a contest. People gather to watch the action. Regina wins first prize. After the contest, Andres and Regina leave the park.

2. Rachel bakes large rolls in the kitchen. She bakes bread and rolls early in the morning. Rachel slices bread with a large knife and serves good bread at each meal. Rachel sells baked goods in the village.

3. Large fish swim slowly in the creek. Bruce wades into the water and casts his fishing line. Then he slowly reels out his line and waits for a fish to bite. Through the long sunny day, Bruce catches bass and perch.

4. Eddie chases a thief, and Nick runs after Eddie. Nick hides behind a trash can and grabs the thief. Eddie searches the thief's pockets for stolen goods. Nick waits with the handcuffs.

5. Kyle gets a big shovel and digs a large hole in the ground. He plants a tree in the hole and waters it often. He watches the tree as the sun shines and the rain falls. Every day, the tree slowly grows.

3 Reinforce and Extend

LEARNING STYLES

Logical/Mathematical

Some students may benefit from a structured approach to the writing process, for example, brainstorming in a group for the prewrite section or consistently trading papers with a partner in the editing portion of the process.

Lesson at a Glance

Chapter 5 Lesson 9

Overview This lesson focuses on punctuation used in possessive pronouns and with interjections.

Objectives

- To add apostrophes to possessive nouns in sentences
- To punctuate sentences with interjections
- To match words with their meanings

Student Pages 108–109

Teacher's Resource Library

Workbook Activity 45

Activity 45

Alternative Activity 45

1 ▸ Warm-Up Activity

Ask students to share what they have learned about forming owner nouns. Then invite volunteers to write examples of singular and plural owner nouns on the board.

2 ▸ Teaching the Lesson

Review with students the concepts of singular and plural possessives and of interjections. As students prepare for Activity B, remind them that they will be carefully proofreading errors as well as using their knowledge of interjections.

Activity A Answers

1. The man's suit hangs in the closet. 2. Many trucks' tires littered the road. 3. Fran's brother owns a theater. 4. Four ships' sails snapped in the wind. 5. A bird's nest fell from the branch.

Lesson 9 Writing Mechanics

You have learned to form owner nouns with apostrophes. Use apostrophe and *-s* to show one owner. Use *-s* and an apostrophe to show more than one owner.

Activity A Write each sentence correctly on your paper. Remember that every sentence begins with a capital letter and ends with a punctuation mark.

1. the mans suit hangs in the closet
2. many trucks tires littered the road
3. frans brother owns a theater
4. four ships sails snapped in the wind
5. a birds nest fell from the branch

An exclamation point or a comma follows interjections that begin a sentence.

An exclamation point is a punctuation mark used when you want to show strong feeling. Use an exclamation point after an interjection that shows strong feelings.

> **EXAMPLE** Yikes! I almost fell off the chair.
> Aha! We caught the dog.

Use a comma after an interjection that shows mild feelings.

> **EXAMPLE** Gee, that book ended sadly.
> Well, we finished our project on time.

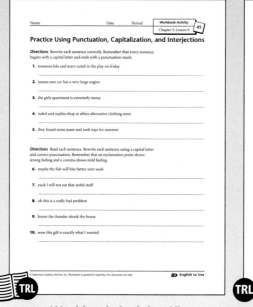

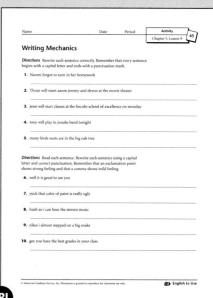

Activity B Decide what feeling you want the interjection to show. Then write each sentence correctly.

1. well i found my house
2. ouch you stepped on my foot
3. quick turn on the lights
4. ah i found my shoe
5. oh i fell across the coffee table
6. boom thunder rattled the house
7. crack lightning hit the roof
8. zzzt lightning zapped the stereo the TV and the CD player
9. oh the lightning could have started a fire
10. wow Krista will never forget that terrible night

Activity C Match the words with their meanings. Write the number and its correct letter on your paper.

Words	Meanings
1. apostrophe	A shows feelings
2. interjection	B !
3. owner pronouns	C tells word order
4. sentence pattern	D mark that shows ownership
5. exclamation point	E my, his, her, its, your, their

Using What You've Learned

Write a paragraph about something that frightened or surprised you or someone else. Use an interjection in at least three sentences.

Activity B Answers

Answers will vary. Possible answers are given. **1.** Well, I found my house. **2.** Ouch! You stepped on my foot. **3.** Quick! Turn on the lights. **4.** Ah, I found my shoe. **5.** Oh! I fell across the coffee table. **6.** Boom! Thunder rattled the house. **7.** Crack! Lightning hit the roof. **8.** Zzzt! Lightning zapped the stereo, the TV, and the CD player. **9.** Oh! The lightning could have started a fire. **10.** Wow! Krista will never forget that terrible night.

Activity C Answers

1. D **2.** A **3.** E **4.** C **5.** B

Using What You've Learned

Have students brainstorm a list of interjections that they might use in scary situations, such as "Oh, my!" and "Careful!" In addition, tell students that they can refer to the list of prepositions on page 104 as they begin their paragraphs.

3 Reinforce and Extend

ONLINE CONNECTION

Schoolhouse Rock's song "Interjections!" first aired on television in the 1970s, and offers a collection of interjections in an amusing context. See the words for "Interjections!" at *www.apocalypse.org/pub/u/gilly/ schoolhouse_Rock/html/grammar/ interjection.html.*

TEACHER ALERT

Remind students that interjections should not be overused. Point out that interjections have the most impact when they are used sparingly.

LEARNING STYLES

LEP/ESL

To help language learners understand whether to use a comma or an exclamation point with an interjection, ask them to offer examples of different interjections from languages they know. (Make sure that the interjections are appropriate for the classroom.) Have students explain which interjections show strong and mild emotion, and discuss the proper punctuation for each example.

Chapter 5 Review

Use the Chapter Review to prepare students for tests and to reteach content from the chapter.

Chapter 5 Mastery Test

The Teacher's Resource Library includes two parallel forms of the Chapter 5 Mastery Test. The difficulty level of the two forms is equivalent. You may wish to use one form as a pretest and the other form as a posttest.

REVIEW ANSWERS

Part A

1. owner noun 2. writing process 3. apostrophe 4. write 5. owner pronoun 6. rewrite 7. owner object 8. prewrite 9. understood subject 10. edit 11. understood *you* 12. interjection

Part B

13. Gee, Carlo still wants this car for work and school.

14. His

15. (car's) doors; (door's) dents; (Carlo's) friend

Word Bank
apostrophe
edit
interjection
owner noun
owner object
owner pronoun
prewrite
rewrite
understood subject
understood *you*
write
writing process

Part A Read each sentence below. Fill in each blank with a vocabulary word that correctly completes each sentence.

1. An _____ is a noun that shows ownership in a sentence.
2. The process that helps you use the four writing steps to present your ideas in writing is called the _____.
3. Use an _____ plus -s to form an owner noun.
4. You _____ when you put your ideas on paper.
5. A pronoun used to show ownership in a sentence is called an _____.
6. To write again until the meaning is clear is to _____.
7. An _____ is a noun following an owner pronoun or owner noun.
8. To talk, think, or read about a topic before writing is to _____.
9. A subject that cannot be seen in a sentence is called an _____.
10. You _____ when you check written work for mistakes.
11. The _____ is *you* as a subject that cannot be seen in a sentence.
12. You use an _____ when you want to show feelings.

Part B Read this paragraph. Answer the questions on your paper.

After work, Carlo looks at the used car for sale. The car's doors have dents. The door's dents are not bad though. Carlo's friend bought a car. His car has a dent, too. Gee, Carlo still wants this car for work and school.

13. Write the sentence that has an interjection.
14. Write the owner pronoun.
15. Write all the owner nouns with their owner objects. Circle the owner nouns.

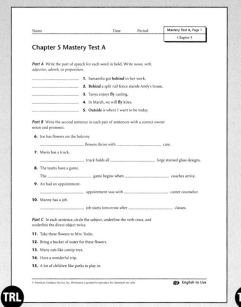

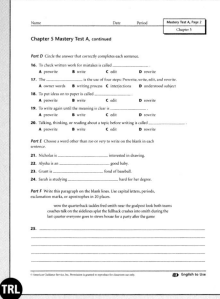

Chapter 5 Mastery Test A

Part C Write these sentences correctly.

16. wow look at that beautiful sunset
17. several spiders webs filled the old barn
18. the red cars door fell off during the race

Part D Write the correct part of speech for each word in bold.

19. Adrienne and Julie **talk** to each other by e-mail.
  A verb   B noun   C adjective   D adverb

20. One night they had a long **talk** about TV shows.
  A adverb   B verb   C adjective   D noun

21. They discussed a **talk** show about rap music.
  A adverb   B adjective   C verb   D preposition

Part E Write the understood subject, the verb, and the direct object for each sentence.

22. See the new models in the showroom.
23. Send both boxes to me.
24. Wow! Feel the beat of the music.

Part F Add adverbs, adjectives, compounds, and prepositional phrases to these sentences. Use the writing process to write a short story.

25. Dog walks.
26. Cat runs.
27. Dog chases.
28. Cat turns.
29. Cat hides.
30. Dog barks.

Test-Taking Tip Take time to organize your thoughts before writing answers to short-answer questions.

REVIEW ANSWERS

Part C

16. Wow! Look at that beautiful sunset. **17.** Several spiders' webs filled the old barn. **18.** The red car's door fell off during the race.

Part D

19. A **20.** D **21.** B

Part E

22. S—you; V—See; D.O.—models
23. S—you; V—Send; D.O.—boxes
24. S—you; V—Feel; D.O.—beat

Part F

Answers for items 25–30 will vary.

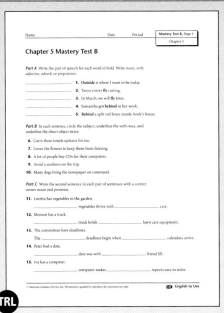

Planning Guide

More Sentence Patterns

	Student Pages	Student Text Lesson			Language Skills	
		Vocabulary	Practice Activities	Identification Skills	Writing Skills	Punctuation Skills
Lesson 1 Indirect Objects	114–115	✔	✔	✔	✔	✔
Lesson 2 Indirect Objects in Long Sentences	116–117		✔	✔	✔	✔
Lesson 3 Object Complements	118–119	✔	✔	✔	✔	✔
Lesson 4 Object Complements in Long Sentences	120–121		✔	✔	✔	✔
Lesson 5 Appositives	122–123	✔	✔	✔	✔	✔
Lesson 6 Writing Practice	124–125		✔	✔	✔	✔
Lesson 7 Writing Mechanics	126–127		✔	✔	✔	✔

Chapter Activities

Teacher's Resource Library
Community Connection 6:
Plan and Prepare a Meal
English in Your World 6:
Sentence Patterns in the Newspaper

Assessment Options

Student Text
Chapter 6 Review

Teacher's Resource Library
Chapter 6 Mastery Tests A and B
Midterm Mastery Test

	Student Text Features					Teaching Strategies					Learning Styles						Teacher's Resource Library				
ASL Illustration	Communication Connection	Notes	Using What You've Learned	Writing Tips	Teacher Alert	Online Connection	Applications (Home, Career, Community, Global)	Speaking Practice	Writing Practice	Auditory/Verbal	Body/Kinesthetic	Interpersonal/ Group Learning	Logical/Mathematical	Visual/Spatial	LEP/ESL	Workbook Activities	Activities	Alternative Activities	Sentence Diagramming Activities	Self-Study Guide
115		✔					115			115						46	46	46	33	✔
		✔				117				117						47	47	47		✔
119					119		119		119							48	48	48	34	✔
				✔									121		121	49	49	49		✔
				✔		123	123									50	50	50	35	✔
						125						125		125		51	51	51		✔
	126		127		127							127				52	52	52		✔

Pronunciation Key

a	hat	e	let	ī	ice	ô	order	ù	put	sh	she
ā	age	ē	equal	o	hot	oi	oil	ü	rule	th	thin
ä	far	ėr	term	ō	open	ou	out	ch	child	ϮH	then
â	care	i	it	ȯ	saw	u	cup	ng	long	zh	measure

ə { a in about
      e in taken
      i in pencil
      o in lemon
      u in circus

Alternative Activities

The Teacher's Resource Library (TRL) contains a set of lower-level worksheets called Alternative Activities. These worksheets cover the same content as the regular Activities but are written at a second-grade reading level.

Skill Track Software

Use the Skill Track Software for English to Use for additional reinforcement of this chapter. The software program allows students using AGS textbooks to be assessed for mastery of each chapter and lesson of the textbook. Students access the software on an individual basis and are assessed with multiple-choice items.

Chapter 6: More Sentence Patterns
pages 112–129

Lessons

1. **Indirect Objects**
   pages 114–115

2. **Indirect Objects in Long Sentences**
   pages 116–117

3. **Object Complements**
   pages 118–119

4. **Object Complements in Long Sentences**
   pages 120–121

5. **Appositives**
   pages 122–123

6. **Writing Practice**
   pages 124–125

7. **Writing Mechanics**
   pages 126–127

Chapter 6 Review
pages 128–129

Skill Track Software for English to Use

Teacher's Resource Library

Workbook Activities 46–52

Activities 46–52

Alternative Activities 46–52

Sentence Diagramming
   Activities 33–35
   (Optional sentence activities
   accompany lessons.)

Community Connection 6

English in Your World 6

Chapter 6 Self-Study Guide

Chapter 6 Mastery Tests A and B

Chapters 1–6 Midterm
   Mastery Test

(Answer Keys for the Teacher's
Resource Library begin on page 308
of this Teacher's Edition.)

Community Connection 6

Name _____ Date _____ Period _____ | Community Connection 6 | Chapter 6

Plan and Prepare a Meal

Think of a meal that you would like to prepare for someone that you know. What would you make for that person? Have you ever prepared that meal before? What ingredients will you need?

Directions Prepare the meal for the person that you chose. Answer the questions below using complete sentences. Remember to use indirect objects, object complements, and appositives in your answers.

1. What are you making for your meal?

2. Who are you making your meal for?

3. What ingredients will you need?

4. Ask the person that you cooked for to describe how the food tasted. Write down the description.

5. Write a description telling about how you planned and prepared a meal for someone using the answers from the questions above. Remember to use indirect objects, object complements, and appositives.

© American Guidance Service, Inc. Permission is granted to reproduce for classroom use only. | English to Use

---

English in Your World 6

Name _____ Date _____ Period _____ | English in Your World 6 | Chapter 6

Sentence Patterns in the Newspaper

You learned about four sentence patterns in Chapter 6:

- Sentences with indirect objects
- Sentences with indirect objects with compound parts and prepositional phrases
- Sentences with object complements
- Sentences with object complements with compound parts and prepositional phrases

Learn to recognize these patterns by looking for them in the newspaper. Follow these steps:

Step 1 Get the news section of your local newspaper. Use it to find these four sentence patterns. Find two of each kind of sentence.

Step 2 Write down each sentence in the space below.

1.
2.
3.
4.
5.
6.
7.
8.

© American Guidance Service, Inc. Permission is granted to reproduce for classroom use only. | English to Use

Chapter

6 More Sentence Patterns

Patterns, whether in nature or in writing, can lead you to look at something more closely. Patterns attract the eye and grab your attention. They demonstrate a sense of order. Look at the intricate patterns in this garden photograph. Every item in the garden has its place. Nothing is random. Color, contrast, and shape make the garden appealing.

Likewise, the parts of a sentence are not random; each part of a sentence has its proper place. Sentences follow certain patterns just like the patterns in the garden. In Chapter 6, you will learn about sentence patterns. You can make your writing more appealing and give it color, contrast, and shape by using what you learn about sentence patterns.

Goals for Learning

◆ To identify indirect objects and object complements

◆ To recognize sentences with indirect objects and object complements

◆ To identify and write appositives

◆ To identify and write sentences that use different sentence patterns

◆ To use correct punctuation with appositives

113

Introducing the Chapter

Ask students to examine the photograph. Ask them to describe the types of patterns they see. Discuss how the variety of patterns makes the photograph interesting. Point out that variety in sentences makes writing more interesting to read. This chapter will provide two more sentence patterns that can add variety to students' writing.

TEACHER'S RESOURCE

The AGS Teaching Strategies in English Transparencies may be used with this chapter. The transparencies add an interactive dimension to expand and enhance the *English to Use* program content.

CAREER INTEREST INVENTORY

The AGS Harrington-O'Shea Career Decision-Making System–Revised (CDM) may be used with this chapter. Students can use the CDM to explore their interests and identify careers. The CDM defines career areas that are indicated by students' responses on the inventory.

Writing Tips and Notes

Ask volunteers to read the tips and notes that appear in the margins throughout the chapter. Then discuss them with the class.

CHAPTER PROJECT

Have the class work as a group to write a short story. First have the class put together a list of words centered on a particular theme. Build the short story over a couple of weeks, adding one or two new sentences each day. Have students decide each day which new sentence parts they want to include in their sentences: appositives, object complements, or indirect objects.

TRL   **TRL**

Chapter 6 Self-Study Guide

Lesson at a Glance

Chapter 6 Lesson 1

Overview This lesson explains the function of indirect objects in sentences with direct objects.

Objectives

- To identify indirect objects in sentences
- To distinguish between direct and indirect objects in sentences

Student Pages 114–115

Teacher's Resource Library

Workbook Activity 46

Activity 46

Alternative Activity 46

Sentence Diagramming Activity 33

Vocabulary

indirect object

1 Warm-Up Activity

Write the following sentence on the board: *Joel gave _____ a present.* Ask students to fill in the blank with a noun or a pronoun, and write their suggestions on the board. Help students identify the sentence's subject (*Joel*), verb (*gave*), and direct object (*present*). Explain that the word they added to the sentence is known as the *indirect object.*

2 Teaching the Lesson

Read aloud the definition of indirect object, and discuss the information and examples. Students may confuse the indirect object with the direct object. Remind them that they will not if they restate the sentence, placing *to* or *for* in front of a noun or pronoun that they think is an indirect object. Model the second group of example sentences, explaining that a sentence's indirect object often will be a person.

Lesson 1 Indirect Objects

Indirect object
A noun or pronoun that takes action from the verb indirectly

Sentences with direct objects may also have **indirect objects.** An indirect object is a noun or pronoun that takes action from the verb indirectly. An indirect object answers the question *to whom, to what, for whom,* or *for what* about the verb.

> **EXAMPLE**
>
> The teacher reads a story.
>
> **Parts of speech** adj. noun verb adj. noun
> **Sentence pattern** subject + verb + direct object
>
> The same sentence can have an indirect object.
>
> The teacher reads us a story.
>
> **Parts of speech** adj. noun verb pron. adj. noun
> **Sentence pattern** subject + verb + indirect object + direct object
>
> (The teacher reads the story to whom? The teacher reads the story *to us. Us* is a pronoun used as an indirect object. *Story* is the direct object.)

Notice that the indirect object usually comes between the verb and the direct object.

Example
The teacher reads **us** a story.

If you are not sure which word in the sentence is the indirect object, try this: Put *to* or *for* in front of the noun or pronoun. If the sentence still makes sense, the noun is the indirect object.

> **EXAMPLE**
>
> The teacher gave Jack extra credit.
> **Try** The teacher gave extra credit *to* Jack.
>
> Ellie saved Anna the last bottle of water.
> **Try** Ellie saved the last bottle of water *for* Anna.
>
> (The sentences make sense both ways. In the first pair of sentences, *Jack* is the indirect object of the verb *gave. Credit* is the direct object. In the second pair of sentences, *Anna* is the indirect object of the verb *saved. Bottle* is the direct object.)

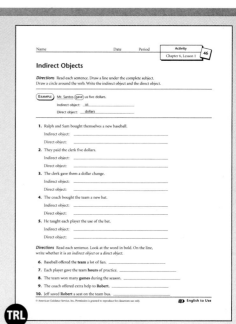

Workbook Activity 46   **Activity 46**

Story

Teacher

Read

We

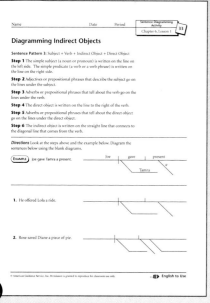
Finish

Activity A On your paper, write the indirect object in each of these sentences. Remember that an indirect object answers the question *to whom, to what, for whom,* or *for what* about the verb.

1. Alejandro asked Ms. Wilson some questions about the lesson.

2. She gave Alejandro the answers.

3. Homework provides students extra practice.

4. The teacher hands Alejandro a report card.

5. The new term offers Alejandro new things to learn.

Activity B Write the word in bold on your paper. Then write whether it is a *direct object* or an *indirect object.*

Example Jenny bought **Fran** lunch at the restaurant.
Fran—indirect object

1. Mr. Tan paid **Jenny** twenty dollars for mowing his lawn.

2. The clerk handed Jenny the **bill** for lunch.

3. She paid the **clerk** six dollars.

4. The clerk gave her a little **change.**

5. Jenny lent Fran **money.**

6. Fran bought **them** drinks.

7. She gave **Jenny** a cold bottle of juice.

8. Jenny's friend told **her** a silly joke.

9. Jenny gave her friend a wide **smile.**

10. Fran's brother Lou offered the girls a **ride** home.

The teacher read us a story.

More Sentence Patterns Chapter 6 **115**

Activity A Answers
1. Ms. Wilson 2. Alejandro
3. students 4. Alejandro
5. Alejandro

Activity B Answers
1. Jenny—indirect object 2. bill—direct object 3. clerk—indirect object 4. change—direct object
5. money—direct object 6. them—indirect object 7. Jenny—indirect object 8. her—indirect object
9. smile—direct object 10. ride—direct object

 3 Reinforce and Extend

LEARNING STYLES

 Body/Kinesthetic
Ask pairs of students to hand classroom objects to each other while the class provides sentences that tell about the exchanges. Help students identify the direct objects and indirect objects in each sentence.

GLOBAL CONNECTION

 Encourage students who know another language to write a sentence in that language and translate it word for word. Then have students point out the differences in structure between the sentence in that language and the same sentence in English. Find out how other languages convey the information found in the English indirect object.

ASL ILLUSTRATION

Have students practice making the ASL signs on the page. Discuss the way in which ASL word order is different from the word order of the sentence in English.

Diagramming Indirect Objects

Sentence Pattern 3: Subject + Verb + Indirect Object + Direct Object

Step 1 The simple subject (a noun or pronoun) is written on the line on the left side. The simple predicate (a verb or a verb phrase) is written on the line on the right side.

Step 2 Adjectives or prepositional phrases that describe the subject go on the lines under the subject.

Step 3 Adverbs or prepositional phrases that tell about the verb go on the lines under the verb.

Step 4 The direct object is written on the line to the right of the verb.

Step 5 Adverbs or prepositional phrases that tell about the direct object go on the lines under the direct object.

Step 6 The indirect object is written on the straight line that connects to the diagonal line that comes from the verb.

Directions Look at the steps above and the example below. Diagram the sentences below using the blank diagrams.

EXAMPLE Joe gave Tamra a present.

1. He offered Lola a ride.

2. Rose saved Diane a piece of pie.

TRL Sentence Diagramming Activity 33

Lesson at a Glance

Chapter 6 Lesson 2

Overview This lesson explains how to identify indirect objects in sentences with compound parts and prepositional phrases.

Objectives

■ To identify the indirect object in lengthy sentences

■ To identify the subject, verb, indirect object, and direct object in sentences

Student Pages 116–117

Teacher's Resource Library

Workbook Activity 47

Activity 47

Alternative Activity 47

 1 Warm-Up Activity

Discuss with students strategies for locating prepositional phrases in a sentence. Tell them that they can draw a line through prepositional phrases to locate other parts of speech. Then write a sentence on the board that includes an indirect object: *The store manager in the shoe department on the second floor gave Leon a job with very flexible hours on weekends.* Have volunteers take turns marking through the four prepositional phrases. When volunteers have finished, have the class identify the indirect object (*Leon*).

 2 Teaching the Lesson

Discuss with students how they can identify sentence patterns in long sentences by looking at the sentences part by part. Discuss the first example sentence with students, helping them identify the adjectives and prepositional phrases.

Sentences with indirect objects may have compound parts and prepositional phrases that add information to the sentence. By identifying the basic parts of the sentence, you can identify the indirect object.

> **EXAMPLE** The principal and the student with the blue backpack on her shoulders asked the basketball coach a question at the same time.
>
> **Compound subject** principal, student
> **Verb** asked
> **Indirect object** coach
> **Direct object** question

Although the example sentence appears long and complicated, it follows the basic sentence pattern of *subject + verb + indirect object + direct object*. Remove the adjectives and prepositional phrases, and you can easily recognize the sentence pattern.

> **EXAMPLE** The principal and student asked the coach a question.
>
> **Sentence pattern** subject + verb + indirect obj. + direct obj.

Activity A Write the indirect object in these sentences on your paper. (Hint: To find the indirect object, find the verb. Ask *to whom, to what, for whom,* or *for what* about the verb.)

1. The boy and girl in the back seat of the car told their mom riddles during the long ride home.

2. The frisky little puppy with the red collar brought the young boy on the porch the ball.

3. The radio announcer offered listeners of his early morning program a free holiday turkey.

4. Passengers on the flight from Boston to Denver handed the flight attendant at the boarding gate their tickets.

5. The football coach on the bus taught the team plays before the game.

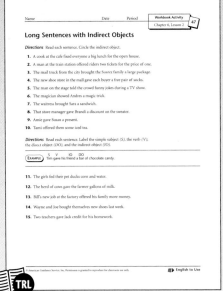

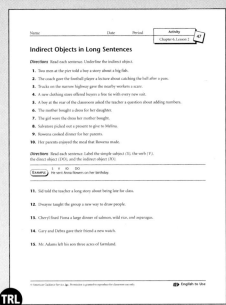

An indirect object does not follow a preposition. When a noun or pronoun follows a preposition it is the object of the preposition.

Example
The teacher read the book **to** the **class**.

Activity B Write these sentences on your paper. Label the simple subject *S*, the verb *V*, the direct object *DO*, and the indirect object *IO*. Some sentences may have compound parts.

<pre>
           S   V   IO   DO
</pre>
Example   Jack drew Emily a picture on a large piece of white paper.

1. The other students in the room asked Jack a question about his picture.

2. Jack taught the group his art style and showed Emily his picture.

3. Some of the students gave Jack a pat on the back for his efforts.

4. Jack gave shy Emily his drawing of her.

5. She sent him her thanks with a smile.

6. Gus and Rose Thompson bought themselves a farm.

7. The Thompson family's hard work on the farm brought them a good life.

8. The herd of cows gave the family good, rich milk.

9. Gus fed the chickens lots of mash and seed.

10. The hens gave the family dozens of eggs.

11. The oldest daughter fixed the younger children large breakfasts of eggs, bacon, and milk.

12. Rose taught her oldest daughter the farm chores.

13. Rose's work in the city brought the farm more money for repairs.

14. Their son built the animals a new barn with large stalls for the horses.

15. Farm life offered Gus, Rose, and their children joy and profit.

More Sentence Patterns Chapter 6 **117**

ONLINE CONNECTION

The Pennsylvania College of Technology offers a grammar site that features essays on teaching grammar, a selection of instructional materials, and a grammar game. Visit the KISS Grammar Site at *curie.pct.edu/ courses/evavra/ KISS.htm.*

Activity A Answers

1. mom 2. boy 3. listeners 4. attendant 5. team

Activity B Answers

1. S—students; V—asked; IO—Jack; DO—question 2. S—Jack; V—taught; IO—group; DO—style; V—showed; IO—Emily; DO—picture 3. S—Some; V—gave; IO—Jack; DO—pat 4. S—Jack; V—gave; IO—Emily; DO—drawing 5. S—She; V—sent; IO—him; DO—thanks 6. S—Gus, Rose Thompson; V—bought; IO—themselves; DO—farm 7. S—work; V—brought; IO—them; DO—life 8. S—herd; V—gave; IO—family; DO—milk 9. S—Gus; V—fed; IO—chickens; DO—lots 10. S—hens; V—gave; IO—family; DO—dozens 11. S—daughter; V—fixed; IO—children; DO—breakfasts 12. S—Rose; V—taught; IO—daughter; DO—chores 13. S—work; V—brought; IO—farm; DO—money 14. S—son; V—built; IO—animals; DO—barn 15. S—life; V—offered; IO—Gus, Rose, children; DO—joy, profit

 3 **Reinforce and Extend**

LEARNING STYLES

Auditory/Verbal
Ask students to add adjectives and prepositional phrases to sentences from Activities A and B in Lesson 1. Have students read aloud the original sentences as well as the new sentences containing adjectives and prepositional phrases. Discuss how the additions make sentences more interesting.

More Sentence Patterns Chapter 6 **117**

Chapter 6 Lesson 3

Overview This lesson introduces object complements. It explains the function of adjective object complements and noun object complements in sentences.

Objective

■ To identify and write object complements in sentences

Student Pages 118–119

Teacher's Resource Library **TRL**

Workbook Activity 48

Activity 48

Alternative Activity 48

Sentence Diagramming Activity 34

Vocabulary

adjective object complement
noun object complement
object complement

 1 Warm-Up Activity

Write these sentences on the board: *The music makes the room <u>noisy</u>. They called the firefighter a <u>hero</u>.* Ask volunteers to identify the subject, verb, and direct object in the first sentence. Then ask students to identify the part of speech for *noisy*. Direct discussion to help students see how the adjective *noisy* adds information about the direct object *room*. Repeat the procedure with the second sentence. Tell students that, in this sentence pattern, the adjective *noisy* and the noun *hero* are called object complements.

2 Teaching the Lesson

Review the definitions and sample sentences with students. Discuss the way that this sentence pattern builds on the noun + verb + direct object pattern. Have volunteers suggest noun + verb + direct object sentences and then work with the class to add object complements.

> **Object complement**
> A word or words that follow the direct object and describe or rename it
>
> **Adjective object complement**
> An adjective that describes the direct object
>
> **Noun object complement**
> A noun that renames the direct object

Sentences with direct objects may also have **object complements.** An object complement is an adjective, a noun, or a pronoun that describes or renames the direct object. An object complement follows the direct object. Like other sentence parts, an object complement may be compound.

An **adjective object complement** follows the direct object and describes it.

> **EXAMPLE**
>
> The girl painted the flower red.
> **Sentence parts**   *subj.*   *v.*   *d. obj.*   *adj. compl.*
> (The adjective *red* describes the direct object *flower*.)
>
> The hikers found the children uninjured and safe.
> **Sentence parts**   *subj.*   *v.*   *d. obj.*   *adj. compl.*
> (The adjectives *uninjured* and *safe* describe the direct object *children*.)

A **noun object complement** is a noun or pronoun that follows the direct object and renames it.

> **EXAMPLE**
>
> My cousin named the fish Goldie.
> **Sentence parts**   *subj.*   *v.*   *d. obj.*   *noun compl.*
> (The proper noun *Goldie* renames the direct object *fish*.)
>
> They consider that player a talented one.
> **Sentence parts** *subj.*   *v.*   *d. obj.*   *noun compl.*
> (The pronoun *one* renames the direct object *player*.)

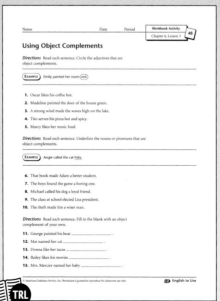

Workbook Activity 48

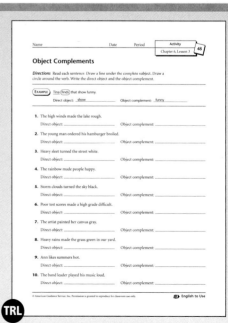

Activity 48

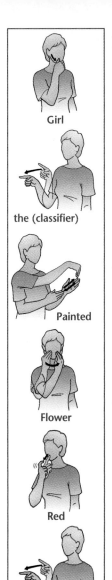

Girl

the (classifier)

Painted

Flower

Red

the (classifier)

Activity A Write the adjectives that are object complements in these sentences on your paper.

1. Jane likes her soup hot.
2. Most people prefer crackers crisp.
3. Cinnamon makes cereal tasty.
4. Andreas likes his soup hot and his sandwiches cold.
5. He wants his salads fresh and his apples crunchy.
6. Stella painted her car blue and gold.
7. Max liked his car red and white.
8. Mitsu built her bike low and sleek.
9. Janet wanted her car beautiful and fast.
10. She got a car that was rusty and slow.

Activity B Write the nouns or pronouns that are object complements in these sentences on your paper.

1. The young man called his old uncle a true friend.
2. The voters in his state elected José senator.
3. Jane called her friends good sports.
4. That movie made the actor a famous person.
5. Many people find that movie an exciting one.

Activity C Fill in the blank with an object complement. Write each completed sentence on your paper.

1. Spice makes food _____ .
2. Phil likes his bread _____ .
3. The man called his friend _____ .
4. Rita named her puppy _____ .
5. Sun turned her skin _____ .

The girl painted the flower red.

Activity A Answers

1. hot **2.** crisp **3.** tasty **4.** hot, cold
5. fresh, crunchy **6.** blue, gold
7. red, white **8.** low, sleek
9. beautiful, fast **10.** rusty, slow

Activity B Answers

1. friend **2.** senator **3.** sports
4. person **5.** one

Activity C Answers

Answers will vary. Make sure that students use object complements.

TEACHER ALERT

Sentences with object complements are relatively rare. Suggest that students watch carefully for this construction.

3 Reinforce and Extend

CAREER CONNECTION

Have students ask people to describe their jobs and how they feel about their work. Ask students to list some of the adjectives and nouns they hear. They can then choose one or two adjectives or nouns to complete a sentence such as this: *(Name) finds (his or her) job (object complement)*. Provide an example by having a student ask you how you feel about teaching. Then ask the student to choose one of the words you used to write the sentence on the board, for example, *Mr. Hernandez finds his job interesting*. Post students' sentences on the bulletin board.

Writing Practice

Ask students to use the sentences in Activity C as models for new sentences with object complements. Then have students choose one sentence from Activity A, B, or C to use as the first sentence of a paragraph. Encourage students to review and apply the four steps of the writing process described in Chapter 5, Lesson 8 as they write their paragraphs.

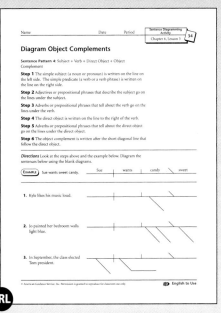

TRL

Sentence Diagramming Activity 34

ASL ILLUSTRATION

Discuss with students how American Sign Language uses the symbol "classifier" to help clarify meaning. Tell students that English language may provide this information by the positioning of words in a sentence. Have each student practice signing the sentence with a partner.

Lesson at a Glance

Chapter 6 Lesson 4

Overview This lesson explains how to identify object complements in sentences with compound parts and prepositional phrases.

Objectives

- To identify object complements in sentences and determine their parts of speech
- To identify the subject, verb, direct object, and object complement in sentences
- To identify direct objects, indirect objects, objects of prepositions, and object complements in sentences

Student Pages 120–121

Teacher's Resource Library

Workbook Activity 49

Activity 49

Alternative Activity 49

1 Warm-Up Activity

Write the example sentence on the board, and have volunteers draw lines through the adjectives and prepositional phrases. Then have students help you identify the basic sentence parts, including subject, verb, direct object, and object complement.

2 Teaching the Lesson

Discuss with students how this lesson asks them to combine two different skills: 1. to identify object complements and 2. to find sentence patterns in long sentences. Review with students the definition of an object complement, and discuss strategies for identifying adjectives and prepositional phrases in sentences.

Sentences with object complements may have compound parts and prepositional phrases. By identifying the basic parts of the sentence, you can identify the object complement.

> **EXAMPLE** On their vacation, the boy and his parents named the rented house in the woods beside the lake Home Base.
>
> | Compound subject | boy, parents |
> |---|---|
> | Verb | named |
> | Direct object | house |
> | Object complement | Home Base |

Although the example sentence has compound parts, adjectives, and adjective phrases, it still follows the basic sentence pattern of *subject + verb + direct object + object complement.* Remove the adjectives and prepositional phrases, and you can easily recognize the sentence pattern.

> **EXAMPLE** The boy and his parents named the house Home Base.
>
>   subject   verb   d. obj.   noun complement

Activity A On your paper, write the object complement in each sentence. Write whether the complement is an *adjective*, a *noun*, or a *pronoun*.

1. In the moonlight over the water, a pilot finds the night a lonely one.
2. At sunset on the pier, a crowd calls the band terrific.
3. By the gate in the park, the girls found a picnic table empty.
4. Down the rutted road through the woods, the driver in the old truck found the road a bumpy mess.
5. Lots of training made the dog a good hunter.

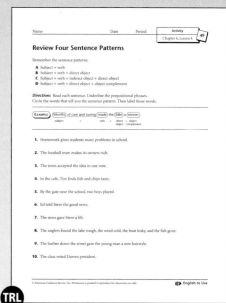

Workbook Activity 49

Activity 49

Activity B On your paper, make a chart like the one shown. In the chart write the words that form the basic sentence pattern in these sentences.

Example Hours of practice in the pool made the swimmer fast and strong.

subject + verb + direct object + object complement			
Hours	made	swimmer	fast, strong

1. The new houses and the park made that street a pretty part of town.

2. The quick mechanic kept his tools handy.

3. Some flowering plants need their soil moist.

4. Herds of cattle and horses made the rancher a rich woman.

5. The people in Westown elected Sam Saltz mayor for two years.

Activity C On your paper, write whether the word in bold is a *direct object,* an *indirect object,* an *object of a preposition,* or an *object complement.*

1. Miguel told **him** the final score of the swim meet.

2. Steven quickly passed the news to the **class.**

3. The wonderful news gave the whole class a **thrill.**

4. The boys on the swim team told their **friends** the news.

5. The news made everyone at school and around town **happy.**

The swimmers race to be the fastest.

Activity A Answers

1. one—pronoun 2. terrific—adjective 3. empty—adjective 4. mess—noun 5. hunter—noun

Activity B Answers

1. S—houses, park; V—made; DO—street; OC—part
2. S—mechanic; V—kept; DO—tools; OC—handy
3. S—plants; V—need; DO—soil; OC—moist 4. S—Herds; V—made; DO—rancher; OC—woman
5. S—people; V—elected; DO—Sam Saltz; OC—mayor

Activity C Answers

1. indirect object 2. object of a preposition 3. direct object 4. indirect object 5. object complement

 3 Reinforce and Extend

LEARNING STYLES

 Logical/Mathematical

Creating a chart can help students recognize patterns and organize information. Ask students to create a chart for Activity C with the following headings: *Subject, Verb, Direct Object, Object Complement,* and *Prepositional Phrase.* Have students log information from Activity C in their charts. Instruct students to complete the final column first, shortening the sentence and making it easier to work with.

LEARNING STYLES

LEP/ESL

Identifying the patterns in long sentences may be difficult for English language learners. Make sure that these students understand the steps required for completing this lesson: 1. They must shorten the sentences to manageable length by identifying (and marking through) prepositional phrases. 2. They must find the subject + verb + direct object pattern in order to locate the object complement. Help check students' understanding of vocabulary by defining any unfamiliar words.

Lesson at a Glance

Chapter 6 Lesson 5

Overview This lesson introduces appositives and explains their function in sentences.

Objectives
- To identify appositives in sentences and the nouns they rename
- To identify whether the appositive explains or renames the subject or direct object of a sentence
- To write appositives for existing sentences

Student Pages 122–123

Teacher's Resource Library **TRL**

Workbook Activity 50

Activity 50

Alternative Activity 50

Sentence Diagramming Activity 35

....

Vocabulary
appositive

....

 1 Warm-Up Activity

Hold up an object such as a pen, and ask students to name it (*pen*). Then ask students to think of other names for a pen, such as *writing tool*. Next, place the pen on the desk, and write on the board: *The pen, a writing tool, sits on the desk.* Point out that the words *writing tool* rename the noun *pen*. Tell students that a word or group of words that renames an object is called an *appositive*. Call on volunteers to repeat the exercise with other familiar objects.

 2 Teaching the Lesson

Review the examples of appositives with students, discussing the instances when the appositives are and are not set off by commas. Discuss with students how appositives can vary in length from one word to many words that may include prepositional phrases.

122 *Chapter 6   More Sentence Patterns*

> **Appositive**
> *A word or group of words that follows a noun and explains the noun or gives another name to the noun*

An **appositive** explains a noun or gives another name to a noun. An appositive may be a single word or a group of words. When an appositive is a group of words, commas usually set it off from the rest of the sentence.

> **EXAMPLE**
> My uncle Antonio works at a bank.
> (*Antonio* is an appositive that gives another name to the noun *uncle*.)
>
> Ms. Levo, the school principal, walked down the hall.
> (*The school principal* is an appositive that explains who Ms. Levo is. Commas set off the appositive from the rest of the sentence.)

An appositive follows a noun in a sentence. The noun may be the subject, the direct object, the indirect object, or the object of a preposition.

> **EXAMPLE**
> His sister Kara moved to Toronto.
> (The appositive *Kara* renames the subject *sister*.)
>
> Emiko got a present, a bicycle.
> (The appositive *a bicycle* explains the direct object *present*.)
>
> Maria sent my cousin Maya a new coat.
> (The appositive *Maya* renames the indirect object *cousin*.)
>
> The boys climbed into the back seat of the car, a convertible.
> (The appositive *a convertible* explains *car*, the object of the preposition *of*.)

An appositive may have a prepositional phrase.

> **EXAMPLE**
> The dress, a fancy one with lace, tore.
> (*A fancy one with lace* is the appositive. *With lace* is a prepositional phrase that is part of the appositive.)

122   *Chapter 6   More Sentence Patterns*

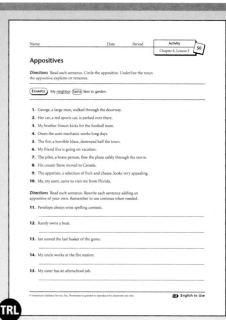

Writing Tip

Keep your writing tight. Use appositives to combine ideas in one sentence.

Example
The dress tore. It was a fancy one with lace.

The dress, a fancy one with lace, tore.

Activity A On your paper, write each sentence. Circle the appositive. Underline the noun the appositive explains or renames. Some sentences may have more than one appositive.

1. The grassy yard, part of a large ranch, glistened in the early morning dew.
2. A barn, the largest building, sits behind the house.
3. Frank, a rancher, gives Joe, the ranch foreman, instructions.
4. A green tractor, one of five, sits near the barn.
5. George, a ranch worker, began to plow the field, a large area.

Activity B On your paper, write the appositive in each sentence. Then write whether it names the *subject*, the *direct object*, or the *object of preposition*.

1. The pirates, a group of thieves, counted their treasure.
2. Big Bart, the leader, buried the huge chest.
3. Bart sailed his boat, a fast ship, into the night.
4. Jenny dug up the chest, a rich prize.
5. Jenny yelled to Amy, her friend, to come and help her.

Activity C Add an appositive to each sentence to rename or explain the noun in bold. Write the sentences on your paper. Use commas where needed to set off appositives.

Example   Anna received an invitation to a **party.**
            Anna received an invitation to a party, a surprise birthday celebration for Melissa.

1. **Anna** went to a wonderful party in the city.
2. She met a tall **boy.**
3. They listened to the music of a great **band.**
4. The **music** was lively and fun.
5. Two dancers taught a new line **dance.**

More Sentence Patterns   Chapter 6   **123**

Activity A Answers

1. The grassy <u>yard</u>, (part of a large ranch,) glistened in the early morning dew.

2. A <u>barn</u>, (the largest building,) sits behind the house.

3. <u>Frank</u>, (a rancher,) gives <u>Joe</u>, (the ranch foreman,) instructions.

4. A green <u>tractor</u>, (one of five,) sits near the barn.

5. <u>George</u>, (a ranch worker,) began to plow the <u>field</u>, (a large area.)

Activity B Answers

1. a group of thieves—S 2. the leader—S 3. a fast ship—DO 4. a rich prize—DO 5. her friend—Obj. of Prep.

Activity C Answers

Answers will vary. Make sure that students add appositives to the sentences.

Speaking Practice

Have students take turns reading aloud the sentences in Activities A and B. Have students observe how the commas that set off appositives create natural pauses when students read the sentences. Have students close their eyes as a volunteer reads aloud a sentence, and ask them to identify the appositive by listening for the pauses in the sentence.

3 Reinforce and Extend

IN THE COMMUNITY

Help students list nouns that can refer to a building, such as *structure, skyscraper,* or *apartment.* Invite students to look carefully at some of the buildings in their community. Ask students to write sentences with appositives that will describe the buildings. Remind them that an appositive is a word or group of words that renames or explains a noun. Encourage students to share their sentences in class.

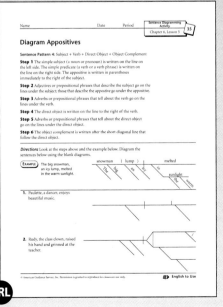

TRL

Sentence Diagramming Activity 35

More Sentence Patterns   Chapter 6   **123**

Chapter 6 Lesson 6

Overview This lesson provides lists of words to inspire students to create sentences and a short story.

Objectives

- To write interesting, well-constructed sentences from categorized lists of words
- To apply the four-step writing process to write a short story based on a list of nouns and appositives

Student Pages 124–125

Teacher's Resource Library

Workbook Activity 51

Activity 51

Alternative Activity 51

1 Warm-Up Activity

To illustrate the wide variety of sentences that writers can create from the same set of words, write the following on the board: *man, friend, paper,* and *secret.*

Ask volunteers to write sentences on their papers using at least two of the words. Then invite students to read aloud their sentences. Discuss the different ideas that students developed from the four original words.

2 Teaching the Lesson

Discuss with students the way the lesson asks them first to write sentences; then to build on their sentences by adding adjectives, adverbs, and prepositional phrases; and finally to combine ideas into a short story. Tell students that the process will seem easier if they organize it into steps. Review the four steps in the writing process introduced in Chapter 5: prewrite, write, rewrite, and edit.

Lesson **6** **Writing Practice**

Writing is hard but fun. You never know where your thoughts might lead you. You can start with a list of words and end with a story. Another student can begin with the same list of words but write a very different story.

Activity A Using the following list of subjects and direct objects, write ten clear sentences on your paper using action verbs. You may use any subject with any direct object.

Subjects	
horse	hero
cat	pitcher
writer	friend
grandmother	sister
teacher	monster

Direct Objects	
money	grass
dinner	television
book	paper
tree	job
game	ball

The pitcher tosses the ball to the batter.

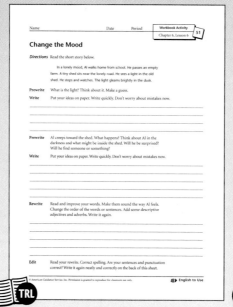

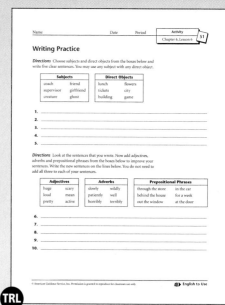

Activity B Using the sentences you wrote in Activity A, add adjectives, adverbs, and prepositional phrases to improve your sentences. Choose from this box, or write your own.

Adjectives	
huge	kind
bleak	friendly
fast	ugly
old	young
brave	beautiful

Adverbs	
slowly	quietly
quickly	wildly
often	poorly
well	gladly
loudly	gently

Prepositional Phrases	
over the hill	on the chair
to the batter	at the desk
under the table	behind a tree
for a month	in the house
from the fire	around the bend

Activity C Write a story using the list of nouns and appositives below. Before you begin, think about what you want to write. Be sure to use the four-step writing process.

Nouns	Appositives
Buddy	cat
kitten	a lively animal
Grace	a lonely child

Activity A Answers

Answers will vary. Students should write clear, well-constructed sentences that begin with a capital letter and end with the appropriate punctuation mark.

Activity B Answers

Answers will vary.

Activity C Answers

Answers will vary.

3 Reinforce and Extend

LEARNING STYLES

Visual/Spatial

Ask students to look at the photograph on page 124 and to think about the action in the photo as the pitcher throws, the batter waits, and the umpire watches. With the class, talk about the different stories that the picture might tell, such as the pitcher's breaking a record or the batter's winning the game. You might want to draw a baseball diamond on the board and have students draw out the events in their stories as they explain.

LEARNING STYLES

Interpersonal/Group

When students have finished their short stories for Activity C, ask them to work in pairs to make one final set of additions and revisions. This time, have student pairs add or rewrite sentences, using the parts of a sentence students learned in this chapter—indirect objects, object complements, and appositives. Emphasize that students may choose to leave their story structures intact and simply revise their sentences or to add new sentences and expand their stories.

Lesson at a Glance

Chapter 6 Lesson 7

Overview This lesson focuses on punctuation marks, reinforcing the use of commas with appositives and items in a series. It reviews previously taught punctuation.

Objectives

- To identify appositives and set off appositives with commas when needed
- To use commas, periods, exclamation marks, and capital letters to punctuate sentences correctly
- To review vocabulary introduced in the chapter

Student Pages 126–127

Teacher's Resource Library

Workbook Activity 52

Activity 52

Alternative Activity 52

1 Warm-Up Activity

Discuss the introductory examples, and review with students when to use commas with appositives. Emphasize that while commas are correct with one-word appositives, as shown in the example, one-word appositives often are not set off with commas.

2 Teaching the Lesson

Review with students the different types of end punctuation and when to use each one. Review the definitions of the parts of speech learned in this chapter: indirect object, noun object complement, adjective object complement, and appositive.

Use commas with appositives that are more than one word long. One-word appositives do not usually need commas, but you can use them.

> **Communication Connection**
>
> People use e-mail to send each other e-cards. E-cards have become a popular way to send birthday and holiday greetings. E-cards can even include music for the occasion. Have you ever received an e-card?

EXAMPLE

Ian, my cousin from Alberta, sent me an e-card.
(The long appositive *my cousin from Alberta* needs commas to set it off.)

Correct My cousin Ian sent me an e-card.

Correct My cousin, Ian, sent me an e-card.
(The one-word appositive *Ian* does not need commas to set it off, but you can use them.)

Activity A Write these sentences on your paper. Add any needed commas. Remember that long appositives need commas.

1. Tony's bike a rocket with wheels roared.
2. Two rabbits scared animals stared into the headlights.
3. They jumped into the ditch a safer place.
4. The moon a beaming light shone on the bikers' helmets.
5. Ann and her best friend Tony rode home together.

Use commas with items in a series. A series is a list of three or more words or phrases connected by a conjunction, such as *and*, *but*, or *or*. Do not put a comma after the last item in a series.

EXAMPLE

Dave, Anita, and Salma enjoyed their trip to Calgary.
(*Dave, Anita,* and *Salma* are nouns in a series.)

They rode down the highway, over a mountain, and through a city on their journey.
(*Down the highway, over a mountain,* and *through a city* are prepositional phrases in a series.)

126 *Chapter 6 More Sentence Patterns*

Using What You've Learned

Write a letter to someone you know who lives far away. Tell about what you, your family, and friends have been doing lately. Use as many appositives and series of items as you can. Be sure to put commas in the correct places.

Activity B Write these sentences correctly on your paper. Use commas, periods, exclamation points, and capital letters. You might wish to review what you have learned about writing sentences in previous lessons.

1. wow the batter the teams star hitter knocked the ball over the fence out of the park and down the street

2. down the alley a chill raw winter wind blew

3. bill and senator jacobs visited friends in new york city

4. ms adams mr smith and dr young sat near the stage at the play

5. bills mother a nice woman had us over for dinner

Activity C Match the items with their descriptions. Write the number and its correct letter on your paper.

Items
1. indirect object
2. noun object complement
3. adjective object complement
4. appositive
5. comma

Descriptions
A noun or pronoun that renames the direct object
B needed with a long appositive
C takes action from the verb indirectly
D adjective that describes the direct object
E gives a noun a new name

Activity A Answers

1. Tony's bike, a rocket with wheels, roared. 2. Two rabbits, scared animals, stared into the headlights. 3. They jumped into the ditch, a safer place. 4. The moon, a beaming light, shone on the bikers' helmets. 5. Ann and her best friend Tony rode home together.

Activity B Answers

1. Wow! The batter, the team's star hitter, knocked the ball over the fence, out of the park, and down the street. 2. Down the alley, a chill, raw, winter wind blew. 3. Bill and Senator Jacobs visited friends in New York City. 4. Ms. Adams, Mr. Smith, and Dr. Young sat near the stage at the play. 5. Bill's mother, a nice woman, had us over for dinner.

Activity C Answers

1. C 2. A 3. D 4. E 5. B

 3 Reinforce and Extend

LEARNING STYLES

 Interpersonal/Group
Have students complete an exercise about appositives by working in pairs. Student partners should take turns choosing an object or person and then giving two nouns for that object or person. The other partner will then use those words to write a sentence that contains an appositive. Help student pairs get started by writing the following examples on the board:

Homework   Paper
My homework, a paper for English class, is lying on my desk.

Friend   Student
I met my friend, another English student, after class.

Remind student pairs that appositives can explain or rename nouns in any part of a sentence.

Using What You've Learned

Remind students that their letters will combine many different skills and that they should look in the text for review if needed. If students would like to share their letters, invite them to trade with partners and proofread one another's work.

 TEACHER ALERT

Ask students to return to earlier chapters in the text and find sentences that can be improved with appositives.

Chapter 6 Review

Use the Chapter Review to prepare students for tests and to reteach content from the chapter.

Chapter 6 Mastery Test

The Teacher's Resource Library includes two parallel forms of the Chapter 6 Mastery Test. The difficulty level of the two forms is equivalent. You may wish to use one form as a pretest and the other form as a posttest.

Midterm Mastery Test

The Teacher's Resource Library includes the Midterm Mastery Test. This test is pictured on page 305 of this Teacher's Edition. The Midterm Mastery Test assesses the major learning objectives for Chapters 1–6.

REVIEW ANSWERS

Part A

1. appositive 2. object complement 3. noun object complement 4. indirect object 5. adjective object complement

Part B

6. pigs—IO; apples—Obj. of Prep.
7. anglers—S; cloudy—OC
8. threw—V; look—DO
9. mailed—V; Elisha—IO
10. window—DO; open—OC
11. Andrea—S; chickens—IO
12. job—Obj. of Prep.; employee—OC 13. Patty—DO; sad—OC

Part C

14. The (cowboy,) a thin dude, played a tune at the ranch.

15. The (sky,) a mass of black clouds, closed over the ranch.

16. The (cook,) a friendly person, greets ranch guests at the door.

17. The (guests,) nature lovers, hoped for clear weather.

Chapter 6   R E V I E W

Word Bank

adjective object complement

appositive

indirect object

noun object complement

object complement

Part A Use the words from the Word Bank to complete sentences 1–5.

1. A word or group of words that follows a noun and explains the noun or gives another name to the noun is an _____ .

2. An _____ is a word or words that follow the direct object and describe or rename it.

3. A noun that renames the direct object is a _____ .

4. A noun or pronoun that takes action from the verb indirectly is an _____ .

5. An _____ is an adjective that describes the direct object.

Part B Write the words in bold in these sentences. Next to each word write its sentence part.

Example   The club sent my **brother** a **letter**.
        brother—indirect object, letter—direct object

6. The farmer fed the **pigs** a bushel of **apples**.

7. Some **anglers** like the sky **cloudy**.

8. The pitcher **threw** the catcher a **look**.

9. Jeffrey **mailed Elisha** a package of CDs.

10. Adam likes the kitchen **window open**.

11. **Andrea** gave the **chickens** some water.

12. Years on the **job** at the factory made Dennis a skillful **employee**.

13. The TV program left **Patty sad**.

Part C Write each sentence correctly on your paper. Underline each appositive, and circle the word it describes.

14. the cowboy a thin dude played a tune at the ranch

15. the sky a mass of black clouds closed over the ranch

16. the cook a friendly person greets ranch guests at the door

17. the guests nature lovers hoped for clear weather

TRL   TRL

Chapter 6 Mastery Test A

Part D Use the sentence in parentheses to add an appositive to each sentence. Write the revised sentences on your paper.

Example   Emilio scored six goals. (Emilio is a fine athlete.)
                  Emilio, a fine athlete, scored six goals.

18. Jenny's computer solved the problem easily. (The computer is a powerful machine.)

19. Tony serves the best lobster in town. (Tony is a great cook.)

20. Jerome Cullen steered his ship. (Jerome Cullen is a captain.)

21. Concetta burned a fast ball to the catcher. (Concetta is the best pitcher in the league.)

22. Alejandro e-mailed Holly. (Holly is his best friend.)

Part E Read each sentence. Write the letter of the correct sentence pattern.

23. The students find this computer game easy.

A subject + verb
B subject + verb + direct object
C subject + verb + indirect object + direct object
D subject + verb + direct object + object complement

24. Isaiah sold his computer.

A subject + verb
B subject + verb + direct object
C subject + verb + indirect object + direct object
D subject + verb + direct object + object complement

25. That computer program gives me problems.

A subject + verb
B subject + verb + direct object
C subject + verb + indirect object + direct object
D subject + verb + direct object + object complement

 When you take a test, be sure to read each question carefully before answering.

Part D

18. Jenny's computer, a powerful machine, solved the problem easily. **19.** Tony, a great cook, serves the best lobster in town. **20.** Jerome Cullen, a captain, steered his ship. **21.** Concetta, the best pitcher in the league, burned a fast ball to the catcher. **22.** Alejandro e-mailed Holly, his best friend.

Part E

23. D **24.** B **25.** C

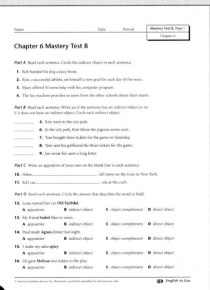

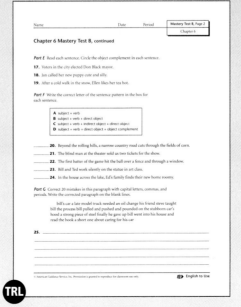

Chapter 6 Mastery Test B

Chapter 7

Planning Guide

Sentences with Linking Verbs

	Student Pages	Vocabulary	Practice Activities	Identification Skills	Writing Skills	Punctuation Skills
		Student Text Lesson		**Language Skills**		
Lesson 1 Noun Subject Complements	132–133	✔	✔	✔	✔	
Lesson 2 Nouns that Give New Names	134–135		✔	✔	✔	✔
Lesson 3 Adjective Subject Complements	136–137	✔	✔	✔	✔	✔
Lesson 4 Adjectives Always Describe Nouns	138–139		✔	✔	✔	✔
Lesson 5 Adjective or Adverb?	140–141		✔	✔	✔	
Lesson 6 Subject Complements in Long Sentences	142–143	✔	✔	✔	✔	✔
Lesson 7 Pronouns in Subject Complement Sentences	144–145		✔	✔	✔	
Lesson 8 More Pronouns	146–147		✔	✔	✔	
Lesson 9 Reviewing Sentence Patterns	148–149		✔	✔	✔	✔
Lesson 10 Writing Practice	150–151		✔	✔	✔	✔
Lesson 11 Writing Mechanics	152–153	✔	✔	✔	✔	✔

Chapter Activities

Teacher's Resource Library

Community Connection 7:
Write Job Interview Questions

English in Your World 7:
Finding Linking Verbs in Catalogs

Assessment Options

Student Text
Chapter 7 Review

Teacher's Resource Library
Chapter 7 Mastery Tests A and B

130A

Student Text Features					Teaching Strategies					Learning Styles						Teacher's Resource Library				
ASL Illustration	Communication Connection	Notes	Using What You've Learned	Writing Tips	Teacher Alert	Online Connection	Applications (Home, Career, Community, Global)	Speaking Practice	Writing Practice	Auditory/Verbal	Body/Kinesthetic	Interpersonal/Group Learning	Logical/Mathematical	Visual/Spatial	LEP/ESL	Workbook Activities	Activities	Alternative Activities	Sentence Diagramming Activities	Self-Study Guide
		✔					133			133						53	53	53	36	✔
				✔				135						135		54	54	54		✔
		✔							137				137			55	55	55	37	✔
139						139						139				56	56	56		✔
	140				141										141	57	57	57		✔
										143	143					58	58	58		✔
										145	145					59	59	59	38	✔
				✔	147					147						60	60	60		✔
						149									149	61	61	61		✔
							151					151				62	62	62		✔
153			153	✔		153								153		63	63	63		✔

Pronunciation Key

a	hat	e	let	ī	ice	ô	order	ù	put	sh	she	a	in about
ā	age	ē	equal	o	hot	oi	oil	ü	rule	th	thin	e	in taken
ä	far	ėr	term	ō	open	ou	out	ch	child	ŦH	then	ə ⟨ i	in pencil
â	care	i	it	ò	saw	u	cup	ng	long	zh	measure	o	in lemon
												u	in circus

Alternative Activities

The Teacher's Resource Library (TRL) contains a set of lower-level worksheets called Alternative Activities. These worksheets cover the same content as the regular Activities but are written at a second-grade reading level.

Skill Track Software

Use the Skill Track Software for English to Use for additional reinforcement of this chapter. The software program allows students using AGS textbooks to be assessed for mastery of each chapter and lesson of the textbook. Students access the software on an individual basis and are assessed with multiple-choice items.

Chapter 7: Sentences with Linking Verbs

pages 130–155

Lessons

1. **Noun Subject Complements**
   pages 132–133

2. **Nouns that Give New Names**
   pages 134–135

3. **Adjective Subject Complements**
   pages 136–137

4. **Adjectives Always Describe Nouns**
   pages 138–139

5. **Adjective or Adverb?**
   pages 140–141

6. **Subject Complements in Long Sentences**
   pages 142–143

7. **Pronouns in Subject Complement Sentences**
   pages 144–145

8. **More Pronouns**
   pages 146–147

9. **Reviewing Sentence Patterns**
   pages 148–149

10. **Writing Practice**
    pages 150–151

11. **Writing Mechanics**
    pages 152–153

Chapter 7 Review
pages 154–155

Skill Track Software for English to Use

Teacher's Resource Library (TRL)

Workbook Activities 53–63

Activities 53–63

Alternative Activities 53–63

Sentence Diagramming Activities 36–38
(Optional sentence activities accompany lessons.)

Community Connection 7

English in Your World 7

Chapter 7 Self-Study Guide

Chapter 7 Mastery Tests A and B

(Answer Keys for the Teacher's Resource Library begin on page 308 of this Teacher's Edition.)

Community Connection 7

English in Your World 7

7 Sentences with Linking Verbs

How might you describe this scene? First, you could say that the girl's reflection is in the window. A reflection is a mirror image. It looks almost the same as the real object, but it is slightly different. The girl's hand seems to connect her to her image. In a similar way, certain words in a sentence reflect on the subject. Predicate nouns rename the subject in different words. Like the girl's hand, linking verbs connect the subject with the predicate noun that renames, or reflects, it.

The girl's reflection shows how she looks, but it reverses her image. You can see her face in a new way. Some sentences have adjectives in the predicate that describe the subject. These predicate adjectives reflect the subject, but they show it in a new light.

In this chapter, you will study more about how words give detailed information and help you reflect, or think back, on what comes before them.

Goals for Learning

◆ To identify linking verbs and sentence patterns that use them

◆ To identify and use subject complements in sentences

◆ To distinguish between adjectives and adverbs

◆ To use pronouns in subject complement sentences

◆ To use comparative and superlative adjectives correctly

131

Introducing the Chapter

Students are now familiar with different types of sentences. They know their separate parts and their collective meanings. This chapter introduces the last two sentence patterns, each of which casts a new light on the personality of the basic sentence.

TEACHER'S RESOURCE

The AGS Teaching Strategies in English Transparencies may be used with this chapter. The transparencies add an interactive dimension to expand and enhance the *English to Use* program content.

CAREER INTEREST INVENTORY

The AGS Harrington-O'Shea Career Decision-Making System–Revised (CDM) may be used with this chapter. Students can use the CDM to explore their interests and identify careers. The CDM defines career areas that are indicated by students' responses on the inventory.

Writing Tips and Notes

Ask volunteers to read the tips and notes that appear in the margins throughout the chapter. Then discuss them with the class.

CHAPTER PROJECT

Divide the class into small writing groups. Have the groups decide on a theme or topic. Then ask each group to write a new sentence that relates to the theme or topic for each of the six sentence patterns. When the groups have finished, have them share the sentences with the rest of the class. The class should critique one another's sentences and identify the sentence patterns. Have groups combine their sentences into a short story, changing words when necessary to fit the story.

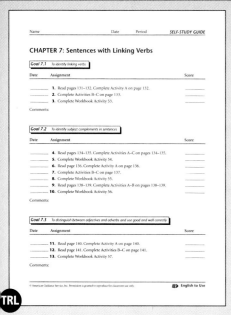

Chapter 7 Lesson 1

Overview This lesson introduces linking verbs, subject complements, and the sentence pattern subject + linking verb + noun subject complement. It also explains how to use *good* and *well* correctly.

Objectives

- To identify and write subject complements in sentences
- To identify linking verbs
- To use *good* and *well* correctly
- To identify sentence patterns

Student Pages 132–133

Teacher's Resource Library

Workbook Activity 53

Activity 53

Alternative Activity 53

Sentence Diagramming Activity 36

Vocabulary

linking verb
noun subject complement
subject complement

 Warm-Up Activity

Write these sentences on the board: *Mr. Gray is a teacher. Julio and Amelia are students.* Ask students to point out the nouns in each sentence. Discuss how the nouns in the second part of the sentence (predicate) rename the subject noun. Explain that *is* and *are* connect nouns in the subject and predicate.

 Teaching the Lesson

Remind students that they can think of linking verbs that appear with noun subject complements as equal signs (=) because the words on one side of the verb rename, or equal, the words on the other.

A **subject complement** describes the subject of a sentence. A **noun subject complement** is a noun or pronoun in the predicate that gives a new name to the subject, along with any words that describe the noun or pronoun. Remember that a sentence has two parts: the subject and the predicate. A noun (or pronoun) in the predicate may rename the subject. A **linking verb** links the predicate with the subject.

Subject complement
One or more words in the predicate that describe the subject

Noun subject complement
A noun or pronoun in the predicate that renames the subject, as well as any words that describe the noun or pronoun

Linking verb
A verb that connects the subject to a word in the predicate

 EXAMPLE   This soup is a favorite snack.

Sentence parts	subject | predicate
Sentence pattern	subject + linking verb + noun subject complement

(The linking verb *is* in this sentence links the subject *soup* with a noun in the predicate *snack*. A favorite snack is the noun subject complement.)

A noun subject complement has another name: predicate nominative. The word *nominative* refers to the subject of a sentence.

Activity A On your paper, write the subject in each sentence. Then write the noun in the predicate that is linked to the subject by the linking verb. The linking verb is in bold.

Example   That police officer **is** my neighbor.
             officer—neighbor

1. Tennis **is** your favorite game.
2. Football **is** my best sport.
3. Haley **is** a speedy worker.
4. Jacob and Isaac **are** fast runners.
5. Sophia and David **were** neighbors.

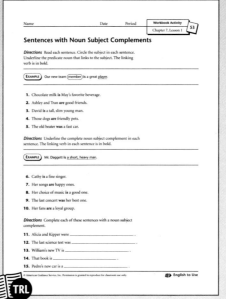

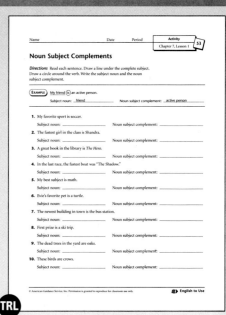

Workbook Activity 53   **Activity 53**

Activity B On your paper, write the noun subject complement in each sentence. The linking verb in each sentence is in bold.

Example Samuel **is** a busy director.
a busy director

1. Many of his movies **are** exciting adventures.
2. He **is** a popular movie director.
3. Most of his movies **are** box office hits.
4. My friends and I **are** loyal fans.
5. Emilio **is** the band's leader.
6. This band **is** a good one.
7. Melita, Jenny, and Christa **are** marchers.
8. The school band **is** a talented group.
9. The plot of this book **is** an exciting one.
10. The book's hero **was** a doctor.
11. Her friends **were** scientists.
12. Their enemy **was** fever.
13. Their job **was** a hard one.
14. A new medicine **was** their discovery.
15. Their victory **was** a breakthrough.

Activity C Complete each of these sentences with a noun subject complement. Write the sentences on your paper.

1. Their trip to Africa was _____ .
2. My aunt and uncle are _____ .
3. That story is _____ .
4. Good friends are _____ .
5. Lincoln and Grant were _____ .

1. Tennis—game 2. Football—sport 3. Haley—worker 4. Jacob, Isaac—runners 5. Sophia, David—neighbors

Activity B Answers

1. exciting adventures 2. a popular movie director 3. box office hits 4. loyal fans 5. the band's leader 6. a good one 7. marchers 8. a talented group 9. an exciting one 10. a doctor 11. scientists 12. fever 13. a hard one 14. their discovery 15. a breakthrough

Activity C Answers

Sentences will vary. Check to see that students have completed sentences with an appropriate noun.

3 **Reinforce and Extend**

LEARNING STYLES

Auditory/Verbal
Encourage students to use one of the sentences in Activity C to start a short paragraph. Tell students to use at least three more sentences with noun subject complements in their paragraphs. Have students read their paragraphs aloud, and ask the audience to listen for the noun subject complements, noting each time that they hear one in the story.

GLOBAL CONNECTION

Write the following Spanish sentence above its English translation on the board: *Mi casa es su casa. / My house is your house.* Point out the linking verbs (*es, is*) in both languages, or invite a Spanish-speaking student to do so. Point out that *casa* means "house," *mi* means "my," and *su* means "your." Explain that people use this expression to welcome others to their homes. Invite students to suggest similar expressions in English.

Diagram Noun Subject Complements

Sentence Pattern 5: Subject + Linking Verb + Noun Subject Complement

Step 1 The simple subject (a noun or pronoun) is written on the line on the left side. The simple predicate (a verb or a verb phrase) is written on the line on the right side.

Step 2 Adjectives or prepositional phrases that describe the subject go on the lines under the subject.

Step 3 Adverbs or prepositional phrases that tell about the verb go on the lines under the verb.

Step 4 The noun subject complement is written after the short diagonal line that follows the linking verb.

Step 5 Adjectives or prepositional phrases that tell about the noun subject complement go on the lines under the noun subject complement.

Directions Look at the steps above and the example below. Diagram the sentences below using the blank diagrams.

Example Tom is a good friend.

1. Jane's friend is a helpful person.

2. A ski trip was the first prize at the shopping mall.

Lesson at a Glance

Chapter 7 Lesson 2

Overview This lesson reviews object complements, appositives, and subject complements.

Objectives

■ To identify nouns used as object complements, appositives, and subject complements in sentences

■ To write sentences with nouns used as object complements, appositives, and subject complements

Student Pages 134–135

Teacher's Resource Library

Workbook Activity 54

Activity 54

Alternative Activity 54

 1 Warm-Up Activity

Write the following sentence on the board as a model: *Our veterinarian, a compassionate woman, is a skillful surgeon.* Ask students to name the relationship between the three nouns in the sentence: *veterinarian, woman, surgeon.* Discuss with students how the sentence uses two different structures to rename the subject: a noun subject complement and an appositive.

 2 Teaching the Lesson

Discuss the text and the examples, and review the difference between a noun object complement and a noun subject complement. Invite students to provide additional examples of sentences with noun object complements, appositives, and noun subject complements. After discussing the example sentences, challenge students to provide sentences that contain both appositives and noun subject complements.

There are three ways that a noun or a pronoun can give a new name to another noun in the sentence. Notice the different ways to rename the noun *salad* in each of the following examples.

> **EXAMPLE**
>
> | Noun object complement | I made the salad a big one. |
> | Appositive | The salad, a tropical fruit mix, chilled in the refrigerator. |
> | Noun subject complement | The fruit salad was a nice treat. |

Sometimes you can rename a noun in the subject in more than one place in a sentence.

> **EXAMPLE**
>
> The manager, a clever woman, is an amazing worker.
>   subject   appositive   noun subject complement
> (The subject noun *manager* is renamed twice: first, by the noun *woman* in the appositive *a clever woman;* and second, by the noun *worker* in the noun subject complement *an amazing worker.*)

Activity A On your paper, write each noun in bold. Next to each noun, write the noun object complement, appositive, or noun subject complement that renames it.

Example My **boss**, an organized man, straightened out his office.
boss—an organized man

1. **Takeo** and **Helen,** our new neighbors, are a busy couple.

2. The **coach,** a happy guy, is also our teacher and friend.

3. The country **woman,** a shy person, found the city a noisy place.

4. The **library,** a room full of books, was a quiet place.

5. Those two young **men,** clerks at the store, are helpful people.

---

134 *Chapter 7 Sentences with Linking Verbs*

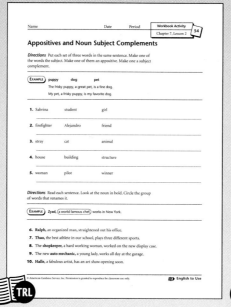

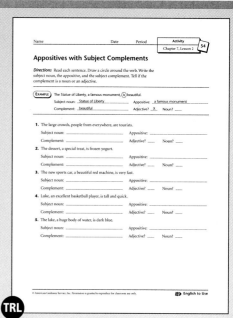

Writing Tip

In your own writing, provide added details about the subject by using both a noun subject complement and an appositive in one sentence.

You can write sentences with appositives and subject complements. Follow these steps:

1. Identify the parts of the sentence.
   Subject: girl
   Appositive: student
   Subject complement: writer

2. Write the sentence. Use the linking verb *is* or *was*.
   The girl, a student, is a writer.

3. Add adjectives to describe the nouns.
   The quiet girl, a bright student, is a good writer.

Activity B Use each group of words below to write a sentence with an appositive and a subject complement. Follow the steps described above.

1. cat, pet, friend
2. woman, singer, dancer
3. building, house, home
4. dog, puppy, animal
5. skater, athlete, winner
6. man, worker, carpenter
7. woman, neighbor, pilot
8. parrot, bird, pet
9. book, favorite, thriller
10. actor, star, performer

Activity C Write the groups of words in bold on your paper. Then write whether the group of words in bold is a *noun object complement*, an *appositive*, or a *noun subject complement*.

Example The baseball game was **an important one.**
an important one—noun subject complement

1. Michael, **the coach,** was very nervous.
2. The coach knew the game was **a big event.**
3. His players were **hard workers.**
4. His team, **the home team,** won the game.
5. The players were **the city champions.**

Sentences with Linking Verbs   *Chapter 7*   **135**

Activity A Answers

1. Takeo, Helen—our new neighbors, a busy couple **2.** coach— a happy guy, our teacher, friend **3.** woman—a shy person; city—a noisy place **4.** library—a room full of books, a quiet place **5.** men— clerks at the store, helpful people

Speaking Practice

Have volunteers take turns reading aloud the sentences in Activity A. Point out to students that the commas on each side of the appositive create short pauses in the sentences. Have students repeat the Activity A sentences until they recognize the rhythm of an appositive.

Activity B Answers

Students' sentences will vary. Check to see that each sentence has an appositive and a subject complement.

Activity C Answers

1. the coach—appositive **2.** a big event—noun object complement **3.** hard workers—noun subject complement **4.** the home team— appositive **5.** the city champions— noun subject complement

 3 Reinforce and Extend

LEARNING STYLES

 Visual/Spatial
Have students look through magazines to find three different images of a similar item. Ask each student to write on the board a sentence that renames the item three times, using an appositive, a noun object complement, and a noun subject complement. Then have students cut out the images they found and use them as nouns in the sentences, taping them into their places in the sentences. Students may want to modify the images they found— drawing on them or adding other images—to make them fit the meaning of the sentence more accurately.

Sentences/Linking Verbs   *Chapter 7*   **135**

Lesson at a Glance

Chapter 7 Lesson 3

Overview This lesson introduces adjective subject complements; it also presents a list of linking verbs.

Objectives

- To identify and write adjective subject complements in sentences
- To identify linking verbs

Student Pages 136–137

Teacher's Resource Library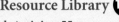

Workbook Activity 55

Activity 55

Alternative Activity 55

Sentence Diagramming Activity 37

....

Vocabulary

adjective subject complement

....

 1 Warm-Up Activity

Write on the board the following sentence: *This bread is an expensive brand.* Beneath it, write the example sentence from this lesson. Ask students to identify the difference between the two. Help students recognize that the noun *brand* is missing from the subject complement in the second sentence. Point out that the adjective *expensive* is called an adjective subject complement. It follows the linking verb is and tells what kind of bread.

2 Teaching the Lesson

Ask students to write sentences that contain adjectives and to underline the adjectives. Tell students that this lesson combines what they know about adjectives with what they know about linking verbs to create a new sentence pattern: Noun + linking verb + adjective subject complement. Have students use the adjectives they underlined in their sentences to build a sentence in the noun + linking verb + adjective subject complement sentence pattern.

Adjective subject complement
One or more adjectives in the predicate that describe the subject

An adjective in the predicate of a sentence may describe the subject noun. The adjective is an **adjective subject complement.**

 EXAMPLE

Parts of speech	This bread is expensive.
	adj. noun verb adj.
Sentence pattern	subject + linking verb + adjective subject complement

(The linking verb *is* links the subject noun *bread* to the adjective in the predicate *expensive*. *Expensive* is the adjective subject complement.)

Some linking verbs are also action verbs. To check a verb's use in a sentence, replace it with a form of *be* or *seem*. If the sentence still makes sense, the verb is a linking verb.

An adjective subject complement always follows a linking verb. Remember that a linking verb connects the predicate with the subject.

Here is a list of linking verbs:

am	been	is	sound
appear	being	look	taste
are	feel	seem	was
be	grow	smell	were

Activity A On your paper, write the adjective subject complement in each sentence.

1. These two good friends are close.
2. Their clothes are old and worn.
3. Their pockets and stomachs are empty.
4. Their travels were exciting.
5. Their smiles are warm and friendly.

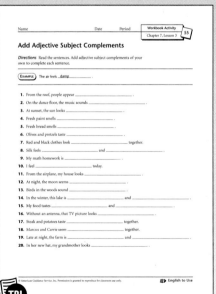

Workbook Activity 55

Activity 55

Activity B Write these sentences on your paper. Underline the linking verb in each sentence. Draw an arrow from the adjective subject complement to the subject in bold.

Example The **soup** at that restaurant <u>tastes</u> delicious.

1. Their fresh **vegetables** are terrific.
2. The **salads** look great.
3. The **bread** smells wonderful.
4. Each **customer** seems happy.
5. The **wait** seems long.

Activity C Complete each sentence with an adjective subject complement. Write the sentences on your paper.

1. The country seems _____ .
2. The farms appear _____ .
3. The breeze feels _____ .
4. The mountains look _____ .
5. The country food tastes _____ .
6. The city is _____ .
7. The crowded streets are _____ .
8. City people are _____ .
9. City lights are _____ .
10. City life is _____ .

In the city, people rush to and from work.

Activity A Answers

1. close 2. old and worn 3. empty
4. exciting 5. warm and friendly

Activity B Answers

1. Their fresh **vegetables** <u>are</u> terrific.
2. The **salads** <u>look</u> great. 3. The **bread** <u>smells</u> wonderful. 4. Each **customer** <u>seems</u> happy. 5. The **wait** <u>seems</u> long.

Activity C Answers

Answers will vary. Check that students have completed each sentence with an appropriate adjective subject complement.

Writing Practice

Have students use the sentences they created in Activity C to write a short paragraph that tells about life in the country or in the city. Tell students to use as many of their sentences as they can, changing them as needed to tell a story or to make a comparison.

3 Reinforce and Extend

LEARNING STYLES

Logical/Mathematical
Ask students to make lists of three kinds of words: nouns, linking verbs, and adjectives. Have students write the lists in three columns. Then ask them to pick a word from each, changing the linking verbs when necessary to agree with plural or singular subjects. Tell students to be as creative as they like with their sentences, but to make sentences correct. The point is to help students see the noun + linking verb + adjective structure.

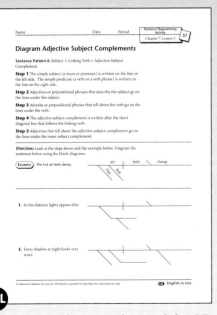

TRL

Sentence Diagramming Activity 37

Lesson at a Glance

Chapter 7 Lesson 4

Overview This lesson reviews different placements of adjectives in sentences.

Objectives

- To identify adjectives that modify specific nouns in sentences
- To write sentences with adjective object complements and sentences with adjective subject complements

Student Pages 138–139

Teacher's Resource Library

Workbook Activity 56

Activity 56

Alternative Activity 56

 1 Warm-Up Activity

Discuss the text and the examples. Invite students to provide additional examples of sentences with adjectives that come before nouns, with adjective object complements, and with adjective subject complements. After discussing the sentences in the examples, challenge students to provide sentences that contain adjectives before and after the nouns they describe.

 2 Teaching the Lesson

Emphasize that the descriptive words students discuss in this chapter describe nouns—people, places, and things. Tell students that other descriptive words (adverbs) describe actions but that adjectives describe only nouns. Remind students that more than one adjective can describe a noun. Clear up any confusion that students may have about adjective object complements and adjective subject complements.

Activity A Answers

1. large, fun **2.** big, exciting
3. bright, pretty **4.** good, great
5. chicken, spicy

An adjective always describes a noun in a sentence. Most adjectives come right before the nouns they describe. An adjective may, however, follow the noun it describes or be separated from the noun by a linking verb.

Notice the placement of the adjectives that describe the noun *bear* in these sentences.

> **EXAMPLE**
>
> | Adjectives before a noun | The hungry, brown **bear** growled. |
> | Adjective object complement | Someone called the **bear** large. |
> | Adjective subject complement | To me, the **bear** seemed huge. |

More than one adjective may describe a noun. These adjectives may come before or after the noun.

> **EXAMPLE**
>
> I find the young **pianist** clever.
> (The adjectives *young* and *clever* both describe the noun *pianist. Clever* is an adjective object complement.)

Activity A On your paper, write the adjectives that describe the nouns in bold in these sentences.

1. Tasha finds large **cities** fun.
2. Night makes the big **city** exciting.
3. She finds the bright **lights** pretty.
4. Shane, the chef, makes good **food** great.
5. He makes the chicken **stir-fry** spicy.

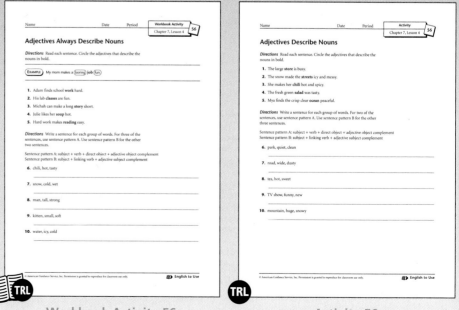

Workbook Activity 56   Activity 56

Me

Bear

(Huge Seemed)

You can write sentences with adjectives like those in Activity A. Follow these steps:

1. Choose a noun.
   Noun: student

2. Choose two or more adjectives to describe the noun.
   Adjectives: young, bright

3. Decide on a sentence pattern, and write the sentence.
   A subject + verb + d. object + adj. obj. complement
      Leslie called the young student bright.
   B subject + linking verb + adj. subj. complement
      The young student is bright.

Activity B On your paper, write a sentence for each group of words. Use an adjective object complement in five sentences (pattern **A** above). Use an adjective subject complement in the other five sentences (pattern **B** above).

1. snow, soft, cold
2. sun, bright, shiny
3. woman, careful, busy
4. car, old, broken
5. soccer player, active, quick
6. elephant, trained, strong
7. cat, fussy, hungry
8. boat, wooden, leaky
9. bike, loud, fast
10. student, smart, eager

To me, the bear seemed huge.

Activity B Answers

Sentences will vary. Check that students wrote five sentences with adjectives used as object complements and five sentences with adjectives used as subject complements.

 3 Reinforce and Extend

LEARNING STYLES

 Interpersonal/Group

Have students work in groups to create a short story using the sentences they formed for Activity B. Ask students to share the 10 sentences they wrote and link them to form a narrative. When students have completed their sentences, have them share their stories with the class.

AT HOME CONNECTION

Encourage students to make frequent efforts to improve their writing skills. Suggest that they check recent writing assignments as well as personal writing for incomplete sentences, capitalization errors, and missing end punctuation. Also have students identify object and subject complements in their sentences.

ASL ILLUSTRATION

Have the class practice making the signs for "To me, the bear seemed huge." Point out to students that the sign for "huge" is made in two parts. The first part of the sign shows height; the second part of the sign shows width.

Lesson at a Glance

Chapter 7 Lesson 5

Overview This lesson explains how to distinguish between adjectives and adverbs in sentences. It reviews the correct use of *good* and *well.*

Objectives

- To distinguish between adjectives and adverbs
- To choose correctly between *good* and *well*

Student Pages 140–141

Teacher's Resource Library

Workbook Activity 57

Activity 57

Alternative Activity 57

1   Warm-Up Activity

Model for students a conversation in which you praise someone's performance by saying "You did well!" In another instance, say "You did good!" Ask students which of the sentences they have heard in conversation. Tell them that in this lesson, they will learn how to tell *good,* an adjective, from *well,* an adverb, and will learn how to use the two words correctly.

2   Teaching the Lesson

Focus students' attention on the examples and explanations of how to distinguish between an adjective and an adverb. Then write the following sentences on the board: *Esperanza is <u>gentle</u>. She speaks <u>gently</u>.* Ask students to read the sentences aloud and to tell the part of speech for each underlined word. Suggest that students apply the strategies described in the examples to figure out which word is an adjective and which is an adverb.

Activity A Answers

1. adjective 2. adverb 3. adjective
4. adjective 5. adverb

Communication Connection

When using the Internet, people often use emoticons in place of adjectives to express emotions. An emoticon is a group of symbols that can be keyboarded to show a feeling.

- :-) means "happy."
- :-(means "sad."
- =:o means "confused."

Some adjectives become adverbs when you add *-ly.*

EXAMPLE   **Adjectives**   quiet, soft, quick, noisy
                 Adverbs   quietly, softly, quickly, noisily

To figure out whether a word is an adjective or an adverb, look carefully at the whole sentence. If the word comes right before a noun or follows a linking verb, it is probably an adjective. If the word ends in *-ly* and follows an action verb, it is probably an adverb.

Remember that an adjective always describes a noun. An adverb tells about a verb, an adjective, or another adverb.

EXAMPLE   **Adjective**   The child seems happy.
(The linking verb *seems* links the adjective *happy* to the noun *child. Happy* is an adjective subject complement.)
            Adverb   The child plays happily.
(The adverb *happily* answers the question *how* about the action verb *plays.*)

Activity A On your paper, write whether the word in bold is an *adjective* or an *adverb.* (You may wish to refer to the list of linking verbs in Lesson 3 on page 136.)

1. The birds in the park appeared **loud.**
2. The birds sang **loudly.**
3. It was a **happy** day for everyone.
4. The winter wind felt **brisk** and cold.
5. Mr. Stillman walked **briskly** to his car.

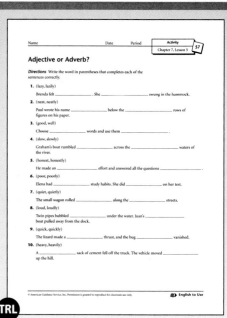

           Workbook Activity 57   Activity 57

Activity B On your paper, write the word in parentheses that completes each of these sentences correctly. Next to the word, write whether it is an *adjective* or an *adverb*.

Example Al stacked boxes in a (neat, neatly) row.
          neat—adjective

1. The (heavy, heavily) load shifted.
2. The load fell (heavy, heavily) to the street.
3. The boat moved (slow, slowly) out of the harbor.
4. The skipper handled the sailboat (careful, carefully).
5. Then a (strong, strongly) south wind moved the boat along (swift, swiftly).

The adjective *good* and the adverb *well* are often used incorrectly. Use *good* after a linking verb to describe the subject. Always use *good* to describe a noun or pronoun. Use *well* after an action verb to tell about the verb.

EXAMPLE	Adjective	That movie was good. We ate a good dinner.
	Adverb	They ate well after their game.

Activity C Write each sentence on your paper. Fill in each blank with either *good* or *well* to complete each sentence correctly.

1. That dress looks _____ on her.
2. She slept _____ during the storm.
3. The old house is in _____ shape.
4. A cold drink tastes _____ on a hot day.
5. Mateo works _____ under pressure.

Activity B Answers

1. heavy—adjective 2. heavily—adverb 3. slowly—adverb 4. carefully—adverb 5. strong—adjective, swiftly—adverb

Activity C Answers

1. That dress looks good on her.
2. She slept well during the storm.
3. The old house is in good shape.
4. A cold drink tastes good on a hot day. 5. Mateo works well under pressure.

 Reinforce and Extend

Lesson at a Glance

Chapter 7 Lesson 6

Overview This lesson defines compound subject complement. It also explains how to find the basic sentence pattern in sentences with compound parts and prepositional phrases.

Objectives

- To find subject complements in sentences with compound parts and prepositional phrases
- To identify sentence parts in sentences with compound parts and prepositional phrases
- To expand sentences by adding adjectives, adverbs, compounds, and prepositional phrases

Student Pages 142–143

Teacher's Resource Library **TRL**

Workbook Activity 58

Activity 58

Alternative Activity 58

Vocabulary
compound subject complement

1 Warm-Up Activity

Write on the board a long sentence containing a subject complement and several prepositional phrases. For example: *On a miserably hot, muggy day in July, the clear water at the natural spring in the center of the city is clear and icy cool.* Invite volunteers to mark out prepositional phrases in the sentence. Remind students that they can find the subjects, verbs, and subject complements even in complex sentences by eliminating adjectives and prepositional phrases.

2 Teaching the Lesson

Discuss the definition of compound subject complement. After discussing the example sentence and how to identify its basic sentence pattern, invite volunteers to write on the board additional long sentences with compound subject complements. Have the class point out the subject complements in each sentence.

142 *Chapter 7   Sentences/Linking Verbs*

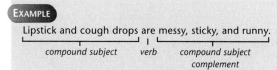

Lesson 6 — Subject Complements in Long Sentences

Compound subject complement

Two or more subject complements joined by a conjunction

Sentences with subject complements may have compound parts and prepositional phrases. Two or more subject complements make a **compound subject complement**.

EXAMPLE   On a hot summer afternoon, lipstick and cough drops in a warm car are messy, sticky, and runny.

Compound subject	lipstick, cough drops
Linking verb	are
Compound subject complement	messy, sticky, runny

Although the example sentence has compound parts, adjectives, and prepositional phrases, it still follows the basic sentence pattern of *subject + linking verb + subject complement*. Remove the adjectives and prepositional phrases, and you can easily recognize the sentence pattern.

EXAMPLE

Lipstick and cough drops are messy, sticky, and runny.

    compound subject   *verb*   *compound subject complement*

Activity A On your paper, write the subject complement in each sentence. Write whether the complement is a *noun subject complement* or an *adjective subject complement*.

1. Of all the town's cooks, Juan is the most talented chef.
2. For meats, Juan's own gravy recipe is a great one.
3. Over steaming rice, Juan's pepper beef stew with gravy and vegetables tastes spicy and terrific.
4. For a side dish, Juan's dinner rolls and salads of mixed greens are extremely fresh and tasty.
5. On Friday nights, Juan's restaurant in the city is full of happy diners.

Workbook Activity 58

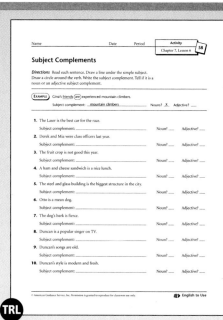

Activity 58

Activity B On your paper, make a chart like the one shown. Write the words that form the basic sentence pattern in these sentences in the chart.

Example The student with top honors in medical school became a doctor and then chief of staff.

subject	+	linking verb	+	subject complement
student		became		doctor, chief of staff

1. Most of the stores in town are bargain shops with good values at low cost.
2. The price of that blue coat in the store on Elm Street looks good to me.
3. The bus with the red sign was late on its way to the station.
4. The fine athlete is a major player on the team and a good student at his school in New York.
5. My brand new computer is a wonderful machine and a useful tool for almost any job.

Activity C Add adjectives, adverbs, compounds, and prepositional phrases to each sentence. Write the sentences on your paper.

1. Josh's car is a wreck.
2. The hood is dented.
3. Two windows are broken.
4. The tires appear flat.
5. That boy is an unhappy person.

LEARNING STYLES

Interpersonal/Group
Ask students to work in small groups and write complete stories using the sentences they wrote in Activity C. Each group's story should explain how the accident happened and what the car's owner will do about his vehicle. Groups should make sure that the sentences they use to expand their stories include subject complements.

Activity A Answers

1. the most talented chef—noun subject complement 2. a great one—noun subject complement 3. spicy and terrific—adjective subject complement 4. extremely fresh and tasty—adjective subject complement 5. full of happy diners—adjective subject complement

Activity B Answers

(Answers are shown as follows: subject/linking verb/subject complement.) 1. Most/are/shops 2. price/looks/good 3. bus/was/late 4. athlete/is/player, student 5. computer/is/machine, tool

Activity C Answer

Sentences will vary.

 3 **Reinforce and Extend**

LEARNING STYLES

Body/Kinesthetic
After students have completed Activity C, have them work in small groups and select several of their sentences to write on construction paper. Tell them to label the parts of speech, writing *subject, verb, adjective, adverb,* and *prepositional phrase* above the correct words in each sentence. Next, have them cut apart the sentences, according to their parts of speech. Have each member of the group stand and hold a different part of speech; group members should read the sentence aloud together. Then have students holding the descriptive parts of the sentence sit down until only the subject, verb, and compound subject complement remain.

Lesson at a Glance

Chapter 7 Lesson 7

Overview This lesson presents sentences that begin with pronoun subjects and with the adverbs *here* and *there*.

Objectives

- To identify the basic parts of the subject + linking verb + subject complement pattern
- To identify the subject in sentences beginning with *here* and *there*

Student Pages 144–145

Teacher's Resource Library

Workbook Activity 59

Activity 59

Alternative Activity 59

Sentence Diagramming Activity 38

1 Warm-Up Activity

Ask students to supply sentences beginning with the pronouns *it, this, that, these,* and *those.* Point out the example sentence and suggest that students model their sentences after it. Some students may suggest sentences in which the demonstrative pronouns *this, that, these,* and *those* are adjectives. Remind students that *this, that, these,* and *those* are pronouns when they are used alone; they are adjectives when used with a noun.

2 Teaching the Lesson

Model the sample sentence with students, and review the subject + linking verb + subject complement pattern. Remind students that in this pattern, the linking verb is similar to an equal sign (=), and the subject complement renames the subject. By checking whether the subject complement is singular or plural, students will know whether the subject is a singular pronoun such as *it* and *that,* or a plural pronoun such as *those* and *these.*

Pronouns are often subjects of sentences with linking verbs. Here are examples of pronouns used as subjects with linking verbs.

it	that	these	this	those

EXAMPLE This is a new song by your favorite singer.

Sentence pattern   subject + linking verb + subject complement

(The pronoun *this* is the subject of the sentence.)

Activity A Write each sentence on your paper. Write *S* above the subject pronoun, *LV* above the linking verb, and *NSC* above the noun subject complement.

             S   LV   NSC

Example Those were the best sheep on the farm.

1. This is the time for the picnic.
2. That is the dog with the sore foot.
3. These are the hottest months of the year.
4. That is a very common problem.
5. That was our last chance for help.
6. It was a neat deal.
7. This is a sea turtle from Florida.
8. It is an animal in trouble.
9. Those were my shoes in the box.
10. This is Leah's new telephone.

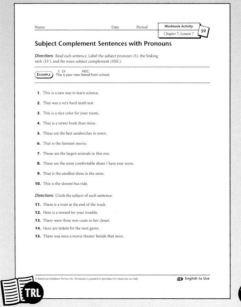

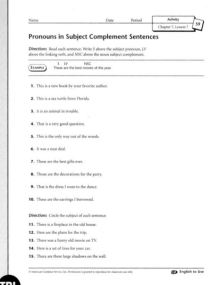

Workbook Activity 59   **Activity 59**

The adverbs *here* and *there* often appear first in sentences with linking verbs. To find the subject in sentences that begin with *here* or *there*, try turning the sentence around so that the noun or pronoun subject comes before the verb.

EXAMPLE

Here is the weekly magazine.
There is the morning train.

Parts of speech   *adv. verb adj. adj. noun*

To find the subjects, reverse the word order.

The weekly magazine is here.
The morning train is there.

Sentence pattern   subject + verb

(The subject of the first sentence is *magazine*. The subject of the second sentence is *train*. The sentence pattern of the original sentences is *subject + verb* even though the order of the words is reversed.)

Activity B On your paper, write the subject of each sentence. If you have trouble finding the subject, try turning the sentence around. Two sentences have a compound subject.

1. There is a sailboat at the end of the lake.

2. Here is the key to the old chest.

3. There is a low, black car on the hilly road.

4. There are a herd of cattle and some sheep on the grassy hill.

5. There was a campfire near the lake.

6. There were bright flashes of lightning and loud cracks of thunder during the storm.

7. Here is a hot cup of coffee.

8. Here are the movie tickets to the next show.

9. There is a silver jet on the runway.

10. There was a moving van in front of his house.

Sentences with Linking Verbs   *Chapter 7*   **145**

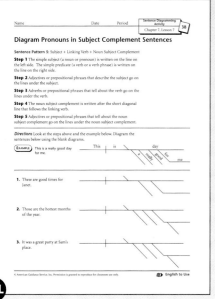
Activity A Answers

1. S—This; LV—is; NSC—time 2. S—That; LV—is; NSC—dog 3. S—These; LV—are; NSC—months 4. S—That; LV—is; NSC—problem 5. S—That; LV—was; NSC—chance 6. S—It; LV—was; NSC—deal 7. S—This; LV—is; NSC—turtle 8. S—It; LV—is; NSC—animal 9. S—Those; LV—were; NSC—shoes 10. S—This; LV—is; NSC—telephone

Activity B Answers

1. sailboat 2. key 3. car 4. herd, sheep 5. campfire 6. flashes, cracks 7. cup 8. tickets 9. jet 10. van

3   Reinforce and Extend

LEARNING STYLES

Auditory/Verbal
Have each student use five sentences from Activity A as the basis for a brief story. Tell students to expand the sentences by adding adjectives, adverbs, and prepositional phrases. Students can write additional sentences of their own if they wish. Have several volunteers read their stories to the class.

LEARNING STYLES

Body/Kinesthetic
Have students write the sentences in Activity B on note cards, with each word on a separate card. Have students arrange the sentences in order and read them aloud. Then have volunteers rearrange the note cards, positioning the subject at the beginning of the sentence. Model the first sentence for the class, arranging the note cards to read: *A sailboat is there at the end of the lake.* Discuss with students how they can help themselves find the subject of the sentence by physically moving the adverbs *here* and *there* out of the subject position.

Chapter 7 Lesson 8

Overview This lesson explains the use of nominative case pronouns and possessive pronouns as subject complements in sentences.

Objectives

- To use the correct form of pronouns in sentences
- To write possessive pronouns as subject complements

Student Pages 146–147

Teacher's Resource Library

Workbook Activity 60

Activity 60

Alternative Activity 60

1 Warm-Up Activity

Hold up a book and say, "I own this book. The book belongs to me. It is my book. The book is mine." Then write the sentences on the board. Discuss with students how all four sentences express the same idea in a different way. Ask students to identify the pronoun in each sentence and to locate each in the pronoun chart in this lesson.

2 Teaching the Lesson

Focus students' attention on the text, reviewing example sentences and the pronouns in the chart. Before students begin Activity A, discuss with them the problem with choosing pronouns that "sound" right in certain spots. In order to use pronouns correctly when we write, we must recognize which pronouns can stand for a subject and which pronouns must be used in the predicate. Create short sentences such as "_____ whistled." or "Jim gave _____ a surprise." Have students practice filling in nominative and objective pronouns.

Lesson **8** More Pronouns

You have learned that pronouns can take the place of nouns in a sentence.

Pronouns			
	Nominative	Objective	Owner
One	I	me	my, mine
	you	you	you, yours
	he, she, it	him, her, it	his, her, hers, its
Two or	we	us	our, ours
More	you	you	your, yours
	they	them	their, theirs

Use nominative pronouns as subjects and as subject complements in sentences with linking verbs. Use objective pronouns as direct objects and indirect objects in sentences with action verbs and as objects of prepositions.

EXAMPLE

Subject	I am happy.
Subject complement	It is I.
Direct object	Gabriel saw me.
Indirect object	Gabriel gave me a book.
Object of preposition	Gabriel gave a book to me.

Use owner pronouns as subject complements in sentences with linking verbs. These owner pronouns are

hers	his	its	mine	ours	theirs	yours

EXAMPLE

	That chair is his.
Parts of speech	adj. n. v. pronoun
Sentence parts	subject I predicate
Sentence pattern	subject + linking verb + subject complement

146 Chapter 7 Sentences with Linking Verbs

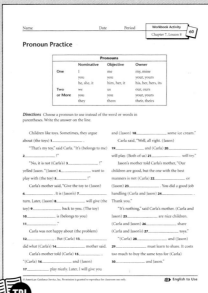

Workbook Activity 60

Activity 60

Activity A On your paper, write the correct pronoun in parentheses. Then write how each pronoun is used in the sentence.

Example Elena gave (he, him) and (I, me) coupons for the restaurant.
him, me—compound indirect object

1. (He, Him) and (I, me) sat together during the show.
2. Ahmad met (he, him) and (she, her) after the play.
3. The four of (we, us) ate at Jake's.
4. (He, Him) and (I, me) liked the play, but Cora did not.
5. The best tennis players are (he, him) and (she, her).
6. (Her, She) slams the ball across the net to (him, he).
7. The winners of the match are (they, them).
8. Afterward, (he, him) asked (she, her) for a ride home.
9. The waiter served lunch to (she, her) and (I, me).
10. The person in the picture is (she, her).

Activity B On your paper, write the second sentence of each set. Fill in the blank with an owner pronoun.

Example Those dishes belong to me.
They are <u>mine</u>.

1. Those clothes belong to Brigette. They are _____ .
2. Mr. and Mrs. Lee own the store. It is _____ .
3. That car belongs to Rob. It is _____ .
4. The books belong to you. They are _____ .
5. We own the table. It is _____ .

Activity A Answers

1. He, I—compound subject 2. him, her—compound direct object 3. us—object of preposition 4. He, I—compound subject 5. he, she—compound noun subject complement 6. She—subject, him—object of preposition 7. they—noun subject complement 8. he—subject, her—direct object 9. her, me—compound object of preposition 10. she—noun subject complement

Activity B Answers

1. They are hers. 2. It is theirs. 3. It is his. 4. They are yours. 5. It is ours.

3 Reinforce and Extend

Lesson at a Glance

Chapter 7 Lesson 9

Overview This lesson presents a review of all six sentence patterns.

Objectives

- To identify the six sentence patterns
- To write sentences for each of the six patterns

Student Pages 148–149

Teacher's Resource Library

Workbook Activity 61

Activity 61

Alternative Activity 61

1 Warm-Up Activity

Review the list and sample sentence patterns on page 148. Then write two sentences on the board: *Telephones ring.* (sentence pattern number 1) *The telephone is loud.* (sentence pattern number 6) Divide the class into two groups. Have one group begin with the first sentence, building on it by writing five sentences that represent the other five patterns in the order presented on page 148. Ask the other group to start with the second sentence and build on it by writing five more sentences that represent the other patterns, going backward from the sixth pattern to the first pattern. When students have finished, have the two groups compare the sentences they have written in the six sentence patterns.

2 Teaching the Lesson

Remind student that they have studied six different sentence patterns. Read and discuss the examples of each pattern, and invite volunteers to create other sentences for each pattern.

Activity A Answers

Answers will vary. Check whether students wrote words that correctly fit the sentence pattern.

Remember, there are six sentence patterns.

Sentence Patterns
(1) subject + verb The salad chills.
(2) subject + verb + direct object The salad dressing stained the carpet.
(3) subject + verb + indirect object + direct object He served her a salad.
(4) subject + verb + direct object + object complement I find this salad tasty.
(5) subject + linking verb + noun subject complement This salad is a healthy choice.
(6) subject + linking verb + adjective subject complement The salad is big.

Activity A Write each sentence on your paper. Fill in the blank with a word of your own choosing.

Example Soccer is my favorite _____ sport _____ .
                                          noun subject complement

1. _____ smiled.
              subject

2. Rose gave _____ a present.
                    indirect object

3. Carol watched a _____ .
                          direct object

4. This CD is _____ .
              adjective subject complement

5. One girl called the concert _____ .
                                    object complement

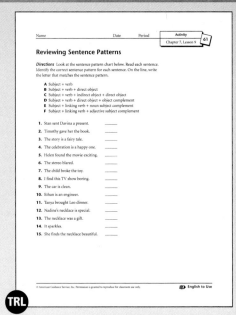

Activity B Identify the correct sentence pattern for each sentence. On your paper, write the number that matches one of the sentence patterns from the chart on page 148.

Example The group of students opened their textbooks to the lesson on sentence patterns.
2 (subject + verb + direct object)

1. Todd was late again.

2. Ms. Costa turned to the class and asked the students a question.

3. Steven gave the right answer.

4. Steven felt smart, and he was proud of himself.

5. He smiled happily.

6. Then she taught the class another grammar lesson.

7. Ms. Costa is a good English teacher.

8. Most students thought the lesson an easy one.

9. Several began their work.

10. Ms. Costa allowed them ten minutes.

11. Everyone finished on time.

12. Well, Todd was a little slow with his paper.

13. Later, the teacher corrected the papers quickly.

14. After school, Todd offered Gina a ride home.

15. Todd's old car is a rare model.

Ms. Costa answers Todd's question.

Activity B Answers

1. 6 (subject + linking verb + adjective subject complement)
2. 3 (subject + verb + indirect object + direct object) 3. 2 (subject + verb + direct object) 4. 6 (subject + linking verb + adjective subject complement) 5. 1 (subject + verb)
6. 3 (subject + verb + indirect object + direct object) 7. 5 (subject + linking verb + noun subject complement) 8. 4 (subject + verb + direct object + object complement)
9. 2 (subject + verb + direct object)
10. 3 (subject + verb + indirect object + direct object) 11. 1 (subject + verb) 12. 6 (subject + linking verb + adjective subject complement)
13. 2 (subject + verb + direct object)
14. 3 (subject + verb + indirect object + direct object) 15. 5 (subject + linking verb + noun subject complement)

 3 Reinforce and Extend

LEARNING STYLES

 LEP/ESL

Some of the sentence patterns in Lesson 9 may be difficult for English language learners if these patterns are not part of their native languages. For example, pattern number 1 and pattern number 2 might be difficult for a student whose native language does not use these patterns. Review the sentence patterns with English language learners, and determine which ones may require more review.

ONLINE CONNECTION

 For more suggestions on writing and speaking exercises for English language learners, visit the National Council of Teachers of English site. "Practical Teaching Ideas on ESL" *www.ncte.org/teach/ esl.shtml* includes numerous second-language teaching ideas selected from NCTE publications and submitted by teachers.

Lesson at a Glance

Chapter 7 Lesson 10

Overview This lesson provides lists of words and asks students to use the words to write clear sentences.

Objectives

- To apply the steps of the writing process
- To create simple sentences and improve them with adjectives, adverbs, and prepositional phrases
- To create descriptive narratives with sentences that include appositives, adjectives, prepositional phrases, and noun and adjective complements

Student Pages 150–151

Teacher's Resource Library

Workbook Activity 62

Activity 62

Alternative Activity 62

1 Warm-Up Activity

Ask students to brainstorm a list of adjectives and nouns. Write the words on the board under the headings *Adjectives* and *Nouns.* Then, write these sentence patterns on the board: *Subject + linking verb + noun subject complement* and *Subject + linking verb + adjective subject complement.* Ask students to select words from their lists to create a sentence for each pattern. Point out that students applied the first two steps of the writing process as they completed this exercise.

2 Teaching the Lesson

Suggest that having a fresh pair of eyes review work can be a great aid in completing a writing assignment.

Activity A Answers

Answers will vary. Be sure students have used the appropriate patterns.

You know that a sentence is a group of words arranged in a certain pattern to express an idea. You and a friend may start with the same list of words, but you will probably write totally different sentences that express different ideas. Your choice of words and how you arrange them will create a different picture in a reader's mind than your friend's sentence will.

Look at the following list of words. Think about an idea for a sentence using some of these words. Then compare your idea with other students' ideas.

Subjects	Adjectives	Subject Complements
morning	bright	gloomy
evening	dark	one
	new	
	starry	
	lovely	

Activity A Using the list of subjects, adjectives, and subject complements below, write five clear sentences using linking verbs on your paper. Add other words as needed.

Subjects	Adjectives	Noun and Adjective Subject Complements
sandwich	tangy	cheap
vegetables	cold	one
orange	hot	dinner
juice	crispy	great
lasagna	juicy	drink

Activity B Improve the sentences you wrote in Activity A by adding adverbs and prepositional phrases. Write your revised sentences on your paper.

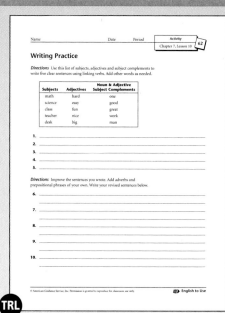

Workbook Activity 62   **Activity 62**

Activity C Use the sentences from Activity B to write a short story about food. Proofread and edit your story.

Activity D Use the list of subjects, adjectives, and subject complements below to write on your paper five clear sentences using linking verbs. Add other adjectives as needed.

Subjects	Adjectives	Noun and Adjective Subject Complements
spider	cute	angry
tiger	hairy	pet
cat	scary	beast
elephant	toothy	noisy
gorilla	strong	huge

Activity E Improve the sentences you wrote in Activity D by adding adverbs and prepositional phrases. Write your revised sentences on your paper.

Activity F Use the sentences from Activity E to write a short story about zoo animals. Proofread and edit your story.

Activity G Now it's your turn. Think about a topic: for example, cars, sports, movies, music, computer games, or anything else that interests you. Next, make a list of words that you might use to describe your topic. You might wish to list the words in a chart similar to the charts shown in this lesson. Finally, follow the steps in the writing process to write a short story on your topic.

Activity B Answers

Answers will vary. Make sure student sentences contain adverbs and prepositional phrases.

Activity C Answers

Answers will vary. Make sure students write about food and that they proofread and edit their stories.

Activity D Answers

Answers will vary. Make sure students use the words in the box to write five clear sentences that contain linking verbs.

Activity E Answers

Answers will vary. Make sure students added adverbs and prepositional phrases to the sentences they wrote for Activity D.

Activity F Answers

Answers will vary. Make sure students write about zoo animals and that they proofread and edit their stories

Activity G Answers

Answers will vary. Have students share and discuss their stories in small groups.

 3 **Reinforce and Extend**

LEARNING STYLES

 Interpersonal/Group
Write a short story as a class. Draw from the class sentences for a first paragraph. Then place students in small groups to complete the story by writing one or two more paragraphs. Remind students to rewrite and edit. Ask each group to share their results with the class.

CAREER CONNECTION

 Students need to explore their interests in relation to the requirements of various jobs. Ask students to follow the writing process as they develop two paragraphs. In the first, they are to summarize their current interests, such as hobbies and leisure activities. In the second, they are to describe some kind of job they would like to have someday that relates to what they like to do.

Chapter 7 Lesson 11

Overview This lesson introduces regular and irregular forms of comparative and superlative adjectives.

Objectives

■ To choose correctly between comparative and superlative forms of adjectives in sentences

Student Pages 152–153

Teacher's Resource Library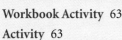

Workbook Activity 63

Activity 63

Alternative Activity 63

Vocabulary

comparative
superlative

 1 Warm-Up Activity

Using three books of different sizes, hold up the appropriate sizes as you say "This is a big book, this is a bigger book, and this is the biggest book." Then hold up one book at a time as you say, "This is a good book, this is a better book, and this is the best book." Invite students to make up similar sentences for other objects.

 2 Teaching the Lesson

Focus on the text and the two examples. Discuss the definitions of comparative and superlative. Be sure students understand the differences before assigning activities in this lesson.

Activity A Answers

1. fastest 2. funnier 3. fattest
4. tallest 5. older

Lesson 11 Writing Mechanics

Comparative
An adjective that compares two nouns

Superlative
An adjective that compares three or more nouns

Writing Tip

Beware of double comparisons. Do not add *more* or *most* when you use the *-er* or *-est* form of an adjective.

Adjectives compare people, places, and things. When you compare two things, the adjective usually has an *-er* added to it. **Comparatives** are adjectives that compare two things. When you compare more than two things, the adjective usually has an *-est* added to it. **Superlatives** are adjectives that compare more than two things.

EXAMPLE

Mariah is	Of the two, Ines is	Of the three, Estella is
quick	quicker	quickest
tall	taller	tallest
early	earlier	earliest
hungry	hungrier	hungriest
happy	happier	happiest

Some adjectives change completely to form their comparative and superlative forms.

EXAMPLE

Adjective	Comparative	Superlative
bad	worse	worst
good	better	best
little	less	least
many	more	most

Activity A On your paper, write the correct form of the adjective in parentheses for each sentence.

1. Javier is the (faster, fastest) runner on the whole team.
2. Of the two comics, she is the (funnier, funniest).
3. Coco is the (fatter, fattest) cat on the block.
4. Sophie is the (taller, tallest) student in her class.
5. Maria is the (older, oldest) of the two sisters.

Workbook Activity 63

Activity 63

Bad

Worse

Good

Better

Activity B On your paper, write the correct form of the adjective in parentheses for each sentence.

1. Of the mother and daughter, the daughter is (tallest, taller).
2. The pig is the (smarter, smartest) of all the animals in that story.
3. My test scores are high, but Jeff's are (higher, highest).
4. Tela's computer is fast, but Maiya's computer is (fastest, faster).
5. That store carries the (fresher, freshest) vegetables of any store in town.

Activity C On your paper, write the correct form of the adjective in parentheses for each sentence.

1. Many people find her the (more, most) talented of all stage actors.
2. In all the family, she is (more, most) famous.
3. Of the two sisters, her acting is (better, best).
4. Her singing is (worse, bad), but she has the (best, better) voice of all the sisters.
5. Of the two problems, this is (less, least) difficult.
6. It is my (least, less) favorite of all.
7. My grades are (good, better), but yours are (best, better).
8. Of the five team members, Pauline has scored the (more, most) points.
9. The Eagles had a bad season, but the Blazers had the (worse, worst) record in the league.
10. Of the two teams, their record is (worse, worst).

Using What You've Learned

Write five sentences comparing two or more movies, TV programs, or books. Compare the items with adjectives. When you have finished writing, check to make sure that you have used the correct comparative or superlative form of each adjective.

Activity B Answers

1. taller 2. smartest 3. higher
4. faster 5. freshest

Activity C Answers

1. most 2. most 3. better 4. bad, best 5. less 6. least 7. good, better
8. most 9. worst 10. worse

3 Reinforce and Extend

LEARNING STYLES

Visual/Spatial
Write the words *Comparative* and *Superlative* on the board. Above *Comparative*, write *only two*. Above *Superlative*, write *3,4, 5 (etc.), of all, of any*. Then suggest adjectives, and have volunteers write the comparative and superlative forms under the appropriate words. You might want to encourage visual learners to circle words in sentences that indicate number or to write the number of items being compared in the margin of their papers.

IN THE COMMUNITY

Buildings offer opportunities for comparison. Ask students to study several buildings and to write sentences with comparatives and superlatives describing the buildings.

ASL ILLUSTRATION

Have students examine the signs for comparative adjectives on page 153. Ask students to look at the ways the comparative adjectives make the signs for "bad" and "good" seem bigger. Have students speculate on what the signs for "worst" and "best" might be, and have students research ASL signs to find out what the superlative signs are.

Using What You've Learned

Point out to students that they will need to locate the number of things being compared when they are deciding whether to use a comparative or superlative form. Tell students that sentences may contain a specific number, but they also may use words or phrases such as *all*, *both*, or *some*. Sentences also may refer to groups with phrases such as *on the team* or *in the company*. Write these words and phrases on the board and review with students which ones would use a comparative or superlative form.

Chapter 7 Review

Use the Chapter Review to prepare students for tests and to reteach content from the chapter.

Chapter 7 Mastery Test

The Teacher's Resource Library includes two parallel forms of the Chapter 7 Mastery Test. The difficulty level of the two forms is equivalent. You may wish to use one form as a pretest and the other form as a posttest.

REVIEW ANSWERS

Part A

1. compound subject complement 2. noun subject complement 3. subject complement 4. linking verb 5. superlative 6. adjective subjective complement 7. comparative

Part B

8. C 9. E 10. F 11. A 12. B 13. D

Part C

14. huge 15. large, interesting 16. large 17. hot

Word Bank
adjective subject complement
comparative
compound subject complement
linking verb
noun subject complement
subject complement
superlative

Part A Read each sentence below. Fill in each blank with a vocabulary word that correctly completes each sentence.

1. Two or more subject complements make a _____ .
2. A _____ is a word in the predicate renaming the subject.
3. A word in the predicate describing the subject is a _____ .
4. A verb connecting the subject to a word in the predicate is a _____ .
5. A _____ compares more than two things.
6. An adjective in the predicate describing the subject is an _____ .
7. An adjective that compares two things is a _____ .

Part B Read this paragraph.

Devon's truck is good for long trips. His truck carries heavy loads. Two of Devon's friends are his partners. They split the costs of each trip. Truck travel pays well for all of them. Devon feels proud that he owns a truck.

Find these words in the paragraph. Match them with the correct labels. On your paper, write the numbers and letters.

Words		Labels
8. They	**A**	linking verb
9. partners	**B**	adjective subject complement
10. well	**C**	pronoun as a subject
11. feels	**D**	pronoun as an object of a preposition
12. good	**E**	noun subject complement
13. them	**F**	adverb

Part C Write the adjectives that describe the nouns in bold.

14. In the park, the **trees** are huge.
15. He finds the large **statues** interesting.
16. On weekends, the **crowds** seem large.
17. There is a cafe that serves the **food** hot.

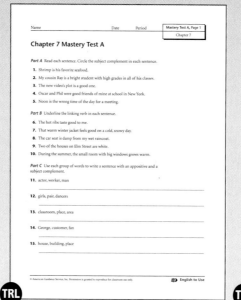

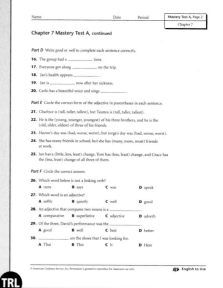

Chapter 7 Mastery Test A

Part D Write the word in parentheses that correctly completes each of these sentences.

18. People drive (quick, quickly) on this road.

19. (He, Him) and (I, me) drive together in the morning.

20. Later, (her, she) asked (he, him) for a ride.

21. Rush hour is the (worse, worst) time of day for traffic.

22. That street has (bad, worse) potholes, but the potholes on this street are (worse, worst).

23. Several of (we, us) rode the bus.

24. Choose (good, well) words, and use them (good, well).

Part E Choose the owner pronoun that correctly completes each set of sentences.

25. Jason owns the computer. It is _____ .

    A him's   **B** he's   **C** his   **D** him

26. The newspaper belongs to the club members. It is _____ .

    A there's   **B** theirs   **C** them's   **D** their

27. Perla owns these videos. They are _____ .

    A hers'   **B** her's   **C** her   **D** hers

Part F Identify and write on your paper the sentence pattern for each of these sentences. Look back at the list of sentence patterns and example sentences in Lesson 9 on page 148 for help. Underline any linking verbs.

28. His dogs are healthy.

29. Terry and Jamilla are good friends.

30. Patrick bought her a ticket to the rodeo.

 Read test questions carefully to identify those questions that require more than one answer.

REVIEW ANSWERS

Part D

18. quickly **19.** He, I **20.** she, him
21. worst **22.** bad, worse **23.** us
24. good, well

Part E

25. C **26.** B **27.** D

Part F

28. subject + linking verb + adjective subject complement; His dogs <u>are</u> healthy.

29. subject + linking verb + noun subject complement; Terry and Jamilla <u>are</u> good friends.

30. subject + verb + indirect object + direct object

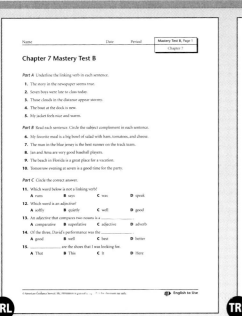

8

Planning Guide
Verbs Tell Time

	Student Pages	Vocabulary	Practice Activities	Identification Skills	Writing Skills	Punctuation Skills
		Student Text Lesson		**Language Skills**		
Lesson 1 Another Look at Verbs	158–159	✔	✔	✔	✔	
Lesson 2 Helping Verbs	160–161	✔	✔	✔	✔	✔
Lesson 3 The Present Tense	162–163	✔	✔	✔	✔	✔
Lesson 4 The Past Tense	164–165	✔	✔	✔	✔	✔
Lesson 5 The Future Tense	166–167	✔	✔	✔	✔	✔
Lesson 6 Negatives	168–169	✔	✔	✔	✔	✔
Lesson 7 Verbs That Change Form	170–171	✔	✔	✔	✔	✔
Lesson 8 Writing Practice	172–173		✔	✔	✔	✔
Lesson 9 Writing Mechanics	174–175	✔	✔	✔	✔	✔

Chapter Activities

Teacher's Resource Library
Community Connection 8:
Talk with Your Neighbors About
Improvements in the Community
English in Your World 8:
Using Action Verbs

Assessment Options

Student Text
Chapter 8 Review

Teacher's Resource Library
Chapter 8 Mastery Tests A and B

ASL Illustration	Communication Connection	Notes	Using What You've Learned	Writing Tips	Teacher Alert	Online Connection	Applications (Home, Career, Community, Global)	Speaking Practice	Writing Practice	Auditory/Verbal	Body/Kinesthetic	Interpersonal/Group Learning	Logical/Mathematical	Visual/Spatial	LEP/ESL	Workbook Activities	Activities	Alternative Activities	Sentence Diagramming Activities	Self-Study Guide
159		✔								159						64	64	64		✔
	160	✔												161		65	65	65		✔
				✔	163		163								163	66	66	66	39	✔
		✔					165		165			165				67	67	67	40	✔
167				✔			167				167					68	68	68	41	✔
								169				169				69	69	69		✔
										171					171	70	70	70		✔
			173			173				173						71	71	71		✔
				✔			175							175		72	72	72		✔

Pronunciation Key

a	hat	e	let	ī	ice	ô	order	ù	put	sh	she	a in about
ā	age	ē	equal	o	hot	oi	oil	ü	rule	th	thin	e in taken
ä	far	ėr	term	ō	open	ou	out	ch	child	ᴛʜ	then	ə { i in pencil
â	care	i	it	ȯ	saw	u	cup	ng	long	zh	measure	o in lemon
												u in circus

Alternative Activities

The Teacher's Resource Library (TRL) contains a set of lower-level worksheets called Alternative Activities. These worksheets cover the same content as the regular Activities but are written at a second-grade reading level.

Skill Track Software

Use the Skill Track Software for English to Use for additional reinforcement of this chapter. The software program allows students using AGS textbooks to be assessed for mastery of each chapter and lesson of the textbook. Students access the software on an individual basis and are assessed with multiple-choice items.

Chapter 8: Verbs Tell Time
pages 156–177

Lessons

1. **Another Look at Verbs**
   pages 158–159

2. **Helping Verbs**
   pages 160–161

3. **The Present Tense**
   pages 162–163

4. **The Past Tense**
   pages 164–165

5. **The Future Tense**
   pages 166–167

6. **Negatives**
   pages 168–169

7. **Verbs That Change Form**
   pages 170–171

8. **Writing Practice**
   pages 172–173

9. **Writing Mechanics**
   pages 174–175

Chapter 8 Review
pages 176–177

**Skill Track Software for
English to Use**

Teacher's Resource Library **TRL**

Workbook Activities 64–72

Activities 64–72

Alternative Activities 64–72

Sentence Diagramming
  Activities 39–41
  (Optional sentence activities
  accompany lessons.)

Community Connection 8

English in Your World 8

Chapter 8 Self-Study Guide

Chapter 8 Mastery Tests A and B

(Answer Keys for the Teacher's
Resource Library begin on page 308
of this Teacher's Edition.)

8 Verbs Tell Time

How important is it to know when something happened or is going to happen? For example, timing is important in nature. As things grow, they have a past, a present, and a future. This photograph shows some stages in a tree's growth. In the past, the tree grew buds, and the buds bloomed. Now—in the present—the tree has apples on it. You can predict what will happen to the apple tree in the future. Birds and people might eat the apples. Maybe the apples will fall to the ground.

Sentences also indicate time. Readers want to know when something happened. The verb in a sentence tells whether something happened in the past, whether it is happening now, or whether it will happen in the future.

In this chapter, you will learn how verbs can tell time in your own writing. You will practice using verbs to indicate when something happened.

Goals for Learning

◆ To use verbs in past, present, and future forms
◆ To use helping verbs and negative adverbs
◆ To use correct forms of irregular verbs
◆ To identify and use contractions

157

Introducing the Chapter

Remind students that verbs in sentences can indicate both long and short periods of time. A verb can describe the brief moment in which a flower bud opens. A verb can also describe the long process during which fruit ripens.

TEACHER'S RESOURCE

The AGS Teaching Strategies in English Transparencies may be used with this chapter. The transparencies add an interactive dimension to expand and enhance the *English to Use* program content.

CAREER INTEREST INVENTORY

The AGS Harrington-O'Shea Career Decision-Making System–Revised (CDM) may be used with this chapter. Students can use the CDM to explore their interests and identify careers. The CDM defines career areas that are indicated by students' responses on the inventory.

Writing Tips and Notes

Ask volunteers to read the tips and notes that appear in the margins throughout the chapter. Then discuss them with the class.

CHAPTER PROJECT

After students have looked over the irregular verbs in Lesson 7, have them mark the verbs that they use frequently. Then have students identify words on the list with which they are unfamiliar or that they use incorrectly. Tell students that they will work in pairs for three minutes at the beginning of each class to review unfamiliar irregular verbs and use them in sentences. During this opening period, introduce other irregular verbs and review correct usages. At the end of the unit, students should have a list of irregular verbs that they have reviewed and mastered.

TRL   **TRL**

Chapter 8 Self-Study Guide

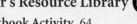
Chapter 8 Lesson 1

Overview This lesson reviews verbs and introduces the concept of verb tense.

Objectives

■ To distinguish between action and linking verbs

■ To label verbs as present, past, or future tense

Student Pages 158–159

Teacher's Resource Library TRL

Workbook Activity 64

Activity 64

Alternative Activity 64

Vocabulary

regular verb
tense

1 Warm-Up Activity

On the board, write the column heads *Past, Present,* and *Future.* Ask volunteers for sentences that tell about something they did yesterday. Write the sentences under *Past.* Repeat this process, having the students provide sentences describing what they are doing now (*Present*) and what they plan to do tomorrow (*Future*). Circle the verbs and help students recognize that the verbs indicate past, present, or future action.

2 Teaching the Lesson

Read the definition of *tense.* Ask volunteers to name the three tenses. Read the definition of *regular verb.* Then ask students to brainstorm a short list of regular verbs. Have students change all the verbs to the past tense by adding *-d* or *-ed.* Discuss how the future tense verb requires the word *will.* Explain that a verb's tense tells readers when an event happened. Discuss other clues in a sentence that can indicate time, for example, the words *today, yesterday,* or *next year.*

> **Tense**
> *Present, past, or future time expressed by a verb*
>
> **Regular verb**
> *A verb that adds -d or -ed to form the past tense*

> There are six verb tenses in all:
> • present
> • past
> • future
> • present perfect
> • past perfect
> • future perfect

Verbs show action or a state-of-being. An action verb tells what the subject of a sentence is doing. Linking, or state-of-being, verbs link the subject to nouns or adjectives in the predicate. Linking verbs help the predicate tell more about the subject.

Activity A On your paper, write the verb in each sentence. Next to each verb, write whether it is an *action verb* or a *linking verb.*

1. The wet streets shine under the light.
2. Francisco works the late shift.
3. He seems really sick today.
4. Andy feels awful, too.
5. Both men left work early.

A verb's **tense** refers to the period of time expressed by the verb. The tense of a verb tells you whether something

• happened in the past
• is happening in the present, or
• will happen in the future.

Regular verbs form their past tense by adding *-d* or *-ed* at the end. Add *-d* to regular verbs that end in *-e.* Add *-ed* to regular verbs that end in other letters.

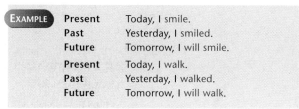

EXAMPLE	Present	Today, I smile.
	Past	Yesterday, I smiled.
	Future	Tomorrow, I will smile.
	Present	Today, I walk.
	Past	Yesterday, I walked.
	Future	Tomorrow, I will walk.

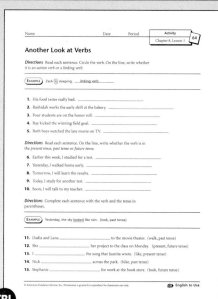

Workbook Activity 64

Activity 64

Smile

(Smile + Finish)
Smiled

(Smile + Will)
Will Smile

Activity B On your paper, write the verbs in these sentences. (Include the word *will* with future tense verbs.) Write whether the verb is in the *present, past,* or *future* tense.

1. Yesterday, I changed schools.
2. Today, I talk with my teacher.
3. Yesterday, I started class.
4. Tomorrow, I will learn about verbs.
5. Yesterday, I learned about sentences.
6. Yesterday, I jumped rope.
7. Tomorrow, I will play basketball with my friends.
8. Today, I watch TV at home.
9. Yesterday, you looked sad about something.
10. Today, you appear fine.

Activity C Complete each sentence using the bold verb in the tense given in parentheses. Write the sentence on your paper. Each of the verbs given is a regular verb.

Example The dogs _____ louder than usual.
(**bark**, past tense)
The dogs **barked** louder than usual.

1. Lin _____ quite happy about her test grade.
(**seem**, past tense)
2. The sauce _____ quite spicy. (**taste**, past tense)
3. The girls _____ about their plans for the summer.
(**talk**, future tense)
4. I _____ for a happy ending to the story.
(**wish**, past tense)
5. She _____ the steps for the directions in order.
(**list**, future tense)

Activity A Answers

1. shine—action verb 2. works—action verb 3. seems—linking verb 4. feels—linking verb 5. left—action verb

Activity B Answers

1. changed—past 2. talk—present 3. started—past 4. will learn—future 5. learned—past 6. jumped—past 7. will play—future 8. watch—present 9. looked—past 10. appear—present

Activity C Answers

1. Lin seemed quite happy about her test grade. 2. The sauce tasted quite spicy. 3. The girls will talk about their plans for the summer. 4. I wished for a happy ending to the story. 5. She will list the steps for the directions in order.

 3 **Reinforce and Extend**

LEARNING STYLES

 Auditory/Verbal
Ask students to create new sentences in the present, past, and future tenses. Refer them to the verbs and sentences in Activities B and C to use as models. Tell students that they may need to change words such as *today, tomorrow,* and *yesterday* when they change the verbs' tenses. Have students read their sentences aloud to the class. Ask students to listen for the verb's tense as well as other clues about time that the sentence contains. Have the class identify the tenses in the new sentences.

ASL ILLUSTRATION

Help students understand how verbs show tense in ASL. In each of the three examples on page 159, the sign for smile remains the same. Adding the sign for finished indicates past tense, and adding the sign for will indicates future tense.

Lesson at a Glance

Chapter 8 Lesson 2

Overview This lesson introduces helping verbs and verb phrases.

Objectives

- To identify main verbs and helping verbs in verb phrases
- To write verb phrases in sentences

Student Pages 160–161

Teacher's Resource Library

Workbook Activity 65

Activity 65

Alternative Activity 65

Vocabulary

helping verb
verb phrase

---

1 Warm-Up Activity

Have students brainstorm items that must be part of a group in order to work. After students have suggested some examples (such as chair legs, telephone lines, or pages of a book), discuss with them how *helping verbs* complete a main verb. Review the list of helping verbs with students and have them indicate any that are unfamiliar. Focus students' attention on the explanation of helping verbs and verb phrases. Point out that the sentence pattern of each sentence in Activity A is subject + verb.

2 Teaching the Lesson

After students have reviewed the list of helping verbs on page 160, encourage them to create verb phrases using one or more helping verbs from the list. Write these verb phrases on the board. Correct any mistakes in verb forms as you write the verb phrases. Then invite volunteers to use each verb phrase in a sentence. Have the volunteers write their sentences on the board. Then ask them to circle the helping verbs in the verb phrases they used.

Lesson 2 Helping Verbs

> **Helping verb**
> A verb that comes before the main verb. Together, the two verbs form a verb phrase
>
> **Verb phrase**
> A verb and its helpers

A **helping verb** is a verb that comes before the main verb. A helping verb *helps* the main verb show action or state a fact. A main verb with one or more helping verbs is a **verb phrase**.

> **EXAMPLE** I was dreaming.
> He could be dreaming.
> You must have been dreaming.
> (In each of the verb phrases, *dreaming* is the main verb. *Was, could, be, must, have,* and *been* are all helping verbs.)

Communication Connection

In the Braille system, raised dots represent letters, combinations of letters, numbers, and punctuation marks. People learn Braille by remembering what each group of dots stands for, just as people with sight learn the alphabet. The word *Braille* written in Braille looks like this:

Forms of the verbs *be, have,* and *do* often serve as helping verbs. Here is a list of common helping verbs:

am	can	doing	is	should
are	could	had	may	was
be	did	has	might	were
been	do	have	must	will
being	does	having	shall	would

Verbs in the future tense always use a helping verb.

> **EXAMPLE** Megan **will go** to the movies later.
> (The verb phrase *will go* consists of the main verb *go* and the helping verb *will.*)

Activity A On your paper, write the bold verb phrase in each sentence. Draw one line under the main verb. Circle the helping verb.

1. Hannah **has packed** her bags.
2. She **will be leaving** tomorrow.
3. Steve and his friends **are listening** to music.
4. They **have been looking** for information about Braille.
5. Kerry **did read** a book in Braille.

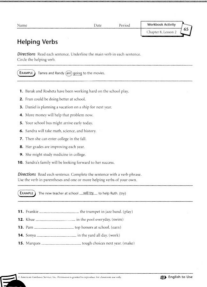

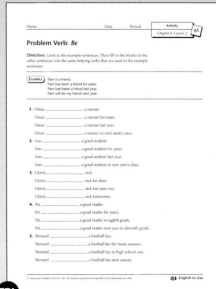

Workbook Activity 65   Activity 65

> The perfect tenses use a helping verb with a past form of the verb.
>
> **Present perfect**
> I have packed.
>
> **Past perfect**
> I had packed.
>
> **Future perfect**
> I will have packed.

Activity B On your paper, write the verb phrase in each sentence. Draw one line under the main verb. Circle the helping verb.

1. David will earn extra money at his job.
2. Then he can buy a Mother's Day gift.
3. The store does deliver gifts for its best customers.
4. The gift should surprise David's mother.
5. Probably she will be smiling happily all day.
6. Pamela did go to the dentist.
7. Her brother must visit the dentist, too.
8. They could have been checked at the same time.
9. Pamela has been taking good care of her teeth.
10. The dentist will praise her.

Activity C Complete each sentence with a verb phrase. Use the verb in parentheses and one or more helping verbs from the list on page 160. Write the completed sentences on your paper.

Example   Ben, a grain and cattle farmer, _____ hard. (work)
Ben, a grain and cattle farmer, has been working hard.

1. He _____ many acres of corn. (plant)
2. He _____ his corn in that tall silo. (store)
3. He _____ some of his corn to his cattle. (feed)
4. Ben _____ his fields carefully. (tend)
5. Ben _____ on his farm for a long time. (live)
6. Luisa _____ the most beautiful quilt by hand. (stitch)
7. She _____ her quilt at the fair. (show)
8. She _____ it in the craft contest. (enter)
9. Her quilt _____ the first prize. (award)
10. Luisa certainly _____ proud of her skills as a quilter. (feel)

Activity A Answers

1. (has) packed 2. (will be) leaving 3. (are) listening 4. (have been) looking 5. (did) read

Activity B Answers

1. (will) earn 2. (can) buy 3. (does) deliver 4. (should) surprise 5. (will be) smiling 6. (did) go 7. (must) visit 8. (could have been) checked 9. (has been) taking 10. (will) praise

Activity C Answers

Answers may vary. Possible answers follow. **1.** He must plant many acres of corn. **2.** He will store his corn in that tall silo. **3.** He could feed some of his corn to his cattle. **4.** Ben has tended his fields carefully. **5.** Ben can live on his farm for a long time. **6.** Luisa is stitching the most beautiful quilt by hand. **7.** She should show her quilt at the fair. **8.** She did enter it in the craft contest. **9.** Her quilt will be awarded the first prize. **10.** Luisa certainly should feel proud of her skills as a quilter.

3 Reinforce and Extend

LEARNING STYLES

Visual/Spatial

Provide students with magazines, and ask them to find pictures that illustrate different types of actions. Have students cut out the pictures and tape them to the board. Next, have each student write a sentence using the picture instead of the main verb. Students will need to fill in helping verbs and add -ed for past tenses. When students have finished, have them read their sentences to the rest of the class.

Present tense
The verb tense that tells about action in the present

Verbs that tell about action that takes place now or continues to take place are in the **present tense.** There are four present tense verb forms.

EXAMPLE
Emily plays soccer.
Emily is playing on a team.
Emily has played well all season.
Emily has been playing soccer for three years.

The helping verbs for present tense are *am, is, are, have, has, has been,* and *have been.*

EXAMPLE
I am running.   You have run.
He is running.   She has run.
They are running.   We have been running.

Activity A Number your paper from 1 to 4. Rewrite the following sentence four times. Each time, use a different form of the present tense for the verb *wait.*

Hulk, the dog, _____ for a bone.

Verbs must agree with their subjects. Many verbs add an *-s* or *-es* to their present tense form when the subject of a sentence is singular.

EXAMPLE
Singular subject   Aram looks.   He watches.
Plural subject   Aram and Joe look.   They watch.

In sentences with verb phrases, the helping verbs must agree with the subjects.

EXAMPLE
Singular subject   Juanita does look.   She is watching.
Plural subject   I do look.   We are watching.

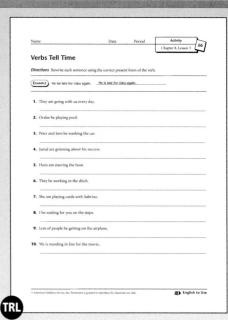

Writing Tip

A change in tense shows a change in the time of action. Do not change from one tense to another while writing unless you need to show the order of events.

Never use *be* as a helping verb in present tense verbs. Never use *been* alone as a helping verb or as a main verb. Use *has* or *have* with *been*.

EXAMPLE

Incorrect	They be waiting for a letter.
Correct	They are waiting for a letter.
Incorrect	They been waiting for a month.
Correct	They have been waiting for a month.

Activity B Write these sentences using the correct present tense forms of the verbs.

1. I be going to the street fair.
2. They am going with me.
3. I been walking down the road.
4. We has been talking with friends.
5. Danny am shopping at the store.
6. He be shopping with her.
7. We is riding the bus uptown.
8. Terri been sitting by the window.
9. We was working all evening.
10. She am studying for a test.
11. I been looking out the window.
12. They is looking for a place to live.
13. Michiko and Tim has been driving all night.
14. She be in class all day.
15. Joe work at the gas station.

Activity A Answers

Accept answers in any order.
1. Hulk, the dog, waits for a bone. 2. Hulk, the dog, is waiting for a bone. 3. Hulk, the dog, has waited for a bone. 4. Hulk, the dog, has been waiting for a bone.

Activity B Answers

Answers may vary, but all verbs should be in the correct present tense form. Possible answers follow. 1. am going 2. are going 3. have been walking 4. have been talking 5. is shopping 6. is shopping 7. are riding 8. has been sitting 9. were working 10. is studying 11. have been looking 12. are looking 13. have been driving 14. is 15. works

 3 **Reinforce and Extend**

LEARNING STYLES

 LEP/ESL
Different languages use a variety of styles to express ongoing action and present tense forms. Invite students who speak a different language to translate the sentences in the example and to write the translations on the board. Discuss the ways that different languages express the concept of tenses and ongoing action.

TEACHER ALERT

 Notice that Lessons 3, 4, and 5 are parallel in their presentation of present, past, and future tenses.

GLOBAL CONNECTION

In most languages, the verb *be* is irregular. Some languages have different words or forms for different situations. For example, the Spanish verb *estar* appears in sentences that tell location. *Ser* appears in sentences describing a person. Both verbs have irregular forms. Both *soy* and *estoy* mean "I am." Ask students who speak Spanish or other languages to provide examples of *be* verbs for the class.

TRL
Sentence Diagramming Activity 39

Chapter 8 Lesson 4

Overview This lesson presents four forms of the past tense and reminds students about subject/verb agreement.

Objectives

- To write correct forms of a verb in the past tense
- To correct improper forms of past tense verbs

Student Pages 164–165

Teacher's Resource Library

Workbook Activity 67

Activity 67

Alternative Activity 67

Sentence Diagramming Activity 40

Vocabulary

past tense

1 Warm-Up Activity

Ask volunteers to use the verb *eat* to describe an event that happened in the past. Have students write their sentences on the board and circle the verb forms. Then ask students when each event happened. Discuss with students how the past tense can describe a variety of activities that happen over time.

Say and write on the board: *Yesterday you learned. Yesterday you were learning. Yesterday you had learned. Yesterday you had been learning.* Change the pronouns in the sentences. With each new pronoun, help students recognize any changes in the form of the helping verb *be.*

2 Teaching the Lesson

Focus students' attention on the first example box. Note that the helping verb *had* does not change the form of the main verb unless another helping verb (*been*) follows *had.* Model sentences in the next two example boxes for students.

Lesson 4 | The Past Tense

Verbs that tell about action that happened in the past are in the **past tense.** There are four past tense verb forms.

Past tense
The verb tense that tells about action in the past

> **EXAMPLE**
> Emily played soccer.
> Emily was playing well.
> Emily had played many times.
> Emily had been playing goalie.

The helping verbs for past tense are *was, were, had,* and *had been.*

> **EXAMPLE**
> I was running.   You were running.
> She had run.   They had been running.

Activity A Number your paper from 1 to 4. Rewrite the following sentence four times. Each time, use a different form of the past tense for the verb *wait.*

Hulk, the dog, _____ for a bone.

Use the correct form of the helping verb *be* in past tense verbs. Remember that a singular subject takes a singular form of the verb. *You* is always a plural subject.

> **EXAMPLE**
> **Singular subject**   I was looking.
>   He was watching.
> **Plural subject**   You were looking.
>   Holly and Kentaro were watching.

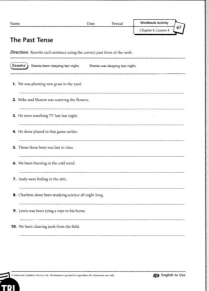

Workbook Activity 67

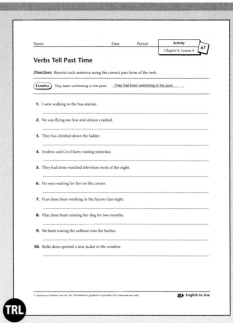

Activity 67

Signal words and phrases also help make the time of the action clear. Words and phrases such as *yesterday, today, tomorrow, this year,* and *this summer* tell about time.

Do not use *done* as a helping verb in past tense verbs. The combination *done been* is never correct. Use the helping verb *had* with *been* in past tense verbs.

 EXAMPLE

Incorrect	They done waited for a month.
Correct	They waited for a month.
Correct	They were waiting for a month.
Incorrect	They done been waiting for a letter.
Correct	They had been waiting for a letter.

Activity B Write these sentences using the correct past tense forms of the verbs.

1. They was heading for home.
2. They had done fished all day.
3. I were fishing, too.
4. We was talking about movies.
5. Ellen been walking with her folks.
6. I been waiting for them.
7. I done helped them.
8. Lucy have bowled a perfect game.
9. Jeff been working at the post office.
10. You was waiting at the station.
11. They had done been gone since yesterday.
12. We been waiting for you.
13. He done seen that video three times.
14. The girls was swimming in the pool.
15. I were helping Brad load the truck.

Verbs Tell Time Chapter 8 **165**

Writing Practice

Draw students' attention to the note on signal words and phrases on page 165. Then ask students to think back to their last birthday and ahead to their next birthday. Have each student write a short paragraph about the events that have happened and will happen between the two birthdays. Remind students to mark the passage of months with signal words and phrases.

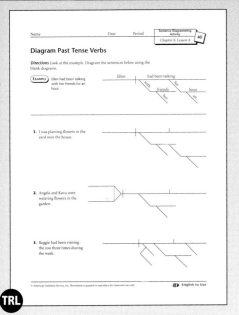

Activity A Answers

Accept answers in any order.
1. Hulk, the dog, waited for a bone.
2. Hulk, the dog, was waiting for a bone. 3. Hulk, the dog, had waited for a bone. 4. Hulk, the dog, had been waiting for a bone.

Activity B Answers

Answers may vary, but all verbs should be in the correct past tense form. Possible answers follow.
1. were heading 2. had fished
3. was fishing 4. were talking
5. had been walking 6. was waiting
7. helped 8. had bowled 9. worked
10. were waiting 11. had been gone 12. had been waiting 13. saw
14. were swimming 15. was helping

 3 **Reinforce and Extend**

LEARNING STYLES

Interpersonal/Group
Have students work in pairs. Assign each student pair a particular verb. Then have student pairs write a short story using the four forms of the verb's present tense and the four forms of the verb's past tense. Challenge students to use as many of the eight verb forms as they can.

IN THE COMMUNITY

Ask students to keep daily notes about the places they pass or visit during the course of a week, such as stores, offices, parks, restaurants, and schools. Have each student write two sentences about each place, using different past tense verb forms. Here are some examples: *I visited Ron's Grocery Store. I bought an orange. We had been passing the library all week. On Wednesday, we went in and checked out some books.*

Lesson at a Glance

Chapter 8 Lesson 5

Overview This lesson presents four forms of the future tense.

Objectives

- To write correct forms of a verb in the future tense
- To correct improper forms of future tense verbs

Student Pages 166–167

Teacher's Resource Library TRL

Workbook Activity 68

Activity 68

Alternative Activity 68

Sentence Diagramming Activity 41

Vocabulary

future tense

1 Warm-Up Activity

Ask students to name some of the activities in which they will participate during an upcoming vacation. Ask students to determine the number of days or weeks that will pass before a particular event takes place. Discuss with students how they can use future tense to discuss events that will happen right away, as well as events that will not take place for years.

Write on the board the future tense forms of the verb *dance*: *I will dance. I will be dancing. I will have danced. I will have been dancing.* Ask students to use one of the future tense verb forms to create sentences that describe activities they might do during an upcoming vacation. Have volunteers write their sentences on the board and underline each future tense verb.

2 Teaching the Lesson

Ask students to look at the first example box. Tell them that the helping verb *will* can go with all future tense verb forms. Point out that *been* always comes after *will have* in future tense forms.

Future tense
The verb tense that tells about action in the future

Verbs that tell about action that has not yet happened are in the **future tense.** There are four future tense verb forms.

> **EXAMPLE**
> Emily will play soccer again.
> Emily will be playing hard.
> Emily will have played more games.
> Emily will have been playing goalie all season.

Writing Tip

You can also use the phrases *about to* and *going to* to tell about action in the future. Just combine the phrase with a form of *be* and a verb.

Example I am about to leave. I am going to play.

All forms of verbs in the future tense need the helping verb *will*. Some future forms need other helping verbs, too. The helping verbs for future tense are *will, will be, will have,* and *will have been.*

> **EXAMPLE**
> I will run.
> She will have run.
> You will be running.
> They will have been running.

Activity A Number your paper from 1 to 4. Rewrite the following sentence four times. Each time, use a different form of the future tense for the verb *wait.*

> Hulk, the dog, _____ for a bone.

Never use *be* as a helping verb in future tense verbs. Always use *will have* with *been* in future tense verbs.

> **EXAMPLE**
> | Incorrect | The bus be coming soon. |
> | Correct | The bus will be coming soon. |
> | Incorrect | In a few days, they been waiting for a month. |
> | Correct | In a few days, they will have been waiting for a month. |

Workbook Activity 68

Activity 68

B

U

S

Soon

Coming

Will

The bus will be
coming soon.

Activity B Write these sentences using the correct future tense forms of the verbs. Remember that all verbs in future tense use the helping verb *will*.

1. Brenda and Sam be doing well.
2. I be doing well next year.
3. The whole group be needing some food.
4. Everyone eating really well.
5. We be working with him.
6. Her car be needing new tires soon.
7. They work hard next year.
8. The dark clouds drop rain later this afternoon.
9. Stan be taking three tests tomorrow.
10. Midori work nights next week.
11. He be sorry tomorrow.
12. Mike be doing better in school next year.
13. I be ready for anything next week.
14. We be early for school tomorrow.
15. Jane be planning a surprise for her friend Chris.

Activity A Answers

Accept answers in any order.
1. Hulk, the dog, will wait for a bone. **2.** Hulk, the dog, will be waiting for a bone. **3.** Hulk, the dog, will have waited for a bone. **4.** Hulk, the dog, will have been waiting for a bone.

Activity B Answers

Answers may vary, but all verbs should be in the correct future tense form. Possible answers follow. **1.** will do **2.** will do **3.** will be needing **4.** will eat **5.** will have worked **6.** will need **7.** will work **8.** will drop **9.** will be taking **10.** will be working **11.** will be **12.** will do **13.** will be **14.** will be **15.** will plan

3 **Reinforce and Extend**

LEARNING STYLES

Body/Kinesthetic
Have students work in groups of three to write a short story that involves past, present, and future tenses. Assign each student one of the verb tenses to act out when he or she uses the tense in the story. Each student should read aloud the sentence that includes his or her verb tense, using gestures to show the action, if appropriate.

AT HOME

In Lessons 3–5, the sentences in Activity B include nonstandard speech patterns that students may use or hear in informal conversation. Encourage students to note occasions when they use nonstandard English and to consider why it is important to know and use standard English.

ASL ILLUSTRATION

Draw students' attention to the way this ASL sentence spells out *bus* rather than providing a sign for it. In addition, you may want to review the ASL feature on page 159 so that students can compare the future tense verbs *will be coming* and *will smile*. Point out that ASL uses the sign for *soon* to convey the idea of *will be coming*.

| Name | Date | Period | Sentence Diagramming Activity 41 |
Chapter 8, Lesson 5

Diagram Future Tense Verbs

Directions Look at the example. Diagram the sentences below using the blank diagrams.

EXAMPLE Jack will play softball tonight.   Jack | will play | softball / tonight

1. You will find it soon.

2. He will receive a much higher grade in this class.

3. Brenna will be moving today.

4. Kelly will be cooking all day.

English to Use

Sentence Diagramming Activity 41

Lesson at a Glance

Chapter 8 Lesson 6

Overview This lesson defines negatives and explains how they affect the meaning of verbs.

Objectives

- To identify verb phrases and negatives
- To recognize that negatives are not part of the verb phrase
- To identify the tenses of verbs with negatives

Student Pages 168–169

Teacher's Resource Library

Workbook Activity 69

Activity 69

Alternative Activity 69

Vocabulary

negative

 1 Warm-Up Activity

Say and write on the board: *I am going on vacation soon.* Ask students to identify the verb phrase and its tense (*am going*, present tense). Then write: *I am not going on vacation soon.*

Have students identify the word you added to the sentence and ask them how that word changes the meaning of the sentence. Discuss with students how the word *not* makes the sentences contradict each other. Emphasize that *not* does not change the construction of the sentence or the tense of the verb phrase *am going*.

 2 Teaching the Lesson

Discuss the definition of negatives, as well as the examples on page 168. Help students find the verb phrases (*is giving, had met, will know*).

Review the past, present, and future tenses and ask volunteers to create sentences containing each of these tenses used with a negative.

Negative
A word that means "no" or "not" and that stops the action of the verb

A **negative** is a word that means "no" or "not." Negatives, such as *not* and *never*, often come between the helping verb and the main verb in a verb phrase. Negatives may go with present, past, and future tense verb forms.

EXAMPLE

Present tense	Oliva is *not* giving guitar lessons this summer.
Past tense	We had *never* met our new coach.
Future tense	She will *not* know our names.

(The verb phrase in each example sentence is in color. *Not* and *never* are adverbs. *Not* and *never* are never part of a verb phrase.)

Activity A Write these sentences on your paper. Underline the verb phrases in the sentences. Circle the negatives.

1. The storm will not be blowing from the east.
2. They will never walk on the beach again.
3. The waves had not covered the whole beach.
4. Waves have not been smashing against the shore for very long.
5. The stores near the beach were not opening their doors.
6. Many people will not forget that awful storm.
7. John has never gone to the beach before, and he has not seen a big storm on the coast.
8. The storm has not arrived yet, but it will not cause much damage.
9. People will not pull their boats from the water.
10. This coast will never be the same.

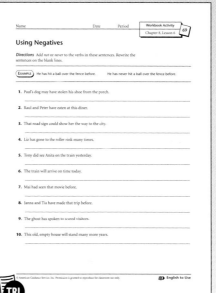

Workbook Activity 69 — Activity 69

Activity B Add *not* or *never* to the verbs in these sentences. Write the sentences on your paper. Underline the verb phrases. Then write whether the verb is in *present tense*, *past tense*, or *future tense*.

Example   The lighthouse had been warning ships about the rocks.

The lighthouse <u>had</u> not <u>been warning</u> ships about the rocks.—past tense

1. Small houses are clustered around the lighthouse.
2. The keeper of the lighthouse is living there.
3. He has been staying in the lighthouse most nights.
4. He will have lived near the lighthouse for seven years.
5. She will hold the meeting here.
6. Others will be coming to her office for the meeting.
7. She will make a deal.
8. She will be building the new place in another six months.
9. Phil and his horse are riding in many events of the rodeo.
10. His horse has jumped over barrels.
11. Phil had roped calves.
12. Phil had won prizes at the rodeo.
13. Alfredo has been using his computer every day.
14. He is playing video games with his friends.
15. This computer will solve all of Alfredo's problems.

The lighthouse stands on the shore.

Verbs Tell Time   Chapter 8   **169**

---

 3 Reinforce and Extend

LEARNING STYLES

Interpersonal/Group

Ask each student to write a positive sentence and then to exchange his or her paper with a partner. Have partners rewrite the original sentences as negative statements. Ask students to read both versions aloud for class critique or in writing response groups.

Speaking Practice

Have students work in pairs. Ask them to read aloud each of the sentences in Activity B. One partner should make the sentence negative by adding *never*, and the other should make the sentence negative by adding *not*. After students read the sentences aloud, have them compare the placement of *never* and *not* and the word order of the sentences.

Activity A Answers

1. The storm <u>will</u> (not) be <u>blowing</u> from the east. 2. They <u>will</u> (never) <u>walk</u> on the beach again. 3. The waves <u>had</u> (not) <u>covered</u> the whole beach. 4. Waves <u>have</u> (not) <u>been smashing</u> against the shore for very long. 5. The stores near the beach <u>were</u> (not) <u>opening</u> their doors. 6. Many people <u>will</u> (not) <u>forget</u> that awful storm. 7. John <u>has</u> (never) <u>gone</u> to the beach before, and he <u>has</u> (not) <u>seen</u> a big storm on the coast. 8. The storm <u>has</u> (not) <u>arrived</u> yet, but it <u>will</u> (not) <u>cause</u> much damage. 9. People <u>will</u> (not) <u>pull</u> their boats from the water. 10. This coast <u>will</u> (never) <u>be</u> the same.

Activity B Answers

Some answers may vary. 1. Small houses <u>are</u> not <u>clustered</u> around the lighthouse.—present tense 2. The keeper of the lighthouse <u>is</u> not <u>living</u> there.—present tense 3. He <u>has</u> not <u>been staying</u> in the lighthouse most nights.—present tense 4. He <u>will</u> not <u>have lived</u> near the lighthouse for seven years.—future tense 5. She <u>will</u> never <u>hold</u> the meeting here.—future tense 6. Others <u>will</u> not <u>be coming</u> to her office for the meeting.—future tense 7. She <u>will</u> never <u>make</u> a deal.—future tense 8. She <u>will</u> not <u>be building</u> the new place in another six months.—future tense 9. Phil and his horse <u>are</u> not <u>riding</u> in many events of the rodeo.—present tense 10. His horse <u>has</u> never <u>jumped</u> over barrels.—present tense 11. Phil <u>had</u> not <u>roped</u> calves.—past tense 12. Phil <u>had</u> never <u>won</u> prizes at the rodeo.—past tense 13. Alfredo <u>has</u> not <u>been using</u> his computer every day.—present tense 14. He <u>is</u> not <u>playing</u> video games with his friends.—present tense 15. This computer <u>will</u> never <u>solve</u> all of Alfredo's problems.—future tense

Chapter 8 Lesson 7

Overview This lesson introduces irregular verbs.

Objective

■ To write the correct form for irregular verbs in sentences

Student Pages 170–171

Teacher's Resource Library **TRL**

Workbook Activity 70

Activity 70

Alternative Activity 70

Vocabulary

irregular verb

1 Warm-Up Activity

Write the following verbs on the board: *eat, throw,* and *sing.* Now add *-ed* to the words and use each of them in a sentence, such as *Yesterday, I singed.* Ask students whether that sentence sounds correct. Tell students that most past tense verbs end in *-ed* but that this rule does not apply to irregular verbs. Ask students to create sentences that correctly use the past tense of *eat, throw,* and *sing.*

2 Teaching the Lesson

Discuss the information presented in the definition and example box. Focus on the list of irregular verbs. Allow students to practice using each form of the verbs in sentences. Emphasize that if students are not sure of how to form a tense, they can check the dictionary. Have students use the dictionary to check the verb forms of these irregular verbs: *keep, teach,* and *find.*

Review with students the irregular forms of the verb *be* and ask them for instances in which they may have heard *be* used incorrectly in everyday conversation.

Irregular verb
A verb that changes its form to form past tenses

You have learned that regular verbs form their past tense by adding *-d* or *-ed* to their present form. Some regular verbs such as *burn* and *dream* can also add *-t* to form their past tense.

EXAMPLE

Present tense	burn	dream
Past tense	burned or burnt	dreamed or dreamt

Irregular verbs do not add *-d* or *-ed* to form their past tenses. They form their tenses in other ways. Study this list of irregular verbs. These verbs do not follow any pattern. The only way that you can remember their different forms is to memorize them.

Present	Past	With a Helping Verb
break	broke	(has) broken
bend	bent	(has) bent
burst	burst	(has) burst
catch	caught	(has) caught
come	came	(has) come
drink	drank	(has) drunk
drive	drove	(has) driven
eat	ate	(has) eaten
know	knew	(has) known
ride	rode	(has) ridden
run	ran	(has) run
see	saw	(has) seen
spring	sprang	(has) sprung
swim	swam	(has) swum
take	took	(has) taken
throw	threw	(has) thrown
write	wrote	(has) written

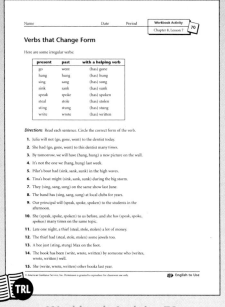

Workbook Activity 70

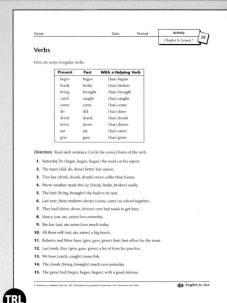

Activity 70

Activity A On your paper, write the correct form of each verb in these sentences. Then write whether the verb is *present tense,* *past tense,* or *future tense.*

1. The three friends have never _____ out to the island. (swim)

2. They _____ some practice laps yesterday. (swim)

3. Sharon will not _____ to the lake with us. (come)

4. The friends have _____ many large fish in that lake. (catch)

5. Over the years, much bait has been _____ into the lake. (throw)

6. The cowboys must have _____ the cattle across the ranch. (drive)

7. They had _____ long and hard for weeks. (ride)

8. At camp, Frank has _____ one calf to the ground. (throw)

9. A cowboy's life has always _____ a lot of hard work. (take)

10. Yesterday, Frank _____ his rope around many cattle. (throw)

11. Next time, we will _____ it in a bucket. (catch)

12. Rita had never _____ anyone as talented as her dance teacher. (know)

13. Rita has _____ of dancing in Broadway shows. (dream)

14. She had _____ her leg badly as a young child. (broke)

15. Afterward, she _____ dancing lessons for therapy. (take)

Students in the dance class practice their steps.

Activity A Answers

1. swum—present tense 2. swam—past tense 3. come—future tense 4. caught—present tense 5. thrown—present tense 6. driven—present tense 7. ridden—past tense 8. thrown—present tense 9. taken—present tense 10. threw—past tense 11. catch—future tense 12. known—past tense 13. dreamed—present tense (*or* dreamt—present tense) 14. broken—past tense 15. took—past tense

3 Reinforce and Extend

LEARNING STYLES

LEP/ESL

Have students who speak other languages translate a few of the irregular verbs from the list on page 170 into their first languages. Ask volunteers to translate both the present and the past tenses so that that the rest of the class can see whether these verbs are regular or irregular. If possible, ask a volunteer to translate a word that takes a special form, as do the irregular verbs in English. Have volunteers discuss whether irregular forms are difficult for them to learn or remember and what strategies help them learn these words.

LEARNING STYLES

Auditory/Verbal

Ask students to choose one or two of the irregular verbs from the chart on page 170 and write sentences in the past tense, present tense, and future tense with helping verbs. Have students say the sentences aloud. As students read their sentences, have them identify verb forms that are particularly difficult for them to use correctly. In addition, students can indicate when nonstandard verb forms may "sound" more correct. Give special time and attention to these problem verb forms and have students model the correct forms more than once.

Lesson at a Glance

Chapter 8 Lesson 8

Overview This lesson challenges students to practice verb tenses in creative writing activities.

Objectives
- To apply the writing process
- To practice writing creatively

Student Pages 172–173

Teacher's Resource Library **TRL**

Workbook Activity 71

Activity 71

Alternative Activity 71

---

 1 Warm-Up Activity

Discuss with students the types of subjects that they enjoy writing about and have them give examples of writing projects they have enjoyed. Then ask them about writing projects that they have found difficult. Ask them to explain why certain projects have been frustrating, while others have given them a feeling of success. Tell students that all writers work hard and that even for professional writers, writing can be a difficult task.

2 Teaching the Lesson

Remind students that they will probably be less frustrated about writing if they do not try to do the entire project all at once. Review the steps in the writing process—prewrite, write, rewrite, and edit—and ask students which of these steps they find most difficult or most enjoyable. Have students share strategies that have helped them work through these steps in the past.

Tell students that being interested in a topic can greatly improve the writing experience. Have students brainstorm ideas for Activity A, discussing different ways that they could approach writing a children's story about a dragon. Help students see that there are many approaches to such a story and discuss with them how they could write it as a mystery, a comedy, or a love story.

Your writing should create images in the minds of others. A good writer can make readers think they are taking part in the story.

Activity A Write a children's story about a dragon. Have your story take place in the past. Follow the four steps in the writing process.

1. **Prewrite.** Think about stories that children enjoy. Think about dragons, and pretend they really did exist sometime in the past.

   > **List words to describe the dragon. Ask:**
   > Is the dragon friendly? clumsy? brave or not? Does it have a funny tail? fiery breath? Does it laugh? giggle? growl?

2. **Write.** Give your dragon a name. Write about what it saw and where it went. Write about what it did. Use your list of describing words.

   > **Example of a beginning:**
   > howard was a sily dragon with a funny tail. he meets a little boy who wanted a ride.

3. **Rewrite.** Look at what you wrote. Would a young child enjoy your story? Is it exciting? funny? scary? Can you make it more interesting?

   > **Example of a beginning rewrite:**
   > Once upon a time, a very sily dragon named howard meets a little boy. the boy looks at the big dragon and says in a small brave voice may I have a ride.

4. **Edit.** Check to make sure that the verbs are all in the past tense. Check for spelling, end marks, and commas.

172 *Chapter 8   Verbs Tell Time*

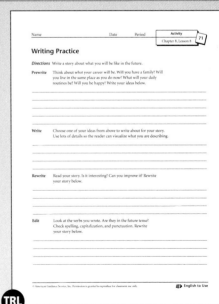

Workbook Activity 71   Activity 71

---

172 *Chapter 8   Verbs Tell Time*

Review a classmate's story. Do the verbs agree in number with their subjects? Are negatives correct? Are past forms of irregular verbs correct? Give suggestions for corrections. Share ideas about other ways to improve the story.

Example of an edited beginning:
Once upon a time, a very silly dragon named Howard met a little boy. The boy looked at the big dragon and said in a small, brave voice, "May I have a ride?"

Activity B Write a story about something that is happening right now. Follow the steps of the writing process.

1. **Prewrite.** Think about a man driving a car, a woman working, or a child playing a game. Choose one of these people to be the main character in your story.

2. **Write.** Write about what the person is doing now. Where is the person? What's happening? Is the person happy or sad? laughing or crying? running or sitting? eating or sleeping? What will happen to the person by the end of the story?

3. **Rewrite.** Read your story. Is it interesting? Can you improve it? Try to make it better.

4. **Edit.** Look at the verbs you wrote. The story happens in the present time. Are your verbs all in present tense? Check spelling, end marks, and commas.

Activity C Write a story that takes place in the future. Follow the steps of the writing process.

1. **Prewrite.** Think about ways people will travel in the future. Think about spaceships. Pretend a spaceship will take tourists to Jupiter.

2. **Write.** Write about a trip to Jupiter. Who will be on the trip? What funny or scary things will happen on the way?

3. **Rewrite.** Read your story. Is it exciting? Can you make it more interesting? Rewrite sentences to improve your story.

4. **Edit.** Look at the verbs you wrote. Your story takes place in the future. Are your verbs correct? Check spelling, end marks, and commas.

Verbs Tell Time *Chapter 8* **173**

Activity A Answers

Stories will vary. Make sure that students have used past tense verbs correctly.

Activity B Answers

Stories will vary. Make sure that students have used present tense verbs correctly.

Activity C Answers

Stories will vary. Make sure that students have used future tense verbs correctly.

Using What You've Learned

Discuss with students different strategies for reviewing other people's stories. For example, students might want to read the story through once, looking only at the punctuation. They may want to skim the story a second time as they check the verbs. Remind students that checking all of the elements of mechanics and punctuation would be difficult to do in one reading.

3 Reinforce and Extend

LEARNING STYLES

Auditory/Verbal
Arrange for students to read their dragon stories to children and their other stories to appropriate audiences. Discuss with students how they can modulate their voices—speeding up, slowing down, speaking more loudly or softly—to maintain audience interest.

ONLINE CONNECTION

The National Council of Teachers of English site has a list of teaching ideas submitted by teachers and selected from NCTE publications. To see their suggestions for writing activities, visit *www.ncte.org/teach/write.shtml.*

Lesson at a Glance

Chapter 8 Lesson 9

Overview This lesson explains how to form contractions.

Objectives

- To add apostrophes to existing contractions
- To form contractions
- To choose correct definitions for terms

Student Pages 174–175

Teacher's Resource Library

Workbook Activity 72

Activity 72

Alternative Activity 72

Vocabulary

contraction

1 Warm-Up Activity

Introduce contractions by saying and writing on the board: *I am a teacher. You are a student.* Ask students to provide contractions for the underlined words (*I'm, You're*). Write the contractions in place of the underlined words on the board, pointing out the apostrophe in each example. Then review the list of contractions. Ask students to note the letters that the apostrophe replaces in each contraction. Invite volunteers to use contractions in sentences.

2 Teaching the Lesson

Discuss with students how we use contractions in everyday speech. Ask volunteers to read the example sentences without using contractions and then talk about why the sentences that use full words sound more formal.

Bring to students' attention the contraction *won't* and discuss how it is different from the other contractions on the list. Point out to students that the vowel changes from *i* to *o* in this instance.

A **contraction** is one word made from two words. A contraction needs an apostrophe. Remember that an apostrophe is a punctuation mark. It takes the place of letters that you leave out when you form a contraction.

Contraction
A word formed when two words are put together and letters are left out

EXAMPLE

| let + us = let's | Let's go swimming. |
| that + is = that's | That's a good idea. |

A pronoun + a helping verb:
I + am = I'm
you + are = you're
we + are = we're
they + are = they're
she, he, it + is = she's, he's, it's

I + will = I'll
you + will = you'll
we + will = we'll
they + will = they'll
she, he, it + will = she'll, he'll, it'll

I + have = I've
you + have = you've
we + have = we've
they + have = they've

I + would = I'd
you + would = you'd
we + would = we'd
they + would = they'd
she, he, it + would = she'd, he'd, it'd

A verb + the adverb *not*:
are + not = aren't
were + not = weren't
has + not = hasn't
is + not = isn't
do + not = don't
does + not = doesn't
did + not = didn't
will + not = won't
could + not = couldn't
would + not = wouldn't
should + not = shouldn't

174 *Chapter 8   Verbs Tell Time*

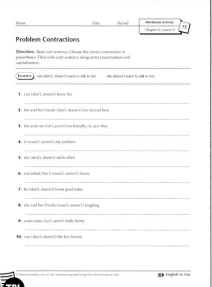

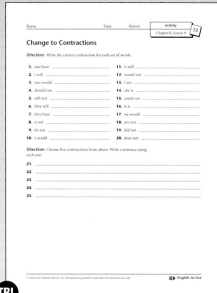

Workbook Activity 72   Activity 72

Writing Tip

We often use contractions when speaking. For this reason, we think of them as informal. In general, you should avoid using contractions in formal writing, such as reports and essays.

Find *will* + *not* on the chart on page 174. Notice that the contraction *won't* does not follow the usual pattern for forming contractions. Remember *will* + *not* = *won't*.

Activity A On your paper, write the contractions in these sentences correctly.

1. Its here somewhere.
2. Ive lost it, and its not on the table now.
3. Shell look on that other table for me.
4. It couldnt just walk away.
5. Ill find it soon, and I wont lose it again.

Activity B Change each pair of underlined words to a contraction. Write the contractions on your paper.

1. <u>He is</u> having a problem and <u>does not</u> know it.
2. He <u>should not</u> lose things.
3. <u>You are</u> going to keep track of your papers.
4. He <u>did not</u> find that last sheet of paper.
5. He <u>has not</u> looked in the desk, and <u>that is</u> where it is.

Activity C Match the words with their meanings. Write the number and its correct letter on your paper.

Words	Meanings
1. present	**A** yesterday
2. past	**B** tomorrow
3. future	**C** helping verb plus main verb
4. contraction	**D** today
5. verb phrase	**E** needs an apostrophe

Activity A Answers

1. It's **2.** I've; it's **3.** She'll
4. couldn't **5.** I'll; won't

Activity B Answers

1. He's; doesn't **2.** shouldn't
3. You're **4.** didn't **5.** hasn't; that's

Activity C Answers

1. D **2.** A **3.** B **4.** E **5.** C

 3 Reinforce and Extend

LEARNING STYLES

 Logical/Mathematical
Help students understand contraction patterns by asking them to create word clusters around the omitted letters. Have students make a list of the letters that are missing from words used in contractions: for example, the *o* from *not*, the *oul* from *would*, *should*, and *could*, and the *i* from *is*. Then have students list as many words that include that deleted letter as they can.

CAREER CONNECTION

 Many workplaces post lists of rules for employees. These rules can relate to safety issues, customer relations, employee relations, company policies, and so on. Ask students to read some company rules at their own or another's workplace. Ask them to note the use or absence of contractions in the rules and to report on which contractions occur most frequently.

Chapter 8 Review

Use the Chapter Review to prepare students for tests and to reteach content from the chapter.

Chapter 8 Mastery Test

The Teacher's Resource Library includes two parallel forms of the Chapter 8 Mastery Test. The difficulty level of the two forms is equivalent. You may wish to use one form as a pretest and the other form as a posttest.

REVIEW ANSWERS

Part A

1. present tense 2. verb phrase
3. negative 4. regular verb
5. tense 6. future tense
7. contraction 8. irregular verb
9. past tense 10. helping verb

Part B

11. (had) begun—past
12. (has been) going—present
13. (will have) broken—future
14. (have) given—present

Part C

15. ridden 16. eaten 17. drunk
18. see

Part D

19. makes 20. uses 21. costs
22. feeds; weighs

Chapter 8 R E V I E W

Part A Use the words from the Word Bank to complete sentences 1–10.

Word Bank
contraction
future tense
helping verb
irregular verb
negative
past tense
present tense
regular verb
tense
verb phrase

1. The tense that tells about action in the present is _____ .
2. A _____ is a verb and its helpers.
3. A _____ is a word that means "no" or "not."
4. A verb that adds -d or -ed to form the past tense is a _____ .
5. The present, past, or future time expressed by a verb is its _____ .
6. The tense that tells about action in the future is _____ .
7. A _____ is one word made from two words.
8. An _____ changes its form in the past tense.
9. The tense that tells about action in the past is _____ .
10. A _____ is a verb that comes before the main verb.

Part B On your paper, write the verb phrase in each sentence. Label it *past, present,* or *future.* Circle the helping verbs, and underline the main verbs.

11. The trip had begun miles away and months ago.
12. Adam has been going through wild country.
13. The wagon will have broken down many times.
14. Heat and cold have given him a bad time.

Part C Write the correct form of each verb in parentheses.

15. By tonight, Adam will have _____ late. (ride)
16. He will have _____ by the campfire. (eat)
17. His mules will have _____ from a stream. (drink)
18. During the day, Adam will _____ many things. (see)

Part D Write the correct present tense form of each verb.

19. Ted (make) phone calls from his desk.
20. By the end of the season, Ted (use) his large machines.
21. Each machine (cost) a lot of money.
22. One machine (feed) his cattle, while another (weigh) them.

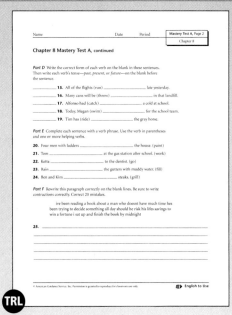

Chapter 8 Mastery Test A

Part E Number your paper from 23 to 26. Change all the verbs in Part D to past tense. Add helping verbs as needed.

Part F Number your paper from 27 to 30. Change all the verbs in Part D to future tense. Add helping verbs as needed.

Part G Add *not* or *never* to change the meaning of these sentences. Label each verb *action* or *linking*.

31. Denzel has been there.　　**34.** You will enjoy it.

32. It was fun.　　**35.** My friends are there.

33. Jane does like the place.

Part H Write these sentences correctly on your paper.

36. sometimes edna cant find the trail

37. she doesnt have a map

38. he doesnt have the energy left

39. we dont have a camp for the night

Part I Write these sentences correctly on your paper. Form contractions with the underlined words.

40. the tent <u>will not</u> stay up　　**42.** this trip <u>has not</u> been fun

41. oh <u>it is</u> raining hard now

Part J Write the letter of the correct word or group of words.

43. The football player _____ find his helmet.

　　A couldnt　　**B** couldn't　　**C** could'nt　　**D** coudn't

44. My favorite store at the mall _____ a sale next week.

　　A will have　　**B** has had　　**C** will had　　**D** had

45. The teacher had _____ the class on a field trip.

　　A took　　**B** tooken　　**C** taked　　**D** taken

If you will have to define terms on a test, write each term on one side of a card. Write its definition on the other. Then test yourself, or work with a partner.

REVIEW ANSWERS

Part E

23. made **24.** used (or had used)
25. had cost **26.** fed; weighed

Part F

27. will make **28.** will use (or will have used) **29.** will cost **30.** will feed; will weigh

Part G

Answers may vary. Possible answers follow. **31.** Denzel has never been there. **32.** It was not fun. **33.** Jane does not like the place. **34.** You will not enjoy it. **35.** My friends are never there.

(LINKING, LINKING, ACTION, ACTION, LINKING labels above respective verbs)

Part H

36. Sometimes, Edna can't find the trail. **37.** She doesn't have a map. **38.** He doesn't have the energy left. **39.** We don't have a camp for the night.

Part I

40. The tent won't stay up.
41. Oh, it's raining hard now.
42. This trip hasn't been fun.

Part J

43. B **44.** A **45.** D

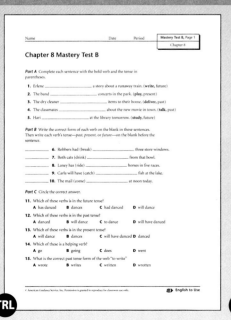

Chapter 8 Mastery Test B

Planning Guide

Be Exact

	Student Text Lesson			Language Skills		
	Student Pages	Vocabulary	Practice Activities	Identification Skills	Writing Skills	Punctuation Skills
Lesson 1 Writing for Yourself	180–181		✔	✔	✔	✔
Lesson 2 *Accept, Except; Teach, Learn*	182–183		✔	✔	✔	✔
Lesson 3 Pronouns or Contractions?	184–185		✔	✔	✔	✔
Lesson 4 *Lie, Lay; Sit, Set; Rise, Raise*	186–187		✔	✔	✔	
Lesson 5 *To, Too, Two; Let, Leave*	188–189		✔	✔	✔	
Lesson 6 Say *No* Only Once	190–191	✔	✔	✔	✔	✔
Lesson 7 Writing Practice	192–193		✔	✔	✔	✔
Lesson 8 Writing Mechanics	194–195	✔	✔	✔	✔	✔

Chapter Activities

Teacher's Resource Library
Community Connection 9:
Observing Your Surroundings
English in Your World 9:
Look It Up!

Assessment Options

Student Text
Chapter 9 Review

Teacher's Resource Library
Chapter 9 Mastery Tests A and B

Student Text Features					Teaching Strategies					Learning Styles						Teacher's Resource Library				
ASL Illustration	Communication Connection	Notes	Using What You've Learned	Writing Tips	Teacher Alert	Online Connection	Applications (Home, Career, Community, Global)	Speaking Practice	Writing Practice	Auditory/Verbal	Body/Kinesthetic	Interpersonal/ Group Learning	Logical/Mathematical	Visual/Spatial	LEP/ESL	Workbook Activities	Activities	Alternative Activities	Sentence Diagramming Activities	Self-Study Guide
				✔	181		181					181				73	73	73		✔
				✔					183		183					74	74	74		✔
185		✔			185								185			75	75	75		✔
		✔			187	187									187	76	76	76		✔
		✔						189				189				77	77	77		✔
	190				191		191							191		78	78	78		✔
				✔	193					193						79	79	79		✔
195			195				195									80	80	80		✔

Pronunciation Key

a	hat	e	let	ī	ice	ô	order	ù	put	sh	she		a	in about
ā	age	ē	equal	o	hot	oi	oil	ü	rule	th	thin		e	in taken
ä	far	ėr	term	ō	open	ou	out	ch	child	ŦH	then	ə	i	in pencil
â	care	i	it	ȯ	saw	u	cup	ng	long	zh	measure		o	in lemon
													u	in circus

Alternative Activities

The Teacher's Resource Library (TRL) contains a set of lower-level worksheets called Alternative Activities. These worksheets cover the same content as the regular Activities but are written at a second-grade reading level.

Skill Track Software

Use the Skill Track Software for English to Use for additional reinforcement of this chapter. The software program allows students using AGS textbooks to be assessed for mastery of each chapter and lesson of the textbook. Students access the software on an individual basis and are assessed with multiple-choice items.

Chapter 9: Be Exact
pages 178–197

Lessons

1. **Writing for Yourself**
   pages 180–181

2. *Accept, Except; Teach, Learn*
   pages 182–183

3. **Pronouns or Contractions?**
   pages 184–185

4. *Lie, Lay; Sit, Set; Rise, Raise*
   pages 186–187

5. *To, Too, Two; Let, Leave*
   pages 188–189

6. Say *No* Only Once
   pages 190–191

7. **Writing Practice**
   pages 192–193

8. **Writing Mechanics**
   pages 194–195

Chapter 9 Review
pages 196–197

Skill Track Software for English to Use

Teacher's Resource Library (TRL)

Workbook Activities 73–80

Activities 73–80

Alternative Activities 73–80

Community Connection 9

English in Your World 9

Chapter 9 Self-Study Guide

Chapter 9 Mastery Tests A and B

(Answer Keys for the Teacher's Resource Library begin on page 308 of this Teacher's Edition.)

Community Connection 9

English in Your World 9

Chapter

9

Be Exact

Have you ever looked closely at stained glass windows? They are made of hundreds of tiny pieces of glass that fit together perfectly to form an image. People who make stained glass windows must have the skill and the patience to fit the pieces of glass together like pieces of a puzzle.

Creating a stained glass window requires precision—using exactly the right piece in exactly the right spot. Similarly, it is important to use exact language when we speak and write. If we know exactly the right words to use, our ideas will be clear and easy to understand: our readers won't have to "fill in the blanks" to imagine what we meant.

In this chapter you will study ways to be more exact when you speak and write.

Goals for Learning

◆ To practice journal writing and note-taking

◆ To choose between easily confused words such as *accept/except* and *lie/lay*

◆ To use correctly words that sound alike but have different spellings

◆ To correct sentences with double negatives

◆ To practice writing a comparison and contrast paragraph

◆ To use correctly abbreviations for time of day and year

179

The editing process is a little like carving—you whittle away the rough or awkward parts of your writing, leaving only what is smooth and polished. Like whittling, editing is a process of being exact and expressing just what you mean.

In this chapter, you will study ways to be more exact when speaking and writing.

TEACHER'S RESOURCE

The AGS Teaching Strategies in English Transparencies may be used with this chapter. The transparencies add an interactive dimension to expand and enhance the *English to Use* program content.

CAREER INTEREST INVENTORY

The AGS Harrington-O'Shea Career Decision-Making System–Revised (CDM) may be used with this chapter. Students can use the CDM to explore their interests and identify careers. The CDM defines career areas that are indicated by students' responses on the inventory.

Writing Tips and Notes

Ask volunteers to read the tips and notes that appear in the margins throughout the chapter. Then discuss them with the class.

CHAPTER PROJECT

Have small groups describe a person or community group they admire. Have them use contrasting words to compare and contrast what the community would be like without that person or group. If time allows, students may want to interview the people and find out more about their work. Then have each group write a short comparison and contrast paragraph.

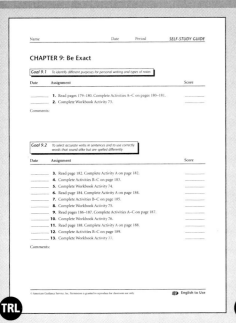

| Name | Date | Period | SELF-STUDY GUIDE |

CHAPTER 9: Be Exact

Goal 9.1   To identify different purposes for personal writing and types of notes

Date	Assignment	Score
	1. Read pages 179–180. Complete Activities A–C on pages 180–181.	
	2. Complete Workbook Activity 73.	

Comments:

Goal 9.2   To select accurate verbs in sentences and to use correctly words that sound alike but are spelled differently

Date	Assignment	Score
	3. Read page 182. Complete Activity A on page 182.	
	4. Complete Activities B–C on page 183.	
	5. Complete Workbook Activity 74.	
	6. Read page 184. Complete Activity A on page 184.	
	7. Complete Activities B–C on page 185.	
	8. Complete Workbook Activity 75.	
	9. Read pages 186–187. Complete Activities A–C on page 187.	
	10. Complete Workbook Activity 76.	
	11. Read page 188. Complete Activity A on page 188.	
	12. Complete Activities B–C on page 189.	
	13. Complete Workbook Activity 77.	

Comments:

© American Guidance Service, Inc. Permission is granted to reproduce for classroom use only.   **English to Use**

| Name | Date | Period | SELF-STUDY GUIDE |

CHAPTER 9 Be Exact, continued

Goal 9.3   To correct sentences with double negatives

Date	Assignment	Score
	14. Read page 190. Complete Activity A on page 191.	
	15. Complete Workbook Activity 78.	
	16. Read pages 192–193. Complete Activities A–B on page 193.	
	17. Complete Activities C–D on page 193.	
	18. Complete Workbook Activity 79.	

Comments:

Goal 9.4   To use abbreviations for time of day and year correctly

Date	Assignment	Score
	19. Read page 194. Complete Activity A on page 194.	
	20. Complete Activities B–C on pages 194–195.	
	21. Complete Workbook Activity 80.	
	22. Complete the Chapter 9 Review, Parts A–H on pages 196–197.	

Comments:

Student's Signature _____ Date _____

Instructor's Signature _____ Date _____

© American Guidance Service, Inc. Permission is granted to reproduce for classroom use only.   **English to Use**

TRL   TRL

Chapter 9 Self-Study Guide

Chapter 9 Lesson 1

Overview This lesson presents journal entries and note taking.

Objectives

■ To practice writing a journal entry
■ To select important facts for notes

Student Pages 180–181

Teacher's Resource Library

Workbook Activity 73
Activity 73
Alternative Activity 73

1 Warm-Up Activity

Bring to class a number of different types of note-taking materials such as the following: sticky notes, "while-you-were-out" memo pads, and odd pieces of scratch paper that may have notes written on them. Ask students which of the note-taking materials they are familiar with, and ask them to suggest any others that they can think of. Ask the class what type of information they might jot down as they take notes, and discuss with them the types of notes that they find most helpful in their daily activities.

2 Teaching the Lesson

Ask students to list times when they write for themselves. Through discussion, help students to talk about the diaries, journals, or class notes they may take. Other suggestions may include writing shopping lists, directions, addresses, and telephone messages.

Activity A Answers

Journal entries will vary. Check to make sure that students have used the suggested ideas. Remind students to write so that they can read entries at some later date.

Lesson 1 Writing for Yourself

Writing Tip

When you take notes, try to use your own words. Putting what you read in your own words is especially important if you plan to use your notes to write a report.

Have you ever seen an interesting looking person and thought he or she would make a great story character? Have you ever heard a joke and said to yourself, "I should write that down so I don't forget it"? Writing your ideas in a journal is one way to record your thoughts and preserve important memories. You can use any kind of notebook for a journal. Write in it as often as you like.

Activity A On your paper, practice writing a journal entry. Use these ideas.

• Put today's date on the top of the page.
• Write about the best part of today.
• Write about the worst part of today.
• Describe something you saw today in as much detail as you can recall. It can be anything—a bird in its nest, a dark rain cloud, a person you passed on the street.

When you want to remember facts and details from class, you can take notes. Notes should include the most important words and ideas. In order to be helpful, reminder notes need to be complete. They also should be neat enough to read and understand.

Activity B On your paper, write reminder notes using only important words from each sentence.

Example Abraham Lincoln, one of the wisest leaders of this country, was the sixteenth president.
Abraham Lincoln—16th president

1. In 1861, he became president of the United States during a time of trouble between the states.
2. His leadership during the Civil War made Lincoln famous.
3. Lincoln wanted all people to be free.
4. He signed a paper and gave African slaves their freedom.
5. People called him foolish, but he won the war.

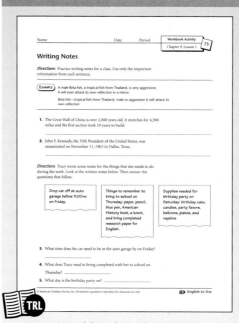

Workbook Activity 73

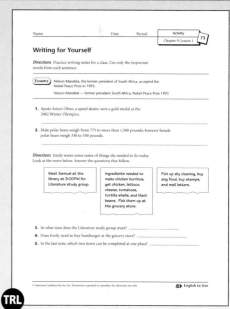

Activity 73

Activity C Write the letter of the note that has more information in each set on your paper. Then use the information in that note to write a more exact sentence.

1. Mary has an appointment.

   A   B

   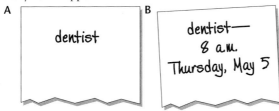

   dentist   dentist—
                     8 a.m.
                   Thursday, May 5

2. Paul has an errand to do.

   A   B

   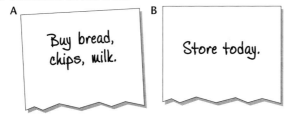

   Buy bread,   Store today.
   chips, milk.

3. Sasha is going downtown.

   A   B

   Meet a friend in   Meet Trina —
   front of store   4 p.m.
   this afternoon.   at 306 Walnut.

Activity B Answers

Answers will vary. Possible responses include the following: Lincoln, president—1861; Civil War—leadership made him famous; Lincoln—wanted all people free; Gave African slaves freedom; Was called foolish—won war

Activity C Answers

Answers will vary. Possible responses follow. **1.** B; Mary has a dentist appointment at 8:00 A.M. on Thursday, May 5. **2.** A; Paul is going to the store today to buy bread, chips, and milk. **3.** B; Sasha will meet Trina at 4:00 P.M. downtown at 306 Walnut Street.

3   **Reinforce and Extend**

LEARNING STYLES

Interpersonal/ Group Learning

Group students into pairs. Ask them to close their books and use their notes from Activity B as material to write a paragraph about Lincoln. If students have trouble remembering a fact or idea, they may ask a question of the entire class to see if others have that information.

AT HOME

Missed communication is often a problem in families. Phone messages are forgotten or shopping lists are left at home. Invite students to offer examples of missed communication that could have been avoided if someone had taken notes. Suggest that students talk with their family members about home situations calling for clearly written notes.

CAREER CONNECTION

Some companies have training programs for new employees and/or for employees promoted to new positions. A promotion often depends upon an employee's writing and speaking skills. Have students create a fictitious character with a position in a local company. Work with students to write a letter to the person's supervisor that explains everything that the person has learned while working at the company, how he or she learned these things, and what the person expects to learn if promoted and accepted into the training program.

TEACHER ALERT

Plagiarism is now harder to detect because of the availability of online resources for direct downloading. Emphasize that original materials are good sources for note-taking activities but that it is not legal or ethical to copy materials without naming the source.

Lesson at a Glance

Chapter 9 Lesson 2

Overview This lesson explains the correct usage of *accept* and *except*, *teach* and *learn*.

Objective

- To select the correct words for use in sentences

Student Pages 182–183

Teacher's Resource Library

Workbook Activity 74

Activity 74

Alternative Activity 74

1 Warm-Up Activity

Say and write on the board: *I accept all your ideas, except for the last one.* Discuss the meanings of *accept* and *except* and the differences in their spellings. Point out that because *accept* and *except* sound almost the same they are often confused.

Then say and write on the board: *Amy is learning Spanish; Juan is teaching her.* Ask students to explain the difference in meanings of the underlined verbs. Help students understand that *learn* is "to acquire knowledge" while *teach* is "to share knowledge."

2 Teaching the Lesson

Tell students that the words in this lesson are commonly confused and that, until they learn the words automatically, they probably ought to double-check their usage each time they use one. Tell students to think of *accept* as a word indicating that something is being included into a group. The word *except*, on the other hand, indicates that something is left out. It may help students learning the proper usage of *teach* and *learn* to remember the prepositions that often accompany these two words: "learn from" and "teach to."

Writing Tip

The word *accept* sometimes means "to agree to."

If you have to respond in writing to an invitation, use *accept*, not *except*.

People often confuse the words *accept* and *except*. *Accept* is a verb that means "to take" or "to receive."

EXAMPLE Guadalupe will accept the call.

Except can be a verb that means "to leave out." It can also be a preposition that means "but."

EXAMPLE

Verb	My father was happy all day, if you except the early morning.
Preposition	No one likes mornings except my mother.

Activity A On your paper, write the word in parentheses that completes each sentence correctly.

1. The teacher will (except, accept) Sam's answers on the test.
2. He answered all the questions correctly (except, accept) three in the math section.
3. All of the students (except, accept) Sam did well in math.
4. Sam will have to (except, accept) a grade of C.
5. He likes school (except, accept) for math.

People sometimes mix up the verbs *learn* and *teach*. *Teach* means "to give new facts." *Learn* means "to get new facts."

EXAMPLE

Yolanda teaches history to Felipe.
(Yolanda is giving facts.)
Felipe learns history from Yolanda.
(Felipe is getting facts.)

Workbook Activity 74

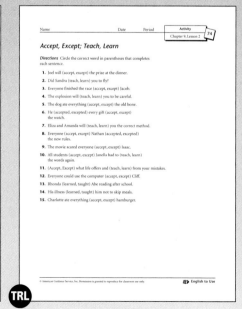

Activity 74

Activity B On your paper, write the word in parentheses that completes each sentence correctly.

1. The booklet will (teach, learn) David a skill.
2. David (taught, learned) a skill from the booklet.
3. Mr. Santos (taught, learned) Peter the violin for three years.
4. I will (teach, learn) you how to play the flute.
5. Lisa will (teach, learn) Ricky some songs.

Activity C On your paper, write the word in parentheses that completes each sentence correctly.

1. Clem (learned, taught) piano to all his sisters (accept, except) the littlest one.
2. Bill will (accept, except) payment from everyone (accept, except) Sara.
3. Those students (learned, taught) every subject from Mr. Adams (accept, except) science.
4. Everyone (accept, except) Tom (learned, taught) something from that last defeat.
5. The bank clerk (accepted, excepted) checks from every student (accept, except) Myra.

Selecting accurate verbs takes practice.

Activity A Answers

1. accept 2. except 3. except
4. accept 5. except

Activity B Answers

1. teach 2. learned 3. taught
4. teach 5. teach

Activity C Answers

1. taught, except 2. accept, except
3. learned, except 4. except, learned 5. accepted, except

 3 **Reinforce and Extend**

LEARNING STYLES

 Body/Kinesthetic
Because the sound and the meaning of the four words in the lesson are so similar, you may want to have students act out the words' meanings to help them internalize the concepts. For example, have a student hold a book, which represents knowledge. Then have the student pass the book to another student, saying, "I *teach* the lesson to (student's name)." The student receiving the book should say, "I *learn* the lesson from (student's name.)" Have students stand in a group, and identify a number of different distinguishing characteristics. Then list the characteristics, saying phrases such as "All the students are wearing jackets *except* (students' names)." Tell students mentioned in the *except* group to step away briefly from the others.

Writing Practice

Draw students' attention to the Writing Tip on page 182. Have students work in pairs to write an invitation asking a friend to a gathering in the future. One partner will suggest several dates and indicate times that he or she is and is not available, using the words *accept* and *except*. The other partner will write back accepting the invitation for a day when he or she can attend.

Lesson at a Glance

Chapter 9 Lesson 3

Overview This lesson explains the correct use of *their, they're, there; you, you're; its,* and *it's.*

Objective

■ To choose the correct homonyms for use in sentences

Student Pages 184–185

Teacher's Resource Library

Workbook Activity 75

Activity 75

Alternative Activity 75

1 Warm-Up Activity

Review with students the text and the words in the chart. After discussing the differences in the spelling and meaning of each set of homonyms, encourage students to use the words in sentences. Write examples on the board and discuss whether the words have been used correctly. Leave the corrected sentences on the board for students to look back on as they complete the activities in the lesson.

2 Teaching the Lesson

Have three students read aloud sentence 1 in Activity A, and have each student choose one of three answers provided. Ask the rest of the class if they could tell any difference in the answers read aloud. Remind students that the distinctions made in the lessons apply entirely to writing, not to spoken language, since the words discussed all sound alike. Before students begin the activities, model spelling out the words that are shortened by the contractions. Show students how saying aloud the words included in the contractions can quickly show them whether the contraction makes sense.

Many people confuse these words: *their, there,* and *they're; your* and *you're; its* and *it's. Their, your,* and *its* are owner pronouns. They do not have apostrophes. *They're, you're,* and *it's* are contractions. Contractions do have apostrophes.

Owner Pronouns	Contractions	Adverb
their	they're = they are	there
your	you're = you are	
its	it's = it is	

There is an adverb that tells where an action takes place.

EXAMPLE We can walk there after practice.

Activity A On your paper, write the words in parentheses that complete the sentences correctly.

1. Andy pulled his boat into (their, they're, there) dock.
2. Twin pipes gurgled beneath (its, it's) stern.
3. (Its, It's) a fast one, and (your, you're) lucky.
4. (Their, They're, There) here to see (your, you're) boat.
5. The boat cost more than (their, they're, there) house.
6. (Their, They're, There) go (your, you're) cousin Jessie and her sister.
7. (Their, They're, There) cruising in (their, they're, there) new car.
8. (Their, They're, There) having a great time with (you're, your) friend Emma.
9. (Your, You're) going (their, they're, there) with them later.
10. (Their, They're, There) is math homework on (your, you're) desk.

> You can use the word *there* with a form of the verb *to be* at the beginning of a sentence.
>
> **Example**
> *There* is the book.
>
> The words *there* and *is* can form the contraction *there's.*
>
> **Example**
> *There's* the book.

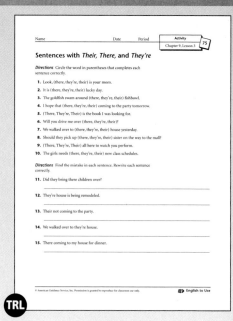

There

Their

Your

Activity B On your paper, write the words in parentheses that complete the sentences correctly.

1. (Your, You're) puppy is sleeping in (its, it's) new doghouse.
2. (Its, It's) time for the dog's dinner, and (its, it's) dish is gone.
3. (Its, It's) collar is new.
4. (Its, It's) collar sparkles, and (its, it's) leather.
5. After (your, you're) walk, put (its, it's) leash away.
6. (There, They're) goes (your, you're) airplane.
7. (Its, It's) a new plane.
8. (Its, It's) cockpit is full of gadgets.
9. Now (its, it's) landing near (its, it's) hangar.
10. (Your, You're) the lucky owner of the plane.
11. (There, They're, Their) sits (your, you're) surprise.
12. (Its, It's) in a big red box.
13. Inside, (there, they're, their) are noisy sounds.
14. People listen. (There, Their, They're) surprised by (its, it's) loud sounds.
15. (Your, You're) careful when you lift (its, it's) lid.

Activity C Find the sentences with mistakes in word usage. Write the sentences correctly on your paper. If a sentence is correct, write *C*.

1. Rob and Lena put they're books over their on the shelf.
2. The dog is taking it's time with you're newspaper.
3. Wait your turn, please.
4. Your too late for dinner, but its not too late for dessert.
5. The look on there faces was one of shock.

Be Exact   Chapter 9   **185**

Activity A Answers

1. their 2. its 3. It's, you're 4. They're, your 5. their 6. There, your 7. They're, their 8. They're, your 9. You're, there 10. There, your

Activity B Answers

1. Your, its 2. It's, its 3. Its 4. Its, it's 5. your, its 6. There, your 7. It's 8. Its 9. it's, its 10. You're 11. There, your 12. It's 13. there 14. They're, its 15. You're, its

Activity C Answers

1. Rob and Lena put their books over there on the shelf. 2. The dog is taking its time with your newspaper. 3. C 4. You're too late for dinner, but it's not too late for dessert. 5. The look on their faces was one of shock.

 3 Reinforce and Extend

LEARNING STYLES

 Logical/Mathematical

So that students may distinguish between *their* and *there,* help them understand the word patterns to which these two homonyms belong. On the board, write *I put it over <u>there</u>,* and have students list as many words as they can to substitute for the adverb there. Then write the sentence, *She borrowed <u>their</u> program,* and have students list other pronouns that fit. Have students read through the *there/their* sentences in Activities A and B and reflect on correct responses. Ask students to explain the reasons for their word choices.

TEACHER ALERT

 The word *homonym* is not taught in this lesson. It is taught in Chapter 12, Lesson 2. In this lesson, you may wish to refer to words that sound alike but have different spellings.

Lesson at a Glance

Chapter 9 Lesson 4

Overview This lesson provides practice in distinguishing between *lie* and *lay*, *sit* and *set*, *rise* and *raise*.

Objectives

■ To differentiate between the meanings of *lie* and *lay*, *sit* and *set*, *rise* and *raise*

■ To use the words correctly in sentences

Student Pages 186–187

Teacher's Resource Library

Workbook Activity 76

Activity 76

Alternative Activity 76

1 Warm-Up Activity

Place a book on a desk and say, "I set this book on the desk. The book sits on the desk." Write both sentences on the board. Then ask students to identify the sentence with the direct object and tell what the direct object is (*in the first sentence*: book).

2 Teaching the Lesson

Discuss the information and examples presented in the text. Encourage students to provide sentences for each part of the verbs in the second chart. Work with students to write sentences using the six verbs from the lesson, as well as the past tenses of those verbs.

People often misuse the verbs *lie* and *lay*, *sit* and *set*, and *rise* and *raise*. To avoid confusion with these verbs, it is important to know the meaning of each word.

Word	Meaning
lie	"to recline" or "to be in a resting position"
lay	"to put" or "to place something"
sit	"to put oneself in a sitting position"(as on a chair)
set	"to place something down"
rise	"to get up" or "to go up"
raise	"to make something go up"

To use these verbs correctly, it is also helpful to know the parts of each verb.

Present	Past	With Helpers
lie	lay	(is) lying, (has) lain
lay	laid	(is) laying, (has) laid
sit	sat	(is) sitting, (has) sat
set	set	(is) setting, (has) set
rise	rose	(is) rising, (has) risen
raise	raised	(is) raising, (has) raised

Finally, it helps to know that *lay, set,* and *raise* may each take a direct object. *Lie* and *rise* never take an object. *Sit* almost never takes an object.

> **EXAMPLE**
>
> **No direct object**   The lion lay in front of the lake.
> **Direct object**   The lion laid his tail on the ground.
> (The lion was in a resting position in front of the lake. The lion placed his tail on the ground. *Tail* is the direct object of *laid*.)

186   *Chapter 9   Be Exact*

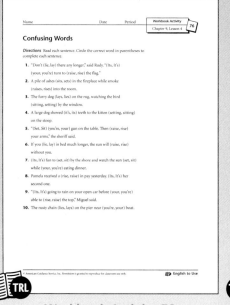

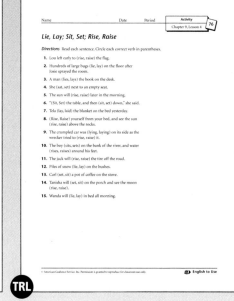

| No direct object | Marisa is sitting on the chair. |
| Direct object | Joaquin set the pen on the desk. |

(Marisa is in an upright position on the chair. Joaquin put the pen on the desk. *Pen* is the direct object of *set*.)

| No direct object | Adah rarely has risen before ten. |
| Direct object | Kalifa and Armando have raised the price. |

(Adah has rarely gotten up before ten. Kalifa and Armando have made the price go up. *Price* is the direct object of *have raised*.)

> The past form of *lie* and the present form of *lay* are the same. Remember, though, the meanings of the verbs *lie* and *lay* are not the same.

Activity A On your paper, write the verb that completes each sentence correctly. Write the direct object if there is one.

1. The sick child had (lain, laid) in bed for weeks.
2. Her nurse (lay, laid) medicine beside the bed.
3. Her cats are (lying, laying) beside the bed.
4. Books (lay, laid) on the floor all over the room.
5. She will (lie, lay) the papers on the table.

Activity B On your paper, write the verb that completes each sentence correctly. Write the direct object if there is one.

1. Enrique had been (sitting, setting) at the head of the table.
2. Together, the men have (sat, set) a plan on paper.
3. The four men (sit, set) around the table and talk.
4. After the meeting, they (sit, set) business aside.
5. They (set, sat) outside, and watched the sun (set, sit).

Activity C On your paper, write the verb that completes each sentence correctly. Write the direct object if there is one.

1. The sun will (rise, raise) in another hour.
2. Joaquin has always (risen, raised) before dawn.
3. He will (rise, raise) the flag at the courthouse.
4. Soon the temperature will (rise, raise) to 100 degrees.
5. His boss will (rise, raise) his hourly pay.

ONLINE CONNECTION

Capital Community College in Hartford, Connecticut, hosts a Guide to Grammar and Writing site with help for word and sentence mechanics problems, as well as essay guidelines and grammar quizzes. They offer help with "Notorious Confusables" at *cctc2.commnet.edu/grammar/notorious.htm.*

Activity A Answers

1. lain **2.** laid—medicine **3.** lying **4.** lay **5.** lay—papers

Activity B Answers

1. sitting **2.** set—plan **3.** sit **4.** set—business **5.** sat, set

Activity C Answers

1. rise **2.** risen **3.** raise—flag **4.** rise **5.** raise—pay

---

TEACHER ALERT

The verbs *lie* and *lay* are particularly difficult to use correctly. Suggest that students ask themselves these questions when using forms of *lie* and *lay* in sentences: *Do I mean "to rest" or "to put something down"? Am I talking about a past, present, or future action?*

---

 3 **Reinforce and Extend**

LEARNING STYLES

 LEP/ESL

English language learners may need extra practice with pronouncing and spelling the words in this lesson because the words are so easily confused. To help ESL students distinguish which verbs take a direct object, write sentences on the board describing items in the classroom and have language learners manipulate the items that are direct objects. For example: *I lay the eraser down,* or *I set the book on the shelf.* Help students understand that the verbs *lay, set,* and *raise* appear in sentences that take direct objects.

Lesson at a Glance

Chapter 9 Lesson 5

Overview This lesson explains the differences between *to*, *too*, and *two* and between *let* and *leave*.

Objectives

- To differentiate between the use of *to*, *too*, and *two* and between *let* and *leave*
- To use these words correctly in sentences

Student Pages 188–189

Teacher's Resource Library TRL

Workbook Activity 77

Activity 77

Alternative Activity 77

1 Warm-Up Activity

Say and write on the board: *The two friends came to the game too early.* Point out the underlined words and elicit their parts of speech. Then ask students to provide additional example sentences for each word and part of speech.

2 Teaching the Lesson

Discuss the text and examples with students. Ask them which words in the lesson they have problems understanding. Tell students that people often use *let/leave* incorrectly in conversation; therefore, the wrong usage can "sound" correct.

Activity A Answers

1. too 2. two 3. to 4. too 5. two

Lesson 5   To, Too, Two; Let, Leave

People often confuse *to*, *too*, and *two*. These words sound alike but mean different things. *To* is a preposition. *Too* is an adverb that means "also" or "too much." *Two* is a number word that can be an adjective or a noun.

EXAMPLE

Preposition	Sitara and I went to the mall.
Adverb	We were too late for the big sale.
Adjective	Luckily, there were two sales.
Noun	The two of us enjoyed shopping.

Activity A On your paper, write the word in parentheses that completes each sentence correctly.

1. The stores on Tenth Avenue close (to, too, two) early.
2. Amanda's bike has seats for (to, too, two).
3. Andy's store moved from Fourth Street (to, too, two) Third Avenue.
4. Pete's company moved (to, too, two).
5. My (to, too, two) best friends are Anita and Connie.

People often confuse the verbs *let* and *leave*. *Let* means "to allow." *Leave* means "to go away." *Leave* can also mean "to stop" or "to let something stay as it is."

EXAMPLE   Let me into the house. (Allow me into the house.)
Halim will leave the house. (Halim will go away from the house.)
Leave the gate closed. (Let the gate stay in that position.)

188 *Chapter 9   Be Exact*

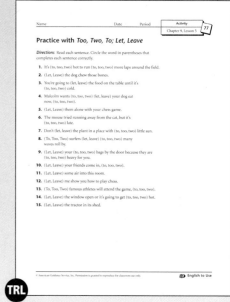

Workbook Activity 77   **Activity 77**

188 *Chapter 9   Be Exact*

Activity B On your paper, write the word in parentheses that completes each sentence correctly.

1. (Leave, Let) Juanita go to the bus station.
2. The bus will (leave, let) early tonight.
3. Kathy didn't (leave, let) the dog out of the house.
4. Both men (leave, let) the office late on Mondays.
5. The small window doesn't (leave, let) the breeze into the office.
6. (Let, Leave) the dog out now for his walk.
7. Bruce always (lets, leaves) food on his plate.
8. (Let, Leave) me work in peace!
9. (Let, Leave) the window open.
10. You should not (let, leave) anyone disturb you.

Activity C On your paper, write the words in parentheses that complete the sentences correctly.

1. (Let, Leave) the light on so I can see (to, too, two).
2. (To, Too, Two) more names have been added (to, too, two) this list.
3. Don't (let, leave) those animals escape from their cages!
4. Anna (let, leave) the airplane engine warm up.
5. (To, Too, Two) many drivers (let, leave) home at seven o'clock.
6. (Let, Leave) Laura go to the hockey game (to, too, two).
7. (Let, Leave) the cat and the monkey come into the house (to, too, two).
8. (Let, Leave) him alone so he can study.
9. Lightning struck Mr. Smith's house (to, too, two) times.
10. (To, Too, Two) many people tried to (let, leave) through the (to, too, two) doors.

> The adverb *too* means "also" when it appears at the end of a sentence. A comma usually comes before *too* in that position.
>
> **Example**
> The stores on the next street close early, *too*.

Activity B Answers

1. Let 2. leave 3. let 4. leave 5. let
6. Let 7. leaves 8. Let 9. Leave
10. let

Activity C Answers

1. Leave, too 2. Two, to 3. let 4. let
5. Too, leave 6. Let, too 7. Let, too
8. Leave 9. two 10. Too, leave, two

 3 Reinforce and Extend

LEARNING STYLES

 Interpersonal/Group
Have students work in pairs to write sentences using the five words studied in this lesson. When the pairs have finished, have them compare their work with another pair. Have the four students review one another's work and correct any errors in usage.

Speaking Practice

Have students take turns reading aloud the sentences in Activity B, helping students to hear the "sound" of correct and incorrect responses. You may also want to use *let/leave* sentences in Activity C as a read-aloud activity. In addition, emphasize that *too* means "too many" or "too much," if the answer comes at the beginning of a sentence. Refer students to the comparison of *too* and *also* in the box on page 189, and ask students to read aloud the word *also* to determine whether *too* fits at the end of a sentence.

Overview This lesson presents double negatives and explains how to avoid using them.

Objective

■ To correct sentences containing double negatives

Student Pages 190–191

Teacher's Resource Library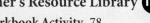

Workbook Activity 78

Activity 78

Alternative Activity 78

Vocabulary

double negative

 Warm-Up Activity

Say and write on the board: *He hardly never went nowhere.* Ask students to find the three negatives, or "no" words, in the sentence (*hardly, never, nowhere*). Ask students to change the sentence so that it has only one negative: for example, *He hardly went anywhere. He never went anywhere. He went nowhere.*

 Teaching the Lesson

Read aloud with students the ways of correcting the example sentences. Have students point out the single negative in each correct sentence. Finally, read the list of negative words in the chart and discuss how to form negative contractions.

> **Double negative**
> *The mistake of using two words that mean "no" in one sentence*

You have learned about negatives—words that say *no*. Never use two negatives in the same sentence. A **double negative** is two negatives in one sentence. Double negatives are always incorrect.

EXAMPLE

Incorrect	I am not never going there.
Correct	I am not going there.
Correct	I am not ever going there.
Correct	I am never going there.

Here is a list of common negative words. Remember that one negative word in a sentence is enough.

hardly	nobody	not	nowhere
never	none	nothing	scarcely
no	no one		

Not often forms part of a contraction. Do not use another negative word in a sentence that has a *not (n't)* contraction.

EXAMPLE

Incorrect	We don't hardly see Paulita anymore.
Correct	We don't see Paulita much anymore.
Correct	We hardly see Paulita anymore.

Here is a list of contractions with *not (n't)*.

aren't	don't	wasn't
can't	hasn't	weren't
couldn't	haven't	won't
didn't	isn't	wouldn't
doesn't	shouldn't	

Communication Connection

Using a double negative is always wrong in English. In some languages, however, a double negative calls attention to a negative idea. Think about how you call attention to ideas, negative or positive. In e-mail, for example, capital letters make a word or phrase stand out.

Activity A Each of these sentences has two or more negative words. Write each sentence correctly on your paper. There may be more than one way to correct each sentence. Write only one correct sentence for each item.

Example	Incorrect	We couldn't see hardly nothing in the dark room.
	Correct	We couldn't see anything in the dark room.
	Correct	We could see nothing in the dark room.
	Correct	We could hardly see anything in the dark room.

1. Carlos and Amy didn't see nobody on the street.

2. It don't have no power for hills.

3. The brakes doesn't work no more.

4. She will not buy no more old cars.

5. Mr. Burton won't never live in an old apartment again.

6. His heater don't give no heat.

7. His neighbor never gives him no peace.

8. The owner can't afford no repairs.

9. The owner won't tell Mr. Burton nothing.

10. Mr. Burton won't pay no more money out of his pocket for rent.

Negatives do not travel in pairs.

Activity A Answers

Answers will vary. Possible answers follow. **1.** Carlos and Sheila didn't see anybody on the street. **2.** It doesn't have power for hills. **3.** The brakes don't work anymore. **4.** She will not buy any more old cars. **5.** Mr. Burton won't ever live in an old apartment again. **6.** His heater doesn't give any heat. **7.** His neighbor never gives him any peace. **8.** The owner can't afford any repairs. **9.** The owner won't tell Mr. Burton anything. **10.** Mr. Burton won't pay any more money out of his pocket for rent.

 3 Reinforce and Extend

LEARNING STYLES

 Visual/Spatial Learning
Help students recognize the number of negative words in a sentence by having them find and highlight different forms of the word *not* in Activity A with a highlighter pen. Tell students that most contractions (those with *n't*) contain a negative. Have students scan the sentences and highlight contractions. Then have students look for words that start with *no* (*nowhere, nobody,* etc.) and highlight those words. Finally, have students skim the sentences for more complex negatives, highlighting words such as *scarcely, hardly,* and *never.* After students have identified these different types of "no" words, they can look back at the sentences and choose which negatives to eliminate.

TEACHER ALERT

Nonstandard English often features double negatives. As necessary, remind students of the importance of using standard English when speaking and writing.

GLOBAL CONNECTION

 Some languages emphasize the negative in sentences by using two or more words that mean *no. No quiero nada* translates literally from Spanish as "I don't want nothing." Although this construction is correct in Spanish, it is not correct in English. Ask students with knowledge of other languages to provide additional sentences containing double negatives or other constructions that do not translate exactly into English.

Chapter 9 Lesson 7

Overview This lesson practices the use of comparison and contrast in writing.

Objectives

- To review the writing process
- To apply techniques of comparison and contrast in writing

Student Pages 192–193

Teacher's Resource Library

Workbook Activity 79

Activity 79

Alternative Activity 79

1 Warm-Up Activity

On the board, write two words or ideas that can be compared and contrasted: for example, *watermelon* and *cantaloupe*. Then help students identify how the two types of melon are similar and different. Guide students to think about categories such as color, size, weight, texture, and taste, and help students use comparative words such as *bigger, sweeter,* and *heavier.* When students have finished, tell them that they have successfully compared and contrasted the two items.

2 Teaching the Lesson

Discuss students' progress with the four-step writing process. Review the step-by-step examples and make sure students understand the comparison and contrast process. If students have problems getting started on any of the activities, encourage them to work with a partner to talk through a comparison such as the *watermelon/cantaloupe* activity noted in the paragraph above.

Lesson 7 Writing Practice

Writing Tip

When writing about contrasts, use words and phrases such as *however* and *on the other hand* to make your point clear.

Example
The pace of baseball is easy to follow. *However,* the fast action of football is more exciting.

Writers use contrasting words and ideas to help readers understand the differences between two or more things or ideas. For example, you might enjoy one school activity but dislike another. You could contrast the positive points of the activity you like to the negative points of the activity you dislike. On the other hand, you might enjoy both activities but for different reasons. Then you would contrast the reasons each activity appeals to you.

The following is a review of the four steps of the writing process. The example is a contrast between two sports—baseball and football.

1. **Prewrite** The first thing you do before writing is decide what you want to write about. Gather your thoughts and arrange them so that your ideas are easy to understand.

   EXAMPLE

baseball?	football?
slow pace	fast action
easy to follow	

2. **Write** Put your thoughts on paper. Write as quickly as you can. Don't worry about mistakes. Just write the ideas. You can correct mistakes later.

   EXAMPLE Which do I like to watch the best? Football or baseball? Baseball is slow. Football has lots of action. I like both. One is easy to follow. I like both sports.

3. **Rewrite** You want your writing to express your meaning. Go back and read what you wrote. How can you improve it? Rewrite sentences that are unclear.

   EXAMPLE I like both football and baseball, Its hard for me to decide which one I like best Footbal has more action but baseball is easiest to follow

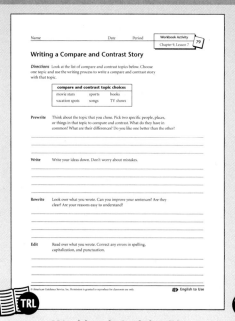

Workbook Activity 79

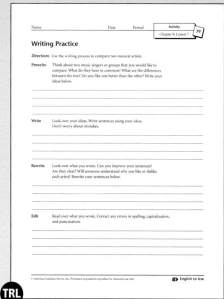

Activity 79

4. **Edit** Now read your work and correct any mistakes you find. Be sure to check for correct spelling and clear sentences.

> **EXAMPLE** I like both football and baseball. It's hard to decide which one I like better. Football has more action, but baseball is easier to follow.

Activity A Use the writing process to compare cars. Think about two kinds of cars. Which car do you like better? Why do you like it better? Rewrite and edit your comparison to make it better and easier to understand.

Activity B Use the writing process to write a short story about where you would like to live—on a farm, in a city, or in a small town. Which place would make you the happiest? Why is that place best for you? Describe the features of the place that make it better than the others. Write ideas as they come to you. Then rewrite and edit your short story.

Activity C Use the writing process to write a short story about the kind of movies you like. Think about comedies, action movies, horror movies, or science fiction. Which do you enjoy most? Why do you think that type of movie is the best? Write ideas as you think of them. Then rewrite and edit.

Activity D Use the writing process to describe an actor on TV or in the movies. Think about the person and the kinds of things he or she says and does. What does the actor do that you like? Why? What does he or she do that you don't like? Do your friends like the same actor? Why, or why not? Write ideas as quickly as they come to you. Then rewrite and edit.

Activity A Answers

Paragraphs will vary. Check to see that students have presented at least one good reason for their preferences.

Activity B Answers

Short stories will vary. Check to see that students have presented at least one good reason for their preferences.

Activity C Answers

Short stories will vary. Check to see that students have presented at least one good reason for their preferences.

Activity D Answers

Descriptions will vary. Check to see that students have presented at least one good reason for liking a particular personality.

 3 Reinforce and Extend

LEARNING STYLES

 Auditory/Verbal
Have students engage in a brief verbal debate about a specific topic. (For example: *school should be in session all year* versus *students need summer vacations.*) While students are giving their opinions, have them jot down notes on key points made during the discussion. They should then use their notes to write a short paragraph expressing their views. Invite students to express their opinions, but check to make sure that they support their opinions with specific reasons.

TEACHER ALERT

 Students may begin writing with a specific idea in mind but finish with a story that is unfocused. Tell them to find a comfortable topic and focus their ideas by revisiting the four-step writing process on pages 192–193 as they write.

Chapter 9 Lesson 8

Overview This lesson focuses on punctuation and abbreviations used in times of day, days of the week, and dates.

Objectives

- To punctuate hours of the day and dates
- To abbreviate and capitalize days and months

Student Pages 194–195

Teacher's Resource Library **TRL**

Workbook Activity 80

Activity 80

Alternative Activity 80

Vocabulary

abbreviation
colon

---

1 Warm-Up Activity

Write the current time, day, and date on the board, leaving out punctuation and capital letters. Ask students to help you correct each item.

2 Teaching the Lesson

Review the styles of writing time (*six o'clock, 6 o'clock, 6:00 A.M.*). For extra practice, bring a clock that can be easily manipulated. Have students take turns selecting and writing different times.

Activity A Answers

1. His flight left on Saturday at 7:30 A.M. **2.** It arrived in Texas at 4:03 P.M. **3.** The last flight left at 4 o'clock. **4.** James made the trip last summer on July 15. **5.** The 10:05 A.M. train is running late.

Lesson 8 Writing Mechanics

Abbreviation
Short form of a word

Colon (:)
A punctuation mark used in time

You can write about time in several ways. Days of the week and months of the year begin with capital letters. Seasons do not begin with capital letters. The days of the week and some months of the year have **abbreviations.** An abbreviation is a short form of a word. You should never use abbreviations for the days and the months when writing sentences.

One way to write the time of day is with a **colon (:)**. A colon is a punctuation mark that separates the hour from the minutes in time.

EXAMPLE

Time	It's 5:00 A.M. It's 5 o'clock. It's five o'clock.
Days	Tuesday, Wednesday, Thursday
Dates and Special Days	April 1 is April Fool's Day.
Seasons	spring, summer, autumn, winter
Date	Saturday, July 5, 2005

Activity A On your paper, write these sentences correctly. Put in the missing punctuation marks and capital letters.

1. his flight left on saturday at 730 AM
2. it arrived in texas at 403 PM
3. the last flight left at 4 oclock
4. james made the trip last summer on july 15
5. the 1005 AM train is running late

Activity B Write the full word for each abbreviation.

1. Sun.	**5.** Thurs.	**9.** Feb.	**13.** Sept.
2. Mon.	**6.** Fri.	**10.** Mar.	**14.** Oct.
3. Tues.	**7.** Sat.	**11.** Apr.	**15.** Nov.
4. Wed.	**8.** Jan.	**12.** Aug.	**16.** Dec.

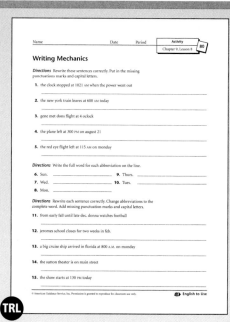

Workbook Activity 80

Abbreviations, Capitalization, and Punctuation Marks

Directions Rewrite these sentences correctly. Put in the missing punctuations marks and capital letters.

1. during the winter the eight o clock bus does not run
2. that flight arrives in florida on new years day
3. Tamras watch always shows 11:15am because the battery stopped
4. both afternoon flights to boston on sunday are full
5. juanita left for mexico on the last tuesday of the year

Directions Write the full word for each abbreviation.

6. Feb. _____   9. Aug. _____
7. Mar. _____   10. Apr. _____
8. Sept. _____

Directions Rewrite each sentence correctly. Change abbreviations to the complete word. Add missing punctuation marks and capital letters.

11. our play will open on jan. 3 and run two weeks
12. joes barber shop is open all day mon. through fri.
13. during aug. it closes at 1 pm on sat.
14. tela has a class at 930am and a lab at 130pm today
15. she has a meeting with her professor at 530pm on thurs.

Activity 80

Writing Mechanics

Directions Rewrite these sentences correctly. Put in the missing punctuations marks and capital letters.

1. the clock stopped at 1021 AM when the power went out
2. the new york train leaves at 600 AM today
3. gene met dons flight at 4 oclock
4. the plane left at 300 PM on august 21
5. the red eye flight left at 115 AM on monday

Directions Write the full word for each abbreviation on the line.

6. Sun. _____   9. Thurs. _____
7. Wed. _____   10. Tues. _____
8. Mon. _____

Directions Rewrite each sentence correctly. Change abbreviations to the complete word. Add missing punctuation marks and capital letters.

11. from early fall until late dec. donna watches football
12. jeromes school closes for two weeks in feb.
13. a big cruise ship arrived in florida at 800 A.M. on monday
14. the sutton theater is on main street
15. the show starts at 130 PM today

Tuesday

Wednesday

Thursday

Spring

Summer

Winter

Activity C Write each sentence correctly. Change abbreviations to the complete word. Add missing punctuation marks and capital letters.

1. joe set his alarm for 8 oclock on june 1 2005
2. it rang on time every mon. through fri. that summer
3. on nov. 12 his clock stopped at 437 AM
4. every fall squirrels gather nuts in oct. and nov. from the tree outside joes window
5. the noisy animals woke joe at 5 AM one mon.
6. aug. 8 1935 was a thur.
7. my parents flight from rome arrived promptly at 630 PM
8. the theater opens the first fri. in oct.
9. it closes after the winter season on the last tue. in mar.
10. tony made a phone call last wed. at 1130 AM
11. summer school ended on july 28 2006
12. in that state farmers plant crops in late mar. and harvest them in early oct.
13. joan closed the cottage for the winter at noon on sept. 15
14. next wed. the 1115 AM flight to detroit will leave at 2 oclock
15. drama students perform their fall play in nov. and their spring play in apr.

Using What You've Learned

Write a description of your schedule for the coming week. Tell what you will be doing each day. Also tell what time you will be doing it. Include the date with each day. Use capital letters and correct punctuation. Share your schedule with a family member.

ASL ILLUSTRATION

After students have practiced the signs on page 195, ask them to analyze the ways the ideas are conveyed. Have students discuss the sequence of the days of the week and imagine what a sign for "Friday" could be. Then have students check reference materials to learn the actual ASL sign.

3 Reinforce and Extend

IN THE COMMUNITY

Stores and offices often have signs stating their opening and closing times, sometimes with abbreviated days of the week. The use of one and two letters to abbreviate the days of the week is becoming more popular. Signs may read: M, Tu (or T), W, Th (or T), F, Sa (or S), Su (or S). Ask students to notice signs in their community and to record the styles of abbreviation for days to discuss in class.

Using What You've Learned

Tell students that their schedules can include events taking place at school, such as tests, field trips, and programs. In addition, it may include appointments and events taking place in the community, such as volunteer work and neighborhood gatherings.

Answers to Using What You've Learned: Schedules will vary.

Chapter 9 Review

Use the Chapter Review to prepare students for tests and to reteach content from the chapter.

Chapter 9 Mastery Test

The Teacher's Resource Library includes two parallel forms of the Chapter 9 Mastery Test. The difficulty level of the two forms is equivalent. You may wish to use one form as a pretest and the other form as a posttest.

REVIEW ANSWERS

Part A

1. colon 2. double negative
3. abbreviation

Part B

4. accept 5. any 6. Too, to
7. there 8. Its, it's, they're, their
9. there 10. You're, there, your
11. let

Part C

Answers will vary. Possible answers follow. 12. The man on the street never saw a pot of flowers. 13. Our bus stops here at 4:45 P.M. every day but Saturday. 14. I haven't ever seen anything like it. 15. Tom went to the cabin on Sunday, December 14, 2002. 16. Nobody ever meant to hurt him. 17. Cara finishes work in the summer at 5 o'clock.

Part D

Responses for items 18–19 will vary. Responses should include the following: Monday, March 24–Frank, dentist appointment, 10:00 A.M.; Anna—buy groceries, peas, bread, dog food, napkins/pet store—hamster food

---

Word Bank
abbreviation
colon
double negative

Part A On a sheet of paper, write the correct word or words from the Word Bank to complete sentences 1–3.

1. A _____ is a punctuation mark used in time.
2. Using two words that mean "no" in one sentence is a _____ .
3. An _____ is a short form of a word.

Part B On your paper, write the word in parentheses that completes each sentence correctly.

4. Adam will (accept, except) a job at the laundry.
5. There weren't (no, any) other jobs.
6. (Too, To, Two) many people wanted (too, to, two) work at the laundry.
7. Adam stayed (there, their, they're) until he got the job.
8. (It's, Its) hours are tough, and (it's, its) true that the owners do not pay well; however, (their, they're, there) nice to (their, they're, there) workers.
9. Adam will go (they're, their, there) early in the morning.
10. (Your, You're) going (there, they're, their) with him; don't forget (your, you're) lunch.
11. Please (leave, let) me go to the zoo.

Part C Write the following sentences correctly.

12. the man on the street never saw no pot of flowers
13. our bus stops here at 445 PM every day but sat.
14. I haven't never seen nothing like it
15. tom went to the cabin on sun. dec. 14 2002
16. nobody didn't never mean to hurt him
17. cara finishes work in the summer at 5 oclock

Part D Write notes using important words from each sentence.

18. On Monday, March 24, Frank has an appointment with the dentist at 10:00 A.M.

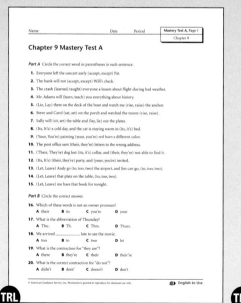

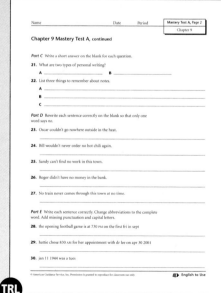

19. When Anna goes to the grocery store, she needs to buy canned peas, bread, dog food, and a large package of napkins. At the pet store, she needs to buy hamster food.

Part E Use the following notes to write sentences.

20. errands today: grocery store, library, bank

21. meeting 6 P.M.—bring notebook

Part F Write each sentence correctly.

22. after you (sit, set) the table, (sit, set) down near the window

23. a poor test score last sept. (learned, taught) fred a lesson

24. before 1000 AM the temperature inside the house will (rise, raise) 25 degrees

25. (your, you're) remote control (lies, lays) under the sofa

26. last wed. the mail carrier had (laid, lain) a box at the door

Part G

27. Use the writing process to write a short story comparing the most exciting day you can remember to the most boring day you can remember.

Part H On your paper, write the letter of the word that correctly completes each sentence.

28. I don't need _____ help with my chores.

   A no   **B** any   **C** none   **D** not

29. It happened at _____ on Wednesday.

   A 900 PM   **B** 900 P.M.   **C** 9:00 PM   **D** 9:00 P.M.

30. He didn't _____ learn how to whistle.

   A ever   **B** never   **C** not   **D** hardly

 Sometimes it is easier to learn vocabulary words if you break them into their word parts.

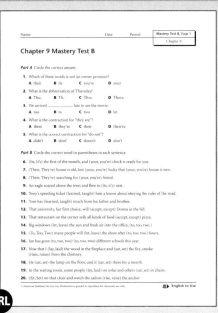

Chapter 9 Mastery Test B

10

Planning Guide

Making Sentences Work

	Student Text Lesson			Language Skills	
	Student Pages	Vocabulary	Practice Activities	Identification Skills	Writing Skills	Punctuation Skills
Lesson 1 Tone of Voice	200–201	✔	✔	✔	✔	✔
Lesson 2 What Sentences Can Do	202–203		✔		✔	✔
Lesson 3 Questions	204–205	✔	✔	✔	✔	✔
Lesson 4 Compound and Complex Sentences	206–207	✔	✔	✔		
Lesson 5 More About Complex Sentences	208–209		✔	✔	✔	✔
Lesson 6 Punctuating Quotations	210–211	✔	✔	✔	✔	✔
Lesson 7 Writing Practice	212–213		✔	✔	✔	✔
Lesson 8 Writing Mechanics	214–215		✔		✔	✔

Chapter Activities

Teacher's Resource Library
Community Connection 10:
Find Out About the Environment in
Your Community
English in Your World 10:
Searching for Complex Sentences
in Manuals

Assessment Options

Student Text
Chapter 10 Review

Teacher's Resource Library
Chapter 10 Mastery Tests A and B

ASL Illustration	Communication Connection	Notes	Using What You've Learned	Writing Tips	Teacher Alert	Online Connection	Applications (Home, Career, Community, Global)	Speaking Practice	Writing Practice	Auditory/Verbal	Body/Kinesthetic	Interpersonal/ Group Learning	Logical/Mathematical	Visual/Spatial	LEP/ESL	Workbook Activities	Activities	Alternative Activities	Sentence Diagramming Activities	Self-Study Guide
				✔			201	201		201						81	81	81		✔
		✔									203			203		82	82	82		✔
205		✔			205		205									83	83	83		✔
				✔		207			207						207	84	84	84		✔
	209				209							209				85	85	85		✔
					211	211							211			86	86	86		✔
		✔				213						213				87	87	87		✔
215			215			215										88	88	88		✔

Pronunciation Key

a	hat	e	let	ī	ice	ô	order	ù	put	sh	she
ā	age	ē	equal	o	hot	oi	oil	ü	rule	th	thin
ä	far	ėr	term	ō	open	ou	out	ch	child	ŦH	then
â	care	i	it	ȯ	saw	u	cup	ng	long	zh	measure

$$\mathrm{\vartheta} \begin{cases} a & \text{in about} \\ e & \text{in taken} \\ i & \text{in pencil} \\ o & \text{in lemon} \\ u & \text{in circus} \end{cases}$$

Alternative Activities

The Teacher's Resource Library (TRL) contains a set of lower-level worksheets called Alternative Activities. These worksheets cover the same content as the regular Activities but are written at a second-grade reading level.

Skill Track Software

Use the Skill Track Software for English to Use for additional reinforcement of this chapter. The software program allows students using AGS textbooks to be assessed for mastery of each chapter and lesson of the textbook. Students access the software on an individual basis and are assessed with multiple-choice items.

Chapter at a Glance

Chapter 10: Making Sentences Work
pages 198–217

Lessons

1. Tone of Voice
   pages 200–201
2. What Sentences Can Do
   pages 202–203
3. Questions
   pages 204–205
4. Compound and Complex Sentences
   pages 206–207
5. More About Complex Sentences
   pages 208–209
6. Punctuating Quotations
   pages 210–211
7. Writing Practice
   pages 212–213
8. Writing Mechanics
   pages 214–215

Chapter 10 Review
pages 216–217

Skill Track Software for English to Use

Teacher's Resource Library **TRL**

Workbook Activities 81–88

Activities 81–88

Alternative Activities 81–88

Community Connection 10

English in Your World 10

Chapter 10 Self-Study Guide

Chapter 10 Mastery Tests A and B

(Answer Keys for the Teacher's Resource Library begin on page 308 of this Teacher's Edition.)

Find Out About the Environment in Your Community

Air and water are parts of your natural environment. The environment can affect your health. How good is your environment? How can you help protect your environment? Environmental problems can be a matter of life and death. See what you can find out about your community's environment.

Directions Look in the Yellow Pages of your telephone book. There may be groups or businesses under each of these names: "Environmental, Conservation & Ecological Organizations," "Environmental Consultants," "Environmental & Ecological Services." Call or visit one of the groups or businesses. Ask someone who knows about the company the questions below. Write your answers on this page. Remember to use various types of sentences and correct punctuation when writing your answers. When finished, go back and underline all of the complex, compound, and complex-compound sentences.

1. What problems in the environment does your group work on? _____
2. How long has your group been working? _____
3. What is your group doing to help protect the environment? _____
4. Does your group charge a fee to help clean up the environment?
   Yes _____ No _____
   If "No": Where do you get your funding? _____
5. What advice do you have to help our community improve the environment? _____

Searching for Complex Sentences in Manuals

When something needs fixing, some people look in how-to manuals. These manuals can be found at a library. They give step-by-step instructions on how to fix something. Another kind of manual is an operator's manual. It is a set of instructions for using something like a watch, computer, or camera. Use these kinds of manuals to practice what you have learned about complex sentences. Follow these steps.

Step 1 Find a how-to or operator's manual. Make sure the manual is written in complete sentences.

Step 2 Find five complete sentences that show something you learned in Chapter 10 about complex sentences. Try to find examples of simple, compound, and complex sentences.

Step 3 Write each sentence on the lines below. After each sentence, explain how the sentence is an example of what you have learned in Chapter 10.

EXAMPLE The watch is waterproof, but it should not be used in saltwater.
(This is a compound sentence.)

1. _____
2. _____
3. _____
4. _____
5. _____

Step 4 Team up with at least two other classmates. Share your sentences.

10 Making Sentences Work

What makes a winning team? A successful team is a product of teamwork, a process that requires excellent communication. Teammates can communicate in a number of ways. They can convey different kinds of information just through the tone of voice that they choose. Team leaders give instructions, and players ask questions to make sure they understand the shared information.

When we communicate in writing, we cannot "hear" the sound of our teammates' voices. As writers, we must work carefully to make certain that our readers understand the tone in our writing. Since readers cannot ask us verbal questions, we must make sure that our instructions are clear and understandable. On a team, we can communicate through just the sounds of our voices; as writers, we have to depend on word choice, punctuation, and a variety of sentence structures.

In this chapter, you will study how to communicate people's spoken words and feelings in your writing.

Goals for Learning

◆ To use punctuation to show tone or mood

◆ To write statements, questions, commands, and requests

◆ To analyze question pronouns and the structure of question sentences

◆ To punctuate direct and indirect quotations correctly

◆ To punctuate and capitalize quotations correctly

199

Introducing the Chapter

Ask students how they think the members of the team in the picture are communicating. Are they gesturing or talking to one another? Discuss how people on a team communicate their messages and feelings to one another through language, gestures, and tone of voice. Point out that writers also use specific techniques to communicate their ideas and feelings to readers.

TEACHER'S RESOURCE

The AGS Teaching Strategies in English Transparencies may be used with this chapter. The transparencies add an interactive dimension to expand and enhance the English to Use program content.

CAREER INTEREST INVENTORY

The AGS Harrington-O'Shea Career Decision-Making System–Revised (CDM) may be used with this chapter. Students can use the CDM to explore their interests and identify careers. The CDM defines career areas that are indicated by students' responses on the inventory.

Writing Tips and Notes

Ask volunteers to read the tips and notes that appear in the margins throughout the chapter. Then discuss them with the class.

CHAPTER PROJECT

Ask students to keep a log of passages, sayings, or quotations they read or hear that show strong feelings. The log may contain passages from well-known people or quotations from classmates. At the end of the chapter, have students choose their favorite quotations and record them in a class album, using correct capitalization and punctuation for direct and indirect quotations.

Lesson at a Glance

Chapter 10 Lesson 1

Overview This lesson focuses on punctuation that expresses voice tone or mood.

Objectives

- To use end punctuation to express tone
- To use punctuation to express tone in sentences with interjections

Student Pages 200–201

Teacher's Resource Library

Workbook Activity 81

Activity 81

Alternative Activity 81

....

Vocabulary

tone of voice

....

 Warm-Up Activity

Write on the board: *"Yes." "Yes?" "Yes!"* Read each word, changing expression and tone of voice to reflect the punctuation used. Point out that in each case, the punctuation indicates how the word should be said. Have students choose other words and change their expression by adding a period, question mark, or exclamation point.

 Teaching the Lesson

Discuss the importance of tone in understanding what people mean. Make the point that in writing, one way we attempt to convey vocal expression and meaning is through punctuation.

Focus on the material presented in the text. Have students read the example sentences with the appropriate expression.

Tone of voice
The sound of speech

Writing Tip

Choose different end punctuation marks to express what you mean. Different kinds of sentences add variety to your writing. They also keep your writing interesting.

A speaker's words send one message. The **tone of voice,** or sound of the speaker's voice, can reinforce the message or change its meaning. One way to communicate a speaker's tone of voice in writing is through end punctuation.

A sentence that ends in a period makes a statement. The speaker's tone of voice is quiet or neutral. The speaker communicates his or her message mainly through the meaning of the words.

A sentence that ends in an exclamation point shows excitement or strong feeling. The speaker's tone of voice expresses extreme joy, sorrow, horror, surprise, or another strong feeling. An exclamation point tells readers to pay attention. The speaker is saying something that is important to him or her.

A sentence that ends in a question mark asks a question. The speaker's tone of voice is curious. It asks *why, what, how, when,* or *who.* A question mark makes the reader wonder, "What next?"

Notice how different end punctuation changes the meaning and tone of voice of the following sentence.

EXAMPLE

Louisa won the prize.
(The period shows that the speaker's tone of voice is neutral. The speaker is stating a fact without expressing any particular feeling.)

Louisa won the prize!
(The exclamation point shows that the speaker's tone of voice is expressing strong feeling, such as happiness or surprise.)

Louisa won the prize?
(The question mark shows that the speaker's tone of voice is expressing curiosity, perhaps even disbelief.)

200 *Chapter 10 Making Sentences Work*

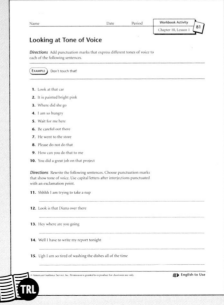

Activity A On your paper, rewrite each of the following sentences. Add end punctuation marks that express different tones of voice.

1. What is going on here
2. I've told you about this before
3. I won't be going to camp this year
4. Thank you for the beautiful gift
5. What a great gift this is

Interjections can also express tone of voice. Interjections followed by a comma express mild feelings. Interjections followed by an exclamation point show strong feelings.

> **EXAMPLE** Well, look at the time.
> (The comma after the interjection shows that the speaker is mildly concerned about the time.
> Well! Look at the time!
> (The exclamation points show that the speaker is excited or upset about the time.)

Activity B On your paper, rewrite these sentences. Choose punctuation marks that show the tone of voice. Use capital letters after interjections punctuated with an exclamation point.

1. What we have a test today
2. Well I didn't know about it
3. Okay I'll do the best I can
4. Look a new movie is in town
5. Hey it has the biggest stars

Students meet in the hall to discuss the test.

Answers will vary. When students have finished, ask volunteers to read sentences aloud with expression, telling what punctuation they used and why.

Activity B Answers

Answers will vary.

 3 Reinforce and Extend

LEARNING STYLES

 Auditory/Verbal
Briefly discuss a topic, such as sports or homework, that will raise strong feelings in your students. Ask students to write a sentence or two about the topic, expressing their strong feelings. Then have students read their sentences aloud to the class.

GLOBAL CONNECTION

The Spanish language uses question marks and exclamation points at both ends of sentences. Marks are upside down at the beginning of the sentence, giving the reader a clue about the tone of voice. *¡Viva!* literally means "live," but is equivalent to the English word *Hurrah!* *¿Está aquí?* means "Is he (or she or it) here?" Ask students who know other languages to explain how changes in tone of voice are expressed in writing.

Speaking Practice

After students have rewritten the sentences in Activity B, have them take turns reading the activity aloud. Have students identify the type of voice inflection used for each statement, question, and exclamation and discuss the tones that are especially surprising or effective.

Lesson at a Glance

Chapter 10 Lesson 2

Overview This lesson explains the purposes of sentences. It also defines *can* and *may*.

Objectives

- To write sentences with different purposes
- To use *can* and *may* correctly in sentences
- To analyze shades of meaning in sentences

Student Pages 202–203

Teacher's Resource Library

Workbook Activity 82

Activity 82

Alternative Activity 82

---

1 Warm-Up Activity

Say to a student: *Bring me that book.* Then write the sentence on the board. Ask students to explain the purpose of the sentence. Then ask students what other purpose a sentence might have and ask them to give examples. Elicit through discussion that sentences give information, ask for information, and give orders or make requests.

2 Teaching the Lesson

Focus students' attention on the text and discuss the examples. Make certain that students understand that a request has a different shade of meaning than a command. A strong request or command is even more emphatic.

Activity A Answers

Sentences will vary. Check to see that students have used appropriate punctuation.

A sentence can make a statement, ask a question, give a command, or make a request.

> **EXAMPLE**
>
> | Statement | I can help you. |
> | Question | May I help you? |
> | Command or request | Help me, please. |
> | Strong command or request | Help me, now! |

Activity A Follow the directions, and write your own sentences on your paper. Use the examples above to help you.

1. Write a statement using the word *save*.
2. Write a question using the word *save*.
3. Write a command using the word *save*.
4. Write a strong request using the word *stop*.
5. Write a statement using the word *stop*.

> Here is a quick way to remember how to use *can* and *may* correctly. Think of the words *able* and *possible*.
>
> can = able
> may = possible

We often use the words *can* and *may* in place of each other, but they have different meanings. To use *can* and *may* correctly, remember to:

- Use *can* to show that someone is able to do something.
- Use *may* to show that someone is allowed to do something or to show the possibility that something will happen.

> **EXAMPLE**
>
> Michelle can ride her bicycle now.
> (Michelle is able to ride her bicycle now.)
>
> Michelle may ride her bicycle now.
> (Michelle has permission to ride her bicycle now, or maybe Michelle will ride her bicycle now.)

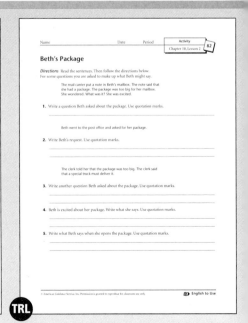

Workbook Activity 82   Activity 82

Activity B On your paper, use *can* or *may* to write a sentence for each of these ideas.

I am able to:	Maybe I will:
run	go to a store
play games	do my chores
stand	wash my face
read	read
eat dinner	eat dinner

Activity C On your paper, write one question, one statement, one request, and one strong request for each group of words below.

1. John has money problems.
2. Angelina was offered a job.
3. The computer is broken.
4. Susan left for Dallas today.
5. William won a prize on a game show.

Activity D On your paper, write the letter of the correct meaning of each sentence.

A The person is giving a strong command.

B The person is able.

C The person is giving or asking permission.

D The person is making a mild request.

1. She may work at the store.
2. He can work at the store.
3. Get to work now!
4. May I work at the store?
5. I can go to the dance with you.

Activity B Answers

Sentences may vary somewhat, but those expressing "I am able to" should use *can*, and those expressing "Maybe I will" should use *may*.

Activity C Answers

Answers will vary but should be based on the information in each sentence.

Activity D Answers

1. C 2. B 3. A 4. D 5. B

3 Reinforce and Extend

LEARNING STYLES

Visual/Spatial

Ask students to draw or find a cartoon that uses exclamation points or questions marks. Discuss the expressions on characters' faces. Some students may wish to sketch a cartoon sequence illustrating one set of sentences they create in Activity C.

LEARNING STYLES

Body/Kinesthetic

Help students understand the meanings of different types of sentences by having them "act out" sentences from Activities C and D. Have students take turns dramatizing sentences for the rest of the class. Using gestures, actions, and voice inflections, the speakers should "act out" the sentences. Ask the class to determine from the actions and inflections whether each is a statement, a command, or a request.

Chapter 10 Lesson 3

Overview This lesson presents words used to form questions. It explains how to identify the subject in questions.

Objectives

- To identify the subject and verb in questions
- To use question pronouns, adverbs, and helping and linking verbs to write questions

Student Pages 204–205

Teacher's Resource Library

Workbook Activity 83

Activity 83

Alternative Activity 83

Vocabulary

question pronoun

---

1 Warm-Up Activity

Say and write on the board: *What are we doing?* Ask students to identify the complete verb (*are doing*) and notice how the verb phrase is split. Then help students find the subject (*we*) in the sentence. Point out that in most questions, the subject is not found at the beginning of the sentence.

2 Teaching the Lesson

Focus students' attention on the text and the sentences in the example boxes. Discuss how to find the subject in questions, and provide additional examples on the board if necessary. Model your sentences on those in the text.

Lesson 3 Questions

> **Question pronoun**
>
> A pronoun that asks a question

A sentence that asks a question ends with a question mark. Some questions begin with pronouns. A **question pronoun** is a pronoun that forms a question. The pronouns *who, whom, whose, what,* and *which* are question pronouns.

EXAMPLE
Who wrote on the table?
Whose is that?

> If you are not sure whether to use *who* or *whom,* try this. Put *he* or *she* where *who* would go. If it sounds right, use *who.*

Other words that form questions include the adverbs *when, where, why,* and *how* and helping verbs such as *will, can, do, have, could, should,* and *would.*

EXAMPLE
When will the guests leave?
Did you see my catch?

When the pronoun *who* begins a question with an action verb, *who* is usually the subject of the sentence. Other question pronouns may also be the subject of action verbs, or they may describe the subject.

EXAMPLE
Who wrote on the table?
What made that sound?
Which of these cabinets holds the papers?
Whose glove fell on the ground?

In questions with linking verbs, the subject often follows the verb. The subject of a question may also come between the helping verb and the main verb. Keep in mind that *whom* is an objective case pronoun and can never be the subject of a sentence.

EXAMPLE
What is your name?
Whom did Dad see at the office?
Why were you so early?
Are Renaldo and Chad at school?

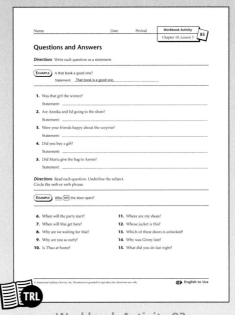

Workbook Activity 83

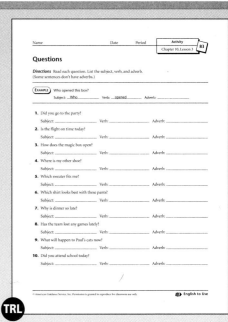

Activity 83

What

Your

Name

?

What is your name?

To find the subject in a question, follow these steps:

1. Find the verb or verb phrase.
2. Ask who or what about the verb.
3. Try to form a statement from the question.
4. Identify the subject.

Activity A Write each question on your paper. Use the above steps to find the subject and verb of each question. Underline the subject. Circle the verb or verb phrase.

1. Did your friends sit near you?
2. Will that stack of books help you with the test?
3. Has Evan parked his car by the pool?
4. Could you bring that book over here?
5. Who runs the old store in town?
6. When does the corner store open?
7. Who bought all that cereal?
8. What will Ilana and Michael find upstairs?
9. Is your class a good one?
10. Are the students in your class friendly?

Activity B Use these words to form questions. Write each question on your paper and underline its subject.

1. who
2. what
3. whose
4. which
5. when
6. where
7. why
8. how
9. will
10. did

Activity A Answers

1. S—friends, V—Did sit 2. S—stack, V—Will help 3. S—Evan, V—Has parked 4. S—you, V—Could bring 5. S—Who, V—runs 6. S—store, V—does open 7. S—Who, V—bought 8. S—Ilana and Michael, V—will find 9. S—class, V—Is 10. S—students, V—Are

Activity B Answers

Answers will vary.

3 **Reinforce and Extend**

TEACHER ALERT

 Students have learned that a pronoun can be the subject of a sentence. Remind students that question pronouns appear at the beginning of a sentence in the subject position but that these pronouns do not function as other pronouns do.

IN THE COMMUNITY

 Suggest that students think about their community as they travel through it. What unanswered questions do they have about the way their community works? For example, *Why isn't there a stoplight in front of the shopping mall?* and *When is the library open?* Ask students to compile and bring to class several questions they and others have about various aspects of community life.

In class, students may consider ways of finding the answers to their questions.

ASL ILLUSTRATION

Have students practice the signs illustrated on page 205, noticing that the sentence ends in a sign for "question mark." Ask students to review other signs they have learned and try to form new questions, ending them with a "question mark" sign.

Chapter 10 Lesson 4

Overview This lesson presents complex sentences, using compound sentences as a contrast.

Objectives

- To distinguish between compound, complex, and compound-complex sentences
- To identify the dependent and independent clauses in compound and complex sentences

Student Pages 206–207

Teacher's Resource Library

Workbook Activity 84

Activity 84

Alternative Activity 84

Vocabulary

complex sentence
compound-complex sentence
dependent clause
independent clause

 Warm-Up Activity

Write on the board the words *dependent* and *independent*. Ask students to define the words. Tell students that independent clauses can stand on their own, and they are used to build compound sentences. Dependent clauses must be connected to an independent thought, and they are used to build complex sentences.

 Teaching the Lesson

Focus students' attention on the second example. Have students identify the subject and verb in the independent and dependent clauses. Suggest that students read each clause aloud. They should be able to hear that the dependent clause does not express a complete thought even though it has a subject and verb (*because he loves music*).

Lesson 4 Compound and Complex Sentences

You learned in Chapter 3 that a compound sentence has two complete thoughts joined by a conjunction or by a semicolon. Conjunctions such as *and, but,* and *or* join main ideas in a compound sentence.

Complex sentence
A sentence that includes both an independent clause and a dependent clause

Independent clause
A complete sentence

Dependent clause
A group of words that does not form a complete thought and cannot stand alone

EXAMPLE

Compound sentence

Alan loves cats, but his cousin is allergic to cat fur.
complete thought   complete thought

A **complex sentence** has an **independent clause** and a **dependent clause.** An independent clause expresses a complete thought and is a sentence. A dependent clause does not express a complete thought. It is not a sentence and cannot stand alone.

EXAMPLE

Complex sentence	Alan works at a radio station on the weekends because he loves music.
Independent clause	Alan works at a radio station on the weekends (a complete thought)
Dependent clause	because he loves music (not a complete thought)

Dependent clause conjunctions join dependent clauses to independent clauses.

Dependent Clause Conjunctions			
after	before	so that	whenever
although	if	unless	where
as	once	until	wherever
because	since	when	while

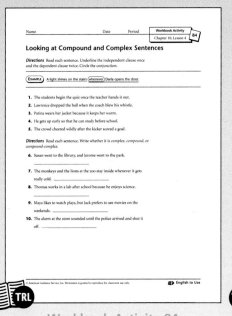

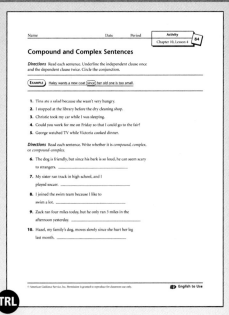

Workbook Activity 84   Activity 84

Activity A Write each complex sentence on your paper. Underline the independent clause once and the dependent clause twice. Circle the conjunction.

Example Andre's van doesn't work well (since) it is so old.

1. He watches for engine overheating if the hill is steep.
2. His van struggles up the hill while traffic waits.
3. An old van can't climb a steep hill unless it's in good shape.
4. He is surprised whenever his van starts.
5. He will buy a new van when he has more money.

A sentence can be both compound and complex. A **compound-complex sentence** has two or more independent clauses and at least one dependent clause.

EXAMPLE

Compound-complex sentence

Alan went home, and I went to the library after school ended.

two independent clauses — dependent clause

Activity B On your paper, write whether each sentence is *compound, complex,* or *compound-complex.*

1. Madalena's grocery cart was full; she shopped for the month.
2. The clerk rang up Madalena's order, which filled twenty bags.
3. We got out of the car, and the dog, which had been asleep on the front porch, sat up and barked.
4. Madalena and I talked while we prepared dinner.
5. Because Madalena bought so much food, the cabinets were full and her whole family was happy.

Activity A Answers

1. He watches for engine overheating (if) the hill is steep.
2. His van struggles up the hill (while) traffic waits.
3. An old van can't climb a steep hill (unless) it's in good shape.
4. He is surprised (whenever) his van starts.
5. He will buy a new van (when) he has more money.

Activity B Answers

1. compound 2. complex
3. compound-complex 4. complex
5. compound-complex

Writing Practice

Refer students to the writing tip on page 207, explaining that compound-complex sentences appear more frequently in written speech than in conversation. Then ask student pairs to briefly discuss what they will do after school that day, listing their activities as they talk. Have students use the information in their lists to create compound-complex sentences.

3 Reinforce and Extend

LEARNING STYLES

LEP/ESL

English language learners may need additional practice in order to distinguish between independent and dependent clauses. Ask students who speak other languages to write down examples from their own language of words that mean *after*, *before*, and *since*. Ask them to use the words to create dependent clauses and then translate the clauses into English. Have the students practice removing the dependent clause conjunctions to create independent clauses.

ONLINE CONNECTION

Capital Community College's "Guide to Grammar and Writing" Web site provides interactive quizzes on topics such as independent clauses, dependent clauses, and types of sentences. See *www.ccc.commnet.edu/grammar/.*

Lesson at a Glance

Chapter 10 Lesson 5

Overview This lesson focuses on the construction and punctuation of complex sentences. It distinguishes between a dependent clause and a prepositional phrase.

Objectives

- To identify dependent clauses in complex sentences and add commas where needed
- To distinguish between dependent clauses and prepositional phrases
- To combine ideas to write complex sentences

Student Pages 208–209

Teacher's Resource Library **TRL**

Workbook Activity 85

Activity 85

Alternative Activity 85

 1 Warm-Up Activity

Write a short list of topics on the board. Have students come to the board in pairs and individually write single sentences on the same topic. Ask the class to use what they know about complex sentences to combine the sentences into one complex sentence. Have students practice placing the dependent clause at both the beginning and the end of each new sentence.

2 Teaching the Lesson

Read the list of relative pronouns and the example sentence. Provide examples of sentences that use the other pronouns, or ask students to give examples.

Then discuss the different placement of dependent clauses in complex sentences and the appropriate punctuation.

In some complex sentences, pronouns relate or tie a dependent clause to the rest of the sentence. The pronoun is the subject of the clause.

Pronouns That Begin Dependent Clauses				
that	what	whatever	which	who

EXAMPLE Brandi, who lives on my block, almost won the match.

A dependent clause can appear at the beginning, in the middle, or at the end of a complex sentence. Use a comma when the dependent clause comes at the beginning or in the middle of the sentence. Do not use a comma when the dependent clause comes at the end of the sentence.

EXAMPLE Because he was hungry, Nigel went out for lunch.
Nigel, who was hungry, went out for lunch.
Nigel went out for lunch because he was hungry.

Activity A On your paper, write each sentence. Underline the dependent clause. Add commas where needed.

1. Unless his brother goes with him Matthew won't go out.
2. Napoli's Pizza Place which has the best pizza in town is their favorite restaurant.
3. Matthew who loves video games plays and eats at the same time.
4. They stay at Napoli's until their friends arrive.
5. Because it has the best pizza the friends always meet at Napoli's.

Some conjunctions that introduce dependent clauses are also prepositions or part of two-word prepositions. These include *after, before, since, until, as of,* and *because of.*

---

208 *Chapter 10 Making Sentences Work*

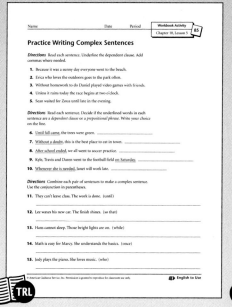

Workbook Activity 85

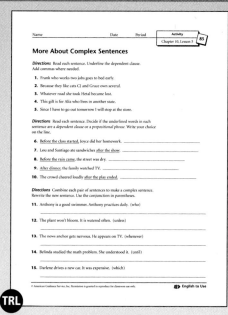

Activity 85

Do not confuse a prepositional phrase with a dependent clause. A dependent clause has a subject and a verb. A prepositional phrase does not.

EXAMPLE

| Dependent clause | We met for dinner after the game ended. |
| Prepositional phrase | We met for dinner after the game. |

Activity B On your paper, write whether the underlined words in each sentence are a dependent clause or a prepositional phrase.

1. Before the game, Jon and Sheri studied.
2. Before the game began, Jon and Sheri studied at the library.
3. After the game ended, Jon and Sheri went to the park.
4. After the game, Austin and Dave went to the pool.
5. During the evening, they watched a movie that had captioning.

Communication Connection

Captioning helps people who are hard of hearing enjoy television, films, and videos. Open captioning translates words and sounds into text. The text appears on the screen in a black box.

Complex sentences combine related ideas. Writers use complex sentences to add interest and variety.

EXAMPLE

| Related ideas | The baseball season is over. We talked about it. |
| Complex sentence | Although the baseball season is over, we talked about it. |

Activity C Combine each pair of sentences to make a complex sentence. Use the dependent clause conjunction in parentheses. Write the sentences on your paper.

1. Athletes can't win. They practice often. (unless)
2. They trained hard. They felt ready. (until)
3. The athletes are heroes. They travel. (wherever)
4. Dave has a new TV set. It has captioning. (because)
5. His mother watches it often. She is hard of hearing. (who)

Making Sentences Work   *Chapter 10*   **209**

Activity A Answers

1. <u>Unless his brother goes with him</u>, Matthew won't go out. 2. Napoli's Pizza Place, <u>which has the best pizza in town</u>, is their favorite restaurant. 3. Matthew, <u>who loves video games</u>, plays and eats at the same time. 4. They stay at Napoli's <u>until their friends arrive</u>. 5. <u>Because it has the best pizza</u>, the friends always meet at Napoli's.

Activity B Answers

1. prepositional phrase
2. dependent clause 3. dependent clause 4. prepositional phrase
5. prepositional phrase

Activity C Answers

Answers will vary. Possible responses are given.

1. Athletes can't win unless they practice often. 2. They trained hard until they felt ready.
3. Wherever they travel, the athletes are heroes. 4. Dave has a new TV set because it has captioning. 5. His mother, who is hard of hearing, watches it often.

3 Reinforce and Extend

LEARNING STYLES

Interpersonal/Group
Ask each student to write a simple sentence. Then pair students or form writing response groups. Have students exchange papers and add dependent clauses to one another's sentences to form complex sentences. Then have students create a second sentence, adding another independent clause to create a compound-complex sentence. Ask students to discuss one another's work.

TEACHER ALERT

Tell students that the dependent clause is separated from the independent clause with two commas, rather than just one, when it is placed in the middle of the sentence. Remind students that even if the dependent clause is removed from the independent clause, the independent clause will still make sense.

Lesson at a Glance

Chapter 10 Lesson 6

Overview This lesson explains direct and indirect quotations and their punctuation.

Objectives

- To identify direct and indirect quotations
- To change indirect quotations into direct quotations
- To punctuate direct quotations

Student Pages 210–211

Teacher's Resource Library

Workbook Activity 86

Activity 86

Alternative Activity 86

Vocabulary

direct quotation
indirect quotation
quotation marks

 1 Warm-Up Activity

Ask two or three volunteers for their favorite sayings. Write each saying on the board first as a direct quotation; then reword them as indirect quotations.

Ask students which sentences use speakers' exact words. Then ask how students can tell where a speaker's exact words begin and end. *(quotation marks appear at the beginning and end of the speaker's exact words)*

 2 Teaching the Lesson

Tell students that direct quotations require specialized punctuation and capitalization.

Activity A Answers

1. direct 2. indirect 3. indirect
4. direct 5. direct

Direct quotation
The exact words that someone says

Quotation marks ("")
Punctuation used to begin and end a direct quotation

Indirect quotation
What someone says but not his or her exact words

A **direct quotation** is the exact words that someone says. Use **quotation marks** ("") to enclose the words of a direct quotation. An **indirect quotation** uses other words to tell what someone says. Do not use quotation marks with an indirect quotation.

EXAMPLE

| Direct quotation | Matt said, "That was a great book!" |
| Indirect quotation | Matt told Max that the book was great. |

Activity A On your paper, write whether the underlined words in each sentence are a *direct quotation* or an *indirect quotation*.

1. Darnay said, "Let's go see a movie."
2. Ray said that he would ask Erica to go.
3. Erica said that she would love to see that movie.
4. "If you pay for the movie, I'll pay for the popcorn," she said.
5. Darnay said, "That's a great idea."

When writing sentences with direct quotations, remember to:

- Capitalize the first word of a direct quotation that is a complete sentence. Always capitalize the first word of a direct quotation that begins a sentence, even if it is not a complete sentence.

- Place a comma right after the words that identify the speaker when the speaker's name comes before the quotation. Place the comma before the final quotation mark when the speaker's name follows the quotation.

- Place the period before the final quotation mark when the quotation ends a sentence that is a statement.

EXAMPLE   Angela said, "Playing volleyball makes me hungry."
"Everything makes you hungry," Max joked.

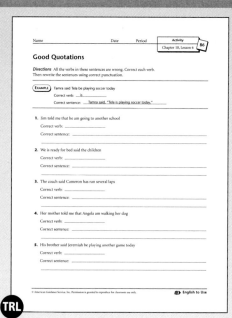

Activity B On your paper, rewrite the following indirect quotations as direct quotations.

1. Kim said that Candace knows a good play we should see.

2. Candace said that the play will run another month.

3. Andy and Aiesha said that they were going to visit next month.

4. They said that they would like to see the play, too.

5. Candace said that she would like to see the play again.

A direct quotation can be more than one sentence long. Use only one set of quotation marks to enclose the speaker's entire speech.

> **EXAMPLE**   Angela said, "The soup was good. Now I want a sandwich."

Activity C On your paper, rewrite the following indirect quotations as direct quotations.

1. Sierra said that she is tired of movies. She prefers TV shows.

2. Madelyn said that she prefers movies. She likes an evening at the theater.

3. Sierra said that it is easier to change channels. She said that she can watch a couple of shows at the same time.

4. Madelyn said that she can't do that. She said that she gets confused.

5. Sierra said that Madelyn should come and spend an evening with her. Sierra said that she would show Madelyn her method of watching two TV shows.

Sierra and Madelyn watch TV together.

Making Sentences Work   *Chapter 10*   **211**

Activity B Answers

1. Kim said, "Candace knows a good play we should see." 2. Candace said, "The play will run another month." 3. Andy and Aiesha said, "We are going to visit next month." 4. They said, "We would like to see the play, too." 5. Candace said, "I would like to see the play again."

Activity C Answers

1. Sierra said, "I am tired of movies. I prefer TV shows." 2. Madelyn said, "I prefer movies. I like an evening at the theater." 3. Sierra said, "It is easier to change channels. I can watch a couple of shows at the same time." 4. Madelyn said, "I can't do that. I get confused." 5. Sierra said, "You should come and spend an evening with me. I will show you my method of watching two TV shows."

 3   Reinforce and Extend

LEARNING STYLES

 Logical/Mathematical

To help students identify a pattern in direct and indirect quotations, show them an illustration of a cartoon in which a character's words appear in a bubble. Tell students that material within quotation marks will make sense in such a bubble. Model this pattern with the sentences in the example on page 211.

AT HOME

 Ask students to take notes the next time they watch a program or movie on television. Ask them to write down a short section of dialogue and the character's name. When the program is over, they can rewrite the dialogue into sentences containing direct or indirect quotations. Have students bring the quotations to class, and have the class review their punctuation and capitalization.

TEACHER ALERT

 Tell students that an important function of quotation marks is to give speakers proper credit for their words. Quoting speakers accurately is not just a courtesy; precision is especially important when writers quote people on controversial subjects.

Lesson at a Glance

Chapter 10 Lesson 7

Overview This lesson reinforces the use of the writing process and offers practice in grammar, usage, and mechanics.

Objectives

- To review grammar terms
- To proofread and edit sentences
- To write compound, complex, and compound-complex sentences
- To write a short story

Student Pages 212–213

Teacher's Resource Library **TRL**

Workbook Activity 87

Activity 87

Alternative Activity 87

1 Warm-Up Activity

Write on the board:

From the vender the manager ordered twenty-three boxes of paper folders for the Tues. presentation.

Have students correct the sentence on the board, adding punctuation and spelling out words as needed. (*From the vendor, the manager ordered twenty-three boxes of paper folders for the Tuesday presentation.*)

2 Teaching the Lesson

Tell students that this lesson provides opportunities to review and sharpen their grammar, punctuation, and capitalization skills.

Activity A Answers

1. prewrite, write, rewrite, edit
2. subject and predicate (or verb)
3. period, question mark, exclamation point 4. noun, pronoun, verb, adverb, adjective, preposition, conjunction, interjection 5. An adjective modifies a noun, and an adverb modifies a verb, an adjective, or another adverb.

> Proofreading marks show where to make corrections. A caret (^) is a common proofreading mark. It shows where to add a word or punctuation mark.

It is important to edit your writing carefully. Here are some helpful hints for proofreading your work.

- Look for mistakes in grammar, punctuation, and spelling.
- Check to see that every sentence has a subject and verb and that it expresses a complete thought.
- Make sure that every sentence begins with a capital letter and ends with a punctuation mark.
- Check that the subject and the verb agree. (Singular subjects take singular verbs. Plural subjects take plural verbs.)
- Make sure to use the correct form of a verb to tell about past, present, and future time.

Activity A On your paper, answer each of the following questions.

1. What are the parts of the writing process?
2. What are the two main parts of a sentence?
3. What are three punctuation marks that end sentences?
4. What are the eight parts of speech?
5. What is the difference between an adjective and an adverb?

Activity B Find and edit the mistakes in each sentence. Write the corrected sentence on your paper.

1. claudio called come and eat dinner
2. after people works hard their hungry
3. claudio a good cook grills thick steaks
4. helen told us that she took a trip to her uncles ranch in texas
5. uncle keshawn and helen talked about there horses while claudio grilled steaks potatoes and fresh corn

---

212 *Chapter 10 Making Sentences Work*

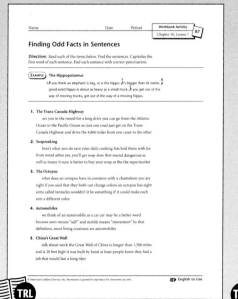

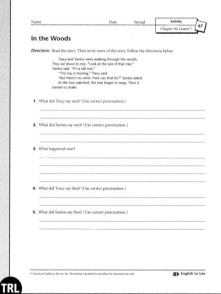

When you write, try to include a variety of sentence types. Remember that you can combine ideas in compound, complex, or compound-complex sentences.

> **EXAMPLE**
>
> **Simple**
> The snow fell. The snow melted. The temperature rose.
> **Compound**
> The snow fell, and then it melted; the temperature rose.
> **Complex**
> The snow melted as the temperature rose.
> **Compound-complex**
> The snow fell and, as the temperature rose, the snow melted.

Activity C Combine the ideas in these simple sentences into compound, complex, or compound-complex sentences. Write at least one sentence of each type on your paper.

1. The dog barked. The cat scratched. They fought.
2. The ball bounced. The player jumped. The game ended.
3. Lights dimmed. Music played. The movie started.
4. Monkeys screech. Lions roar. The zoo opens.
5. A rooster crows. A robin sings. A new day dawns.

Activity D Use the steps in the writing process to write a short story about Ellen on your paper. Use a variety of sentence types and quotations in your story. Use this information.

> Serena asked Ellen to a party. Ellen said she would go. She doesn't know many of the people who will be at the party. Later, her best friend asks her to another party. She talks to her friends about the problem.

1. What do Ellen's friends say? What does Ellen decide to do? What does she tell Serena and her best friend?
2. Rewrite and edit your short story about Ellen.

Making Sentences Work Chapter 10 **213**

Activity B Answers

Some answers may vary.

1. Claudio called, "Come and eat dinner!" 2. After people work hard, they're hungry. 3. Claudio, a good cook, grills thick steaks. 4. Helen told us that she took a trip to her uncle's ranch in Texas. 5. Uncle Keshawn and Helen talked about their horses while Claudio grilled steaks, potatoes, and fresh corn.

Activity C Answers

Answers will vary. Sample responses are given.

1. The dog barked and the cat scratched when they fought. 2. The ball bounced and the player jumped as the game ended. 3. Lights dimmed, music played, and the movie started. 4. Monkeys screech and lions roar as the zoo opens. 5. As a new day dawns, a rooster crows and a robin sings.

Activity D Answers

Short stories will vary.

 3 Reinforce and Extend

Lesson at a Glance

Chapter 10 Lesson 8

Overview This lesson focuses on the punctuation of quotations. It also reviews capitalization and punctuation in compound and complex sentences.

Objectives

- To add punctuation and capitalization in existing sentences
- To write direct quotations using appropriate verbs

Student Pages 214–215

Teacher's Resource Library

Workbook Activity 88

Activity 88

Alternative Activity 88

---

1 Warm-Up Activity

Write the following passage on the board:

Have you read the new issue of los angeles magazine serena asked. No declan replied I didn't know it had arrived in the library. What great photographers that magazine has juana exclaimed. They're the best in the state.

Have the class identify the speakers and quotations in the passage above. Discuss with the class how the proper capitalization and punctuation of quotations makes them much easier to understand. Then have the class correct the passage's punctuation and capitalization.

2 Teaching the Lesson

Discuss the different placement of the speaker tag in the sentences in the second example and the correct use of commas with each construction.

Next, discuss the placement of question marks and exclamation points in quotations, using the example sentences as a guide. Remind students that when a quotation that is not a question or an exclamation ends a sentence, the period is always inside the final quotation mark.

A direct quotation may stand alone.

> **EXAMPLE** "The day we quit is the day we lose."

The name of the person quoted can come before, after, or in the middle of the quotation. Notice the placement of the commas that separate the speaker from the quotation in each of these examples.

> **EXAMPLE**
> Mr. Hackett said, "The day we quit is the day we lose."
> "The day we quit," said Mr. Hackett, "is the day we lose."
> "The day we quit is the day we lose," said Mr. Hackett.

If a quotation is a question or an exclamation, place the question mark or exclamation point before the final quotation mark.

> **EXAMPLE**
> "Where have you been?" Kerry asked.
> Susan exclaimed, "What an exciting time we had!"
> (Notice that no comma comes before Kerry's name. No end punctuation comes after the quotation marks that enclose an exclamation or a question that ends a sentence.)

Activity A Write these sentences correctly on your paper.

1. Melanie said welcome to my cafe
2. Where is the meal I ordered asked Travis
3. Tom asked quietly zack are you asleep
4. justin's father yelled I thought you were working on the lawn
5. I was working said justin but I took a break

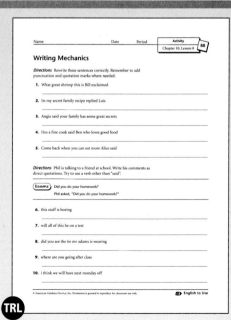

Workbook Activity 88

Activity 88

Yell

Ask

Declare

Repeating the verb *said* in sentences can make your writing sound dull. Here is a list of other verbs to use in place of *said* when writing direct quotations.

ask	exclaim	mumble
call out	gasp	whisper
declare	laugh	yell

Activity B Tia is at a ball game. On your paper, write Tia's comments as direct quotations. Try not to repeat the word *said* in your sentences. Look at the list above for words you can use in place of *said*.

Example   Let's play harder
             Tia yelled, "Let's play harder!"

1. when will this game begin
2. I hope it doesn't rain
3. that was a nice catch
4. don't stop run for third base
5. send in a new pitcher

Activity C Write these compound and complex sentences on your paper. Add capital letters and punctuation.

1. the day was a long one and now i am very tired
2. new york is a nice city but i prefer san diego
3. january is cold june is warm
4. as i sit here i think about my friends and my family
5. when class began mary wasn't there

Using What You've Learned

Write a conversation between yourself and a friend or family member. The conversation can be real or imaginary. Place names of the speakers before, after, or in the middle of quotations. Use a variety of verbs that mean "say." Make sure you have used end punctuation and quotation marks correctly.

Activity A Answers

1. Melanie said, "Welcome to my cafe." 2. "Where is the meal I ordered?" asked Travis. 3. Tom asked quietly, "Zack, are you asleep?" 4. Justin's father yelled, "I thought you were working on the lawn!" 5. "I was working," said Justin, "but I took a break."

Activity B Answers

Answers will vary.

Activity C Answers

1. The day was a long one, and now I am very tired. 2. New York is a nice city, but I prefer San Diego. 3. January is cold; June is warm. 4. As I sit here, I think about my friends and my family. 5. When class began, Mary wasn't there.

3 ▶ Reinforce and Extend

CAREER CONNECTION

As part of students' efforts to explore future career options, suggest that they ask workers they know, "Do you like your job? Why, or why not?" Have them write the responses as direct quotations, without worrying about retaining every word. They might pretend the worker is a character in a story and write his or her thoughts as a conversation. In class, discuss the reasons people give for liking or not liking their jobs.

Using What You've Learned

Some writers, such as journalists, have to be especially sure that their quotations are accurate. Some students may enjoy recording short conversations (with the permission of the people involved) and then writing down the quotations. By referring to the recording, students can be sure that each quotation is exact.

Chapter 10 Review

Use the Chapter Review to prepare students for tests and to reteach content from the chapter.

Chapter 10 Mastery Test

The Teacher's Resource Library includes two parallel forms of the Chapter 10 Mastery Test. The difficulty level of the two forms is equivalent. You may wish to use one form as a pretest and the other form as a posttest.

REVIEW ANSWERS

Part A

1. dependent clause
2. quotation marks 3. complex sentence 4. indirect quotation
5. tone of voice 6. independent clause 7. question pronoun
8. direct quotation
9. compound-complex sentence

Part B

Answers will vary. Sample responses are given.

10. Well, you should have looked both ways! 11. Look! There is my math teacher! 12. Hey! Can you go ask him a question?

Part C

13–15 Sentences will vary but should be based on the information in each sentence.

Part D

16. S—Zachary, V—does use
17. S—he, V—Has written
18. S—Zachary, V—did buy
19. S—he, V—will sell

Chapter 10 R E V I E W

Word Bank

complex sentence
compound-complex sentence
dependent clause
direct quotation
independent clause
indirect quotation
question pronoun
quotation marks
tone of voice

Part A Read each sentence below. Fill in each blank with a vocabulary word that correctly completes each sentence.

1. A group of words that does not form a complete thought and cannot stand alone is a _____ .
2. Place _____ around the words in a direct quotation.
3. A _____ contains both an independent clause and a dependent clause.
4. An _____ uses words other than the speaker's to tell what the speaker says.
5. The sound of a speaker's voice is called _____ .
6. An _____ expresses a complete thought and is a sentence.
7. A pronoun that forms a question is called a _____ .
8. A _____ is the speaker's exact words.
9. A sentence with two or more independent clauses and one or more dependent clauses is a _____ .

Part B Rewrite these sentences, choosing punctuation that shows the tone of voice.

10. Well you should have looked both ways
11. Look there is my math teacher
12. Hey can you go ask him a question

Part C Write one question, one statement, one command, and one strong command for each group of words below.

13. Your neighbor has three dogs
14. I can eat dinner early tonight
15. The computer is fixed.

Part D On your paper, write the subject and the complete verb for each question.

16. Why does Zachary still use that old computer?
17. Has he written good stories on it?
18. Where did Zachary buy it?
19. When will he sell it?

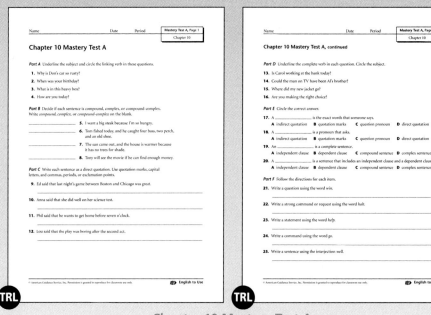

Chapter 10 Mastery Test A

Part E Read each sentence below. Choose the letter next to the word that tells the part of speech of the word in bold.

20. **Which** of the books did you write?
- A question pronoun
- C adverb
- B verb
- D subject

21. Why **is** the cat fat?
- A subject
- C linking verb
- B helping verb
- D adverb

22. How **can** you learn about the contest?
- A subject
- C adverb
- B helping verb
- D linking verb

Part F Write these sentences correctly on your paper. Use punctuation and capital letters.

23. where does the dirt road lead garret asked

24. alice yelled the last movie begins in two minutes

25. you can do it lena exclaimed if you try

Part G Write these sentences on your paper. Underline the independent clause once and the dependent clause twice.

26. The team that won the championship was from Atlanta.

27. Whatever happens, the play will open Saturday.

Part H Write whether each sentence is compound, complex, or compound-complex.

28. When the class bell rang, some students were in the hall.

29. Because the day was hot, Bryan went home early, and Jana went swimming.

30. I am going to the beach, and Tanya is going shopping.

 If you are having trouble solving a problem on a test, go on to the next problem and come back to any skipped problems.

Part E

20. A 21. C 22. B

Part F

23. "Where does the dirt road lead?" Garret asked. 24. Alice yelled, "The last movie begins in two minutes!" 25. "You can do it," Lena exclaimed, "if you try!"

Part G

26. The team that won the championship was from Atlanta.
27. Whatever happens, the play will open Saturday.

Part H

28. complex 29. compound-complex 30. compound

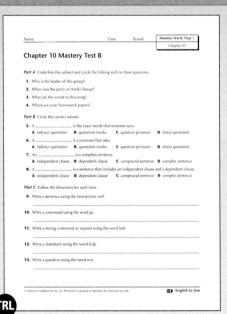

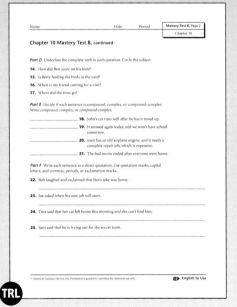

Chapter 10 Mastery Test B

Making Sentences Work   *Chapter 10*   **217**

Planning Guide

Writing for Others

	Student Pages	Student Text Lesson		Language Skills		
		Vocabulary	Practice Activities	Identification Skills	Writing Skills	Punctuation Skills
Lesson 1 Write the Facts	220–221	✔	✔	✔	✔	✔
Lesson 2 Facts Make News	222–223	✔	✔	✔	✔	✔
Lesson 3 Write a Paragraph to Describe	224–225	✔	✔	✔	✔	✔
Lesson 4 Writing a Process Paragraph	226–227	✔	✔	✔	✔	✔
Lesson 5 Writing a Paragraph to Persuade	228–229	✔	✔	✔	✔	✔
Lesson 6 Writing a Story	230–231	✔	✔	✔	✔	✔
Lesson 7 Writing a Review	232–233	✔	✔	✔	✔	✔
Lesson 8 Writing a Letter to a Friend	234–235	✔	✔	✔	✔	✔
Lesson 9 Writing Mechanics	236–237		✔	✔	✔	✔

Chapter Activities

Teacher's Resource Library

Community Connection 11:
Talk with a Senior Citizen

English in Your World 11:
The Parts of a Memo

Assessment Options

Student Text

Chapter 11 Review

Teacher's Resource Library

Chapter 11 Mastery Tests A and B

	Student Text Features				Teaching Strategies					Learning Styles						Teacher's Resource Library				
ASL Illustration	Communication Connection	Notes	Using What You've Learned	Writing Tips	Teacher Alert	Online Connection	Applications (Home, Career, Community, Global)	Speaking Practice	Writing Practice	Auditory/Verbal	Body/Kinesthetic	Interpersonal/Group Learning	Logical/Mathematical	Visual/Spatial	LEP/ESL	Workbook Activities	Activities	Alternative Activities	Sentence Diagramming Activities	Self-Study Guide
		✔				221				221						89	89	89		✔
223				✔			223				223					90	90	90		✔
				✔			225								225	91	91	91		✔
227		✔					227	227						227		92	92	92		✔
				✔			229						229			93	93	93		✔
		✔							231	231						94	94	94		✔
	233									233						95	95	95		✔
			235		235							235				96	96	96		✔
					237									237		97	97	97		✔
					239															

Pronunciation Key

a	hat	e	let	ī	ice	ô	order	ù	put	sh	she	ə	a	in about
ā	age	ē	equal	o	hot	oi	oil	ü	rule	th	thin		e	in taken
ä	far	ėr	term	ō	open	ou	out	ch	child	ᴛH	then		i	in pencil
â	care	i	it	ò	saw	u	cup	ng	long	zh	measure		o	in lemon
													u	in circus

Alternative Activities

The Teacher's Resource Library (TRL) contains a set of lower-level worksheets called Alternative Activities. These worksheets cover the same content as the regular Activities but are written at a second-grade reading level.

Skill Track Software

Use the Skill Track Software for English to Use for additional reinforcement of this chapter. The software program allows students using AGS textbooks to be assessed for mastery of each chapter and lesson of the textbook. Students access the software on an individual basis and are assessed with multiple-choice items.

218B

Chapter 11: Writing for Others

pages 218–239

Lessons

1. **Write the Facts**
   pages 220–221

2. **Facts Make News**
   pages 222–223

3. **Writing a Paragraph to Describe**
   pages 224–225

4. **Writing a Process Paragraph**
   pages 226–227

5. **Writing a Paragraph to Persuade**
   pages 228–229

6. **Writing a Story**
   pages 230–231

7. **Writing a Review**
   pages 232–233

8. **Writing a Letter to a Friend**
   pages 234–235

9. **Writing Mechanics**
   pages 236–237

Chapter 11 Review
pages 238–239

Skill Track Software for English to Use

Teacher's Resource Library

Workbook Activities 89–97

Activities 89–97

Alternative Activities 89–97

Community Connection 11

English in Your World 11

Chapter 11 Self-Study Guide

Chapter 11 Mastery Tests A and B

(Answer Keys for the Teacher's Resource Library begin on page 308 of this Teacher's Edition.)

Talk with a Senior Citizen

Older people have interesting stories to tell. What was it like when they were young! What did they do for fun? What memories do they have about the places they lived?

Directions Talk with an older person in your community. Ask the questions below. Write the answers on this page.

1. Where did you live when you were growing up? _____
2. What did you do for fun? _____
3. What work did you do? Did you like it? _____
4. What is your happiest memory? _____

5. What is the biggest difference between your life as a younger person and the way younger people live now? _____

6. Write a paragraph to your teacher about your conversation with this person. _____

The Parts of a Memo

A memorandum, or memo for short, is an informal message written in a special form. It is used most often by businesses. At the top of most memos are four bits of information: who the memo is to, who it is from, the date, and the subject.

Learning how to read and write memos is an important skill to have when you begin to work. A memo is the main way to communicate for most companies. Writing an unclear memo or not reading a memo correctly can cause mistakes.

To get an idea of what memos look like, study actual memos. Follow the steps below.

Step 1 Get at least two copies of memos from a friend or family member who works. You could also ask for a copy of a memo from a local business.

Step 2 Answer the questions below about the two memos.

1. Who are the memos to? _____
2. Who are the memos from? _____
3. What is the subject for each memo? _____
4. What information is being communicated in the body of each memo? _____
5. Do the memos ask for someone to do something? _____

11 Writing for Others

Do you enjoy writing letters? You write letters mainly to communicate with others. How do you make your letters interesting and fun for the people who read them? Do you share important details of your life and the lives of those close to you? Do you include humorous stories about yourself?

A letter is one form of written communication. There are other forms, such as memos, invitations, news articles, directions, stories, and reviews. Whenever you write, your goal is to share information and ideas with readers. To be sure readers understand your ideas, you must present them in a clear, organized way.

In this chapter, you will study different forms of written communication.

Goals for Learning

◆ To write facts in memos, invitations, and news stories
◆ To write paragraphs that describe, that give directions, and that persuade
◆ To write a story, a review, and a letter

219

Introducing the Chapter

Discuss with students the writing that they create for others to read. Remind them of letters, invitations to events, or papers for assignments they may have written. Ask students to talk about the person or persons for whom they were writing and to discuss how formal or casual their writing style was in each example. Tell students that this chapter will provide guidelines and practice for various forms of written communication.

TEACHER'S RESOURCE

The AGS Teaching Strategies in English Transparencies may be used with this chapter. The transparencies add an interactive dimension to expand and enhance the *English to Use* program content.

CAREER INTEREST INVENTORY

The AGS Harrington-O'Shea Career Decision-Making System–Revised (CDM) may be used with this chapter. Students can use the CDM to explore their interests and identify careers. The CDM defines career areas that are indicated by students' responses on the inventory.

Writing Tips and Notes

Ask volunteers to read the tips and notes that appear in the margins throughout the chapter. Then discuss them with the class.

CHAPTER PROJECT

Ask students to bring in direct mail letters they have received in the mail at home. The letters can be advertisements, solicitations, or public service announcements. Students can analyze the type of message in the letters and discuss how effectively the message is delivered. In addition, students review the address forms used on the envelopes.

Lesson at a Glance

Chapter 11 Lesson 1

Overview This lesson focuses on the format and elements of memos and invitations.

Objective

■ To select essential facts for memos and invitations

Student Pages 220–221

Teacher's Resource Library

Workbook Activity 89

Activity 89

Alternative Activity 89

Vocabulary

invitation
memo

1 Warm-Up Activity

Have students give examples of messages they have forgotten to pass along or of times when they have missed an important message. Discuss how problems might have been avoided and the importance of writing down essential information. You may want to bring examples of telephone message pads.

2 Teaching the Lesson

Point out that taking clear, accurate notes is an important skill that students will use in their daily lives. Ask students to offer other examples of situations in which note taking is required.

Discuss the information in the sample memo. Point out that telephone messages usually are handwritten on preprinted memo pads but that they also may be sent by e-mail.

220 *Chapter 11 Writing for Others*

Memo

A clear, organized record of important facts and details

Imagine this scene: The phone rings. You answer it. It's for your sister who is out. You take a message, making sure that you write the information clearly and accurately.

People in offices handle situations like this every day. An important part of their jobs is their ability to take and give messages clearly and accurately.

Memo is short for *memorandum*. The word *memorandum* comes from Latin. It means "something that must be remembered." A memo's brief, clear form makes details easy to see and remember.

Many office workers record important messages in **memos.** A memo records facts and details in a clear, organized way. The person reading the memo should not have any questions about the message or its purpose. Look at the example memo below.

EXAMPLE On January 15 at 2:00 P.M., Mark called. Troy answered the phone. Mark told Troy that it was very important that Kendrell call him back that night before 8:00 P.M. at 945-555-2216.

MEMO	
To:	Kendrell
From:	Troy
Subject:	Phone call from Mark
Date:	Jan. 15
Time:	2:00 P.M.

He says it is important that you call him back before 8:00 P.M. tonight at 945-555-2216.

Activity A On your paper, write a memo for each of these phone calls. Use the example as your model.

1. Linda called Joey on December 1 at 3:30 P.M. She wants him to meet her at 5th and State Streets at 5:00 P.M.

2. Peter called for Aaron on January 7 at 7:00 P.M. He wants to borrow one of Aaron's cassette tapes.

3. Kim called on April 2 at 8:00 P.M. She wants Karen to call her tomorrow at work. The number is 766-555-7011.

220 *Chapter 11 Writing for Others*

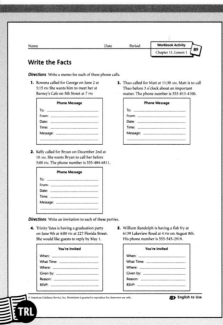

Workbook Activity 89   **Activity 89**

Invitation
A written request

An **invitation** is a written request. An invitation asks someone to attend a party, a meeting, a lunch, or other event. Like a memo, an invitation presents important information in a clear, organized way. Invitations tell

- what the event is and, usually, its purpose
- when, where, and at what time the event will take place
- who is arranging the event

Most invitations also include a telephone number for an RSVP. This means "please reply" to tell whether you can or cannot attend the event. Often, an invitation gives a date by which to reply. This helps the person planning the event know how many people will attend. Here is an example of an invitation.

> **You're invited to a celebration!**
>
> | **When:** | June 3 |
> |---|---|
> | **What Time:** | 4:00 P.M. |
> | **Where:** | 1340 Dustpath Way |
> | **Given by:** | Helen Waite |
> | | To celebrate Tom Waite's graduation |
> | **RSVP:** | 502-555-2072, by May 15 |

Activity B On your paper, write an invitation to each of these parties.

1. Everett Hull is having a New Year's Eve party on December 31 at 9:00 P.M. at 16 Holland Street. He would like guests to reply by December 20. His phone number is 223-555-7102.

2. Katie Thomas is having a graduation party on June 2 at 2:00 P.M. at 201 South Fourth Street. Her phone number is 678-555-4003.

3. Bill McKay and Jill Johnson just got engaged. Jill's younger sister Amy is having a party for them at 7:00 P.M. on March 4 at 601 West Main. Amy's phone number is 811-555-1767. She wants guests to reply by February 15.

 3 **Reinforce and Extend**

LEARNING STYLES

 Auditory/Verbal

Ask students to form groups of three. Ask one group member to whisper a message to a second group member, who must write a memo about the message for the third person. The person receiving the memo can check with the first student to see whether the memo is accurate.

ONLINE CONNECTION

 For more ideas on teaching students about taking notes, see "Teaching Students to Take Better Notes: Notes on Notetaking" featured on the University of Nebraska-Lincoln's Teaching & Learning Center Web site, *www.unl. edu/teaching/notetakingtips.html*.

Activity A Answers

1. To: Joey
   From: [Student's name]
   Subject: Phone call from Linda
   Date: Dec. 1
   Time: 3:30 P.M.
   Linda will meet you at the corner of 5th and State Streets at 5:00 P.M.

2. To: Aaron
   From: [Student's name]
   Subject: Phone call from Peter
   Date: Jan. 7
   Time: 7:00 P.M.
   Peter wants to borrow one of your cassette tapes.

3. To: Karen
   From: [Student's name]
   Subject: Phone call from Kim
   Date: Apr. 2
   Time: 8:00 P.M.
   Kim wants you to call her tomorrow at work—766-555-7011.

Activity B Answers

Wording may vary. Invitations should include the following details.

1. When: December 31
   What Time: 9:00 P.M.
   Where: 16 Holland Street
   Given by: Everett Hull, to celebrate the New Year
   RSVP: 223-555-7102 by December 20

2. When: June 2
   What Time: 2:00 P.M.
   Where: 201 South Fourth Street
   Given by: Katie Thomas, to celebrate graduation
   RSVP: 678-555-4003

3. When: March 4
   What Time: 7:00 P.M.
   Where: 601 West Main
   Given by: Amy Johnson, to celebrate the engagement of Bill McKay to her sister Jill Johnson
   RSVP: 811-555-1767 by February 15

Lesson at a Glance

Chapter 11 Lesson 2

Overview This lesson focuses on the elements in a lead paragraph of a news article.

Objectives

■ To identify facts in the lead paragraph of a news article

■ To write a lead paragraph from given facts

Student Pages 222–223

Teacher's Resource Library TRL

Workbook Activity 90

Activity 90

Alternative Activity 90

Vocabulary

lead paragraph

---

 1 Warm-Up Activity

Read aloud the first paragraph of a newspaper story. Then ask what the paragraph was about and what facts students learned. List the facts on the board. Help students identify *who, what, when, where, why,* and *how.*

2 Teaching the Lesson

Ask students to discuss why lead paragraphs include the most important facts in a story. Point out that newspaper articles are cut for fit from the bottom up. By putting the most important facts at the beginning, writers make sure that essential parts of the article won't be cut.

Activity A Answers

1. Who: Miguel Rivera **2.** What: All-State Pitcher **3.** Where: at a State Baseball Association conference **4.** When: last Monday **5.** Why: he pitched five shutouts **6.** How: with his fastball

---

Lesson 2 Facts Make News

Lead paragraph
A paragraph that introduces a news article; it tells who, what, when, where, why, and sometimes, how

Writing Tip
When you write a news story, make the first sentence of your lead paragraph engaging. The first sentence is called the hook. It should catch the reader's attention.

News stories give us facts about current events. We hear news reports on radio and television. We read news articles in newspapers and magazines. The **lead paragraph** in a news article answers the questions *who, what, where, when, why,* and sometimes, *how.*

EXAMPLE

> ### Local Girl Wins Award
>
> Maya Lewis, 1206 Rock Road, won an award at the county festival last Sunday for her giant tomatoes. The tomatoes raised by Lewis were as large as basketballs. When asked how she grew such big tomatoes, Lewis replied, "Water, luck, and my secret plant food."

Who:	Maya Lewis
What:	won an award
Where:	at the county festival
When:	last Sunday
Why:	for her tomatoes
How:	water, luck, secret plant food

Activity A Read this lead paragraph for a news article. Find the facts that answer the questions below. Write the facts on your paper.

> ### Rivera Wins Sports Honor
>
> Miguel Rivera, 409 Bluewave Blvd., was named "All-State Pitcher" by the State Baseball Association at a conference last Monday. Rivera's fastball helped him pitch five shutouts for the Centerpoint Mustangs last year. The Mustangs finished undefeated.

1. Who?
2. What?
3. Where?
4. When?
5. Why?
6. How?

Workbook Activity 90   Activity 90

Who

What

Where

Why

The Writing Process

1. **Prewrite** The facts are given for you to use.
2. **Write** Turn the facts into sentences. Write quickly.
3. **Rewrite** Improve your sentences.
4. **Edit** Read your work and correct all mistakes.

Activity B Use the steps above to write a lead paragraph for an article about the events outlined below.

1. *Who:* Joshua Hirsch
   What: arrived from Israel
   When: Tuesday
   Where: New York City
   Why: to see a brother he hasn't seen in fifty years

2. *Who:* Enzo Santos
   What: won Dry Gulch Auto Race
   When: Saturday
   Where: Reno, Nevada
   Why: best time for the track
   How: fastest car and best pit crew

3. *Who:* Elisa Harper
   What: slept on her roof
   When: Thursday night
   Why: to escape floodwaters when dam broke
   How: "I climbed out the attic window and onto the roof."

4. *Who:* Ella Schmidt
   What: won music contest
   When: Friday
   Where: Park College
   Why: played guitar and drums
   How: played original songs and well-known favorites

5. *Who:* Florita Wilson
   What: caught a 20-pound catfish
   When: Thursday evening
   Where: Black Lagoon, Memphis
   Why: to win contest for biggest fish
   How: used old-fashioned bait—ordinary earthworms

Writing for Others   Chapter 11   **223**

Activity B Answers

Answers will vary, but each should contain the basic facts in sentence form.

 Reinforce and Extend

LEARNING STYLES

 Body/Kinesthetic
Ask student pairs to find examples of good lead paragraphs in newspapers or magazines. Have the pairs work together to act out the event described in the paragraph. Have other class members question the student pairs about the event, asking them *Who? What? Where? When? Why?* and *How?*

AT HOME

Ask students to read, listen to, or watch a news story at home, writing the basic facts that answer the questions *Who? What? Where? When? Why?* and *How?* Assure students that identifying these specific facts enables people to grasp quickly the content of a news story.

ASL ILLUSTRATION

Ask students to practice making the signs illustrated on page 223. Then ask students to look back at previous chapters to find examples of ASL sentences. Ask students to turn the ASL sentences into questions by using the signs on page 223. Suggest that students use reference tools to find the ASL sign for *how*.

Lesson at a Glance

Chapter 11 Lesson 3

Overview This lesson defines and explains how to write a descriptive paragraph.

Objectives

- To understand the purpose of a topic sentence
- To use the writing process to write a descriptive paragraph

Student Pages 224–225

Teacher's Resource Library

Workbook Activity 91

Activity 91

Alternative Activity 91

....

Vocabulary

descriptive paragraph
paragraph
topic
topic sentence

....

 1 Warm-Up Activity

Ask students to define *paragraph*. Record their definitions on the board. Then ask students what they think the purpose of a descriptive paragraph might be. Compare students' definitions to those in the lesson.

 2 Teaching the Lesson

Go over the steps of the writing process for a descriptive paragraph and discuss the example. Invite volunteers to make up other facts and sentences to go with the edited paragraph. Write the facts and sentences on the board and ask students to decide whether they do or do not relate to the topic sentence.

Activity A Answers

Paragraphs will vary. Monitor students' use of the writing process.

A **paragraph** is a group of sentences that tells about one **topic**, or main idea. The **topic sentence** states the main idea of the paragraph. The other sentences in the paragraph relate to, or support, the main idea.

A **descriptive paragraph** describes a person, place, or thing. Use the steps of the writing process to write a descriptive paragraph.

1. **Prewrite** Think about a topic. Write it down. List facts about your topic, along with some descriptive adjectives.
2. **Write** Write a topic sentence. Then write a sentence for each fact on your list.
3. **Rewrite** Improve the paragraph. Combine short sentences into longer ones. Check to see that all the sentences are about the topic. Change the order of sentences if you wish.
4. **Edit** Check your spelling, punctuation, and word use. Make changes for your final copy.

> **EXAMPLE** **Topic sentence**
> The hillside was beautiful that June morning.
> **Facts**
> 1. big trees in the field
> 2. summer wind
> 3. flowers in the field
> 4. puffy, white clouds
> 5. clear, blue sky
>
> **Edited Paragraph**
> The hillside was beautiful that June morning. A summer wind warmed us. We watched the flowers in the field swaying under puffy, white clouds. Everything glistened under a clear blue sky.

Activity A Use the steps in the writing process to write a paragraph that describes your favorite place. Write your paragraph on your paper.

Paragraph
A group of sentences about one topic
Topic
The main idea of an essay or paragraph
Topic sentence
A sentence that states the main idea of a paragraph
Descriptive paragraph
A paragraph that describes a person, place, or thing

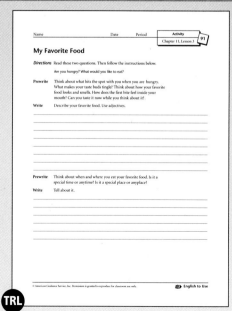

Workbook Activity 91   Activity 91

Writing Tip

To write a paragraph, you will probably need at least three facts. If you do not have enough facts, choose a different topic.

Activity B Write a paragraph about Gregory Ramos. Use the following topic sentence and supporting facts and details:

> **Topic sentence**
> Gregory Ramos was a well-liked person.
>
> **Facts and details**
> 1. friendly   4. helpful
> 2. polite   5. sense of humor
> 3. good listener   6. honest

Activity C Write a paragraph that describes your dream house. What does it look like? What special features does it have? Be as creative as you wish. Use the steps in the writing process to write your paragraph.

Activity D Write a paragraph about a special moment in time. Use the steps in the writing process as you create a descriptive paragraph with the following information:

> **Topic sentence**
> The senator from Ohio spoke to the class.
>
> **Facts and details**
> 1. on the lawn in front of school   4. senator talked
> 2. students gathered   5. people asked questions
> 3. principal introduced senator   6. warm afternoon in April

Activity E Write a paragraph about the best or most important moment in your life. Use the steps in the writing process to write your paragraph.

Students gather to listen to a speech.

Writing for Others   Chapter 11   **225**

Activity B Answers

Paragraphs will vary. Check to see that students have included the supporting facts and details.

Activity C Answers

Paragraphs will vary. Have each student switch paragraphs with a classmate to complete the "edit" step in the writing process.

Activity D Answers

Paragraphs will vary.

Activity E Answers

Paragraphs will vary.

3   Reinforce and Extend

LEARNING STYLES

LEP/ESL

English language learners may need more structure as they begin to add description in the Chapter 11 activities. For Activity C, for example, make sure that language learners have the vocabulary necessary to name the different parts of a house. Begin by asking language learners to name different parts of a house and listing the words on the board. Then ask students to think of descriptive details for each part.

GLOBAL CONNECTION

Display a scenic picture of another region or country. After you identify the place and locate it on a map or globe, ask students for words and phrases about the place. Record students' responses on the board. Then ask students to use the ideas on the board to write a descriptive paragraph about the place. Encourage students to follow the steps of the writing process. Invite students to share their edited paragraphs with the class.

Lesson at a Glance

Chapter 11 Lesson 4

Overview This lesson defines and explains how to write a process paragraph.

Objectives
- To write a process paragraph
- To reorder the steps in a process paragraph

Student Pages 226–227

Teacher's Resource Library

Workbook Activity 92

Activity 92

Alternative Activity 92

....

Vocabulary

process paragraph

....

 Warm-Up Activity

Ask students to explain step-by-step how to play a game or sport. Write the steps on the board in the order that students describe them. Have students review the steps to make sure none are missing. Then cover up one of the steps so it is hidden. Ask students whether a reader could follow the steps if one was missing or out of order.

 Teaching the Lesson

Discuss the example and the edited paragraph. Encourage students who bowl to add steps that might be helpful to someone who has never bowled.

Activity A Answers

Paragraphs will vary. Look for a clear topic sentence. Check to see that no steps are missing and that there are logical supporting steps.

Lesson 4 Writing a Process Paragraph

Process paragraph
A paragraph that tells how to do something

You can write a paragraph to explain how to do something. A **process paragraph** explains step-by-step how to do something. When you are writing a process paragraph, it is important to include each step of the process and to order the steps in the correct sequence.

1. Prewrite Think about a topic sentence. Write it down. Add a list of steps.

2. Write Write a sentence for each step on your list. Keep your sentences about the steps short and easy to follow.

3. Rewrite Improve the paragraph. Check to see that you have not left out any steps. Be sure your sentences are in the right order.

4. Edit Check your spelling, punctuation, and word use. Make changes for your final copy.

Words that tell the order of steps are important. Help readers follow your order by using words such as *first, second, third, next, last, then, before,* and *after.*

EXAMPLE

Topic sentence
Bowling can be fun when you relax and follow these simple directions.

Steps
1. Hold the ball in front of you.
2. Take three steps toward the pins.
3. Roll the ball down the alley on your last step.

Edited paragraph
Bowling can be fun when you relax and follow a few simple directions. First, hold the ball in front of you. Next, take three steps toward the pins. Finally, roll the ball down the alley on your last step.

Activity A Write a process paragraph about sharpening a pencil. Watch someone sharpen a pencil. List each step. Then follow the rest of the writing process to complete your paragraph.

226 *Chapter 11 Writing for Others*

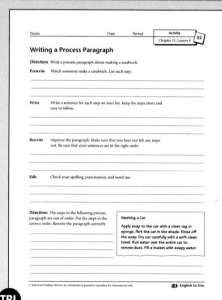

Workbook Activity 92   Activity 92

Plate

Dishwashing

Washing the dishes

Riding a bicycle

Activity B The steps in the following process paragraph are out of order. Put the steps in the correct order. Then rewrite the paragraph correctly on your paper.

Changing a Lightbulb

The lightbulb in the table lamp has burned out, and the lamp needs a new bulb. Twist the new lightbulb into the socket. Remove the lamp shade. Take the old lightbulb out of the socket by twisting the bulb counterclockwise, or starting toward the left. Put the lamp shade back on the lamp. Unplug the lamp from the wall. Plug the lamp into the wall outlet again. Now the lamp is fixed.

Activity C Choose three of the following topics. On your paper, write a process paragraph about each topic. Be sure to follow the steps in the writing process.

Riding a Bicycle	Playing a Video Game
Making a Sandwich	Fixing a Flat Tire
Selecting a Library Book	Making Cookies
Dialing Long Distance	Setting an Alarm Clock
Washing the Dishes	Wrapping a Present
Planting a Tree	Playing a Sport
Ironing a Shirt	Playing a Musical Instrument
Walking on Ice	Shopping for Shoes
Waxing a Car	Making Breakfast
Mowing the Lawn	Planning a Party

Activity B Answers

(Students might logically reverse the second and third sentences and the sixth and seventh sentences in the following paragraph.)

The lightbulb in the table lamp has burned out, and the lamp needs a new bulb. Unplug the lamp from the wall. Remove the lamp shade. Take the old lightbulb out of the socket by twisting the bulb counterclockwise, or starting toward the left. Twist the new lightbulb into the socket. Put the lamp shade back on the lamp. Plug the lamp into the wall outlet again. Now the lamp is fixed.

Activity C Answers

Paragraphs will vary.

3   Reinforce and Extend

LEARNING STYLES

Visual/Spatial

Gather directions from recipe books, game boxes, electronic equipment, and so on. Do students find the instructions clear? Do they think they could prepare the recipe, play the game, or assemble the product by following the instructions?

Speaking Practice

Have students read aloud the paragraphs they have written for Activity C. Ask them to emphasize the words that tell the order of steps, such as *first, next,* and *later.* Ask the class how the emphasis helped them follow the step-by-step process.

ASL ILLUSTRATION

Have students practice the signs illustrated on page 227. Ask students who wrote paragraphs on riding a bicycle or washing dishes to identify two or three of the most important steps in those processes. Then have students use online or other resources to find the ASL signs to describe these processes.

Lesson at a Glance

Chapter 11 Lesson 5

Overview This lesson outlines the steps for writing persuasive paragraphs.

Objective

■ To write persuasive paragraphs

Student Pages 228–229

Teacher's Resource Library

Workbook Activity 93

Activity 93

Alternative Activity 93

....

Vocabulary

persuasive paragraph

 Warm-Up Activity

Display several advertisements from newspapers and magazines. Ask students to study the ads and explain the purpose of each one. Have students talk about how the ads encourage readers to take an action or buy a particular product. Explain that advertising is a form of persuasive writing.

 Teaching the Lesson

Discuss the information presented in the text. Review how the writing process is used to write persuasive paragraphs. Ask students to study the example, pointing out Justin's reason for writing. Note that his topic sentence gets right to the point and that his last sentence sums up his position. Also note that, as in previous examples, the edited paragraph arranges the list of facts to make an effective argument.

Writing a Paragraph to Persuade

Persuasive paragraph
A paragraph that tries to make readers believe something or do something

Have you ever made up your mind to do something or believe something because you're sure that you are right? Then, you may have read something that persuaded you to change your mind. A **persuasive paragraph** tries to convince readers to think or act a certain way. When you write a persuasive paragraph, include language that will make people think and feel as you do.

1. **Prewrite** Write down something you would like to persuade others to do. List reasons why others should believe the way you do about this topic.

2. **Write** Write a topic sentence that states your purpose (to persuade readers to do something). Then write sentences for each reason you listed.

3. **Rewrite** Check to see that you have listed all the reasons you can think of to support your topic. Change or add words that will make your paragraph more persuasive.

4. **Edit** Check your spelling, punctuation, and word use. Make changes for your final copy.

> **EXAMPLE** Justin's manager has decided to lay him off to cut costs at work. Justin must persuade his manager not to lay him off.
>
> **Topic sentence**
> I am a good employee for this company.
>
> **Facts**
> 1. finish tasks quickly
> 2. arrive early
> 3. work after hours sometimes
> 4. skills worth my wage
>
> **Edited paragraph**
> I am a good employee for this company. I believe my skills are worth the wage I receive. I always arrive at work early; often, I work after hours. I complete my tasks quickly. I believe I should continue working here.

Name _____ Date _____ Period _____ | **Workbook Activity** Chapter 11, Lesson 5 **93**

They Get a Kick Out of Football

Directions Read this paragraph. Then follow the instructions for each step that follows.

Many people love football. They love to cheer for their favorite team.

Prewrite What are your thoughts about football? How well do you like it?

Write If you like the game, write a persuasive paragraph about the importance of football in America. If you don't like football, write a persuasive paragraph about why it's not important.

© American Guidance Service, Inc. Permission is granted to reproduce for classroom use only.   English to Use

Workbook Activity 93

Name _____ Date _____ Period _____ | **Activity** Chapter 11, Lesson 5 **93**

Are Cats Doggone Good?

Directions Suppose that you feel cats make the best pets. Write a paragraph to persuade your reader that cats are the number-one pet. Or, if you don't like cats, persuade your reader that another pet is better. Follow the writing process. Prewrite and write here.

© American Guidance Service, Inc. Permission is granted to reproduce for classroom use only.   English to Use

Activity 93

Activity A On your paper, write a persuasive paragraph about why your friends should study with you tonight. Use the steps of the writing process to write your paragraph. Here are some possible reasons you might use to support the topic that you and your friends should study together. You can add reasons of your own.

- There is a test tomorrow.
- We can share ideas.
- We can read one another's notes.
- We can practice saying facts out loud.
- We can correct one another's work.

Here is a possible topic sentence:

Our group of friends should study together.

Activity B Rewrite and edit this persuasive paragraph to improve it. You may change the order of the sentences. You may combine sentences, and you may write additional sentences.

> My dog Monty is not dangerous. He has never bites. He doesn't growls at strangers. He a friendly dog Monty likes peple. When he jumps up on other's he's just saying helo. I keep Monty on a leash. When we walk But, it's not because he's a mean dog. very nice Every one likes Monty.

Activity C Choose two of these topics. Write a persuasive paragraph for each one.

1. Your favorite sports team is the best.
2. People should vote in elections.
3. Your town (or city or state) has more to offer than other places in the country.
4. Being a child (or teenager, young adult, or senior citizen) is better than being in any other age group.
5. Regular exercise is important for good health.

Activity A Answers

Paragraphs will vary. Students' paragraphs should offer reasons that support the topic.

Activity B Answers

Paragraphs will vary. Possible response:

My dog Monty is not dangerous. He never bites or growls at strangers. He is a friendly dog. When he jumps up on others, he's just saying hello. I keep Monty on a leash when we walk, but it's not because he's a mean dog. Monty likes people. He's very nice. Everyone likes Monty. He is a great pet.

Activity C Answers

Paragraphs will vary.

3 **Reinforce and Extend**

LEARNING STYLES

Logical/Mathematical

Help students write a persuasive paragraph about a current school or community issue. First, identify a topic that students would like to examine. Then make *pro* and *con* columns on the board. Have the class discuss different reasons for and against the position and write them in the columns. Ask students to write a persuasive paragraph based on the ideas discussed.

IN THE COMMUNITY

Help students create a list of reasons why their community should be awarded a fictitious prize, such as their state's "Community of the Year" award. Have students work in small groups to write a paragraph that convinces the members of the award committee to vote for their town. Have each group read its paragraph. Ask the class to vote for the most persuasive paragraph.

Lesson at a Glance

Chapter 11 Lesson 6

Overview This lesson presents the elements of a story and explains how writers make stories interesting.

Objectives

■ To analyze the content and form of a narrative

■ To practice writing dialogue

■ To write the middle and end of a story

Student Pages 230–231

Teacher's Resource Library

Workbook Activity 94

Activity 94

Alternative Activity 94

....

Vocabulary

dialogue

narrative

....

1 Warm-Up Activity

Bring to class a history book and a work of historical fiction. Discuss the difference between fiction and nonfiction. Talk about how historical fiction adapts historical events to form a story. Point out that in stories as well as in other kinds of writing, events must flow in logical order.

2 Teaching the Lesson

Discuss the example story with students, examining both its form and content. Ask students how dialogue adds to the narrative's effectiveness. Have students offer their ideas about what qualities are found in an interesting story and why readers are drawn to tales that have a strong beginning, an effective middle, and a satisfying end.

Activity A Answers

1. 1; Jerod, Cordell **2.** Jerod's yard; 2 **3.** Jerod wants to walk on a rope; Cordell said, "That trick is not easy." **4.** 1, 4, 6 **5.** Cordell laughs because Jerod is still shaking and his rope was only two feet off the grass.

Narrative

A series of paragraphs that go together to tell a story

A **narrative** is a series of paragraphs that tell what happens in a story. Notice how each paragraph in the following narrative helps tell the story.

EXAMPLE **Jerod's Balancing Trick**

1   Jerod and his friend Cordell went to a carnival. A woman in a costume walked on a rope high above the ground. Jerod thought this trick looked easy.

2   The next day, Jerod stretched a rope in the air between two trees in his yard. "Anybody can do this," Jerod said.

3   "That trick is not easy," replied Cordell.

4   Jerod grabbed a pole and walked proudly to the rope. He put one foot on the rope, then the other foot. He felt like the woman in the show.

5   "Go, go!" Cordell yelled. He waved his arms and grinned.

6   Jerod's legs shook. The rope shook. Jerod shook. His legs wobbled trying to keep straight. He dropped the pole and fell on the grass.

7   Later, Jerod said, "You were right, Cordell. This trick is for experts. It's scary business. I'm still shaking!"

8   Cordell laughed. "Your balancing trick was only two feet off the grass!" he said.

Activity A Write the answer to each question about the example narrative.

1. Which paragraph introduces the story characters? What are the characters' names?

2. Where does most of the story take place? Which paragraph tells you this?

3. What does Jerod want to do? What does Cordell say to try to get Jerod to change his mind?

4. Which paragraphs have descriptive details only and no words spoken by the characters?

5. Why does Cordell laugh at the end?

Name _____ Date _____ Period _____ | Workbook Activity | 94 |
Chapter 11, Lesson 6

The Group

Directions Read this paragraph. Then follow the instructions in the steps that follow.

One day some friends, Joe, Tim, and Eli, get together to talk things over. They have a problem, and they're looking for a way to solve it.

Prewrite What's their problem? _____

What's their solution? _____

Write What do they say to each other about the problem and the solution?

_____

_____

_____

_____

_____

_____

_____

_____

_____

_____

_____

_____

English to Use

Workbook Activity 94

Name _____ Date _____ Period _____ | Activity | 94 |
Chapter 11, Lesson 6

A New Friend

Directions Read this paragraph. Then follow the instructions below.

The door of the classroom opens. A new student walks in. The person looks interesting. Maybe you can make a new friend.

Prewrite Think about the new student. What would make a new student look interesting to you? What would the person look like? Is the person tall or short? What would the person be wearing? Would the person be carrying something?

Write Describe the new student. Use adjectives.

_____

_____

_____

_____

Prewrite Class is over. Now you can talk to the new student. Think about what you would say.

Write Write your first words to the person.

_____

_____

_____

_____

English to Use

Activity 94

One way writers make a story interesting is by using **dialogue.** Dialogue is conversation between two or more characters. Dialogue helps readers know what the characters are like and why they act the way they do. A new paragraph begins each time the speaker changes or the topic changes.

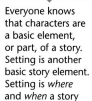

Dialogue

Conversation between two or more characters in a story

Another way writers make a story interesting is by adding a twist at the end that surprises or shocks readers.

Activity B On your paper, list ways that the writer made "Jerod's Balancing Trick" interesting for you.

Activity C Write the following as a story. Remember to begin a new paragraph each time the speaker changes.

> "Hi," said Valerie. "Well, hello," said Maurice. "It's nice to see you again," said Valerie. "Thanks," said Maurice. "I'm heading for the mall," said Valerie. "Me, too," said Maurice. "I'll go with you, but let's stop for lunch before we go." "Great idea! I'm hungry," said Valerie. "Maybe we could go to the theater later." Then Maurice said, "Maybe we should skip the mall and catch a movie."

Every story has a beginning, a middle, and an ending. The beginning introduces the setting, the characters, and the main character's goal. The middle tells how the main character tries to achieve the goal. The ending tells what happens when the main character reaches the goal.

Everyone knows that characters are a basic element, or part, of a story. Setting is another basic story element. Setting is *where* and *when* a story takes place.

Activity D Here is the beginning of a story. Use the writing process to write a middle and an ending. Be creative.

> **The Fortune Hunter**
>
> Each day at 8:00 A.M., Olindo is at the river. He dips his bucket into the cold, swirling water. Slowly, he pours mud and rocks from his bucket. His hands search for bits of treasure. Time passes, and the heat drains his strength.
> One afternoon . . .
>
> *What happens to Olindo? What does he do? Are any other people involved?*

Activity B Answers

Answers will vary but could include the use of dialogue and the amusing, surprising ending.

Activity C Answers

"Hi," said Valerie.

"Well, hello," said Maurice.

"It's nice to see you again," said Valerie.

"Thanks," said Maurice.

"I'm heading for the mall," said Valerie.

"Me, too," said Maurice. "I'll go with you, but let's stop for lunch before we go."

"Great idea! I'm hungry," said Valerie. "Maybe we could go to the theater later."

Then Maurice said, "Maybe we should skip the mall and catch a movie."

Activity D Answers

Middle and end paragraphs will vary.

 3 Reinforce and Extend

LEARNING STYLES

 Auditory/Verbal

Direct students to the box on page 231 that describes *setting.* Then ask volunteers to read aloud their stories from Activity D. Have members of the class name the details that helped them identify the setting of each volunteer's story.

Writing Practice

To provide more practice in writing dialogue, return to the activities in Lesson 6 of Chapter 10. Have students change indirect quotations to direct quotations and write the sentences as dialogue.

Lesson at a Glance

Chapter 11 Lesson 7

Overview This lesson demonstrates how to write a review.

Objective

- To write reviews with well-supported opinions

Student Pages 232–233

Teacher's Resource Library

Workbook Activity 95

Activity 95

Alternative Activity 95

Vocabulary

review

---

1 Warm-Up Activity

Ask students to briefly explain why they did or did not enjoy a recent popular book or film. Note any differences of opinion, pointing out areas in which students can cite different examples. Tell students that by stating and supporting their opinions, they have formed the basis of a review.

2 Teaching the Lesson

Discuss how the writing process can be applied to writing a review. Go over the example, pointing out that writers must support their opinions with valid evidence or reasons if they want to be taken seriously. Tell students that reviewers, like other persuasive writers, attempt to persuade readers of their opinions.

Lesson 7 Writing a Review

Review
A writer's opinion about a movie, TV show, book, or play

Have you recently seen a movie that you really liked? Perhaps you saw a TV program that you disliked. You can write your ideas about a movie or a television program as a **review.** A review tells one person's opinion about a movie, TV program, play, or written work.

1. **Prewrite** Think about something you read or saw recently. Write it down. Did you like it or not? List your reasons for liking or disliking this work.

2. **Write** Write a topic sentence that states your opinion. Write a sentence for each supporting reason on your list.

3. **Rewrite** Improve the paragraph as you rewrite it.

4. **Edit** Correct your spelling, punctuation, and word use.

EXAMPLE **Topic sentences stating different opinions**
1. This movie was fun and entertaining.
2. This movie didn't have a point.

Reasons

First opinion	Second opinion
real characters	no plot
good jokes	bad acting
lively music	boring

Edited paragraphs
1. This movie was fun and entertaining. It had characters who seemed real. They told some good jokes. I also thought the music was lively and original.
2. This movie didn't have a point. It had no plot. The actors spoke with no expression, and the movie was boring.

232 *Chapter 11 Writing for Others*

Workbook Activity 95

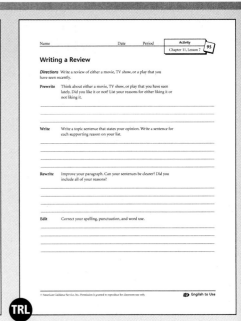

Activity 95

Activity A Read the story below. Then, on your paper, write a review of the story. State your opinion clearly. Give at least three reasons for your opinion.

> When Carl was eight years old, he got trapped in an old well. Carl and his cousin Simon were playing in a field on the family farm. They spotted the old well and went over to look at it. Simon dared Carl to go down into the well. Carl climbed down into the well. He went about six feet down and stood on a ledge inside the well. Simon looked down at him and waved. Carl waved back. Suddenly, the ledge crumbled beneath Carl and he fell down deeper into the well. Carl and Simon both screamed with fear! Carl's father, Edward, heard the screams and came running over to Simon. Simon told him that Carl had fallen down in the well. Edward looked down into the well and called to Carl. Carl yelled back to his father. He had fallen about six more feet down. Edward ran to the barn and got a ladder. He quickly returned and lowered the ladder into the well. Carl climbed up the ladder and jumped into his father's arms. He had suffered some bumps and bruises when he fell, but otherwise he was all right. Carl and Simon decided never to dare each other again.

Communication Connection

People use body language to show their opinion of a live performance, such as a play or concert. If you like a performance, when it is over you can clap your hands. If you really love it, you can stand up and clap your hands. This is called a standing ovation.

Activity B Write a review paragraph for one of these events.

1. a concert

2. a TV show

3. a club activity

4. a sports activity

5. a play

Activity C Write a review about one of these topics.

1. a book you have read

2. a movie or TV show you have seen

3. a song you have sung or heard

4. a favorite activity of your friends

5. a computer game you have played

Writing for Others Chapter 11 **233**

Activity A Answers

Paragraphs will vary. Check for a topic sentence and supporting reasons for the student's opinion.

Activity B Answers

Paragraphs will vary. Students' paragraphs should lead with a topic sentence and inlude supporting reasons.

Activity C Answers

Paragraphs will vary. Check for a topic sentence and supporting reasons.

3 **Reinforce and Extend**

LEARNING STYLES

Auditory/Verbal

Ask all students to review the same TV program, short story, or song. Have volunteers read their reviews aloud. Discuss how students' opinions are similar and different.

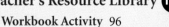

Chapter 11 Lesson 8

Overview This lesson explains the form of a friendly letter.

Objectives

- To analyze the format of friendly letters
- To write a friendly letter

Student Pages 234–235

Teacher's Resource Library TRL

Workbook Activity 96

Activity 96

Alternative Activity 96

Vocabulary

body
closing
greeting
heading
signature

1 Warm-Up Activity

Ask students how they correspond with out-of-town family or friends. Find out how many call, send e-mail, or write a letter. Discuss with students the advantages and disadvantages of each method of communication, considering the speed and the cost of each one.

2 Teaching the Lesson

Have students look at the letter outline. Review each term in relation to its position on the form. You may want to compare the way a letter includes this information with the way an e-mail presents it. Print out an e-mail and have students compare how the time, sender, and subject line of an e-mail compare with different parts of a letter.

Heading
The address of the person writing the letter

Greeting
Word or phrase used before the name or title of the person to whom a letter is sent

Body
The message part of a letter

Closing
Word or phrase used before the signature in a letter

Signature
The name signed by the writer of the letter

You write friendly letters to people you know. Friendly letters share news about yourself and let people know you care about them.

Friendly letters follow a form that includes a **heading**, a **greeting**, a **body**, a **closing**, and a **signature.** The heading gives the address of the writer; the date follows it. The greeting addresses the person receiving the letter. *Dear Mary* is an example of a greeting. The body of the letter contains the message. The closing is a polite word or phrase that ends the letter. The signature is the name of the person writing the letter.

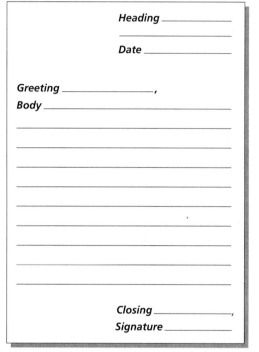

Read the letter on the next page from Melinda to her friend Larissa.

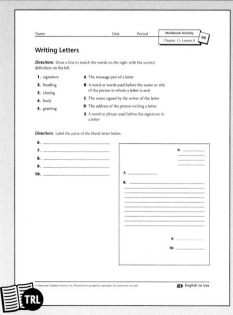

Workbook Activity 96

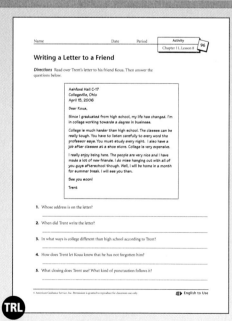

Activity 96

```
                              36 Plains Avenue
                              Minneapolis, Minnesota
                                            55406
                              January 17, 2004

   Dear Larissa,

        It's always nice to get a message from you.
   I enjoy hearing about your town. Your new neighbors
   sound like nice friends.
        Your old classmates here miss you. We often
   wish that you were here. We missed your help at the
   party last month. You think of funny games.
        The school is planning a trip to Williamsburg
   next year. Everybody is excited. We earned some
   money from book sales and painting. I hope you
   and I can meet when we are there. I'll write again
   when I have more ideas, and we can plan.
        Everyone is hoping you'll come for a week next
   year. We'd love to have you stay with us.

                              Sincerely,
                              Melinda
```

Activity A On your paper, answer the following questions about Melinda's letter.

1. What is Melinda's address? Why is her address in the letter?

2. When did Melinda write the letter?

3. What greeting does Melinda use? What end punctuation mark follows the greeting?

4. What closing does Melinda use? What end punctuation mark follows the closing?

5. How does Melinda let Larissa know that she cares about her?

Using What You've Learned

Write a friendly letter to someone you have not seen for a while. Tell him or her what you have been doing lately. Use the correct form for a friendly letter.

Activity A Answers

1. 36 Plains Avenue, Minneapolis, Minnesota 55406; so Larissa will know where to send her reply **2.** January 17, 2004 **3.** Dear Larissa; a comma **4.** Sincerely; a comma **5.** Melinda tells Larissa that her old friends miss her and that they missed her help at the party. Melinda also invites Larissa to visit.

 Reinforce and Extend

LEARNING STYLES

 Interpersonal/Group
Pair students and have them write letters to each other. Have students discuss each letter's tone as well as the qualities that make a letter interesting.

Using What You've Learned

As students practice writing friendly letters, they also may enjoy writing letters to classmates or other students in school. For privacy reasons, have students write to classmates in care of the school. Make sure that students record the school's correct address.

TEACHER ALERT

Some students may be more familiar with e-mail communication than with written letters. Discuss with students the occasions for which a written letter might be more appropriate. Have the class talk about times when a person might want to send a written letter, which can be more formal or more friendly than an e-mail.

Lesson at a Glance

Chapter 11 Lesson 9

Overview This lesson explains how to address an envelope.

Objectives
- To write addresses for envelopes
- To match terms with their definitions
- To edit sentences

Student Pages 236–237

Teacher's Resource Library

Workbook Activity 97

Activity 97

Alternative Activity 97

1 Warm-Up Activity

Display several addressed envelopes. Point out the correct position of the address and return address on each envelope. Ask students to identify different elements of the addresses. Ask volunteers to explain why they think letters contain return addresses. (*The letter will be returned to the sender if it cannot be delivered.*)

2 Teaching the Lesson

Discuss the importance of having clear, legible addresses on envelopes. Remind students that because mail is automated, machines, rather than people, may read addresses at several stages of the sorting process. Explain that neatly addressed envelopes are likely to be delivered more quickly and easily than ones that are difficult to read.

Lesson 9 Writing Mechanics

It is important to address an envelope correctly. This will ensure that your letter reaches the person to whom you are writing.

Put two addresses on the outside of an envelope. Print your return address in the upper left-hand corner. Print the address of the person to whom you are writing in the center of the envelope. The person's title and name are on the first line. The street address is on the second line. The city, state or province, and ZIP or postal code are on the third line.

Use the short or full form for state or province names. Print clearly or type the entire address on the envelope.

EXAMPLE

Activity A Write each address as it should appear on an envelope.

1. Dr. John Hall, 708 Center Terrace Drive, Columbus, Ohio 43201–5986
2. Mrs. Ellen Park, 5 Allen Street, Vance, South Carolina 29163–6983
3. Dr. Rita Ponce, 289 Superior Avenue, Winnipeg, Manitoba, Canada R3T 3XI
4. Mr. Marco Perry, 16 Henry Place, Omega, Georgia 31775–3911
5. Ms. Jane Smith, 25 Northfield Avenue, Port Charlotte, Florida 33952–1164

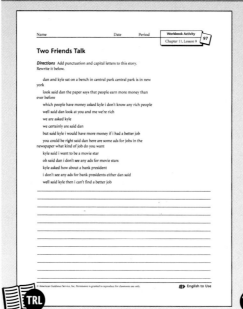

Workbook Activity 97

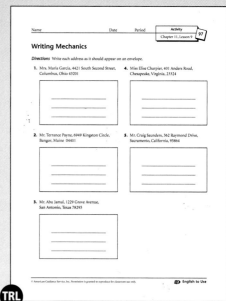

Activity 97

Activity B Match the words with their meanings. Write each number and its correct letter on your paper.

Words	Meanings
1. paragraph	A goes in the upper right-hand part of a letter
2. topic sentence	B goes just above the signature
3. heading	C group of sentences about one topic
4. date	D tells the main idea of a paragraph
5. closing	E goes under the heading

Activity C Edit the following sentences. Write the edited sentences on your paper.

1. Helenas house hasn't no yard

2. School start in a few week I hope I do good

3. I gets up early when I go to work lorena said

4. Kelly wisht she had wait for her frend on main street

Many people keep in touch with friends by writing letters.

5. too baby lions arrived at the washington zoo arent they cute

6. that music is much too loud shouted tom

7. you're new computer program wont never fit this machine

8. what you doing kerry asked

9. Im writing a letter to me friend in detroit said susan to kerry

10. Susan went to mailing off a letter

Writing for Others   Chapter 11   **237**

Activity A Answers

1. DR JOHN HALL
   708 CENTER TERRACE DRIVE
   COLUMBUS OH 43201–5986

2. MRS ELLEN PARK
   5 ALLEN STREET
   VANCE SC 29163–6983

3. DR RITA PONCE
   289 SUPERIOR AVENUE
   WINNIPEG MANITOBA CANADA
   R3T 3XI

4. MR MARCO PERRY
   16 HENRY PLACE
   OMEGA GA 31775–3911

5. MS JANE SMITH
   25 NORTHFIELD AVENUE
   PORT CHARLOTTE FL 33952–1164

Activity B Answers

1. C   2. D   3. A   4. E   5. B

Activity C Answers

Some answers may vary. Possible responses follow.

1. Helena's house doesn't have a yard. 2. School starts in a few weeks. I hope I do well. 3. "I get up early when I go to work," Lorena said. 4. Kelly wished she had waited for her friend on Main Street. 5. Two baby lions arrived at the Washington Zoo. Aren't they cute? 6. "That music is much too loud!" shouted Tom. 7. Your new computer program will never fit on this machine. 8. "What are you doing?" Kerry asked. 9. "I'm writing a letter to my friend in Detroit," said Susan to Kerry. 10. Susan went to mail a letter.

 3   **Reinforce and Extend**

LEARNING STYLES

Logical/Mathematical
Have students bring in envelopes with different types of addresses. Then group the addresses by the information they provide so that students can see the different patterns of addresses. Have students first separate business addresses from residential addresses and then compare the type of information included in three-line addresses with what is included in addresses of four or more lines.

TEACHER ALERT

The two-letter abbreviations for states are preferable to the full names on envelopes. If you have access to a list of state abbreviations, share it with students and ask them to use it when completing Activity A. Also note that many people still use lowercase letters and commas in addresses. Explain that although this style is acceptable, the style preferred by the U.S. Postal Service is capital letters and no punctuation.

Writing for Others   Chapter 11   **237**

Chapter 11 Review

Use the Chapter Review to prepare students for tests and to reteach content from the chapter.

Chapter 11 Mastery Test

The Teacher's Resource Library includes two parallel forms of the Chapter 11 Mastery Test. The difficulty level of the two forms is equivalent. You may wish to use one form as a pretest and the other form as a posttest.

REVIEW ANSWERS

Part A

1. M 2. E 3. I 4. A 5. K 6. J 7. Q
8. L 9. B 10. F 11. D 12. N 13. H
14. P 15. O 16. G 17. C

Part B

18. Answers will vary. Answers should closely relate to the topic. Paragraphs should exhibit correct grammar, punctuation, and spelling.

Chapter 11 R E V I E W

Part A Match each of the following vocabulary words with its definition.

Words		Definitions
1. body	A	a conversation between two or more characters
2. closing	B	a record of important facts or details
3. descriptive paragraph	C	a sentence that states the main idea
4. dialogue	D	a group of sentences about one topic
5. greeting	E	the words before the signature in a letter
6. heading	F	a series of paragraphs that tell a story
7. invitation	G	the main idea of a paragraph or essay
8. lead paragraph	H	a paragraph that tells how to do something
9. memo	I	a paragraph that describes someone or something
10. narrative	J	the address of the person writing a letter
11. paragraph	K	the words before the name of the person who receives a letter
12. persuasive paragraph	L	a paragraph that introduces a news article
13. process paragraph	M	the message part of a letter
14. review	N	a paragraph that tries to make readers believe or do something
15. signature	O	the signed name of the writer of a letter
16. topic	P	a writer's opinion about something
17. topic sentence	Q	a written request

Part B

18. Imagine that you fell asleep today and woke up in twenty years. Write a five-sentence paragraph to describe the things you might see.

238   *Chapter 11   Writing for Others*

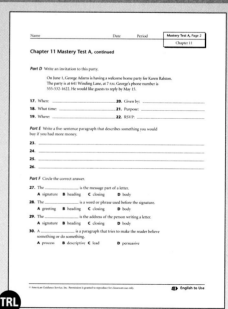

Chapter 11 Mastery Test A

Part C On your paper, write these sentences as a conversation between Jordan and Arisa.

19. hello jordan said arisa hi arisa said jordan arisa said i am moving to kansas city missouri i will miss you said jordan we will still be friends arisa said

Part D Write the answers for each item on your paper.

20. List the facts you need for a party invitation.

21. List the facts you need for a news story.

Part E

22. Write a memo for this phone call. Include these things: To whom, From whom, Subject, Date, Time, and Message.

Saul called on October 15 at 5:15 P.M. He wants Ramone to call him about the time and place of the tennis game.

Part F Choose the letter that correctly answers each question.

23. A pretend person who appears in a story is a _____ .

  A writer   **B** fact   **C** character   **D** hero

24. All appear on an envelope EXCEPT _____ .

  A the writer's telephone number
  B the ZIP or postal code
  C the return address
  D the title of the person who will receive the letter

25. The words "Love, Yasmine" in a letter are _____ .

  A a closing and a signature   **C** a closing
  B a greeting   **D** a heading

Test-Taking Tip When a test question asks you to write a paragraph, make a plan first. Write the main idea for your paragraph. List the supporting details you can include. Then write the paragraph.

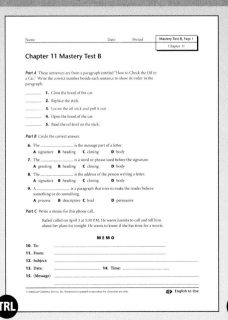

Chapter 11 Mastery Test B

Chapter

Planning Guide

Spelling

	Student Text Lesson			Language Skills	
	Student Pages	Vocabulary	Practice Activities	Identification Skills	Writing Skills	Punctuation Skills
Lesson 1 Practice Spelling	242–243		✔	✔	✔	✔
Lesson 2 Homonyms—Words That Sound Alike	244–245	✔	✔	✔	✔	✔
Lesson 3 More Homonyms	246–247		✔	✔	✔	✔
Lesson 4 Plurals—Two or More	248–249	✔	✔	✔	✔	✔
Lesson 5 Other Word Endings	250–251		✔	✔	✔	✔
Lesson 6 Words with *ie* or *ei*	252–253		✔	✔	✔	✔
Lesson 7 Words That Look Similar	254–255		✔	✔	✔	✔
Lesson 8 Writing Mechanics	256–257		✔	✔	✔	✔

Chapter Activities

Teacher's Resource Library
Community Connection 12:
Visit the U.S. Post Office
English in Your World 12:
Using the Dictionary to
Check Spelling

Assessment Options

Student Text
Chapter 12 Review

Teacher's Resource Library
Chapter 12 Mastery Tests A and B

240A

Student Text Features					Teaching Strategies					Learning Styles						Teacher's Resource Library				
ASL Illustration	Communication Connection	Notes	Using What You've Learned	Writing Tips	Teacher Alert	Online Connection	Applications (Home, Career, Community, Global)	Speaking Practice	Writing Practice	Auditory/Verbal	Body/Kinesthetic	Interpersonal/Group Learning	Logical/Mathematical	Visual/Spatial	LEP/ESL	Workbook Activities	Activities	Alternative Activities	Sentence Diagramming Activities	Self-Study Guide
		✔				243						243				98	98	98		✔
				✔			245							245		99	99	99		✔
							247			247						100	100	100		✔
		✔			249								249			101	101	101		✔
251				✔		251										102	102	102		✔
		✔					253		253						253	103	103	103		✔
			255	✔				255			255					104	104	104		✔
257	257				257											105	105	105		✔

Pronunciation Key

a	hat	e	let	ī	ice	ô	order	ù	put	sh	she	a	in about
ā	age	ē	equal	o	hot	oi	oil	ü	rule	th	thin	e	in taken
ä	far	ėr	term	ō	open	ou	out	ch	child	ᴛʜ	then	ə { i	in pencil
â	care	i	it	ȯ	saw	u	cup	ng	long	zh	measure	o	in lemon
												u	in circus

Alternative Activities

The Teacher's Resource Library (TRL) contains a set of lower-level worksheets called Alternative Activities. These worksheets cover the same content as the regular Activities but are written at a second-grade reading level.

Skill Track Software

Use the Skill Track Software for English to Use for additional reinforcement of this chapter. The software program allows students using AGS textbooks to be assessed for mastery of each chapter and lesson of the textbook. Students access the software on an individual basis and are assessed with multiple-choice items.

Chapter 12: Spelling
pages 240–259

Lessons

1. **Practice Spelling**
   pages 242–243

2. **Homonyms—Words That Sound Alike**
   pages 244–245

3. **More Homonyms**
   pages 246–247

4. **Plurals—Two or More**
   pages 248–249

5. **Other Word Endings**
   pages 250–251

6. **Words with *ie* or *ei***
   pages 252–253

7. **Words That Look Similar**
   pages 254–255

8. **Writing Mechanics**
   pages 256–257

Chapter 12 Review
pages 258–259

Skill Track Software for English to Use

Teacher's Resource Library

Workbook Activities 98–105

Activities 98–105

Alternative Activities 98–105

Community Connection 12

English in Your World 12

Chapter 12 Self-Study Guide

Chapter 12 Mastery Tests A and B

(Answer Keys for the Teacher's Resource Library begin on page 308 of this Teacher's Edition.)

Name _____ Date _____ Period _____   **Community Connection** 12
Chapter 12

Visit the U.S. Post Office

The people at the U.S. Post Office do more than sell stamps. They make letters and packages move on their way quickly. A visit to your post office can give you an idea about the different kinds of services offered to the public.

Directions Visit the post office and look around at the posters and signs on the wall. Read the information. Answer the questions below. Remember to check over your answers for any spelling mistakes.

1. What is the best way to wrap a package for the mail?

2. How long does it take to deliver:
   A Express Mail? _____   **C** First Class Mail? _____
   B Priority Mail? _____   **D** Parcel Post? _____

3. The Post Office offers four special services. Write the letter of the description beside the name.
   A Insurance coverage for merchandise
   B Confirms delivery of merchandise
   C Secure delivery for mail with significant value, such as jewelry
   D Ensures receipt of official documents, such as tax forms
   ____ Certified Mail   ____ Return Receipt   ____ Insured   ____ Registered Mail

4. Look in the National Zip Code Directory. Choose a place and write its name and zip code here.
   Name of place: _____   Zip code: _____

5. Read the bulletin board. Write four things you learn.
   A _____
   B _____
   C _____
   D _____

© American Guidance Service, Inc. Permission is granted to reproduce for classroom use only.   **English to Use**

TRL   **Community Connection 12**

Name _____ Date _____ Period _____   **English in Your World** 12
Chapter 12

Using the Dictionary to Check Spelling

Some words are hard to spell. Sometimes special rules can help you to spell a word correctly. But for other words, you simply have to know which spelling is right. You can use a dictionary to help with spellings of these kinds of words. Follow these steps.

Step 1 Go back to Chapter 12 in the textbook. The chapter discusses words such as *brake—break, glass—glasses, knife—knives, stop—stopping, either,* and *grammar.* Write down five words from the chapter that are difficult for you to spell. Use the lines below.

1. _____
2. _____
3. _____
4. _____
5. _____

Step 2 Use a dictionary to look up each word. After each word, write the part of speech for the word.

(**EXAMPLE**) piece (noun)

Step 3 After the part of speech, write the definition.

Step 4 Get into a group with two of your classmates. Share with one another the problems you have with spelling the words correctly. Talk about tricks or hints that can help you use the correct spelling.

© American Guidance Service, Inc. Permission is granted to reproduce for classroom use only.   **English to Use**

TRL   **English in Your World 12**

Chapter

12 Spelling

You probably recognize the two small animals shown in the picture. But do you know how to spell this animal's name? Is it "deer," or is it "dear"? One of these words is a noun that names a four-legged mammal, and one is an adjective used to show affection.

Correct spelling can be a challenge. Many English words, such as *deer* and *dear* or *brake* and *break,* have the same sounds but different spellings. Other words, such as "though" or "rough," are not spelled the way they sound. In addition, many words have irregular plural forms and do not end in *-s* or *-es.* For example, you see two animals in the illustration but you would not say, "I see two deers." Since "deer" is a plural word as well as a singular one, the proper usage is "I see two deer."

Certain rules will help you spell most English words correctly. However, you may have to memorize some spellings that are exceptions to these rules.

In this chapter, you will study ways to help you spell better.

Goals for Learning

◆ To practice spelling common problem words
◆ To choose the correct spelling of words that sound alike
◆ To learn rules for forming plurals
◆ To practice spellings of word endings
◆ To learn rules for words that use *ie* and *ei*

241

Ask students whether they have ever confused the words *deer* and *dear* and invite them to discuss other experiences with spelling. Talk about whether they consider themselves good spellers or simply adequate spellers. Ask students about spell checkers on computers and discuss why spell checkers might not spell all words correctly.

Tell students that this chapter includes tips that can help improve their spelling. Suggest that students refer to the chapter as needed when they are writing.

TEACHER'S RESOURCE

The AGS Teaching Strategies in English Transparencies may be used with this chapter. The transparencies add an interactive dimension to expand and enhance the *English to Use* program content.

CAREER INTEREST INVENTORY

The AGS Harrington-O'Shea Career Decision-Making System–Revised (CDM) may be used with this chapter. Students can use the CDM to explore their interests and identify careers. The CDM defines career areas that are indicated by students' responses on the inventory.

Writing Tips and Notes

Ask volunteers to read the tips and notes that appear in the margins throughout the chapter. Then discuss them with the class.

CHAPTER PROJECT

Have class members keep a list of words they find difficult to spell or words they confuse with other words. Students should record the words, along with a brief description of when or how they heard them. Ask students to review troublesome words as they make additions to their lists.

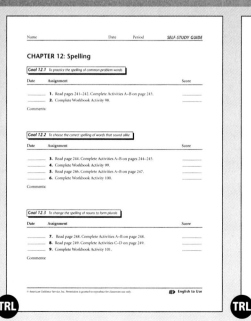

Chapter 12 Lesson 1

Overview This lesson presents a strategy for spelling difficult and new words.

Objective

■ To practice the correct spelling of commonly misspelled words

Student Pages 242–243

Teacher's Resource Library

Workbook Activity 98

Activity 98

Alternative Activity 98

1 Warm-Up Activity

On the board, write several pairs of easily misspelled words along with the correct spellings, for example, *thier* and *their*. Ask students to discuss whether they have ever misspelled any of the word pairs. Then ask how they learned the correct spellings, either through practice, mnemonic devices, or use of the dictionary. Have students identify the correct spelling of the words on the board. Have a dictionary handy if students need extra help. Discuss with students the importance of correcting misspelled words when writing information that will be shared with others.

2 Teaching the Lesson

Focus students' attention on the spelling strategy presented in the text. Have students apply this method to words listed on the board. Emphasize that this strategy is a suggestion; any strategy that helps them spell correctly is acceptable.

Ask students to look over the list of commonly misspelled words. Have them identify words in the list that cause them problems. Suggest that students practice spelling those words, using the four-step method described in the text.

It can be easier to spell some words if you break them into smaller parts. Learn to spell the word part by part. Try spelling the word *accident* this way: *ac-ci-dent*.

The more you practice a skill, the easier that skill becomes. Spelling is a skill that takes practice. Focus your practice on words that give you trouble. Soon you will be able to spell those words with ease.

Here are four steps that you can use to practice spelling a new or difficult word.

1. Copy the word on your paper correctly.
2. Write the word again while you say it aloud.
3. Cover the word. Say it. Then write it as you spell it aloud.
4. Check your spelling. If you have spelled the word incorrectly, return to steps 2 and 3.

People often misspell the following words. You may find that learning their spellings is easier if you study the words in small groups.

Group 1	Group 3	Group 5	Group 7	Group 9
accident	disturb	instead	once	study
arctic	doctor	judge	paid	thought
athletic	February	knock	pleasant	toward
beggar	finally	maybe	pretty	trail
beginning	forgot	minute	probably	trial
boundary	forty	misspell	review	Wednesday
Group 2	**Group 4**	**Group 6**	**Group 8**	
calendar	fourteen	necessary	safety	
children	government	nickel	sentence	
consider	grammar	nineteen	shovel	
curious	guard	ninety	since	
decide	history	occur	speak	
destroy	hundred	often	speech	

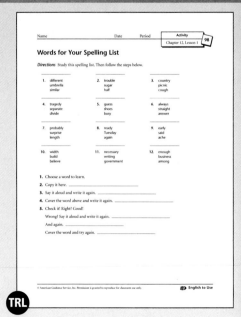

Activity A Find the misspelled word in each sentence. Write the word correctly on your paper.

1. The artic cold froze my toes.

2. Alec's car was in an acident, but he had the car fixed.

3. Our school has the best atletic teams in the state.

4. He was once a poor begger; now he's rich and famous.

5. This is the begining of a long movie.

6. The fence marks the boundry of our property.

7. Lots of childern play in the park during the summer.

8. The members of the jury will concider the case in private.

9. I was cureous about the contents of the big box.

10. The results of this test will diside my grade for the term.

Activity B Find the misspelled word in each sentence. Write the word correctly on your paper.

1. The raging fire will destory the forest lands.

2. My mother was quiet so she would not desturb my sleep.

3. Call the docter if your fever gets any higher.

4. Valentine's Day is on Febuary 14.

5. The letter from my best friend finaly arrived.

6. Over fourty people came to the big party.

7. My sister will be forteen years old next May.

8. Members of goverment meet in the capitol building.

9. Sue earns high grades on her grammer tests.

10. Adam is in trouble; he fourgot his homework.

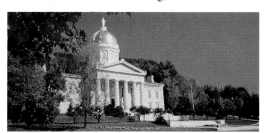

Remember that a capitol building is spelled with an o.

1. arctic 2. accident 3. athletic
4. beggar 5. beginning 6. boundary
7. children 8. consider 9. curious
10. decide

Activity B Answers

1. destroy 2. disturb 3. doctor
4. February 5. finally 6. forty
7. fourteen 8. government
9. grammar 10. forgot

 3 **Reinforce and Extend**

LEARNING STYLES

 Interpersonal/Group
Assign each student three spelling words from the list of commonly misspelled words. Ask students to write an interesting sentence for each word. Have them exchange sentences with partners, who should check for correct spelling as well as for correct punctuation and grammar.

ONLINE CONNECTION

 LD OnLine offers teaching support at *www.ldonline.org*. See "Five Guidelines for Learning to Spell and Six Ways to Practice Spelling" at *www.ldonline.org/ld_indepth/teaching _techniques/spelling_studying.html*.

Lesson at a Glance

Chapter 12 Lesson 2

Overview This lesson introduces homonyms.

Objective

■ To use homonyms correctly in sentences

Student Pages 244–245

Teacher's Resource Library

Workbook Activity 99

Activity 99

Alternative Activity 99

Vocabulary

homonym

 1 Warm-Up Activity

Write on the board: *break* and *brake.* Ask students to say the words and tell what they notice about them. Elicit that the words sound alike but have different spellings and different meanings. Ask students to use each word in a sentence, identifying which word makes sense in that context.

Next, read aloud the definition of *homonym* in the text. Ask volunteers to read each pair of homonyms, the parts of speech, and the definitions. Challenge students to use each homonym in a sentence that clearly demonstrates its meaning.

 2 Teaching the Lesson

Review the definition of *homonym* and make sure that students understand the concept. In addition, make sure that students understand the vocabulary used in the exercises. Students may be unfamiliar with words such as *bin* and *fare.* In addition, students who are more familiar with oral than with written language may not recognize that a final *d* is missing in the word *close* in Activity B.

Review the four-step spelling strategy from the previous lesson.

Homonym

A word that sounds like another word but has a different meaning and spelling

Writing Tip

Because they sound alike, it is easy to confuse homonyms. The one sure way to use the word with the correct meaning is to learn which meaning goes with which spelling.

Homonyms are words that sound alike but have different meanings and different spellings. You can figure out which homonym to use by thinking about the meaning of the other words in the sentence.

EXAMPLE

Homonyms		Definitions
been	(verb)	past form of *be*
bin	(noun)	a box used for storage
blue	(adjective)	a color; feeling sad
blew	(verb)	past form of *blow*
break	(verb)	to destroy
	(noun)	time off
brake	(noun)	used to stop a car, bike, truck, or other vehicle
buy	(verb)	to pay for something
by	(preposition)	beside; near; within a certain time
dear	(adjective)	loved
deer	(noun)	animal
fair	(noun)	a show with amusements
	(adjective)	pleasing; average; just
fare	(noun)	the price of a ride
for	(preposition)	used to show the purpose or a reason
four	(noun)	a number

Activity A Write the homonym in parentheses that completes each sentence correctly.

1. Jon put trash in the (been, bin).
2. She has (been, bin) here before.
3. Jennifer has a new (blue, blew) bike.
4. The wind (blue, blew) hard all night.

---

244 *Chapter 12 Spelling*

---

5. Kerry feels (blue, blew) because her friend Amahl is moving to Detroit.

6. Be careful, or you will (break, brake) the glass.

7. Put your foot on the (break, brake) right now and stop this car.

8. Juanita was tired, so she took a (break, brake) from studying.

9. The new calf stands (buy, by) its mother.

10. Derek will (buy, by) a new suit for his grandmother's birthday party.

11. His grandmother is a (dear, deer) person; everyone loves her.

12. The (dear, deer) are shy and run back into the woods whenever anyone comes near them.

13. We had (fair, fare) skies today with lots of sunshine.

14. Jill got on the bus and paid her (fair, fare).

15. Sarah won a blue ribbon for her apple pie at the county (fare, fair).

16. Tamra said that she would be back home (buy, by) dinnertime.

17. That toy is very (dear, deer) to the little boy.

18. Do you think these new game rules are (fair, fare)?

19. Max bought (for, four) apples.

20. He wants a hot dog (for, four) lunch.

Activity B Rewrite and edit this paragraph. Correct the spelling, grammar, and punctuation. Try to improve the paragraph by adding words and combining ideas.

> Peg said It isnt fare I by a TV set it doesn't work I didn't brake it It just blue up buy the time I got back to the store it was close i went home and threw my new TV in the trash been. It just isnt fare.

Spelling *Chapter 12* **245**

Activity A Answers

1. bin 2. been 3. blue 4. blew
5. blue 6. break 7. brake 8. break
9. by 10. buy 11. dear 12. deer
13. fair 14. fare 15. fair 16. by
17. dear 18. fair 19. four 20. for

Activity B Answers

Answers will vary. A possible response follows.

Peg said, "It isn't fair. I buy a TV set, and it doesn't work. I didn't break it; it just blew up! By the time I got back to the store, it was closed. I went home and threw my new TV in the trash bin. It just isn't fair!"

3 **Reinforce and Extend**

LEARNING STYLES

Visual/Spatial
Help students match homonyms by creating a homonym memory game. Pair students and give each group six blank cards. Ask students to write three homonym pairs, one word per card. Flip over the cards so that the words do not show and arrange them in a grid. Then have students take turns flipping over the cards to find the matching homonym pairs.

GLOBAL CONNECTION

Some words in other languages look very much like English words, but they are usually pronounced differently. For example, a word meaning "big" or "large" is *grand* in English and *grande* in Spanish. Ask students who know other languages to identify words that are similar to English words. Perhaps they can also share spelling problems they have in those languages.

Lesson at a Glance

Chapter 12 Lesson 3

Overview This lesson expands on the previous lesson on homonyms.

Objective

- To use homonyms correctly in sentences

Student Pages 246–247

Teacher's Resource Library

Workbook Activity 100

Activity 100

Alternative Activity 100

 1 Warm-Up Activity

Write on the board: *hair* and *hare*. Have students say the words and tell them that they sound alike but have different meanings and spellings. Ask students to use each word in a sentence that demonstrates its meaning. You may ask students to play a brief game of "charades" and act out the different meanings of different homonyms.

 2 Teaching the Lesson

Focus students' attention on the text. Review the three-step strategy for knowing which homonym to use in a sentence. Then ask volunteers to read each pair of homonyms listed, the parts of speech, and the definitions. Challenge students to use each homonym in a sentence that clearly demonstrates its meaning.

Recognize that students' pronunciation of words may influence the way they interpret homonyms. Some students may pronounce the *our/hour* or *weather/whether* homonyms differently, according to their regional speech patterns.

Lesson 3 More Homonyms

Remember that homonyms are words that sound alike but have different meanings and spellings. Follow these steps to know which homonym to use in a sentence:

1. Think about the meaning of the other words in the sentence.
2. Think about the meaning of the homonyms.
3. Choose the homonym that makes sense in the sentence.

Practice using these homonyms in sentences.

EXAMPLE

Homonyms		Definitions
hear	(verb)	to listen to
here	(adverb)	this place
hoarse	(adjective)	harsh, scratchy
horse	(noun)	an animal
hour	(noun)	60 minutes; time
our	(pronoun)	belonging to us
knew	(verb)	past form of *know*; understood
new	(adjective)	recent; fresh
know	(verb)	to understand
no	(adjective)	not any
plain	(adjective)	not fancy
	(noun)	flat, wide-open land
plane	(noun)	airplane
so	(adverb)	very
	(conjunction)	in order that
sew	(verb)	to stitch cloth with thread
son	(noun)	male child
sun	(noun)	source of heat and light
weather	(noun)	climate
whether	(conjunction)	if (used with *or*)

Workbook Activity 100

Activity 100

Activity A Write the homonym in parentheses that completes each sentence correctly.

1. She didn't (hear, here) me call her name.

2. (Hear, Here) is the money I owe you.

3. Anna will ride the black (hoarse, horse) to the ranch.

4. The coach's voice is (hoarse, horse) from yelling.

5. We met (hour, our) parents for dinner.

6. I'll meet you in one (hour, our).

7. I (knew, new) all the answers but one.

8. We moved into a (knew, new) house.

9. She does not (know, no) the answer to the last question.

10. We were late for dinner, and there was (know, no) food left.

11. They rode in a covered wagon across the grassy (plain, plane).

12. A small silver (plain, plane) landed at the airport.

13. Maria wore a (plain, plane) black dress to the party.

14. Tim baby-sat (sew, so) his parents could go out.

15. She will (sew, so) the tear in her pants.

16. I'm (sew, so) sorry you can't come with us to the movies.

17. The (son, sun) will set at 6:30 P.M.

18. Adam is Shelby's (son, sun).

19. He could not decide (weather, whether) he should go home early or stay late.

20. Today's (weather, whether) will be cloudy and warm.

Activity B Rewrite and edit this paragraph. Correct the spelling, grammar, and punctuation. Try to improve the paragraph by adding words and combining ideas.

> it was the middle of the night I new there was something wrong. I could here the sound of a horse voice It was almost an our before I learnt the cause of the problem Hour knew neighbor has for big parrots and they talk to each other. Now that I no, I can sleep

---

Activity A Answers

1. hear 2. Here 3. horse 4. hoarse
5. our 6. hour 7. knew 8. new
9. know 10. no 11. plain 12. plane
13. plain 14. so 15. sew 16. so
17. sun 18. son 19. whether
20. weather

Activity B Answers

Answers will vary. A possible response follows.

   It was the middle of the night. I knew there was something wrong. I could hear the sound of a hoarse voice. It was almost an hour before I learned the cause of the problem. Our new neighbor has four big parrots, and they talk to each other. Now that I know, I can sleep.

3 **Reinforce and Extend**

LEARNING STYLES

Auditory/Verbal
Ask students to write their own sentences for the homonyms introduced in the lesson. Tell them to write the pair of homonyms in parentheses as in Activity A. Have students trade papers with partners who can fill in the blanks. Partners can discuss answers. In addition, students may read their sentences aloud and ask their partners to spell the correct homonym in the sentence.

CAREER CONNECTION

Consider the problems poor spellers have in their careers. Ask students to list careers that require good spelling skills. (Students might mention secretarial and clerical work, writing, editing, teaching, advertising—any career that requires the writing of reports, proposals, and so on.) Point out that many jobs require good writing skills, including spelling.

Lesson at a Glance

Chapter 12 Lesson 4

Overview This lesson presents the rules for regular and irregular plurals.

Objective

■ To change singular nouns into plural nouns

Student Pages 248–249

Teacher's Resource Library

Workbook Activity 101

Activity 101

Alternative Activity 101

Vocabulary

plural
singular

....

1 Warm-Up Activity

Write these sentences on the board: *This is her pencil. These are her pencils. She made a wish. She made three wishes.* Ask students to read each pair of sentences aloud and tell what they notice about the sentences. Elicit that the first sentence in each pair talks about one object; the second talks about more than one. Ask volunteers to circle the noun that means more than one in each set of sentences. Note the *-s* and *-es* endings in these words.

Next, discuss the definitions and the words in the first example in the text. Point out that *-es* is usually added to nouns that end in *-s, -ss, -ch, -sh,* and *-x*.

2 Teaching the Lesson

Review the definitions of *plural* and *singular* in the text. You may want to read aloud the words in Activity C to make sure that students can clearly hear the differences between the *f* and *v* sounds. Discuss with students whether they have heard any of the words in Activity D made plural with an *-s*, for example, *foots* or *tooths*.

248   *Chapter 12   Spelling*

Singular
One
Plural
More than one

A **singular** noun names one person, place, or thing. A **plural** noun names more than one person, place, or thing. Add *-s* or *-es* to most singular nouns to form their plurals.

EXAMPLE	Singular	Plural
	door	doors
	rake	rakes
	inch	inches
	wish	wishes
	dress	dresses

Activity A Write each singular noun on your paper. Next to each noun, write its plural.

1. hat		**6.** school		**11.** box
2. frog		**7.** building		**12.** pass
3. fire		**8.** truck		**13.** watch
4. town		**9.** bike		**14.** bush
5. rock		**10.** road		**15.** bus

To form the plural of most nouns that end in *-y*, change the *y* to *i* and add *-es*. To form the plural of nouns that end in a vowel plus *-y*, add *-s*.

EXAMPLE	Singular	Plural
	hobby	hobbies
	way	ways

Activity B Write each singular noun on your paper. Next to each noun, write its plural.

1. sky		**6.** library		**11.** guy
2. toy		**7.** daisy		**12.** bakery
3. glossary		**8.** family		**13.** copy
4. fly		**9.** key		**14.** valley
5. lady		**10.** day		**15.** monkey

248   *Chapter 12   Spelling*

A dictionary is handy when you cannot remember the plural of a noun. Look up the singular noun. The dictionary often gives the plural spelling if it is unusual.

Add -s to some words that end in -f or -fe to form their plurals. For other words that end in -f or -fe, change the f or fe to v and add -es.

EXAMPLE

Singular	Plural
chief	chiefs
life	lives

Activity C Write each singular noun on your paper. Next to each noun, write its plural.

1. leaf
2. shelf
3. calf
4. loaf
5. thief

6. half
7. yourself
8. wolf
9. elf
10. wife

Some nouns form their plurals in irregular ways. Some nouns do not change at all to form their plurals.

EXAMPLE

Singular	Plural
child	children
man	men
woman	women
foot	feet
mouse	mice
goose	geese
tooth	teeth
sheep	sheep
deer	deer

Activity D Write each sentence correctly on your paper. Change the singular nouns in bold to plural nouns.

1. The two **man** were diving from **cliff**.
2. Their **tooth** chattered from the cold.
3. Two **mouse** ran across both of her **foot**.
4. Three **child** each paid five **penny** to pet the **sheep**.
5. Both **library** are closed on **Sunday**.

Activity A Answers

1. hat, hats 2. frog, frogs 3. fire, fires 4. town, towns 5. rock, rocks 6. school, schools 7. building, buildings 8. truck, trucks 9. bike, bikes 10. road, roads 11. box, boxes 12. pass, passes 13. watch, watches 14. bush, bushes 15. bus, buses/busses

Activity B Answers

1. sky, skies 2. toy, toys 3. glossary, glossaries 4. fly, flies 5. lady, ladies 6. library, libraries 7. daisy, daisies 8. family, families 9. key, keys 10. day, days 11. guy, guys 12. bakery, bakeries 13. copy, copies 14. valley, valleys 15. monkey, monkeys

Activity C Answers

1. leaf, leaves 2. shelf, shelves 3. calf, calves 4. loaf, loaves 5. thief, thieves 6. half, halves 7. yourself, yourselves 8. wolf, wolves 9. elf, elves 10. wife, wives

Activity D Answers

1. The two men were diving from cliffs. 2. Their teeth chattered from the cold. 3. The mice ran across both of her feet. 4. Three children each paid five pennies to pet the sheep. 5. Both libraries are closed on Sundays.

 3 Reinforce and Extend

TEACHER ALERT

Review with students the information about dictionaries given in the margin of page 249. Then show students a copy of a dictionary page on an overhead projector. Point out the section in which a dictionary definition indicates the plural endings of nouns. Make sure that students can use the dictionary to identify irregular plurals.

LEARNING STYLES

 Logical/Mathematical

Have students analyze the list of irregular plural forms. After students look at the words, have them determine the patterns that are represented in the list, for example, "added -en" or "change *oo* to *ee*."

Lesson at a Glance

Chapter 12 Lesson 5

Overview This lesson presents two spelling rules for adding endings to words.

Objective

■ To spell words with endings correctly

Student Pages 250–251

Teacher's Resource Library

Workbook Activity 102

Activity 102

Alternative Activity 102

1 Warm-Up Activity

Write on the board the following sets of words and endings: *stop + ed*, *end + ed*, *happen + ing*, *begin + ing*. Ask volunteers to add the endings to the words. Tell volunteers that they may have to add letters to spell each new word correctly. Then have volunteers look up the new words in a dictionary to see whether they spelled the words correctly. Discuss the changes that were made to spell *stopped* and *beginning* correctly.

2 Teaching the Lesson

Discuss the first spelling rule and the four examples that follow. Ask students to explain why the first two words keep the final *e* and the last two drop the *e*. Help students see that the endings of the first two words begin with consonants; the endings of the last two words begin with vowels.

Discuss the second rule and the examples that follow. If necessary, explain that a syllable is a word part. Review short vowel sounds if necessary.

Focus on words that do not conform to the spelling rules. Suggest that students memorize these irregular words and think of strategies to remember their spellings. Reinforce the concept that students can check a dictionary if they are unsure of a word's spelling.

Writing Tip

Never guess about the spelling of a word. Say the word aloud. List some possible spellings. Look for each spelling in the dictionary. Use the correct spelling when you find it.

You can add endings to many words to make new words.

When adding an ending to a word that ends in -*e*, drop the final *e* if the ending starts with a vowel. Do not drop the *e* if the ending starts with a consonant.

EXAMPLE

love + less	=	loveless
love + ly	=	lovely
love + ing	=	loving
love + able	=	lovable

When adding an ending that begins with a vowel to one-syllable words with a short vowel sound, double the final consonant before adding the ending.

EXAMPLE

drop + ed	=	dropped
skip + ed	=	skipped
bat + ing	=	batting
plan + ing	=	planning

Some words do not follow the spelling rules. If you are not sure how to spell a word with an ending added, check the dictionary.

EXAMPLE

awe + ful	=	awful
courage + ous	=	courageous
wax + ing	=	waxing
mile + age	=	mileage

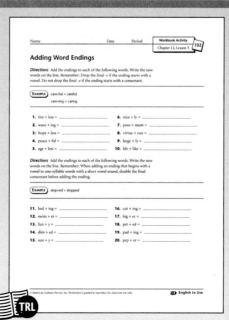

Workbook Activity 102

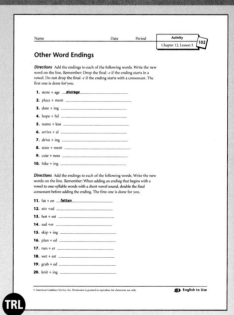

Activity 102

Lovely

Careful

Careless

Hopping

Activity A Add the endings to each of the following words. Write the new words on your paper.

1. care + ful
2. care + ing
3. care + less
4. fame + ous
5. flame + less
6. prime + ary
7. safe + ty
8. bride + al
9. like + ly
10. like + ness

Activity B Add the endings to each of the following words. Write the new words on your paper.

1. flag + ed
2. hit + ing
3. hop + ing
4. let + ing
5. step + ed
6. spin + ing
7. slap + ing
8. shop + ed
9. rub + ing
10. win + er

Activity C Rewrite and edit this paragraph. Correct the spelling, grammar, and punctuation. Try to improve the paragraph by adding words and combining ideas.

> The bater steped to the plate he is planing on hiting a home run. The pitcher is rubing the ball. the pitcher is the hotest, fasttest player in the league. The ball is spining. The bater carefuly conects with the ball fans in the stands make an aweful noise. The ball skipps across the fence for a home run. It realy is a good game

Activity A Answers

1. careful 2. caring 3. careless
4. famous 5. flameless 6. primary
7. safety 8. bridal 9. likely
10. likeness

Activity B Answers

1. flagged 2. hitting 3. hopping
4. letting 5. stepped 6. spinning
7. slapping 8. shopped 9. rubbing
10. winner

Activity C Answers

Answers will vary. A possible response follows.

   The batter stepped to the plate. He is planning on hitting a home run. The pitcher is rubbing the ball. The pitcher is the hottest, fastest player in the league. The ball is spinning. The batter carefully connects with the ball. Fans in the stands make an awful noise. The ball skips across the fence for a home run. It really is a good game.

3 Reinforce and Extend

IN THE COMMUNITY

A dictionary is an important reference tool in school, at home, and in the workplace. Ask students to make a list of different kinds of dictionaries available at the public or school library. Tell them to include foreign language dictionaries and dictionaries for specific fields such as science or geography. Students can also check out the dictionary shelf in local bookstores. Ask students to share their dictionary lists in class and point out the most interesting or unusual dictionaries on their lists.

ASL ILLUSTRATION

Have students practice making the signs illustrated on page 251. When students are proficient with the signs, ask them to compare the signs for "careful" and "careless." Ask them to identify what the sign for "care" might be. Then have them compare the way English adds suffixes with the way sign language adds the idea of *-ful* and *-less* to an idea.

Lesson at a Glance

Chapter 12 Lesson 6

Overview This lesson presents rules for spelling words with the vowel pairs *ie* and *ei*. It also provides practice for skills learned in earlier lessons.

Objectives

- To spell words with *ie* and *ei* correctly
- To review previously presented rules

Student Pages 252–253

Teacher's Resource Library TRL

Workbook Activity 103

Activity 103

Alternative Activity 103

1 Warm-Up Activity

Focus students' attention on the rules and examples in the text. Ask students to share any rhymes or techniques they know and use for spelling words that have *ie* and *ei* together. Most students will probably recall the rhyme:

I before *e* except after *c* or in words that say *a,* as in *neighbor* and *weigh.*

Point out that this rhyme is especially helpful because it states the rule and then gives exceptions to the rule and examples.

2 Teaching the Lesson

In Activity A, students may not immediately be able to identify the word they are being asked to complete. You may want to have students work in pairs to identify what sounds need to be added to the incomplete words before choosing *ie* or *ei.*

Words with the vowel pairs *ie* and *ei* often cause spelling problems.

Write *i* before *e* when the vowel sound is long *e* except after the letter *c.*

EXAMPLE	believe	field	receive	deceit
Exceptions	either	seize	weird	

Write *e* before *i* when the vowel sound is not long *e.*

EXAMPLE	weigh	eight	forfeit	neighbor
Exceptions	view	friend	conscience	

Activity A Add *-ei* or *-ie* to each of the following words. Write the words on your paper.

1. rel_ _f
2. f_ _ld
3. rec_ _ve
4. n_ _ghbor
5. ch_ _f
6. dec_ _ve
7. pr_ _st
8. rec_ _pt
9. gr_ _ve
10. n_ _ce
11. c_ _ling
12. l_ _sure
13. for_ _gn
14. bel_ _f
15. _ _ght

Activity B Find the misspelled words in these sentences. Write the words correctly on your paper. A sentence may have one or more mistakes.

1. Ken plays iether first base or right feild.
2. He has a batting avrage of .300.
3. Tom has been hiting the ball hard latly, to.
4. A fast inside pitch nocked off his glases.
5. The picher through another fastball.
6. Ken told the coaches that he needed some releif as he droped his bat.

Workbook Activity 103

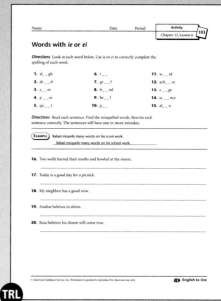

Activity 103

7. Woodcrest is one of the busyest towns in the whole state.

8. People try seting new records buy doing some very wierd things.

9. The doctor wrote down Hakim's hight and weight at his yearly physical.

10. Alice went to three scools last year because her famaly moved so offen.

11. The dentist said that Jane's wisdom tooths had to be pulled.

12. Hour nieghbor's dog has ieght of the cutest little puppys you ever saw.

13. I like to play with them in my liesure time.

14. My friend Toshiro peted one of the puppys.

15. Wendy is learning a foriegn language.

16. He recieved the funnyest letter from his neice.

17. Six mouses made a nest behind the stove.

18. The three mans fixed the crack in the cieling.

19. Suri holds strong believes about that topic.

20. I read an aweful reveiw of his lattest play.

Remember to change the y to an i and add -es to make the word puppies.

Activity A Answers

1. relief **2.** field **3.** receive
4. neighbor **5.** chief **6.** deceive
7. priest **8.** receipt **9.** grieve
10. niece **11.** ceiling **12.** leisure
13. foreign **14.** belief **15.** eight

Activity B Answers

1. either, field **2.** average **3.** hitting, lately, too **4.** knocked, glasses
5. pitcher, threw **6.** coaches, relief, dropped **7.** busiest **8.** setting, by, weird **9.** height **10.** schools, family, often **11.** teeth **12.** Our, neighbor's, eight, puppies
13. leisure **14.** petted, puppies
15. foreign **16.** received, funniest, niece **17.** mice **18.** men, ceiling
19. beliefs **20.** awful, review, latest

Writing Practice

Ask students to write sentences for the words they completed in Activity A. Then have students work in groups to select sentences and combine them into a short paragraph. Encourage student groups to make their paragraphs as funny or silly as possible.

 3 **Reinforce and Extend**

LEARNING STYLES

 LEP/ESL
English language-learners may have difficulty pronouncing words with *ei* and *ie* combinations because each letter combination can take on the sound of another vowel. Create lists of words with *ei* and *ie* that are grouped together by sounds, such as "Long *a* sound: *weigh, eight, neighbor*" or "Long *e* sound: *receive, believe, either*." Have English language-learners practice pronouncing the words correctly and help them see the patterns of the different vowel sounds.

AT HOME

 The *i* before *e* rhyme is one of the most familiar mnemonic devices—or memory tricks—used to recall a spelling rule. Other examples include "*Loose* lost an *o* and became *lose*" and "I see no *end* to our *friendship*." Encourage students to make up other memory tricks for words that cause them spelling problems. Emphasize that if a rhyme or a saying helps them remember how a word is spelled, then it doesn't matter how silly it sounds to others.

Lesson at a Glance

Chapter 12 Lesson 7

Overview This lesson focuses on words that are easily and frequently confused.

Objective

■ To choose the correct word for use in a sentence

Student Pages 254–255

Teacher's Resource Library

Workbook Activity 104

Activity 104

Alternative Activity 104

1 Warm-Up Activity

Write on the board: *all together* and *altogether*. Say the words aloud, emphasizing the separation between *all* and *together*. Then explain that *all together* and *altogether* are examples of words that are easy to confuse because they sound alike and have similar spelling patterns. Ask students whether they can tell you which of the words means "everyone located in the same place" (*all together*) and which means "completely" or "entirely" (*altogether*). Then ask students to use the words in sentences that demonstrate their meanings.

2 Teaching the Lesson

Discuss the words listed in the text. Invite volunteers to read each set of words, their parts of speech, and their definitions. Note the different pronunciations of *desert* (land without water) and *desert* (to leave alone).

Discuss with students the importance of proofreading to identify words that look similar. Tell them that spell checker programs will not identify incorrect usage of the words in the example list. When students confuse these words, they often spell the words correctly but use them incorrectly. Computer programs will not be able to identify, for example, that a writer should have used *quiet* rather than *quit*.

254 *Chapter 12 Spelling*

Some words with similar spelling patterns and similar sounds can cause spelling problems. People often confuse these words. Be careful when using them.

Writing Tip

Always proofread your writing for spelling errors. Be careful with spell checkers. You may want *loose* but write *lose*. Since *lose* is spelled correctly, the spell checker may not help you.

EXAMPLE

Words		Definitions
already	(adverb)	by this time
all ready	(adjective)	prepared
breath	(noun)	air
breathe	(verb)	to inhale and exhale air
close	(verb)	shut
	(adjective)	near; dear
clothes	(noun)	items to wear
cloths	(noun)	pieces of fabric
dairy	(noun)	shop where milk products are sold
diary	(noun)	daily record or journal
desert	(noun)	land without water
	(verb)	to leave alone
dessert	(noun)	last course of a meal; sweets
loose	(adjective)	free; not held tightly
lose	(verb)	to misplace; to fail to win
quiet	(adjective)	not noisy
quit	(verb)	to stop or leave
quite	(adverb)	completely; rather

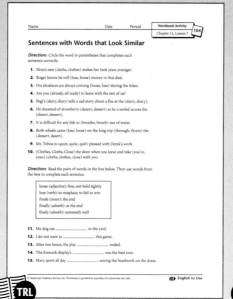

Workbook Activity 104

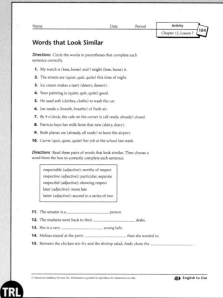

Activity 104

Activity A Write the word or words in parentheses that complete each sentence correctly.

1. We've packed our things, and we're (already, all ready) for our trip.

2. The train was (already, all ready) at the station when we got there.

3. I cannot hold my (breath, breathe) for very long.

4. Open your mouth and (breath, breathe) in the fresh, country air.

5. Please (close, clothes, cloths) the window.

6. You can dust the furniture with one of the old dusting (close, clothes, cloths).

7. Don't sit too (close, clothes, cloths) to the open window.

8. Brittany writes in her (dairy, diary) every night.

9. I bought some cheese at the (dairy, diary).

10. I served the fruit for (desert, dessert).

11. I would never (desert, dessert) you in your time of need.

12. He will (loose, lose) his job if business doesn't pick up soon.

13. The clown's pants were so (loose, lose) they kept falling down.

14. There is nothing (quiet, quit, quite) as refreshing as a morning swim in the sea.

15. Ben will (quiet, quit, quite) his job if he does not get a raise.

Using What You've Learned

Correct the spelling of the underlined words in this paragraph.

The diner is <u>quite</u> most <u>afternoones.</u> In the evening, however, people talk <u>noisyly.</u> Jean and Al often <u>meat four</u> lunch <u>hear.</u> Last <u>weak,</u> on <u>Febuary</u> 9, Al <u>stoped</u> in late. Jean was <u>worryed,</u> but she felt <u>relieved</u> when her <u>freind</u> arrived. Al told Jean not to worry since he would never <u>dessert</u> her. He had gone <u>shoping</u> to buy something <u>four</u> his <u>nieghbor's childern.</u> Al also bought some new <u>close</u> to wear to work next week. Jean had <u>all ready</u> eaten and was having <u>friut</u> for <u>desert.</u> Al ordered iced tea because he cannot have <u>diary</u> products.

Spelling   *Chapter 12*   **255**

Speaking Practice

Some students may be confused by words with similar sounds and spelling patterns because they are unclear about proper pronunciation. Have students take turns reading the words in the example on page 254 aloud and using them in sentences. Have students listen carefully to the subtle differences between *loose/lose* and *quiet/quit/quite.* In addition, you may want students to read Activity A aloud when they have completed the exercise.

3 Reinforce and Extend

LEARNING STYLES

Body/Kinesthetic

Have students write words from the example list on flashcards, with the definition of each word on the back of the card. Hand out the flashcards to volunteers and have the class work together to complete Activity A, with members of the class calling on the volunteer needed to complete the sentence correctly. The volunteer should stand as the class reads the complete sentence aloud and then turn over his or her flashcard and read the definition. The class can check to see whether the definition makes sense in the context of the sentence.

Using What You've Learned

Some students may be overwhelmed by the number of errors presented in the activity. Tell students that they may want to work through the paragraph several times, reading for different types of errors each time. For example, they may want to make one pass through the text looking for incorrect plural forms. A second time, they could look for incorrect endings, such as *-ed, -ing,* and *-ly.*

Answers to Using What You've Learned: The diner is quiet most afternoons. In the evening, however, people talk noisily. Jean and Al often meet for lunch here. Last week, on February 9, Al stopped in late. Jean was worried, but she felt relieved when her friend arrived. Al told Jean not to worry since he would never desert her. He had gone shopping to buy something for his neighbor's children. Al also bought some new clothes to wear to work next week. Jean had already eaten and was having fruit for dessert. Al ordered iced tea because he cannot have dairy products.

Lesson at a Glance

Chapter 12 Lesson 8

Overview This lesson introduces comparative and superlative adverbs.

Objectives

- To use the comparative and superlative forms of adverbs correctly
- To make comparisons with adverbs that end in *-ly*

Student Pages 256–257

Teacher's Resource Library TRL

Workbook Activity 105

Activity 105

Alternative Activity 105

1 Warm-Up Activity

Ask students to name a musician or an athlete who performs well. Does he or she perform better than other musicians or athletes? Of all the musicians or athletes, who performs best? Write *well, better,* and *best* on the board and explain that these words are adverbs that show comparisons.

2 Teaching the Lesson

Focus students' attention on the text. Discuss the adverbs in the examples and ask volunteers for sentences that use each adverb. Be sure students are using the words as adverbs. If necessary, remind students that adverbs answer the questions *When? Why? Where?* and *How?* about verbs, adjectives, or other adverbs.

Activity A Answers

1. well 2. better 3. best 4. well 5. better

Adverbs can compare when, where, and how things happen. Add *-er* to an adverb to compare one thing to one other thing. Add *-est* to an adverb to compare two or more things.

EXAMPLE

Adverb	Comparing with One	Comparing with Two or More
quick	quicker	quickest
slow	slower	slowest

Some adverbs change their form to make comparisons. The adverb *well* means "in the right way." Don't confuse the adverb *well* with the adjective *good*.

EXAMPLE

Adverb	Comparing with One	Comparing with Two or More
well	better	best

Activity A On your paper, write the correct form of the adverb in parentheses to complete each sentence.

1. Andy spoke (good, well) in the first round of the speech competition.
2. He did a little (better, best) in the next round.
3. He spoke the (better, best) in the final round.
4. Amy did (good, well) in math on Monday.
5. Her friend did (better, best) than she did on Tuesday.

Communication Connection

Many people are scared to speak in front of a group. Here are three ways to feel more comfortable speaking in front of others:

- On a sheet of paper, write what you are going to say.
- Practice your speech in front of a mirror until you know all of the words. Then, practice in front of one or two people.
- Relax before you give your speech

Workbook Activity 105

Activity 105

More

Most

Less

Least

Use *more* and *most* and *less* and *least* to make comparisons with adverbs that end in *-ly*.

EXAMPLE

Adverb	Comparing with One	Comparing with Two or More
easily	more easily less easily	most easily least easily
suddenly	more suddenly less suddenly	most suddenly least suddenly
neatly	more neatly less neatly	most neatly least neatly

Activity B Write the correct form of the adverb in parentheses to complete each sentence.

1. Mario's new car runs (more, most) smoothly than his old car.
2. It reached 65 miles per hour (more, most) quickly than his old car.
3. It burns oil (less, least) rapidly than his old car, too.
4. Mario's friends like his old car, but they like his new car (better, best).
5. Beth finishes her homework (faster, fastest) than I do.
6. Of all the teams in the league, our team worked (harder, hardest).
7. Joanna works (more, most) happily at her job than Ellie does.
8. Paul moves swiftly; Josh moves (more, most) swiftly.
9. When the four team members ran around the track, Brenda ran the distance (more, most) easily.
10. Jack handles eggs (more, most) carefully than he handles bread.

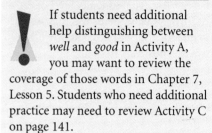

3 **Reinforce and Extend**

TEACHER ALERT

If students need additional help distinguishing between *well* and *good* in Activity A, you may want to review the coverage of those words in Chapter 7, Lesson 5. Students who need additional practice may need to review Activity C on page 141.

ASL ILLUSTRATION

Have students practice making the signs illustrated on page 257. Have students find sentences in Activity B that include *more/most* and *less/least* and ask them to make the signs as they read the sentences aloud. Ask students to review which signs compare two elements and which compare more than two elements.

Chapter 12 Review

Use the Chapter Review to prepare students for tests and to reteach content from the chapter.

Chapter 12 Mastery Test

The Teacher's Resource Library includes two parallel forms of the Chapter 12 Mastery Test. The difficulty level of the two forms is equivalent. You may wish to use one form as a pretest and the other form as a posttest.

REVIEW ANSWERS

Part A

1. singular 2. plural 3. homonym

Part B

4. calves, bushes 5. mice, teeth, kernels 6. Flies 7. children, buses, schools 8. Days, leaves 9. geese 10. knives 11. monkeys, trees 12. libraries, copies, notes 13. hills, valleys

Part C

14. argument 15. skipped 16. awful 17. lovely 18. famous 19. Either 20. mischief 21. ceiling 22. doctor, vein 23. receive, friend

---

Chapter 12 REVIEW

Word Bank

homonym

plural

singular

Part A Use the words from the Word Bank to complete sentences 1–3.

1. A word that means "one" is _____.
2. A word that means "more than one" is _____.
3. A _____ is a word that sounds like another word but has a different meaning and spelling.

Part B Change the nouns in bold to plural nouns. Write the plural nouns on your paper.

4. Behind the barn, two **calf** chewed on some **bush**.
5. Inside the barn, **mouse** sank their **tooth** into stray **kernel** of corn.
6. **Fly** buzz.
7. Some **child** ride **bus** to their **school**.
8. **Day** go by, and the **leaf** turn red and yellow.
9. During the summer, the lake is full of **goose**.
10. The chef bought three new **knife** at the cooking store.
11. The **monkey** climbed to the top of the **tree**.
12. Ty checked both **library** and made **copy** of his **note**.
13. Beyond those **hill** lie two large **valley**.

Part C Write the word in parentheses that has the correct spelling.

14. Craig and Lucy had an (arguement, argument).
15. Anton's two sisters (skiped, skipped) rope in the park.
16. Sharon thought the computer game was (awful, aweful).
17. "What a (lovly, lovely) idea," said Ruth.
18. At the party, Zoe saw three (famous, fameous) people.
19. (Either, Iether) we go to the movies now or we go later.
20. As a boy, Mr. Cho was always into (mischeif, mischief).
21. The walls are white, and the (cieling, ceiling) is blue.
22. The (doctor, docter) took blood from Allen's (vien, vein).
23. Tammy will (receive, recieve) news from her (friend, freind).

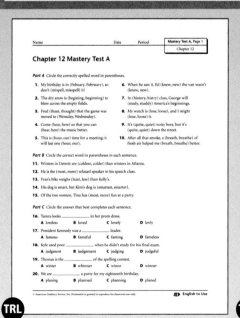

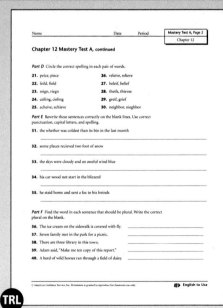

Chapter 12 Mastery Test A

Part D Rewrite the paragraph. Choose the word in parentheses that has the correct spelling and that completes the sentence correctly.

Adam and Caroline traveled west **24.** (threw, through) the hot **25.** (desert, dessert). **26.** (Sum, Some) **27.** (families, familys) in the wagon train were **28.** (weak, week) from hunger and thirst. Adam **29.** (new, knew) few wild animals were **30.** (hear, here).

The **31.** (skies, skys) were clear. **32.** (Their, There) was no **33.** (break, brake) in the heat during the **34.** (dais, days). Later, at the water **35.** (whole, hole), **36.** (their, there) was **37.** (piece, peace) and **38.** (quite, quiet) among the **39.** (hoarses, horses).

At night, the travelers **40.** (heard, herd) **41.** (wolfs, wolves) beyond the light of the campfires. The sleep of these **42.** (mans, men) and women was **43.** (breif, brief), and they were **44.** (carful, careful) about their **45.** (safety, safty). At least, they **46.** (received, recieved) cool night air for **47.** (relief, releif).

Part E Choose the letter of the word or phrase that correctly completes each sentence.

48. My sister smiled _____ than I did.
  A cheerfullier   C most cheerfully
  B cheerfulliest   D more cheerfully

49. This is the _____ movie I have ever seen.
  A best   B better   C good   D well

50. The students sang _____ than they did yesterday.
  A more louder   C louder
  B less louder   D loudest

 If you have to choose the correct word to complete a sentence, read the sentence using each of the choices given. Then choose the word that fits the sentence best.

REVIEW ANSWERS

Part D

24. through 25. desert 26. Some
27. families 28. weak 29. knew
30. here 31. skies 32. There
33. break 34. days 35. hole
36. there 37. peace 38. quiet
39. horses 40. heard 41. wolves
42. men 43. brief 44. careful
45. safety 46. received 47. relief

Part E

48. D 49. A 50. C

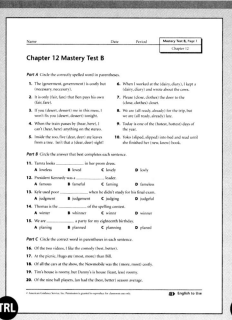

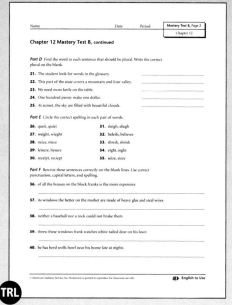

TRL

TRL

Chapter 12 Mastery Test B

13

Planning Guide

Fine-Tuning Your Writing

	Student Pages	Student Text Lesson		Language Skills		
		Vocabulary	Practice Activities	Identification Skills	Writing Skills	Punctuation Skills
Lesson 1 Subject-Verb Agreement	262–263	✔	✔	✔	✔	✔
Lesson 2 More About Subject-Verb Agreement	264–265		✔	✔	✔	✔
Lesson 3 Verb Agreement with Pronoun Subjects	266–267	✔	✔	✔	✔	✔
Lesson 4 Pronoun-Noun Agreement	268–269		✔	✔	✔	✔
Lesson 5 *Don't* and *Doesn't*	270–271		✔	✔	✔	✔
Lesson 6 Misplaced Words and Phrases	272–273		✔	✔	✔	✔
Lesson 7 Standard English	274–275		✔	✔	✔	✔
Lesson 8 Writing Mechanics	276–277		✔	✔	✔	✔

Chapter Activities

Teacher's Resource Library
Community Connection 13:
Nonstandard English in Your World
English in Your World 13:
Correct Sentences

Assessment Options

Student Text
Chapter 13 Review

Teacher's Resource Library
Chapter 13 Mastery Tests A and B
Final Mastery Test

ASL Illustration	Communication Connection	Notes	Using What You've Learned	Writing Tips	Teacher Alert	Online Connection	Applications (Home, Career, Community, Global)	Speaking Practice	Writing Practice	Auditory/Verbal	Body/Kinesthetic	Interpersonal/ Group Learning	Logical/Mathematical	Visual/Spatial	LEP/ESL	Workbook Activities	Activities	Alternative Activities	Sentence Diagramming Activities	Self-Study Guide
263					263		263									106	106	106		✔
				✔			265			265						107	107	107		✔
						267					267					108	108	108		✔
269							269	269					269			109	109	109		✔
		✔		✔			271								271	110	110	110		✔
	273			✔								273		273		111	111	111		✔
		✔			275											112	112	112		✔
		✔	277		277				277							113	113	113		✔

Pronunciation Key

a	hat	e	let	ī	ice	ô	order	ú	put	sh	she		a in about
ā	age	ē	equal	o	hot	oi	oil	ü	rule	th	thin	ə	e in taken
ä	far	ėr	term	ō	open	ou	out	ch	child	₮H	then		i in pencil
â	care	i	it	ȯ	saw	u	cup	ng	long	zh	measure		o in lemon
													u in circus

Alternative Activities

The Teacher's Resource Library (TRL) contains a set of lower-level worksheets called Alternative Activities. These worksheets cover the same content as the regular Activities but are written at a second-grade reading level.

Skill Track Software

Use the Skill Track Software for English to Use for additional reinforcement of this chapter. The software program allows students using AGS textbooks to be assessed for mastery of each chapter and lesson of the textbook. Students access the software on an individual basis and are assessed with multiple-choice items.

Chapter 13: Fine-Tuning Your Writing
pages 260–279

Lessons

1. **Subject-Verb Agreement**
   pages 262–263

2. **More About Subject-Verb Agreement**
   pages 264–265

3. **Verb Agreement with Pronoun Subjects**
   pages 266–267

4. **Pronoun-Noun Agreement**
   pages 268–269

5. ***Don't*** and ***Doesn't***
   pages 270–271

6. **Misplaced Words and Phrases**
   pages 272–273

7. **Standard English**
   pages 274–275

8. **Writing Mechanics**
   pages 276–277

Chapter 13 Review
pages 278–279

Skill Track Software for English to Use

Teacher's Resource Library TRL

Workbook Activities 106–113

Activities 106–113

Alternative Activities 106–113

Community Connection 13

English in Your World 13

Chapter 13 Self-Study Guide

Chapter 13 Mastery Tests A and B

Final Mastery Test

(Answer Keys for the Teacher's Resource Library begin on page 308 of this Teacher's Edition.)

Chapter

13 Fine-Tuning Your Writing

Look around you. Is there something you would like to change or improve? Is your car in good shape? It might run better if it had a tune-up. New spark plugs will fire at the right time to help the car get better mileage and prevent engine damage. Clean battery terminals might help the car start more easily. Changing the oil will protect the engine. A wax and polish could make the car shine.

You can fine-tune your writing so that it works better and flows more smoothly. Changing words and adding details can make your sentences more interesting. Rearranging sentences in a paragraph can make your ideas easier to follow and understand. Correcting mistakes in punctuation, spelling, and grammar will add polish to your writing and make it shine.

In this chapter, you will practice ways to improve your writing.

Goals for Learning

◆ To make subjects agree with verbs and pronouns agree with nouns

◆ To identify improperly written sentences

◆ To rewrite sentences to improve them

◆ To avoid the use of nonstandard English

◆ To use standard English to speak and to write

261

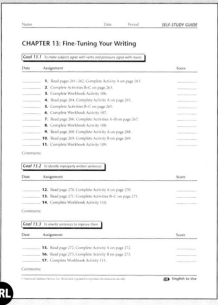

Name ___ Date ___ Period ___ SELF-STUDY GUIDE

CHAPTER 13: Fine-Tuning Your Writing

Goal 13.1 To make subjects agree with verbs and pronouns agree with nouns

Date | Assignment | Score

___ 1. Read pages 261–262. Complete Activity A on page 263.
___ 2. Complete Activities B–C on page 263.
___ 3. Complete Workbook Activity 106.
___ 4. Read page 264. Complete Activity A on page 265.
___ 5. Complete Activities B–C on page 265.
___ 6. Complete Workbook Activity 107.
___ 7. Read page 266. Complete Activities A–B on page 267.
___ 8. Complete Workbook Activity 108.
___ 9. Read page 268. Complete Activity A on page 268.
___ 10. Read page 269. Complete Activity B on page 269.
___ 11. Complete Workbook Activity 109.

Comments:

Goal 13.2 To identify improperly written sentences

Date | Assignment | Score

___ 12. Read page 270. Complete Activity A on page 270.
___ 13. Read page 271. Complete Activities B–C on page 271.
___ 14. Complete Workbook Activity 110.

Comments:

Goal 13.3 To rewrite sentences to improve them

Date | Assignment | Score

___ 15. Read page 272. Complete Activity A on page 272.
___ 16. Read page 273. Complete Activity B on page 273.
___ 17. Complete Workbook Activity 111.

Comments:

© American Guidance Service, Inc. Permission is granted to reproduce for classroom use only. English to Use

Name ___ Date ___ Period ___ SELF-STUDY GUIDE

CHAPTER 13 Fine-Tuning Your Writing, continued

Goal 13.4 To avoid the use of nonstandard English and to use standard English to speak and write

Date | Assignment | Score

___ 18. Read pages 274–275. Complete Activities A–B on page 275.
___ 19. Complete Workbook Activity 112.
___ 20. Read page 276. Complete Activity A on page 276.
___ 21. Complete Activities B–C on page 276.
___ 22. Read page 277. Complete Activity D on page 277.
___ 23. Complete Activity E on page 277.
___ 24. Complete Workbook Activity 113.
___ 25. Complete the Chapter 13 Review, Parts A–F on pages 278–279.

Comments:

Student's Signature ___ Date ___
Instructor's Signature ___ Date ___

© American Guidance Service, Inc. Permission is granted to reproduce for classroom use only. English to Use

TRL   TRL

Chapter 13 Self-Study Guide

Introducing the Chapter

Ask students whether they ever tuned up a car or updated a computer's screen-saver. Have they tweaked a dance routine or adjusted roller blades? Then ask about personal skills they've fine-tuned or improved. Help students see that fine-tuning involves smoothing out and refining.

Explain that in this chapter, students will learn to fine-tune writing and speaking skills.

TEACHER'S RESOURCE

The AGS Teaching Strategies in English Transparencies may be used with this chapter. The transparencies add an interactive dimension to expand and enhance the *English to Use* program content.

CAREER INTEREST INVENTORY

The AGS Harrington-O'Shea Career Decision-Making System–Revised (CDM) may be used with this chapter. Students can use the CDM to explore their interests and identify careers. The CDM defines career areas that are indicated by students' responses on the inventory.

Writing Tips and Notes

Ask volunteers to read the tips and notes that appear in the margins throughout the chapter. Then discuss them with the class.

CHAPTER PROJECT

Have students work in groups to record several short conversations about topics that interest them. Have them transcribe selected parts of the conversation that demonstrate use of subject-verb agreement and pronoun usage. Ask students to rewrite some sections of their conversation in standard English.

Fine-Tuning Writing Chapter 13 **261**

Chapter 13 Lesson 1

Overview This lesson explains subject-verb agreement.

Objectives
- To identify singular and plural subjects and verbs
- To choose a verb that agrees with a singular or plural subject

Student Pages 262–263

Teacher's Resource Library

Workbook Activity 106

Activity 106

Alternative Activity 106

Vocabulary
agreement

1 Warm-Up Activity

Write sentences on the board that include the names of students in the class, but use a verb that does not agree in number with the subject: *Darleen and Joycelyn sits by the window. Chu wear a yellow coat.* Discuss with the class how a subject and verb must agree in number, balancing one another like a seesaw. Talk with students about how the examples on the board do not balance. Have volunteers take turns changing either the subjects or the verbs to make the sentences agree in number.

2 Teaching the Lesson

Read with students the explanation of subject-verb agreement, and ask them to provide additional sentences modeled on the examples in the first box. Then discuss the remaining text and examples. Review singular and plural forms of verbs and nouns, including collective nouns. In addition, help students identify the prepositional phrase, the dependent clause, and the appositive in the sentences in the last example box.

Lesson 1 Subject-Verb Agreement

Agreement
The rule that a singular subject has a singular verb and a plural subject has a plural verb

You have learned that every sentence has a subject and a verb. The rule of **agreement** states that a verb must agree in number with its subject. A singular subject takes a singular verb. A plural subject takes a plural verb.

EXAMPLE

Singular	He eats.
Plural	They eat.
Singular	Aziza plays the guitar.
Plural	The two friends play the guitar.
Singular	The tiger runs fast.
Plural	Tigers run fast.

Do not be confused by plural nouns in titles. The title of a book, poem, song, movie, or play is singular.

EXAMPLE *Purple Bunnies* is a silly TV show.
(Although *bunnies* is a plural noun, the subject *Purple Bunnies* names one TV show. The singular subject takes the singular verb *is*.)

Do not be confused by plural nouns in phrases, clauses, or appositives that come between the subject and verb.

EXAMPLE The neighbor of my two cousins teaches history at our school.
(*Neighbor* is the singular subject. It takes the singular verb *teaches*.)

A jar that contains nails falls off the shelf.
(*Jar* is the singular subject. It takes the singular verb *falls*.)

The girl, one of three performers, smiles proudly for the audience.
(*Girl* is the singular subject. It takes the singular verb *smiles*.)

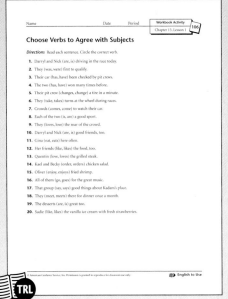

Classifier
(He, Him)

Eats

He eats.

Activity A Copy the sentences on your paper. Underline the subject, and circle the verb. Then write whether the subject and verb are *singular* or *plural*.

1. A small child plays with the toy.
2. Many children ride on the bus.
3. His store, which sells chairs, opens for business today.
4. Alice, a swim teacher for young children, works for the town.
5. Sheep from Ted's ranch graze on the grassy hill.

Activity B On your paper, write the verb in parentheses that agrees with the subject.

1. A woman with twin boys (buy, buys) a dozen eggs.
2. The eggs (come, comes) from a local farm.
3. Many hens (lays, lay) eggs.
4. A farmer (collects, collect) the eggs.
5. Farmers (sells, sell) the eggs to grocery stores.

Activity C Rewrite and edit this paragraph. Correct the agreement of subjects and verbs. Improve the sentences by combining them or changing their order.

> The roads across America is busy. Vehicles of all kinds drives on the highways. A trip to distant places are fun for families. People likes all the parks and beach and mountain in our country Some national parks has a few wolf and bear. When people respects wildlife, all living things is safe. Then people enjoys the outdoor life.

Activity A Answers

1. A small <u>child</u> (plays) with the toy—singular 2. Many <u>children</u> (ride) on the bus—plural 3. His <u>store</u>, which sells chairs, (opens) for business today—singular 4. <u>Alice</u>, a swim teacher for young children, (works) for the town—singular 5. <u>Sheep</u> from Ted's ranch (graze) on the grassy hill—plural

Activity B Answers

1. buys 2. come 3. lay 4. collects 5. sell

Activity C Answers

Paragraphs will vary. Check that subjects and verbs agree. Also check for correct spelling of plurals and for end punctuation. One possible version follows.

The roads across America are busy. Vehicles of all kinds drive on the highways. Trips to distant places are fun for families, who like the beaches and mountains that our country has to offer. People who enjoy the outdoor life also like the national parks, some of which are homes to wolves and bears. When people respect wildlife, all living things are safe.

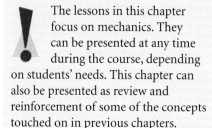 **3** **Reinforce and Extend**

TEACHER ALERT

The lessons in this chapter focus on mechanics. They can be presented at any time during the course, depending on students' needs. This chapter can also be presented as review and reinforcement of some of the concepts touched on in previous chapters.

ASL ILLUSTRATION

Remind students that the "classifier" in ASL can be either a subject pronoun *(he)* or an object pronoun *(him)*. Volunteers might want to research ASL to learn the "classifier" sign for "she/her." Have students practice making the ASL signs.

GLOBAL CONNECTION

 Ask students who are bilingual or multilingual to explain the rules for subject-verb agreement in languages other than English. If possible, have them provide examples of sentence constructions that cause problems with subject-verb agreement. These problems would be similar to those that occur in English when plural nouns appear in prepositional phrases, clauses, and appositives that come between the subject and verb.

Chapter 13 Lesson 2

Overview This lesson focuses on subject-verb agreement in sentences with compound subjects and in inverted subject-verb construction.

Objective

■ To use the correct verb form in sentences with compound subjects, in sentences that begin with *here* or *there*, and in questions

Student Pages 264–265

Teacher's Resource Library

Workbook Activity 107

Activity 107

Alternative Activity 107

1 Warm-Up Activity

Place two items on your desk, and ask students to name them. Then have students ask you what is on your desk. Name only one item: *A book is on my desk.* Have students ask you again to identify the items on your desk, and name two items, using the same verb: *A pencil and a book is on my desk.* Tell students that it can be easy to overlook a part of a compound subject, and discuss the importance of making a verb agree with *all* the subjects in a sentence. Have students correct the verb in the sentence you created with a compound subject.

2 Teaching the Lesson

Focus students' attention on the text and the first example box. Note that in the second sentence, *teacher* is singular but that the compound subject (*students* and *teacher*) takes a plural verb. Ask students to provide other sentences modeled on those in the example box.

Review the remaining rules and example boxes with students. Stress that no matter what word begins a sentence or question, the subject and verb must still agree.

Lesson **2** More About Subject-Verb Agreement

There are some things to keep in mind to avoid making common mistakes with subject-verb agreement.

A compound subject connected by *and* always takes a plural verb. Pay careful attention when the first part of a compound subject is plural and the second part is singular.

> **EXAMPLE** The singers and the musicians are performing.
> The students and their teacher listen carefully.

In a sentence that begins with the adverb *here* or *there*, the subject follows the verb. Find the subject. If the subject is singular, it takes a singular verb. If the subject is plural, it takes a plural verb.

> **EXAMPLE**
> | Singular | There goes a very long train. |
> | Plural | There go two very long trains. |
> | Plural | There go a train and a bus. |

In a question, the subject often follows the verb or comes between the helping verb and main verb. Find the subject. If the subject is singular, it takes a singular verb. If the subject is plural, it takes a plural verb.

> **EXAMPLE**
> | Singular | Is your brother coming with us? |
> | Plural | Where are the girl and her cat? |
> | Plural | Do the students know the words of the poem? |

Writing Tip

To check subject-verb agreement in sentences starting with *here* or *there* or in questions, try this. Switch the word order so the subject comes first.

Example
A very long train goes there.

Your brother is coming with us?

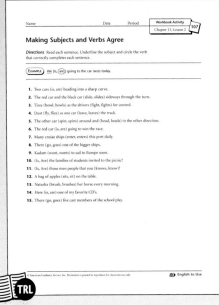

Workbook Activity 107

Activity 107

Activity A Write each sentence. Underline the subject. Choose the verb in parentheses that agrees with the subject.

1. Louis and Tim (is, are) in the choir.
2. (Do, Does) the members of the choir sing this Saturday?
3. Louis and Tim (have, has) been singing in the choir for five years.
4. Here (come, comes) Mr. Whithall, the band leader.
5. When (is, are) the choir and band practicing?

Activity B On your paper, write the verb in parentheses that agrees with the subject.

1. Here (come, comes) the tow truck.
2. (Is, Are) there many cars and trucks on the highways?
3. There (has, have) been several accidents this winter.
4. There (was, were) some people stranded by the storm.
5. (Is, Are) there more snow in the weather forecast?
6. There (stand, stands) the tallest statue in the city.
7. Here (is, are) your test scores.
8. There (is, are) several large motels in the next town.
9. There (is, are) one motel with a good restaurant.
10. (Do, Does) your family and friends eat there?

Activity C Rewrite and edit this paragraph. Correct the agreement of subjects and verbs. Improve the sentences by combining them or changing their order.

> Here is my friends. Here is the place where we has parties. There are the table for snacks. Here come more friends. There is a big crowd now. Are there enough food? Is there too many people? Are there room for everyone? Well, we always has good times together.

Activity A Answers

1. <u>Louis</u> and <u>Tim</u> are in the choir.
2. Do the <u>members</u> of the choir sing this Saturday? 3. <u>Louis</u> and <u>Tim</u> have been singing in the choir for five years. 4. Here comes <u>Mr. Whithall</u>, the band leader. 5. When are the <u>choir</u> and <u>band</u> practicing?

Activity B Answers

1. comes 2. Are 3. have 4. were 5. Is 6. stands 7. are 8. are 9. is 10. Do

Activity C Answers

Paragraphs will vary. Check that subjects and verbs agree. Also check to see that students have made an attempt to improve the paragraph. One version follows.

Here are my friends, and here come some more. This is the place where we have parties. There is a big crowd now. Are there too many people? Is there room for everyone? This is the table for snacks. Is there enough food? We always have good times together.

3 Reinforce and Extend

LEARNING STYLES

Auditory/Verbal

Have students work in groups to write sentences beginning with *here* and *there,* as well as sentences that contain compound subjects. Ask members of the groups to read the sentences aloud to the rest of the class, with both a singular and plural verb in the sentence. Have listeners identify clues that can help them select the correct verb. For example, members of the group can listen for the word *and,* which connects the parts of a compound subject.

CAREER CONNECTION

Invite someone whose job requires excellent writing skills to speak to your class about the rewriting and editing aspects of his or her work. Alternatively, obtain (or ask students to get) information from a guidance or career counselor about careers that require writing. Point out that writers work in advertising, on newspaper staffs, in public relations offices, in publishing companies, in political campaign offices, in television and radio, and in many other industries.

Chapter 13 Lesson 3

Overview This lesson focuses on subject-verb agreement with indefinite pronouns.

Objective

■ To choose the verb that agrees with a pronoun subject

Student Pages 266–267

Teacher's Resource Library

Workbook Activity 108

Activity 108

Alternative Activity 108

1 ▸ Warm-Up Activity

Say and write the following sentence on the board: *Are the class ready?* Ask students to identify and correct the error. Ask them what kind of noun *class* is *(a group noun)*, what kind of verb many group nouns take *(singular)*, and what kinds of pronouns replace many group nouns *(singular)*.

Read the list of pronouns and sentences in the first example box. Be sure that students understand the difference between singular and plural pronouns.

2 ▸ Teaching the Lesson

Make sure that students can distinguish between plural and singular pronouns, and give examples of singular and plural pronouns that do and do not agree with verbs. Then read the pronouns that can be both singular and plural. Discuss the example sentences and ask volunteers to provide additional example sentences for the five pronouns listed. Have students explain why the verb is singular or plural in each of their example sentences.

Lesson 3   Verb Agreement with Pronoun Subjects

Some pronouns that refer to people and things in general are always singular. Some are always plural. Remember that a singular subject takes a singular verb. A plural subject takes a plural verb.

Singular		Plural
anybody	everything	both
anyone	neither	few
each	no one	many
either	nobody	others
everybody	somebody	several
everyone	someone	

> **EXAMPLE**   **Singular**   Does anybody want lunch?
> **Plural**   Many want lunch.

Some pronouns that refer to people and things in general can be either singular or plural.

all	any	most	none	some

If the noun that the pronoun refers to is singular, the pronoun is singular. If the noun is plural, the pronoun is plural.

> **EXAMPLE**   **Singular**   Most of the lunch has been eaten.
> **Plural**   Most of the lunches have been eaten.

The singular pronouns *everybody, everyone,* and *everything* cause special problems with subject-verb agreement. Try to think of each of these words as a group. A noun that names a group usually takes a singular verb.

> **EXAMPLE**   Everyone is hungry.
> Everybody wants lunch.
> Everything in the lunches was fresh.

266   *Chapter 13   Fine-Tuning Your Writing*

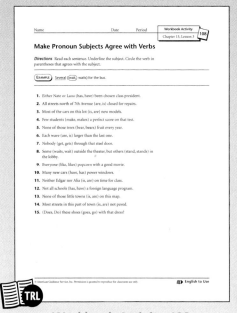

Workbook Activity 108

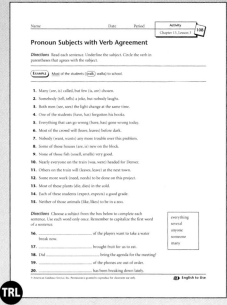

Activity 108

Activity A Write each sentence. Underline the subject. Choose the verb in parentheses that agrees with the subject.

1. Several (stand, stands) in line.
2. Few (leave, leaves) the line.
3. No one (is, are) pushing and shoving.
4. Many (wait, waits) for hours.
5. Each of the women (get, gets) concert tickets.
6. Others in line (is, are) not so lucky.
7. Everyone (want, wants) tickets for the show.
8. Neither of the lines (is, are) shorter than the other.
9. (Does, do) anyone look unhappy?
10. Everybody from our group (has, have) a ticket now.

Activity B Write each sentence. Underline the subject. Choose the verb in parentheses that agrees with the subject.

1. Several of the choir members (was, were) practicing.
2. (Have, Has) any of the members gone home yet?
3. None of that song (sound, sounds) good.
4. All of the singers (was, were) tired.
5. Each of the farmer's fields (need, needs) extra work.
6. Most of the work (has, have) been finished.
7. Some of the dogs (is, are) barking.
8. Nobody in the barns (know, knows) about the cattle contest.
9. (Do, Does) anybody know the words to this song?
10. There (is, are) some of the pizza left for you.

Many people enjoy singing in a choir.

Activity A Answers

1. <u>Several</u> stand in line. 2. <u>Few</u> leave the line. 3. <u>No one</u> is pushing and shoving. 4. <u>Many</u> wait for hours. 5. <u>Each</u> of the women gets concert tickets. 6. <u>Others</u> in line are not so lucky. 7. <u>Everyone</u> wants tickets for the show. 8. <u>Neither</u> of the lines is shorter than the other. 9. Does <u>anyone</u> look unhappy? 10. <u>Everybody</u> from our group has a ticket now.

Activity B Answers

1. <u>Several</u> of the choir members were practicing. 2. Have <u>any</u> of the members gone home yet? 3. <u>None</u> of that song sounds good. 4. <u>All</u> of the singers were tired. 5. <u>Each</u> of the farmer's fields needs extra work. 6. <u>Most</u> of the work has been finished. 7. <u>Some</u> of the dogs are barking. 8. <u>Nobody</u> in the barns knows about the cattle contest. 9. Does <u>anybody</u> know the words to this song? 10. There is <u>some</u> of the pizza left for you.

 3 Reinforce and Extend

LEARNING STYLES

Body/Kinesthetic
Have students write sentences describing classroom activities; the sentences should use pronouns that can be both singular and plural. Then have small groups act out the activities in the sentences. Have the class decide whether the pronoun refers to a noun that is singular or plural, and have them help select the correct verb form.

ONLINE CONNECTION

 The Writing Center at Tidewater Community College offers online assistance for students, including grammar and punctuation guidelines, a practical punctuation guide, and other self-help handouts. Visit the site at *www.tc.cc.va.us/writcent/*.

Lesson at a Glance

Chapter 13 Lesson 4

Overview This lesson focuses on noun-pronoun agreement with possessive pronouns and on subject-verb agreement with compound subjects connected by *either-or*, *neither-nor*.

Objectives

■ To complete sentences with possessive pronouns that agree with subjects

■ To choose verbs that agree with compound subjects connected by *either-or*, *neither-nor*

Student Pages 268–269

Teacher's Resource Library

Workbook Activity 109

Activity 109

Alternative Activity 109

1 Warm-Up Activity

Say and write on the board: *We are in our classroom. Each of us is in his or her classroom. All of us are in our classroom.* Help students find and underline each subject. Then ask whether each is singular or plural. Point out the effect of a singular or plural pronoun on the choice of verb.

2 Teaching the Lesson

Focus students' attention on the text and discuss the sentences in the example boxes. Emphasize the importance of locating the simple subject of the sentence before choosing a pronoun that agrees with it.

Activity A Answers

1. Brenda sprained her ankle.
2. I gave Brenda my help.
3. Together, we made our way down the cliff. 4. Josh called home on his cellular phone. 5. Kevin, Josh, and Brenda remember their day on the mountain.

An owner pronoun and the noun it refers to should agree in number and gender.

EXAMPLE Carmelita hooked her cable to the rock.
(The pronoun *her* refers to the singular feminine noun *Carmelita*.)

Stefano and Jamilla hooked their cables to the rock.
(The pronoun *their* refers to the compound subject *Stefano* and *Jamilla*. A compound subject is plural, so the pronoun is plural.)

Each of the men took his dog to Dr. Velasquez.
(The pronoun *his* refers to the singular pronoun *each*. The masculine form appears because *each* refers to *men*, a masculine noun that is the object of the preposition *of*.)

If you are not sure whether you should use *her* or *his*, try these choices.

• Use both *his* and *her*.

• Reword the sentence.

• Do not use a pronoun at all.

EXAMPLE Each student liked his or her book.
The students liked their books.
Each student liked a book.

Activity A On your paper, write each sentence with an owner pronoun. Underline the word to which the pronoun refers.

1. Brenda sprained _____ ankle.
2. I gave Brenda _____ help.
3. Together, we made _____ way down the cliff.
4. Josh called home on _____ cellular phone.
5. Kevin, Josh, and Brenda remember _____ day on the mountain.

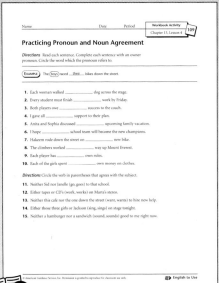

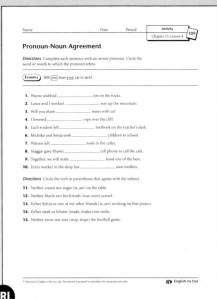

Workbook Activity 109

Activity 109

A compound subject connected by *and* is plural. It takes a plural verb. A compound subject connected by *or* can be singular or plural.

> **EXAMPLE**
> **Plural**   Julio and Keiko work.
> **Singular**   Julio or Keiko works.
> **Plural**   Her cousins or her aunts work.

You can connect a compound subject with the conjunctions *either-or* or *neither-nor*.

If both parts of a compound subject are singular, use a singular verb.

> **EXAMPLE**
> Either Benjiro or Paulita is singing tonight.
> Neither Benjiro nor Paulita is singing tonight.

If both parts of a compound subject are plural, use a plural verb.

> **EXAMPLE**
> Either the sisters or their parents are singing.
> Neither the sisters nor their parents are singing.

If one part of a compound subject is singular and the other part is plural, the verb usually agrees with the part closest to the verb.

> **EXAMPLE**
> Either the sisters or Paulita is singing.
> Neither Paulita nor the sisters are singing.
> Paulita or the sisters are singing.

Activity B Write the verb in parentheses that agrees with the subject.

1. Neither wolves nor tigers (live, lives) in that country.
2. Neither science nor math (is, are) my favorite subject.
3. Either tools or a flashlight (fit, fits) into the space.
4. Neither the women nor Chuck (know, knows) the way.
5. Neither Ron nor his friends (was, were) hungry.

The students liked their books.

Book

Their

Student

Like

Finish

Fine-Tuning Your Writing   Chapter 13   **269**

ASL ILLUSTRATION

As students review the sign language feature, have them notice how the word order of the signs differs from the English rendering of the sentence. Discuss with students the sign for "finish," asking them how we convey that concept in both spoken and written language. Have students practice using the ASL signs.

IN THE COMMUNITY

Have partners play a guessing game about an item at a local store. First, write down an item he or she has seen in a store: for example, a school supply or a favorite magazine. Then have that student give his or her partner clues about the item. Students should present clues in an *either-or, neither-nor* format: for example, *I am thinking of an item in the stationery department at Blank-Mart that is neither a notebook nor a pen.* When the first partner has guessed the item, tell students to switch partners and let the other person guess.

Activity B Answers

1. live **2.** is **3.** fits **4.** knows **5.** were

Speaking Practice

Have students take turns reading aloud the sentences in Activity B. Ask students to use their voice inflection to emphasize the *either-or/neither-nor* constructions. Have students listen for plural and singular subjects that are closest to the verb. If necessary, model an example for students, and help them understand what the correct agreement "sounds" like in these constructions.

3 Reinforce and Extend

LEARNING STYLES

Logical/Mathematical
Have student groups write sentences with compound subjects that contain *and, either-or,* and *neither-nor*. Tell students to omit the verbs. Then have groups switch sentences and insert verbs following this pattern:

1. First circle all *ands*. Groups should insert plural verbs in these instances.

2. In the remaining *either-or* and *neither-nor* sentences, groups should underline the two parts of the subject. They should write *P* or *S* above the subject to indicate whether the noun is plural or singular.

3. In sentences where both parts of the *either-or, neither-nor* subjects are plural, students should write a plural verb. In sentences where both parts are singular, students should write a singular verb.

4. In the remaining sentences, which contain both singular and plural verbs, students should make the verb match the closest subject noun.

Lesson at a Glance

Chapter 13 Lesson 5

Overview This lesson focuses on subject-verb agreement with *don't* and *doesn't*.

Objectives

■ To use *don't* and *doesn't* correctly in sentences

■ To use *this*, *that*, *these*, and *those* correctly in sentences with *don't* or *doesn't*

Student Pages 270–271

Teacher's Resource Library **TRL**

Workbook Activity 110

Activity 110

Alternative Activity 110

---

1 Warm-Up Activity

Discuss the rules presented in the text for using *doesn't* and *don't*. Go over the examples. Then write sentence pairs such as the following on the board: *She doesn't have any homework. She don't have any homework. Don't he want any supper? Doesn't he want any supper?* Have students identify the correct sentence in each pair and explain why it is correct.

2 Teaching the Lesson

Provide students with a reference for plural and singular forms by writing on the board: *Plural: don't, do not, these, those; Singular: doesn't, does not, this, that.* Remind students to substitute *do not* and *does not* if they are unsure of the correct contraction.

Lesson 5 — Don't and Doesn't

There is an easy way to check whether you have used *don't* or *doesn't* correctly. Replace with *do not* or *does not* in the sentence.

Doesn't is a contraction for *does not*. *Does* and *doesn't* go with singular subjects except *I* and *you*.

Don't is a contraction for *do not*. *Do* and *don't* go with plural subjects.

EXAMPLE

Singular	Plural
Maria doesn't swim.	Maria and Rosita don't swim.
The dog does swim.	The dogs do swim.
I don't swim.	We don't swim.
Don't you swim?	You two don't swim.

Activity A Complete each sentence with *don't* or *doesn't*. Write the sentences on your paper.

1. You _____ need money at the picnic.
2. She _____ look very happy.
3. They _____ want any dinner.
4. It _____ look good to me.
5. He _____ say very much.
6. We _____ play video games at the mall.
7. A hot summer _____ seem short.
8. Sandy and Ed _____ own a fax machine.
9. A pleasant vacation _____ seem long.
10. It _____ matter.
11. Grass and flowers _____ grow well in this dry climate.
12. A big truck _____ stop fast.
13. They _____ live in this town.
14. He _____ go to this school.
15. _____ she want breakfast?

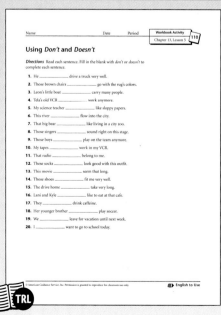

Workbook Activity 110

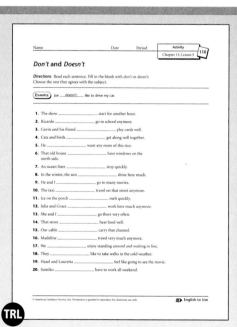

Activity 110

Writing Tip

Using *this, that, these,* and *those* can make your sentences more interesting.

Remember not to use the contractions *doesn't* and *don't* in reports and other formal writing.

Use *doesn't* with *this* and *that.*

EXAMPLE That window doesn't open easily.
This plant doesn't have flowers.

Use *don't* with *these* and *those.*

EXAMPLE These tables don't match each other.
Those pictures don't hang straight.

Activity B Complete each sentence with *don't* or *doesn't.* Write the sentences on your paper.

1. This book _____ belong to me.

2. That one _____ belong to me, either.

3. These_____ look good.

4. Those _____ look very good, either.

5. This _____ look much better.

6. _____ that seem like a good idea?

7. This room _____ look good.

8. That lamp _____ work.

9. These drapes _____ go with the sofa.

10. That carpet _____ go with anything.

Activity C Rewrite and edit this paragraph. Correct the agreement of subjects and verbs. Improve the sentences by combining them or changing their order.

> My computer don't work good. Either the program or the machine aren't working right. When I call a repair service, they doesn't know nothing. My computer teacher at school help me. Now my computer do work. My printer are jammed. Neither my teacher nor my friends knows about that problem.

Fine-Tuning Your Writing Chapter 13 **271**

---

3 Reinforce and Extend

LEARNING STYLES

LEP/ESL
Pay close attention to speakers of languages in which the double negative is correct. For example, *No es nada* (Spanish) would translate as "I want nothing" (or "I don't want anything") rather than "I don't want nothing." Have English learners work in pairs and write or say a negative sentence in their native languages and translate it into standard English.

AT HOME

Newspaper reporters often write stories in a hurry to meet a deadline. Editors must check closely to catch any mistakes in grammar or usage. Ask students to look through a local newspaper for mistakes editors may have missed or for sentences that could be improved. Suggest that students focus on the news and sports sections, since articles for these sections are often written at the last moment. Ask students to bring their example sentences to class.

Activity A Answers

1. You don't need money at the picnic. 2. She doesn't look very happy. 3. They don't want any dinner. 4. It doesn't look good to me. 5. He doesn't say very much. 6. We don't play video games at the mall. 7. A hot summer doesn't seem short. 8. Sandy and Ed don't own a fax machine. 9. A pleasant vacation doesn't seem long. 10. It doesn't matter. 11. Grass and flowers don't grow well in this dry climate. 12. A big truck doesn't stop fast. 13. They don't live in this town. 14. He doesn't go to this school. 15. Doesn't she want breakfast?

Activity B Answers

1. This book doesn't belong to me. 2. That one doesn't belong to me, either. 3. These don't look good. 4. Those don't look very good, either. 5. This doesn't look much better. 6. Doesn't that seem like a good idea? 7. This room doesn't look good. 8. That lamp doesn't work. 9. These drapes don't go with the sofa. 10. That carpet doesn't go with anything.

Activity C Answers

Paragraphs will vary. Check that subjects and verbs agree and that all other mistakes in grammar and usage have been corrected. One version follows.

My computer didn't work well; either the program or the machine wasn't working properly. Neither my family nor my friends know about computer problems. When I called a repair service, no one knew anything. However, my computer teacher at school was able to help me. He saw that my printer was jammed. Now my computer does work.

Lesson at a Glance

Chapter 13 Lesson 6

Overview This lesson focuses on the placement and meaning of the words *only* and *just* in sentences and on misplaced adjective and adverb phrases.

Objectives

■ To determine the difference in meaning between sentences with *just* and *only* in different positions

■ To identify and correctly revise sentences with misplaced modifiers

Student Pages 272–273

Teacher's Resource Library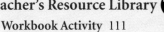

Workbook Activity 111

Activity 111

Alternative Activity 111

 Warm-Up Activity

Say and write on the board: *I was only taking a nap. Only I was taking a nap.* Ask students to identify the difference between the two sentences. Help them recognize how the placement of *only* changes the meaning of the sentences. Have students repeat the sentences, substituting the word *just* for *only*.

 Teaching the Lesson

Discuss with students how our use of phrases, as well as *just* and *only,* can be casual and inexact in everyday conversation. Ask volunteers to offer sentences with *just, only,* and misplaced phrases that could be confusing and to offer examples of gestures, intonation, or body language that might make their messages clear. Tell the class that written language must be exact, since writers cannot clarify their meanings with gestures or other non-verbal clues.

Writing Tip

Always proofread your writing carefully to make sure you have really said what you mean. Are words and phrases near the words and phrases they describe? Would the placement of any words or phrases confuse your reader?

The meaning of an entire sentence can change when you move a word or a phrase. Read over your sentences. Be sure the sentence means what you want it to mean.

EXAMPLE Consuela just met Abdul at the library.
(Here *just* tells when Consuela met Abdul at the library. They met *just* now.)

Consuela met just Abdul at the library.
(Here *just* tells whom Consuela met at the library. She met *just* Abdul and no one else.)

Only Emiko knows the third answer.
(Here *only* means no one but Emiko knows the third answer.)

Emiko knows only the third answer.
(Here *only* means Emiko knows the third answer, but she does not know any other answers.)

Emiko knows the only answer.
(Here *only* means there is one answer, and Emiko knows it.)

Activity A On your paper, explain the difference in meaning between the sentences in each group.

1. Only Jenny looked out the window.
   Jenny looked only out the window.
   Jenny looked out the only window.

2. Sarah just suggested that Janine have a sandwich.
   Sarah suggested that Janine have just a sandwich.

3. I just brought in the CD player.
   I brought in just the CD player.

4. Dee earned just twenty dollars.
   Just Dee earned twenty dollars.
   Dee just earned twenty dollars.

5. That bank stays open late only on Thursdays.
   Only that bank is open late on Thursdays.

272 Chapter 13 *Fine-Tuning Your Writing*

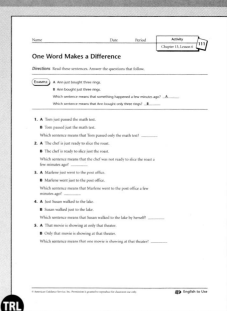

Try to place phrases close to the words they describe. A sentence may not make sense or its meaning may be unclear if you misplace a phrase.

> **EXAMPLE**
>
> | Unclear | The reporters talked about cooking at work. (Did the reporters want to cook at work? Probably they did not.) |
> | Clear | The reporters talked at work about cooking. |
> | Unclear | The boy saw an elephant on the way home. (Was the elephant on its way home? It's not likely.) |
> | Clear | On the way home, the boy saw a elephant. |

Activity B Find the misplaced phrase in each sentence. Rewrite the sentence so that its meaning is clear.

1. Mom drove Alice to the party in her car.
2. A present was brought by Alice in brown paper.
3. The children told stories about ghosts in the room.
4. Alice wandered into the room acting shy and nervous.
5. Casey asked Alice to sit next to her smiling.
6. The animals looked at me in the zoo through the bars.
7. The rabbit hid under the bush with the little white tail.
8. The elephant sprayed the man on the bench with a trunkful of water.
9. Some people waited beside the lion cage with strollers.
10. The monkeys watched Kate swinging on the tree branches.

You can see a variety of animals at the zoo.

Communication Connection

People use body language to show how they feel. A shy, nervous person might hold his or her head down. Smiling is a sign that a person is happy and friendly.

---

3 Reinforce and Extend

LEARNING STYLES

Interpersonal/Group

Have students work in pairs to present a short dialogue that demonstrates how word order can affect meaning. Students may want to expand on one of the groups of sentences presented in Activity A, elaborating on the scenario to show the type of confusion that can arise from inexact language use.

LEARNING STYLES

Visual/Spatial

Have students write the sentences in Activity B on construction paper. Then have them cut out the phrases that are misplaced and paste them in the correct position. Students may find that the phrases can be repositioned in more than one spot. Students may want to work in pairs in order to discuss possible placements for the phrases.

Activity A Answers

Wording will vary. **1.** In the first sentence, no one but Jenny looked out the window. In the second sentence, Jenny looked nowhere but out the window. In the third sentence, there was just one window out of which to look. **2.** In the first sentence, Sarah either made a casual suggestion or made a suggestion very recently. In the second sentence, she is suggesting that Janine have no more than one sandwich. **3.** In the first sentence, the person brought in the CD player very recently. In the second sentence, the CD player was the only item the person brought in. **4.** In the first sentence, Dee earned no more than twenty dollars. In the second sentence, no other person but Dee earned twenty dollars. In the third sentence, Dee earned twenty dollars recently. **5.** The first sentence means that the bank is not open late on any day except Thursday. The second sentence means that no other bank is open late on Thursdays.

Activity B Answers

Answers may vary. **1.** Mom drove Alice in her car to the party. **2.** Alice brought a present in brown paper. **3.** The children in the room told stories about ghosts. **4.** Acting shy and nervous, Alice wandered into the room. **5.** Smiling, Casey asked Alice to sit next to her. **6.** The animals in the zoo looked through the bars at me. **7.** The rabbit with the little white tail hid under the bush. **8.** The elephant sprayed a trunkful of water on the man on the bench. **9.** Some people with strollers waited beside the lion cage. **10.** The monkeys swinging on the tree branches watched Kate.

Lesson at a Glance

Chapter 13 Lesson 7

Overview This lesson contrasts standard and nonstandard English.

Objectives

■ To identify standard English usage

■ To rewrite nonstandard English sentences in standard English

Student Pages 274–275

Teacher's Resource Library

Workbook Activity 112

Activity 112

Alternative Activity 112

1 Warm-Up Activity

Ask volunteers to read aloud the three sentences in the first example box. Ask students what they notice about the speaker's speech patterns in each sentence. Whom do students think the speakers are addressing? Does the language seem appropriate to these situations? Discuss with students how speakers are using a relaxed, or nonstandard, form of English in situations where standard English might be more appropriate.

2 Teaching the Lesson

Ask students to read aloud the corrected sentences in the second example box. Have students discuss which of the sentence pairs is easier to understand in a written format. Ask students what impression the second sentences might have on listeners as opposed to the impression the first set of sentences might give. Emphasize the difference between formal language and informal conversation, in which speakers clarify potentially confusing usages through voice inflection and gesture.

You probably speak differently to your teachers and your boss than you do to your friends. Most people tend to use a more relaxed form of the English language when speaking to family and friends. In some cases, however, this relaxed attitude results in dialogue that has little or no meaning for listeners.

> "Well, I'd like this job and, well, I think you should hire me and, well, I hope you will."
>
> "So, like, if you hire me and, like, I'm sick, like, do I get, like, sick leave?"
>
> "You know, I think we need longer, you know, breaks, you know, because, you know, we're on our feet, you know, all day."

The repetition of *well, like,* and *you know* in the examples gets in the way of the speaker's message. Notice how the removal of these words makes the speaker's meaning clear.

EXAMPLE

> "I'd like this job, and I think you should hire me. I hope you will."
>
> "If you hire me, and I get sick, do I get sick leave?"
>
> "I think we need longer breaks because we're on our feet all day."

You might also find nonstandard English in friendly letters or e-mail. You should never use nonstandard English in reports, presentations, or business letters.

People sometimes divide the English language into two types.

- Standard English is the English you read in most textbooks and hear on TV and radio news programs. Standard English follows the rules of English grammar. It is always acceptable and correct.

- Nonstandard English is the English you may use with your friends. You may also hear characters in TV shows and movies speaking it. Writers may use it in dialogue to make their characters sound like real people. Nonstandard English follows current styles of speech. It often contains slang and regional expressions. It does not always follow the rules of grammar. For these reasons, it is not acceptable to use nonstandard English in formal situations.

274 Chapter 13 *Fine-Tuning Your Writing*

Here are examples of standard and nonstandard English.

Standard English	Nonstandard English
She isn't here.	She ain't here.
Where were you?	Where were you at?
Jorge did well.	Jorge done good.
He might have done it.	He might of done it.
She will try to go.	She will try and go.
He's been everywhere.	He's been everywheres.
Serafina went all the way down the street.	Serafina went a ways down the street.

Activity A Read what Pam tells her friend Beth about Ben, who works with her. Rewrite Pam's dialogue on your paper. Use standard English.

> I saw Ben in Shipping. So I go, "Hi," and he goes, "Hi yourself." Then he goes, "How you doing?" and I go, "Not bad. How about you?" So he goes, "Okay, sorta. I'm sorta hanging loose between things."

Activity B On your paper, rewrite the following dialogue. Use standard English.

> Colleen has done collected dolls from all over the world. She says, "I ain't never gonna stop. Like, I like dolls from everywheres on earth."
>
> Then I says, "Where did you find this one at?"
>
> Then she says, "Like, you know, in a store in New York. It's from like Tibet."
>
> Then I says, "I should of started a doll collection, too."
>
> Then she says, "I ain't too busy to try and help you."
>
> Then I says, "Thanks. You done real good with your set."

Activity A Answers

Answers may vary but should feature standard English. A possible answer follows.

> I saw Ben in Shipping. I said, "Hi." He said, "Hi, yourself. How are you doing?" I said, "Not bad. How about you?" He said, "Okay. I'm hanging loose between things."

Activity B Answers

Answers may vary but should feature standard English. A possible answer follows.

> Colleen has collected dolls from all over the world. She said, "I'm not ever going to stop. I like dolls from everywhere on earth."
>
> I asked, "Where did you get this one?"
>
> She said, "In a store in New York. It's from Tibet."
>
> Then I said, "I should have started a doll collection, too."
>
> She said, "I'm not too busy to try to help you."
>
> Then I said, "Thanks. You did very well with your set."

 Reinforce and Extend

TEACHER ALERT

 Make sure that students understand that the usage called "standard English" describes a particular type of formal writing and speech. Many students may write or speak in a particular regional or ethnic dialect that is entirely appropriate in its context. They should not be made to feel that such regional, ethnic language (*Gullah, "Spanglish"*) is a nonstandard or inappropriate usage for their home or community.

Chapter 13 Lesson 8

Overview This lesson focuses on the rewriting stage of the writing process.

Objectives

- To rewrite and edit a rough draft and sentences with nonstandard English
- To choose verbs that agree with subjects
- To match terms with definitions

Student Pages 276–277

Teacher's Resource Library

Workbook Activity 113

Activity 113

Alternative Activity 113

1 Warm-Up Activity

Have volunteers act out an on-the-job meeting involving a trainee and a supervisor. Ask the volunteer acting as supervisor to read aloud the letter in Activity A. Have the volunteers act out how the supervisor might respond to the trainee's concerns as written in the letter, and ask the trainee to clarify verbally his or her requests for changes. Ask the class to discuss whether the letter helped or hindered the trainee in conveying the need for changes.

2 Teaching the Lesson

Tell students that this lesson provides an opportunity to act as editors. Explain that they will correct a rough draft of a letter and sentences containing errors in grammar, punctuation, and spelling. Emphasize to students that they are proofreading materials to find errors.

Lesson 8 Writing Mechanics

Good writers may edit and rewrite a story or an article several times before they are satisfied. The edit and rewrite stages of the writing process are important, and you should never rush or skip them.

You may not be sure what to edit or rewrite. Ask a classmate, teacher, friend, or family member to read your story or article. Readers often have valuable suggestions about what to change or correct.

Activity A Read the first draft of a letter by an unhappy worker to her boss. On your paper, rewrite the paragraph to improve it. Use standard English. Correct mistakes in grammar, spelling, and punctuation.

> I got several problems with my job I ain't had enough time to do it right. I got too much to do. I beleive I need more time to complete this job well. Maybe two more weeks. I can do it, but I needs more time. I no the company wants good work and like I wants more time so's its done good.

Activity B Write the verb in parentheses that agrees with the subject.

1. "Smiles" (is, are) a nice song.
2. Smiles (is, are) nice.
3. "Rainy Days" (is, are) a sad piece of music.
4. *Happy Guys* (was, were) a funny movie.
5. The happy guys (was, were) played by good actors.

Activity C Match the terms with their descriptions. Write the number and its correct letter on your paper.

Terms	Descriptions
1. several	A follows current styles of speech
2. everybody	B names an entire group
3. agree	C names more than one
4. standard English	D follows rules of grammar in writing and speaking
5. nonstandard English	E what subjects and verbs need to do

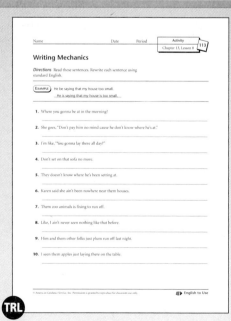

Workbook Activity 113   Activity 113

Try to avoid using sentences that ask *where* someone or something is by using the word *at*.

> **EXAMPLE**
>
> | | |
> |---|---|
> | Nonstandard English | She knows where it's at. |
> | Standard English | She knows where it is. |
> | Nonstandard English | Where is the office at? |
> | Standard English | Where is the office? |

Activity D Rewrite these sentences on your paper. Use standard English.

1. I know where it's at.
2. Where you at?
3. Let me know where you're at tonight.
4. Tell me where Joe's going to be at tomorrow.
5. Look where I'm at now!
6. Where are you at with your homework?
7. If you want good music, that radio station is where it's at.
8. Where have Ben and Todd been at lately?
9. Where have you been at while I was gone?
10. How can I know where you're at if you don't call?

Activity E Edit and rewrite these sentences. Use standard English.

1. I ain't never been nowhere in my life.
2. I'm like, "Where you at?"
3. He don't go there no more.
4. So I go, "No way! I ain't doing that!"
5. We doesn't set on the porch no more.

Using What You've Learned

Write a paragraph about a conversation that you had with a friend. Edit and rewrite your work, checking for nonstandard English and incorrect grammar, spelling, and punctuation.

---

 3 Reinforce and Extend

TEACHER ALERT

Remind students that in this lesson, the job of editor involves several different tasks. They will have to use what they know about mechanics and grammar, but they will also have to use their ears to listen for nonstandard English. Encourage students to go over the sentences in Activities A, D, and E more than once as they proofread for different types of errors.

Using What You've Learned

Tell students that their paragraphs can contain nonstandard English that is part of a dialogue. Remind students that they can use quotation marks to indicate the exact words of the conversation.

Activity A Answers

Paragraphs will vary. A sample response follows.

I have several problems with my job. I haven't had enough time to do it right. I have too much to do. I believe I need more time to complete this job well. I can do it, but I need about two more weeks. I know the company expects good work, and I want more time to do the job well.

Activity B Answers

1. is 2. are 3. is 4. was 5. were

Activity C Answers

1. C 2. B 3. E 4. D 5. A

Activity D Answers

1. I know where it is. 2. Where are you? 3. Let me know where you are tonight. 4. Tell me where Joe's going to be tomorrow. 5. Look where I am now! 6. Where are you with your homework? 7. If you want good music, that radio station is where it is. 8. Where have Ben and Todd been lately? 9. Where have you been while I was gone? 10. How can I know where you are if you don't call?

Activity E Answers

Answers may vary. Possible answers follow. 1. I have never been anywhere in my life. 2. I asked, "Where are you?" 3. He doesn't go there anymore. 4. I said, "I'm not doing that!" 5. We don't sit on the porch anymore.

Writing Practice

Have students brainstorm facts they might like to learn about a business, a product, a job, or non-profit organization. Then have students write a short letter asking for this information. Have students review one another's letters. Encourage students to mail their letters when they have finished the editing process. Help them find the proper addresses.

Chapter 13 Review

Use the Chapter Review to prepare students for tests and to reteach content from the chapter.

Chapter 13 Mastery Test

The Teacher's Resource Library includes two parallel forms of the Chapter 13 Mastery Test. The difficulty level of the two forms is equivalent. You may wish to use one form as a pretest and the other form as a posttest.

Final Mastery Test

The Teacher's Resource Library includes the Final Mastery Test. This test is pictured on pages 306–307 of this Teacher's Edition. The Final Mastery Test assesses the major learning objectives of this text, with emphasis on Chapters 7–13.

REVIEW ANSWERS

Part A

1. are 2. have 3. are 4. do 5. has

Part B

6. Someone has answered all the questions. 7. Others have not finished the test. 8. Most study hard for that class. 9. Many earn good grades. 10. Each member of our class takes three tests today. 11. All of the tests are an hour long. 12. One of the tests covers science. 13. Rod and his friends learn what the teacher expects from the class. 14. Each of the cooks is trained well. 15. No one complains about this food.

Part C

16. In the first sentence, Graciana gave a present to no one but Kareem. In the second sentence, Graciana recently gave a present to Kareem. In the third sentence, Graciana gave Kareem nothing but a present.

Part A Write the verb in parentheses that agrees with the subject.

1. Bill and Jenny (is, are) two old friends.
2. They (have, has) flown jets for several years.
3. Both (are, is) checked out for carrier landings.
4. Bill and Jenny (do, does) most of their flying together.
5. Their teamwork (have, has) earned them a fine military record.

Part B Copy each sentence. Underline each subject. Choose the correct form of the verb. Do not be confused by nouns in prepositional phrases.

6. Someone (has, have) answered all the questions.
7. Others (has, have) not finished the test.
8. Most (study, studies) hard for that class.
9. Many (earn, earns) good grades.
10. Each member of our class (take, takes) three tests today.
11. All of the tests (is, are) an hour long.
12. One of the tests (cover, covers) science.
13. Rod and his friends (learn, learns) what the teacher expects from the class.
14. Each of the cooks (is, are) trained well.
15. No one (complain, complains) about this food.

Part C On your paper, explain the difference in meaning between the sentences.

16. Graciana gave just Kareem a present on his birthday.
    Graciana just gave Kareem a present on his birthday.
    Graciana gave Kareem just a present on his birthday.

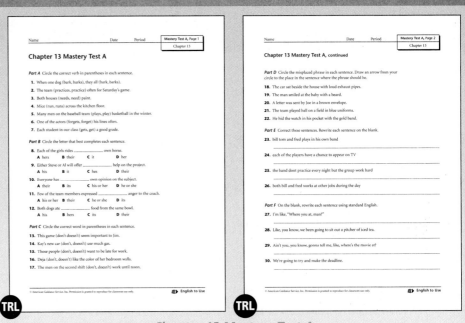

Chapter 13 Mastery Test A

Part D Rewrite these sentences correctly on your paper.

17. jill says that its fun surfing the internet but she don't know where shes at

18. antonio says your right but i ain't got no modem

19. by one of them modems at the big store next to the park with the red neon sign said jill

20. their like easy to use said jill.

21. she said that alls you have to do is like plug it in

22. the computer recieves all them signals jill told antonio

23. antonio said i no where the store's at and I'm gonna go

Part E Write the pronoun in parentheses that agrees with the subject.

24. One of the men has (his, their) own service station.

25. Each of the women gave (her, their) thanks for the good job the men did.

26. Most of the people give (his, their) support to local shops.

Part F Write the letter of the word or phrase that correctly completes each sentence.

27. The rule of _____ says that a singular subject has a singular verb and a plural subject has a plural verb.
    A verbs   B number   C action   D agreement

28. That movie _____ terrible.
    A were   B are   C is   D am

29. Neither this store nor that one _____ DVDs.
    A sell   B sells   C are selling   D have sold

30. Either the twins or their sister _____ a TV.
    A owns   B own   C have owned   D do own

When studying for a test, use a highlighter to mark things you want to remember. To review your notes quickly, look at the highlighted words.

REVIEW ANSWERS

Part D

17. Jill says that it's fun surfing the Internet, but she doesn't know where she is. **18.** Antonio says, "You're right, but I don't have a modem." **19.** "Buy one of those modems at the big store with the red neon sign next to the park," said Jill. **20.** "They're easy to use," said Jill. **21.** She said that all you have to do is plug it in. **22.** "The computer receives all those signals," Jill told Antonio. **23.** Antonio said, "I know where the store is, and I'm going to go."

Part E

24. his **25.** her **26.** their

Part F

27. D **28.** C **29.** B **30.** A

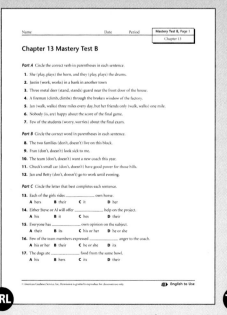

Chapter 13 Mastery Test B

Appendix A

The Writing Process

Overview This section may be used to review the steps of the writing process and to reinforce writing strategies.

Objectives

- To identify stages in the writing process
- To use the writing process when writing

Student Pages 280–286

Teacher's Resource Library (TRL)
Preparing for Writing Tests 1–4

Prewriting

Have students read the first paragraph on page 280. Encourage them to think about the strategies they use when they write. Help them make a list.

Read the Prewriting section on pages 280–282. On the board or a transparency, draw a two-column chart. Label one column *Choose a topic* and the other *Develop the topic.* Have students list in the appropriate columns procedures that will enable them to complete the prewriting procedure.

Writing for Tests

Today many tests are designed to assess students' ability to communicate in writing. The writing process can be adapted to help students organize and write in testing situations.

Point out to students that writing tests provide writing prompts that ask students to entertain, to inform, to persuade, to tell a story, or to describe. Emphasize that these are the purposes for writing. Knowing the purpose for writing will enable students to focus their writing. The prompt may also ask students to write in a particular format, such as letter, journal entry, paragraph, and poem.

Distribute copies of Preparing for Writing Tests 1. Ask students to read the prompts and identify what their writing purpose is. Also have them identify the format they are being asked to use.

The word *process* makes writing sound as if it is a simple set of steps every writer follows. In fact, every writer follows his or her own set of steps. But every writer must answer the same questions: *What do I write about? How do I organize my ideas? What do I leave in? What do I take out? How can I make my writing better?* Answering these questions is part of every writer's writing process. The process discussed below gives you guidelines to follow when you write.

Prewriting

Choosing a Topic

Some writers think this is the hardest part of writing. Certainly it is a very important part. Without a good topic, you have nowhere to go with your writing. Here are some ways to look for a topic:

- Think about people you know, places you have seen, and activities you enjoy.
- Think about memories or experiences from your past.
- Read newspapers and magazines. Listen to the radio. Watch TV.
- Write down anything that comes to mind. You may find an idea as you freewrite. When you freewrite, you write topics as you think of them. This is also called *brainstorming.*
- Talk to other people about your ideas. They may offer suggestions.
- Ask questions about a subject. A question can be a good topic to investigate.

Writing Tests 1

- Choose a topic that you feel strongly about. It may be something you like. It may be something you dislike.
- Use a graphic organizer such as a map, diagram, chart, or web. The details in a graphic organizer may provide a good topic. Here is an example of a graphic organizer you can use as you prewrite.

Four-Column Chart

Main Topic

Subtopic	Subtopic	Subtopic	Subtopic
details about the main topic	details about the main topic	details about the main topic	details about the main topic

You can use a four-column chart to organize your thoughts before you begin writing. It will help you see the relationship among ideas. Write your main topic as the title of the chart. Then write a subtopic at the top of each column. Use the columns beneath each subtopic to record details that you can use to support your main topic.

Once students have chosen a topic, they must develop ideas that support the topic. Using a four-column chart will enable them to list subtopics and details to support that topic. Draw a four-column chart on the board. Ask students to choose a topic that they might like to write about. Then demonstrate how to use the chart to identify subtopics and supporting details for that topic.

Remind students of the variety of reference sources available for research. Display encyclopedia volumes, almanacs, atlases, dictionaries, thesauruses, and other resources that students can use to research information. Have students identify the type of information each resource provides.

Be sure to suggest the Internet as a reference source. Remind students that electronic versions of standard resources such as encyclopedias and almanacs, as well as numerous other sources, are available on the Internet.

Developing a Topic

Once you have chosen your topic, you need to find information about it. There are several kinds of details:

- Facts
- Reasons
- Examples
- Sensory images
- Stories or events

Where do you get these details? First, look back at anything you wrote when you were thinking about topics—notes, charts, webs, maps, and so on. To find more details, you might do the following:

- Research
- Interview
- Observe
- Remember
- Imagine

Before you begin to write your first draft, you need to answer two more questions:

- What is my reason for writing?
- Who is my audience?

Your reason for writing may be to entertain, to inform, to persuade, or a combination of these purposes. Your audience may be your classmates, your friends, or any other group of people. Knowing your reason for writing helps you focus. Knowing your audience helps you choose the information to include.

Drafting

Now it is time to write your first draft. In a first draft, you put down all your ideas on paper. Some writers make an outline or a plan first and follow it as they write. Other writers write their ideas in no particular order and then rearrange them later. Use whatever method works best for you.

Try to write the whole draft at once. Do not stop to rearrange or change anything. You can do that after you have finished the draft. Remember, a first draft will be rough.

How can you arrange your details? Here are some suggestions:

- Main idea and supporting details
- Chronological, or time, order
- Order of importance
- Comparison and contrast

How can you begin and end your writing? A good introduction should tell readers what they will be reading about. It should also catch their attention. You might begin with:

- A story
- A fact
- A question
- A quotation

A good conclusion tells readers that the writing is coming to a close. Generally, it makes a statement about what you have written. You might end with:

- A summary
- A suggestion
- The last event in a sequence

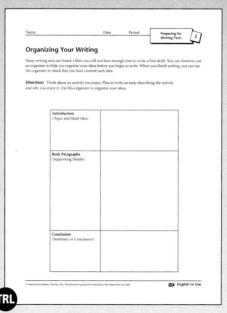

Writing Tests 2

Drafting

Ask students to read the Drafting section on page 283. Explain that the first draft gives students an opportunity to jot down all their ideas. Remind them that when writing a first draft, they need not worry about writing a polished written work. They can rework, reorganize, and edit in later drafts. The goal of the first draft is to record ideas.

Writing for Tests

Many writing tests are timed. Students may not have the opportunity to produce a complete first draft. However, they may have time to use a graphic organizer to help them organize ideas for the introductory paragraph, supporting paragraphs, and summary or concluding paragraph.

Distribute Preparing for Writing Tests 2. Show students how to complete the chart by developing ideas for a topic such as "what we are studying in social studies this week."

Suggest that students use graphic organizers to outline their ideas briefly when they are writing for tests.

Revising

Read with students the Revising section on page 284. Discuss the suggestions for reviewing their writing to identify what needs to be revised.

Have students use samples of their writing from their writing portfolios. Ask them to implement one or more suggestions given in the Revising section to review and revise their written work.

Proofreading

Read with students the Proofreading section on pages 284–285. Explain to students the importance of carefully proofreading their work. Errors in usage, spelling, capitalization, and punctuation can confuse readers or make a written work harder to understand. Remind students that effective written communication conveys the writer's ideas to the readers. Errors in organization and mechanics can interfere with the message, making writing less effective.

Revising

Now it is time to revise your draft. When you revise, you try to improve what you have written. You decide what you like and do not like. You decide what you want to change and how you will change it. You might add or take out words. You might rearrange sentences or paragraphs. Here are some tips for revising:

- Set your draft aside for a while. Then read it. This will help you see your writing in a new way.
- Read your draft aloud. This will help you hear awkward sentences and see places where information is missing.
- Ask someone else to read your draft. Encourage the reader to tell you what you have done well and what needs work.
- Ask yourself (and your reader) questions about your draft. For example:
    —Is my main idea clear?
    —Have I arranged my ideas in a way that makes sense?
    —Is there any information that I should include?
    —Is there any information that I should leave out?

Now, using your comments and your reader's comments, rewrite your draft. Then read your second draft and revise it. You may have to write several drafts before you have one that you like.

Proofreading

Once you have a draft you like, proofread it. When you proofread, you look for and correct mistakes in spelling, grammar, punctuation, and capitalization. These kinds of mistakes distract your reader. Remember, you want your reader to notice your ideas, not your mistakes. Here are some suggestions to help you proofread:

- Make a checklist of things to look for. For example:
    —Did I spell words correctly?
    —Did I write complete sentences?
    —Did I vary my sentences?
    —Did I use vivid verbs and specific details?
    —Do my subjects and verbs agree?
    —Did I use correct capitalization?
    —Did I use correct end punctuation?

- Use a computer spell checker, but remember, it cannot catch some spelling errors.
- Ask someone else to proofread your work.
- Proofread more than once. Look for a different kind of mistake each time.
- Read your work aloud. You may hear mistakes.
- Set your writing aside. Proofread it later. You may see mistakes more clearly.
- Keep a thesaurus nearby. It will help you replace words that you have used too frequently.
- Keep a dictionary and a grammar reference book nearby. You may have questions that they can help answer.

To make your proofreading faster and easier to follow, use proofreaders' marks. Draw the mark at the place where you want to make the correction. Here are some common proofreaders' marks.

Proofreaders' Marks

ℒ	Delete or take out	⩗	Insert an apostrophe
⑤℗	Spell out	⩔	Insert quotation marks
∧	Insert	ℓc	Change to lowercase
#	Insert space	≡	Change to capital letter
⊙	Insert a period	⌒	Close up; take out space
⋏	Insert a comma	¶	Begin a paragraph
⋏	Insert a semicolon	tr	Transpose letter or words

Together with students, review the Proofreaders' Marks. Then have students use these marks to proofread newspaper columns or magazine articles. After proofing the pages, students can share with the class the errors they found.

Writing for Tests

When taking a writing test, students will want to review and proofread their writing carefully and quickly. They may wish to read their paper silently twice.

Suggest that they first read paragraphs for sense, making sure each paragraph contains the information or ideas essential to convey the intended message. Students can then reread each paragraph for mechanical corrections. Ask them to study each sentence separately, checking for correct spelling and usage, sentence structure, punctuation, and capitalization.

To help students practice their proofreading skills, have them complete Preparing for Writing Tests 3. Explain that they should look in each sentence for spelling, punctuation, grammar and usage, and capitalization errors.

Name ___ Date ___ Period ___ Preparing for Writing Tests 3

Proofreading for Errors

When taking a timed writing test, be sure to allow enough time to read and proofread what you have written. When you proofread, you check for errors in mechanics including spelling, grammar and usage, capitalization, and punctuation. Proofreading practice helps reinforce your proofreading skills.

Directions Read each sentence. Circle any error you find in the sentence and rewrite the sentence so that it does not contain the error.

1. Jason and Rico were trying to deside what to due on Saturday afternoon?

2. Earth is the three planet from the son.

3. Do you knew where they have hung there poster?

4. Abraham Lincoln delivered the gettysburg Address at the dedication of the cemetery in Gettysburg, Pennsylvania.

5. Anita and Terry lives in the some apartment building.

© American Guidance Service, Inc. Permission is granted to reproduce for classroom use only. *English to Use*

TRL

Writing Tests 3

English to Use Appendix A **285**

Publishing

Read the Publishing section on page 286. Discuss the publishing ideas identified in the text. Then ask students to brainstorm additional ways they can publish their writing. List their ideas on the board.

Suggest that students select favorite written pieces from their portfolios. Encourage them to publish their work using one of the publishing methods identified.

Writing for Tests

The more students write, the better writers they will become and the better prepared they will be to write effectively on tests.

Distribute Preparing for Writing Tests 4. You can use this resource to simulate a writing test experience. You may wish to make this a timed test. Suggest ways that students can allocate their time. For example, if the test time is 20 minutes, they might spend 5 minutes in the prewriting and drafting phase, 10 minutes writing, and 5 minutes proofing and correcting their written work.

Publishing

Think of publishing as presenting and sharing your writing with others. Many writers get their writing published in a newspaper or magazine or as a book. However, there are other ways to publish your writing:

- Get together with other writers. Take turns reading your work aloud and discussing it.
- Send your writing to a school or community newspaper or magazine.
- Give copies of your work to anyone who is interested in reading it, including family members and friends.
- Post your work on the classroom bulletin board.
- Make a classroom newspaper or magazine several times a year. Use the newspaper or magazine to present things that you and your classmates write.

Each time you write, think about the writing process you used. Ask yourself the following questions: *What would I do the same next time? What would I do differently? What parts of the process do I need to work on?* Use the answers to these questions to help you the next time you write.

Writing Tests 4

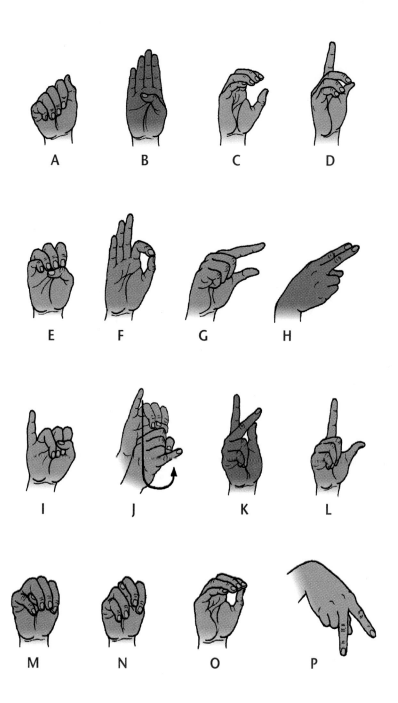

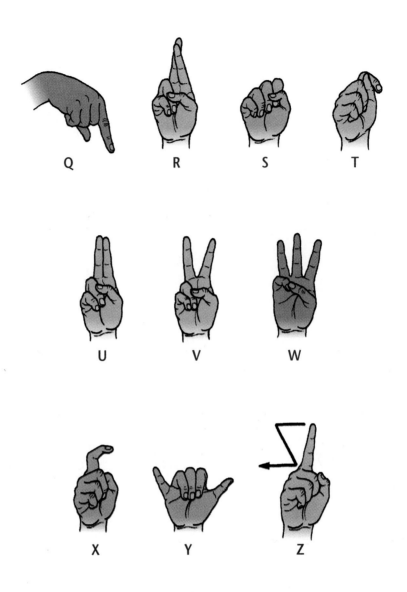

Across   Ask   Bad   Better

Between   Canada   Careful

Careless   Day   Declare

Detroit   Good   Holiday

Hopping

In

Less

Least

Lovely

More

Most

President

Spring

Summer

Telephones

Their

There

Thursday

Towns

Tuesday

Wednesday

What

Where

Who

Why

Winter

With

Worse

Yell

Your

Glossary

A

Abbreviation—(ə brē vē ā´ shən) short form of a word (p. 194)

Abstract noun—(ab´ strakt noun) a word that names something that cannot be seen or touched (p. 77)

Action verb—(ak´ shən vėrb) a word that tells what the subject of a sentence does (p. 10)

Adjective—(aj´ ik tiv) a word that describes a noun (p. 8)

Adjective object complement—(aj´ ik tiv ob´ jikt kom´ plə mənt) an adjective that describes the direct object (p. 118)

Adjective prepositional phrase—(aj´ ik tiv prep ə zish´ ə nəl frāz) a prepositional phrase that describes a noun (p. 30)

Adjective subject complement—(aj´ ik tiv sub´ jikt kom´ plə mənt) one or more adjectives in the predicate that describe the subject (p. 136)

Adverb—(ad´ vėrb) a word that describes a verb, an adjective, or another adverb (p. 12)

Adverb prepositional phrase—(ad´ vėrb prep ə zish´ ə nəl frāz) a prepositional phrase that describes a verb (p. 34)

Agreement—(ə grē´ mənt) the rule that a singular subject has a singular verb and a plural subject has a plural verb (p. 262)

Apostrophe—(ə pos´ trə fē) a punctuation mark in an owner's name (p. 94)

Appositive—(ə poz´ ə tiv) a word or group of words that follows a noun and explains the noun or gives another name to the noun (p. 122)

Article—(är´ tə kəl) a word that points out a noun (p. 9)

B

Body—(bod´ ē) the message part of a letter (p. 234)

C

Capital letter—(kap´ ə təl let´ ər) a letter that is uppercase. *A* is a capital or uppercase letter; *a* is a lowercase letter (p. 4)

Capitalize—(kap´ ə tə līz) to use capital letters (p. 86)

Closing—(klō´ zing) word or phrase used before the signature in a letter (p. 234)

Colon—(kō´ lən) a punctuation mark used in time (p. 194)

Comma—(kom´ ə) a punctuation mark used to set apart one or more words (p. 22)

Common noun—(kom´ ən noun) the name of a general type of person, place, or thing (p. 44)

Comparative—(kəm par´ ə tiv) an adjective that compares two nouns (p. 152)

Complete predicate—(kəm plēt´ pred´ ə kit) the whole part of a sentence that tells what the subject is doing (p. 18)

Complete subject—(kəm plēt´ sub´ jikt) the whole part of a sentence that tells who or what the sentence is about (p. 18)

Complex sentence—(kom´ pleks sen´ təns) a sentence that includes both an independent clause and a dependent clause (p. 206)

Compound—(kom´ pound) two or more words, phrases, or ideas joined by a conjunction (p. 60)

Compound-complex sentence—(kom´ pound kom´ pleks sen´ təns) a sentence with two or more independent clauses and one or more dependent clauses (p. 207)

Compound direct object—(kom´ pound də rekt´ ob´ jikt) two or more direct objects joined by a conjunction (p. 70)

Compound object of preposition—(kom´ pound ob´ jikt ov prep ə zish´ ən) two or more objects of one preposition joined by a conjunction (p. 56)

Compound predicate—(kom´ pound pred´ ə kit) two or more verbs joined by a conjunction (p. 54)

Compound sentence—(kom´ pound sen´ təns) a sentence made up of two or more complete sentences joined by a conjunction (p. 58)

Compound subject—(kom´ pound sub´ jikt) two or more subjects joined by a conjunction (p. 52)

Compound subject complement—(kom´ pound sub´ jikt kom´ plə mənt) two or more subject complements joined by a conjunction (p. 142)

Concrete noun—(kon´ krēt noun) a word that names something that can be seen or touched (p. 77)

Conjunction—(kən jungk´ shən) a word that joins two or more words, phrases, or ideas in a sentence (p. 50)

Contraction—(kən trak´ shən) a word formed when two words are put together and letters are left out (p. 174)

D

Dependent clause—(di pen´ dənt klȯz) a group of words that does not form a complete thought and cannot stand alone (p. 206)

Descriptive paragraph—(di skrip´ tiv par´ ə graf) a paragraph that describes a person, place, or thing (p. 224)

Dialogue—(dī´ ə lȯg) conversation between two or more characters in a story (p. 231)

Direct object—(də rekt´ ob´ jikt) a noun or pronoun that receives action directly from the verb (p. 68)

Direct quotation—(də rekt´ kwō tā´ shən) the exact words that someone says (p. 210)

Double negative—(dub´ əl neg´ ə tiv) the mistake of using two words that mean "no" in one sentence (p. 190)

E

Edit—(ed´ it) checking written work for mistakes (p. 106)

Exclamation point—(ek´ sklə mā´ shən point) a punctuation mark showing strong feeling (p. 4)

F

Fragment—(frag´ mənt) a group of words that is not a complete sentence (p. 20)

Future tense—(fyü´ chər tens) the verb tense that tells about action in the future (p. 166)

G

Greeting—(grē´ ting) word or phrase used before the name or title of the person to whom a letter is sent (p. 234)

H

Heading—(hed´ ing) the address of the person writing the letter (p. 234)

Helping verb—(hel´ ping vėrb) a verb that comes before the main verb. Together, the two verbs form a verb phrase (p. 160)

Homonym—(hom´ ə nim) a word that sounds like another word but has a different meaning and spelling (p. 244)

I

Independent clause—(in di pen´ dənt klȯz) a complete sentence (p. 206)

Indirect object—(in də rekt´ ob´ jikt) a noun or pronoun that takes action from the verb indirectly (p. 114)

Indirect quotation—(in də rekt´ kwō tā´ shən) what someone says but not his or her exact words (p. 210)

Interjection—(in tər jek´ shən) a word that shows feelings (p. 104)

Invitation—(in və tā´ shən) a written request (p. 221)

Pronunciation Key						
a hat	e let	ī ice	ȯ order	u̇ put	sh she	a in about
ā age	ē equal	o hot	oi oil	ü rule	th thin	ə { e in taken
ä far	ėr term	ō open	ou out	ch child	ŦH then	i in pencil
â care	i it	ȯ saw	u cup	ng long	zh measure	o in lemon
						u in circus

Irregular verb—(i reg´ yə lər vėrb) a verb that changes its form to form past tenses (p. 170)

L

Lead paragraph—(lēd par´ ə graf) a paragraph that introduces a news article; it tells who, what, when, where, why, and sometimes, how (p. 222)

Linking verb—(lingk´ ing vėrb) a verb that connects the subject to a word in the predicate (p. 132)

M

Memo—(mem´ ō) a clear, organized record of important facts and details (p. 220)

N

Narrative—(nar´ ə tiv) a series of paragraphs that go together to tell a story (p. 230)

Negative—(neg´ ə tiv) a word that means "no" or "not" and that stops the action of the verb (p. 168)

Nominative pronoun—(nom´ ə nə tiv prō´ noun) a pronoun used as the subject of a sentence (p. 78)

Noun—(noun) a word that names a person, place, or thing (p. 6)

Noun object complement—(noun ob´ jikt kom´ plə mənt) a noun that renames the direct object (p. 118)

Noun subject complement—(noun sub´ jikt kom´ plə mənt) a noun or pronoun in the predicate that renames the subject, as well as any words that describe the noun or pronoun (p. 132)

O

Object complement—(ob´ jikt kom´ plə mənt) a word or words that follow the direct object and describe or rename it (p. 118)

Object of the preposition—(ob´ jikt ov тнə prep ə zish´ ən) the noun or pronoun that follows the preposition in a prepositional phrase (p. 28)

Objective pronoun—(əb jek´ tiv prō´ noun) a pronoun that is the direct object or object of the preposition (p. 78)

Owner noun—(ō´ nər noun) a noun that owns something in a sentence (p. 94)

Owner object—(ō´ nər ob´ jekt) a noun following an owner pronoun or owner noun (p. 96)

Owner pronoun—(ō´ nər prō´ noun) a pronoun that owns something in a sentence (p. 96)

P

Paragraph—(par´ ə graf) a group of sentences about one topic (p. 224)

Past tense—(past tens) the verb tense that tells about action in the past (p. 164)

Period—(pir´ ē əd) the punctuation mark ending a sentence that makes a statement or gives a command (p. 4)

Persuasive paragraph—(pər swā´ siv par´ ə graf) a paragraph that tries to make readers believe something or do something (p. 228)

Plural—(plùr´ əl) more than one (p. 248)

Predicate—(pred´ ə kit) the part of a sentence that tells what the subject is doing (p. 4)

Preposition—(prep ə zish´ ən) a word that ties or relates a noun or pronoun to another part of the sentence (p. 28)

Prepositional phrase—(prep ə zish´ ə nəl frāz) a group of words that begins with a preposition and ends with a noun or pronoun (p. 28)

Present tense—(prez´ nt tens) the verb tense that tells about action in the present (p. 162)

Prewrite—(prē´ rīt) talking, thinking, or reading about a topic before writing (p. 106)

Process paragraph—(pros´ es par´ ə graf) a paragraph that tells how to do something (p. 226)

Pronoun—(prō´ noun) a word that takes the place of a noun (p. 78)

Proper noun—(prop´ ər noun) the name of a specific person, place, or thing (p. 44)

Punctuation—(pungk chü ā´ shən) marks in a sentence that tell readers when to pause or stop (p. 22)

Q

Question mark—(kwes´ chən märk) a punctuation mark that ends a sentence asking a question (p. 4)

Question pronoun—(kwes´ chən prō´ noun) a pronoun that asks a question (p. 204)

Quotation marks—(kwō tā´ shən märks) punctuation used around the title of a part of a large work; punctuation used to begin and end a direct quotation (pp. 63, 210)

R

Regular verb—(reg´ yə lər vėrb) a verb that adds -*d* or -*ed* to form the past tense (p. 158)

Review—(ri vyü´) a writer's opinion about a movie, TV show, book, or play (p. 232)

Rewrite—(rē´ rīt) writing again until the meaning is clear (p. 106)

S

Semicolon—(sem´ i kō lən) a punctuation mark that separates two related ideas not connected by a conjunction (p. 62)

Sentence—(sen´ təns) a group of words that forms a complete thought; a sentence begins with a capital letter and ends with a period, question mark, or exclamation point (p. 4)

Sentence pattern—(sen´ təns pat´ ərn) the basic form of a sentence (p. 5)

Signature—(sig´ nə chər) the name signed by the writer of the letter (p. 234)

Simple predicate—(sim´ pəl pred´ ə kit) one or more verbs in a sentence (p. 18)

Simple subject—(sim´ pəl sub´ jikt) one or more subject nouns or pronouns in a sentence (p. 18)

Singular—(sing´ gyə lər) one (p. 248)

State-of-being verb—(stāt ov bē´ ing vėrb) a verb that tells that the subject exists, but does not show action (p. 40)

Subject—(sub´ jikt) the part of a sentence that tells who or what the sentence is about (p. 4)

Subject complement—(sub´ jikt kom´ plə mənt) one or more words in the predicate that describe the subject (p. 132)

Superlative—(sə pėr´ lə tiv) an adjective that compares three or more nouns (p. 152)

T

Tense—(tens) present, past, or future time expressed by a verb (p. 158)

Tone of voice—(tōn ov vois) the sound of speech (p. 200)

Topic—(top´ ik) the main idea of an essay or paragraph (p. 224)

Topic sentence—(top´ ik sen´ təns) a sentence that states the main idea of a paragraph (p. 224)

U

Understood subject—(un´ dər stŏŏd´ sub´ jikt) a subject that cannot be seen in a sentence (p. 100)

Understood *you*—(un´ dər stŏŏd´ yōō) *you* as a subject that cannot be seen in a sentence (p. 100)

V

Verb—(vėrb) a word that shows action (p. 10)

Verb phrase—(vėrb frāz) a verb and its helpers (p. 160)

W

Write—(rīt) putting ideas on paper (p. 106)

Writing process—(rī´ ting pros´ es) the use of four steps: prewrite, write, rewrite, and edit (p. 106)

Pronunciation Key

a hat	e let	ī ice	ȯ order	u̇ put	sh she
ā age	ē equal	o hot	oi oil	ü rule	th thin
ä far	ėr term	ō open	ou out	ch child	ᵀH then
â care	i it	ȯ saw	u cup	ng long	zh measure

ə { a in about / e in taken / i in pencil / o in lemon / u in circus }

Index

A

A/an, 9
  as noun indicators, 77
Abbreviations
  punctuation of, 86
  of time, 194
Abstract nouns, 77, 86, 94
Accept/except, 182
Action verbs
  definition of, 10
  direct object and, 68
  function of, 158
  pronouns and, 146
  state-of-being verb vs., 41
  who as subject of, 204
Addresses, 236
Adjective object complement,
  118, 138
Adjective prepositional phrases,
  30–31
  definition of, 30
  direct object and, 74
  placement of, 42
  use in sentences, 38
Adjectives, 8–9
  adverbs and, 12–13, 140
  articles as, 9
  comma separating, 22
  comparative, 152
  definition of, 8
  direct objects and, 69
  good as, 13, 141, 256
  nouns and, 138–39
  as object complement, 118
  placement of, 138–39
  in predicate, 136–37
  in prepositional phrases,
    31–33
  prepositional phrases as,
    31–33, 38, 42
  pronoun vs., 82
  superlative, 152

this/that/these/those as, 84–85
  use in sentences, 92
  verb forms used as, 93
Adjective subject complement,
  136–37, 138
Adverb prepositional phrase,
  34–37
  confusion with adverb, 37
  definition of, 34
  placement of, 42
  questions answered by, 34
  state-of-being verb and, 40
  use in sentences, 38
Adverbs, 102–03
  adjectives and, 102–03, 140
  comma following, 22
  comparison with, 256–57
  confusion with preposition,
    36
  definition of, 12
  forming questions, 204
  interjections vs., 105
  with *-ly* ending, 13
  not ending in *-ly,* 13
  placement of, 12–13, 15
  prepositional phrases as,
    30, 34–37, 38, 42
  questions answered by,
    12–17, 14–17
  use in sentences, 92
  verbs and, 102
  well as, 30, 140, 141
After, 206, 208
Agreement
  pronoun-noun, 268–69
  subject-verb, 162, 164,
    262–67, 269, 270–71
All ready/already, 254
Although, 206
Am, 162
And
  compound sentences and, 58
  function of, 50

series and, 126
  subject-verb agreement and,
    52, 264, 269
Apostrophe
  in contractions, 174, 184
  more than one owner and, 98
  owner nouns and, 94, 108
  owner pronouns and, 96
Appositive, 122–23
  commas around, 126
  definition of, 122
  with noun subject
    complement, 134–35
  plural nouns as, 262
  punctuation of, 122
Are, 162
Articles, 9, 77
Article titles, 63
As, 206
As of, 208
As well as, 50
At, 277

B

Be
  forms used in past tenses, 164
  forms used in present tenses,
    162, 163
  future tense and, 166
  as helping verb, 160
  pronouns used with, 80
  as state of being verb, 40
  subject complements and,
    132–33, 136
Because, 206
Because of, 208
Been
  future tense and, 166
  as helping verb for present
    tense, 162
  use of *has/have* with, 163

Been/bin, 244

Before, 206, 208

Besides, 87

Blew/blue, 244

Blindness, 97, 160

Body language, 233, 273

Body of letter, 234

Book title, 63, 262

Both-and, 51

Braille system, 97, 160

Brake/break, 244

Breath/breathe, 254

But, 50, 126

Buy/by, 244

C

Can, 202, 204

Capitalization
  on envelopes, 236
  of first word of sentence,
    4, 22, 45
  of person's name, 86
  of proper names, 63
  of proper nouns, 44–45, 86
  in quotations, 210
  of time words, 194
  of titles, 63, 86

Capitalize, definition of, 86

Capital letters, 4

Cases of pronouns, 78–79

CD title, 63

Chapter titles, 63

Characteristics, names of, 77

Characters, 231

Clauses, 206–07, 262

Close/clothes/cloths, 254

Closing of letter, 234

Colon, 194

Comma
  appositives and, 122, 126
  after beginning adverb, 22
  after beginning prepositional
    phrase, 44–45

compound parts and, 62
in compound sentences,
  58, 87
definition of, 22
dependent clauses and, 208
interjections and, 108, 201
in quotations, 210, 214
semicolon and, 87
separating adjectives, 22
in series, 126
before *too,* 189

Commands, 202

Common noun, 44–45, 94

Comparative, definition
  of, 152

Comparative adjectives, 152

Comparison, 256–57

Complete predicate
  adverb prepositional phrase
    and, 34
  definition of, 18
  direct object as part of, 71
  prepositional phrases and, 34

Complete subject, 18, 30

Complex sentences, 206–09

Compound, 60–61
  definition of, 60
  object complements and, 120
  punctuation of, 62
  subject complements and, 142

Compound-complex sentences,
  207

Compound direct object, 70–71,
  72, 73

Compound object complement,
  118

Compound object of
  preposition, 56–57, 62

Compound predicate
  confusion with compound
    sentence, 72
  direct object and, 73
  with other compound parts,
    54–55
  punctuation of, 62

Compound sentences, 206–07
  confusion with compound
    parts, 72
  with direct objects, 70
  punctuation of, 87
  sentence parts of, 58–59

Compound subject, 52–53
  compound sentences and, 72
  definition of, 52
  in long sentences, 116
  punctuation of, 62
  subject-verb agreement and,
    264, 269

Compound subject
  complements, 142–43

Computers
  e-cards, 126
  emoticons, 140
  instant messaging with, 37
  newsgroups on, 17
  using e-mail, 62

Concrete noun, 77

Conjunctions, 50–51
  comma and, 62
  compound direct object
    and, 70
  compound predicates and,
    54–55
  compounds and, 60
  in compound sentences,
    58–59, 62, 72, 206
  compound subjects and, 52
  definition of, 50
  dependent clauses and,
    206, 208
  semicolon and, 62
  semicolon and comma
    with, 87
  in series, 126
  in sets, 51

Contractions, 174–75
  confusion with owner
    pronouns, 184
  definition of, 174
  doesn't/don't as, 270–71
  with *not,* 190

Correlative conjunctions, 51
Could, 204

D

Dairy/diary, 254
Days of week, 194
Deafness, 80, 209
Dear/deer, 244
Dependent clause, 206–07, 208, 208–09
Dependent clause conjunctions, 206, 208–09
Descriptive paragraph, 224–25
Desert/dessert, 254
Dialogue, 231
Dictionary, 250
Direct object, 67–75
    adjectives and, 69
    appositive of, 122
    compound, 70–71, 72, 73
    compound verb and, 73
    definition of, 68
    indirect object and, 114
    lay/set/raise and, 186–87
    object complement and, 118
    objective pronoun as, 78
    as part of complete predicate, 71
    placement of, 71
    prepositional phrase and, 74–75
    pronouns as, 146
Direct quotation, 210–11, 214–15
Do, 160, 204
Done, 165
Done been, 165
Don't/doesn't, 270–71
Double negatives, 190–91

E

Each other/one another, 82–83
Editing, 106, 212–13, 276–77
    of descriptive paragraph, 224

    of news stories, 223
    of persuasive paragraph, 228
    of process paragraph, 226
    of review, 232
Either-or, 51, 269
E-mail
    e-cards, 126
    instant messaging, 37
    use of, 62
Emoticons, 140
Envelopes, 236
-er/-est, 256
Everybody/everyone/everything, 266
Except/accept, 182
Exclamation point
    at end of sentences, 4, 22
    interjections and, 108
    in quotations, 214
    tone of voice and, 200–201

F

Fair/fare, 244
Fast, 13
Feelings
    names of, 77
    written expression of, 108, 200–201
First person pronoun, 78
For/four/four, 244
Form
    for envelope addressing, 236
    for letters, 234
Forms of pronouns, 78–79
Forms of verbs, 93
Fragment, 20–21
Friendly letters, 219, 234–35
Future perfect tense, 158, 161
Future tenses, 158, 166–67
    helping verbs of, 160–61
    negatives and, 168

G

Gender, 268–69
Good/well, 13, 141, 256
Greeting in letters, 234
Group nouns, 99

H

Had, 162, 164
Had been, 162, 164–65
Hard, 13
Hardly, 190
Has, 162, 163
Have, 160, 162, 163, 204
Have been, 162
Heading of letters, 234
Hear/here, 246
Helping verbs, 160–61
    agreement with subject, 162
    be/been not used as, 163
    contractions with pronouns, 174
    for future tense, 160, 166
    negatives and, 168
    for past tense, 164, 165
    for perfect tenses, 161
    for present tense, 162, 162–63
Her, 96, 268
Here
    hear and, 246
    with linking verbs, 145
    sentences beginning with, 100, 101
    subject-verb agreement and, 264
His, 96, 268
Hoarse/horse, 246
Homonyms, 244–47
Homophones, 188–89
Hour/our, 246
How, 204, 222
However, 87

I

ie/ei, 252–53

If, 206

Indefinite pronoun, 81

Independent clause, 206–07

Indirect object, 114–17
  appositive of, 122
  definition of, 114
  identification of, 114, 116–17
  in long sentences, 116
  pronouns as, 146
  questions answered by, 114

Indirect quotation, 210, 214

Instead, 87

Interjections, 104–05, 108, 201

Internet newsgroups, 17

Invitations, 221

Irregular nouns, 249

Irregular verbs, 170–71

Is, 162

Italic type, 63

It/its, 96, 99, 144

Its/it's, 184

J

Journals, 180

K

Knew/new, 246

Know/no, 246

L

Lead paragraph, 222

Learn/teach, 182

Less/least, 257

Let/leave, 188–89

Letters, friendly, 219, 234–35

Lie/lay, 186–87

Like, 274

Linking verbs, 131–55
  adjective subject complement
    and, 136–37

definition of, 132
function of, 158
with *here/there*, 145
list of, 136
noun subject complements
  and, 132–33
pronouns and, 144, 146

Loose/lose, 254

-ly, 256

M

Magazine title, 63, 262

Main verb
  been not used as, 163
  helping verb and, 160
  negatives and, 168
  as simple predicate, 18, 34

May/can, 202

Memos (memorandums), 220

Messages, 220

Misplaced words/phrases, 272–73

Months, 194

More/most, 257

Movie title, 262

My, 96

N

Names, 6, 44–45. *See also* Nouns

Narrative, 230–31

Negatives, 168–69, 190 91

Neither-nor, 51, 269

Never, 168, 190

New/knew, 246

Newsgroups, 17

Newspaper title, 63

News stories, 222–23

Nobody, 190

No/know, 246

Nominative pronouns, 78, 146

None, 190

No/not, 190

Nonstandard English, 274–75

No one, 190

Nor, 52

Not, 168, 174

Note-taking, 180

Nothing, 190

Not only-but also, 51

Noun object, 38

Noun object complement,
  118, 134

Noun-pronoun agreement,
  268–69

Nouns
  abstract, 77, 86, 94
  adjective prepositional
    phrases and, 30, 42
  adjectives and, 8, 138, 140
  appositives and, 122–23
  common, 44–45, 94
  concrete, 77
  definition of, 6
  as direct object, 68, 76
  ending in
    -f or *-fe*, 249
    -y, 248
  following owner pronoun, 96
  group, 99
  identification of, 77
  as indirect object, 114
  irregular, 249
  naming groups, 33, 99
  as object complement, 118
  as object of preposition, 28, 76
  owner, 94–95, 98, 108
  plural, 248–49
  prepositional phrase as, 32
  pronouns and, 78, 80, 99,
    266–69
  proper, 44–45, 63, 86, 94
  singular, 248
  as subject complement, 132
  as subject of sentence, 6, 18,
    30, 76
  that give new names, 134–35
  use in sentences, 92

Noun subject complements,
  132–35

Nowhere, 190

O

Object complement, 118–21
Objective pronouns, 78, 146, 204
Object of preposition
    adjective prepositional
        phrases and, 38
    appositive of, 122
    compound, 56–57
    confusion with subject,
        32–33, 100
    definition of, 28
    pronouns as, 78, 146
Once, 206
One another/each other, 82–83
Open captioning, 209
Or
    compound sentences and, 50
    series and, 126
    subject-verb agreement and,
        52, 269
Our, 96, 246
Owner nouns, 94–95, 108
Owner object, 96
Owner pronouns, 96–97
    agreement with noun, 268–69
    confusion with contractions,
        184
    definition of, 96
    group nouns and, 99
    owner objects and, 96–97
    as subject complement, 146

P

Paragraphs
    descriptive, 224–25
    dialogue and, 231
    lead of news story, 222
    persuasive, 228–29
    process, 226–27
Parts of speech, 91–105
    examples of, 6, 8, 10, 12, 14,
        28, 30, 31, 34, 62, 69, 70,
        92, 102, 114, 145, 146
    use in sentence and, 92–93
    See also Adjectives;
        Adverbs; Conjunctions;
        Interjections; Nouns;
        Prepositions; Pronouns;
        Verbs
Past form of verb, 161
Past perfect tense, 158, 161
Past tense, 164–65
    helping verbs used in, 164, 165
    of irregular verbs, 170
    negatives and, 168
    of regular verbs, 158, 170
Pattern 1 sentences, 5–16, 148
    examples of, 6, 10, 12, 14, 16,
        40, 100, 145
Pattern 2 sentences, 68, 68–77,
    100, 148
    examples of, 100
Pattern 3 sentences, 114, 116, 148
Pattern 4 sentences, 118–21, 148
Pattern 5 sentences, 132–33,
    142, 144, 146, 148
Pattern 6 sentences, 136, 142,
    144, 146, 148
Perfect tenses, 158, 161
Period
    at end of sentence, 4, 22, 45
    interjections and, 108
    in quotations, 210
    after shortened form of
        title, 86
    tone of voice and, 200
Person
    name of, 6, 44–45, 86
    title of, 86
Persuasive paragraph, 228–29
Phrases
    conjunctions and, 50, 60
    misplaced, 272–73
    plural nouns in, 262
    See also Prepositional phrase;
        Verb phrase
Place, name of, 6, 44–45
Plain/plane, 246
Play title, 262
Plural nouns, 248–49, 262
Plural owner nouns, 98
Plural owner pronouns, 96, 98
Plural pronouns, 78, 146,
    268–69
Plural subject
    agreement with verb, 162,
        164, 262–71
    you as, 164
Plural verb
    agreement with subject, 162,
        164, 262–71
    compound verb as, 264
Poem title, 262
Predicate
    adverbs as part of, 12
    complete and simple, 18, 34
    compound, 54–55
    definition of, 4
    direct object as part of, 71
    in fragments, 20–21
    linking verbs and, 136, 158
    verb as part of, 10
Predicate nominative, 132
Prepositional phrase, 27–47
    as adjective, 31–33
    adjective within, 31
    as adverb, 34–37
    in appositive, 122
    confusion with verb, 40
    definition of, 28
    dependent clause vs., 209
    direct object and, 74–75
    in long sentences, 116
    object of, 76
    as part of complete subject,
        30, 56
    placement of, 32, 42
    use in sentences, 38
    verb and, 74
Prepositions, 27–47
    confusion with adverb, 36
    confusion with dependent
        clause conjunctions, 208
    definition of, 28
    list of, 28
    sentence meaning and, 28–29
    use in sentences, 92
Present perfect tense, 158, 161
Present tenses, 158, 162–63, 168

Prewriting, 106
    of descriptive paragraph, 224
    of news stories, 223
    of persuasive paragraph, 228
    of process paragraph, 226
    of review, 232

Process paragraph, 226–27

Pronouns, 78–85
    adjective vs., 82
    case of, 146
    contractions of, 174, 184
    definition of, 78
    as direct object, 68
    forming questions, 204–05, 222
    forms (cases) of, 78
    group nouns and, 99
    indefinite, 81
    as indirect object, 114
    noun replaced by, 80, 146, 266–69
    as object complement, 118
    as object of preposition, 28
    owner, 96–97, 98, 184
    with -self ending, 81
    singular/plural, 78, 146, 266, 268–69
    as subject, 18, 30, 144
    subject complements and, 132, 144–45
    subject-verb agreement and, 266–67
    that begin dependent clauses, 208
    this/that/these/those as, 84–85
    of two words, 82
    ways to use, 79, 80

Proofreading, 106, 212–13
    of descriptive paragraph, 224
    of news stories, 223
    of persuasive paragraph, 228
    of process paragraph, 226
    of review, 232

Proper noun, 86, 94
    capitalization of, 44–45
    titles as, 63

Public speaking, 256

Punctuation
    of abbreviations, 86
    apostrophe, 94, 96, 98, 108, 174
    of appositives, 122, 126
    capitalization, 44–45, 63, 86, 194, 210
    colon, 194
    comma, 22, 44–45, 62, 86, 108, 122, 126, 189, 208, 210
    of compounds, 62
    after conjunctions, 87
    of contractions, 174
    definition of, 22
    of dependent clauses, 208
    at end of sentences, 4, 45, 204, 210–11, 214
    on envelopes, 236
    exclamation point, 4, 108, 200–201, 214
    interjections and, 108
    italic type, 63
    of owner nouns, 94, 98, 108
    period, 4, 45, 86, 108, 200–201, 210
    question mark, 4, 200, 204–05, 214
    quotation marks, 63, 210–11, 214
    of quotations, 210–11, 214
    semicolon, 62, 87, 206
    of series, 126
    of time words, 194
    of titles, 63
    tone of voice and, 200–201
    before too, 189
    underlining, 63

Q

Qualities, names of, 77

Question mark
    at end of sentence, 4, 22, 204
    in quotations, 214
    tone of voice and, 200

Question pronouns, 204–05

Questions, 202–05

Quiet/quite/quit, 254

Quotation marks, 63, 210–11, 214–15

Quotations, 210–11, 214–15

R

Regular verb, 158

Relationship
    complex sentences and, 209
    owner nouns showing, 94
    prepositions showing, 28
    pronouns showing, 208

Requests, 202

Return address, 236

Reviews, 232–33

Revising, 106, 276–77
    descriptive paragraphs, 224
    news stories, 223
    persuasive paragraphs, 228
    process paragraphs, 226
    reviews, 232

Rewriting, 106, 276–77
    of descriptive paragraph, 224
    of persuasive paragraph, 228
    of process paragraph, 226
    of review, 232

Rise/raise, 186–87

RSVP, 221

S

Said, 215

Scarcely, 190

Second person pronoun, 78

-self pronouns, 81

Semicolon, 62, 87, 206

Sentence fragments, 20–21

Sentence patterns, 113–29
    definition of, 5
    review of, 148
    subject + linking
        verb + adjective subject
        complement, 136, 142, 144–45, 146
    subject + linking verb + noun
        subject complement, 132, 142, 144–45, 146

subject + verb, 5–16, 40, 78, 100, 145
subject + verb + direct object, 68–77, 100, 114
subject + verb + direct object + object complement, 118–21
subject + verb + indirect object + direct object, 114, 116
Sentences, 3–25, 199–217
combining, 53, 55
complex, 206–07, 208–09
compound, 58–59, 70, 206–07
compound-complex, 207
compound parts of, 60–61
definition of, 4
fragments of, 20–21
function of, 202–05
with linking verbs, 131–55
with here/there, 145
with pronoun subjects, 144
subject complements and, 132–33, 136–37
prepositional phrases in, 28–29, 38
punctuation of, 4, 45, 87
as questions, 204–05
with quotations, 210–11
starting with here/there, 145
tone of voice revealed in, 200–201
Series, punctuation of, 126
Setting, 231
Sew/so, 246
Should, 204
Signal words/phrases, 165
Signature on letter, 234
Simple predicate, 18, 34
Simple subject, 18, 30, 56
Since, 206, 208
Singular nouns, 94, 98, 248
Singular owner nouns, 94, 98
Singular owner pronouns, 96

Singular pronouns, 78, 96, 146, 266, 268–69
Singular subject, 162, 164, 262–71
Singular verb, 162, 164, 262–71
Sit/set, 186–87
Slang, 274–75
Song titles, 63, 262
Son/sun, 246
So that, 206
Speaker
of quotations, 214
tone of voice of, 200–201
Spelling, 241–59
adding endings, 250–51
commonly misspelled words, 242
homonyms, 244–47
plural nouns, 248–49
similar-looking words, 254–55
steps to practicing, 242–43
words with ie or ei, 252–53
Standard English, 274–75
Statements, 202
State-of-being verb, 40–41, 158
Story writing, 230–31
Subject
adjective prepositional phrase and, 38
agreement with verb, 162, 164, 262–71, 270–71
appositive of, 122
complete and simple, 18, 30
compound, 52–53, 72, 264, 269
in compound sentences, 58
confusion with object of preposition, 32–33
definition of, 4
in dependent clause, 209
in fragments, 20–21
identification of, 32, 56, 100, 145
linking verbs and, 136, 158
nominative pronoun as, 78

noun as, 6
nouns naming groups as, 33
object of preposition and, 56, 100
plural, 162, 164, 262–71
prepositional phrase as part of, 30
pronouns as, 144, 144–45, 146
in questions, 264
singular, 162, 164, 262–71
subject complements and, 132
understood you as, 100
who as, 204
Subject + linking verb + adjective subject complement pattern (6), 136, 146, 148
Subject + linking verb + noun subject complement pattern (5), 132, 144, 146, 148
Subject + verb + direct object + object complement pattern (4), 118–21, 148
Subject + verb + direct object pattern (2), 68–77, 99, 148
Subject + verb + indirect object + direct object pattern (3), 114, 116, 148
Subject + verb pattern (1), 5, 145, 148
examples of, 6, 10, 12, 14, 16, 18, 40, 78, 100
Subject complement, 132–33
compound, 142
in long sentences, 142–43
pronouns and, 144–45
pronouns as, 146–47
Subject-verb agreement, 262–71
compound subjects and, 264, 269
doesn't/don't and, 270–71
here/there and, 264
in past tense, 164
plural nouns and, 262–63
in present tense, 162
pronoun subjects and, 266–67

in questions, 264
  titles and, 262–63
Superlative, definition of, 152
Superlative adjectives, 152
Synonyms
  for *said,* 215
  for *too/very,* 102

T

Teach/learn, 182
Tenses
  definition of, 158
  future, 166
  negatives and, 168
  past, 164–65
  perfect, 158, 161
  present, 162–63
That, 222
The, 9, 77
Their, 96
Their/there/they're, 184
There
  with linking verbs, 145
  sentences beginning with,
    100, 101
  subject-verb agreement
    and, 264
Therefore, 87
Thing, name of, 6, 44–45
Third person pronoun, 78
This/that/these/those
  doesn't/don't and, 271
  as subjects with linking
    verbs, 144
  use of, 84–85
Time
  abbreviations of, 194
  signal words and, 165
  verbs telling, 157–77
  ways to write, 194
Titles
  of people, 86
  punctuation of, 63
  as singular, 262

Tone of voice, 200–201
Too, 102
Topic, 224
Topic sentence, 224
To/too/two, 188–89

U

Underlining, 63
Understood subject, 100–101
Unless, 206
Until, 206, 208
Upper case letters, 4. *See also*
  Capitalization

V

Verb forms, 93
Verb phrase
  agreement with subject, 162
  definition of, 160
  negatives and, 168
Verbs, 10–11, 157–77
  action, 10, 158, 204
  adverb prepositional phrase
    and, 34, 42
  adverbs and, 12, 13,
    15–17, 140
  agreement with subject,
    162, 164, 262–71
  compound, 72, 73
  in compound predicates,
    54–55
  in compound sentences, 58
  compound subjects and, 52
  confusion with prepositional
    phrases, 40
  contractions with *not,* 174
  in dependent clauses, 209
  direct object and, 68, 71
  forming questions, 204
  forms of, 186–87
  helping, 160–61
    for past tenses, 164
    for present tenses, 162–63
  irregular, 170–71

linking, 131–55, 158
  adjective subject
    complement and,
    136–37
  definition of, 132
  list of, 136
  noun subject complements
    and, 132
main, 160
negatives and, 168
as part of predicate, 10
past tense, 164–65
perfect tenses, 158, 161
plural, 262–63, 264
prepositional phrases and, 74
present tense, 162–63
pronoun case and, 146
in questions, 264
regular, 158, 170
as simple predicate, 18, 34
singular, 262–63
state-of-being, 40–41, 158
tenses, 158
use in sentences, 92
with *who* as subject, 204
Very, 102
Voice, 200–201

W

Was, 162, 164
Weather/whether, 246
Well, 274
Well/good, 13, 141, 256
Were, 162, 164
What, 208, 222
Whatever, 208
When, 206
Whenever, 206
When/why/where/how, 204
Where, 206, 277
Wherever, 206
Which, 208
While, 206
Who, 204, 208, 222

Index

Who/what/why/when/where/how, 222

Who/whom/whose/what/which, 204

Will, 166, 204

Will be, 166

Will have, 166

Will have been, 166

Won't, 175

Word endings, 250–51

Word order, 5
   of adverbs, 12, 13, 15
   in questions, 264
   reversing to find subject, 145
   sentence meaning and, 272–73
   See also Sentence patterns

Words, 50, 60

Would, 204

Write, 106

Y

Yet, 50

You, 100, 164

You know, 274

Your, 96, 184

You're/your, 184

Z

ZIP code, 236

Photo Credits

Midterm Mastery Test

Midterm Mastery Test Page 1

Midterm Mastery Test, Chapters 1–6

Part A Read each sentence. Draw a vertical line between the complete subject and the complete predicate. Underline the noun and the verb.

1. The baseball player hit the ball.
2. The new car engine runs smoothly and quietly.
3. The young clerk sold us three tickets.
4. The tired truck driver found the heavy fog a problem.
5. Carol, a proud owner, washed and waxed her bike carefully.

Part B Label each word in these sentences. Above each word, write one of these abbreviations:

N for noun	*Adj* for adjective	*P* for pronoun	*C* for conjunction
V for verb	*Adv* for adverb	*Prep* for preposition	*I* for interjection

6. Wow! A basketball dropped through the hoop and the noisy crowd cheered.
7. Ann and Tom gladly sold us three more tickets to the new play.
8. Oh, that huge truck carries a really heavy load, but it moves quickly.
9. Hours of very hard work made his engine a smooth one.
10. Quickly, he landed the airplane on a runway and hopped out.

Part C Circle every prepositional phrase in each sentence. Draw an arrow from each circle to the word the phrase describes.

11. At the zoo, a little boy stares at the huge lion.
12. Beside the river, four ducks sit in the sun.
13. A pretty lamp with a gold base stands on the table.
14. Smoke rises from the chimney on the roof.
15. A large horse with a new saddle trots smartly in the parade.

English to Use

Midterm Mastery Test Page 2

Midterm Mastery Test, Chapters 1–6, continued

Part D Circle the subject in each sentence. Underline the appositive in each sentence.

16. The fireworks, a beautiful display, filled the sky with color.
17. Harsha must study chapter three, a tough one, for the quiz on Monday.
18. His cousin Bert, a lucky man, won big money in the lottery.
19. Ben's party, a happy event, lasted into the night.

Part E Circle the answer that describes the word in bold.

20. Latasha **planted** flowers on her balcony.
    A noun　　B adverb　　C verb　　D adjective
21. **Planted** pots lined the sidewalk.
    A noun　　B preposition　　C verb　　D adjective
22. Jassmine got **behind** in her studies.
    A noun　　B adverb　　C preposition　　D adjective
23. **Behind** a couch hides the cat.
    A noun　　B adverb　　C preposition　　D adjective
24. **Roaming** is what I like to do best.
    A noun　　B adverb　　C verb　　D adjective
25. We were **roaming** around the lake in the boat.
    A noun　　B adverb　　C verb　　D adjective

Part F Read each sentence. Decide if the direct object is simple or compound. Write *simple* or *compound* on the blank.

_____ 26. Les ordered a cheeseburger and soft drink.
_____ 27. Juanita and Elsa bought the newspaper.
_____ 28. Tonya heard the thunder and the rain in the night.
_____ 29. The chef cut the chicken and vegetables for the stir fry recipe.
_____ 30. His brother buys and sells used computers.

English to Use

Midterm Mastery Test Page 3

Midterm Mastery Test, Chapters 1–6, continued

Part G Circle the verb in each sentence. Decide if it is an action verb or a state-of-being verb. Write *Action* or *Being* on the blank.

31. I like watermelon. _____
32. He is a short person. _____
33. We drove to the mountains. _____
34. Ronda grabbed the pencil. _____
35. The cat is cuddly and warm. _____

Part H Write *and, or, but, yet,* or *as well as,* to complete each sentence correctly. Use each conjunction only once.

36. The book _____ the pen dropped on the floor.
37. Noah polished _____ shined his car.
38. The dog went to its bowl to eat, _____ it was empty.
39. A petal broke off from a flower, _____ it did not fall to the ground.
40. You can either cut the grass _____ clean the garage.

Part I Circle the question that the adverb in the sentence is answering.

41. The long train arrives today.
    A When?　　B How often?　　C What direction?　　D Where?
42. The tree fell down in the yard.
    A When?　　B Where?　　C How long?　　D How?
43. Snow often falls in the spring.
    A When?　　B Where?　　C How long?　　D How?
44. Jack usually works on Saturdays.
    A When?　　B Where?　　C How long?　　D How?
45. Maddie swims twice a day.
    A When?　　B Where?　　C How often?　　D How long?

English to Use

Midterm Mastery Test Page 4

Midterm Mastery Test, Chapters 1–6, continued

Part J Read each sentence. Circle the indirect object in each sentence.

46. Too much sun gives Louie a bad sunburn.
47. Polly, a singer in the chorus, sold Mandy three tickets to the concert.
48. Ranisha gave her sister a ride to the bus stop.
49. Today, Charles bought himself a new modem.
50. A friend of theirs sent them an invitation to her cabin for the weekend.

Part K Write these sentences correctly on the blank lines.

51. at thomas lake a power boat stops near the shore
_____
52. on the shore the boat captain says joe i have something for you
_____
53. he gives joe an article called how to ski on water
_____
54. joe a hard worker wants to ski well
_____
55. hey joe is the best skier on that great big lake
_____

Part L Circle the answer that correctly completes each sentence.

56. Darte and _____ saw you at the movies.
    A we　　B me　　C I　　D you
57. Joanna and _____ ate lunch together.
    A we　　B his　　C her　　D us
58. _____ went to the park with Randy and Jody.
    A Them　　B They　　C Us　　D Her
59. _____ and Lou gave a party for our family.
    A Us　　B Them　　C His　　D She
60. At the game, _____ bought me a baseball poster.
    A we　　B them　　C he　　D her

English to Use

Midterm Mastery Test 305

Final Mastery Test

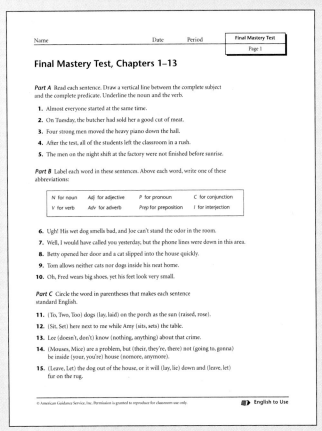

Final Mastery Test, Chapters 1–13

Part A Read each sentence. Draw a vertical line between the complete subject and the complete predicate. Underline the noun and the verb.

1. Almost everyone started at the same time.
2. On Tuesday, the butcher had sold her a good cut of meat.
3. Four strong men moved the heavy piano down the hall.
4. After the test, all of the students left the classroom in a rush.
5. The men on the night shift at the factory were not finished before sunrise.

Part B Label each word in these sentences. Above each word, write one of these abbreviations:

N for noun	*Adj* for adjective	*P* for pronoun	*C* for conjunction
V for verb	*Adv* for adverb	*Prep* for preposition	*I* for interjection

6. Ugh! His wet dog smells bad, and Joe can't stand the odor in the room.
7. Well, I would have called you yesterday, but the phone lines were down in this area.
8. Betty opened her door and a cat slipped into the house quickly.
9. Tom allows neither cats nor dogs inside his neat home.
10. Oh, Fred wears big shoes, yet his feet look very small.

Part C Circle the word in parentheses that makes each sentence standard English.

11. (To, Two, Too) dogs (lay, laid) on the porch as the sun (raised, rose).
12. (Sit, Set) here next to me while Amy (sits, sets) the table.
13. Lee (doesn't, don't) know (nothing, anything) about that crime.
14. (Mouses, Mice) are a problem, but (their, they're, there) not (going to, gonna) be inside (your, you're) house (nomore, anymore).
15. (Leave, Let) the dog out of the house, or it will (lay, lie) down and (leave, let) fur on the rug.

English to Use

Final Mastery Test Page 1

Final Mastery Test, Chapters 1–13, continued

Part D Circle every prepositional phrase in each sentence. Draw an arrow from each circle to the word the phrase describes.

16. In the store, a man shops for a new computer.
17. Under the bridge, two people in shorts paddle.
18. A lady with blue shoes waits beside the car.
19. Steam rises from the pavement on the driveway.
20. A small pony with a shaggy mane trots slowly around the track.

Part E Circle the verb in each sentence. Decide if it is an action verb or a state-of-being verb. Write *Action* or *Being* on the blank.

21. I like bananas. _____
22. Luis is a kind person. _____
23. Rosie walked five miles today. _____
24. Dave caught the pop fly gracefully. _____
25. The puppies are frisky and curious. _____

Part F Read each sentence. Circle the indirect object in each sentence.

26. Too much rain gave me a big cleanup job in the basement.
27. Sally, a watercolor artist, sold Austin two paintings.
28. Sam handed his brother the bat.
29. Yesterday, Charlene bought herself a fax machine.
30. A man on the bus gave the lady next to him his newspaper.

Part G Read each sentence. Decide if the direct object is simple or compound. Write *simple* or *compound.*

_____ 31. Hal chose a salad and steak for dinner.
_____ 32. Carlos and Rafael sold their motorcycle.
_____ 33. Tassie heard the crashing and banging of the shutters.
_____ 34. The waiter brought the dessert tray and coffee to our table.
_____ 35. Her mother buys and sells antiques.

English to Use

Final Mastery Test Page 2

Final Mastery Test, Chapters 1–13, continued

Part H Underline the linking verb in each sentence.

36. The hot soup tasted so delicious.
37. The fire in the fireplace feels good on a cold winter night.
38. The carpet is wet from the rain.
39. The music at the bandshell by the lake sounds soothing on a summer evening.
40. The dog appears pretty frisky to me.

Part I Underline the complete verb in each sentence. Write the tense of the verb on the blank—*past, present,* or *future.*

_____ 41. Mr. Adams has been teaching sixth grade math for ten years.
_____ 42. By spring, Andy will have played baseball for four years.
_____ 43. The police had been warning drivers about the flooded roads.
_____ 44. Good grades have always taken a lot of hard work.
_____ 45. The windows over the alley had been broken for six months.
_____ 46. That river had not flooded in a long time.
_____ 47. We will have been waiting for this moment for four years.
_____ 48. George will take the exam again on Tuesday.
_____ 49. You are playing in the final game.
_____ 50. Jan was traveling to the city on a bus with her friends.

Part J Circle the subject complement in each sentence.

51. Turkey is my favorite poultry.
52. Katie is a good friend to older people.
53. That concert was certainly a good one.
54. The two doors on that house are bright red.
55. Early morning is a good time to read books.

English to Use

Final Mastery Test Page 3

Final Mastery Test, Chapters 1–13, continued

Part K Underline each independent clause in these sentences.

56. Tom's plate is still full because he took too much food.
57. The snow was falling heavily when we arrived at Jan's house, a nice warm place.
58. If the oil isn't changed, the car doesn't run well.
59. Floodwater closed many of the city streets, but our school stayed open.
60. When I opened the door of the cage, the bird flew away.

Part L Circle the answer that describes the word in bold.

61. Tela walked **around** the track.
   A preposition   B adverb   C verb   D adjective
62. The children ran **around** in the park.
   A noun   B preposition   C adverb   D adjective
63. The **paint** is too thick.
   A noun   B adverb   C preposition   D adjective
64. I **paint** pictures of wildlife as a hobby.
   A noun   B adverb   C verb   D adjective
65. The **paint** mixture is the wrong color.
   A noun   B adverb   C verb   D adjective

Part M Circle the correct word in parentheses in each sentence.

66. The (fare, fair) for a ride at the (fare, fair) in the park is (to, too) high, and (it's, its) not (fare, fair).
67. You can (here, hear) Alfonso's stereo from (here, hear).
68. At the picnic, four (families, familys) waited for the (skys, skies) to clear.
69. Her throat is sore and her voice is (horse, hoarse), but her (horse, hoarse) came when she called.
70. The (ladies, ladys) swatted (flies, flys), and they felt (relief, releif) when they (recieved, received) some flypaper.

English to Use

Final Mastery Test Page 4

Final Mastery Test

Final Mastery Test Page 5
Final Mastery Test Page 6

Page 5

Final Mastery Test, Chapters 1–13, continued

Part N Correct these sentences using standard English. Rewrite each sentence on the blank.

71. do you has carrots on the menu dan asked the waiter

_____

72. i dont know nobody who like carrots the waiter said

_____

73. mary looked at the menu and asked do you have liver

_____

74. nobody been likeing liver the waiter said angrily

_____

75. dan and mary closed they're menus and stood up

_____

Part O Circle the misplaced phrase in each sentence. Rewrite the sentences so they make sense.

76. The gift was mailed by Joe in a large box.

_____

77. A group of men talked about hunting in the living room.

_____

78. A large dog entered the yard with a long tail.

_____

79. A black horse walked toward the little girl with white spots.

_____

80. A cowboy climbed on his horse with thick glasses.

_____

Page 6

Final Mastery Test, Chapters 1–13, continued

Part P Circle the answer that correctly completes each sentence.

81. Tran and _____ ran into them at the mall.
A we **B** her **C** she **D** they

82. Hannah and _____ had a picnic by the lake.
A me **B** I **C** we **D** they

83. _____ drove to the city with Mai.
A Him **B** Them **C** He **D** Us

84. _____ threw a party for our grandparents.
A Us **B** Them **C** Me **D** We

85. Between you and I, Leo did not tell _____ the truth.
A them **B** we **C** she **D** he

86. Each of the boys has applied for _____ driver's license.
A her **B** our **C** his **D** their

87. Neither Pegi nor Brittany know _____ test score.
A his **B** their **C** we **D** her

88. Everybody has _____ calendar full by now.
A his or her **B** their **C** we **D** our

89. Several have brought _____ own computer.
A our **B** his or her **C** their **D** we

90. Others think _____ ideas are the best ones.
A their **B** our **C** we **D** his or her

Part Q Some of these words are not spelled correctly. Write each misspelled word correctly on the blank. If the word is spelled correctly, write *correct*.

91. nickle _____ **96.** safetey _____

92. neccessary _____ **97.** occur _____

93. goverment _____ **98.** beginning _____

94. grammer _____ **99.** tooths _____

95. atheletic _____ **100.** niece _____

Teacher's Resource Library Answer Key

Activities

Activity 1–Make a Sentence

1–10. Answers may vary. Check to make sure that subjects agree with predicates.

11–20. Answers may vary. Check to make sure that predicates agree with subjects.

Activity 2–Find the Nouns

1. <u>Children</u> shout. **2.** <u>Truckers</u> drive. **3.** <u>cats</u> hiss. **4.** <u>Fire</u> burns **5.** <u>Diamonds</u> sparkle. **6.** <u>Snakes</u> slither. **7.** <u>Adults</u> talk. **8.** <u>Lions</u> roar. **9.** <u>Cars</u> race. **10.** <u>Teens</u> dance.

Circle the nouns. On the line write if the noun is a *person, place* or *thing*.

11. (Scissors) cut—thing 12. (Volcanoes) erupt—thing **13.** (Cities) grow—place **14.** (Singers) hum—person **15.** (Trucks) rumble—thing.

Circle the noun in each group.

16. lakes, shore **17.** trees, birds **18.** puddle **19.** sun **20.** music, song **21.** phones, bells **22.** pen, paper **23.** mall, clothes **24.** band, drums **25.** artists, pencil

Activity 3–Adjectives

Circle the adjective and underline each noun.

1. (Cold) <u>rain</u> falls. **2.** (Wide) <u>rivers</u> flow. **3.** (Large) <u>eagles</u> fly. **4.** (Scared) <u>horses</u> buck. **5.** (Fast) <u>swimmers</u> race. **6.** (Quick) <u>players</u> score. **7.** (Young) <u>people</u> dance. **8.** (Hungry) <u>children</u> eat. **9.** (Noisy) <u>frogs</u> croaked. **10.** (Glass) <u>bottles</u> broke. **11.** A **12.** The **13.** The **14.** An **15.** A **16.** The **17.** A **18.** A **19.** An **20.** The

Activity 4–Action Verbs

Draw a line under each action verb.

1. Happy people <u>laugh.</u> **2.** Cold winds <u>blow.</u> **3.** Big trees <u>sway.</u> **4.** Heavy snow <u>falls.</u> **5.** Huge grasshoppers <u>jump.</u> **6.** A large seal <u>plays.</u> **7.** Small guppies <u>swim.</u> **8.** The tired baby <u>cries.</u> **9.** The old computer <u>froze.</u> **10.** Loud alarms <u>blare.</u> **11.** noun **12.** verb **13.** adjective **14.** noun **15.** adjective **16.** verb **17.** adjective **18.** noun **19.** verb **20.** adjective

Activity 5–Adverbs

Circle each adverb and underline the verb.

1. The river <u>runs</u> (rapidly.) **2.** The girl <u>spoke</u> (quietly.) **3.** Huge dinosaurs <u>move</u> (slowly.) **4.** Small animals <u>run</u> (quickly.) **5.** The young man <u>works</u> (hard.) **6.** The woman <u>walked</u> (fast.) **7.** The ship <u>sailed</u> (easily.) **8.** The bell <u>rang</u> (sharply.) **9.** The man <u>arrived</u> (promptly.) **10.** The branches <u>swayed</u> (silently.) **11.** Loudly, the dogs bark. **12.** Suddenly, the shuttle lands. **13.** Nervously, the woman sang. **14.** Steadily, the climber moved. **15.** Happily, the children played.

Activity 6–Adverbs That Tell "When"

Circle the adverb. Underline each verb.

1. The big crowd <u>yelled</u> (often.) **2.** (Sometimes) the tiny bird <u>chirps.</u> **3.** The school choir <u>practiced</u> (daily.) **4.** The old car <u>traveled</u> (often.) **5.** The students <u>arrived</u> (first.) **6.** (Today) a large ship <u>sailed.</u> **7.** The teacher <u>arrives</u> (now.) **8.** (Yesterday) two trains <u>left.</u> **9.** The bell <u>rings</u> (soon.) **10.** The young man <u>arrived</u> (last.) **11–20.** Answers may vary. Check to make sure that the adverb makes sense in the sentence.

Activity 7–Kinds of Adverbs

Write the adverb on the line. Mark if the adverb tells *how, when* or *where*.

1. again, when **2.** nearby, where **3.** noisily, how **4.** today, when **5.** rapidly, how **6.** brightly, how **7.** quickly, how **8.** tomorrow, when **9.** upstairs, where **10.** here, where

Activity 8–Subject and Predicate, Adjective and Adverb

Draw a line under the complete subject. Circle the complete predicate. Adjectives are bolded. Adverbs are italicized.

1. <u>The **cold, wet** mud</u> (oozes *silently*.) **2.** <u>A **large, golden** sun</u> (sank *slowly*.) **3.** <u>Laura</u> (*always* finishes *first*.) **4.** <u>The **high** school</u> (opens *early*.) **5.** <u>Jose,</u> (*often* sleeps *late*.) **6.** <u>The **large, black** birds</u> (*usually* stay *near*.) **7.** <u>The **green** boat,</u> (handles *nicely*.) **8.** <u>The **fast** car,</u> (runs *smoothly*.) **9.** <u>The **old fat** cat,</u> (ran *away*.) **10.** <u>**Three** airplanes,</u> (*smoothly* land *here*.)

Activity 9–Sentence or Fragment?

1. fragment **2.** sentence **3.** fragment **4.** fragment **5.** sentence **6.** fragment **7.** fragment **8.** sentence **9.** sentence **10.** fragment **11–20.** Answers will vary. Check to make sure that all are complete sentences.

Activity 10–Practicing Punctuation

Add commas to separate adjectives.

1. The bright, hot fire crackled. **2.** Soft, mushy marshmallows cooked. **3.** Tired, happy campers sang. **4.** Small, loud crickets chirped. **5.** A light, cool breeze blew. **6.** Large, bright lights shine. **7.** The small, red bugs ran. **8.** The happy, pretty girl smiled. **9.** The tall, young man sang. **10.** Loud, shrill alarms rang. **11.** Big, fluffy clouds float. **12.** The old, blue car crashed. **13.** Quietly, the cat crept away. **14.** Small, cute dogs play .**15.** Sleek, shiny airplanes fly.

Activity 11–Prepositional Phrases

1–10. Answers will vary. Check to make sure that the preposition makes sense in the sentence. **11–15.** Answers will vary. Possible answers follow. **11.** against the fence. **12.** under the table. **13.** during the game. **14.** along the beach. **15.** behind the tree.

Activity 12–Adjective Prepositional Phrases

Underline the complete subject. Draw a circle around the verb. Write the prepositional phrase in each sentence. Write the word it describes.

1. <u>The sun behind some clouds</u> (shines) weakly—behind some clouds—sun **2.** <u>Janice and Sarah aboard a small boat</u> (paddle) away—aboard a small boat—Janice and Sarah **3.** <u>Janice in the leaky boat</u> (rows) hard—in the leaky boat—Janice **4.** <u>The small boat of friends</u> (drifts) away—of friends—boat **5.** <u>Clouds with rain</u> (move) briskly—with rain—clouds

Underline the adjective prepositional phrase. Circle the noun it describes.

6. (Sarah) <u>with Janice</u> heads back. **7.** The (boat) <u>without a rudder</u> slides sideways. **8.** The poor (friends) <u>inside the boat</u> shiver. **9.** The two friends <u>with wet clothes</u> jump and run. **10.** The (fire) <u>in the cabin</u> burns brightly.

Activity 13–Confusing Subjects

Circle the prepositional phrase. Underline the simple subject.
1. The pipes (on the new boat) gurgle softly. **2.** A boat (at the dock) rocks gently. **3.** Light (from the sun) shines brightly. **4.** A boat (on the lake) roars past. **5.** Shadows (from tall trees) grow quickly. **6.** A tall pile (of books) falls. **7.** A group (of men) sing loudly. **8.** A box (of candy) slowly melts. **9.** People wait (in line) early. **10.** Crowds (of children) giggle noisily. **11–15.** Answers will vary. Possible answers follow.
11. near the window **12.** with a backpack **13.** with a hat on **14.** in the yard **15.** in the field

Activity 14–Adverb Prepositional Phrases

Underline the complete subject. Draw a circle around the verb. Write the prepositional phrase.
1. Andy (left) during the game—during the game **2.** His friends (looked) around the stadium—around the stadium **3.** Wolves (howl) loudly in the woods—in the woods **4.** A group of teens (drove) around the city—around the city **5.** The stars (shone) brightly across the sky—across the sky **6.** The flower pot (fell) off the ledge—off the ledge **7.** The car (went) through a tunnel—through a tunnel **8.** The large rubber ball (bounced) off a wall—off a wall **9.** Lightning (flashed) across the dark sky—across the dark sky **10.** The tired hikers (stopped) near a river—near a river

Activity 15–Preposition or Adverb?

Underline the verb. Decide if the bold word is an adverb or preposition then write either on the line.
1. The cat wakes up **in** the empty house.—adverb **2.** the cat plays **with** the string.—preposition **3.** The string lays **on** the floor.—preposition **4.** The big ball **of** string sits on the table.— preposition **5.** **Then** the cat jumped on the chair.—adverb **6.** He looked **at** the ball of string.—preposition **7.** His paw reached **out** for the ball.—adverb **8.** The cat and the string fell **under** the table.—preposition **9.** A tangle of string twists **around** the big chair.—preposition **10.** The small ball **of** string lays under the table. —preposition
Draw a line under the adverb, bold the prepositional phrase and circle the verb.
11. The bicyclist (rode) quickly **around the lake. 12.** He (stopped) across **from the park. 13.** The bicyclist (looked) around **for the drinking fountain. 14.** The children (ate) happily **in the park. 15.** They (played) freely **on the playground.**

Activity 16–Adjective and Adverb Prepositional Phrases

Underline the simple subject, draw a circle around the verb, and write the prepositional phrase.
1. A tall man in a white suit (climbed) into the taxi—in a white suit, adj.—into the taxi, adv. **2.** Her new ring (sparkled) in the light—in the light, adv. **3.** Chuck (stepped) over the log in the woods—over the log, adv.—in the woods, adj. **4.** The building with the glass front (shines) in the sunlight—with the glass front, adj.—in the sunlight, adv. **5.** The ice on the street (melted) during the day—on the street, adj.—during the day, adv.
Underline the prepositional phrase.
6. A deep blue liquid shone inside the test tube. **7.** The test tube fell out of his hands. **8.** The glass container shattered on the countertop. **9.** The liquid dripped onto the floor. 10. The doctor wiped up the spill.

Activity 17–Hidden Verbs

State-of-being verb is bolded. Circle the prepositional phrase.
1. Alicia **is** a great student (at school.) **2.** Brandon **became** a good player (on his team.) **3.** They **are** the best team (at the school.) **4.** That new show **is** (on TV.) **5.** The tired dog **remains** (on the floor.)
Circle the prepositional phrase. Draw a line under the subject noun. Bold the state-of-being verb.
6. Antonio **was** (outside near the fence.) **7.** Maria **appears** tired (at work.) **8.** Thao and Reggie **were** (on the soccer team.) **9.** Soon, Mai **will be** (in Manitoba.) **10.** That school **is** on (Second Street near the park.) **11.** Lola and Jamal **are** (in the store.) **12.** The rabbit **is** (behind the tree.) **13.** A red car **was** (on the street.) **14.** The large dog (around the block) **seems** friendly. **15.** The girls **are** (by the fence.)

Activity 18–Two Kinds of Prepositional Phrases

Circle each prepositional phrase. Draw an arrow from the phrase to the word it describes.
1. (At the shopping mall,) the girls buy the dresses (with glitter.) **2.** The boys went (to the arcade) with their parents. **3.** Ramon helped clean (up the park.) **4.** Tabitha (with her dog) walked (to the lake.) **5.** The woman (at the store) yelled (at the robber.) **6.** A **7.** A **8.** B **9.** B **10.** B

Activity 19–Writing Mechanics

1. x **2.** **3.** x **4.** **5.** Virginia **6.** **7.** x **8.** Demetrius **9.** x **10.** Indiana **11.** Central Park **12.** x **13.** Vancouver **14.** x **15.** Houston **16.** x **17.** Samuel **18.** x **19.** Mars **20.** x **21.** Beyond the hill, the sun shone brightly. **22.** Under the water, moss grows. **23.** On the street, music plays. **24.** During the long cold winter, this lake freezes. **25.** At the party, people dance happily.

Activity 20–Conjunctions

Answers may vary. Possible answers follow.
1. and **2.** or **3.** as well as **4.** as well as **5.** but **6.** or **7.** yet **8.** and **9.** and **10.** as well as **11.** Both, and **12.** Not only, but also **13.** either, or **14.** Neither, nor **15.** Both, and **16.** not only, but also **17.** Neither, nor **18.** either, or **19.** both, and **20.** Not only, but also

Activity 21–Compound Subjects

Underline the simple subjects. Circle the conjunction.
1. The desk (and) the computer look nice there. **2.** The paper (and) pencils are on the table. **3.** LaToya (and) Annika went to the art museum. **4.** Mario (and) Kyle shopped for school clothes. **5.** Families (and) friends gathered at the park. **6.** Marques (and) Anthony went to summer camp. **7.** The cat (and) the dog slept on the floor. **8.** Harold (and) Julie walked to the library. **9.** Hector (and) Pilar swim in the water. **10.** Patrick (and) Rudy paint the house.
Underline the compound subject. Circle the conjunction.
11. A robin, a cardinal, (and) a bluebird flew by the house. **12.** Two young women (and) one man get off of the bus. **13.** Camels, zebras, (and) elephants live at the zoo. **14.** Two blue cars, one yellow car, (and) two red cars raced around the track. **15.** Two squirrels (and) an owl are in the tree.

Activity 22–Compound Subjects and Predicates

1–10. Answers will vary. **11–20.** Answers will vary.

Activity 23–Compound Objects of Prepositions

1–10. Answers will vary.
Underline the objects of prepositions. Circle the preposition.
11. The car (with) a cracked window and a broken headlight broke down. **12.** A large dog ran (through) the streets and the yard.

13. The visitor (with) the long <u>coat</u> and the dark <u>hat</u> entered the house.
14. Natasha likes her sandwich (with) <u>lettuce</u> and <u>tomatoes.</u> **15.** The girls walked (around) the <u>lake</u> and the <u>park.</u>

Activity 24–Compound Sentences
1–10. Answers will vary.

Activity 25–Compounds
Draw a circle around each prepositional phrase in the story.
Circle *in the pool , on the tennis court, in the sun, to the radio, over the pool and lawn, into the ball, over the net, off the court, through the day, in the sun*
1. lazily   up
    hard   high
2. Fred and Sonia
3. Swims and plays   sails and bounces
    lies and listens
4. pool and lawn
5. Answers will vary. Check for the use of compounds.

Activity 26–Writing Mechanics
1. Actors run, jump, and dance on the stage. **2.** Flies, bugs, and mice hide under the old house. **3.** Math, science, and music are on the schedule for today. **4.** Fans often yell, jump, and stomp at a big game. **5.** Sofas, desks, and tables sit in the store window.
6–10. Answers will vary. Check to make sure three sentences use a conjunction and two sentences use a semicolon.

Activity 27–Subject + Verb + Direct Object
1. broke → window **2.** watched → truck **3.** planted → flowers **4.** plays → trumpet **5.** sent → letters **6.** watched → television **7.** struck → tree **8.** fixed → tire **9.** played → chess **10.** tossed → ball

Activity 28–Find and Combine the Parts
1. Drum, horn, music, and hands. **2.** Across the grass, on the band, at the quiet park **3.** away **4.** Answers will vary. **5.** Answers will vary.

Activity 29–More Compounds
1. NC **2.** C **3.** C **4.** C **5.** NC **6.** CDO **7.** CV **8.** CV **9.** Both **10.** CV **11.** C sentence **12.** CDO **13.** CV **14.** CS **15.** CV

Activity 30–Direct Objects and Prepositions
Underline each verb. Draw a circle around each direct object. Write each prepositional phrase.
1. The spotted cat <u>carried</u> the (mouse) into the kitchen—into the kitchen **2.** The mouse <u>ran</u> toward the door —toward the door **3.** A dog <u>grabbed</u> the (mouse). **4.** The cat <u>swiped</u> at the dog—at the dog **5.** The dog <u>pulled</u> the (cat) toward the sink—toward the sink **6.** The cat <u>hissed</u> at the dog—at the dog **7.** The cat <u>bit</u> the (dog) and <u>jumped</u> into the air—into the air **8.** The dog <u>ran</u> from the mouse—from the mouse **9.** The cat <u>chased</u> the (dog) around the kitchen—around the kitchen **10.** The cat <u>climbed</u> up the curtain and <u>crawled</u> out the window—up the curtain—out the window

Activity 31–Nouns in a Sentence
Circle the nouns that are subjects. Underline the nouns that are direct objects. Draw a box around the nouns that are objects of a preposition.
1. (Esteban) throws his <u>hook</u> into the [water.] **2.** A (fish) watches the big <u>hook</u> above [him.] **3.** The (fish) sniffs the <u>bait</u> on the [hook.] **4.** A long (line) in the [water] warns the <u>fish.</u> **5.** The (fish) swims away, and (Esteban) lifts the <u>bait</u> from the [water.] **6.** concrete

7. abstract **8.** concrete **9.** abstract **10.** concrete **11.** abstract **12.** abstract **13.** abstract **14.** concrete **15.** abstract

Activity 32–Pronouns in a Sentence
Circle the correct pronoun.
1. we **2.** He, them **3.** him **4.** us, them **5.** them **6.** We **7.** He, I **8.** I, them **9.** He **10.** She, them **11.** OP **12.** OP **13.** NP **14.** OP **15.** NP

Activity 33–Using Pronouns
1. Beth chatted with her. **2.** He walked Oma and Rita to the car. **3.** Melinda bought an apple and ate it on the bus. **4.** Daniel saw them at the concert. **5.** Otto bought a book and left it at school. **6.** herself **7.** itself **8.** myself **9.** himself **10.** themselves **11.** yourself **12.** ourselves **13.** yourselves **14.** myself **15.** herself

Activity 34–Pronoun or Adjective?
Underline each adjective and draw an arrow to the noun it describes.
1. <u>Many</u> → families; <u>two</u> → cars **2.** <u>Some</u> → people; <u>many</u> → cars; **3.** <u>Each</u> → person; <u>favorite</u> → car; **4.** <u>One</u> → man; <u>sports</u> → car; **5.** <u>Another</u> → man; <u>all</u> → cars **6.** adjective **7.** adj. **8.** pronoun **9.** pronoun **10.** adjective **11.** pronoun **12.** adjective **13.** adjective **14.** pronoun **15.** adjective

Activity 35–This, That, These, Those
1. this **2.** these **3.** that **4.** that **5.** those **6.** adjective **7.** adj. **8.** adjective **9.** adjective **10.** pronoun **11.** Those **12.** These **13.** That **14.** This **15.** This

Activity 36–Writing Mechanics
1–10. Answers will vary **11.** Ms. Graham **12.** Nelson Mandela **13.** Senator Adams **14.** Toronto SkyDome **15.** Dr. Koua Nguyen **16.** Mr. Thomas called for my father, but he was not at home. **17.** Dr. Suarez spoke with Dr. Reed, Dr. Hely, and Dr. Rahamim at the conference. **18.** Barak wanted to go to the dance; however, he had to work that night. **19.** Ms. Dai went to dinner with Ms. Abel, Ms. Elias, and Ms. Ato-Case. **20.** The thunder boomed; the lightning flashed.

Activity 37–What Are the Parts?
1. verb, preposition **2.** noun, preposition **3.** conjunction, verb **4.** noun, noun **5.** adjective, adverb **6.** noun or pronoun, verb, noun **7.** verb, adverb **8.** verb, adjective **9.** noun, noun **10.** adjective, adjective

Activity 38–Owners
1. Alec's **2.** woman's **3.** Isaac's **4.** dog's **5.** Maria's **6.** Felipe's **7.** Tomas' **8.** Alyssa's **9.** man's **10.** family's

Activity 39–Owner Pronouns
1. (her) → sister **2.** (his) → team and (its) → place **3.** (Our) → boat **4.** (Your) → friend, (his) → brother, and (my) → cousin. **5.** (your) → friend and (my) → car. **6.** its **7.** her **8.** their **9.** its **10.** your **11.** our **12.** his **13.** their **14.** their **15.** her

Activity 40–More Than One Owner
1. flowers' **2.** houses' **3.** yards' **4.** boys' **5.** cats' **6.** It won the contest **7.** They stayed late at the factory. **8.** It jumps out of the water and into the boat. **9.** He ran down the street **10.** She flew a kite over the big field.

Activity 41–Where is the Subject?
Write the subject. Then write the complete sentence.
1. you—You watch the scary movie. **2.** You—You dig a deeper hole. **3.** You—You kick the starter on your dirt bike. **4.** You—You look at the dog. **5.** You—You eat hot dogs and onions. **6.** Watch, dig, kick, look, eat **7.** movie, hole, starter, hot dogs, onions **8.** on your dirt bike, at the dog **9.** Answers will vary. **10.** Answers will vary.

Activity 42–More About Adverbs
1. awfully—deep, adjective **2.** So—long, adjective **3.** quite—slowly, adverb **4.** rather—quickly, adverb **5.** really—serious, adjective **6–15.** Answers will vary. Possible answers follow. **6.** extremely **7.** awfully **8.** truly **9.** unusually **10.** quite **11.** so **12.** somewhat **13.** almost **14.** rather **15.** terribly

Activity 43–Interjections
1–10. Answers will vary. Possible answers follow. **1.** Wow **2.** Ouch **3.** Hey **4.** Gee **5.** Oh **6.** Yikes **7.** Hello **8.** Hooray **9.** Boy **10.** Well **11–15.** Answers will vary. **16.** adverb **17.** interjection **18.** adverb **19.** interjection **20.** interjection

Activity 44–Write About Your Day
Answers will vary.

Activity 45–Writing Mechanics
1. Naomi forgot to turn in her homework. **2.** Thran will meet Aaron, Jeremy, and Devon at the movie theater. **3.** Jesse will start classes at the Lincoln School of Excellence on Monday. **4.** Tony, a great drummer, will play in Jonah's band tonight. **5.** Many birds' nests are in the big oak tree. **6–10.** Answers will vary. Possible answers follow. **6.** Well, it is good to see you. **7.** Yuck! That color of paint is really ugly! **8.** Hush, so I can hear the stereo's music. **9.** Yikes! I almost stepped on a big snake! **10.** Gee, you have the best grades in your class.

Activity 46–Indirect Objects
Draw a line under the complete subject. Draw a circle around the verb. Write the indirect object and the direct object.
1. Ralph and Sam (bought) themselves a new baseball—Indirect object: themselves—Direct object: baseball **2.** They (paid) the clerk five dollars.—Indirect object: clerk—Direct object: dollars **3.** The clerk (gave) them a dollar change.—Indirect object: them—Direct object: change **4.** The coach (bought) the team a new bat.—Indirect object: team—Direct object: bat **5.** He (taught) each player the use of the bat.—Indirect object: player—Direct object: use **6.** indirect object **7.** direct object **8.** direct object **9.** direct object **10.** indirect object

Activity 47–Indirect Objects in Long Sentences
Underline the indirect object.
1. boy **2.** player **3.** workers **4.** buyers **5.** teacher **6.** daughter **7.** mother **8.** Melina **9.** parents **10.** Rowena **11.** An S above **Sid**, a V above **told**, an IO above **teacher**, a DO above **story** **12.** An S above **Dwayne**, a V above **taught**, an IO above **group**, a DO above **way**. **13.** An S above **Cheryl**, a V above **fixed**, an IO above **Fiona**, a DO above **dinner**. **14.** An S above **Gary & Debra**, a V above **gave**, an IO above **friend**, a DO above **watch**. **15.** An S above **Adams**, a V above **left**, an IO above **son**, a DO above **acres**.

Activity 48–Object Complements
Draw a line under the complete subject. Draw a circle around the verb. Write the direct object and object complement.
1. The high winds (made) the lake rough-Direct object: **lake** Object complement: **rough 2.** The young man (ordered) his hamburger broiled. Direct object: **hamburger** Object complement: **broiled 3.** Heavy sleet (turned) the street white. Direct object: **street** Object complement: **white 4.** The rainbow (made) people happy. Direct object: **people** Object complement: **happy 5.** Storm clouds (turned) the sky black Direct object: **sky** Object complement: **black 6.** Poor test scores (made) a high grade difficult. Direct object: **grade** Object complement: **difficult 7.** The artist (painted) her canvas gray. Direct object: **grass** Object complement: **gray 8.** Heavy rains (made) the grass green in our yard. Direct object: **grass** Object complement: **green 9.** Ann (likes) summers hot. Direct object: **summers** Object complement: **hot 10.** The band leader (played) his music loud. Direct object: **music** Object complement: **loud**

Activity 49–Review Four Sentence Patterns
Underline the prepositional phrases, circle the words that tell you the sentence pattern.
1. Homework gives students many problems in school.—subject + verb + direct object + object complement **2.** The football team makes its owners rich—subject + verb + direct object + object complement **3.** The town accepted the idea in one vote.—subject + verb + direct object **4.** In the cafe, Tim finds fish and chips tasty—subject + verb + direct object + direct object + object complement **5.** By the gate near the school, two boys played.—subject + verb **6.** Ed told Steve the good news.—subject + verb + indirect object + direct object **7.** The news gave Steve a lift.—subject + verb + indirect object + direct object **8.** The anglers found the lake rough, the wind cold, the boat leaky, and the fish gone.—subject + verb + direct object + object complement + direct object + object complement + direct object + object complement + direct object + object complement **9.** The (barber) down the street (gave) the young (man) a new (hairstyle) —subject + verb + indirect object + direct object **10.** The (class) (voted) (Darren) (president.) —subject + verb + direct object + object complement

Activity 50–Appositives
Circle the appositive, underline the noun.
1. George, (a large man,) walked through the doorway. **2.** Her car, (a red sports car,) is parked over there. **3.** My brother (Simon) kicks for the football team. **4.** Owen (the auto mechanic) works long days. **5.** The fire, (a horrible blaze,) destroyed half the town. **6.** My friend (Eva) is going on vacation. **7.** The pilot, (a brave person,) flew the plane safely through the storm. **8.** His cousin (Steve) moved to Canada. **9.** The appetizer, (a selection of fruit and cheese,) looks very appealing. **10.** Ida, (my aunt,) came to visit me from Florida. **11–15.** Answers will vary. Check for an appositive in each sentence.

Activity 51–Writing Practice
1–5. Answers will vary. Check to see if each sentence contains a subject and a direct object. **6–10.** Answer will vary.

Activity 52–Punctuate and Capitalize
Rewrite the sentences correctly. End punctuation may vary.
1. Patrick's car, an older model, wins prizes everywhere. **2.** Wow! Its paint looks new. **3.** The car won four prizes, a real honor. **4.** Patrick and his friend, Helena, washed the car each week. **5.** They tuned the engine, too. **6.** Oh! Listen to the twin pipes rumble. **7.** Each Sunday, the friends drive to Indianapolis. **8.** There, among other fine cars, Patrick's car sits proudly. **9.** Patrick puts hard work, care, and money into his car. **10.** Patrick, a hard worker, earns his prizes.

Activity 53–Noun Subject Complements

Draw a line under the complete subject. Draw a circle around the verb. Write the subject noun and the noun subject complement.
1. My favorite sport (is) soccer—Subject Noun: **Sport**—Noun subject complement: **soccer 2.** The fastest girl in the class (is) Shandra—Subject Noun: **girl**—Noun subject complement: **Shandra 3.** A great book in the library (is) *The Hero.* —Subject Noun: **book**—Noun subject complement: *The Hero* **4.** In the last race, the fastest boat (was) "The Shadow"—Subject Noun: **boat**—Noun subject complement: "The Shadow" **5.** My best subject (is) math. —Subject Noun: **subject**—Noun subject complement: **math 6.** Evie's favorite pet (is) a turtle. —Subject Noun: **pet**—Noun subject complement: **turtle 7.** The newest building in town (is) the bus station. —Subject Noun: **building**—Noun subject complement: **bus station 8.** First prize (is) a ski trip. —Subject Noun: **prize**—Noun subject complement: **ski trip 9.** The dead trees in the yard (are) oaks. —Subject Noun: **trees**—Noun subject complement: **oaks 10.** These birds (are) crows. —Subject Noun: **birds**—Noun subject complement: **crows**

Activity 54–Appositives with Subject Complements

Draw a circle around the verb. Write the subject noun, the appositive, and the subject complement. Tell if the complement is a noun or an adjective.
1. Circle *are*—Subject noun: crowds—Appositive: people from everywhere—Complement: tourists—noun **2.** Circle *is*—Subject noun: dessert—Appositive: A special treat—Complement: frozen yogurt—noun **3.** Circle *is*—Subject noun: car—Appositive: a beautiful red machine—Complement: fast—adjective **4.** Circle *is*—Subject noun: Luke—Appositive: An excellent basketball player—Complement: tall and quick—adjective **5.** Circle *is*—Subject noun: lake—Appositive: a huge body of water—Complement: dark blue—adjective

Activity 55–Adjective Subject Complements

Draw a line under the complete subject. Draw a circle around the verb. Write the subject noun and the adjective subject complement.
1. The clouds over the sunset (are) golden.—Subject noun: clouds—Adjective subject complement: golden **2.** Sandy's beautiful new watch (was) expensive.—Subject noun: watch—Adjective subject complement: expensive **3.** His computer (is) new. —Subject noun: computer—Adjective subject complement: new **4.** Those big waves beyond the reef (are) high.—Subject noun: waves—Adjective subject complement: high **5.** The rain during this month (is) heavy.—Subject noun: rain—Adjective subject complement: heavy **6.** Rosie's new blue shoes (are) tight.—Subject noun: shoes—Adjective subject complement: tight **7.** The math classroom (is) always too hot.—Subject noun: classroom—Adjective subject complement: hot **8.** Our new science course (is) very hard.—Subject noun: course—Adjective subject complement: hard **9.** The weeds in the yard (are) tall.—Subject noun: weeds—Adjective subject complement: tall **10.** The big dogs in Ellie's yard (are) hungry.—Subject noun: dogs—Adjective subject complement: hungry

Activity 56–Adjectives Describe Nouns

Circle the adjectives that describe the nouns in bold.
1. large, busy **2.** icy, messy **3.** hot, spicy **4.** fresh, green, tasty **5.** crisp, clear, peaceful **6–10.** Answers will vary. Check to see if two sentences use sentence pattern A and two sentences use sentence pattern B.

Activity 57–Adjective or Adverb

1. lazy, lazily **2.** neatly, neat **3.** good, well **4.** slowly, slow **5.** honest, honestly **6.** poor, poorly **7.** quietly, quiet **8.** loudly, loud **9.** quick, quickly **10.** heavy, heavily

Activity 58–Subject Complements

Draw a line under the simple subject. Draw a circle around the verb. Write the subject complement. Tell if it is a noun or an adjective subject complement.
1. The Laser (is) the best car for the race.—Subject complement: best car—Noun **2.** Derek and Mia (were) class officers last year.—Subject complement: class officers—Noun **3.** The fruit crop (is) not good this year.—Subject complement: not good—Adjective **4.** A ham and cheese sandwich (is) a nice lunch.—Subject complement: nice lunch—Noun **5.** The steel and glass building (is) the biggest structure in the city.—Subject complement: biggest structure—Noun **6.** Otto (is) a mean dog.—Subject complement: mean dog—Noun **7.** The dog's bark (is) fierce.—Subject complement: fierce—Adjective **8.** Duncan (is) a popular singer on TV.—Subject complement: popular singer—Noun **9.** Duncan's songs (are) old.—Subject complement: old—Adjective **10.** Duncan's style (is) modern and fresh.—Subject complement: modern and fresh—Adjective

Activity 59–Pronouns in Subject Complement Sentences

Write S above the subject pronoun, LV above the linking verb and NSC above the noun subject complement.
1. S: This, LV: is, NSC: book **2.** S: This, LV: is, NSC: sea turtle **3.** S: Its, LV: is, NSC: animal **4.** S: That, LV: is, NSC: question **5.** S: This, LV: is, NSC: way **6.** S: It, LV: was, NSC: deal **7.** S: These, LV: are, NSC: gifts **8.** S: Those, LV: are, NSC: decorations **9.** S: That, LV: is, NSC: dress **10.** S: These, LV: are, NSC: earrings
Circle the subject of each sentence.
11. There **12.** Here **13.** There **14.** Here **15.** There

Activity 60–More Pronouns

1. him **2.** her **3.** us **4.** They **5.** it **6.** our **7.** his **8.** you **9.** you **10.** me **11.** mine **12.** hers **13.** ours **14.** his **15.** theirs

Activity 61–Reviewing Sentence Patterns

1. C **2.** C **3.** E **4.** E **5.** B **6.** A **7.** B **8.** D **9.** F **10.** E **11.** C **12.** F **13.** E **14.** A **15.** D

Activity 62–Writing Practice

1–5. Answers will vary. Check to see if subjects, adjectives, and subject complements are present. **6–10.** Answers will vary.

Activity 63–Adjectives that Compare

1. handiest **2.** faster **3.** smallest **4.** tall, taller **5.** wet, wetter **6.** faster **7.** loudest **8.** bad, better **9.** many, more **10.** bigger **11.** hungriest **12.** happier **13.** prettier **14.** worst **15.** more **16.** least **17.** harder **18.** better **19.** early, earlier **20.** better

Activity 64–Another Look at Verbs

Circle the verb. Write whether it is an action or a linking verb.
1. tastes–linking verb **2.** works–action verb **3.** are–linking verb **4.** kicke–action verb **5.** watched–action verb **6.** past tense **7.** past tense **8.** future tense **9.** present tense **10.** future tense **11.** walked **12.** will present **13.** like **14.** biked **15.** will look

Activity 65–Problem Verb: Be

1. is, has been or was, had been or was, will be **2.** is, has been, had been, will be **3.** is, has been, had been or was, will be **4.** is, has been, had been or was, will be **5.** is, has been or was, had been or was, will be

Activity 66–Verbs Tell Time

1. They are going with us every day. **2.** Oralee is playing pool. **3.** Peter and Joni are washing the car. **4.** Jamal is grinning about his success. **5.** Hans is steering the boat. **6.** They are working in the ditch. **7.** She is playing cards with Sabrina. **8.** I am waiting for you on the steps. **9.** Lots of people are getting on the airplane. **10.** We are standing in line for the movie.

Activity 67–Verbs Tell Past Time

1. I was walking to the bus station. **2.** We were flying too low and almost crashed. **3.** They (had) climbed down the ladder. **4.** Andrew and Cecil were visiting yesterday. **5.** They (had) watched television most of the night. **6.** He was waiting for her on the corner. **7.** Fran had been working in the factory last night. **8.** Pilar had (or has) been missing her dog for two months. **9.** We were towing the sailboat into the harbor. **10.** Rollo (had) spotted a new jacket in the window.

Activity 68–The Future Tense

1. Sue Ann will be sewing a new dress tomorrow. **2.** Piedro will be cooking steak and potatoes. **3.** Lots of people will be going to that party on Friday. **4.** Everyone will be laughing tonight at the movie. **5.** Sandra will be moving away soon. **6.** Jerry will be sleeping well tonight. **7.** The new play will have opened later this month. **8.** She will be planning a surprise party for her friend. **9.** Mrs. Garcia will be leaving for Detroit next week. **10.** The team will be ready for opening day.

Activity 69–Negatives

1–10. Answers will vary. Check to make sure that not or never is placed correctly in the answer.

Activity 70–Verbs

1. began **2.** did **3.** drunk **4.** break **5.** brought **6.** came **7.** driven **8.** ate **9.** eaten **10.** eat **11.** given **12.** gave **13.** caught **14.** brought **15.** begun

Activity 71–Writing Practice

Answers will vary.

Activity 72–Change to Contractions

1. you've **2.** I'll **3.** you'd **4.** shouldn't **5.** won't **6.** they'll **7.** they've **8.** isn't **9.** don't **10.** I'd **11.** it'll **12.** wouldn't **13.** I'm **14.** she's **15.** couldn't **16.** it's **17.** we'd **18.** aren't **19.** didn't **20.** doesn't **21–25.** Answers will vary. Check to make sure a contraction is used in each sentence.

Activity 73–Writing for Yourself

1. Apolo Anton Ohno—speed skater, gold medal at 2002 Winter Olympics **2.** Male polar bears—weigh 775–1,500 pounds; female polar bears—weigh 330–550 pounds **3.** 3:00 P.M. **4.** no **5.** buy stamps and mail letters

Activity 74–Accept, Except; Teach, Learn

1. accept **2.** teach **3.** except **4.** teach **5.** except **6.** accepted, except **7.** teach **8.** except, accepted **9.** except **10.** except, learn **11.** Accept, learn **12.** except **13.** taught **14.** taught **15.** except

Activity 75–Sentences with *Their, There,* and *They're*

1. there **2.** their **3.** their **4.** they're **5.** There **6.** there **7.** their **8.** their **9.** They're **10.** their **11.** Did they bring their children over? **12.** Their house is being remodeled **13.** They're not coming to the party. **14.** We walked over to their house. **15.** They're coming to my house for dinner.

Activity 76–*Lie, Lay, Sit, Set; Rise, Raise*

1. raise **2.** lay **3.** lays **4.** sat **5.** rise **6.** Set, sit **7.** lie **8.** Raise, rise **9.** lay, raise **10.** sits, rises **11.** raise **12.** lie **13.** set **14.** sit, rise **15.** lie

Activity 77–Practice with *Too, Two, To; Let, Leave*

1. too, two **2.** Let **3.** leave, too **4.** to, let, too **5.** Leave **6.** too **7.** leave, too **8.** Two, let, too **9.** Leave, two, too **10.** Let, too **11.** Let **12.** Let **13.** Two, too **14.** Leave, too **15.** Leave

Activity 78–Double Negatives

1. any **2.** any **3.** any **4.** anything **5.** any **6.** ever **7.** has **8.** any **9.** anything **10.** anywhere **11.** any **12.** anything **13.** anymore **14.** anywhere **15.** any

Activity 79–Writing Practice

Answers will vary.

Activity 80–Writing Mechanics

1. The clock stopped at 10:21 A.M. when the power went out. **2.** The New York train leaves at 6:00 A.M. today. **3.** Gene met Don's flight at 4 o'clock. **4.** The plane left at 3:00 P.M. on August 21. **5.** The red-eye flight left at 1:15 A.M. on Monday. **6.** Sunday **7.** Wednesday **8.** Monday **9.** Thursday **10.** Tuesday **11.** From early fall until late December, Donna watches football. **12.** Jerome's school closes for two weeks in February. **13.** A big cruise ship arrived in Florida at 3:00 A.M. on Monday. **14.** The Sutton Theater is on Main Streeet. **15.** The show starts at 1:30 P.M. today.

Activity 81–Tone of Voice

1–15. Answers will vary. Check to make sure that end punctuation is used correctly.

Activity 82–Beth's Package

1–5. Answers will vary. Check to make sure quotation marks are used correctly.

Activity 83–Questions

	Subject	Verb	Adverb
1.	Subject: you	Verb: did go	
2.	Subject: flight	Verb: is	
3.	Subject: box	Verb: does open	
4.	Subject: shoe	Verb: is	Adverb: where
5.	Subject: sweater	Verb: fits	
6.	Subject: shirt	Verb: looks	Adverb: best
7.	Subject: dinner	Verb: is	Adverb: late
8.	Subject: team	Verb: has lost	Adverb: lately
9.	Subject: cats	Verb: will happen	Adverb: now
10.	Subject: you	Verb: atttend	Adverb: today

Activity 84–Compound and Complex Sentences

Underline the independent clause, bold the dependent clause, and circle the conjunction.

1. <u>Tina ate a salad</u> (because) **she wasn't very hungry.**
2. <u>I stopped at the library</u> (before) **the dry cleaning shop.**
3. <u>Christie took my car</u> (while) **I was sleeping.**
4. <u>Could you work for me on Friday</u> (so) **that I could go to the fair?**
5. <u>George watched</u> TV (while) **Victoria cooked dinner.**
6. compound-complex **7.** compound **8.** compound **9.** compound
10. complex

Activity 85–More About Complex Sentences

1. Frank, <u>who works two jobs</u>, goes to bed early. **2.** <u>Because they like cats</u>, CJ and grace own several. **3.** <u>Whatever road she took</u>, Hetal became lost. **4.** This gift is for Alia, <u>who lives in another state.</u>
5. <u>Since I have to go out tomorrow</u>, I will stop at the store.
6. dependent clause **7.** prepositional phrase **8.** dependent clause
9. prepositional phrase **10.** prepositional phrase. **11.** Anthony, who is a good swimmer, practices daily. **12.** The plant won't bloom unless it is watered often. **13.** The news anchor gets nervous whenever he appears on TV. **14.** Belinda studied the math problem until she understood it. **15.** Darlene drives a new car, which was expensive.

Activity 86–Good Quotations

Correct each verb. Then rewrite the sentences using correct punctuation.
1. is—Jim told me that he is going to another school. **2.** are—"We are ready for bed," said the children. **3.** run—The coach said, "Cameron has run several laps." **4.** is—Her mother told me that Angela is walking her dog. **5.** is—His brother said, "Jeremiah is playing another game today."

Activity 87–In the Woods

1–5. Answers will vary. Check to make sure that correct punctuation is used.

Activity 88–Writing Mechanics

1. "What great shrimp this is," Bill said **2.** "It's my secret family recipe," replied Luis. **3.** Angie said, "Your family has some great secrets." **4.** "He's a fine cook," said Ben, who loves good food.
5. "Come back when you can eat more," Alice said. **6–10.** Answers will vary. Check to make sure the verbs vary.

Activity–89 Ricky Found Something

Answers will vary.

Activity–90 Facts Make News

Answers will vary.

Activity 91–My Favorite Food

Answers will vary.

Activity 92–Writing a Process Paragraph

Answers will vary. Check to make sure that all steps are in the correct order.

Activity 93–Are Cats Doggone Good?

Answers will vary. Check to make sure that the writing process is followed.

Activity 94–A New Friend

Answers will vary.

Activity 95–Writing a Review

Answers will vary. Check to make sure that the writing process is followed.

Activity 96–Writing a Letter to a Friend

1. Trent's **2.** April 15, 2006 **3.** Answers will vary. **4.** Answers will vary. **5.** See you soon!, an exclamation point.

Activity 97–Writing Mechanics

1.   MRS MARIA GARCIA
     4421 SOUTH SECOND STREET
     COLUMBUS OH 43201
2.   MR TERRENCE PAYNE
     6949 KINGSTON CIRCLE
     BANGOR ME 04401
3.   MR ABU JAMAL
     1229 GROVE AVENUE
     SAN ANTONIO TX 78295
4.   MISS ELISE CHARPIER
     401 ANDERS ROAD
     CHESAPEAKE VA 23324
5.   MR CRAIG SAUNDERS
     362 RAYMOND DRIVE
     SACRAMENTO CA 95864

Activity 98–Words for Your Spelling List

1–5. Answers will vary.

Activity 99–Homonyms

1. sea **2.** see **3.** buy **4.** by **5.** deer **6.** dear **7.** break **8.** brake **9.** blue
10. blue

Activity 100–Words that Sound Alike

1. piece **2.** peace **3.** read **4.** red **5.** some, sum **6.** threw **7.** some
8. through **9.** piece **10.** red

Activity 101–Plurals—Two or More

1. boys **2.** ties **3.** donkeys **4.** foxes **5.** shoes **6.** halves **7.** yourselves
8. wolves **9.** elves **10.** knives **11.** The divers hit the water between two waves. **12.** I read four books about deer this summer. **13.** The police chiefs met to talk about the thieves with knives. **14.** Three calves ran from two wolves. **15.** Both children have problems with their teeth.

Activity 102–Other Word Endings

1. storage **2.** placement **3.** daring **4.** hopeful **5.** nameless **6.** arrival
7. driving **8.** statement **9.** cuteness **10.** hiking **11.** fatten **12.** stirred
13. hottest **14.** sadder **15.** skipping **16.** planned **17.** runner
18. wettest **19.** grabbed **20.** knitting

Activity 103–Words with *ie* or *ei*

1. sl<u>ei</u>gh **2.** dr<u>ie</u>d **3.** s<u>ei</u>ze **4.** p<u>ie</u>ce **5.** qu<u>ie</u>t **6.** t<u>ie</u> **7.** gr<u>ie</u>f **8.** fr<u>ie</u>nd
9. br<u>ie</u>f **10.** p<u>ie</u> **11.** w<u>ei</u>rd **12.** ach<u>ie</u>ve **13.** s<u>ie</u>ge **14.** sc<u>ie</u>nce **15.** al<u>ie</u>n
16. Two wolves bared their teeth and howled at the moon.
17. Today is a good day for a picnic. **18.** My neighbor has a good view. **19.** Analise believes in aliens. **20.** Russ believes his dream will come true.

Activity 104–Words that Look Similar

1. loose, lose **2.** quiet **3.** dessert **4.** quite **5.** cloths **6.** breath
7. already **8.** dairy **9.** all ready **10.** quit **11.** respectable
12. respective **13.** respectful **14.** later **15.** latter

Activity 105–Writing Mechanics

1. well **2.** good **3.** good **4.** well, better **5.** best **6.** better **7.** more
8. more, harder **9.** fastest **10.** most **11.** most **12.** best **13.** more
14. more **15.** fewer

Activity 106–Make Verbs Agree with Subjects

1. wants **2.** slices **3.** fall **4.** drop **5.** play **6.** curls **7.** clatter **8.** read
9. shine **10.** rumble **11.** shoots **12.** slams **13.** stay **14.** fall **15.** cuts
16. burns **17.** lifts **18.** works **19.** graze **20.** shops

Activity 107–Subject and Verb Agreement

1. are **2.** have **3.** are **4.** were **5.** are **6.** has **7.** is **8.** were **9.** are **10.** was
11. are **12.** handle **13.** were **14.** are **15.** is **16.** squeal **17.** Are
18. Does **19.** go **20.** play

Activity 108–Pronoun Subjects with Verb Agreement

1. Underline **Many**, circle **are**, underline **few**, circle **are 2.** Underline
Somebody, circle **tells 3.** Underline **Both**, circle **see 4.** Underline
One, circle **has 5.** Underline **Everything**, circle **has 6.** Underline
Most, circle **leave 7.** Underline **Nobody**, circle **wants 8.** Underline
Some, circle **are 9.** Underline **None**, circle **smells 10.** Underline
everyone, circle **was 11.** Underline **Others**, circle **leave**
12. Underline **Some**, circle **needs 13.** Underline **Most**, circle **die**
14. Underline **Each**, circle **expects 15.** Underline **Neither**, circle
likes 16–20. Answers will vary. Check to make sure each word is
used only once.

Activity 109–Pronoun-Noun Agreement

Complete each sentence with an owner pronoun. Circle the word(s)
to which the pronoun refers.
1. circle Wayne—his **2.** circle Lance and I—our **3.** circle you—your
4. circle I—my **5.** circle student—his or her **6.** circle Michiko and
Sonja—their **7.** circle Warren—his **8.** circle Maggie—her **9.** circle
we—our **10.** circle worker—his or her **11.** are **12.** were **13.** is
14. makes **15.** stops

Activity 110–*Don't* and *Doesn't*

1. doesn't **2.** doesn't **3.** don't **4.** don't **5.** doesn't **6.** doesn't **7.** doesn't
8. doesn't **9.** don't **10.** doesn't **11.** doesn't **12.** don't **13.** don't
14. doesn't **15.** doesn't **16.** doesn't **17.** don't **18.** don't **19.** don't
20. doesn't

Activity 111–One Word Makes a Difference

1. B **2.** A **3.** A **4.** A **5.** B

Activity 112–Fine-Tune this Story

Answers will vary.

Activity 113–Writing Mechanics

Answers will vary. Check to make sure that standard English is used.

Alternative Activities

Alternative Activity 1–Make a Sentence

1–8 Answers may vary. Check to make sure that subjects agree with
predicates. **9–15** Answers may vary. Check to make sure that
predicates agree with subjects.

Alternative Activity 2–Find the Nouns

1. Children shout. **2.** Truckers drive. **3.** Cats hiss. **4.** Fire burns
5. Diamonds sparkle.
Circle the nouns. On the line write if the noun is a *person, place* or
thing.
6. Dogs bark.—thing **7.** Teens skate—person **8.** Cities grow—
place **9.** Singers hum—person **10.** Trucks move—thing.
Circle the noun in each group.
11. Lakes, beach **12.** trees, birds **13.** puddle **14.** sun **15.** song

Alternative Activity 3–Adjectives

Circle the adjective and underline each noun.
1. Cold rain falls. **2.** Wide rivers flow. **3.** Large eagles fly. **4.** Fast
swimmers race. **5.** Young people dance. **6.** Hungry children eat.
7. Noisy frogs croaked.
8. The **9.** The **10.** An **11.** A **12.** The **13.** A **14.** A **15.** The

Alternative Activity 4–Action Verbs

Draw a line under each action verb.
1. Happy people laugh. **2.** Cold winds blow. **3.** Big trees sway.
4. Heavy snow falls. **5.** A large seal plays. **6.** The tired baby cries.
7. Loud alarms blare. **8.** noun **9.** adjective **10.** noun **11.** adjective
12. adjective **13.** noun **14.** verb **15.** adjective

Alternative Activity 5–Adverbs

Circle each adverb and underline the verb.
1. The river runs rapidly. **2.** The girl spoke quietly. **3.** Small
animals run quickly. **4.** The young man works hard. **5.** The ship
sailed easily **6.** Loudly, the dogs bark. **12.** Suddenly, the plane
lands. **8.** Nervously, the woman sang. **9.** Steadily, the climber moved.
10. Happily, the children played.

Alternative Activity 6–Adverbs That Tell "When"

Circle the Adverb. Underline each verb.
1. The big crowd yelled often. **2.** Sometimes the tiny bird chirps.
3. The old car traveled often. **4.** Today a large ship sailed.
5. Yesterday two trains left. **6–10.** Answers may vary. Check to
make sure that the adverb makes sense in the sentence.

Alternative Activity 7–Kinds of Adverbs

Write the adverb on the line. Mark if the adverb tells *how, when* or
where.
1. today, when **2.** rapidly, how **3.** brightly, how **4.** upstairs, where
5. here, where

Alternative Activity 8–Subject and Predicate, Adjective and Adverb

Draw a line under the complete subject. Circle the complete
predicate. Adjectives are bolded. Adverbs are italicized.
1. **A large, golden** sun, sank *slowly.* **2.** Laura *always* finishes *first.*
3. **The high school** opens *early.* **4.** Jose *often* sleeps *late.*
5. The **fast** car, runs *smoothly.*

Alternative Activity 9–Sentence or Fragment?

1. sentence **2.** fragment **3.** fragment **4.** fragment **5.** sentence
6–10. Answers will vary. Check to make sure that all are complete sentences.

Alternative Activity 10–Practicing Punctuation

Add commas to separate adjectives.
1. The bright, hot fire crackled. **2.** Tired, happy campers sang. **3.** A light, cool breeze blew. **4.** Large, bright lights shine. **5.** The small, red bugs ran **6.** Big, fluffy clouds float. **7.** The old, blue car crashed. **8.** Quietly, the cat crept away. **9.** Small, cute dogs play. **10.** Sleek, shiny airplanes fly.

Alternative Activity 11–Prepositional Phrases

1–5. Answers will vary. Check to make sure that the preposition makes sense in the sentence. **6–10.** Answers will vary. Possible answers follow. **6.** against the fence. **7.** under the table. **8.** during the game. **9.** along the beach. **10.** behind the tree.

Alternative Activity 12–Adjective Prepositional Phrases

Underline the complete subject. Draw a circle around the verb. Write the prepositional phrase in each sentence. Write the word it describes.
1. The sun behind some clouds (shines) weakly—behind some clouds—sun **2.** Janice in the leaky board (rows) hard—in the leaky boat—Janice **3.** Clouds with rain (move) briskly—with rain—clouds
Underline the adjective prepositional phrase. Circle the noun it describes.
4. Sarah with Janice heads back. **5.** The poor friends inside the boat shiver.

Alternative Activity 13–Confusing Subjects

Circle the prepositional phrase. Underline the simple subject.
1. Light (from the sun) shines brightly. **2.** A boat (on the lake) roars past. **3.** Shadows (from tall trees) grow quickly. **4.** A tall pile (of books) falls. **5.** A group (of men) sing loudly. **6–10.** Answers will vary. Possible answers follow. **6.** near the window **7.** with a backpack **8.** with a hat on **9.** in the yard **10.** in the field

Alternative Activity 14–Adverb Prepositional Phrases

Underline the complete subject. Draw a circle around the verb. Write the prepositional phrase.
1. Andy (left) during the game—during the game **2.** A group of teens (drove) around the city—around the city **3.** The stars (shone) brightly across the sky—across the sky **4.** The car (went) through a tunnel—through a tunnel **5.** Lightning (flashed) across the dark sky—across the dark sky

Alternative Activity 15–Preposition or Adverb?

Underline the verb. Decide if the bold word is an adverb or preposition then write either on the line.
1. The cat wakes **up** in the empty house.—adverb **2.** the cat plays **with** the string.—preposition **3.** The string lays **on** the floor.—preposition **4.** His paw reached **out** for the ball.—adverb **5.** The small ball **of** string lays under the table. —preposition
Draw a line under the adverb, bold the prepositional phrase and circle the verb.
6. The bicycle rider (rode) quickly **around the lake. 7.** He (stopped) across **from the park. 8.** The bicycle rider (looked) around **for the picnic area. 14.** The children (ate) happily **in the park. 15.** They (played) freely **on the playground.**

Alternative Activity 16–Adjective and Adverb Prepositional phrases

Underline the simple subject, draw a circle around the verb, and write the prepositional phrase. Decide if they are adverb or adjective phrases.
1. A tall man (climbed) into the taxi—into the taxi, adverb **2.** Her new ring (sparkled) in the light—in the light, adverb **3.** The test tube (fell) out of his hands **4.** The liquid (dripped) onto the floor. **5.** The doctor (wiped) up the spill.

Alternative Activity 17–Hidden Verbs

State-of-being verb is bolded. Circle the prepositional phrase.
1. Alicia **is** a great student at school. **2.** Brandon **became** a good player on his team. **3.** They **are** the best team (at the school.) **4.** That new show **is** (on TV.) **5.** The tired dog **remains** (on the floor.)
Circle the prepositional phrase. Draw a line under the subject noun. Bold the state-of-being verb.
6. Maria **appears** tired (at work.) **7.** Thao and Reggie **were** (on the soccer team.) **8.** Soon, Mai **will be** (in Manitoba.) **9.** The large dog (around the block) **seems** friendly. **10.** The girls **are** (by the fence.)

Alternative Activity 18–Two Kinds of Prepositional Phrases

Circle each prepositional phrase. Draw an arrow from the phrase to the word it describes.
1. The boys went (to the movies) (with their parents.)
2. Tabitha (with her dog) walked (to the lake.) **3.** A **4.** B **5.** B

Alternative Activity 19–Writing Mechanics

1. x **2.** x **3.** Virginia **4.** x **5.** Indiana **6.** Central Park **7.** Houston **8.** x **9.** Mars **10.** x **11.** Beyond the hill, the sun shone brightly. **12.** In the water, fish swim. **13.** On the street, music plays. **14.** During the long cold winter, this lake freezes. **15.** At the party, people dance happily.

Alternative Activity 20–Conjunctions

Answers may vary. Possible answers follow.
1. and **2.** or **3.** as well as **4.** but **5.** and **6.** Both, and **7.** Neither, nor **8.** either, or **9.** both, and **10.** Not only, but also

Alternative Activity 21–Compound Subjects

Underline the simple subjects. Circle the conjunction.
1. The paper (and) pencils are on the table. **2.** LaToya (and) Annika went to the art store. **3.** Mario (and) Kyle shopped for school clothes. **4.** Families (and) friends gathered at the park. **5.** The cat (and) the dog slept on the floor.
Underline the compound subject. Circle the conjunction.
6. A robin, a cardinal, (and) a bluebird flew by the house. **7.** Two young women (and) one man get off of the bus. **8.** Lions, zebras, (and) monkeys live at the zoo. **9.** Two blue cars, one yellow car, (and) two red cars raced around the track. **10.** Two squirrels (and) an owl are in the tree.

Alternative Activity 22–Compound Subjects and Predicates

1–5, 6–10. Answers will vary.

Alternative Activity 23–Compound Objects of Prepositions

1–5. Answers will vary.
Underline the objects of prepositions. Circle the preposition.
6. The house (with) a blue door and a pink fence was sold. **7.** A large dog ran (through) the streets and the yard. **8.** The visitor (with) the long coat and the dark hat entered the house. **9.** Natasha likes her

316   *Answer Key*

sandwich (with) lettuce and tomatoes. **10.** The girls walked (around) the lake and the park.

Alternative Activity 24–Compound Sentences
1–5. Answers will vary.

Alternative Activity 25–Compounds
Draw a circle around each prepositional phrase in the story.
Circle *in the pool, on the tennis court, in the sun, to the radio, over the pool and lawn, into the ball, over the net, off the court, through the day, in the sun*
Possible answers:
1. lazily, up, hard, high
2. Tara and Abria
3. Swims and plays, sails and bounces, lies and listens
4. pool and lawn
5. Answers will vary. Check for the use of compounds.

Alternative Activity 26–Writing Mechanics
1. Actors run, jump, and dance on the stage. **2.** Flies, bugs, and mice hide under the old house. **3.** Fans often yell, jump, and stomp at a big game. **4–5.** Answers will vary. Check to make sure one sentence uses a conjunction and the other uses a semicolon.

Alternative Activity 27–Subject + Verb + Direct Object
1. broke → window **2.** watched → truck **3.** watched → television
4. struck → tree **5.** fixed → tire

Alternative Activity 28–Find and Combine the Parts
1. Circle drum, horn, music, and hands. **2.** Possible answers: Across the grass, on the band, at the quiet park **3.** away **4.** Answers will vary. **5.** Answers will vary.

Alternative Activity 29–More compounds
1. NC **2.** C **3.** C **4.** CDO **5.** CV **6.** both **7.** C sentence **8.** CDO
9. CV **10.** CS

Alternative Activity 30–Direct Objects and Prepositions
Underline each verb. Draw a circle around each direct object. Write each prepositional phrase.
1. The black cat carried the (mouse) into the kitchen—into the kitchen **2.** The dog chased the (cat) toward the sink—toward the sink. **3.** The cat bit the (dog) and jumped into the air—into the air **4.** The cat chased the (dog) around the kitchen—around the kitchen **5.** The cat climbed up the curtain and crawled out the window—up the curtain—out the window

Alternative Activity 31–Nouns in a Sentence
Circle the nouns that are subjects. Underline the nouns that are direct objects. Draw a box around the nouns that are objects of a preposition.
1. (Mario) throws his hook into the water. **2.** A (fish) watches the big hook above him. **3.** The (fish) sniffs the bait on the hook. **4.** A long (line) in the water warns the fish. **5.** The (fish) swims away, and (Mario) lifts the bait from the water. **6.** concrete **7.** abstract
8. abstract **9.** abstract **10.** concrete

Alternative Activity 32–Pronouns in a Sentence
Circle the correct pronoun
1. we **2.** He, them **3.** him **4.** He, I **5.** She, them **6.** OP **7.** OP **8.** NP
9. OP **10.** NP

Alternative Activity 33–Using Pronouns
1. Beth chatted with her. **2.** He walked Oma and Rita to the car.
3. Melinda bought an apple and ate it on the bus. **4.** Daniel saw them at the concert. **5.** Otto bought a book and left it at school
6. herself **7.** myself **8.** themselves **9.** yourself **10.** ourselves

Alternative Activity 34–Pronoun or Adjective?
Underline each adjective and draw an arrow to the noun it describes.
1. Many → families; two → cars **2.** Some → people; many → cars
3. Each → person; favorite → car; **4.** One → man; sports → car;
5. Another → man; all → cars **6.** adjective **7.** pronoun **8.** pronoun
9. pronoun **10.** adjective

Alternative Activity 35–This, That, These, Those
1. this **2.** these **3.** that **4.** adjective **5.** adjective **6.** pronoun **7.** Those
8. These **9.** That **10.** This

Alternative Activity 36–Writing Mechanics
1–8. Answers will vary. **9.** Ms. Graham **10.** Nelson Mandela
11. Toronto SkyDome **12.** Dr. Koua Nguyen **13.** Mr. Thomas called for my father, but he was not at home. **14.** Ms. Dai went to dinner with Ms. Abel, Ms. Elias, and Ms. Ato-Case. **15.** The thunder boomed; the lightning flashed.

Alternative Activity 37–What Are the Parts?
1. verb, preposition **2.** conjunction, verb **3.** noun, noun **4.** verb, adjective **5.** noun, noun

Alternative Activity 38–Owners
1. Alec's **2.** woman's **3.** Isaac's **4.** Tomas' **5.** family's

Alternative Activity 39–Owner Pronouns
1. (her) → sister **2.** (his) → team and (its) → place **3.** (Our) → boat
4. (Your) → friend, (his) → brother, and (my) → cousin.
5. (your) → friend and (my) → car. **6.** its **7.** your **8.** our **9.** his
10. their

Alternative Activity 40–More Than One Owner
1. flowers' **2.** houses' **3.** boys' **4.** cats' **5.** He ran down the street.

Alternative Activity 41–Where is the Subject?
Write the subject. Then write the complete sentence.
1. you—You watch the scary movie. **2.** You—You kick the starter on your dirt bike. **3.** Watch, kick **4.** movie, starter **5.** Answers will vary.

Alternative Activity 42–More About Adverbs
1. awfully—deep, adjective **2.** So—long, adjective **3.** quite—slowly, adverb **4.** rather—quickly, adverb **5.** really—serious, adjective
6–10. Answers will vary. Possible answers follow. **6.** awfully
7. unusually **8.** quite **9.** almost **10.** rather

Alternative Activity 43–Interjections
1–10. Answers will vary. Possible answers follow **1.** Wow **2.** Hey
3. Hello **4.** Hooray **5.** Boy **6–10.** Answers will vary. **11.** adverb
12. interjection **13.** adverb **14.** interjection **15.** interjection

Alternative Activity 44–Write About Your Day
Answers will vary.

Alternative Activity 45–Writing Mechanics
1. Jesse will start classes at the Lincoln School of Excellence on Monday. **2.** Tony will play in Jonah's band tonight. **3–5.** Answer will vary. Possible answers follow. **3.** Well, it is good to see you. **4.** Yikes! I almost stepped on a big snake! **5.** Gee, you have the best grades in your class.

Alternative Activity 46–Indirect Objects
Draw a line under the complete subject. Draw a circle around the verb. Write the indirect object and the direct object.
1. They paid the clerk five dollars.—Indirect object: clerk—Direct object: dollars **2.** The clerk gave them a dollar change.—Indirect object: them—Direct object: change **3.** indirect object **4.** direct object **5.** indirect object.

Alternative Activity 47–Indirect Objects in Long Sentences
Underline the indirect object.
1. daughter **2.** mother **3.** Melina **4.** parents **5.** Rowena **6.** An S above **Sid**, a **V** above **told**, an **IO** above **teacher**, a **DO** above **story** **7.** An S above **Dwayne**, a **V** above **taught**, an **IO** above **group**, a **DO** above **way**. **8.** An S above **Cheryl**, a **V** above **fixed**, an **IO** above **Fiona**, a **DO** above **dinner**. **9.** An S above **Gary & Debra**, a **V** above **gave**, an **IO** above **friend**, a **DO** above **watch**. **10.** An S above **Adams**, a **V** above **left**, an **IO** above **son**, a **DO** above **acres**

Alternative Activity 48–Object Complements
Draw a line under the complete subject. Draw a circle around the verb. Write the direct object and object complement.
1. The rainbow (made) people happy. Direct object: **people** Object complement: **happy 2.** Storm clouds (turned) the sky black Direct object: **sky** Object complement: **black 3.** The artist (painted) her canvas gray. Direct object: **grass** Object complement: **gray 4.** Ann (likes) summers hot. Direct object: **summers** Object complement: **hot 5.** The band leader (played) his music loud. Direct object: **music** Object complement: **loud**

Alternative Activity 49–Review Four Sentence Patterns
Underline the prepositional phrases, circle the words that tell you the sentence pattern.
1. The town accepted the idea in one vote.—subject + verb + direct object **2.** In the cafe, Tim, finds fish and chips tasty—subject + verb + direct object + direct object + object complement **3.** By the gate near the school, two boys, played—subject + verb **4.** Ed told Steve the good news—subject + verb + indirect object + direct object **5.** The anglers found the lake rough, the wind cold, the boat leaky, and the fish, gone—subject + verb + direct object + object complement + direct object + object complement + direct object + object complement + direct object + object complement

Alternative Activity 50–Appositives
Circle the appositive, underline the noun.
1. Her car, (a red sports car,) is parked over there. **2.** My brother (Simon) kicks for the football team. **3.** My friend (Eva) is going on vacation. **7.** The pilot, (a brave person,) flew the plane safely through the storm. **4.** His cousin, (Steve,) moved to Canada. **5.** Ida, (my aunt,) came to visit me from Florida. **6–10.** Answers will vary. Check for an appositive in each sentence.

Alternative Activity 51–Writing Practice
1–3. Answers will vary. Check to see if each sentence contains a subject and a direct object. **4–5.** Answers will vary.

Alternative Activity 52–Punctuate and Capitalize
Rewrite the sentences correctly. End punctuation may vary.
1. Patrick's car, an older model, wins prizes everywhere. **2.** Wow! Its paint looks new. **3.** Patrick and his friend, Helena, washed the car each week. **4.** Patrick puts hard work, care, and money into his car. **5.** Patrick, a hard worker, earns his prizes.

Alternative Activity 53–Noun Subject Complements
Draw a line under the complete subject. Draw a circle around the verb. Write the subject noun and the noun subject complement.
1. The fastest girl in the class (is) Shandra—Subject Noun: **girl**—Noun subject complement: **Shandra 2.** A great book in the library (is) *The Hero.* —Subject Noun: **book**—Noun subject complement: *The Hero* **3.** In the last race, the fastest boat (was) "The Shadow" —Subject Noun: **boat**—Noun subject complement: "The Shadow" **4.** My best subject (is) math. —Subject Noun: **subject**—Noun subject complement: **math 5.** First prize (is) a ski trip. —Subject Noun: **prize**—Noun subject complement: **ski trip**

Alternative Activity 54–Appositives with Subject Complements
Draw a circle around the verb. Write the subject noun, the appositive, and the subject complement. Tell if the complement is a noun or an adjective.
1. (are)—Subject noun: crowds—Appositive: people from everywhere—Complement: visitors—noun **2.** (is)—Subject noun: dessert—Appositive: A special treat—Complement: frozen yogurt—noun **3.** (is)—Subject noun: car—Appositive: a beautiful red machine—Complement: fast—adjective **4.** (is)—Subject noun: Luke—Appositive: A great basketball player—Complement: tall and quick—adjective **5.** (is)—Subject noun: lake—Appositive: a huge body of water—Complement: dark blue—adjective

Alternative Activity 55–Adjective Subject Complements
Draw a line under the complete subject. Draw a circle around the verb. Write the subject noun and the adjective subject complement.
1. Sandy's beautiful new watch (was) expensive.—Subject noun: watch—Adjective subject complement: expensive **2.** The rain during this month (is) heavy.—Subject noun: rain—Adjective subject complement: heavy **3.** Rosie's new blue shoes (are) tight.—Subject noun: shoes—Adjective subject complement: tight **4.** Our new science class (is) very hard.—Subject noun: course—Adjective subject complement: hard **5.** The big dogs in Ellie's yard (are) hungry.—Subject noun: dogs—Adjective subject complement: hungry

Alternative Activity 56–Adjectives Describe Nouns
Circle the adjectives that describe the nouns in bold.
1. hot, spicy **2.** fresh, green, tasty **3–5.** Answers will vary. Check to see if two sentences use sentence pattern A and one sentence uses sentence pattern B.

Alternative Activity 57–Adjective or Adverb
1. good, well **2.** slowly, slow **3.** honest, honestly **4.** quietly, quiet **5.** quick, quickly

Alternative Activity 58–Subject Complements
Draw a line under the simple subject. Draw a circle around the verb. Write the subject complement. Tell if is a noun or an adjective subject complement.
1. The Laser (is) the best car for the race.—Subject complement: best car—Noun **2.** Derek and Mia (were) class officers last year.—Subject

complement: class officers—Noun **3.** The fruit <u>crop</u> (is) not good this year. .—Subject complement: not good—Adjective **4.** <u>Otto</u> (is) a mean dog.—Subject complement: mean dog—Noun **5.** Duncan's <u>songs</u> (are) old.—Subject complement: old—Adjective

Alternative Activity 59–Pronouns in Subject Complement Sentences

Write S above the subject pronoun, LV above the linking verb and NSC above the noun subject complement.
1. Put an *S* above *This*, an *LV* above *is*, an *NSC* above *book* **2.** Put an *S* above *That*, an *LV* above *is*, an *NSC* above *question.* **3.** Put an *S* above *It* an *LV* above *was*, an *NSC* above *deal.* **4.** Put an *S* above *These*, an *LV* above *are*, an *NSC* above *gifts.* **5.** Put an *S* above *That*, an *LV* above *is*, an *NSC* above *dress*
Circle the subject of each sentence.
6. There **7.** Here **8.** There **9.** Here **10.** There

Alternative Activity 60–More Pronouns

1. him **2.** her **3.** us **4.** They **5.** it **6.** mine **7.** hers **8.** ours **9.** his **10.** theirs

Alternative Activity 61–Reviewing Sentence Patterns

1. C **2.** E **3.** E **4.** D **5.** A **6.** B **7.** D **8.** F **9.** A **10.** D

Alternative Activity 62–Writing Practice

1–5. Answers will vary. Check to see if subjects, adjectives and subject complements are present.

Alternative Activity 63–Adjectives that Compare

1. faster **2.** smallest **3.** tall, taller **4.** wet, wetter **5.** loudest **6.** bigger **7.** hungriest **8.** happier **9.** prettier **10.** worst **11.** more **12.** least **13.** harder **14.** better **15.** better

Alternative Activity 64–Another Look at Verbs

Circle the verb. Write whether it is an action or a linking verb.
1. circle tastes-linking verb **2.** circle are-linking verb **3.** circle kicked-action verb **4.** circle watched-action verb **5.** past tense **6.** present tense **7.** future tense **8.** liked **9.** biked **10.** will look

Alternative Activity 65–Problem Verb: *Be*

1. is, had been or was, will be **2.** is, has been, will be **3.** is, has been, had been or was **4.** has been, had been or was, will be **5.** is, has been, will be

Alternative Activity 66–Verbs Tell Time

1. They are going with us every day. **2.** Peter and Joni are washing the car. **3.** I am waiting for you on the steps. **4.** Lots of people are getting on the airplane. **5.** We are standing in the line for the movie.

Alternative Activity 67–Verbs Tell Past Time

1. I was walking to the bus station. **2.** They had climbed down the ladder. **3.** Andrew and Cecil were visiting yesterday. **4.** Pilar had been missing her dog for two months. **5.** Rollo had spotted a new coat in the window.

Alternative Activity 68–The Future Tense

1. Lots of people will be going to that party on Friday. **2.** Everyone will be laughing tonight at the movie. **3.** Sandra will be moving away soon. **4.** Terry will be sleeping well tonight. **5.** Mrs. Garcia will be leaving for Detroit next week.

Alternative Activity–69 Negatives

1–5. Answers will vary. Check to make sure that *not* or *never* is placed correctly in the answer.

Alternative Activity–70 Verbs

1. began **2.** did **3.** drunk **4.** break **5.** brought **6.** came **7.** driven **8.** ate **9.** given **12.** gave **10.** caught

Alternative Activity 71–Writing Practice

Answers will vary.

Alternative Activity 72–Change to Contractions

1. you've **2.** I'll **3.** shouldn't **4.** won't **5.** they'll **6.** They've **7.** isn't **8.** don't **9.** It'll **10.** wouldn't **11.** I'm **12.** she's **13.** couldn't **14.** it's **15.** aren't **16.** doesn't **17–20.** Answers will vary. Check to make sure a contraction is used in each sentence.

Alternative Activity 73–Writing for Yourself

1. Apolo Anton Ohno—speed skater, gold medal at 2002 Winter Olympics **2.** Male polar bears—weigh 775-1500 pounds; female polar bears—weigh 330-550 pounds **3.** 3:00 PM **4.** no **5.** buy stamps and mail letters

Alternative Activity 74–*Accept, Except; Teach, Learn*

1. accept **2.** teach **3.** except **4.** except **5.** accepted, except **6.** except, accepted **7.** except **8.** except, learn **9.** taught **10.** except

Alternative Activity 75–Sentences with *Their, There,* and *They're*

1. there **2.** their **3.** their **4.** they're **5.** There **6.** Did they bring their children over? **7.** Their house is being remodeled **8.** They're not coming to the party. **9.** We walked over to their house. **10.** They're coming to my house for dinner.

Alternative Activity 76–*Lie, Lay, Sit, Set; Rise, Raise*

1. raise **2.** lays **3.** sat **4.** rise **5.** Set, sit **6.** laid **7.** sits, rises **8.** lie **9.** sit, rise **10.** lie

Alternative Activity 77–Practice with *Too, Two, To; Let, Leave*

1. too, two **2.** Let **3.** leave, too **4.** to, let, too **5.** leave, too **6.** Leave, two, too **7.** Let, too **8.** Let **9.** Leave, too **10.** Leave

Alternative Activity 78–Double Negatives

1. any **2.** any **3.** ever **4.** has **5.** anywhere **6.** any **7.** anything **8.** anymore **9.** anywhere **10.** any

Alternative Activity 79–Writing Practice

Answers will vary.

Alternative Activity 80–Writing Mechanics

1. The clock stopped at 10:21 A.M. when the power went out. **2.** The New York train leaves at 6:00 A.M. today. **3.** The plane left at 3:00 P.M. on August 21. **4.** Sunday **5.** Wednesday **6.** Thursday **7.** From early fall until late December, Donna watches football. **8.** A big ship arrived in Florida at 3:00 A.M. on Monday. **9.** The Sutton Theater is on Main Streeet. **10.** The show starts at 1:30 P.M. today.

Alternative Activity 81–Tone of Voice

1–10. Answers will vary. Check to make sure that end punctuation is used correctly.

Alternative Activity 82–Beth's Package

1–5. Answers will vary. Check to make sure quotation marks are used correctly.

Alternative Activity 83–Questions
1. Subject: you   Verb: did go
2. Subject: box   Verb: does open
3. Subject: shoe   Verb: is   Adverb: where
4. Subject: dinner   Verb: is   Adverb: late
5. Subject: team   Verb: has lost   Adverb: lately

Alternative Activity 84–Compound and Complex Sentences
Underline the independent clause, bold the dependent clause, and circle the conjunction.
1. <u>Tina ate a salad</u> (because) **she wasn't very hungry.**
2. <u>I stopped at the library</u> (before) **the dry cleaning shop.**
3. compound-complex 4. compound 5. complex

Alternative Activity 85–More About Complex Sentences
1. Frank, <u>who works two jobs</u>, goes to bed early. 2. This gift is for Alia, <u>who lives in another state. 3. Since I have to go out tomorrow,</u> I will stop at the store. 4. dependent clause 5. prepositional phrase 6. dependent clause 7. prepositional phrase 8. prepositional phrase. 9. Belinda studied the math problem until she understood it. 10. Darlene drives a new car, which cost a lot of money.

Alternative Activity 86–Good Quotations
Correct each verb. Then rewrite the sentences using correct punctuation.
1. is—Tamra said, "Tela is playing soccer today." 2. are—"We are ready for bed," said the children. 3. run—The coach said, "Cameron has run several laps." 4. is—Her mother told me that Angela is walking her dog. 5. is—His brother said, "Jeremiah is playing another game today."

Alternative Activity 87–In the Woods
1–5. Answers will vary. Check to make sure that correct punctuation is used.

Alternative Activity 88–Writing Mechanics
1. "It's my secret family sauce," replied Luis. 2. Angie said, "Your family has some great secrets." 3. "Come back when you can eat more," Luis said. 4–5. Answers will vary. Check to make sure the verbs vary.

Alternative Activity 89–Ricky Found Something
Answers will vary.

Alternative Activity 90–Facts Make News
Answers will vary.

Alternative Activity 91–My Favorite Food
Answers will vary.

Alternative Activity 92–Writing a Process Paragraph
Answers will vary. Check to make sure that all steps are in the correct order.

Alternative Activity 93–Are Cats Doggone Good?
Answers will vary. Check to make sure that the writing process is followed.

Alternative Activity 94–A New Friend
Answers will vary.

Alternative Activity 95–Writing a Review
Answers will vary. Check to make sure that the writing process is followed.

Alternative Activity 96–Writing a Letter to a Friend
1. Bryan's 2. April 15, 2006 3. Answers will vary. 4. Answers will vary. 5. See you soon!, an exclamation point.

Alternative Activity 97–Writing Mechanics
1.   MISS ELISE CHARPIER
     4421 SOUTH SECOND STREET
     COLUMBUS OH 43201
2.   MR CRAIG SAUNDERS
     6949 KINGSTON CIRCLE
     BANGOR ME 04401
3.   MR TERRANCE PAYNE
     1229 GROVE AVENUE
     SAN ANTONIO TX 78295
4.   MRS MARIA GARCIA
     401 ANDERS ROAD
     CHESAPEAKE VA 23324
5.   MR ABU JAMAL
     362 RAYMOND DRIVE
     SACRAMENTO CA 95864

Alternative Activity 98–Words for Your Spelling List
1–5. Answers will vary.

Alternative Activity 99–Homonyms
1. sea 2. see 3. buy 4. by 5. deer 6. dear 7. break 8. brake 9. blue 10. Answers will vary.

Alternative Activity 100–Words that Sound Alike
1. piece 2. peace 3. read 4. red 5. some, sum 6. threw 7. some 8. through 9. piece 10. red

Alternative Activity 101–Plurals-Two or More
1. boys 2. ties 3. donkeys 4. yourselves 5. elves 6. The divers hit the water between two waves. 7. I read four books about deer this summer. 8. The police chiefs met to talk about thieves. 9. Three calves ran from two wolves. 10. Both children have problems with their teeth.

Alternative Activity 102–Other Word Endings
1. placement 2. daring 3. hopeful 4. nameless 5. arrival 6. stirred 7. hottest 8. sadder 9. skipping 10. planned

Alternative Activity 103–Words with *ie* or *ei*
1. sleigh 2. dr<u>ie</u>d 3. s<u>ei</u>ze 4. p<u>ie</u>ce 5. qu<u>ie</u>t 6. w<u>ei</u>rd 7. ach<u>ie</u>ve 8. s<u>ie</u>ge 9. sc<u>ie</u>nce 10. al<u>ie</u>n 11. Rafael misspells many words on his schoolwork. 12. Today is a good day for a picnic. 13. My neighbor has a good view. 14. Analise believes in aliens. 15. Russ believes his dream will come true.

Alternative Activity 104–Words that Look Similar
1. loose, lose 2. quiet 3. dessert 4. quite 5. cloths 6. breath 7. already 8. dairy 9. all ready 10. quit

Alternative Activity 105–Writing Mechanics
1. well 2. good 3. good 4. well, better 5. best 6. better 7. more 8. more, harder 9. fastest 10. most

Alternative Activity 106–Make Verbs Agree with Subjects
1. wants 2. slices 3. fall 4. drop 5. play 6. curls 7. clatter 8. read 9. shine 10. stay 11. burns 12. lifts 13. works 14. graze 15. shops

1. are **2.** are **3.** are **4.** has **5.** is **6.** are **7.** are **8.** was **9.** are **10.** were **11.** is **12.** Are **13.** Does **14.** go **15.** play

Alternative Activity 108–Pronoun Subjects with Verb Agreement

1. Many (are) few (are) **2.** Somebody (tells) **3.** Both (see) **4.** One (has) **5.** Everything (has) **6.** Most (leave) **7.** Nobody (wants) **8.** Some (are) **9.** None (smells) **10.** everyone (was) **11.** Others (leave) **12.** Some (needs) **13.** Most (die) **14.** Each (expects) **15.** Neither (likes) **16-20.** Answers will vary. Check to make sure each word is used only once.

Alternative Activity 109–Pronoun-Noun Agreement

Complete each sentence with an owner pronoun. Circle the word(s) to which the pronoun refers.

1. (Wayne)—his **2.** (Lance) and (I)—our **3.** (myself)—I **4.** (student)—his or her **5.** (Maggie)—her **6.** is **7.** were **8.** is **9.** makes **10.** stops

Alternative Activity 110–*Don't* and *Doesn't*

1. doesn't **2.** doesn't **3.** don't **4.** don't **5.** doesn't **6.** doesn't **7.** don't **8.** doesn't **9.** don't **10.** don't **11.** doesn't **12.** doesn't **16.** doesn't **13.** don't **14.** don't **15.** doesn't

Alternative Activity 111–One Word Makes a Difference

1. B **2.** A **3.** A **4.** A **5.** B

Alternative Activity 112–Fine-Tune this Story

Answers will vary.

Alternative Activity 113–Writing Mechanics

Answers will vary. Check to make sure that standard English is used.

Workbook Activities

Workbook Activity 1–Sentences

1–5. Answers vary. **6.** subject **7.** verb **8.** verb **9.** subject **10.** verb **11.** subject **12.** subject **13.** verb **14.** subject **15.** verb

Workbook Activity 2–Nouns in Place

1. circle *door, thing, car* **2.** circle *paper, tree* **3.** circle s*pider* **4.** circle *night, barn* **5.** circle *wolf* **6.** circle *bike, motorcycle* **7.** circle *street, fall* **8.** circle *picture* **9.** circle *gravel, grass* **10.** circle *city*
11-15. Answers will vary.

Workbook Activity 3–Writing Sentences with Adjectives

1-5. Answers will vary. **6-10.** Answers will vary.

Workbook Activity 4–Sentences with Action Verbs

Draw a line under each action verb. Circle the subject.

1. The blue (car) honked. **2.** A (light) flickered. **3.** The (tiger) roars. **4.** Old (flowers) wilt. **5.** An (owl) hoots. **6.** The (sun) rises. **7.** The large (bear) sleeps. **8.** The red (hammer) pounds. **9.** The (wrench) grips. **10.** The cold (water) drips. Answers will vary. **11.** screams **12.** blares **13.** travels **14.** smiles **15.** dances

Workbook Activity 5–Build a Sentence

1-10. Answers will vary.

Workbook Activity 6–Sentences with Adverbs That Tell "When"

Circle the adverb. Underline each verb.

1. Large planes fly (daily.) **2.** That package came (today.) **3.** The clock chimes (hourly.) **4.** (Often) a green light blinks. **5.** The big bus arrived (late.) **6.** (Today) that new TV show begins. **7.** The sink clogs (often.) **8.** (Yesterday) both computers crashed. **9.** The man runs (nightly.) **10.** The fall festival begins (tomorrow.) Answers will vary. **11.** late **12.** today **13.** twice **14.** soon **15.** now

Workbook Activity 7–Adverbs tell "Where"

Answers will vary. **1.** here **2.** around **3.** nearby **4.** by **5.** down **6.** outside **7.** there **8.** below **9.** near **10.** upstairs
Circle the adverb, underline the verb.
11. The old man sits (outside.) **12.** A guard stood (nearby.) **13.** The students went (inside.) **14.** A police officer talked (there.) **15.** The couple walked (around.)

Workbook Activity 8–Sentence Parts

Write the complete predicate of each sentence. Circle the simple subject and the simple predicate.

1. The hot, yellow (sun) (beats) down
2. Two hungry (boys) (ate) quickly
3. The noisy, dusty, bumpy (ride) (took) forever
4. Our (students) always (work) hard
5. Heavy, wet (snow) (fell) yesterday
6. (John) (swims) fast
7. The fishing (store) (opened) early
8. White sea (gulls) (flew) high
9. The lucky (number) (won) again
10. The exited (group) (traveled) around

Workbook Activity 9–Is it a Sentence or a Fragment?

1. fragment **2.** sentence **3.** sentence **4.** fragment **5.** fragment
Answers may vary. **6.** Missing predicate **7.** Missing predicate **8.** Missing subject **9.** Missing predicate **10.** Missing predicate

Workbook Activity 10–Commas and Periods

Add commas after adverbs.

1. Loudly, the girl called out. **2.** Happily, the children played. **3.** Cautiously, the man walked. **4.** Quickly, the chef cooked. **5.** Slowly, the person typed.

Rewrite the sentences correctly. **6.** Luckily, the movie ended early. **7.** A tall, heavy man walked away. **8.** Soon, a big, long train will arrive. **9.** Later, the girls ate sandwiches. **10.** This long, stringy plant grew quickly.

Workbook Activity 11–March of Prepositions

Answers may vary.

1. during, game **2.** with, cheerleaders **3.** in, street **4.** before, players **5.** around, bleachers **6.** behind, team **7.** down, field **8.** at, park **9.** toward, town **10.** for, crowd

Workbook Activity 12–Sentences with Adjective Prepositional Phrases

Underline the adjective prepositional phrase. Circle the noun it describes.

1. A (bird) in the tree chirped. **2.** A small (child) with a loud toy ran around. **3.** Yellow (fish) in the bowl swim slowly **4.** (Planes) from the air base landed nearby. **5.** The heavy (smoke) from the fire drifted away.

Circle the adjective prepositional phrase. Underline the noun it describes. Draw an arrow from the adjective prepositional phrase to the noun it describes.

6. Light (from the full moon) glows softly. **7.** The big plate (of pizza) disappeared. **8.** Heat (from the bonfire) feels good. **9.** An old man (with a sweater) walks slowly. **10.** Five riders (on red bikes) wave happily. **11.** The woman (with the black bag) walked quickly. **12.** The turkey (in the oven) smells good. **13.** That dog (with the green collar) barked loudly. **15.** The rose bush (near the door) bloomed last week.

Workbook Activity 13–Sentences with Confusing Subjects

Circle the prepositional phrase. Underline the simple subject.

1. Thick dust (on the road) rose slowly. **2.** New leaves (on the plant) grow quickly. **3.** the door (to the house) opened wide. **4.** The light (beside the building) shines brightly. **5.** That star (in the sky) rises early. **6.** Green paint (on the door) looks nice. **7.** A flock (of blackbirds) flew overhead. **8.** Children (on the sidewalk) skip happily. **9.** A bus (from the city) arrived late. **10.** Books (in the library) became dusty. **11.** of ants **12.** across the street **13.** in the river **14.** at the game **15.** in the fountain

Workbook Activity 14–A Short Story with Prepositions

Prepositional phrases: down the street; after his car; along the curb; up a hill; into traffic; through a tunnel; off a wall; into a tree; near a river **1-3.** Answers will vary.

Workbook Activity 15–Change an Adverb to a Preposition

1. Circle in-in, car **2.** Circle around-around, block **3.** Circle down-down, stairs **4.** Circle up- up, street **5.** Circle over-over, bridge

Workbook Activity 16–Lots of Prepositional Phrases

1. in the distance	adj.	mountains	noun
above the sea	adv.	rise	verb
2. with golden edges	adj.	clouds	noun
across the sky	adv.	drift	verb
at sunset	adv.	drift	verb
3. with a noisy bell	adj.	cow	noun
under a tree	adv.	chews	verb
in the field	adv.	chews	verb
4. with a dog	adj.	boy	noun
down the path	adv.	runs	verb
behind the barn	adv.	runs	verb
5. for the bone	adv.	leaps	verb
in my hand	adv.	leaps	verb

Workbook Activity 17–More Hidden Verbs

State-of-being verb is underlined. Circle the prepositional phrase. **1.** Sherrelle and Lola will be (on the team.) **2.** They look nervous (before the game.) **3.** That team is winner (for the school.) **4.** Each girl seems happy (at the school.) **5.** Both girls were (on the honor roll.)

Circle the prepositional phrase. Draw a line under the subject noun. Bold the state-of-being verb.

6. Two swimmers **remain** (near the pier.) **7.** The news **will be** (on TV soon.) **8.** A pot of soup **is** (on the stove.) **9.** Chicken and rice **are** (in the oven.) **10.** Bread (with butter) **is** on the table. **11.** The large alligator **is** (in the swamp.) **12.** We **were** (around the block.) **13.** She **feels** sick (on the boat.) **14.** Tony **was** (across the street.) **15.** He **looks** nice (in that outfit.)

Workbook Activity 18–All Kinds of Prepositional Phrases

1-10. Answers will vary.

Workbook Activity 19–Nouns and Punctuation

Place an X on the line if the word is a common noun. If it is a proper noun, rewrite it correctly.

1. x **2.** x **3.** Michaelina **4.** Pluto **5.** x **6.** x **7.** California **8.** x **9.** x **10.** America **11.** Alicia **12.** x **13.** San Diego **14.** Washington **15.** x **16.** Rhode Island **17.** x **18.** Canada **19.** x **20.** Atlantic **21.** Around the block, the boys ran. **22.** To New York, Teka traveled often. **23.** In the park, three men talked. **24.** At the store, a man shopped. **25.** On the table, a radio played. **26.** In formation, four jets flew. **27.** Beside the fence, a truck waited. **28.** Behind the wall, three boys played. **29.** On a grassy field, the girls rested. **30.** Down the street, two cars drove.

Workbook Activity 20–Sentences with Conjunctions

1. and **2.** or **3.** but **4.** yet **5.** as well as

Circle the conjunction. Underline the words, phrase or ideas that the conjunction connects.

6. Is the dog in the house (or) in the yard? **7.** Bradden missed that class (but) LaToya did not. **8.** Kites (as well as) balloons rose into the sky. **9.** Snow (and) ice make the road slick. **10.** That boat is old (yet) sturdy. **11-15.** Answers will vary.

Workbook Activity 21–Writing Compound Subjects

Underline the compound subjects. Circle the conjunction.

1. A rowboat (and) a sailboat float near a dock. **2.** Boats (and) swimmers move in the water. **3.** Andres (and) Rudy jumped into the lake. **4.** Dark clouds (and) lightning fill the sky. **5.** All swimmers (and) boaters must leave the lake. **6.** A sports car, a truck (and) an old green minivan sit on the sales lot. **7.** Flocks of ducks (and) geese fly across the sky. **8.** A large table, a small desk (and) an old chair sit in the office. **9.** Chicken sandwiches, beef tacos (and) salad are on the menu at school. **10.** A glass of water, two forks, (and) a spoon were left on the table.

Underline the compound subject. Circle the conjunction.

11. Raquel and Chris study in the library. **12.** David and Tanisha are in the marching band. **13.** Mr. Munoz and Mrs. Hely flew to Spain.

322   Answer Key

14. The old pickup truck and the big station wagon turned off the road. **15.** Latore and James work late tonight.

Workbook Activity 22–Compound Predicates
Underline the verbs in the compound predicate. Circle the conjunction.

1. A startled rabbit <u>jumps</u> up (and) <u>runs</u> towards the field. **2.** A stream of water <u>rushes</u> (and) <u>flows</u> over the rocks. **3.** Derek <u>sang</u> (and) <u>danced</u> in the talent show. **4.** The girls <u>shouted</u> (and) <u>waved</u> their arms at their friends on the field. **5.** Dejuan and Travis <u>built</u> (and) <u>raced</u> their own go-cart. **6.** Natalie <u>planted</u> (and) <u>cared</u> for a garden. **7.** The flowers <u>bloomed</u> (and) <u>smelled</u> all summer. **8.** The horse <u>bucked</u> (and) <u>jumped</u> out of the ring. **9.** The volcano <u>erupted</u> (and) <u>spewed</u> lava all over the ground. **10.** The shark <u>swam</u> around (and) <u>trapped</u> the fish.
11. shouted, cheered **12.** skated, performed **13.** fell, landed **14.** raced, flew **15.** posed, shook

Workbook Activity 23–Building Compounds
1-5. Answers will vary. **6-10.** Answers will vary. **6.** day, night **7.** mountain, valley **8.** bridge, tunnel **9.** trip, radio **10.** city, house

Workbook Activity 24–Compounds in Sentences
1-15. Answers will vary.

Workbook Activity 25–Prepositions and Compounds
Draw a line under: *through the woods, over the fallen tree, around a rock, through the darkness and rain, toward a small cabin, against the door, from the sky, through the roof, at the door,* and *in the night.* Circle: *inside, finally*
1. Lightning blazed and a tree fell. (or) The wind screamed and the cabin vanished in the night. **2.** Finally, the scary movie ended. **3.** The men pulled and pushed at the door. Thunder cracked and rumbled. **4.** They jumped over the fallen tree and around a rock. **5.** Two men ran through the woods. Yellow lights pointed toward a small cabin.

Workbook Activity 26–Using Commas, Semicolons, and Quotation Marks
1. The restaurant serves appetizers, dinners, and dessert. **2.** Football players usually run, catch and pass during a game. **3.** Tires, rags, and empy cans sit on the garage floor. **4.** The girls talked, laughed, and listened to music at their sleepover. **5.** Adults, teens, and children all lined up to get tickets for that concert. **6.** Lightning flashed, and thunder boomed. **7.** The large tree fell; the animals scattered. **8.** The book is <u>How to Stay Healthy</u>; the chapter is "Exercise." **9.** The magazine is <u>Fixing Your Own Car</u>; the article is "Exhaust Systems." **10.** The newspaper is <u>Life and Style</u>; the article is "Decorating Your House."

Workbook Activity 27–Verbs and Direct Objects
1. typed→letter **2.** bought→shirt **3.** broke→heart **4.** played→piano **5.** ate→leaves **6.** saw→puppy **7.** hit→pins **8.** painted→picture **9.** struck→twelve **10.** built→house

Workbook Activity 28–Compounds: Write Your Own
1-5. Answers will vary.

Workbook Activity 29–Writing Compounds
1. NC **2.** C **3.** NC **4.** C **5.** NC **6.** CDO **7.** both **8.** CV **9.** CDO **10.** CV **11.** C S **12.** C subject **13.** C direct object **14.** C verb **15.** C subject

Workbook Activity 30–Two Sentence Patterns
New sentences will vary but should show different sentence patterns.
1. Pattern: subject + verb + do
2. Pattern: subject + verb + prep
3. Pattern: subject + verb + do + prep
4. Pattern: subject + verb + do + prep
5. Pattern: subject + verb
6. Pattern: subject + verb + do
7. Pattern: subject + verb + prep + prep
8. Pattern: subject + verb + do
9. Pattern: subject + verb + do + prep
10. Pattern: subject + verb + do

Workbook Activity 31–Looking at Nouns in a Sentence
Circle the nouns. Above each noun label it as subject (S), direct object (DO), or object of a preposition (OP).
1. Circle *Brian,* label *S,* circle *cafe,* label *OP* **2.** Circle *diner,* label *S,* circle *burger,* label *DO,* circle *fries,* label *OP* **3.** Circle *diner,* label *S,* circle *Brian,* label *DO,* circle *ribs,* label *OP,* circle *saucer,* label *OP* **4.** Circle *server,* label *S,* circle *Brian,* label *DO,* circle *salads,* label *DO* **5.** Circle *Brian,* label *S,* circle *door,* label *DO,* circle *night* , label *OP,* circle *work,* label *OP* **6.** concrete **7.** abstract **8.** concrete **9.** concrete **10.** abstract **11.** abstract **12.** abstract **13.** concrete **14.** abstract **15.** concrete

Workbook Activity 32–Using Pronouns in a Sentence
Circle the correct pronoun.
1. She, us **2.** They **3.** We, them **4.** I, him **5.** me **6.** me **7.** They **8.** I, him **9.** I, them **10.** She **11.** NP **12.** OP **13.** OP **14.** NP **15.** OP

Workbook Activity 33–Practice Using Pronouns
1. Marcus watched them sing the song. **2.** Larry bought a new suit and wore it to the dance. **3.** She sat with Alan at the baseball game. **4.** Hector rode his bike to the park and then rode it to the store. **5.** They stay after school often. **6.** DO **7.** S **8.** OP **9.** DO **10.** S

Workbook Activity 34–Identifying Pronoun and Adjectives
Underline each adjective and draw an arrow to the noun it describes.
1. Underline Many, one. Draw an arrow to people, pet **2.** Underline several. Draw an arrow to dogs **3.** Underline three. Draw an arrow to rabbits **4.** Adjective **5.** Pronoun. **6.** Pronoun **7-10.** Answers will vary.

Workbook Activity 35–Using *This, That, These, Those*
1. that **2.** those **3.** these **4.** this **5.** that **6.** pronoun **7.** adjective **8.** adjective **9.** pronoun **10.** adjective **11.** This **12.** These **13.** That **14.** Those **15.** This

Workbook Activity 36–Capitals, Semicolons, Commas, and Periods
1. I saw Mrs. Ann Gomez at the Olympics. **2.** Last Tuesday, she and Dr. Frank Munoz flew to Germany. **3.** Dr. Munoz and Mrs. Gomez speak German. **4.** I like baseball; however, I missed the World Series. **5.** Ms. Ellen Thomas will arrive on the Sunday after the Fourth of July holiday. **6.** Lots of people go to Europe, but I prefer Latin America. **7.** Last spring, Queen Elizabeth went to Kentucky; however, she only looked at horses. **8.** They speak French, Spanish, and German; however, they know English also. **9.** Senator Dawkins and Dr. Soto arrived from Europe on a plane. **10.** Jacob will study Italian at South City High School.

Workbook Activity 37–Parts of Speech
1. verb, adverb **2.** direct object, adjective/article **3.** adverb, verb **4.** verb, adjective **5.** pronoun/subject, preposition **6.** adverb, adverb

7. preposition, adjective **8.** verb, object of the preposition **9.** verb, adjective **10.** adjective, object of the preposition

Workbook Activity 38–Using Owner Words
1. Vivian's **2.** Jason's **3.** Cole's **4.** Marie's **5.** LaToya's **6.** theater's **7.** parked car's **8.** cafe's **9.** building's **10.** store's

Workbook Activity 39–Using Owner Pronouns
1. circle **their**–draw an arrow to **car 2.** circle **his**–draw an arrow to **car 3.** circle **Its**–draw an arrow to **paint 4.** circle **My**–draw an arrow to **friend** ; circle **your**–draw an arrow to **house 5.** circle **Our**–draw an arrow to **team**; Circle **your**–draw an arrow to **team 6.** its **7.** your **8.** its **9.** our/his **10.** their **11.** her **12.** my **13.** our **14.** your **15.** its

Workbook Activity 40–Sentences with More Than One Owner
1. boats' **2.** ladies' **3.** hamsters' **4.** books' **5.** pencils' **6.** Its weight broke through the ice. **7.** Its edge is cracked. **8.** Her purse is blue with gold trim. **9.** His hat blew across the street during the storm. **10.** Their food is in those bags on the floor.

Workbook Activity 41–A Lot
1. Underline *lot*, circle *rose*. **2.** Underline *cat*, circle *eat* **3.** Underline *lot*, circle *left* **4.** Underline *Adrian*, circle *caught* **5.** Underline *lot*, circle *flowed* **6.** Cats eat a lot of mice. Adrian caught a lot of fish. **7.** Adjective prepositional phrases: *of dust, of people, of water*—Adverb Prepositional phrase: behind us, of mice, after the fire, of fish, of the pail **8.** out **9.** Answers will vary. **10.** Answers will vary.

Workbook Activity 42–Sentences with Adverbs
1. really—fast, adverb **2.** quickly—moves, verb **3.** quite—close, adverb **4.** so—easy, adverb **5.** truly—sleek, adjective
Answers will vary
6. quite **7.** completely **8.** somewhat **9.** terribly. **10.** really **11.** truly **12.** rather **13.** so **14.** extremely **15.** almost

Workbook Activity 43–Using Interjections
1-10. Answers will vary. **11.** interjection **12.** interjection **13.** adverb **14.** interjection **15.** adverb

Workbook Activity 44–The Rewrite Sheet
Answers will vary.

Workbook Activity 45–Practice Using Punctuation, Capitalization, and Interjections
1. Towanna, Lola, and Mary acted in the play on Friday. **2.** Jamie's new car has a very large engine. **3.** The girl's (or girls') apartment is extremely messy. **4.** Isabel and Sophia shop at Abby's Alternative Clothing Store. **5.** They found some jeans and tank tops for summer. **6.** Maybe, the fish will bite better next week. **7.** Yuck! I will not eat that awful stuff! **8.** Oh! this is a really bad problem! **9.** Boom! The thunder shook the house! **10.** Wow! This gift is exactly what I wanted!

Workbook Activity 46–Make a Change
1. The pitcher threw the batter a curve ball. **2.** Annika bought the new car and paid the dealer $20,000. **3.** Carter's wife bought him a new suit. **4.** The team gave Darryl an award. **5.** The young woman wrote the newspaper editor a letter about city problems. **6.** The cashier gave the man a receipt. **7.** Hector and Theresa's grandfather in Mexico sent them a check. **8.** Rain brought the farmers relief. **9.** Josie's friends threw her a party. **10.** Martin made his mother a card.

Workbook Activity 47–Long Sentences with Indirect Objects
1. Circle *everyone* **2.** Circle *riders* **3.** Circle *family* **4.** Circle *buyer* **5.** Circle *crowd* **6.** Circle *Andres* **7.** Circle *Sara* **8.** Circle *Brandi* **9.** Circle *Susan* **10.** Circle *them*
Label the simple subject (S), the verb (V), the direct object (D) and the indirect object (IO).
11. An S above **girls**, a V above **fed**, an IO above **ducks**, a DO above **corn, water 12.** An S above **cows**, a V above **gave**, an IO above **farmer**, a DO above **gallons 13.** An S above **job**, a V above **offered**, an IO above **Family**, a DO above **money. 14.** An S above **Wayne & Joe**, a V above **bought**, an IO above **themselves**, a DO above **shoes 15.** An S above **teachers**, a V above **gave**, an IO above **Jack**, a DO above **credit**

Workbook Activity 48–Using Object Complements
1. Circle *hot* **2.** Circle *green* **3.** Circle *high* **4.** Circle *hot,spicy* **5.** Circle *loud* **6.** Underline *student* **7.** Underline *one* **8.** Underline *friend* **9.** Underline *president* **10.** Underline *man* **11-15.** Answers will vary.

Workbook Activity 49–Object Complements in Long Sentences
1. Skater—Noun **2.** cold—Adjective **3.** Blue—Adjective **4.** Shadow—Noun **5.** one —Pronoun **6.** object of the preposition **7.** indirect object **8.** direct object **9.** object compliment **10.** direct object **11.** direct object **12.** object of the preposition **13.** object complement **14.** object of the preposition **15.** object complement

Workbook Activity 50–Combine Sentences
1. Jeff, a terrific guy, had a wonderful party. **2.** The dog down the street, a large animal, is dangerous. **3.** Everyone like that great sport, baseball. **4.** The teacup, my mother's favorite, fell off the table. **5.** Thea, a champion swimmer, won first place. **6.** Zachary Barnes, the father of twins, is a happy man. **7.** A full moon, a big, orange globe, rose over the quiet city. **8.** People rushed outside for the happy event, Walter's return from the army. **9.** The wind, a heavy gust, blew down the palm tree. **10.** Shaunna finished reading the book, a suspense novel.

Workbook Activity 51–Change the Mood
Answers will vary.

Workbook Activity 52–Rewriting Sentences
1. Wow! Alec played well! **2.** Tim and his team, a great group of players, won the state's top honor. **3.** The three judges' decision brought cheers. **4.** The team's pride showed as they accepted the shiny cup. **5.** The big cup, a beautiful trophy, sits in the school's showcase. **6.** Ah, the team's effort earned it. **7.** Alec, Frank, Carlos, and Darnell, the team's top players, practice every Saturday. **8.** Alec also enjoys tennis, golf, swimming and bowling. **9.** Gee! Alec's sports take a lot of time. **10.** Well, Alec's sister Rita likes sports too!

Workbook Activity 53–Sentences with Noun Subject Complements
Circle the subject. Underline the predicate noun that links to the subject.
1. Circle *milk*, underline *beverage*. **2.** Circle *Ashley and Tran*, underline *friends* **3.** Circle *David*, underline *man* **4.** Circle *dogs*, underline *pets* **5.** Circle *beater*, underline *car* **6.** underline *a fine skater* **7.** underline *happy ones* **8.** underline *a good one* **9.** underline *her best one* **10.** underline *a loyal group* **11-15.** Answers will vary.

Workbook Activity 54–Appositives and Noun Subject Complements

1-5. Answers will vary. **6.** Circle *an organized man* **7.** Circle *the best athlete in our school* **8.** Circle *a hard working woman* **9.** Circle *a young lady* **10.** Circle *a fabulous artist*.

Workbook Activity 55–Add Adjective Subject Complements

1-20. Answers will vary.

Workbook Activity 56–Adjectives Always Describe Nouns

Circle the adjectives that describe the nouns in bold.

1. hard **2.** his, lab **3.** long, short **4.** her, hot **5.** easy **6-10.** Answers will vary.

Workbook Activity 57–Adverb or Adjective?

Circle the word that correctly completes each sentence.

1. slowly **2.** rapidly **3.** heavy, well **4.** smoothly, quietly **5.** suddenly, dark **6.** Quickly **7.** dark, large **8.** gently **9.** clear **10.** directly **11.** slowly **12.** quickly **13.** good, well **14.** hard **15.** good

Workbook Activity 58–More Subject Complements

Draw a line under the simple subject. Draw a circle around the verb. Write the subject complement. Tell if is a noun or an adjective. **1.** Pierre's sports car (is) a fast car.—Subject complement: car—Noun **2.** Pierre's sports car (is) very fast.—Subject complement fast—adjective **3.** Its luggage space (is) large.—Subject complement: large—Adjective **4.** Its stereo (is) a good system.—Subject complement: system—Noun **5.** Its stereo (is) the best.—Subject complement: best—Noun **6.** The brakes and steering (are) very good.—Subject complement: good—Adjective **7.** The engine (is) strong.—Subject complement: strong—Adjective **8.** The red paint (is) beautiful.—Subject complement: beautiful—Adjective **9.** Pierre's friends (are) jealous.—Subject complement: jealous—Adjective **10.** Pierre (is) a happy man.—Subject complement: man—Noun

Workbook Activity 59–Subject Complement Sentences with Pronouns

Write S above the subject pronoun, LV above the linking verb and NSC above the noun subject complement.

1. Put an *S* above *This*, an *LV* above *is*, an *NSC* above *way* **2.** Put an *S* above *That*, an *LV* above *was*, an *NSC* above *test*. **3.** Put an *S* above *This*, an *LV* above *is*, an *NSC* above *color*. **4.** Put an *S* above *That*, an *LV* above *is*, an *NSC* above *book*. **5.** Put an *S* above *These*, an *LV* above *are*, an *NSC* above *sandwiches*. **6.** Put an *S* above *That* an *LV* above *is*, an *NSC* above *movie*. **7.** Put an *S* above *Those*, an *LV* above *are*, an *NSC* above *animals*. **8.** Put an *S* above *These*, an *LV* above *are*, an *NSC* above *shoes*. **9.** Put an *S* above *That*, an *LV* above *is*, an *NSC* above *dress*. **10.** Put an *S* above *This*, an *LV* above *is*, an *NSC* above *ride*. Circle the subject of each sentence. **11.** train **12.** reward **13.** coats **14.** tickets **15.** theater

Workbook Activity 60–Pronoun Practice

1. Them **2.** mine **3.** hers **4.** I **5.** it **6.** him **7.** his **8.** he **9.** it **10.** It **11.** yours **12.** it **13.** she **14.** her **15.** her **16.** you **17.** he **18.** him **19.** you **20.** I **21.** we **22.** she **23.** he **24.** them **25.** they **26.** they **27.** their **28.** she **29.** he **30.** her

Workbook Activity 61–Sentence Patterns Practice

1. Pattern: subject + verb + direct object—Your sentence: Answers vary. **2.** Pattern: subject + verb + indirect object + direct object—Your sentence: Answers vary. **3.** Pattern: subject + linking verb +

noun + subject complement—Your sentence: Answers vary. **4.** Pattern: subject + verb —Your sentence: Answers vary. **5.** Pattern: subject + verb + direct object + object complement—Your sentence: Answers vary

Workbook Activity 62–Practice Writing Sentences

1-10. Answers will vary.

Workbook Activity 63–Adjectives Can Compare

Circle the adjective for each sentence.

1. worst **2.** littlest **3.** bigger **4.** worse **5.** most **6.** happier **7.** bigger **8.** smaller **9.** better **10.** worse **11.** bright **12.** least **13.** better **14.** better **15.** best

Workbook Activity 64–Looking at Verbs

Circle the verb. Write whether it is an *action* or a *linking verb*.

1. circle *fills*—linking verb **2.** circle *be*—linking verb **3.** circle *saw*—action verb **4.** circle *jumped*—action verb **5.** circle *walk*—action verb **6.** past tense **7.** future tense **8.** future tense **9.** present tense **10.** future tense **11.** laughed **12.** will ask **13.** talked **14.** will start **15.** likes

Workbook Activity 65–Helping Verbs

Underline the main verb. Circle the helping verb.

1. Circle *have been*, underline *working* **2.** Circle *could be*, underline *doing* **3.** Circle *is*, underline *planning* **4.** Circle *will*, underline *help* **5.** Circle *might*, underline *arrive* **6.** Circle *will*, underline *take* **7.** Circle *can*, underline *enter* **8.** Circle *are*, underline *improving* **9.** Circle *might*, underline *study* **10.** Circle *will be*, underline *looking* **11.** is playing **12.** has been swimming **13.** will earn **14.** has worked **15.** could be making

Workbook Activity 66–Verbs Tell Present Time

1. I am walking in the mud. **2.** I am watching television with them. **3.** You are in our new store. **4.** I am behind the fence all day. **5.** We are waiting for you in the alley. **6.** The school needs new space. **7.** Everybody is working this month. **8.** Everyone is happy for him **9.** I am going away for a long rest. **10.** Many people at the fair are smelling the good food.

Workbook Activity 67–The Past Tense

1. We were planting new grass in the yard. **2.** Mike and Sharon were watering the flowers. **3.** He was watching TV late last night. **4.** He had played in that game earlier. **5.** Those three boys were late to class. **6.** We were freezing in the cold wind. **7.** Andy was hiding in the attic. **8.** Charlene had been studying science all night long. **9.** Lewis has been tying a rope to his horse. **10.** We were clearing junk from the field.

Workbook Activity 68–Verbs Tell Future Time

1. Tomorrow, Dorothy will be going to 10th Avenue to catch a bus. **2.** The buses will stop at every corner where passengers wait. **3.** Juan will be waiting for Dorothy downtown. **4.** They will have lunch at the diner. **5.** Afterward, Bryan will be meeting them. **6.** They all will be going to see a play at their favorite theater. **7.** They will plan to arrive early at the theater. **8.** Their seats will be reserved for them in the center section. **9.** The new play will have opened by tomorrow. **10.** They will be listening to the director's discussion before the play starts.

Workbook Activity 69–Using Negatives

1. Paul's dog may not have stolen his shoe from the porch. **2.** Raul and Peter have never eaten at this diner. **3.** That road sign could not show her the way to the city. **4.** Liz has not gone to the roller rink many times. **5.** Tony did not see Anita on the train yesterday. **6.** The train will not arrive on time today. **7.** Mai had never seen that movie before. **8.** Janna and Tia have never made that trip before. **9.** The ghost has never spoken to scared visitors. **10.** This old, empty house will not stand many more years.

Workbook Activity 70–Verbs that Change Form
Circle the correct form of the verb.
1. go **2.** gone **3.** hung **4.** hung **5.** sunk **6.** sink **7.** sang **8.** sung **9.** speak **10.** spoke, spoken **11.** stole **12.** stolen **13.** stung **14.** written, writes **15.** wrote

Workbook Activity 71–Practice Writing a Story
Answers will vary.

Workbook Activity 72–Problem Contractions
1. Van doesn't know her. **2.** She and her friends don't live around here. **3.** She and Van aren't too friendly, are they? **4.** It wasn't my problem. **5.** She doesn't smile often. **6.** Van joked, but it wasn't funny. **7.** He doesn't know good jokes. **8.** She and her friends weren't laughing. **9.** Some jokes aren't really funny. **10.** Van doesn't like her friends.

Workbook Activity 73–Writing Notes
1. Great Wall of China—over 2,000 years old—4,500 miles—first section built in ten years. **2.** John F. Kennedy—35th U.S. president—assassinated 11/22/63 in Dallas, TX **3.** before 11:00 A.M. **4.** English research paper **5.** Saturday

Workbook Activity 74–Sentences with *Accept, Except; Teach, Learn*
1. accept **2.** teach **3.** learned **4.** except **5.** learned **6.** accepted, taught **7.** accepted, except **8.** accept, learn **9.** taught **10.** except **11.** teach, except **12.** learned **13.** accept **14.** learn **15.** accept

Workbook Activity 75–*Their, There,* and *They're*
1. There **2.** They're **3.** their **4.** there **5.** there **6.** they're **7.** they're **8.** their **9.** they're **10.** there

Workbook Activity 76–Confusing Words
Circle the correct word in parentheses to complete each sentence.
1. lie, It's, your, raise **2.** sits, rises **3.** lies, sitting **4.** it's, sitting **5.** Set, your, raise **6.** lie, rise **7.** It's, sit, set, your're **8.** raise,It's **9.** It's, you're, raise **10.** lies, your

Workbook Activity 77–*Too, Two, To; Let, Leave*
Circle the correct word in parentheses to complete each sentence.
1. Let **2.** too **3.** to, leave **4.** two **5.** leaves, to **6.** too, let **7.** too **8.** Let, to **9.** let **10.** two, to, too **11.** leaves **12.** two **13.** to **14.** too **15.** let **16.** to **17.** to **18.** Let **19.** Let **20.** too

Workbook Activity 78–Say No Only Once
1. They didn't see anybody come out of the burning house. **2.** Nobody saw anything strange during the fire. **3.** They will never go near that house again. **4.** The old car cannot go down the road anymore. **5.** He got no sleep during the last two nights. **6.** That house of yours isn't worth anything. **7.** The windows hardly open. **8.** The doors are scarcely better. **9.** The sofa has no springs. **10.** All that food isn't good for you.

Workbook Activity 79–Writing a Compare and Contrast Story
Answers will vary.

Workbook Activity 80–Abbreviations, Capitalization, and Punctuation Marks
1. During the winter, the eight o'clock bus does not run. **2.** That flight arrives in Florida on New Year's Day. **3.** Tamra's watch shows 11:15 A.M. on Nov. 4, 2005. **4.** Both afternoon flights to Boston on Sunday are full. **5.** Juanita left for Mexico on the last Tuesday of the year. **6.** February **7.** March **8.** September **9.** August **10.** April **11.** Our play will open on January 3 and run two weeks. **12.** Joe's Barber Shop is open all day Monday through Friday. **13.** During August, it closes at 1 P.M. on Saturday. **14.** Tela has a class at 9:30 A.M. and a lab at 1:30 P.M. today. **15.** She has a meeting with her professor at 5:30 p.m. on Thursday.

Workbook Activity 81–Looking at Tone of Voice
1. Look at that car! **2.** It is painted bright pink! **3.** Where did she go? **4.** I am so hungry! **5.** Wait for me here! **6.** Be careful out there! **7.** He went to the store! **8.** Please, do not do that! **9.** How can you do that to me? **10.** You did a great job on t hat project! **11.** Shhh! I am trying to take a nap. **12.** Look! Is that Diana over there? **13.** Hey! Where are you going? **14.** Well, I have to write my report tonight. **15.** Ugh! I am so tired of washing the dishes all of the time!

Workbook Activity 82–What Sentences Can Do
1. *Question:* Do you want to go to the movies with Tara? *Request:* Go to the movies with Tara. *Strong request:* You have to go to the movies with Tara! **2.** *Question:* Raul, did you do your homework? *Statement:* Raul did not do his homework. *Strong request:* Raul, go do your homework now! **3.** *Question:* Did the juice spill all over the carpet? *Statement:* The juice spilled all over the carpet. *Strong request:* Please clean the juice up from the carpet. **4.** *Statement:* The bus is late. *Request:* Tell the bus driver I couldn't wait any longer. *Strong request:* You are late! You need to get me to 4th Street as soon as possible! **5.** *Question:* Amanda, did you break the jar? *Request:* Please tell me who broke the jar. *Strong request:* Tell me who broke the jar now!

Workbook Activity 83–Questions and Answers
1. That girl was the winner! **2.** Annika and Ed are going to the show. **3.** Your friends were happy about the surprise. **4.** You did buy a gift! **5.** Marta did give the bag to Aaron
Underline the subject. Circle the verb or verb phrase.
6. When (will) the party (start)? **7.** When (will) Mai (get) here? **8.** Why (are) we (waiting) for Mai? **9.** Why (are) you so early? **10.** (Is) Thao at home? **11.** Where (are) my shoes? **12.** Whose jacket (is) this? **13.** Which of these doors (is) unlocked? **14.** Why (was) Ginny late? **15.** What (did) you (do) last night?

Workbook Activity 84–Looking at Compound and Complex Sentences
Underline the independent clause, bold the dependent clause, and circle the conjunction.
1. The students begin the quiz (once) **the teacher hands it out.** **2.** Lawrence dropped the ball (when) **the coach blew his whistle.** **3.** Patina wears her jacket (because) **it keeps her warm.** **4.** He gets up early (so that) **he can study before school.** **5.** The crowd cheered wildly (after) **the kicker scored a goal.** **6.** compound **7.** complex **8.** complex **9.** compound **10.** compound-complex

Workbook Activity 85–Practice Writing Complex Sentences

1. <u>Because it was a sunny day</u>, everyone went to the beach. **2.** Erica, <u>who loves the outdoors</u>, goes to the park often. **3.** <u>Without homework to do</u>, Daniel played video games with friends. **4.** <u>Unless it rains today</u>, the race begins at two o'clock. **5.** Sean waited for Zoua <u>until late in the evening</u>. **6.** dependent clause **7.** prepositional phrase **8.** dependent clause **9.** prepositional phrase **10.** dependent clause **11.** They can't leave class until the work is done. **12.** Lee waxes his new car so that the finish shines. **13.** While those bright lights are on, Hans cannot sleep. **14.** Once she understands the basics, math is easy for Marcy. **15.** Jody, who loves music, plays the piano.

Workbook Activity 86–Punctuating Quotations

Correct each verb. Then rewrite the sentences using correct punctuation.
1. are—"We are swimming late tonight," Albert said. **2.** am— Coach Rivera told me that I am the best wrestler in school. **3.** has been— Tina found her book and said, "It has been sitting there all day." **4.** is—They told us that Zach is writing a letter. **5.** was—The newspaper said the moon was full last night.

Workbook Activity 87–Finding Odd Facts in Sentences

1. **A**re you in the mood for a long drive? **Y**ou can go from the Atlantic Ocean to the Pacific Ocean on just one road! **J**ust get on the Trans-Canada Highway**,** and drive the 4,860 miles from one coast to the other. **2.** **H**ere's what you do. Save your daily cooking fats. **B**oil them with lye from wood ashes. **Y**es, you'll get soap! **D**oes that sound dangerous as well as messy? **I**t sure is better to buy your soap at the supermarket. **3.** **W**hat does an octopus have in common with a chameleon? **Y**ou are right if you said that they both can change colors. **A**n octopus has eight arms called tentacles. **W**ouldn't it be something if it could make each arm a different color! **4.** **W**e think of an automobile as a car. **C**ar may be a better word because auto means "self" and mobile means "movement." **B**y that definition, most living creatures are automobiles. **5.** **T**alk about work! **T**he Great Wall of China is longer than 1,500 miles and is 20 feet high. **I**t was built by hand. **A**t least people knew they had a job that would last a long time!

Workbook Activity 88–Monkey Around

Ling the monkey did not like being in the zoo. In fact, he hated it! For one thing, he was too big for his cage.

One day, he got out of his cage, and the zookeeper chased him downtown. Ling climbed to the top of a tall building. He grasped the building tightly.

"If I stay up here, they can't catch me," he said to himself.

People in the top ten floor of the building crowded to the windows.

Ling looked down at the street many feet below. "If I stay here until dark, the man from the zoo will go away," he thought.

After dark, Ling climbed down from the building. I'll never do that again. I guess the zoo is safer," he thought.

Workbook Activity 89–Write the Facts

1. To: George
From: Rowen
Date: June 2
Time: 5:15 P.M.
Message: Meet her at Barney's Café on 5th Street at 7 P.M.

2. To: Bryan
From: Kelly
Date: December 2
Time: 10 A.M.
Message: Call her before 5 P.M. at (555) 484-6811

3. To: Matt
From: Thao
Date: ?
Time: 11:30 A.M.
Message: Call him at (555) 813-4100 before 3 P.M.

4. When: June 9
What Time: 4:00 P.M.
Where: 227 Florida Street
Given by: Trinity Yates
Reason: Graduation
RSVP: May 1

5. When: August 8
What Time: 4:00 P.M.
Where: 6139 Lakeview Rd.
Given by: William Randolph
Reason: fish fry
RSVP: (555) 545-2919

Workbook Activity 90–Why Is This Man Running So Hard?

Answers will vary.

Workbook Activity 91–A Real Winner

Answers will vary.

Workbook Activity 92–How to Play it

Answers will vary.

Workbook Activity 93–They Get a Kick Out of Football

Answers will vary.

Workbook Activity 94–The Group

Answers will vary.

Workbook Activity 95–Writing Another Review

Answers will vary.

Workbook Activity 96–Writing Letters

1. Draw a line to C **2.** Draw a line to D **3.** Draw a line to E **4.** Draw a line to A **5.** Draw a line to B **6.** heading **7.** greeting **8.** body **9.** closing **10.** signature

Workbook Activity 97–Two Friends Talk

Dan and Kyle sat on a bench in Central Park. Central Park is in New York.

"Look!" said Dan. "The paper says that people earn more money than ever before."

"Which people have money?" asked Kyle. "I don't know any rich people.

"Well," said Dan, "look at you and me, we're rich."

"We are? asked Kyle.

"We certainly are," said Dan. "We have lots of time to do the things we like to do.

"But," said Kyle, "I would have more money if I had a better job."

"You could be right," said Dan. "Here are some ads for jobs in the newspaper. What kind of job do you want?"

Kyle said, "I want to be a movie star."

"Oh," said Dan, "I don't see any ads for movie stars."

Kyle asked, "How about a bank president?"

"I don't see any ads for bank presidents either," Dan said.

"Well," said Kyle, "then I can't find a better job. Let's just sit here and rest after that big job search."

Workbook Activity–98 Spelling Practice
1-15. Answers will vary.

Workbook Activity 99–Homonyms—Words that Sound Alike
Circle the homonym in parentheses that completes each sentence.
1. fare, fair **2.** four **3.** been **4.** bin **5.** By, know **6.** buy **7.** break
8. brake **9.** blue **10.** Answers will vary.

Workbook Activity 100–Sound-Alike Words
1. vary **2.** very **3.** wear **4.** where **5.** witch **6.** which **7.** whole **8.** hole
9. write **10.** right **11.** week **12.** weak **13.** sent **14.** cent **15.** scent

Workbook Activity 101–More Than One
New sentences will vary.
1. Women **2.** girls **3.** Ladies **4.** boxes **5.** oxen **6.** sheep **7.** copies
8. papers **9.** Watches **10.** wolves

Workbook Activity 102–Adding Word Endings
1. tireless **2.** waving **3.** hopeless **4.** peaceful **5.** ageless **6.** nicely
7. pavement **8.** virtuous **9.** largely **10.** lifelike **11.** bedding
12. swimmer **13.** funny **14.** dimmed **15.** sunny **16.** cutting
17. bigger **18.** petted **19.** padding **20.** pepper

Workbook Activity 103–Spelling Words with *ie* or *ei*
Circle the correct spelling then write a sentence using that word. Sentences will vary.
1. Neighbor **2.** ceiling, **3.** belief **4.** weight **5.** relief **6.** Those chrome wheels give that car a weird look. **7.** He has a good friend for a neighbor. **8.** Mice in the basement ate the potatoes. **9.** That plane flies in any weather. **10.** The teacher advised her to study a foreign language.

Workbook Activity 104–Sentences with Words that Look Similar
Circle the word in parentheses that completes each sentence correctly.
1. clothes **2.** lose **3.** loose **4.** all ready **5.** diary, dairy **6.** dessert, desert **7.** breathe **8.** loose, desert **9.** quite **10.** close, your, clothes
11. loose **12.** angle **13.** finally **14.** finale **15.** finely

Workbook Activity 105–Using Words that Compare
Circle the correct adverb in parentheses to complete each sentence.
1. higher **2.** most **3.** well **4.** good, through **5.** well, better **6.** highest
7. more **8.** more, **9.** short, funniest **10.** brightest **11.** better **12.** good, best **13.** best **14.** more, most **15.** fastest

Workbook Activity 106–Choose Verbs to Agree with Subjects
Circle the correct verb.
1. are **2.** were **3.** has **4.** have **5.** changes **6.** take **7.** come **8.** is **9.** love
10. are **11.** eats **12.** like **13.** loves **14.** order **15.** enjoys **16.** go **17.** says
18. meet **19.** is **20.** likes

Workbook Activity 107–Subjects and Verbs Agree
Underline the subject and circle the verb that correctly completes each sentence.
1. Two cars (are) heading into a sharp curve **2.** The red car and the black car (slide) sideways through the turn. **3.** Tires (howl) as the drivers (fight) for control. **4.** Dust (flies) as one car (leaves) the track.

5. The other car (spins) around and (heads) in the other direction.
6. The red car (is) going to win the race. **7.** Many cruise ships (enter) this port daily. **8.** There (goes) one of the bigger ships. **9.** Kadam (wants) to sail to Europe soon. **10.** (Are) the families of students invited to the picnic? **11.** (Are) those men people that you (know)?
12. A bag of apples (sits) on the table. **13.** Natasha (brushes) her horse every morning. **14.** Here (is) one of my favorite CD's.
15. There (go) five cast members of the school play.

Workbook Activity 108–Make Pronoun Subjects agree with Verbs
Underline the subject. Circle the verb that agrees with the subject.
1. Either Nate or Lana (has been) chosen class president. **2.** All streets north of 7th Avenue (are) closed for repairs. **3.** Most of the cars on this lot (are) new models. **4.** Few students (make) a perfect score on that test. **5.** None of those trees (bears) fruit every year. **6.** Each wave (is) larger than the last one. **7.** Nobody (gets) through that steel door.
8. Some (wait) outside the theater, but others (stand) in the lobby.
9. Everyone (likes) popcorn with a good movie. **10.** Many new cars (have) power windows. **11.** Neither Edgar nor Alia (is) on time for class. **12.** Not all schools (have) a foreign language program.
13. None of those little towns (are) on this map. **14.** Most streets in this part of town (are) not paved. **15.** Do these shoes (go) with that dress?

Workbook Activity 109–Practicing Pronoun-Noun Agreement
Complete each sentence with an owner pronoun. Circle the word(s) to which the pronoun refers.
1. circle woman—her **2.** circle student—his or her **3.** circle players—their **4.** circle I—my **5.** circle Anita and Sophia—their **6.** circle team—their **7.** circle Hakeem—his **8.** circle climbers—their **9.** circle player—his or her **10.** circle girls—their **11.** circle *goes* **12.** circle *work* **13.** circle *wants* **14.** circle *sings* **15.** circle *sounds*

Workbook Activity 110–*Don't* and *Doesn't*
1. doesn't **2.** don't **3.** doesn't **4.** doesn't **5.** doesn't **6.** doesn't **7.** doesn't
8. don't **9.** don't **10.** don't **11.** doesn't **12.** don't **13.** doesn't **14.** don't
15. doesn't **16.** don't **17.** don't **18.** doesn't **19.** don't **20.** don't

Workbook Activity 111–Misplaced Words and Phrases
1. Eddie's the only person who tried out—Eddie tried out only a few minutes ago. **2.** Mai didn't wait any longer than an hour—Mai's the only person who waited for Anna. **3.** Nekeisha's the only person who knows the answer—Nekeisha knows nothing but the right answer.
4. The bell in the hall sounds the start of class. **5.** The boy in the library reads books about monsters.

Workbook Activity 112–Standard English
1. I will try to get a better grade. **2.** If I had seen it, I would have known about it. **3.** I'm going to relax and lay in the sun. **4.** Where were you when I went for ice cream? **5.** He is missing because I wasn't watching him. **6.** I think I know the answer, but can't say anything. **7.** You have broken one of those lamps. **8.** He said, "I need this job very badly." **9.** If you tell me where you are, I'll come get you. **10.** As soon as my car is running, I'll take you to the store.

Workbook Activity 113–Writing Mechanics
Answers will vary.

Diagramming Activities

Sentence Diagramming Activity 1

1. Dogs | bark

2. Birds | chirp

3. Children | play

4. People | talk

5. Stores | open

Sentence Diagramming Activity 2

1. Stars | shine

2. Horses | trot

3. Deer | run

4. Babies | sleep

5. Dogs | howl

Sentence Diagramming Activity 3

1. men | work — Tough

2. girls | smile — Pretty

3. woman | plans — A, smart

4. sun | rose — The, early, morning

Sentence Diagramming Activity 4

1. child | wins — Some, lucky

2. telephone | rings — The, black, wall

3. student | reads — A, bright, clever

4. teacher | helps — One, nice, smart

Sentence Diagramming Activity 5

1. theater | opened — The, old, movie, early

2. Nikki | runs — Little, fast

3. men | dress — The, three, well

4. rain | fell — cold, wet, yesterday

Sentence Diagramming Activity 6

1. children | sing — Small, daily

2. bus | left — The, early, today

3. box | came — The, huge, first

4. train | arrives — the, Today

Sentence Diagramming Activity 7

1. man | sits — A, big, upstairs

2. woman | came — The, young, downstairs

3. boy | played — A, happy, outside

4. ladies | go — The, out

Sentence Diagramming Activity 8

1. man | stops — The, old, suddenly

2. leaf | drops — A, red, slowly

3. worker | finished — A, fast, early

4. bike | worked — The, new, well

Sentence Diagramming Activity 9

1. Planes | fly — through / clouds

2. People | sleep — during / night, the

3. Children | play — near / house, the

4. dog | crawled — A, under / porch, the

Answer Key 329

Sentence Diagramming Activity 10

1.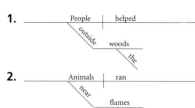

2.

3.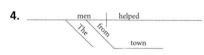

4.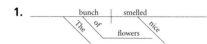

Sentence Diagramming Activity 11

1.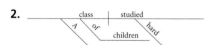

2.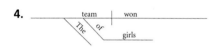

3.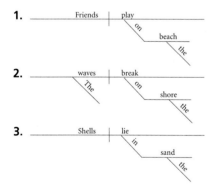

4.

Sentence Diagramming Activity 12

1.

2.

3.

Sentence Diagramming Activity 13

1.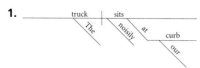

2.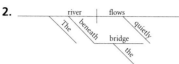

3.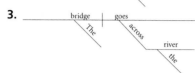

Sentence Diagramming Activity 14

1.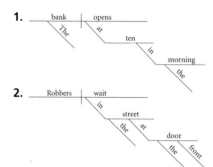

2.

Sentence Diagramming Activity 15

1.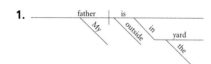

2.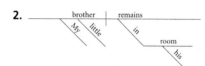

3.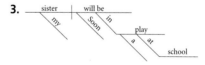

Sentence Diagramming Activity 16

1.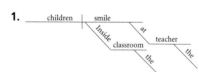

2.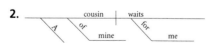

3.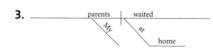

Sentence Diagramming Activity 17

1.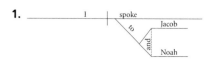

2.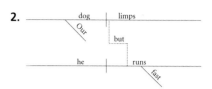

Sentence Diagramming Activity 18

1.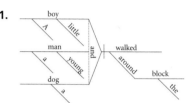

2.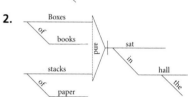

Sentence Diagramming Activity 19

1.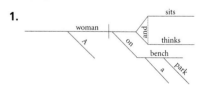

2.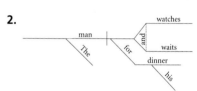

Sentence Diagramming Activity 20

1.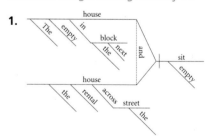

Sentence Diagramming Activity 21

1.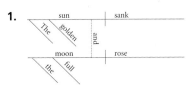

2.

Sentence Diagramming Activity 22

1.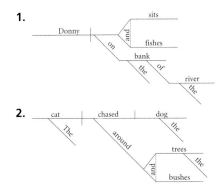

2.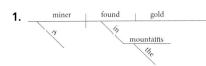

Sentence Diagramming Activity 23

1.

2.

3.

Sentence Diagramming Activity 24

1.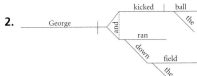

2.

3.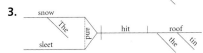

Sentence Diagramming Activity 25

1.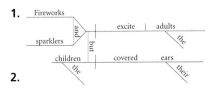

2.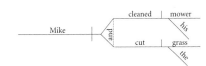

Sentence Diagramming Activity 26

1.

2.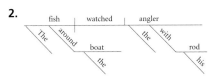

Sentence Diagramming Activity 27

1.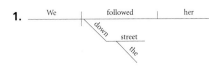

2.

Sentence Diagramming Activity 28

1.

2.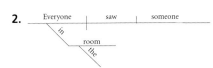

Sentence Diagramming Activity 29

1.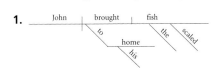

2.

Sentence Diagramming Activity 30

1.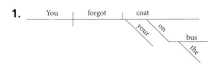

2.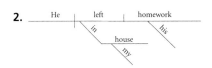

Sentence Diagramming Activity 31

1.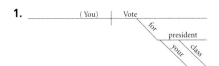

2.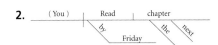

Sentence Diagramming Activity 32

1.

2.

Sentence Diagramming Activity 33

1.

2.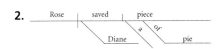

Sentence Diagramming Activity 34

1.

2.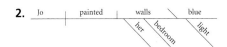

3.

Sentence Diagramming Activity 35

1.

2.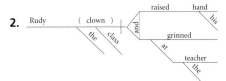

Sentence Diagramming Activity 36

1.

2.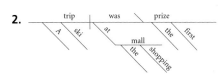

Sentence Diagramming Activity 37

1.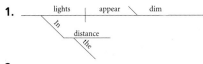

2.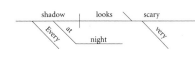

Sentence Diagramming Activity 38

1.

2.

3.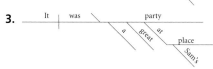

Sentence Diagramming Activity 39

1.

2.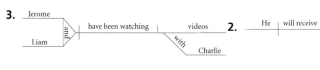

3.

4.

Sentence Diagramming Activity 40

1.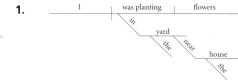

2.

3.

Sentence Diagramming Activity 41

1.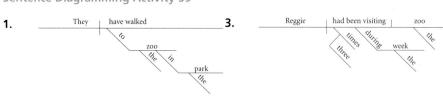

2. He | will receive | grade

3. Brenna | will be moving

4. Kelly | will be cooking

Community Connection

Completed activities will vary for each student. Community Connection activities are real-life activities completed outside of the classroom by the students. These activities give students practical learning and practice of the skills taught in *English to Use*. Check completed activities to see that students have followed directions, filled in all blanks, provided reasonable answers to questions, written legibly, and used proper grammar and punctuation.

English in Your World

Completed English in Your World activities will vary for each student. The activities are meant to help students see how what they learn in *English to Use* applies to the everyday world around them. The activities are meant to be completed outside the classroom. Check completed activities to see that students have followed directions, completed each step, filled in all charts and blanks, provided reasonable answers to questions, written legibly, and used proper grammar and punctuation.

Self-Study Guide

Self-Study Guides outline suggested sections from the text and workbook. These assignment guides provide flexibility for individualized instruction or independent study.

Preparing for Writing Tests

Test 1–Writing Prompts

1. Purpose: to persuade   Format: letter
2. Purpose: to describe   Format: paragraphs
3. Purpose: to inform   Format: list
4. Purpose: to entertain   Format: paragraphs
5. Purpose: to persuade   Format: letter

Test 2–Organizing Your Writing

Information in organizers will vary.

Test 3–Proofreading for Errors

1. Jason and Rico were trying to **decide** what to **do** on Saturday afternoon. 2. Earth is the **third** planet from the **sun**. 3. Do you **know** where they have hung **their** poster? 4. Abraham Lincoln **delivered** the **Gettysburg** Address at the dedication of the cemetery in Gettysburg, Pennsylvania. 5. Anita and Terry **live** in the **same** apartment building.

Test 4–Writing Test Practice

Essays and answers will vary.

Mastery Tests

Chapter 1 Mastery Test A

Part A: 1. F **2.** S **3.** S **4.** F **5.** F **6.** S **7.** F **8.** F **9.** S **10.** S

Part B: 11. Many <u>students</u> | <u>work</u> quickly. **12.** The <u>teacher</u> | <u>speaks</u> rapidly. **13.** A cold <u>rain</u> | <u>falls</u> today. **14.** The young <u>dancer</u> | <u>leaps</u> gracefully. **15.** The new <u>curtains</u> | <u>hang</u> well. **16.** The old <u>man</u> | <u>sits</u> quietly. **17.** The little <u>fish</u> | <u>splashes</u> noisily. **18.** The young <u>man</u> | <u>dresses</u> poorly. **19.** The good <u>student</u> | <u>writes</u> carefully. **20.** The heavy cement <u>bag</u> | <u>falls</u> over.

Part C: 21. B; **22.** D; **23.** C; **24.** A; **25.** D

Part D: 26. slowly—how **27.** often—when **28.** nearby—where **29.** today—when **30.** down—where

Part E: Adverbs are bold. **31.** The big black steam engine (noun) chugs (verb) **noisily. 32.** Chuck (noun) **often** works (verb) **late. 33.** The empty classroom (noun) fills (verb) **quickly. 34.** The new boat (noun) **suddenly** sinks (verb). **35. Quickly,** the first swimmer (noun) splashes (verb) **past.**

Part F: 36. Suddenly, the bell rang. **37.** The tired students left fast. **38.** Some teachers stayed late. **39.** Slowly, the darkness falls. **40.** Good students study hard.

Chapter 1 Mastery Test B

Part A: 1. S **2.** F **3.** F **4.** S **5.** S **6.** F **7.** S **8.** S **9.** F **10.** F

Part B: 11. B; **12.** D; **13.** C; **14.** A; **15.** D

Part C: 16. Many ocean fish | swim slowly. **17.** The little baby | cries loudly. **18.** The orange flagpole | stands tall. **19.** The old dog | snores gently. **20.** The chilly north wind | blows hard. **21.** The young man | leaves early. **22.** The baby bird | sings softly. **23.** The old woman | dresses well. **24.** The strong hiker | walks quickly. **25.** Black smoke rises thickly.

Part D: Adverbs are bold. **26.** The sleek bullet train (noun) glides (verb) **silently. 27.** Anne (noun) **often** arrives (verb) **early. 28.** The new computer person (noun) works (verb) **hard. 29.** The small red bike (noun) parks (verb) **nearby. 30. Slowly,** the big airplane (noun) lands (verb) **safely.**

Part E: 31. Carefully, the man stands up. **32.** Some people watch quietly. **33.** The lights dim slightly. **34.** The cold wind howls shrilly. **35.** Slowly, the man walks away.

Part F: 36. often—when **37.** quickly—how **38.** soon—when **39.** there—where **40.** well—how

Chapter 2 Mastery Test A

Part A: 1. No **2.** Yes **3.** Yes **4.** No **5.** Yes

Part B: 6. adv. **7.** prep. **8.** adv. **9.** prep. **10.** adv.

Part C: 11. D; **12.** A; **13.** C; **14.** A; **15.** B

Part D: 16. action; **17.** being; **18.** action; **19.** action; **20.** being

Part E: 21. with the green door—prep. phrase; house—subject; stood—verb **22.** down the alley—prep. phrase; ball—subject; rolled—verb **23.** Under the bridge—prep. phrase; ducks—subject; sleep—verb

Part F: 24. At football games, students at Springer High School cheer loudly. **25.** In the late afternoons, the Washington Monument catches the glint of the sun. **26.** From New York Harbor, the Statue of Liberty welcomes strangers to our shores.

Part G: Answers will vary but should include prepositional phrases.

Chapter 2 Mastery Test B

Part A: 1. Yes **2.** No **3.** No **4.** Yes

Part B: 5. prep. **6.** prep. **7.** adv. **8.** prep.

Part C: **9.** Being **10.** Action **11.** Being **12.** Being **13.** Action

Part D: **14.** with the old books—prep. phrase; shelf—subject; fell—verb **15.** toward the hole—prep. phrase; ball—subject; rolled—verb **16.** On a tree limb—prep. phrase; owl—subject; hooted—verb **17.** of the team—prep. phrase; member—subject; laughed—verb **18.** near the lake—prep. phrase; boys—subject; waited—verb

Part E: **19.** D; **20.** A; **21.** C; **22.** A; **23.** B

Part F: **24-27.** Answers will vary but should include prepositional phrases.

Part G: **28.** At basketball practice, the Park High School team prepares for Friday's big game. **29.** About 9 A.M., President Sherman will hold a press conference. **30.** During the winter, skiers like the Colorado Rockies near Aspen.

Chapter 3 Mastery Test A

Part A: **1.** and; **2.** but; **3.** or

Part B: Answers will vary. Possible answers are given.

4. Clouds form, and the lightning crackles. **5.** Rain falls, yet the river does not overflow.

Part C: **6.** B; **7.** C; **8.** A

Part D: **9.** The student read an article called "Space Stations" in the <u>All About Space Encyclopedia</u>. **10.** The article "Smart Student" is in a magazine called <u>News for Teens</u>.

Part E: Compound Sentence: The movie plays on, yet the clock ticks slowly. **11.** Conjunctions: and; and; as well as; but; or; yet; neither; nor; or **12.** Compound Subjects: Fred and Steve; cowboy as well as horse; Fred nor Steve **13.** Compound Verbs: glows and flickers; rides but sings **14.** Compound Objects of Prepositions: trails or fields; movie or its stars

Part F: **15.** School opens; students arrive. Bells ring in the halls, classrooms, and gym. Girls and boys rush to class. Teachers and students work hard on reading, writing, science, history, and math skills. School ends; students leave.

Chapter 3 Mastery Test B

Part A: **1.** B; **2.** C; **3.** A

Part B: **4.** but; **5.** and; **6.** or

Part C: Answers will vary. Possible answers are given.

7. Snow falls, yet the ice does not freeze. **8.** Bands play, and people dance.

Part D: **9.** The name of the article is "Practical Home Improvement Projects." **10.** A student read the chapter called "Animal Life" in a book called <u>Science</u>.

Part E: **11.** Summer ends; fall begins. Cold weather arrives early. Red and yellow leaves appear on maple, oak, birch, and sumac trees. In the early morning, the sun shines through frost on the windows. Fall ends; winter begins.

Part F: Compound Sentence: The star quarterback throws hard, but the injured halfback does not kick well. **12.** Conjunctions: as well as; and; and; or; and; but; Neither; nor **13.** Compound Subjects: football players, cheerleaders; quarterback, halfback; coach, principal **14.** Compound Verbs: jump and run; walks . . . or talks **15.** Compound Objects of Prepositions: players, trainers; center, guards

Chapter 4 Mastery Test A

Part A: **1.** subject—dog, verb—grabbed, direct object—bone

2. subject—Harry, verb—bought, direct object— CD

3. subject—boat, verb—hit, direct object— pier

4. subject—Ann, verb—shoveled, direct object—snow

5. subject—people, verb—watched, direct object— show

Part B: **6.** field **7.** dials **8.** kicked **9.** bowls **10.** searched

Part C: **11.** compound **12.** simple **13.** compound **14.** compound **15.** simple

Part D: **16.** C; **17.** B; **18.** D; **19.** A; **20.** B

Part E: **21.** Jon drops a hook into the water from his boat at Lake George. **22.** Dr. Sung and Mrs. Jones were speakers, and Mr. Parks and Senator Cole were guests. **23.** Prince Henry will not be at the Fourth of July event; however, Queen Maria will take his place. **24.** Juanita, Tela, and Rose attend Central City High School. **25.** Gerry and Loni drove to the Grand Canyon, Phoenix, and Las Vegas on their vacation in May.

Chapter 4 Mastery Test B

Part A: **1.** filled **2.** ran **3.** cowboy **4.** twisted **5.** dumped

Part B: **6.** simple **7.** compound **8.** simple **9.** simple **10.** compound

Part C: **11.** C; **12.** B; **13.** D; **14.** A; **15.** B

Part D: **16.** subject—sun, verb—heated, direct object—water

17. subject—snow, verb—covered, direct object—bushes

18. subject—Internet, verb—spans, direct object—globe

19. subject—driver, verb—hit, direct object—brakes

20. subject—water, verb—filled, direct object—bathtub

Part E: **21.** Hurricane Andrea damaged homes; therefore, insurance rates went up July 1. **22.** Five Atlanta Braves players hit home runs during the third World Series game. **23.** Mardi Gras parades in New Orleans stop traffic, entertain visitors, and delight children. **24.** Governor Jones, Senator Long, and Mayor Garcia spoke at Rice University in Houston, Texas. **25.** Their trip takes them to five African countries; however, they will not go to Kenya.

Chapter 5 Mastery Test A

Part A: **1.** adverb **2.** preposition **3.** adjective **4.** verb **5.** noun

Part B: Owner nouns and pronouns are bold. **6.** **Joe's** flowers thrive with **his** care. **7.** **Maria's** truck holds all **her** large stained glass designs. **8.** The **teams'** game begins when **their** coaches arrive. **9.** **Anne's** appointment was with **her** career counselor. **10.** **Manny's** job starts tomorrow after **his** classes.

Part C: Subjects are bold. **11.** (You) <u>Take</u> these flowers to Mrs. Yoder. **12.** (You) <u>Bring</u> a bucket of water for these flowers. **13.** Many **cats** <u>like</u> catnip toys. **14.** (You) <u>Have</u> a wonderful trip. **15.** A lot of **children** <u>like</u> parks to play in.

Part D: **16.** C; **17.** B; **18.** B; **19.** D; **20.** A

Part E: Answers will vary. Sentences should include an adverb other than too or very. Suggested answers are given. **21.** Nicholas is really interested in drawing. **22.** Alysha is an extremely good baby. **23.** Grant is rather fond of baseball. **24.** Sarah is studying terribly hard for her degree.

Part F: Changes are bold. **25.** **W**ow! The quarterback tackles Fred Smith near the goalpost. **L**ook! Both teams' coaches talk on the sidelines. **S**plat! **T**he fullback crashes into **S**mith during the last quarter. **E**veryone goes to Steve's house for a party after the game.

Chapter 5 Mastery Test B

Part A: **1.** noun **2.** adjective **3.** verb **4.** adverb **5.** preposition

Part B: Subjects are bold. **6.** (You) <u>Carry</u> these towels upstairs for me. **7.** (You) <u>Cover</u> the flowers to keep them from freezing. **8.** A lot of **people** <u>buy</u> CDs for their computers. **9.** (You) <u>Avoid</u> a sunburn on the trip. **10.** Many **dogs** <u>bring</u> the newspaper on command.

Part C: Owner nouns and pronouns are bold. **11.** **Loretta's** vegetables thrive with **her** care. **12. Monroe's** truck holds **his** lawn care equipment. **13.** The **committees'** deadlines begin when **their** calendars arrive. **14. Peter's** date was with **his** friend Jill. **15. Iva's** computer makes **her** reports easy to write.

Part D: Answers will vary. Sentences should include an adverb other than too or very. Suggested answers are given. **16.** Reuben wants to go to town quite often. **17.** Sam always arrives so early at school. **18.** Helping with the baking is truly appealing to Lidya. **19.** Joe is completely involved when he plays games.

Part E: 20. C; **21.** B; **22.** B; **23.** D; **24.** A

Part F: 25. Changes are bold. Look! That big bird circles over **M**iller **L**ake. **H**ey! **H**e spots a fish. **S**plash! **T**he bird grabs the fish in his beak. **S**ome of the bird's feathers fall into the water. **T**he bird flies to a tree's branch for a tasty lunch after it catches the fish.

Chapter 6 Mastery Test A

Part A: 1. Jenny **2.** brother **3.** himself **4.** me

Part B: 5. no **6.** yes—Ama **7.** no **8.** yes—him **9.** no

Part C: 10. C; **11.** A; **12.** B; **13.** C; **14.** B

Part D: 15. muddy **16.** one **17.** hot, spicy

Part E: Answers will vary. Check that each sentence has an appositive. Possible answers are given. **18.** Benton, a tiny town in the mountains, has a good view of the valley. **19.** Oscar, a famous author, signed books in a store for his fans.

Part F: 20. B; **21.** D; **22.** A; **23.** C; **24.** B

Part G: 25. Changes are bold. The **A**ndersons' house, the oldest house in **W**estport, burned **S**aturday night. **F**irefighters from **R**iver **C**ity, a good team, smashed through the front door. **T**hey found the fire a hot one. **T**he walls fell onto the ground. **T**he house, once the pride of **W**estport, sat in ruins.

Chapter 6 Mastery Test B

Part A: 1. dog **2.** himself **3.** Al **4.** us

Part B: 5. no **6.** yes—pigeons **7.** no **8.** yes—girlfriend **9.** yes—aunt

Part C: Answers will vary. Check that each sentence has an appositive. Possible answers are given. **10.** Helen, a good friend of mine, left town on the train to New York. **11.** Ed's car, a powerful model, sits at the curb.

Part D: 12. C; **13.** A; **14.** B; **15.** C; **16.** B

Part E: 17. mayor **18.** cute, silly **19.** hot

Part F: 20. A; **21.** C; **22.** B; **23.** A; **24.** D

Part G: 25. Changes are bold. **B**ill's car, a late model truck, needed an oil change. **H**is friend, **S**teve, taught **B**ill the process. **B**ill pulled, pushed, and pounded on the stubborn car's hood, a strong piece of steel. **F**inally, he gave up. **B**ill went into his house and read the book, a short one, about caring for his car.

Chapter 7 Mastery Test A

Part A: 1. seafood **2.** student **3.** one **4.** friends **5.** time

Part B: 6. taste **7.** feels **8.** is **9.** are **10.** grows

Part C: Answers will vary. Possible answers are given. Check that each sentence has an appositive and a subject complement. **11.** The actor, a hard worker, is a talented man. **12.** The little girls, a cute pair of twins, are great tap dancers. **13.** The classroom, a noisy place, has a small area for play practice. **14.** George, a regular customer at the restaurant, is a pizza fan. **15.** The old house, a large empty building, is a scary place at night.

Part D: 16. good **17.** well **18.** good **19.** well **20.** well

Part E: 21. tall, taller **22.** youngest, oldest **23.** bad, worse **24.** more **25.** little, less, least

Part F: 26. A; **27.** D; **28.** A; **29.** C; **30.** D

Chapter 7 Mastery Test B

Part A: 1. seems **2.** were **3.** appear **4.** is **5.** feels

Part B: 6. bowl **7.** runner **8.** players **9.** place **10.** time

Part C: 11. C; **12.** D; **13.** A; **14.** C; **15.** D

Part D: 16. well **17.** good **18.** well **19.** good **20.** good

Part E: 21. more; **22.** bad, worse; **23.** tell, taller; **24.** little, less, least; **25.** youngest, oldest

Part F: Answers will vary. Possible answers are given. Check that each sentence has an appositive and a subject complement. **26.** Peg and Kathy, the new restaurant owners, are great cooks. **27.** The old movie, a hit on cable TV, was a Hollywood classic. **28.** The young doctor, a cheerful man, is a distance swimmer. **29.** The Alaskan husky, a strong sled dog, is a fast runner. **30.** Daniel, a friend of mine, is a singer.

Chapter 8 Mastery Test A

Part A: 1. goes/will go **2.** fills **3.** played **4.** walked **5.** will cook

Part B: 6. D; **7.** A; **8.** B; **9.** C; **10.** A

Part C: Answers may vary. Possible answers are given. **11.** Jan had not been fishing at the lake on Tuesday. **12.** Tomaso is never going there again. **13.** I never saw the car coming toward me. **14.** My parents will not like the video games.

Part D: 15. ran—past **16.** thrown—future **17.** caught—past **18.** swims—present **19.** ridden—past

Part E: Answers will vary. Students should use the verb given and one or more helping verbs. Check that sentences make sense. Possible answers are given. **20.** Four men with ladders were painting the house. **21.** Tom will be working at the gas station after school. **22.** Ketta has gone to the dentist. **23.** Rain must have been filling the gutters with muddy water. **24.** Ben and Kim might be grilling steaks.

Part F: Changes are bold; answers may vary. **25.** I've been reading a book about a man who doesn't have much time. He's been trying to decide something all day. Should he risk his life's savings to win a fortune? I sat up and finish**ed** the book by midnight.

Chapter 8 Mastery Test B

Part A: 1. will write **2.** plays **3.** delivered **4.** talked **5.** will study

Part B: 6. broken—past **7.** drink—present **8.** ridden—present **9.** caught—future **10.** came—past or comes—present

Part C: 11. D; **12.** A; **13.** B; **14.** C; **15.** A

Part D: Answers may vary. Possible answers are given. **16.** They had never invited Margo to the cabin for a weekend. **17.** She was not planning to go there. **18.** My computer will not let me get information from CDs. **19.** Jere did not find information about car prices on the Internet.

Part E: 20. Joe's new car **will** be ready soon. **He**'d ordered it from the dealer. **He**'s be**en** waiting for two weeks. **It**'s a blue sports model**,** and **it has** a CD player and a turbo engine. **H**is friend chose the color.

Part F: Answers will vary. Students should use the verb given and one or more helping verbs. Check that sentences make sense. Possible answers are given. **21.** Lee might be working in the next room. **22.** By tonight, Dan's truck could move six loads to the dump. **23.** Kim must watch two videos and a cable movie Friday. **24.** Three dogs have been barking in the alley behind the house. **25.** With luck, Ahmad should have scored the extra points on his test.

Chapter 9 Mastery Test A

Part A: 1. except **2.** accept **3.** taught **4.** teach **5.** Lie, raise **6.** sat, rise **7.** set, lay **8.** It's, its **9.** You're, your **10.** their **11.** Their, its, they're

12. Its, their, you're **13.** Let, to, too **14.** Leave, too **15.** Let
Part B: 16. C; **17.** D; **18.** A; **19.** B; **20.** D
Part C: Accept answers in any order. **21.** a. journal b. notes **22.** a. Include the most important words and ideas; b. Complete so they are most helpful; c. Neat enough to read and understand.
Part D: Answers will vary. Possible answers are given. **23.** Oscar couldn't go anywhere outside in the beastly heat. **24.** Bill wouldn't ever order hot chili again. **25.** Sandy can find no work in this town. **26.** Roger didn't have any money in the bank. **27.** No train ever comes through this town at any time.
Part E: 28. The opening football game is the first Friday in September at 7:30 P.M. **29.** Hattie chose 8:30 A.M. for her appointment with Dr. Lee on April 30, 2001. **30.** January 11, 1944, was a Tuesday.

Chapter 9 Mastery Test B
Part A: 1. C; **2.** D; **3.** A; **4.** B; **5.** D
Part B: 6. It's, your **7.** Their, you're, your **8.** They're, your **9.** its **10.** taught **11.** learned **12.** accept **13.** except **14.** let, too **15.** Too, leave, two **16.** to, two **17.** laid, set, rises **18.** set, sat **19.** lay, sat **20.** Sit, raise
Part C: Accept answers in any order. **21.** a. Include the most important words and ideas. b. Make complete so they are most helpful. c. neat enough to read and understand. **22.** a. journaling b. notes
Part D: 23. January 11, 1944, was a Tuesday. **24.** The opening football game is the first Friday in September at 7:30 P.M. **25.** Hattie chose 8:30 A.M. for her appointment with Dr. Lee on April 30, 2001.
Part E: Answers will vary. Possible answers are given. **26.** Nobody did anything to save the man in the leaky boat. **27.** Jen didn't have any money for fancy clothes. **28.** The old man can't hear music on the stereo. **29.** Tom went nowhere without his friends. **30.** Nobody ever saw Bill lose a baseball game.

Chapter 10 Mastery Test A
Part A: Subjects and linking verbs are given in that order. **1.** car; is **2.** birthday; was **3.** What; is **4.** you; are
Part B: 5. complex **6.** compound **7.** compound-complex **8.** complex
Part C: 9. Ed said, "Last night's game between Boston and Chicago was great!" **10.** Anna said, "I did well on my science test." **11.** Phil said, "I want to get home before seven o'clock." **12.** Lou said, "The play was boring after the second act."
Part D: 13. Complete verb—Is working; S—Carol **14.** Complete verb—Could have been; S—man; **15.** Complete verb—did go; S—jacket **16.** Complete verb—Are making; S—you
Part E: 17. D; **18.** C; **19.** A; **20.** D
Part F: Sentences will vary. Check that students have used the correct punctuation and type of sentence. Types of sentences and the word to be used are given here. **21.** question—win **22.** strong command or request—halt **23.** statement—help **24.** command—go **25.** interjection—well

Chapter 10 Mastery Test B
Part A: Subjects and linking verbs are given in that order. **1.** leader; is **2.** party; was **3.** What; are **4.** papers; are
Part B: 5. D; **6.** C; **7.** A; **8.** D
Part C: Sentences will vary. Check that students have used the correct punctuation for each type of sentence and the word specified. Types of sentences and the word to be used are given here. **9.** interjection—well **10.** command—go **11.** strong command or request—halt **12.** statement—help **13.** question—win

Part D: 14. Complete verb—did score; S—Ben **15.** Complete verb—Is feeding; S—Betty **16.** Complete verb—is coming; S—friend **17.** Complete verb—did go; S—time
Part E: 18. compound-complex **19.** compound **20.** compound-complex **21.** complex
Part F: 22. Bob laughed and exclaimed, "Ben's joke was funny!" **23.** Joe asked, "When will my new job start?" **24.** Tina said, "My cat left home this morning, and I can't find him." **25.** Sam said, "I am going out for the soccer team."

Chapter 11 Mastery Test A
Part A: 1. 3 **2.** 1 **3.** 5 **4.** 4 **5.** 2
Part B: 6. To: Al **7.** From: Kim **8.** Subject: Date of math test **9.** Date: March 4 **10.** Time: 7:30 P.M. **11.** Messages will vary but should include this information: Call Kim to tell her the date of the math test.
Part C: News stories will vary but should include the five points of information. Give one point each for including these items in the story: **12.** Who: Andy Young **13.** What: Fell out of a fifty-foot tree **14.** When: Saturday night **15.** Where: 1711 Waterfall Drive **16.** Why: Tried to catch his cat
Part D: 17. When: June 1 **18.** What time: 7 p.m. **19.** Where: 641 Winding Lane, Central City, Idaho **20.** Given by: George Adams **21.** Purpose: Welcome home party for Karen Ralston **22.** RSVP: 532-1622, by May 15
Part E: 23-26. Descriptive paragraphs about what students would buy if they had more money will vary. Give one point for each of the five sentences. Check that sentences make sense and flow together as a paragraph.
Part F: 27. D; **28.** C; **29.** B; **30.** D

Chapter 11 Mastery Test B
Part A: 1. 5 **2.** 4 **3.** 2 **4.** 1 **5.** 3
Part B: 6. D; **7.** C; **8.** B; **9.** D
Part C: 10. To: Juanita **11.** From: Rafael **12.** Subject: Plans tonight **13.** Date: April 3 **14.** Time: 5:30 p.m. **15.** Messages will vary but should include this information: Call Rafael to tell him whether you have time for a movie tonight.
Part D: 16. When: November 3 **17.** What time: 8 P.M. **18.** Where: 211 Windsong Road, Green Bay, Wisconsin **19.** Given by: Larry and Jill Thomas **20.** Purpose: Housewarming party for our new home **21.** RSVP: 231-9878, by October 17
Part E: 22-25. Descriptive paragraphs about the student's street, town, or city will vary. Give one point for each of the five sentences. Check that sentences make sense and flow together as a paragraph.
Part F: News stories will vary but should include the five points of information. Give one point each for including these items in the story: **26.** Who: Ed Chan **27.** What: Walked four miles in deep snow and fought off wolves **28.** When: Friday night **29.** Where: Highway 118 **30.** Why: His car broke down

Chapter 12 Mastery Test A
Part A: 1. February, misspell **2.** beginning **3.** thought, Wednesday **4.** here, hear **5.** our, hour **6.** knew, new **7.** history, study **8.** loose, lose **9.** quite, quiet **10.** breath, breathe
Part B: 11. colder **12.** most **13.** less **14.** smarter **15.** more
Part C: 16. C; **17.** A; **18.** A; **19.** D; **20.** C
Part D: 21. piece **22.** field **23.** reign **24.** ceiling **25.** achieve **26.** relieve **27.** belief **28.** thieves **29.** grief **30.** neighbor
Part E: 31. The weather was colder than it's been in the last month. **32.** Some places received two feet of snow. **33.** The skies were

cloudy, and an awful wind blew. **34.** His car would not start in the blizzard. **35.** He stayed home and sent a fax to his friends. **Part F: 36.** flies **37.** families **38.** libraries **39.** copies **40.** daisies

Chapter 12 Mastery Test B

Part A: 1. government, necessary **2.** fair, fare **3.** desert, dessert **4.** here, hear **5.** deer, dear **6.** dairy, diary **7.** close, clothes **8.** all ready, already **9.** hottest **10.** slipped, new

Part B: 11. C; **12.** A; **13.** A; **14.** D; **15.** C

Part C: 16. better **17.** more **18.** most **19.** less **20.** best

Part D: 21. students **22.** valleys **23.** knives **24.** pennies **25.** skies

Part E: 26. quiet **27.** weight **28.** niece **29.** leisure **30.** receipt **31.** sleigh **32.** believes **33.** shriek **34.** eight **35.** seize

Part F: 36. Of all the houses on the block, Frank's is the most expensive. **37.** Its windows, the best on the market, are made of heavy glass and steel wires. **38.** Neither a baseball nor a rock could break them. **39.** Through these windows, Frank watches white-tailed deer on his lawn. **40.** He has heard wolves howl near his home late at night.

Chapter 13 Mastery Test A

Part A: 1. barks, bark **2.** practices **3.** need **4.** run **5.** play **6.** forgets **7.** gets

Part B: 8. D; **9.** A; **10.** C; **11.** B; **12.** D

Part C: 13. doesn't **14.** doesn't **15.** don't **16.** doesn't **17.** don't

Part D: 18. with loud exhaust pipes—car **19.** with a beard—man **20.** in a brown envelope—letter **21.** in blue uniforms—team **22.** with the gold band—watch

Part E: Probable sentences are given. **23.** Bill, Tom, and Fred play in their own band. **24.** Each of the players has a chance to appear on TV. **25.** The band doesn't practice every night, but the group works hard. **26.** Both Bill and Fred work at other jobs during the day.

Part F: Probable sentences are given. **27.** I asked, "Where are you?" **28.** We were going to set out a pitcher of iced tea. **29.** Are you going to tell me where the movie is? **30.** We're going to try to make the deadline.

Chapter 13 Mastery Test B

Part A: 1. plays, play **2.** works **3.** stand **4.** climbs **5.** walks, walk **6.** is **7.** worry

Part B: 8. don't **9.** doesn't **10.** doesn't **11.** doesn't **12.** don't

Part C: 13. D; **14.** A; **15.** C; **16.** B; **17.** D

Part D: Probable sentences are given. **18.** Joe doesn't go to work at Acme Foundry until noon today. **19.** His new job doesn't pay well, but the hours are good. **20.** His friends, Steve and Fred, work there, too. **21.** Their boss, Al, likes them to be on time when they come to work.

Part E: 22. with gold trim—house **23.** in a large pot—cooked **24.** with new blue paint—boat **25.** with wooden canes—men **26.** with long, white teeth and a furry tail—wolf

Part F: Probable sentences are given. **27.** I should have gone anywhere but here. **28.** We're going to try to make the deadline. **29.** I asked, "Where are you?" **30.** We were going to set out a pitcher of iced tea.

Midterm Mastery Test

Part A: 1. The baseball player | hit the ball.
2. The new car engine | runs smoothly and quietly.
3. The young clerk | sold us three tickets.
4. The tired truck driver | found the heavy fog a problem.
5. Carol, a proud owner, | washed and waxed her bike carefully.

Part B: 6. N—basketball, hoop, crowd; V—dropped, cheered; Adj—A, the, the, noisy; Prep—through; C—and; I—Wow **7.** N—Ann, Tom, tickets, play; V—sold; Adj—three, the, new; Adv—gladly, more; P—us; Prep—to; C—and **8.** N—truck, load; V—carries, moves; Adj—that, huge, a, heavy; Adv—really, quickly; P—it; C—but; I—Oh **9.** N—Hours, work, engine, one; V—made; Adj—hard, a, smooth; Adv—very; P—his; Prep—of **10.** N—airplane, runway; V—landed, hopped; Adj—the, a; Adv—Quickly, out; P—he; Prep—on; C—and

Part C: 11. At the zoo—stares, at the huge lion—stares **12.** Beside the river—sit, in the sun—sit **13.** with a gold base—lamp, on the table—stands **14.** from the chimney—rises, on the roof—chimney **15.** with a new saddle—horse, in the parade—trots

Part D: 16. subject—fireworks, appositive—a beautiful display **17.** subject—chapter three, appositive—a tough one **18.** subject—Bert, appositive—a lucky man **19.** subject—party, appositive—a happy event

Part E: 20. C; **21.** D; **22.** B; **23.** C; **24.** A; **25.** C

Part F: 26. compound **27.** simple **28.** compound **29.** compound **30.** simple

Part G: 31. like—Action **32.** is—Being **33.** drove—Action **34.** grabbed—Action **35.** is—Being

Part H: 36. Accept either answer: and or as well as **37.** Accept either answer: and or as well as **38.** but **39.** yet **40.** or

Part I: 41. today—A when **42.** down—B where **43.** often—A when **44.** usually—D how **45.** twice a day—how often

Part J: 46. Louie **47.** Mandy **48.** sister **49.** himself **50.** them

Part K: 51. At Thomas Lake, a power boat stops near the shore. **52.** On the shore, the boat captain talks to Joe. **53.** He gives Joe an article called "How to Ski on Water." **54.** Joe, a hard worker, wants to ski well. **55.** Hey! Joe is the best skier on that great big lake.

Part L: 56. C; **57.** A; **58.** B; **59.** D; **60.** C

Part A: 1. Almost <u>everyone</u> | <u>started</u> at the same time.

2. On Tuesday, the <u>butcher</u> | <u>had sold</u> her a good cut of meat.

3. Four strong <u>men</u> | <u>moved</u> the heavy piano down the hall.

4. After the test, all of the <u>students</u> | <u>left</u> the classroom in a rush.

5. The <u>men</u> on the night shift at the factory | <u>were not finished</u> before sunrise.

Part B: 6. N—dog, Joe, odor, room; V—smells, can stand; Adj—wet, bad, the, the; Adv—n't; P—His; Prep— in; C—and; I—Ugh

7. N—lines, area; V—would have called, were; Adj—the, phone, this; Adv—yesterday, down; P—I, you; Prep—in; C—but; I—Well

8. N—Betty, door, cat, house; V—opened, slipped; Adj—a, the; Adv—quickly; P—her; Prep—into; C—and

9. N—Tom, cats, dogs, home; V—allows; Adj—neat; P—his; Prep—inside; C—neither, nor

10. N—Fred, shoes, feet; V—wears, look; Adj—big, small; Adv—very; P—his; C—yet; I—Oh

Part C: 11. Two, lay, rose **12.** Sit, sets **13.** doesn't, anything **14.** Mice, they're, going to, your, anymore **15.** Let, lie, leave

Part D: 16. In the store—shops, for a new computer—shops **17.** Under the bridge—paddle, in shorts—people **18.** with blue shoes—lady, beside the car—waits **19.** from the pavement—rises, on the driveway—pavement **20.** with a shaggy mane—pony, around the track—trots

Part E: 21. like—Action **22.** is—Being **23.** walked—Action **24.** caught—Action **25.** are—Being

Part F: 26. me **27.** Austin **28.** brother **29.** herself **30.** lady

Part G: 31. compound **32.** simple **33.** compound **34.** compound **35.** simple

Part H: 36. tasted **37.** feels **38.** is **39.** sounds **40.** appears

Part I: 41. has been teaching—present **42.** will have played—future **43.** had been warning—past **44.** have taken—present **45.** had been broken—past **46.** had flooded—past **47.** will have been waiting—future **48.** will take—future **49.** are playing—present **50.** was traveling—past

Part J: 51. poultry **52.** friend **53.** one **54.** red **55.** time

Part K: 56. Tom's plate is still full **57.** The snow was falling heavily **58.** the car doesn't run well **59.** Flood water closed many of the city streets; our school stayed open **60.** the bird flew away

Part L: 61. A; **62.** C; **63.** A; **64.** C; **65.** D

Part M: 66. fare, fair, too, it's, fair **67.** hear, here **68.** families, skies **69.** hoarse, horse **70.** ladies, flies, relief, received

Part N: Sentences may vary. Probable answers are given.

71. "Do you have carrots on the menu?" Dan asked the waiter.

72. "I don't know anybody who likes carrots," the waiter said.

73. Mary looked at the menu and asked, "Do you have liver?"

74. "Nobody likes liver!" the waiter said angrily.

75. Dan and Mary closed their menus and stood up.

Part O: Some answers may vary. Probable answers are given.

76. The gift **in a large box** was mailed by Joe. **77. In the living room**, a group of men talked about hunting. **78.** A large dog **with a long tail** entered the yard. **79.** A black horse **with white spots** walked toward the little girl. **80.** A cowboy **with thick glasses** climbed on his horse.

Part P: 81. C; **82.** B; **83.** C; **84.** D; **85.** A; **86.** C; **87.** D; **88.** B; **89.** C; **90.** B

Part Q: 91. nickel **92.** necessary **93.** government **94.** grammar **95.** athletic **96.** safety **97.** correct **98.** correct **99.** teeth **100.** correct

AGS Teacher Questionnaire

Attention Teachers! As publishers of *English to Use*, we would like your help in making this textbook more valuable to you. Please take a few minutes to fill out this survey. Your feedback will help us to better serve you and your students.

1. What is your position and major area of responsibility? _____
   _____
   _____

2. Briefly describe your setting:
   ____ regular education ____ special education ____ adult basic education
   ____ community college ____ university ____ other _____

3. The enrollment in your classroom includes students with the following (check all that apply):
   ____ at-risk for failure ____ low reading ability ____ behavior problems
   ____ learning disabilities ____ ESL ____ other _____

4. Grade level of your students: _____

5. Racial/ethnic groups represented in your classes (check all that apply):
   ____ African-American ____ Asian ____ Caucasian ____ Hispanic
   ____ Native American ____ Other

6. School location:
   ____ urban ____ suburban ____ rural ____ other _____

7. What reaction did your students have to the materials? (Include comments about the cover design, lesson format, illustrations, etc.)
   _____
   _____
   _____

8. What features in the student text helped your students the most?
   _____
   _____
   _____

OVER ➤

9. What features in the student text helped your students the least? Please include suggestions for changing these to make the text more relevant.

   _____

   _____

10. How did you use the Teacher's Edition and support materials, and what features did you find to be the most helpful?

   _____

   _____

11. What activity from the program did your students benefit from the most? Please briefly explain.

   _____

   _____

   _____

12. Optional: Share an activity that you used to teach the materials in your classroom that enhanced the learning and motivation of your students.

   _____

   _____

   _____

Several activities will be selected to be included in future editions. Please include your name, address, and phone number so we may contact you for permission and possible payment to use the material.

Thank you!

▼ fold in thirds and tape shut at the top ▼

- -

CIRCLE PINES MN 55014-9923
PO BOX 99
4201 WOODLAND ROAD
AGS ATT'N MARKETING SUPPORT

POSTAGE WILL BE PAID BY ADDRESSEE

BUSINESS REPLY MAIL
FIRST-CLASS MAIL PERMIT NO.12 CIRCLE PINES MN

NO POSTAGE
NECESSARY
IF MAILED
IN THE
UNITED STATES

Phone: _____
City/State/ZIP: _____
Address: _____
School: _____
Name: _____